THE NIV APPLICATION COMMENTARY

From biblical text . . . to contemporary life

THE NIV APPLICATION COMMENTARY

From biblical text . . . to contemporary life

DOUGLAS J. MOO

ZONDERVAN

The NIV Application Commentary: Romans
Copyright © 2000 by Douglas J. Moo

Requests for information should be addressed to:

Zondervan, 3900 *Sparks Dr. SE, Grand Rapids, Michigan 49546*

Library of Congress Cataloging-in-Publication Data

Moo, Douglas J.
    Romans / Douglas J. Moo.
       p. cm. — (NIV application commentary)
    Includes bibliographical references and indexes.
    ISBN 978-0-310-49400-3 (hardcover)
    1. Bible. N.T. Romans — Commentaries. I. Title. II. Series.
  BS 2665.3 .M554 2000
  227'.1077 — dc21

00 – 043647

Printed in the United States of America

15 16 17 18 19 20 21 22 23 24 /DCI/ 43 42 41 40 39 38 37 36 35 34 33 32 31 30 29 28

Contents

The NIV Application Commentary Series

When complete, the NIV Application Commentary
will include the following volumes:

Old Testament Volumes

Genesis, John H. Walton

Exodus, Peter Enns

Leviticus/Numbers, Roy Gane

Deuteronomy, Daniel I. Block

Joshua, Robert L. Hubbard Jr.

Judges/Ruth, K. Lawson Younger

1-2 Samuel, Bill T. Arnold

1-2 Kings, Gus Konkel

1-2 Chronicles, Andrew E. Hill

Ezra/Nehemiah, Douglas J. Green

Esther, Karen H. Jobes

Job, Dennis R. Magary

Psalms Volume 1, Gerald H. Wilson

Psalms Volume 2, Jamie A. Grant

Proverbs, Paul Koptak

Ecclesiastes/Song of Songs, Iain Provan

Isaiah, John N. Oswalt

Jeremiah/Lamentations, J. Andrew Dearman

Ezekiel, Iain M. Duguid

Daniel, Tremper Longman III

Hosea/Amos/Micah, Gary V. Smith

Jonah/Nahum/Habakkuk/Zephaniah,
    James Bruckner

Joel/Obadiah/Malachi, David W. Baker

Haggai/Zechariah, Mark J. Boda

New Testament Volumes

Matthew, Michael J. Wilkins

Mark, David E. Garland

Luke, Darrell L. Bock

John, Gary M. Burge

Acts, Ajith Fernando

Romans, Douglas J. Moo

1 Corinthians, Craig Blomberg

2 Corinthians, Scott Hafemann

Galatians, Scot McKnight

Ephesians, Klyne Snodgrass

Philippians, Frank Thielman

Colossians/Philemon, David E. Garland

1-2 Thessalonians, Michael W. Holmes

1-2 Timothy/Titus, Walter L. Liefeld

Hebrews, George H. Guthrie

James, David P. Nystrom

1 Peter, Scot McKnight

2 Peter/Jude, Douglas J. Moo

Letters of John, Gary M. Burge

Revelation, Craig S. Keener

To see which titles are available,
visit our web site at www.zondervan.com

NIV Application Commentary
Series Introduction

THE NIV APPLICATION COMMENTARY SERIES is unique. Most commentaries help us make the journey from our world back to the world of the Bible. They enable us to cross the barriers of time, culture, language, and geography that separate us from the biblical world. Yet they only offer a one-way ticket to the past and assume that we can somehow make the return journey on our own. Once they have explained the *original meaning* of a book or passage, these commentaries give us little or no help in exploring its *contemporary significance*. The information they offer is valuable, but the job is only half done.

Recently, a few commentaries have included some contemporary application as *one* of their goals. Yet that application is often sketchy or moralistic, and some volumes sound more like printed sermons than commentaries.

The primary goal of the NIV Application Commentary Series is to help you with the difficult but vital task of bringing an ancient message into a modern context. The series not only focuses on application as a finished product but also helps you think through the *process* of moving from the original meaning of a passage to its contemporary significance. These are commentaries, not popular expositions. They are works of reference, not devotional literature.

The format of the series is designed to achieve the goals of the series. Each passage is treated in three sections: *Original Meaning, Bridging Contexts*, and *Contemporary Significance*.

THIS SECTION HELPS you understand the meaning of the biblical text in its original context. All of the elements of traditional exegesis—in concise form—are discussed here. These include the historical, literary, and cultural context of the passage. The authors discuss matters related to grammar and syntax and the meaning of biblical words.[1] They also seek to explore the main ideas of the passage and how the biblical author develops those ideas.

---

1. Please note that in general, when the authors discuss words in the original biblical languages, the series uses a general rather than a scholarly method of transliteration.

After reading this section, you will understand the problems, questions, and concerns of the *original audience* and how the biblical author addressed those issues. This understanding is foundational to any legitimate application of the text today.

THIS SECTION BUILDS a bridge between the world of the Bible and the world of today, between the original context and the contemporary context, by focusing on both the timely and timeless aspects of the text.

God's Word is *timely*. The authors of Scripture spoke to specific situations, problems, and questions. The author of Joshua encouraged the faith of his original readers by narrating the destruction of Jericho, a seemingly impregnable city, at the hands of an angry warrior God (Josh. 6). Paul warned the Galatians about the consequences of circumcision and the dangers of trying to be justified by law (Gal. 5:2–5). The author of Hebrews tried to convince his readers that Christ is superior to Moses, the Aaronic priests, and the Old Testament sacrifices. John urged his readers to "test the spirits" of those who taught a form of incipient Gnosticism (1 John 4:1–6). In each of these cases, the timely nature of Scripture enables us to hear God's Word in situations that were *concrete* rather than abstract.

Yet the timely nature of Scripture also creates problems. Our situations, difficulties, and questions are not always directly related to those faced by the people in the Bible. Therefore, God's word to them does not always seem relevant to us. For example, when was the last time someone urged you to be circumcised, claiming that it was a necessary part of justification? How many people today care whether Christ is superior to the Aaronic priests? And how can a "test" designed to expose incipient Gnosticism be of any value in a modern culture?

Fortunately, Scripture is not only timely but *timeless*. Just as God spoke to the original audience, so he still speaks to us through the pages of Scripture. Because we share a common humanity with the people of the Bible, we discover a *universal dimension* in the problems they faced and the solutions God gave them. The timeless nature of Scripture enables it to speak with power in every time and in every culture.

Those who fail to recognize that Scripture is both timely and timeless run into a host of problems. For example, those who are intimidated by timely books such as Hebrews, Galatians, or Deuteronomy might avoid reading them because they seem meaningless today. At the other extreme, those who are convinced of the timeless nature of Scripture, but who fail to discern its timely element, may "wax eloquent" about the Melchizedekian priest-hood to a sleeping congregation, or worse still, try to apply the holy wars of the Old Testament in a physical way to God's enemies today.

The purpose of this section, therefore, is to help you discern what is time-less in the timely pages of the Bible—and what is not. For example, how do the holy wars of the Old Testament relate to the spiritual warfare of the New? If Paul's primary concern is not circumcision (as he tells us in Gal. 5:6), what *is* he concerned about? If discussions about the Aaronic priesthood or Melchizedek seem irrelevant today, what is of abiding value in these passages? If people try to "test the spirits" today with a test designed for a specific first-century heresy, what other biblical test might be more appropriate?

Yet this section does not merely uncover that which is timeless in a passage but also helps you to see *how* it is uncovered. The authors of the commentaries seek to take what is implicit in the text and make it explicit, to take a process that normally is intuitive and explain it in a logical, orderly fashion. How do we know that circumcision is not Paul's primary concern? What clues in the text or its context help us realize that Paul's real concern is at a deeper level?

Of course, those passages in which the historical distance between us and the original readers is greatest require a longer treatment. Conversely, those passages in which the historical distance is smaller or seemingly nonex-istent require less attention.

One final clarification. Because this section prepares the way for dis-cussing the contemporary significance of the passage, there is not always a sharp distinction or a clear break between this section and the one that fol-lows. Yet when both sections are read together, you should have a strong sense of moving from the world of the Bible to the world of today.

 THIS SECTION ALLOWS the biblical message to speak with as much power today as it did when it was first written. How can you apply what you learned about Jerusalem, Ephesus, or Corinth to our present-day needs in Chicago, Los Angeles, or London? How can you take a message originally spoken in Greek, Hebrew, and Aramaic and com-municate it clearly in our own language? How can you take the eternal truths originally spoken in a different time and culture and apply them to the sim-ilar-yet-different needs of our culture?

In order to achieve these goals, this section gives you help in several key areas.

(1) It helps you identify contemporary situations, problems, or questions that are truly comparable to those faced by the original audience. Because

contemporary situations are seldom identical to those faced by the original audience, you must seek situations that are analogous if your applications are to be relevant.

(2) This section explores a variety of contexts in which the passage might be applied today. You will look at personal applications, but you will also be encouraged to think beyond private concerns to the society and culture at large.

(3) This section will alert you to any problems or difficulties you might encounter in seeking to apply the passage. And if there are several legitimate ways to apply a passage (areas in which Christians disagree), the author will bring these to your attention and help you think through the issues involved.

In seeking to achieve these goals, the contributors to this series attempt to avoid two extremes. They avoid making such specific applications that the commentary might quickly become dated. They also avoid discussing the significance of the passage in such a general way that it fails to engage contemporary life and culture.

Above all, contributors to this series have made a diligent effort not to sound moralistic or preachy. The NIV Application Commentary Series does not seek to provide ready-made sermon materials but rather tools, ideas, and insights that will help you communicate God's Word with power. If we help you to achieve that goal, then we have fulfilled the purpose for this series.

The Editors

General Editor's Preface

IN A WORLD OF DIVISIONS—ethnic, racial, national, religious—there has never been a more appropriate time for unity and healing. One of the purposes the apostle Paul has in writing Romans, as Doug Moo so brilliantly shows in the commentary that follows, is to unify a divided Christian community in Rome. The community there was probably started by Jewish Christians, but their numbers were quickly matched by an equal number of Gentile Christians. These two groups are now at loggerheads. The ongoing tendency for old church members to resent newcomers is exacerbated by different ethnic and religious histories.

Paul is at a lull in his work. He wants to break new missionary ground, perhaps in Spain. He desires the support of the most western outpost of Christianity, Rome, to do so. And he does not want to see twenty-five years of missionary work dissolve in factional strife. So for a couple of practical reasons he wants to bring peace among Jewish and Gentile Christians.

It is obvious, however, that his rationale for peace goes beyond the practical. If his reasons were purely practical, his strategies would be different. In order to gain support for his Spanish initiative he would make a presentation of his idea, arguing that unified support is the only way to accomplish the task. He could make what in the first century A.D. passed for "sociological" arguments for solidarity or "psychological" benefits of reconciliation.

Paul, however, chooses neither of those options. Instead, he argues for solidarity and reconciliation using *doctrine* as his rationale. The book of Romans is about healing divisions in the church with doctrine rather than with sociology, psychology, business management, or even reason to do the work. It is as if Paul said to the church at Rome, "Let's stop and think about this in the same way God thinks about this. *Then* let's act."

Using Christian doctrine to solve problems of disunity and strife is fast becoming an endangered methodology. Doing so means one eventually has to make judgments about right and wrong—and calling someone wrong these days is interpreted, in religious circles at least, as intellectual harassment. Using doctrine means being willing to draw boundaries as perimeters for Christian faith, and many consider boundaries to be the equivalent of religious red-lining.

To be sure, the anti-doctrine forces in our society make an important point. Sometimes human reason can be used in our theological discussions as a synonym for biblical teaching. Theology, some suggest, is a reasonable exercise, so let's get together and figure out what God is up to. Unity comes from agreement. This approach is as dangerous an understanding of the church's task as are the sociological and psychological ones.

Paul has a different idea. He makes clear in the sixteen chapters of Romans that the healing of divisions in the church comes from getting in touch with God's plan for humankind: what God has done in the past through Israel, what God is doing now through Jesus (which includes Gentiles), and what God projects for the future of the church. Paul does not present a systematic argument as much as faithfully portrays the gospel story. One does not argue oneself to faith, one accedes to the trajectories of the story. That story, Paul tells us, is that of the church engaging the world in ever widening circles of contact.

Yes, Paul says that unity comes from unifying around an insight: The church as God has intended it is a missionary church. Paul's next wider circle is Spain. He tells Jewish Christians and Gentile Christians that unity comes not from introspective therapy that leads to liking one another or agreeing with one another. It comes, rather, from getting on board the gospel train that is always, everywhere, just now leaving the station. The strong understand this; the weak are in the process of getting on board. To understand Romans, we must during our reading always listen for the voice of the conductor, Paul, telling us it is time to leave.

Terry C. Muck

Abbreviations

AB	Anchor Bible
BAGD	Bauer, Arndt, Gingrich, Danker, *A Greek-English Lexicon of the New Testament*
BECNT	Baker Exegetical Commentary on the New Testament
BBR	*Bulletin for Biblical Research*
BSac	*Bibliotheca Sacra*
CBQ	*Catholic Biblical Quarterly*
EvQ	*Evangelical Quarterly*
ExpTim	*Expository Times*
GTJ	*Grace Theological Journal*
HNTC	Harper New Testament Commentary
ICC	International Critical Commentary
JB	Jerusalem Bible
JBL	*Journal of Biblical Literature*
JETS	*Journal of the Evangelical Theological Society*
JRE	*Journal of Religion and Ethics*
JSNT	*Journal for the Study of the New Testament*
JSNTSup	Journal for the Study of the New Testament Supplement Series
JTS	*Journal of Theological Studies*
J.W.	*Jewish War*
KJV	King James Version
LXX	The Septuagint (Greek translation of the Old Testament)
m.	*Mishnah*
NAB	New American Bible
NASB	New American Standard Bible
NEB	New English Bible
NICNT	New International Commentary on the New Testament
NIV	New International Version
NIVAC	NIV Application Commentary
NJB	New Jerusalem Bible
NLT	New Living Translation
NovT	*Novum Testamentum*
NRSV	New Revised Standard Version
NTS	*New Testament Studies*
PNTC	Pillar New Testament Commentary

Abbreviations

REB	Revised English Bible
RSV	Revised Standard Version
SBL	Society of Biblical Literature
SBLDS	Society of Biblical Literature Dissertation Series
SJT	*Scottish Journal of Theology*
SNTSMS	Society for New Testament Studies Monograph Series
TDNT	*Theological Dictionary of the New Testament*
TEV	Today's English Version
TNTC	Tyndale New Testament Commentaries
TrinJ	*Trinity Journal*
TynBul	*Tyndale Bulletin*
TZ	*Theologische Zeitschrift*
WBC	Word Biblical Commentary
WTJ	*Westminster Theological Journal*

Introduction

FOUR YEARS AGO, my second son, David, went off to a secular college. He had been brought up in the church and attended Sunday school and youth group faithfully. He was raised in a Christian household, where the Bible was read and studied and the things of the Lord were regularly discussed. Yet he had not been at college long before he was deluging me with questions. "How do we Christians respond to the Buddhist view of God? What am I supposed to think about one of the nicest guys on campus—who just happens to be gay? What is wrong with New Age religion? How can I prove that there is such a thing as absolute truth?" Thrown into the cauldron of contemporary pluralism, David was floundering. He did not doubt his own faith, but he had serious problems figuring out just what his Christian convictions meant in the rough-and-tumble of intellectual debate.

David is not alone. Most Christians today are brought into direct touch with other religious options—at work, at school, at social gatherings—in ways that did not happen so often in the past. Meeting the challenge of Islam seemed easy when we learned rote responses out of a book; it may not seem as easy when we enter into discussion with a live Muslim who lives next door. What such conversations often expose is the pitifully shallow understanding of our own faith.

Many evangelical Christians sit in churches in which they are spoon-fed stock answers to current issues. They are against abortion, believe homosexual activity is a sin, and are against environmentalism. All too few put down roots into the soil of Christian theology deeply enough to know *why* they hold such views and to be able to distinguish between which ones are genuinely Christian and which the product of a politically oriented view of Christianity. For instance, opposition to abortion and homosexuality are, I think, genuinely Christian views. But, as a Christian environmentalist, I am distressed to hear brothers and sisters in my own church aping certain prominent radio preachers, lumping all environmentalists into the category of New Age tree huggers, and dismissing the whole movement as a secularist plot.

What we badly need is solid grounding in the Christian worldview. We need to know how to think "Christianly" about everything in our culture, not just what we happen to have been taught. If we are to be prepared to respond to the array of religious options in our culture and to live consistently Christian lives, we must operate from the broad perspective of the Christian understanding of God, the world, and human beings. If the church is to have a meaningful and persuasive voice in the "culture wars," it will also have to enunciate clearly, lovingly, and persuasively the Christian interpretation of reality.

What does all this have to do with Romans? Lots. For Romans is, finally, about worldview. As most Christians know, Romans is "doctrinal." That description scares many off, who are afraid that Romans will be both dry and difficult. It is certainly difficult at times. And preachers and teachers—to our shame—can sometimes make it pretty dry too. But think about what Romans teaches us: what human beings really are like and what they need, what God has done to provide a way of escape from our estrangement and mortality, and what a lifestyle that grows out of a Christian worldview looks like. Such topics should certainly not be dry or boring!

In fact, Romans is one of the most interesting and engaging books in the Bible—precisely because it shapes the way we think about so much of the universe we inhabit. I am convinced that the contemporary church desperately needs to grapple with what is going on in Romans. In the pages that follow, I hope I can help Christians to probe this wonderful book and bring its eternal message into our own situation. I intend to show how the truths that Romans teaches affect the practice of the faith. But, true to the nature and purpose of Romans, I have especially focused on what Romans tells us about how we are to *think*.

Thus far we have talked about Romans as a great doctrinal treatise, which it is. But we will badly misunderstand that doctrine unless we root it in the specific setting of the first-century church. Paul did not sit down one day and decide to write a textbook on doctrine. He wrote a *letter*. He wrote it to a specific church to handle some problems the church was facing. As we will argue below, those circumstances combined to turn Romans into a book that tackles basic issues of the Christian worldview. But only by recognizing the cultural setting for this statement of the Christian worldview will we be able rightly to understand and apply it. So in the pages that follow we will sketch the circumstances that we need to know if we are to apprehend accurately what God wants to teach us today through his inspired words in this letter to the Romans.

Paul

ROMANS CLAIMS TO be written by Paul the apostle (1:1)—or, we might more accurately say, composed by Paul, who uses Tertius as his "amanuensis," or scribe, to "write down" what Paul dictates to him (see 16:22). The apostle tells us clearly what his situation is when he composes the letter. His reference to Cenchrea in 16:1 suggests he is staying in Corinth at the time, for Cenchrea was the seaport next to Corinth. He has finished an important stage of his missionary work; as he puts it in 15:19, "from Jerusalem all the way around to Illyricum, I have fully proclaimed the gospel of Christ." The geography

Paul describes here includes all the churches he has planted on his famous three "missionary journeys" (Acts 13–20), in south Galatia (Pisidian Antioch, Lystra, Iconium, and Derbe), and in the Roman provinces of Asia (Ephesus), Macedonia (Philippi, Thessalonica), and Achaia (Corinth).

Now Paul is ready for a fresh challenge, to plant churches in completely new territory. He has decided that territory will be Spain (Rom. 15:23–24, 28). But before he goes there, he intends to return to Jerusalem to hand over to the church there the money he has been collecting from the Gentile churches (15:25–27). Then on his way from Jerusalem to Spain, Paul plans to stop off in Rome (15:23–24, 29).

From these references, it is clear that Paul writes Romans while in Corinth during the third missionary journey (Acts 20:2–3). This is probably in A.D. 57, give or take a year. What is most significant for our understanding of Romans is the sense Paul gives us of having reached an important transition point in his missionary career. He has been preaching the gospel for almost twenty-five years; he has planted thriving churches over much of the northeastern Mediterranean part of the Roman empire; he has hammered out his theology on the anvil of pastoral problems and debates with opposing factions. He thus writes Romans during a lull in his ministry, at a time when he can reflect on what he has come to believe and what it may mean for the church.

These circumstances help explain why we find so much general doctrinal discussion in Romans. Yet without taking anything away from this point, we must also recall that Romans is "Romans"—that is, Paul sends it as a letter to Christians living in Rome. Surely their circumstances are as important in determining the shape of this letter as are Paul's.

Rome

WHAT DO WE know about these Christians in Rome? The book of Acts tells us nothing about the founding of the church. But Luke does tell us that Jews from Rome were among those who saw the pouring out of the Spirit on the Day of Pentecost (2:10). We may surmise that some of them were among the three thousand converted on that day (2:41) and that they brought their new belief in Jesus as Messiah back with them to Rome. So the church in Rome, as the church father Ambrosiaster later claimed, probably had its origins in the synagogue.[1]

---

1. See *Patrologia Latina*, vol. 17, col. 46. Church tradition in the fourth century (the *Catalogus Liberianus*) names Peter as the founder and first bishop of the Roman church. But earlier tradition has both Peter and Paul involved in the founding of the church (Ireneaus, *Adv. Her.* 3.1.2; 3.3.1). Most modern scholars agree that Peter had no role in founding the church at Rome (see, e.g., Oscar Cullmann, *Peter: Disciple, Apostle, Martyr* [Philadelphia: Westminster, 1962], 72–157).

There were many synagogues in Rome by the first century A.D.; enough Jews had emigrated to Rome to make up a significant portion of the population.[2] But if the church was Jewish in origin, it probably added a significant Gentile element at an early time. Many of the initial Gentile converts would have come from the ranks of the "God-fearers," those Gentiles who were not full-fledged Jews because they were not circumcised, but who attended the synagogue and followed the teachings of Judaism.

The Jewish character of Christianity in Rome suddenly and drastically changed. In A.D. 49 Emperor Claudius, out of exasperation with squabbles among the Jews about *Chrestus* (probably a reference to Jesus' claims to be the "Christ"), issued an edict that required all Jews to leave Rome.[3] Jewish-Christians (like Priscilla and Aquila; cf. Acts 18:2) would have been included. Overnight, therefore, the church in Rome became virtually 100 percent Gentile.

By the time Paul writes, Jews were allowed back into Rome (see, again, Priscilla and Aquila, Rom. 16:3). But they came back to a church dominated by Gentiles. One can imagine the kind of social tension that such a situation would create. Jews, who stand in the heritage from which Christianity has sprung and who were at one time the leaders of the community, now find themselves in a minority. Several key emphases of the letter make good sense against this background: the preoccupation with the Jewish law and its place in the life of Christians (e.g., Rom. 7), Paul's scolding of the Gentile Christians for their arrogance (11:18–23, 25; cf. 13–14), and, most of all, his admonitions to the strong and the weak (14:1–15:13).[4]

The Letter to the Romans

HAVING BRIEFLY SURVEYED the circumstances of Paul and the Roman church, we are now in a position to turn to the letter itself. Six issues relevant to the way we read the letter need to be clarified: its integrity, form, audience, purpose, theme, and structure.

---

2. See Philo, *Embassy to Gaius*. Note the discussions in W. Wiefel, "The Jewish Community in Ancient Rome and the Origins of Roman Christianity," in *The Romans Debate*, ed. K. Donfried (2d ed.; Peabody, Mass.: Hendrickson, 1991), 86–92.

3. Reference to the edict of Claudius comes in Suetonius, *Life of Claudius* 25.2. The date of this decree is debated, some scholars putting it later than A.D. 49. But a strong case for the A.D. 49 date, first mentioned by the fifth-century writer Orosius, can be made (e.g., E. Mary Smallwood, *The Jews Under Roman Rule* [Leiden: Brill, 1976], 210–16). The A.D. 49 date also fits perfectly with the chronology presumed in Acts 18:2.

4. See esp. Wiefel, "Jewish Community," for the implications of this scenario.

Integrity

IN A LITERARY context, a book's integrity refers to its textual coherence. In other words, we inquire about whether the sixteen-chapter text of Romans that we have in our Bibles is a single letter written by Paul on one occasion. A number of scholars have questioned this point, and they have some evidence in the manuscripts to back up their questions. While only a few late and insignificant witnesses leave out any substantial portion of Romans, several early and important manuscripts rearrange the text. One, for instance, puts the doxology (16:25–27) at the end of chapter 15 (the early papyrus 𝔭46), while several others put it after chapter 14 (the uncials A, P, and Y, as well as several minuscules).

These differences have led to various theories about the original form of Romans. The most popular of these holds that Paul's original letter to the Romans consisted of 1:1–15:33. Chapter 16 was added when Paul sent a copy of the letter to the church at Ephesus. This theory explains the many greetings in chapter 16, which seem strange in a letter written to a church Paul has never visited but makes perfect sense in a letter to a church he knows intimately.[5] But few modern scholars follow this theory—or others like it. No significant manuscript of Romans omits chapter 16. The differing placements of the doxology probably reflect the efforts of editors to "generalize" the message of Romans for the church.[6] Paul can greet so many people in Rome because he has encountered so many of them during the time of their exile. Virtually all modern commentators treat the text printed in our modern Greek testaments and translated into our English versions as substantially the original text Paul wrote to the Roman Christians.

Form

ROMANS IS A letter, but what kind of letter? Ancient people wrote many different kinds of letters, ranging from brief family notes ("Dear Dad: Send money") to long, literary compositions intended for publication. Paul's letters clearly fall between these extremes. All of them—even those to individuals, like 1 and 2 Timothy, Titus, and Philemon—have broad pastoral purposes. But none of them has the self-conscious literary preoccupation that marks the "public" letter. They are all written to specific people or churches and deal with issues specific (if not limited to) those addressees.

---

5. See esp. T. W. Manson, "St. Paul's Letter to the Romans—and Others," in *The Romans Debate*, 3–15.

6. See esp. the thorough treatment of Harry Gamble Jr., *The Textual History of the Letter to the Romans: A Study in Textual and Literary Criticism* (Grand Rapids: Eerdmans, 1977).

Yet Romans (we can also add Ephesians) is the letter least ostensibly specific. Its opening (1:1–15) and closing (15:14–16:27) mark it clearly as a letter. But what is remarkable is the way the body of the letter develops by its own internal logic. Paul does not seem to be dealing with issues and problems presented to him by the church but to be mounting an argument that proceeds by its own inertia. Paul clearly thinks his argument has relevance to situations in the Roman community. This becomes explicit in chapter 11, as he uses his argument about Israel's place in salvation history to berate Gentiles in Rome for arrogance. Moreover, 14:1–15:13 is directed to a specific situation in Rome. But even this text, which has a parallel in 1 Corinthians 8–10, focuses more on principles than on specifics.

The body of Romans, then, is in the form of a tractate or treatise. In it Paul addresses basic theological issues against the backdrop of early Christianity and with reference to some affairs in the Roman community. But these contexts do play a large role in dictating the topics he treats. The tradition of viewing Romans as a kind of mini-systematic theology founders on just this selectivity. What systematic theology would omit a significant discussion of Christology, or eschatology, or ecclesiology—as Romans does? And what systematic theology would focus so relentlessly on issues such as Jewish-Gentile relationships and the place of the Mosaic law in the history of salvation?

In other words, Romans is theological through and through—but it is *occasional*, not *systematic* theology. The first-century situation of the church at large and the church in Rome in particular leads Paul to develop his theology on certain particular issues. But in God's providence, those situations are such that Paul ends up addressing issues of perennial theological significance.

Audience

THE CHURCH AT Rome, as we have seen, was made up of both Jews and Gentiles, with Gentiles having recently become the majority group. Paul's letter seems to reflect just this balance.

Paul reflects the Gentile dominance by treating the church as a Gentile community. He addresses himself to "you [Gentiles]" (1:6; cf. comments on 1:5) and treats the Roman church as one that belongs within his province as "minister of Christ Jesus to the Gentiles" (15:15–16; cf. 1:13). He directly addresses Gentile Christians in 11:13–25. Yet he also gives evidence that he has Jewish Christians in view. He greets several of his "relatives" in chapter 16 (vv. 7, 11); and Priscilla and Aquila (16:3–4) are also, of course, Jewish. He calls Abraham *"our* forefather" (4:1) and claims in 7:1 to be addressing "[those] who know the law." And, of course, the letter is shot through with motifs especially significant for Jewish Christians: the failure of the old covenant (ch. 2), the Mosaic law (3:20, 31; 4:15; 5:13–14, 20; 6:14, 15; ch. 7; 9:30–10:8), and Israel's place in salvation history (chs. 9–11).

A few scholars have tried to minimize one side of this evidence or the other, arguing that the letter is addressed only to Jewish Christians[7] or only to Gentile Christians.[8] But such conclusions can only be achieved by suppressing one side of the evidence or the other. With the large majority of modern scholars, therefore, we conclude that Paul's audience in Romans includes both Gentile and Jewish Christians, with Gentile Christians in the majority.[9]

Purpose

WHY DOES PAUL write this particular letter to the Roman church? Since he gives no clear answer to that question in the letter itself, scholars have had a field day in supplying their own answers. We may group the options within two categories: theories that focus on Paul's own circumstances, and theories that focus on the circumstances of the Roman church.

Theories focusing on Paul's circumstances. The three main theories in this category are related to places that Paul mentions, or that are implicit, in Romans 15.

Corinth. As we have seen, Paul writes from Corinth. We have also noted that Paul's stay in Corinth marks a significant transition point in his ministry. He has a kind of "breathing space" after the hectic years of ministry in the east and before he heads on to Jerusalem, Rome, and Spain. One explanation of Romans, then, is that it is a kind of summary of Paul's theological beliefs that he draws up during that hiatus in missionary work.[10] We may agree that Romans reflects the mature thinking of an apostle seasoned by years of ministry and controversy. But this theory does not explain why Paul sends this letter *to Rome.*

Jerusalem. The next stop on Paul's itinerary is Jerusalem, where he plans to deliver to the Jewish Christians the money he has been collecting from the Gentile churches he founded. Paul is clearly concerned about this ministry

---

7. This was the view of the influential nineteenth-century "Tübingen" scholar, F. C. Baur (*Paul the Apostle of Jesus Christ: His Life and Work, His Epistles and His Doctrine* [2d ed.; 2 vols.; London: Williams & Norgate, 1876], 1:331–65). See also, e.g., F. Watson, *Paul, Judaism, and the Gentiles* (SNTSMS 56; Cambridge: Cambridge Univ. Press, 1986), 103–7.

8. See esp. J. Munck, *Paul and the Salvation of Mankind* (London: SCM, 1959), 200–209; A. Jülicher, *Introduction to the New Testament* (London: Smith and Elder, 1904), 112–15.

9. For a representative statement, see Werner Georg Kümmel, *Introduction to the New Testament* (London: SCM, 1975), 309–11.

10. See esp. Gunther Bornkamm, "The Letter to the Romans as Paul's Last Will and Testament," in *The Romans Debate*, 16–28.

and how it will be received (15:30–32). He wants it to be a tangible witness to the unity between Jews and Gentiles in the church. Thus, as J. Jervell has suggested, Paul is so preoccupied with this issue that he delivers in Romans the speech he hopes to make in Jerusalem.[11] Again, there is something to this idea. The collection is important for Paul, and it may have played a role in setting the agenda of Romans. But the collection is not *that* important. Why would Paul choose Rome as the recipient of such a speech?

Spain. Paul's ultimate destination is Spain. As he clearly hints in 15:24, he is coming to Rome, among other things, to get the Romans to help him with that mission. But Paul has never been to Rome. Moreover, he is a controversial figure in the early church. As both a faithful Jew and God's "point man" in opening the Gentile mission, he has been constantly under suspicion. Jewish Christians thought he was giving too much of the old tradition away, whereas Gentile Christians thought he was still too Jewish. A lot of false rumors about what he teaches and does swirl around him (cf. 3:8). Paul therefore probably knows he is going to have to clear the air if he expects the Romans to support him. Thus, it is argued, he writes Romans to clarify just what he believes.

Romans, in other words, is his "doctrinal statement," sent on ahead to demonstrate his orthodoxy and worthiness of missionary support.[12] Most scholars agree that this purpose plays some role in Romans. I, myself, think it is a significant reason for Paul's writing. But it still does not explain everything about Romans. Indeed, any explanation of the letter that does not take into account some of the specifics about the Romans themselves is finally inadequate.

Theories focusing on the Romans' circumstances. Modern scholars insist that Romans, as a real letter, must have been written to respond to the needs of the Roman congregation. That much can be granted, though some scholars—I think, illegitimately—confine those needs to practical ones. Could not the Romans have had a general need to be informed about various Christian beliefs—a need Paul satisfies by writing a theological treatise? One cannot dismiss the possibility that Romans is a theological tractate simply by appealing to its epistolary form.

Nevertheless, the evidence of the letter itself suggests that at least one specific circumstance in the Roman community plays a significant role in Paul's purpose in Romans. I refer to the section on the strong and the weak (14:1–15:13). Contemporary scholars generally agree that the debate between these two groups in Rome reflects the community's division between Gen-

---

11. Jacob Jervell, "The Letter to Jerusalem," in *The Romans Debate*, 53–64.
12. See esp. Morris, *The Epistle to the Romans* (PNTC; Grand Rapids: Eerdmans, 1988), 17.

tile and Jewish Christians. Paul implies that these two groups are divided over whether believers need to obey certain provisions of the Mosaic law. (See comments on this section in the commentary.) A popular theory about the letter's purpose today, then, is that Paul writes Romans to help heal this division. Romans 14:1–15:13 represents the heart of the letter; the theology of the earlier chapters simply prepares the way for this climactic appeal.[13]

The very presence of this section in the letter makes it clear that we must include Paul's desire to reconcile these two parties in Rome as part of his purpose in Romans. Moreover, the theological focus on Jews and Gentiles in many parts of the letter also fits this purpose well. But Paul raises other theological issues in Romans, not so clearly related to this dispute (see esp. chs. 5–8). In addition, if this were Paul's only purpose, it is difficult to explain why he includes the exhortations in chapters 12–13.

Paul's purpose in Romans, therefore, cannot be restricted to any one of these suggestions. He has several "reasons for Romans."[14] But the various purposes share a common denominator: Paul's missionary situation.[15] The past battles to define and defend the gospel, the coming crisis in Jerusalem, the need to secure a logistical base for his outreach in Spain, the importance of unifying the Roman Christians around a common vision of the gospel—all these specific purposes conspire to lead Paul to rehearse his understanding of the gospel.

What is the "good news" of Jesus Christ? Why do people need to hear it? How can they experience it? What will it mean for their future? And what does the good news have to do with everyday life? These large and basic questions form Paul's agenda in Romans—an agenda dictated by a combination of circumstances and purposes. These same purposes force Paul to concentrate attention especially on one particular question: What does the gospel mean for the flow of salvation history? Or, broken down into some of its specific components, does the Old Testament and the good news about Jesus fit into one coherent plan of God? What happens to the law of Moses or to God's promise to Israel? The breaking of the "ethnic boundary" of Israel by the introduction of Gentiles into the people of God makes this question critical to Christian self-definition.

---

13. See esp. Paul S. Minear, *The Obedience of Faith: The Purpose of Paul in the Letter to the Romans* (Naperville, Ill.: Allenson, 1971); Willi Marxsen, *Introduction to the New Testament* (Philadelphia: Fortress, 1968), 92–104; W. S. Campbell, "Why Did Paul Write Romans?" *ExpTim* 85 (1974): 264–69; Karl Donfried, "A Short Note on Romans 16," in *The Romans Debate*, 46–48.

14. The title of A. J. M. Wedderburn's monograph, in which he argues precisely this point (Edinburgh: T. & T. Clark, 1991).

15. See J. A. Jervis, *The Purpose of Romans: A Comparative Letter Structure Investigation* (Sheffield: JSOT, 1991), esp. 158–63.

The salvation-historical issue, with all its various facets, was at the center of the early Christian movement as it sought to define itself over against both Judaism and paganism. Jewish Christians and Gentile Christians, at Rome as elsewhere, have different opinions on these matters. Paul must therefore address in Romans the very nature of the gospel. Because he does so, it has a purpose that transcends its immediate circumstances. By tackling such fundamental theological issues, Paul writes a letter that makes an enduring and vital contribution to Christians' understanding of who they are and what they believe. As Luther therefore said:

> [Romans] is worthy not only that every Christian should know it word for word, by heart, but occupy himself with it every day, as the daily bread of the soul. It can never be read or pondered too much, and the more it is dealt with the more precious it becomes, and the better it tastes.[16]

Theme

WE HAVE INEVITABLY begun to discuss the theme of Romans in examining its purpose. But we now want to address this matter more directly. Two preliminary points should be made. (1) We must beware the danger of reductionism, that is, the assumption that Romans *must* have a single, overarching theme. We frequently oversimplify biblical books by sticking a convenient tag on them. Philippians is "about" joy; Ephesians is "about" the church; 1 Thessalonians is "about" eschatology, etc. While these tags may help us recall some of the key features of these books, they can also become a straightjacket that forces everything in the letter into one narrow channel. A letter need not be about only one thing. Only if we can honestly and fairly fit most of the content of a book under a certain theme should we propose it as a serious option.

(2) In talking about the theme of Romans, we are also opening up an important and controversial issue in current assessments of the letter—and indeed, of all of Paul's theology. The issue could not be more fundamental: What is Romans basically about? Is it about the individual sinner's restoration to fellowship with God? Or is it about the extension of God's grace to Gentiles in the new era of salvation history? Is Romans oriented vertically (God-man) or horizontally (Jew-Gentile)?

Of course, casting the issue in such stark alternatives grossly oversimplifies it. Almost all scholars acknowledge that both play some role in the letter. But these two alternatives do help us to conceptualize the issue by

---

16. Luther, "Preface to the Epistle to the Romans" (1522).

establishing the ends of the spectrum of opinion. Our answer to this question will dictate our reading strategy and have a big impact on our interpretation of text after text. The smaller pieces of the puzzle only make sense in light of the big picture.

A quick historical sketch will introduce some of the key options and issues. The Reformers and their heirs have located the essence of Romans in the individual's relationship to God. "Justification by faith" was often isolated as the key idea of the letter. Many of us have absorbed this way of thinking about Romans. If asked what Romans is basically about, we tend to respond in terms of the old "Romans Road" of salvation: how a person can move from wrath to glory by accepting the completed work of Jesus Christ on the cross by faith.

This way of reading Romans received its first serious challenge in the late 1800s and early 1900s, when a few scholars began arguing that justification is not really an important issue in Romans. It is little more than a "battle doctrine" that Paul formulates in debate with Jews. The real theme of Romans lies not in the justification language of chapters 1–4 but in the "mystical union" concept of chapters 5–8.[17]

But a more serious blow to the individualist approach to Romans is the claim that Paul simply would not think in such personal categories. In a famous article, Krister Stendahl argued that generations of scholars have read into Paul, and Romans, a modern preoccupation with the individual that is simply not present in Paul's day. Luther's question was, "How can a sinner get right with a wrathful God?" But that is not Paul's question. Typical of the corporate way of thinking at that time, he wants to answer the question: "How can Jews and Gentiles cohere in one people of God?"[18]

Stendahl's general approach has been widely adopted in recent scholarship on Romans. The heart of Romans is not found in either chapters 1–4 ("justification by faith") or chapters 5–8 ("mystical union with Christ") but in chapters 9–11: Who now constitutes the people of God? This approach is part of a larger revolution in approaches to Paul and Judaism, dubbed the "new perspective on Paul." One of the best advocates of this approach is James D. G. Dunn, and his commentary in the Word Biblical Commentary series is the most reasonable attempt to explain Romans from that new perspective.

What are we to make of all this? As I write, these questions are still being sharply debated; no consensus has emerged—perhaps because each "side" in

---

17. See esp. Wilhelm Wrede, *Paul* (London: Philip Green, 1907), 123–25; Albert Schweitzer, *The Mysticism of Paul the Apostle* (London: A. & C. Black, 1931), 205–26.

18. Krister Stendahl, "The Apostle Paul and the Introspective Conscience of the West," *Harvard Theological Review* 56 (1963): 199–215.

the debate has some truth. The modern scholars who focus on the "people" issue in Romans have rightly put their finger on a key motif in the letter. Paul is constantly bringing in the issue of Jew and Gentile, from the theme of the letter on ("first for the Jew, then for the Gentile" [1:16]). Hardly a topic goes by without Paul's bringing in this facet of the issue. Romans 9–11 are clearly directed to this issue. It will simply not do, as a few older commentators did, to try to fit these chapters under an "individual" approach by making their topic predestination.

But many modern scholars have gone too far in this direction, unfairly minimizing the great amount of material in Romans that is about the individual. When Paul sketches the human predicament in chapters 1–3, he shows how it specifically affects both Jew and Gentile. But the predicament, at bottom, is a *human* one—not a Jewish or a Gentile one. The salvation offered in Christ through faith (3:21–4:25) is also profoundly individualistic: Each person must accept the gift for himself or herself. Similarly, in chapters 5–8 it is the individual who is rescued from death in Adam by the obedience of Christ and who is promised glory with God in the last day. The individual, of course, is always part of a larger body—whether "in Adam" or "in Christ." I have no desire to minimize the importance of the corporate element in Paul. But Paul is ultimately concerned with the individual.

What, then, is Romans about? I am uncomfortable with both of the "stock" answers. Justification by faith is, I think, an absolutely vital teaching in the letter, but I don't think it is broad enough to "cover" the content of Romans as a whole. Gentile inclusion is likewise a vital part of the letter—but it is more of a motif that runs through the whole than a theme. The best candidate for the theme of Romans, I would argue, is the "gospel." Paul highlights this concept in the opening and closing sections of the letter (1:1, 2, 9, 15; 15:16, 19), and it is the key word in his own statement of the letter's theme: "I am not ashamed of the gospel . . . " (1:16). We require a theme as broad as the gospel to encompass the diversity of topics the apostle handles in the letter. Moreover, as I have argued, Romans grows out Paul's missionary situation, and the gospel he preaches is the heart of that missionary work.

Structure

J. C. BEKER has warned about forcing "architectonic" structures on New Testament letters that were never written with such logical precision in mind.[19] His warning is well-taken. We can easily force material out of the shape that the original author intended by insisting that it fit into the mold of our "outline" form. But for all their drawbacks, outlines do help us get a picture of

---

19. J. C. Beker, *The Theology of Paul the Apostle* (Philadelphia: Fortress, 1980), 64–69.

where a book is going. And Romans, precisely because it is so logical in orientation, invites us to seek its underlying structure and movement.

My own outline of Romans reflects my decision about its theme. I therefore use the "gospel" as the overarching rubric. Most scholars agree on the divisions of the text that you find below, although they do not, of course, agree on the titles I have given the sections. The greatest disagreement over text division comes with chapter 5. Many think this is the concluding part of the first main section of the letter rather than (as I have made it) the beginning of the second main section. Please see comments on chapter 5 for why I have divided it this way.

Outline

I. The Letter Opening (1:1–17)
   A. Prescript (1:1–7)
   B. Thanksgiving and Occasion: Paul and the Romans
      (1:8–15)
   C. The Theme of the Letter (1:16–17)
II. The Heart of the Gospel: Justification by Faith
    (1:18–4:25)
   A. The Universal Reign of Sin (1:18–3:20)
      1. All Persons Are Accountable to God for Sin
         (1:18–32)
      2. Jews Are Accountable to God for Sin (2:1–3:8)
         a. The Jews and the Judgment of God (2:1–16)
         b. The Limitations of the Covenant (2:17–29)
         c. God's Faithfulness and the Judgment of Jews (3:1–8)
      3. The Guilt of All Humanity (3:9–20)
   B. Justification by Faith (3:21–4:25)
      1. Justification and the Righteousness of God
         (3:21–26)
      2. "By Faith Alone" (3:27–4:25)
         a. "By Faith Alone": Initial Statement (3:27–31)
         b. "By Faith Alone": Abraham (4:1–25)
III. The Assurance Provided by the Gospel: The Hope of
     Salvation (5:1–8:39)
   A. The Hope of Glory (5:1–21)
      1. From Justification to Salvation (5:1–11)
      2. The Reign of Grace and Life (5:12–21)
   B. Freedom from Bondage to Sin (6:1–23)
      1. "Dead to Sin" Through Union with Christ (6:1–14)
      2. Freed from Sin's Power to Serve Righteousness
         (6:15–23)
   C. Freedom from Bondage to the Law (7:1–25)
      1. Released from the Law, Joined to Christ (7:1–6)
      2. The History and Experience of Jews under the Law
         (7:7–25)
         a. The Coming of the Law (7:7–12)
         b. Life Under the Law (7:13–25)

D. Assurance of Eternal Life in the Spirit (8:1–30)
   1. The Spirit of Life (8:1–13)
   2. The Spirit of Adoption (8:14–17)
   3. The Spirit of Glory (8:18–30)
E. The Believer's Security Celebrated (8:31–39)

IV. **The Defense of the Gospel: The Problem of Israel (9:1–11:36)**
   A. Introduction: The Tension Between God's Promises and Israel's Plight (9:1–5)
   B. Defining the Promise (1): God's Sovereign Election (9:6–29)
      1. The Israel Within Israel (9:6–13)
      2. Objections Answered: The Freedom and Purpose of God (9:14–23)
      3. God's Calling of a New People: Israel and the Gentiles (9:24–29)
   C. Understanding Israel's Plight: Christ as the Climax of Salvation History (9:30–10:21)
      1. Israel, the Gentiles, and the Righteousness of God (9:30–10:13)
      2. Israel's Accountability (10:14–21)
   D. Summary: Israel, the "Elect," and the "Hardened" (11:1–10)
   E. Defining the Promise (2): The Future of Israel (11:11–32)
      1. God's Purpose in Israel's Rejection (11:11–15)
      2. The Interrelationship of Jews and Gentiles: Warning to Gentiles (11:16–24)
      3. The Salvation of "All Israel" (11:25–32)
   F. Conclusion: Praise to God in Light of His Awesome Plan (11:33–36)

V. **The Transforming Power of the Gospel: Christian Conduct (12:1–15:13)**
   A. The Heart of the Matter: Total Transformation (12:1–2)
   B. Humility and Mutual Service (12:3–8)
   C. Love and Its Manifestations (12:9–21)
   D. The Christian and Secular Rulers (13:1–7)
   E. Love and the Law (13:8–10)
   F. Living in Light of the Day (13:11–14)
   G. A Plea for Unity (14:1–15:13)
      1. Do Not Condemn One Another! (14:1–12)

Annotated Bibliography

THE BIBLIOGRAPHY ON ROMANS, as one might imagine, is immense. I list below only the most important commentaries and a few key monographs. The reader will notice that I have written another commentary on Romans, in the New International Commentary series. This commentary is much longer and more detailed, and has considerable more interaction with scholarly sources. Though I do not refer explicitly to that commentary often, the reader is invited to consult it for elaboration of points I make here.

One other note: Quotations from the Bible, unless otherwise noted, are from the NIV. Translations from the Apocrypha are from the NRSV. Quotations from the Pseudepigrapha are from *The Old Testament Pseudepigrapha*, ed. James H. Charlesworth (2 vols.; New York: Doubleday, 1983, 1985). Quotations of the works of Philo and Josephus are from the Loeb Classical Library series.

Technical Commentaries on the Greek Text

Cranfield, C. E. B. *A Critical and Exegetical Commentary on the Epistle to the Romans*. ICC, new series. 2 vols. Edinburgh: T. & T. Clark, 1975, 1979. Intensive interaction with the Greek text, with careful grammatical analysis. Barthian in its theological stance and written before the "new perspective."

Dunn, James D. G. *Romans 1–8; Romans 9–16*. WBC. Waco, Tex.: Word, 1988. Especially strong on Jewish backgrounds, with constant interaction with other scholarly viewpoints. The best representative of the "new perspective" on Paul in Romans.

Fitzmyer, Joseph. *Romans*. AB. New York: Doubleday, 1993. Good on introductory issues, the history of scholarship, and bibliography. Roman Catholic in theology, but not aggressively so.

Godet, Frederic Louis. *Commentary on Romans*. 1879. Reprint. Grand Rapids: Kregel, 1977. An excellent representative of the older tradition of careful exegetical and logical analysis. Especially important for its Arminian perspective.

Käsemann, Ernst. *Commentary on Romans*. Grand Rapids: Eerdmans, 1980. A translation of a German classic, representing the post-Bultmannian perspective. Difficult to work through, but with many insightful hints at meaning and application.

Sanday, William, and Arthur C. Headlam. *A Critical and Exegetical Commentary on the Epistle to the Romans*. ICC, old series. Edinburgh: T. & T. Clark, 1902.

Good representative of the older critical approach, with brief exegetical and textual comments but with little theology or logical analysis.

Schreiner, Thomas. *Romans.* BECNT. Grand Rapids: Baker, 1998. A fine, balanced treatment, combining exegesis with solid theological insight. An important response to the "new perspective" approach to Romans.

Expositions

Barrett, C. K. *A Commentary on the Epistle to the Romans.* HNTC. San Francisco: Harper & Row, 1957. Frustratingly brief, but direct, exposition from a noted British scholar.

Bruce, F. F. *The Letter of Paul to the Romans.* TNTC. Grand Rapids: Eerdmans, 1985. General treatment by the prince of evangelical Pauline scholars.

Calvin, John. *Commentaries on the Epistle of Paul the Apostle to the Romans.* 1540. Reprint. Grand Rapids: Eerdmans, 1947. Brief exposition from one of the chief Reformers, focusing on the essence of the gospel.

Lloyd-Jones, D. Martyn. *Romans: An Exposition of Chapter 5: Assurance; Romans: An Exposition of Chapter 6: The New Man; Romans: An Exposition of Chapters 7:1– 8:4: The Law: Its Functions and Limits; Romans: An Exposition of Chapter 8:5–17: The Sons of God.* Grand Rapids: Zondervan, 1971, 1973, 1974, 1975. Insightful, theologically oriented exposition.

Moo, Douglas J. *The Epistle to the Romans.* NICNT. Grand Rapids: Eerdmans, 1996.

Morris, Leon. *The Epistle to the Romans.* PNTC. Grand Rapids: Eerdmans, 1988. Clear exposition from a broad evangelical viewpoint.

Murray, John. *The Epistle to the Romans.* 2 vols. NICNT. Grand Rapids: Eerdmans, 1959, 1965. Steady, theologically oriented exposition from a Reformed perspective.

Nygren, Anders. *Commentary on Romans.* 1944. Reprint. Philadelphia: Fortress, 1949. Excellent example of a Lutheran theological approach to the letter, incorporating insightful ideas from the modern "salvation-historical" school.

Stott, John. *Romans: God's Good News for the World.* Downers Grove, Ill.: Inter-Varsity, 1994. Clear exposition with application.

Stuhlmacher, Peter. *Paul's Letter to the Romans.* Louisville: Westminster/John Knox, 1994. Translation of a brief exposition by a key German contemporary Pauline scholar.

Some Significant Monographs

Deidun, T. J. *New Covenant Morality in Paul.* Rome: Pontifical Biblical Institute, 1981. Stimulating theological study of the basic structures of Paul's moral teaching.

Donfried, Karl, ed. *The Romans Debate.* 2d ed. Peabody, Mass.: Hendrickson, 1991. Valuable collection of essays on the purpose and nature of Romans.

Fee, Gordon D. *God's Empowering Presence: The Holy Spirit in the Letters of Paul.* Peabody, Mass.: Hendrickson, 1994. Comprehensive and stimulating analysis of Paul's teaching about the Holy Spirit and the life of the Christian.

Hays, Richard B. *Echoes of Scripture in the Letters of Paul.* New Haven, Conn.: Yale Univ. Press, 1989. Important and insightful approach to a key component of the argument of Romans.

Hultgren, A. J. *Paul's Gospel and Mission: The Outlook from His Letter to the Romans.* Philadelphia: Fortress, 1985. Valuable, though universalist-tending, study of the gospel in Romans.

Laato, Timo. *Paul and Judaism: An Anthropological Approach.* Atlanta: Scholars, 1995. Very helpful response to basic issues raised by the "new perspective" approach to Paul, focusing on the critical issue of anthropology.

Munck, Johannes. *Paul and the Salvation of Mankind.* 1954. London: SCM, 1959. Ground-breaking study of Paul's theological significance within a salvation-historical approach.

Piper, John. *The Justification of God: An Exegetical and Theological Study of Romans 9:1–23.* Grand Rapids: Baker, 1983. Excellent exegetical-theological study from a Calvinistic perspective.

Ridderbos, Herman N. *Paul: An Outline of His Theology.* Grand Rapids: Eerdmans, 1974. The best treatment of Paul's theology from the "salvation-historical" perspective adopted in this commentary.

Watson, Francis. *Paul, Judaism, and the Gentiles: A Sociological Approach.* SNTSMS 56. Cambridge: Cambridge Univ. Press, 1986. Interesting attempt to explain Paul's argument in Romans against the background of social issues in the church.

Westerholm, Stephen. *Israel's Law and the Church's Faith.* Grand Rapids: Eerdmans, 1988. Excellent survey of the "new perspective" on this key theological point with a reasoned defense of a more traditional approach.

_____. *Preface to the Study of Paul.* Grand Rapids: Eerdmans, 1997. A helpful teaching aid, applying the insights of Romans to contemporary postmodern thinking.

Romans 1:1–7

P AUL, A SERVANT of Christ Jesus, called to be an apostle and set apart for the gospel of God—²the gospel he promised beforehand through his prophets in the Holy Scriptures ³regarding his Son, who as to his human nature was a descendant of David, ⁴and who through the Spirit of holiness was declared with power to be the Son of God by his resurrection from the dead: Jesus Christ our Lord. ⁵Through him and for his name's sake, we received grace and apostleship to call people from among all the Gentiles to the obedience that comes from faith. ⁶And you also are among those who are called to belong to Jesus Christ.

⁷To all in Rome who are loved by God and called to be saints:

Grace and peace to you from God our Father and from the Lord Jesus Christ.

ANCIENT LETTERS TYPICALLY began with a simple identification of the sender, the recipients, and a greeting. New Testament letters follow this pattern, but often elaborate by adding distinctly Christian nuances. No New Testament letter shows as much elaboration as Romans. Perhaps because he is writing to a church he has never visited before, Paul spends six verses identifying himself before he mentions the recipients (v. 7a) and extends them a greeting (v. 7b).

Paul (1:1)

PAUL INTRODUCES HIMSELF to the Roman Christians by identifying his master, his office, and his purpose. (1) He is a "servant of Christ Jesus." While clearly revealing Paul's sense of subservience to his Lord (the word "servant" [*doulos*] can also be translated "slave"), this title also suggests his status. For the Old Testament "servant of the Lord" was applied especially to outstanding figures in Israel's history, such as Moses (e.g., Josh. 14:7) and David (e.g., Ps. 18:1).

(2) Paul also points in verse 1 to his office and to its authority: He is "called to be an apostle," one of those whom Jesus himself had appointed to represent him and to provide the foundation for his church (see Eph. 2:20).

(3) The most important point Paul wants to make in this opening verse has to do with his purpose: "set apart for the gospel of God." God may have set apart Paul for the gospel ministry as early as the womb—just as he had done for the prophet Jeremiah (Jer. 1:5). But the "setting apart" probably refers to the time when God called him on the Damascus Road to come into relationship with Christ and to proclaim him to both Jews and Gentiles (Acts 9:1–19, esp. vv. 15–16; note the use of this same verb in 13:2). The "gospel" is the central, unifying motif of Romans, and Paul signals its importance by referring to it three other times in the introduction to the letter (vv. 9, 15, 16). God has appointed Paul to the special task of proclaiming and explaining the good news of God's intervention in Jesus Christ.

Paul and the Gospel (1:2–4)

PAUL NOW ELABORATES his brief introduction, describing the "gospel" in verses 2–4 and his apostolic calling in verses 5–6. The first point Paul makes about the gospel (v. 2) reflects another key theme of Romans. Throughout the letter he is at pains to demonstrate that the good news about Jesus Christ is rooted firmly in the soil of the Old Testament. The "prophets" to which he refers are not just the famous writing prophets, whose books are now found in the Old Testament, but Old Testament authors generally. As Luther put it, in Paul's perspective, "Scripture is completely prophetical." Verses 3–4 describe the content of the gospel: Jesus Christ himself. In two parallel statements, Paul succinctly summarizes the mission of Christ:

Regarding his Son,

verse 3	*verse 4*
who as to his human nature was a descendant of David	who through the Spirit of holiness was declared with power to be the Son of God by his resurrection from the dead:

Jesus Christ, our Lord

The current NIV translation suggests that Paul is contrasting the two "natures" of Christ. He is both fully human, a descendant of David, and fully divine, shown by his resurrection to be the Son of God. But this is probably incorrect. The verb translated "declared" in verse 4 (from *horizo*) is better translated "appointed."[1] Thus, this verse does not mean that the resurrection made clear what Jesus already was; rather, it qualified him to attain an entirely new status. However, this does not mean that Jesus *became* Son of God at the

---

1. See Luke 22:22; Acts 2:23; 10:42; 11:29; 17:26, 31; Heb. 4:7.

time of his resurrection; he always was God's Son. But he did become "Son-of-God-in-power."[2] In his earthly life, Jesus was truly the Messiah, descendant of David, and Paul does not minimize the importance of this status. But Jesus' resurrection, concluding and validating the messianic work of redemption, gave him new power to dispense salvation to all those who would believe in him (see esp. v. 16).

To put it another way, verses 3–4 do not depict two natures of Christ, but two stages in his existence. This is confirmed by one more key contrast in the verses. The word translated in the NIV "human nature" is *sarx* (lit., flesh). "Spirit of holiness" is properly capitalized in the NIV (though see NIV note) to indicate a reference to the Holy Spirit. The flesh/Spirit contrast in Paul is fundamental to his theology and will appear constantly in Romans. What is key to this text is that the contrast is usually a salvation-historical one in Paul. "Flesh" represents the old era that is passing away; "Spirit" denotes the new era inaugurated by Christ's work of redemption and marked by a new, powerful work of God's Spirit.[3]

The relatively few specific references to Christology in the body of Romans do not mean that the person of Christ is not important for the gospel. Verses 3–4, easily overlooked in the prescript of the letter, introduce Christ as the content of the gospel. By quoting a tradition about Jesus that was probably already circulating in the early church (see Bridging Contexts section), Paul both lays the foundation for the gospel he will elaborate in the letter and establishes common ground with the Roman Christians.

Paul's Apostolic Ministry (1:5–6)

IN VERSES 5–6, Paul elaborates briefly on his apostolic status. He has received this "grace of being an apostle" (taking "grace" and "apostleship" closely together) for two purposes. (1) One task is to "call people from among all the Gentiles to the obedience that comes from faith." From the time of his conversion (see Acts 9:15), the Lord made clear that Paul's primary mission was to bring Gentiles to faith in Jesus. But rather than referring simply to "faith," Paul uses an expanded phrase, which literally translates "the obedience of faith." The NIV, following many commentators, takes "faith" (*pistis*) as the *basis* for the obedience: commitment to Christ in faith leads to obedience in life.[4]

---

2. Most recent commentators take *en dynamei* (lit., "in power") with "Son of God" rather than with the participle *horisthentos*, "declared" (see Moo, *The Epistle to the Romans*, 48).

3. For more on the flesh/Spirit contrast in Paul, see esp. the Bridging Contexts section on 8:1–13.

4. The word *pisteos* (the genitive of *pistis*) is then a genitive of source. See, e.g., G. N. Davies, *Faith and Obedience in Romans: A Study in Romans 1–4* (JSNTSup 39; Sheffield: JSOT, 1990), 25–30.

But *pistis* can also *identify* the obedience that Paul has in mind: "the obedience that is faith." Paul sometimes describes faith in terms of obedience, as when he speaks of people "obeying" the gospel (Rom. 10:16 NRSV).[5]

Neither of these alternatives does justice to the interplay between faith and obedience in Paul. The former can imply that faith is the first stage of Christian experience, to be followed by obedience. But faith is central to all stages of the Christian life. The latter improperly collapses obedience into faith, whereas in Paul they are usually distinct ideas. The best alternative, then, is to use the straightforward, though ambiguous, translation "obedience of faith," and to interpret the words in the phrase as mutually interpreting: faith, if genuine, always has obedience as its outcome; obedience, if it is to please God, must always be accompanied by faith (for more on this, see Contemporary Significance section).

Paul probably uses this unusual formulation as a deliberate counter to the Jewish "works of the law." What marks God's people is no longer deeds done in obedience to the law, but an obedience that stems from, accompanies, and displays faith. Significantly, Paul ends this letter on the same note, referring in the doxology again to "the obedience of faith" (16:26; NIV paraphrases it as "believe and obey"). If one purpose of Paul's apostolic ministry is horizontal, the second and ultimate purpose is vertical: Paul ministers "for his name's sake." Bringing glory to God must always be the preeminent purpose of all ministry.

(2) The Christians in Rome, Paul asserts in verse 6, are included among those Gentiles. One of Paul's concerns in this long prescript is to establish his right to address a group of Christians he has never met before. Thus he makes it clear that the Romans belong to the sphere of ministry God has assigned him. God gave Paul the task of calling "people from among all the Gentiles" to the obedience of faith (v. 5). This interpretation rests on an alternative translation to that found in the NIV. The NIV suggests that "also" should be linked with the word "called": Like Paul (cf. v. 1), the Christians in Rome have also been called. But the emphasis of verse 5 makes it more likely that Paul is claiming that the Romans are "also" among those Gentiles to whom Paul has been sent to proclaim the message of "the obedience of faith."[6]

The Roman Christians (1:7)

PAUL FINALLY GETS around to identifying the recipients of the letter. They are all the Christians in Rome, "loved by God and called to be saints." Both

---

5. The word *pisteos* is then an epexegetic genitive. See, e.g., Käsemann, *Commentary on Romans*, 14–15.

6. See Moo, *The Epistle to the Romans*, 53.

descriptions reflect Old Testament language about Israel. Paul, as an important part of his agenda in this letter, is implying that the Roman Christians, Gentiles though most of them may be, have inherited the privileges and promises granted to the Old Testament people of God. "Saints" translates a Greek word (*hagioi*) that means "holy ones." The Roman Christians, like the Israelites of old, are "holy" because God has set them apart to be his own people. The prescript concludes with the typical wish for grace and peace. "Grace" (*charis*) comes from a word (*chairein*) that often appears in Greek letters as a greeting (cf., e.g., James 1:1). "Peace," by contrast, reflects the Semitic world, for behind it lies *shalom*, the Old Testament word for the well-being of the righteous.

IF WE ARE to appreciate Paul's teaching in these first seven verses—and, indeed, throughout this letter—we must have a sense of what the language Paul uses may have meant to the first readers of this letter. Words always have a context, and only by having some sense of that context can we truly appreciate their real significance. Two contexts that we may not be aware of will help us understand more fully Paul's words in these first seven verses.

Early Christian teaching. Paul reflects early Christian teaching about Jesus and his significance. This is especially true in verses 3–4, where most interpreters think Paul is quoting from a hymn or creed about Jesus that circulated widely among the first Christians. As we noted above, these verses can be arranged in two "stanzas" with roughly parallel lines. The parallelism is more striking in Greek than in the English—the kind of parallelism we might expect in a hymn. Moreover, the verses contain some language, such as "Spirit of holiness," that Paul uses nowhere else, and some ideas, such as the Davidic descent of Jesus, that do not feature prominently in his teaching. When we add to these considerations a natural desire on Paul's part to establish common ground with the Roman Christians, whom he has never met, the conclusion he is quoting from another source in these verses seems well established.

To be sure, we must be cautious about this conclusion and any inferences we draw from it. Some interpreters do not think that we have here a quotation at all. Paul may have used some traditional words and ideas in formulating his own semi-poetic Christological statement. Even if we think a quotation does exist, we should recognize that we do not have enough information to justify some of the exegetical conclusions scholars have reached. Some of them, for instance, distinguish between the original form of the quotation and additions or modifications Paul made to it. Paul's "redaction," they suggest, betrays his real purpose in using the quotation and directs our attention to the parts of the quotation that he agrees with and those he may want to reject. Instead, we must interpret the words in the context in which they now appear.[7]

Still, we think it likely that Paul does quote from a hymn or creed, and the procedure is both rhetorically effective and theologically unobjectionable. A good communicator will always try to build a bridge to his or her audience by using words and ideas they are familiar with. Just as the preacher quotes the stanza of a popular hymn to bring a point home, so Paul may well want to cite lines from a well-known early Christian hymn to communicate the truth of Christ to the Roman Christians. But a quotation will often do far more than merely illustrate a point; it will bring it home to an audience in the way a simple prose statement cannot. Because this point is so important in appreciating Romans, we will spend a little time on it.

Let me begin with an example. When my sons were growing up, I regularly played basketball with them on the driveway in front of our house. Now that they are grown, I foolishly try to continue the tradition. Not long ago, I was playing some one-on-one with my third son, 6'6" 240 lb. Lukas, who plays intercollegiate basketball. I taunted him, "Be careful, Luke, I'm going to take the ball to the basket on you." His response: "Go ahead, Dad—make my day." His words, of course, reflect the famous Clint Eastwood line from the *Dirty Harry* movies. Luke could simply have said to me, "If you try that, Dad, I am going to reject your shot." But by using this particular line, he brought to the driveway a sense of the menace and steely determination that was intrinsic to the original cinematic context.

In other words, quotations and allusions generally have the power to conjure up for the reader something of the context from which the words were taken. Putting our finger on the exact nuance is often difficult, because much of the significance may be emotional. (I know Luke's words stirred emotions in me, most of them making me think twice about taking the ball to the basket.) We must recognize that Paul in Romans frequently seeks, through quotation and allusion, to draw his readers into his argument in a way that his own words could never have done.

The Old Testament. Because we have no independent knowledge of the Christian tradition Paul may be citing in verses 3–4, we have no way of determining the precise effect the quotation may have had. But we do have access to another tradition that is far more important for Paul's purposes in Romans: the Old Testament. Because so much of Romans is about the rela-

---

7. See, e.g., Schreiner, *Romans*, 40.

tionship between Christians and the Old Testament, Paul weaves Old Testament quotations and allusions into his argument throughout. Quotations, because they are set off by an introductory formula or change in syntax, are easy to identify. But the casual reader can easily pass right by Old Testament allusions that contribute significantly to Paul's argument.

Consider, for instance, verse 7. Paul identifies his audience as "loved by God" and "called to be saints." Both phrases are used often in the Old Testament to describe Israel. For instance, the famous vineyard analogy in Isaiah 5 begins by identifying Israel as God's "loved one" (Isa. 5:1). "Saints" comes from the same root as the word "holy," one of the most common ways of describing Israel's call before the Lord (see, e.g., Ex. 19:16: "You will be for me a kingdom of priests and a holy nation"). The first readers of Romans, though Gentiles, had a deep familiarity with the Old Testament—perhaps because they had been "God-fearers" before they were converted. They would immediately have identified the background of this terminology and recognized that Paul was here asserting something amazing: that they, so long excluded as Gentiles from God's people, are now included. They may have gone even further, reasoning that if they are now God's saints, Israel must no longer be. Thus already here Paul begins to hint at the problem of Israel that he will address fully in chapters 9–11.

 THE PRESCRIPT, PRECISELY because it acts something like the overture to the opera, sounds many notes that will be heard repeatedly in Romans. Most of these can best be appreciated in the contexts where Paul turns to discuss them at greater length. But two of the notes found in this text are not elaborated directly elsewhere in Romans. Both deserve mention here.

Grace and apostolic calling. The first is Paul's association of "grace" with his apostolic calling (1:5). As we noted above, these words are to be taken closely together. Being an apostle is an act of God's grace. As Paul makes clear elsewhere (e.g., the "gifts" or "acts of grace" of 1 Cor. 12 and Eph. 4), so are all ministries. Serving God and his people in specific ways is a product of God's unmerited favor toward us. When we serve the Lord and the church, we do what we have no right to do on our own: speak in God's name, reach out with his love, and lead his people. Only because God both calls us to minister and gives us the grace to do it can we accomplish anything worthwhile.

Moreover, we must remember that we can serve only out of our own weakness. Any strength we possess in ministry comes from God and gives no basis for any pride (see 2 Cor. 10–13). Ministering to others can easily lead to pride and even arrogance. Reminding ourselves that we minister as a gift from God will help stifle that pride and keep us on our knees.

Obedience and faith. The phrase "the obedience that comes from faith" also needs further unpacking. As noted above, Paul returns to this phrase in 16:26, and he also touches significantly on the issue of the Christian's response to God's grace in chapter 6. But the phrase itself has become almost a slogan for different viewpoints.

As we explained above, neither "the obedience that comes from faith" or "the obedience that is faith" does justice to Paul's intention. The first rendering too easily suggests a kind of two-stage process of discipleship: One first believes the gospel and then afterward commits to Christ as Lord. Such a model has always had its supporters, and it has been argued vigorously again recently (though in a slightly different form) by some who are worried about tying our assurance as Christians to works. If we base our certainty about being Christians on works, these scholars argue, we will never have true assurance, for our works are always imperfect and inconsistent. Thus, "faith" and "obedience" should be kept distinct from one another.

The other extreme is to merge "faith" and "obedience" into one another. This is the danger in the other usual rendering of the phrase in verse 5. We admit that the identification of faith and obedience has some basis in Paul, since he sometimes seems to interchange the two (cf. Rom. 1:8 and 16:19; 10:16a and 10:16b; 11:23; 11:30 and 11:31) and even speaks of "obeying" the gospel (Rom. 10:16 NRSV; 2 Thess. 1:8; 3:14). Most scholars who argue for this interpretation do not conclude that Paul always merges the two concepts. But the phrase in Romans 1:5 has almost programmatic significance for the letter as a whole, and identifying faith and obedience here therefore sets a tone for the letter that minimizes the role of obedience in Paul's argument throughout the letter. By contrast, the obedience of Christians to the Lord who has redeemed them is vital to the gospel Paul preaches, as chapters 6 and 12–15 make clear.

Thus we must avoid two theological extremes: separating faith from obedience in such a way that we can have the one without the other, or identifying them in such a way that obedience is minimized. Paul, along with other New Testament writers, certainly emphasizes the basic importance of faith as the means by which we get into relationship with God (see, e.g., 3:28). But precisely because faith is not exercised in a vacuum but is directed to one who is the Lord, the commitment to obey is inextricably bound up with true faith (see esp. James 2). So faith and obedience are two sides of the same coin. They must be distinguished, but they cannot be separated.

When we come to Christ initially, we come to one who demands total allegiance. This allegiance is something we learn to live out as God begins his work of transforming our minds so that we may do his will (Rom. 12:1–2). But never can we obey without believing. If obedience is implied from the beginning in our faith, faith is always essential for any true obedience. It is true that people can outwardly conform with the demands of the gospel. All of us know non-Christians whose outward conduct appears to be closer to the demands of Scripture than that of some Christians. But without the inward commitment of the heart, such obedience is, in biblical terms, no obedience at all.

We have perhaps loaded Paul's simple phrase "obedience of faith" with more baggage than it can carry. But the phrase, understood in the way we have suggested, is a neat slogan that sums up the essence of Christian living. As we read Scripture, worship God, and pray, our faith in Christ deepens. That deepening faith will inevitably reveal itself in a more consistent and radically Christlike lifestyle. This is the message Paul proclaims to the Gentiles in his "gospel": not just initial conversion, but the transformation of life.

Romans 1:8–15

FIRST, I THANK my God through Jesus Christ for all of you, because your faith is being reported all over the world. ⁹God, whom I serve with my whole heart in preaching the gospel of his Son, is my witness how constantly I remember you ¹⁰in my prayers at all times; and I pray that now at last by God's will the way may be opened for me to come to you.

¹¹I long to see you so that I may impart to you some spiritual gift to make you strong—¹²that is, that you and I may be mutually encouraged by each other's faith. ¹³I do not want you to be unaware, brothers, that I planned many times to come to you (but have been prevented from doing so until now) in order that I might have a harvest among you, just as I have had among the other Gentiles.

¹⁴I am obligated both to Greeks and non-Greeks, both to the wise and the foolish. ¹⁵That is why I am so eager to preach the gospel also to you who are at Rome.

PAUL CONTINUES TO adapt the ancient letter form to his own purposes. Letters often featured an expression of thanks to the gods in the "proem," the second main part of a letter. Paul gives thanks to God for the Roman Christians and assures them that he often prays for them. He uses his petition for his own ministry among them as a transition to a brief description of his plans and motivations. The section is marked by a certain hesitation and deference on Paul's part, as he seeks to avoid "lording it over" these Christians whom he did not convert and has never visited. He writes diplomatically in an effort to win a hearing for his presentation of the gospel.

Thanksgiving and Prayer (1:8–12)

THE "FIRST" THAT begins this section is never followed by a "second" or "third." Paul may simply have forgotten to go on with his enumeration, or the word "first" may indicate priority rather than sequence: "first of all."

Paul's thanksgiving is expressed to "my God" and is mediated "through Jesus Christ." Christ has created the access to God that enables Paul to approach him in thanksgiving.[1] The reason for Paul's thanks is the wide reputation the Roman Christians have gained for their faith. "Reported all over the world" is hyperbole, but it would be natural for Christians throughout the Mediterranean world to be aware that the gospel was planted in the capital of the empire itself. In verses 9–10 Paul reinforces the sense of commitment to the Roman Christians hinted at in verse 8 by emphasizing his constant prayers for them. He reiterates one of the key motifs in this opening part of the letter by asserting again his commitment to the gospel of God's Son.

According to the NIV, Paul claims that he serves this gospel "with my whole heart." But the Greek word here for heart is *pneuma* (spirit), and Fee is probably right to insist that this must be a reference to the Spirit of God resident in Paul.[2] Paul's own spirit has been caught up in God's Spirit, and he now serves the gospel "in" and "by means of" that transformed spirit. When Paul asserts that he "constantly" (v. 9) makes mention of the Roman Christians in his prayers, he means that he brings them regularly before the Lord—testimony to the importance and wide-ranging nature of Paul's prayer life.

One specific focus of Paul's prayer in relationship to the Romans is that he may be able finally to come to Rome to minister (v. 10b). Specifically (v. 11), he wants to go to Rome so that he may "impart to you some spiritual gift to make you strong." What Paul means by "spiritual gift" is not clear. He may have in mind a specific "gift," of the sort he describes in 1 Corinthians 12–14, that he hopes to use for the benefit of the Roman Christians when he arrives.[3] But Paul nowhere else uses the specific language we have here (*charisma pneumatikon*) to denote such a gift, and the indefinite language ("some") makes this view difficult.

The apostle may, then, refer to a general spiritual "blessing" he hopes will result from his work at Rome (see 15:27).[4] But "gift" seems too specific for this interpretation, so perhaps the reference is to an insight or ability given to Paul by the Spirit that he hopes to share with the Romans. In any case, the purpose of sharing the gift is to "strengthen" (see also 1 Thess. 3:2; 2 Thess. 2:17; 3:3) the faith of the Roman Christians.

But Paul immediately qualifies this purpose, revealing again his hesitancy to claim too much authority over a community he has not himself founded. It is not, Paul hastily adds (v. 12), that the spiritual benefit will flow all one direction, from Paul to the Romans. Rather, he anticipates a time of mutual edification with them, as the faith God has given each individual stimulates and encourages spiritual growth in the others.

---

1. Käsemann, *Commentary on Romans*, 17.
2. Fee, *God's Empowering Presence*, 485–86.
3. E.g., Sanday and Headlam, *The Epistle to the Romans*, 21.
4. Cranfield, *The Epistle to the Romans*, 78–79.

Paul's Plans (1:13–15)

As Paul thinks of the ministry he hopes to have in Rome, he turns attention naturally to his plans for such a visit. He is apparently aware that some Christians in Rome may have been critical of him for "ignoring" them for so long. So he wants them to understand that his failure to visit Rome was not because of lack of will but because of lack of opportunity. Paul has often planned to visit them but was prevented from doing so. We do not know for sure what kept him from Rome. But it was probably the pressing needs of the ministry in the eastern Mediterranean, where Paul had been working up to this point. But Paul is still intent on getting to Rome, where he wants to enjoy a time of mutual edification in the gospel.

Paul's desire to preach in Rome is motivated not by a concern to expand his personal "territory" but by his deep sense of obligation to preach the gospel to all kinds of people. "Woe to me if I do not preach the gospel!" Paul exclaims on another occasion (1 Cor. 9:16). The NIV translation suggests a rather loose connection between Romans 1:13 and 14. That is, a sense of obligation to preach to all people, including both "Greeks and non-Greeks," only generally grounds Paul's determination to reap a spiritual harvest among Gentiles in Rome. But a closer connection can be established if we define this first pair of terms in verse 14 differently.

"Greeks" is a faithful translation of the Greek word *Hellen*, but the second word is *barbaros*, from which we get "barbarian." Educated Greeks used this word to mock those who could not pronounce the Greek language as accurately as they did. But Jewish writers usually did not include themselves among the "barbarians." Probably, then, "Greek and non-Greek" is Paul's way of referring to all of Gentile humanity.[5]

The relationship between this first pair of terms and the second ("the wise and the foolish") is not clear, but it probably refers again to Gentiles only. This, then, explains (v. 15) why Paul is so eager to "preach the gospel also to you who are at Rome." Paul has been given a commission from the Lord to be "apostle to the Gentiles," and it is this divine mandate, not any personal benefit or emotional satisfaction or marketing strategy, that impels Paul to travel ever farther afield.

Applying Biblical Narrative. Since Paul is speaking in these verses of his own ministry and plans, application of the overall teaching of the section will depend considerably on the extent to which we can validly use Paul as a model for our own Christian service. In many

---

5. Fitzmyer, *Romans*, 250–51.

ways, of course, Paul's service of the Lord was unique; no one else was, or had been, called the way he was or given a mandate directly from the risen Christ. But are there other ways Paul may serve as a model for us? If so, how can we discern those ways?

The question we raise here is a basic one in the interpretation of Scripture. Much of Scripture comes to us in the form of narrative, stories depicting specific experiences of the people of God. How are we to make such historical narratives relevant for the people of God today? Many preachers, unfortunately, resort to analogy to make the connection: As "x" did in this passage of the Bible, so we today can/should do. But such an approach, if pursued too rigidly, robs the biblical narratives of their power. The point of those narratives is often to portray for us the historical foundation for the faith we now share. God did certain things in history to provide salvation for his people and to reveal his glory and his will. The preacher who fails to see and proclaim these elements in the narrative often misses the essence of these accounts.[6] Taken to its logical conclusion, one can imagine a sermon on the crucifixion that focuses on how we can learn to die gracefully!

But we must also grant that biblical narratives and personal accounts sometimes—perhaps often—have a subsidiary purpose of providing for God's people an example for them to emulate. Thus, the question cannot be avoided: How can we know what is to be modeled and what is not? Some interpreters suggest that virtually everything in a narrative not branded as morally wrong elsewhere in Scripture should be taken over. In other words, we must disciple people just as Jesus did or evangelize people just as Paul did.

There is undoubtedly much to be learned from such examples, but we think the wholesale transfer of virtually everything not morally evil in narratives goes too far. On the one hand, we must remember that the specific culture in which Jesus and Paul ministered plays a fundamental role in the methods and approaches they adopted. They perhaps often did things a certain way simply because that was the most effective way to reach people molded by their distinctive first-century social and religious environment.

A more sound procedure is to scrutinize the details of narratives in light of Scripture elsewhere and draw far-ranging conclusions only when specific teaching or general principles found elsewhere in the Bible legitimize the application. In the case of Paul, then, we should not assume his specific methods are to be imitated unless we have teaching that endorses the methods as universally applicable.

---

6. See on this esp. Sidney Greidanus, *The Modern Preacher and the Ancient Text: Interpreting and Preaching Biblical Literature* (Grand Rapids: Eerdmans, 1989).

On the other hand, Paul often puts himself forward as a person to be imitated by his converts (e.g., 1 Cor. 4:16; 11:1; Phil. 3:17; 2 Thess. 3:7). Some scholars think that this call to imitate him involves only general moral qualities and that Christians are generally called not to active evangelism but to passive evangelism, that is, living good lives as a light that may attract converts. But Peter O'Brien has shown that the call is broader than that, extending to the ministry of evangelism that Paul was himself committed to.[7] Thus, we have good grounds within Paul's writings themselves to conclude that the sense of obligation to preach the gospel to those who have not heard it in Romans 1:13–15 provides us with a model we are to imitate.

ZEAL FOR EVANGELISM. With this solid hermeneutical foundation in place, we can now assert that Paul's zeal for preaching the gospel should serve as a model for us. As this passage reveals, he was motivated to evangelize and plant churches because he was a man under obligation. To be sure, Paul's obligation had at least one unique cause: Christ's commissioning him as "apostle to the Gentiles" on the Damascus Road. This event gave his ministry a clear basis and special direction.

Few of us will have such clear direction about a call to ministry or about the direction our ministry should take. But the imperative to evangelize is an obligation, Paul suggests, that all believers share. In 1 Corinthians 3–4, he describes his dedication to the task of evangelism (3:3–15), a task that brought him much personal hardship (4:8–13). He concludes with a call to the Corinthians to imitate him (4:16). Similarly in 2 Corinthians Paul asserts that, knowing the fear of the Lord, he tries to persuade people to follow Christ (2 Cor. 5:11). And the reason for his commitment? "Christ's love compels us" (5:14).[8] Contemplation of the benefits won for us by Christ should motivate all of us to seek to share these benefits with others.

But another motivation also appears regularly in Paul's discussion of his ministry: the enhancement of God's name and glory. We have seen such a concern already in Romans, as Paul claimed that his apostolic work was "for his [Jesus Christ's] name's sake" (1:5). In a climactic section of Romans, Paul announces that the inclusion of Gentiles within the people of God is so that they "may glorify God for his mercy" (15:9; see also 15:16; 2 Cor. 4:15; Phil. 1:11). Paul's evangelism, his letters suggest, has two great motivations: a

---

7. Peter T. O'Brien, *Gospel and Mission in the Writings of Paul: An Exegetical and Theological Analysis* (Grand Rapids: Baker, 1995).

8. I want to thank Peter Dybvad for drawing my attention to these texts.

sense of obligation derived from what God has done for him and commissioned him to do for others, and a desire that God will be glorified by as great a number of people as possible. We are to imitate Paul by extending God's grace in the gospel just as he did.

Not all of us will be called to engage in evangelism full-time; we may have a tough time deciding whether we have a "call" to ministry and where that call should be discharged. We will struggle as well to balance the demands of life with those of evangelism. But every Christian should have the same sense of obligation that Paul speaks of in Romans 1:14–15. We must pray that God will impress on our hearts such an obligation so as to become imitators of Paul.

Discipleship. Thus far we have used Romans 1:14–15 as a basis for involvement in evangelism. But we can perhaps take this one step further. Easily overlooked in this passage is the fact that Paul announces his intention to preach the gospel "to you who are at Rome" (1:15). What can he mean by this, since he is writing to people who are already Christians (see 1:7)? Some answer that Paul is reflecting here only on his past plans.[9] Others suggest that the "you" is general, so that Paul is simply indicating he wants to evangelize in Rome.[10] But such alternatives do not do justice to the text. What Paul seems rather to hint at is that he includes within the scope of "preaching the gospel" the continuing work of discipleship that follows evangelism.

Certainly Paul modeled such a broad concern throughout his ministry, for his initial evangelistic work in towns was usually followed by teaching, pastoral exhortation, and later visits. As Paul Bowers has argued, "the gospel" in Paul includes "not simply an initial preaching mission but the full sequence of activities resulting in settled churches."[11] Only when a church had reached the point of sufficient maturity as to be self-producing did the apostle feel he could leave to move on to new fields. The point for us is obvious and has been made so often in recent years that it need not detain us for long: Successful evangelism includes follow-up. Discipling those who have "come forward" to receive the gospel is not an optional add-on, but a necessary component of the initial preaching of the gospel itself.

---

9. Stuhlmacher, *Paul's Letter to the Romans*, 26.

10. Godet, *Commentary on Romans*, 90.

11. Paul Bowers, "Fulfilling the Gospel: The Scope of the Pauline Mission," *JETS* 30 (1987): 198.

Romans 1:16–17

I AM NOT ashamed of the gospel, because it is the power of God for the salvation of everyone who believes: first for the Jew, then for the Gentile. ¹⁷For in the gospel a right-eousness from God is revealed, a righteousness that is by faith from first to last, just as it is written: "The righteous will live by faith."

THESE TWO VERSES are transitional. Though not explicitly indicated in the NIV, verse 16 begins with a conjunction "for" (*gar*), connecting it to verses 13–15. The train of thought is: "I am so eager to preach the gospel also to you who are in Rome *because* I am not ashamed of the gospel...." From this perspective, then, verses 16–17 belong to the introduction to the letter.

But these verses are also closely related to the body of the letter that follows, as Paul introduces the theme he will develop in the following chapters. For many interpreters, that theme is enunciated in verse 17: "righteousness that is by faith." However, while this doctrine, as we will show, is critical to Paul's argument in Romans, it is not the overarching theme. For this theme, we need to look at the word that heads these two verses: *gospel*. The argument of these verses proceeds in a "stair-step" movement:

I am not ashamed of the gospel,

    because it is the power of God for the salvation of everyone who believes:

        first for the Jew, then for the Gentile.

    For in the gospel a righteousness from God is revealed, a righteousness

        that is by faith from first to last,

    just as it is written, "The righteous will live by faith."

Picking up the key word "gospel" that has been a basic motif in the introductory verses (see 1:1, 2, 9, 15), Paul now briefly explains why he is so committed to spreading the good news and how that message is able to transform human beings.

The negative formulation of verse 16—"I am *not* ashamed"—may be no more than a literary device (litotes), functioning in a basic positive sense: "I am very proud of...." Paul may have a reason for this way of putting the matter. As his passing reference to people who slander him in 3:8 suggests, he knows he has come under fire for his advocacy of the law-free gospel for Gentiles. One of the reasons he writes such a long and theological letter to the Roman Christians is to disabuse them of some wrong ideas about his own view of the gospel that they have probably heard. Thus, it makes perfect sense for him to go on the defensive here: I am *not* ashamed of this gospel I preach.

Why is he not ashamed? Because he knows the gospel he preaches is the divinely appointed means to bring salvation to the world. "Salvation" (*soteria*; see also 10:1, 10; 11:11; 13:11) and the verb "to save" (*sozo*; 5:9, 10; 8:24; 9:27; 10:9, 13; 11:14, 26) are important words in Romans. We sometimes use this language to describe conversion only ("When were you saved?"), but Paul more often uses it to refer to final deliverance from sin and evil that will come to the believer at death or the Parousia (see esp. 5:9–10; 13:11).

Announcing what will become a key note in this letter, Paul insists that the salvation available in the gospel is for *all* who believe (3:22; 4:11, 16; 10:4, 11–13; cf. 11:32; 16:26). In a significant advance on the Old Testament, which focused on Israel, the gospel is universally available. But also typical of Romans is the qualification Paul immediately adds: This gospel of salvation is "first for the Jew." Some think Paul means by this no more than that the gospel was, historically, first preached to Jews, as the book of Acts makes clear. But the development of this point in Romans reveals that Paul's point is more theological. In some sense, he will affirm, Jews still have a kind of priority in the plan of salvation. Perhaps the closest we can get to the idea is to say that Jews are the first addressees of the good news of Jesus Christ. That is, God worked through them to prepare the way for the coming of Messiah, and the glad tidings about him naturally have them as the primary focus. The juxtaposition of these two statements—"*everyone* who believes" and "*first* for the Jew"—drives the theological dynamic of Romans.

Why does the gospel transmit salvation to those who believe? Paul explains this in verse 17, turning to the language of "righteousness" to make his point. The NIV's "a righteousness from God" reflects one possible interpretation of a debated phrase. The Greek is simply *dikaiosyne theou*, literally, "righteousness of God." Paul uses the phrase only nine times in his letters (see also 3:5, 21, 22, 25, 26; 10:3 [2x]; 2 Cor. 5:21). Since eight of them come in Romans, clearly the phrase is significant for the argument of this letter. Each occurrence must be examined in its own context, but most agree that the references here, in 3:21–22, and in 10:3 have the same meaning and are key to the letter. Three interpretations are popular.

(1) "God's righteousness"—an attribute of God. "Righteousness" can refer to God's justice, but as Luther discovered long ago, it is hardly good news

to disobedient sinners to learn about God's justice. Thus it is more likely, if an attribute of God is in view, that the reference is to God's faithfulness.[1]

(2) "Righteousness *from* God"—a status given to people by God. This interpretation was championed by the Reformers and is the traditional view among Protestant theologians.[2] When God "justifies" (the Gk. verb is *dikaioo*, cognate to the word for "righteousness") the sinner, God gives that person a new legal standing before him—his or her "righteousness."

(3) "Righteousness *done by* God"—an action of "putting in the right" being done by God. This view, held by a growing number of scholars, gives a dynamic sense to "righteousness."[3] It is God's intervention to set right what has gone wrong with his creation.

The context does not point clearly in one direction. The verb "reveal," which has a dynamic sense (come into being, manifest; see 1:18) favors the third view. But the fact that this righteousness, as Paul goes on to say, is based on faith, favors the second view. Perhaps the most important consideration, however, is the use of the language "righteousness of God" in the Old Testament. Here we find that key prophetic texts use this phrase to denote God's eschatological saving activity (see Bridging Contexts section). We think, then, that Paul announces the arrival in history of this saving activity of God. But in the context of his larger teaching and qualified as it is here by human faith, this saving activity takes a specific form: the act by which God puts people who believe in right relationship with himself.

A central motif in Romans, and in Paul's gospel in general, is the insistence that one can experience this righteousness of God *only* through faith. Paul emphasizes this point in two ways. (1) He repeats the word "faith": (lit.) "from [*ek*] faith into [*eis*] faith," which is probably correctly interpreted in the NIV as an emphatic construction, "faith from first to last." (2) Paul cites Habakkuk 2:4 for the connection between the righteous person, faith, and life. The precise relationship among these three that Paul intends is debated. Is he emphasizing that righteous people should live by faith (NIV; NASB; KJV)?[4] Or is he asserting that it is only the person who is righteous by faith who will attain life (NRSV; TEV; REB)?[5] The syntax can go either way, but we think that the argument of the letter, in which Paul again and again asserts that a person is righteous (or justified) only by faith, favors this second reading.

---

1. See esp. Sam K. Williams, "The 'Righteousness of God' in Romans," *JBL* 99 (1980):241–90.

2. See, e.g., Cranfield, *The Epistle to the Romans*, 91–99.

3. See, e.g., Moo, *The Epistle to the Romans*, 70–75; Dunn, *Romans*, 40–43.

4. See, e.g., Godet, *Commentary on Romans*, 98; Murray, *The Epistle to the Romans*, 1:33.

5. See, e.g., Cranfield, *The Epistle to the Romans*, 101–2.

THE RIGHTEOUSNESS OF **God in the Old Testa-ment.** As we pointed out in the Bridging Contexts section of 1:8–15, a thorough understanding of the Old Testament is indispensable to understanding Paul's teaching in Romans. The letter focuses on the question of the way in which the gospel of Christ relates to God's Word in the Old Testament. Paul assumes his readers are well grounded in the Old Testament and so constantly uses its categories and wording to make his points. Many of us who read Romans today do not share that same intimate acquaintance with the Old Testament; we don't naturally "hear" the allusions and references the first readers did. Thus, we must have our Old Testament concordances open as we read in order to trace the undercurrents of Paul's argument.

Nowhere in Romans is this more important than in interpreting Paul's references to "the righteousness of God." Righteousness language (the noun *dikaiosyne*, the adjective *dikaios*, and the verb *dikaioo*) was common enough in normal Greek, but its significance for the New Testament is based on the use of these words to translate Hebrew words from the *sdq* root into the Greek translation of the Old Testament (the LXX). Paul and other New Testament writers grew up hearing and reading this language, and their own use of the terms is decisively colored by this influence. Moreover, Paul implies in Romans that phrases like "the righteousness of God" were familiar to both himself and his readers. It is striking that he does not explain the phrase, but begins by announcing that the "righteousness of God" had been revealed (1:17). He assumes that his readers will know what this "righteousness of God" is—and the Old Testament provides the necessary context.

The phrase *dikaiosyne theou* ("the righteousness of God") never occurs in the LXX, while the phrase "the righteousness of the Lord" occurs twice (cf. 1 Sam. 12:7; Mic. 6:5). But the phrase "his righteousness," where "his" refers to God, is common (forty-eight occurrences). When "righteousness" is used in this way, it has three different meanings.

(1) It can denote God's justice. Psalm 50 speaks of God's summoning both his own people and the wicked to appear before him. Israel is rebuked for its trifling with God, while the wicked are condemned. Verse 6 sets the stage for this judging activity: "And the heavens proclaim *his righteousness*, for God himself is judge" (italics added). God is absolutely just and impartial, equitably and fairly determining the rights and wrongs of every person and situation (see also Ps. 7:17; 97:2; Isa. 59:17).

(2) But God does not deal with his people in a vacuum. He himself has established a covenant relationship with them. This relationship is the context in which God deals with Israel. What is "right" for Israel is set forth in her covenant obligations. Similarly, what is "right" for God to do is enunciated

in his own commitment to his people. In these contexts, therefore, God's righteousness often takes on the notion of "faithfulness," as God reiterates the commitment he has made to his people. The plea of David in Psalm 31:1 is typical: "In you, O LORD, I have taken refuge; let me never be put to shame; deliver me *in your righteousness*" (italics added; see also Ex. 15:13; Ps. 71:2; Isa. 38:19; 63:7).

(3) Most important, God's righteousness can also have a dynamic sense, equivalent to his saving activity. The most important texts are two prophecies from Isaiah:

> I am bringing *my righteousness* near,
>> it is not far away;
>> and my salvation will not be delayed.
> I will grant salvation to Zion,
>> my splendor to Israel. (Isa. 46:13, italics added)

> *My righteousness* draws near speedily,
>> my salvation is on the way,
>> and my arm will bring justice to the nations.
> The islands will look to me
>> and wait in hope for my arm.
> Lift up your eyes to the heavens,
>> look at the earth beneath;
> the heavens will vanish like smoke,
>> the earth will wear out like a garment
>> and its inhabitants die like flies.
> But my salvation will last forever,
>> *my righteousness* will never fail.
> Hear me, you who know what is right,
>> you people who have my law in your hearts:
> Do not fear the reproach of men
>> or be terrified by their insults.
> For the moth will eat them up like a garment;
>> the worm will devour them like wool.
> But *my righteousness* will last forever,
>> my salvation through all generations. (Isa. 51:5—8, italics added)

As the parallelism in both these texts makes clear, God's "righteousness" is equivalent to the "salvation" he promises to bring to his people. "Righteousness" here denotes God's saving activity, in which he upholds what is "right" by vindicating his people and delivering them from their distress. Part of our problem is that we have no verb in English that is cognate to "righteousness," but the idea would be that God "righteouses" his people.

Two considerations lead me to conclude that it is this last meaning of "righteousness" that Paul has in mind in 1:17. (1) As we have seen, he expects his readers to recognize what he means when he announces the arrival of God's righteousness. These prophetic texts just cited predict precisely such an arrival. (2) The prophecy of Isaiah, particularly chapters 40–66, exerted an enormous influence on Paul and the New Testament. Thus, Paul's readers would naturally have "heard" in Paul's announcement in 1:17 the claim that the eschatological intervention of God to save his people has occurred.

But they also would have "heard" two somewhat unexpected notes in Paul's announcement. (1) This vindication of God's people is not just for Israel, as the Old Testament suggests and virtually all Jews assumed; rather, it is for "[all] who believe" (1:16). As we noted in the Original Meaning section, this extension of God's saving activity to Gentiles is a characteristic emphasis in Romans.

(2) The righteous activity of God is "based on" human faith. How can this be? How can God's action be constrained by human response? Here Paul introduces a key modification of the Old Testament idea of God's righteousness. God's righteousness is the "righteousness of faith." The upshot is that "righteousness of God" in Paul is personal and relational. It speaks not just about God's work in Christ on the cross, but more directly of his work in individual human lives, as he puts those who respond to the gospel in faith in right relationship to himself.[6]

 SINCE 1:16–17 ANNOUNCE the theme of the letter, they touch on many of the themes that Paul will develop in this letter: how one is justified by faith in Christ (1:18–4:25), how being justified leads to final salvation (chs. 5–8), and how the gospel is both for everyone and for the "Jew first" (chs. 9–11). This section on Contemporary Significance could therefore be long indeed! But other texts will provide a better basis for exploring the significance of some of these topics; here we will confine ourselves to a few words on justification by faith.

Justification by faith. Verse 17 does not refer, in so many words, to "justification by faith," but the idea is clearly expressed: God's righteousness is "by faith from first to last"; it is the one who is "righteous by faith" who will gain spiritual life. This doctrine of justification by faith has had a checkered history. Virtually ignored until the Reformation, it was elevated to the head of all doctrines by Luther. Lutheran theologians have generally followed

---

6. For more detail on these points, see Moo, *The Epistle to the Romans*, 79–89.

their founder's lead, proclaiming in the oft-quoted phrase that justification by faith is the doctrine "on which the church stands or falls."

While important for the other Reformers, justification by faith did not have quite the same importance as it did for Luther. But the Protestant tradition generally has put great emphasis on the doctrine. Essential to the Protestant interpretation has been the judicial, or forensic, understanding of justification and righteousness language generally. To be "justified" does not mean, Protestant theologians insist, to be "made" righteous, but to be "declared" righteous. What God does for us in justification is similar to what the judge does in a law court: He does not change the defendant by turning him or her into a new kind of person; rather, he declares the defendant innocent of the charges brought against him or her. This *forensic* understanding of justification was often denied by Roman Catholic interpreters, who insisted that righteousness must always include inner transformation. This difference set the battle lines for Protestant-Roman Catholic debate for centuries.

But we live in a new world. Most contemporary Roman Catholic scholars now agree that the Protestant theologians are right to insist that "justification" language in Paul is forensic. At the same time, many Protestant interpreters now want to minimize the significance of the doctrine of justification by faith. New debates have sprung up over the key issue of the basis of God's verdict of justification. Just how can God declare the sinner "innocent" when he or she is really not? We will return to some of these issues later on. But for now, we want briefly to highlight two points: the importance of justification and its essential meaning.

Under the tyranny of being "relevant" many preachers in our day avoid doctrine like the plague. It smells of old books and dusty theologians debating incomprehensible issues. But doctrine is, of course, simply the truth that God has revealed to us in his Word. And if the Christian life is anything, it must be rooted firmly in the truth about God and the world. God makes clear to us that the fundamental human problem is not horizontal (estrangement in human relationships) but vertical (estrangement from the only true God). Justification is God's response to that problem. Through the gospel God unleashes a power to change people, and at the crucial point: in their relationship to him. When people respond in faith to the message of the good news, God "justifies" them; that is, he declares them innocent before him, removing the barrier that exists between all human beings in their natural state and God. Everything else in the Christian life flows from this marvelous experience.

Yet many people do not hear this good news, and many Christians do not understand what has happened to them. Why? Because too many preachers don't think a topic like justification by faith is "relevant." A fresh commitment on the part of all preachers to set before their people what God, in his Word, has deemed relevant will go a long way toward bringing the church to a deeper consciousness of the most important truth in the world: that the God of this universe is willing to accept us as his own simply through our faith.

As we recommit to bringing the truth of justification before our people, we need to be sure to present it accurately. It is vitally important that we emphasize that justification is a forensic action. As we explained above, in justification God does not change us but accepts us as we are. To be sure, he insists on changing us once we have been accepted, but the acceptance always comes first.

Christians who struggle to think of themselves as "worthy" to be in relationship with God need especially to understand this truth. We, in ourselves, are *never* worthy, not the best one of us. The gospel is precisely "good news" (the lit. meaning of the Gk. word *euangelion*) because it announces that God accepts us anyway; all that we have to do is receive his offer in faith—to be sure, a faith that must, by its very nature, always be accompanied by obedience (cf. 1:5). Justification reminds us that our standing with God is by grace and that thankfulness should be the hallmark in all our dealings with him.

Romans 1:18–32

THE WRATH OF God is being revealed from heaven against all the godlessness and wickedness of men who suppress the truth by their wickedness, ¹⁹since what may be known about God is plain to them, because God has made it plain to them. ²⁰For since the creation of the world God's invisible qualities—his eternal power and divine nature—have been clearly seen, being understood from what has been made, so that men are without excuse.

²¹For although they knew God, they neither glorified him as God nor gave thanks to him, but their thinking became futile and their foolish hearts were darkened. ²²Although they claimed to be wise, they became fools ²³and exchanged the glory of the immortal God for images made to look like mortal man and birds and animals and reptiles.

²⁴Therefore God gave them over in the sinful desires of their hearts to sexual impurity for the degrading of their bodies with one another. ²⁵They exchanged the truth of God for a lie, and worshiped and served created things rather than the Creator—who is forever praised. Amen.

²⁶Because of this, God gave them over to shameful lusts. Even their women exchanged natural relations for unnatural ones. ²⁷In the same way the men also abandoned natural relations with women and were inflamed with lust for one another. Men committed indecent acts with other men, and received in themselves the due penalty for their perversion.

²⁸Furthermore, since they did not think it worthwhile to retain the knowledge of God, he gave them over to a depraved mind, to do what ought not to be done. ²⁹They have become filled with every kind of wickedness, evil, greed and depravity. They are full of envy, murder, strife, deceit and malice. They are gossips, ³⁰slanderers, God-haters, insolent, arrogant and boastful; they invent ways of doing evil; they disobey their parents; ³¹they are senseless, faithless, heartless, ruthless. ³²Although they know God's righteous decree that those who do such things deserve death, they not only continue to do these very things but also approve of those who practice them.

VERSE 18 COMES to the reader as quite a surprise. Paul has just announced his theme for the letter: the gospel as God's saving power, revealing his righteousness to all who believe. But instead of the exposition of these wonderful truths, we get dire news about God's wrath against sin. Indeed, it is not until fully two chapters later, in 3:21, that Paul finally picks up on the themes he broached in 1:16–17. Why is this? Apparently Paul thinks it necessary to make clear just why the revelation of God's righteousness in the gospel is necessary. Only by fully understanding the "bad news" can we appreciate the "good news." Thus, Paul goes to some lengths to detail for us the nature and dimension of the human predicament (1:18–3:20).

His argument moves in several clearly marked stages. Heading the entire section is the announcement of God's wrath against sin (1:18–20). But almost as important in this announcement is his insistence that God's wrath is *earned*: Human beings have suppressed God's truth. Paul goes on to show how all people, Gentiles (1:21–32) and Jews (2:1–29) alike, have rejected God's truth and brought justly on themselves God's wrath. In 3:1–8 Paul moves away from the main story line to qualify what he says in chapter 2 about the privileges of the Jews. Then, in 3:9–20, he brings the discussion to a close with a final indictment of humanity.

The particular section we are now dealing with divides into three basic parts: God's wrath against sin and its basis (1:18–20), people's suppression of truth and its consequences (1:21–31), and a concluding indictment (1:32).

God's Wrath against Sin and Its Basis (1:18–20)

VERSE 18 APPEARS at first sight to be closely related to verses 16–17. A *gar* ("for") connects verse 18 with what comes before it, and both verses 17 and 18 use the verb "reveal." On this basis a few interpreters have concluded that the revelation of God's righteousness (v. 17) and the revelation of his wrath (v. 18) are both parts of the gospel (v. 16).[1] But the negative note of God's wrath does not fit Paul's consistently positive use of the word "gospel." Probably, then, the "for" that begins this verse introduces all of the section that follows: It is necessary for God to reveal his righteousness in the gospel *because* God has also found it necessary to reveal his wrath against sin.

Some modern translations use the term "anger" instead of "wrath" for the Greek word used here (*orge*). But "wrath," while a bit old-fashioned, preserves

---

1. See esp. Karl Barth, *A Shorter Commentary on Romans* (Richmond: John Knox, 1959), 42–43; Cranfield, *The Epistle to the Romans*, 106–8.

the more objective sense the Greek word has when applied to God. God's reaction to sin is not the "anger" of an emotional person; it is the necessary reaction of a holy God to sin. The Old Testament regularly speaks of God's inflicting wrath on people, both in the course of history (e.g., Ex. 32:10 – 12; Num. 11:1; Jer. 21:3 – 7) and, especially, at the end of history. Paul usually also depicts God's wrath as coming at the Parousia (see, e.g., Rom. 2:5, 8; 5:9; Col. 3:6; 1 Thess. 1:10). Because of this, some interpreters think that the verb "is being revealed" is a futuristic present, meaning "will be revealed."[2] But Paul is probably referring broadly to the sentence of condemnation that all people stand under — a sentence that God sometimes inflicts in the events of history but will carry out with finality at the end of history.

Especially important for Paul is his insistence that God's wrath falls on people who "suppress the truth." One can only suppress something of which one has knowledge. As a result, Paul goes on in verses 19 – 20 to show that this word is entirely appropriate to use in describing people's relationship to God's truth. Human beings do have knowledge about God. He has revealed it to them (v. 19b), manifesting some of his divine qualities in the world he has created (v. 20). Moreover, these qualities "have been clearly seen" by people.

Paul here establishes the truth of what we sometimes call "natural revelation": God discloses something of his existence and nature to all people in the created natural world (for more on this, see the Contemporary Significance section). Yet the end of verse 20 already anticipates the negative direction that Paul's argument about natural revelation will take: "so that men are without excuse." Rather than bringing people into relationship with God, natural revelation makes them guilty. Why this is so and how it has happened will be the focus of the next section.

Peoples' Suppression of Truth and Its Consequences (1:21 – 31)

THIS SECTION IS dominated by a thrice-repeated sequence:

> "they . . . exchanged" (vv. 22 – 23) — "Therefore God gave them
> over . . ." (v. 24)
> "they exchanged" (v. 25) — "Because of this, God gave them over
> . . ." (v. 26)
> "their women exchanged . . . in the same way the men also" (vv.
> 26b – 27) — "he gave them over . . ." (v. 28b)

In each case, human beings put their own "god" or sin in place of the truth God has revealed to them. God reacts by "handing them over" to the conse-

---

2. See, e.g., Sanday and Headlam, *The Epistle to the Romans*, 41.

quences of the choice they have made. Just who the people are who make these "exchanges" is never clearly stated; throughout Paul uses the general "they."

A few interpreters have suggested Paul may be speaking directly about the decision of the first human pair in the Garden of Eden to turn from God. However, while the story of humankind's original fall into sin has undoubtedly colored Paul's description, what he says goes far beyond this situation. It is better to think that he has in view human beings generally, prone to turn away from God because of the original fall into sin. What he says, in other words, is typical of human beings who have been given some evidence of God's truth in the natural world around them. They choose not to worship God but to worship gods of their own making, falling deeper into sin in the process and earning God's condemnation.

The first "exchange" (1:21—24) focuses explicitly on idolatry. People "knew" God (i.e., they knew about him; cf. v. 20), but they refused to acknowledge him. "Their thinking became futile" (v. 21b), they prided themselves on their own wisdom (v. 22), and they traded the "glory of the immortal God" for their own self-made images (v. 23). Paul echoes language used in the Old Testament to describe Israel's fall into idolatry when the people fashioned a golden calf to worship (see Ex. 32): "They exchanged their Glory for an image of a bull, which eats grass" (Ps. 106:20; see also Jer. 2:11). Paul implies, therefore, that his condemnation of idolatry in this section may extend beyond Gentiles to include, as least in theory, Jews.

As a punishment for this idolatry, God "gave them over." What Paul means by this language is not clear. Some give it a passive sense, as Godet illustrates: "He [God] ceased to hold the boat as it was dragged by the current of the river."[3] But the language suggests a more active involvement of God. He does not simply let go of the boat; rather, he confirms its disastrous course downstream. God reacts to the human decision to turn from him by consigning people to the consequences of their actions. As Paul will show, this involves an ever-increasing cycle of sin, but he highlights sexual sins. The NIV rightly interprets the general word "immorality" (*akatharsia*, lit. "uncleanness") as "sexual impurity." In keeping with a widespread Jewish tradition that Paul is adapting in this passage (see Bridging Contexts section on 2:1—11), he shows how the sin of idolatry leads to the disruption of God's intention in sexual relationships.

The second "exchange sequence" (1:25—26) reiterates the connection between idolatry and sexual sin established in verse 24. The end of verse 26 is then transitional, as Paul both unpacks this sexual sin in terms of homosexuality

---

3. Godet, *Commentary on Romans*, 107. Chrysostom, one of the great patristic commentators on Romans, held a similar view.

and introduces the third "exchange sequence" as well (vv. 26b–28). He there singles out both women and men. Paul uses the Greek words for "female" (*thelys*) and "male" (*arsen*) to underscore the divine creation of human beings into these two categories and the implications about proper sexual conduct that flow from that distinction. The same emphasis on created intention is also conveyed by the language of "nature" in this passage: Women "exchanged natural relationships for unnatural ones" (v. 26b), and men likewise "abandoned natural relations with women" (v. 27). These "natural" relations are the ones God established for human beings in his creation (see Bridging Contexts section for more on this).

The focus on homosexual acts in these verses again reflects Jewish tradition, which often saw in homosexuality particularly striking evidence of the Gentiles' idolatry and depravity. At the end of this section, Paul indicates the consequences of the indulgence in homosexual acts (in this case, among men in particular), that they "received in themselves the due penalty for their perversion" (v. 27b). Since Paul in this passage seems to be detailing various ways in which God's wrath is inflicted on human beings, and since AIDS so often afflicts homosexual men, it is not surprising that some interpreters have thought that this disease is one manifestation of God's wrath against human sin. But such a conclusion is possible only if we recognize that virtually all that is evil or wrong in our world is likewise a manifestation of God's wrath. AIDS is simply one visible and deadly evidence of a world that has turned from God and brought on itself tragedies of all kinds.

At the end of verse 28, Paul finally introduces the "handing over" that corresponds to the "exchanged" of verse 26b. He has muddied their close relationship in his desire in verse 28 to emphasize the correspondence between sin and result. The relationship is intolerably awkward in English, but it would go something like this: Because people did not "approve" (*edokimasan;* NIV, "think it worthwhile") of God's knowledge, he handed them over to "unapproved" (*adokimon;* NIV, "depraved") minds. Sin affects not only our affections (idolatry) and our senses (sex) but our very thinking.

Turning away from true knowledge of God means cutting ourselves off from any ultimately accurate understanding of this world and our place within it. No wonder that people do not understand the moral stances that Christians take on the basis of God's truth! Another result is not surprising either: People end up doing "what ought not to be done" (v. 28b). In verses 29–31, Paul provides several illustrations of this sinful conduct. His list falls into three parts, indicated accurately in the NIV in its three-sentence arrangement:

- "They have become filled with every kind of wickedness, evil, greed and depravity."
- "They are full of envy, murder, strife, deceit and malice."

- "They are gossips, slanderers, God-haters, insolent, arrogant and boastful; they invent ways of doing evil; they disobey their parents; they are senseless, faithless, heartless, ruthless."

The syntactical structure reflects a certain logical order as well. The first sentence contains a list of general terms for sin; the second focuses on basic sins affecting human relationships; and the third list is more a potpourri of sinful conduct. Similar lists of sins—usually called "vice lists"—appear elsewhere in the New Testament (Matt. 15:19; Gal. 5:19–21; Col. 3:5; 1 Tim. 1:9–10; 1 Peter 2:1; 4:3) and imitate a widespread secular form.

While some of the Greek terms in these lists are obviously chosen for their appropriateness to the context, many are cited at random. Paul is simply trying to convey in a general way the different forms that sin can take. After focusing on idolatry and sexual sins, he may have been worried that some readers would conclude that only such "major" sins really were a problem. So he adds at the end of the paragraph a long list of sins, convinced that at least one of them will hit home to every person who reads the letter. We may not be worshiping the statue of an animal, but do we gossip? The latter, while perhaps not as serious to us as the former, is nevertheless just as much an indication of God's wrath against sin.

Concluding Indictment (1:32)

AT THE END of this section, Paul reiterates its key themes. (1) Human beings are in a position to understand God's truth. Earlier Paul focused on what we might call "ontological" knowledge of God, that in creation, people come to understand something of God's existence and nature (v. 20). In verse 32, however, he turns to the "moral" knowledge that people also possess: They "know God's righteous decree that those who do such things deserve death" (cf. 2:14–16, where Paul elaborates on this general idea by introducing the faculty of the "conscience"). Yet Paul makes clear here that people in general (the subject is still the vague "they") have a sense of right and wrong and understand that wrong actions deserve punishment.

(2) The next key theme that Paul expresses one last time is the fact of divine punishment for sin. Sinners "deserve death." Death (*thanatos*) is spiritual death, the condemnation or wrath of God, under which all human beings stand as a result of sin.

(3) The final part of verse 32 introduces something of an unexpected twist in Paul's argument. He suggests it is worse for a person to "approve" those who practice sins than to do them oneself. Paul would be the last to minimize the seriousness of actual sin. But he apparently wants to castigate especially those people who, while not themselves perhaps tempted by a

particular sin, lead others into it by their approval of it. As Murray says, "we are not only bent on damning ourselves but we congratulate others in the doing of those things that we know have their issue in damnation."[4]

PERHAPS THE BIGGEST obstacle to accurate interpretation of Scripture is the conflict in worldview between the biblical author and readers on the one hand and the contemporary reader on the other. Biblical authors will frequently touch on a concept that is everywhere accepted in their own culture but which clashes violently with the culture of the reader. Two important issues raised in these verses are clear examples of such notions: the wrath of God and homosexuality.

Cultural influences on our understanding of God's wrath. One famous scholarly reaction to Paul's teaching on God's wrath in Romans 1:18ff. will help us to put the problem in focus. C. H. Dodd, a British scholar active in the middle of the century, made significant contributions to our understanding of the New Testament. But he struggled with Paul's teaching about God's wrath. Dodd was deeply trained in ancient Greek literature. Throughout this literature (as, indeed, in the literature of many cultures) the "wrath" of the gods is emotional and capricious, often driven by ego rather than by justice.

A person, a family, a town, or a whole nation, for example, might inadvertently offend a god by failing to offer a sacrifice in the right manner or by refusing hospitality to a visitor. Such a "sinful" act may be the cause of the wrath; in this sense, one could say the wrath was "justified." But the degree of wrath inflicted is all out of proportion to the offense. The motivation for the wrath is not a desire on the god's part to establish justice but to assuage his offended pride or dignity. Dodd had a hard time believing that the God of the Bible ever acted in such a way. Thus, to avoid any hint of emotionalism or capriciousness in the biblical concept, he argued that God's wrath was nothing more than "an inevitable process of cause and effect in a moral universe."[5]

But such an understanding of God's wrath is more in keeping with a deistic view of God. For deists, God is little more than the original cause of the

---

4. Murray, *The Epistle to the Romans*, 1:53. Paul may again reflect Jewish tradition here: "The two-faced are doubly punished because they both practice evil and approve of others who practice it; they imitate the spirits of error and join in the struggle against mankind" (*T. Asher* 6:2).

5. C. H. Dodd, *The Epistle of Paul to the Romans* (New York: Harper and Bros., 1932), 50. See also, for a similar approach, A. T. Hanson, *The Wrath of the Lamb* (London: SPCK, 1957), 84–85.

universe. Having set it in a motion, he is now content to let it run its course without intervention (the usual analogy is the watchmaker). But the Bible presents God as a personal being, interested in and intervening in the course of human history in all kinds of ways. To be sure, we must allow for the frequent anthropopathic element in the biblical description of God. The biblical writers often use analogies with human emotions to depict God, and we are wrong if we attribute these emotions to God in the same way as they are present in us. But we cannot avoid the distinctly personal language used to describe God's relationship to his world. He chastises, tests, repents, rejoices, and, yes, he grows angry.

But God's anger is not like ours, nor is it like the wrath of the Greek gods. His anger is like theirs in that it is motivated by an offense against divine standards, but it is never egotistic, as if he feels he needs to defend his dignity. Nor is it capricious, for God always acts justly, on the basis of his own unchangeable standards revealed in his Word to human beings. In fact, rather than dismissing pagan notions of the wrath of the gods entirely, we should perhaps see in them a pale reflection of the truth about the wrath of the real God. In the pagan impulse to appease an angry deity, in both ancient and modern times, we can detect one way in which God has left in the world he created some evidence of himself.

But if immersion in certain cultures leads people to interpret God's wrath inaccurately, immersion in others can lead us to dismiss the concept altogether. Modern materialism, of course, denies the possibility of God's wrath. But perhaps a greater danger to the church is the persistent tendency in the midst of the awakened interest in "spirituality" to view God as a purely benign being. If God exists, so many people seem to reason, then he must be a good God who has our own interests at heart. Surely he could never be angry with us or do anything that might inconvenience us!

This view of God is far from the biblical view of a holy and righteous God whose very nature demands that he react negatively to sin. Ultimately a failure to appreciate the reality of God's holiness and its implication, wrath against sin, warps our understanding of the Christian faith generally. Thus, believers seeking to understand Paul's presentation of the gospel in Romans need to adjust their own perspective to match the biblical worldview. Reading and rereading Scripture is the only practicable way to soak up that biblical worldview.

Cultural influences on our understanding of homosexuality. Most modern cultures have undergone a bewilderingly rapid sea change in views on homosexuality. What was condemned twenty years ago is now accepted—indeed, sometimes advocated—as an "alternative lifestyle." It is not easy for Christians to get their bearings when so sudden and violent a shift occurs.

Some too quickly go with the flow and read the change in culture into the Bible; others so strongly resist the flow that they go beyond what the Bible says. Romans 1:26–27 is one of the three most important passages in the New Testament on homosexuality (see also 1 Cor. 6:9–10; 1 Tim. 1:10). Since understanding the context of Paul's teaching is vital to correct interpretation of the passages, we must treat this matter in the present section.

Interpreters agree that Greek culture, in general, tolerated and sometimes even looked approvingly on homosexual relationships, especially between men, and that Jewish culture universally condemned them. The Jewish viewpoint is well summarized in *Sybilline Oracles* 3.594–600: "Surpassing, indeed, all humans, they [Jewish men] are mindful of holy wedlock and do not engage in evil intercourse with male children, as do Phoenicians, Egyptians, and Romans, spacious Greece and many other nations, Persians, Galatians, and all Asia, transgressing the holy law of the immortal God." The Jews' condemnation of homosexuality is rooted, of course, in the Old Testament, which plainly and repeatedly denounces the practice (see, e.g., Gen. 19:1–28; Lev. 18:22; 20:13; Deut. 23:17–18). Paul seems to take over the typical Jewish viewpoint, highlighting homosexual behavior as an especially obvious indication of the way human beings have turned from the true God.

But modern revisionists, seeking to bring the Bible in line with contemporary culture, argue that this is not the case. They take two different, though sometimes overlapping, tacks. (1) Some interpreters suggest Paul may be citing the Jewish teaching on homosexuality not because he necessarily agrees with it but simply because it is part of the tradition he is using at this point.[6] But would Paul take over teaching he does not agree with? He is not quoting from a source, so he is at liberty to take over whatever part of the tradition he wants and to omit whatever he wants. Surely his inclusion of this part of the tradition shows that he agrees with it.

(2) Other interpreters have seized on the language of "against nature" that Paul uses in 1:26–27 to argue that those whom Paul condemns here are only those who practice homosexuality when it is against their *own* nature.[7] In other words, it would be wrong for a person with a heterosexual orientation to engage in homosexual relations, but not for a person with a "natural" homosexual orientation. The problem with this view is a failure to understand Paul's "nature" language against its proper background. Paul is using this word as other Jewish writers did, to refer to the natural order of things *as ordained by God.* The historian Josephus, for example, writes that "the law [of Moses] knows no

---

6. Robin Scroggs, *The New Testament and Homosexuality* (Philadelphia: Fortress, 1983), 114–15.
7. See John Boswell, *Christianity, Social Tolerance and Homosexuality: Gay People in Europe from the Beginning of the Christian Era to the Fourteenth Century* (Chicago: Univ. of Chicago Press, 1980), 111.

sexual connection but the natural intercourse with a wife" (*Against Apion* 2.24). "Nature" in this passage refers not to individual human nature or orientation but to the world as God has made it. Engaging in homosexual activity is to violate his created intention in making human beings male and female.[8]

Paul therefore endorses the Old Testament and Jewish view: Homosexual relations violate the order of creation established by God for all people. Believers ought to judge our culture by biblical standards and not force the Bible into the mold of our culture. Yet in a laudable insistence on maintaining biblical standards, we should not go further than Scripture. The Bible does not brand as sinful a homosexual orientation as such, only the indulgence of that orientation in lustful attitudes or actual sex.

Nor is it so clear that the Bible presents homosexual activity as a perversion worse than any other—as many Christians have thought. To be sure, Romans 1 singles out homosexual activity for special attention. But Paul's purpose in doing so may not be because he regards it as a more serious sin than others but because he sees it as a particularly clear illustration of the violation of the created order. In any case, we are clearly called on to offer the same love and hope through the gospel to homosexuals that we offer to any caught up in any forms of sin.

IN THE BRIDGING CONTEXTS section, we have already moved into the application of this paragraph to contemporary life. But the passage is rich in implication, and we will explore here the significance of two more issues Paul raises in these verses.

Natural revelation. In what becomes both a fascination and a frustration, the interpreter of Romans is confronted in virtually every chapter with a text that is one of the most important in the Bible on a huge and usually debated theological issue. The fascination comes from getting into issues of such far-reaching significance; the frustration comes from the need to study so much Scripture in order to come to a right understanding of the particular text in Romans. Nothing in Romans 1 stimulates these reactions more than Paul's teaching on natural revelation.

This issue is unclear in the Bible, with many texts to be considered and not all them appearing to move in the same direction. Moreover, the religious

---

8. For an excellent response to Boswell's interpretation (which has been picked up by many other interpreters), see Richard B. Hays, "Relations Natural and Unnatural: A Response to John Boswell's Exegesis of Romans 1," *JRE* 14 (1986): 184–215. See also Hays' larger discussion of homosexuality in *The Moral Vision of the New Testament* (San Francisco: Harper, 1996), 379–406.

pluralism of our culture has put the whole matter of God's revelation in other religions at the top of the theological agenda. We have neither the space nor the expertise to treat this issue adequately. But several points can be drawn from what Paul teaches here in Romans 1.

(1) There is such a thing as natural revelation. A few scholars, notably the important twentieth-century theologian Karl Barth, have denied the existence of any true revelation of God apart from Christ. But Paul seems clear: "For since the creation of the world God's invisible qualities—his eternal power and divine nature—have been clearly seen, being understood from what has been made" (v. 20). Not only has God left clear evidence of himself in the world he has made, but this evidence is actually perceived by people: It is "clearly seen"; "God has made it plain to them" (v. 19).

Most theologians have, therefore, rightly concluded that alongside "special" revelation—God's acts and their authoritative interpretation in Scripture—we must also place "natural" revelation—God's disclosure of information about himself in the world. The reality of natural revelation and its universal availability has consequences for one of the most often-asked questions about God's justice: What about the fate of those who have "never heard"? This is a question I myself asked when people were witnessing to me in my college days. It has no easy answer. But one thing we can say on the basis of Romans 1: All people *have* heard. God has revealed certain truths about himself in the world, and all people have access to that truth. Every person is guilty of rejecting that knowledge of God universally available.

(2) What God reveals to people in nature is limited. In this context, Paul refers to certain "invisible qualities" of God and to a recognition that sinful acts are worthy of death (v. 32). He does not mention any other theological truths as available to people through natural revelation. His silence does not, of course, mean that God might not reveal other truth through this means. But natural revelation is rather limited in the amount of information about God that it conveys.

(3) The results of natural revelation are negative. We must recall the larger purpose of Paul at this point in Romans. He is showing why the revelation of God's righteousness in the gospel is necessary—because all people are locked up under sin's power (3:9) and are helpless to free themselves from its grip. The drastic step God has taken in the gospel—sending his Son to die on a Roman cross—would surely be unnecessary if rescue were available elsewhere. We will pursue this issue further when considering 2:14–16. Suffice it to say here that Paul's whole argument makes any positive role for natural revelation at this point in Romans unlikely.

More important is what Paul explicitly says about natural revelation in this passage. For verse 20 concludes: "so that men are without excuse." Paul presents the reality of natural revelation in order to justify his assertion that people "suppress the truth" (v. 18). His purpose is to vindicate God by proving that he is perfectly just in inflicting his wrath on people. They had some knowledge of God; they turned away from that knowledge; thus, they are "without excuse" before God when he pours his wrath out on them.

Calvin's summary of the matter is worth quoting at length:

> It is therefore in vain that so many burning lamps shine for us in the workmanship of the universe to show forth the glory of its Author. Although they bathe us wholly in their radiance, yet they can of themselves in no way lead us into the right path. Surely they strike some sparks, but before their fuller light shines forth these are smothered.... But although we lack the natural ability to mount up unto the pure and clear knowledge of God, all excuse is cut off because the fault of dullness is within us.[9]

But we must not take this negative point too far. As Calvin has rightly put it, the truths revealed by God in nature "of themselves" cannot bring one to a true knowledge of God. But Paul does not deny that these truths may help lead people to search for true knowledge of God or to illustrate that knowledge. An important passage here is Acts 17:22–34, where Paul uses natural revelation as a stepping-stone to the presentation of the gospel to intellectuals in Athens. Thus, the evidence of Scripture as a whole leads us to conclude that natural revelation has a real, but limited, purpose. The beauty and intricacy of the world can help people understand that there must be a Creator; that religious traditions can reinforce notions of sin, judgment, and atonement; and that history can point to a providential ordering of events. Such things can stimulate in people a search for the true God. But Paul emphasizes how limited such knowledge is. Apart from God's grace, it does not lead people to worship the true God. Without further revelation about Christ and his work on the cross, disclosed in the gospel, it cannot bring salvation.

Idolatry. This point is, perhaps, obvious—but no interpretation of Romans 1 would be complete without reminding ourselves of all the varied shapes that idolatry can take. Paul accuses people of turning from the "glory" and "truth" of God to images and lies of their own making (vv. 23, 25). Few of us worship images, but we are all prone to put something in the place that God alone deserves in our lives. That "idol" may be something evil in itself. But more often, the devil is more insidious, using a perfectly good or innocent pleasure to lure us from the wholehearted devotion to God that he deserves and demands.

---

9. John Calvin, *Institutes* 1.5.14.

Recently, for instance, my old love for photography has reawakened, and I find myself as an almost "empty-nester" with a bit (but only a little bit!) more disposable income than in the last couple of decades. I have therefore been buying some equipment (though, of course, one never has enough equipment) and spending time reading books on photography, chatting with other photographers on the Web, and taking trips and walks where I can take photographs. I am convinced that photography is a good creative outlet, a healthy change-of-pace from reading, studying, and teaching, and a wonderful hobby that my wife and I can share together. But I have also seen that photography is capable of taking up far too much of my time and money. It can, in brute fact, become an "idol" for me.

Idols lurk everywhere, lying in wait for those not fully enough aware of the danger. Liberated from idolatry in the ultimate sense by the work of God in Christ applied to our hearts, we can still fall prey to idols in a weaker sense, allowing people, things, or activities to deflect our worship and service of the true God.

Romans 2:1–11

YOU, THEREFORE, HAVE no excuse, you who pass judgment on someone else, for at whatever point you judge
the other, you are condemning yourself, because you
who pass judgment do the same things. ²Now we know that
God's judgment against those who do such things is based on
truth. ³So when you, a mere man, pass judgment on them and
yet do the same things, do you think you will escape God's
judgment? ⁴Or do you show contempt for the riches of his
kindness, tolerance and patience, not realizing that God's
kindness leads you toward repentance?

⁵But because of your stubbornness and your unrepentant
heart, you are storing up wrath against yourself for the day of
God's wrath, when his righteous judgment will be revealed.
⁶God "will give to each person according to what he has
done." ⁷To those who by persistence in doing good seek glory,
honor and immortality, he will give eternal life. ⁸But for those
who are self-seeking and who reject the truth and follow evil,
there will be wrath and anger. ⁹There will be trouble and distress for every human being who does evil: first for the Jew,
then for the Gentile; ¹⁰but glory, honor and peace for everyone who does good: first for the Jew, then for the Gentile.
¹¹For God does not show favoritism.

<table>
<tr><td>Original Meaning</td></tr>
</table>

Original Meaning

PAUL SIGNALS A SHIFT in his argument at the beginning of chapter 2 by abandoning the third plural
verbs he has used throughout 1:18–32 (i.e., "*they*
knew God"; "*they* exchanged"; "*they* know God's
righteous decree") in favor of the second person singular: "*You*, therefore,
have no excuse." This change suggests he is now turning his attention to a
different group of people. The second person address could, of course, mean
he is now speaking directly to the Roman Christians. But why would he use
a *singular* form of "you" if this were his intention? It seems unlikely that he is
addressing a single person in the church.

In fact, Paul here begins to use a popular ancient literary form, in which
a speaker or writer instructs his audience by letting them listen in on a

discussion between himself and the representative of another viewpoint (see Bridging Contexts, below). What viewpoint does the person Paul here addresses represent? Some interpreters think he has in mind educated pagans, who prided themselves on being superior to the run-of-the-mill people Paul condemns in 1:18−32.[1] But it is more likely that he is now beginning to address Jews.[2]

To be sure, Paul does not directly address his "opponent" as a Jew until 2:17. But the language he uses in verses 1−5 points unmistakably to a Jewish situation. Paul has shown in 1:21−32 that Gentiles have suppressed the truth that God revealed to them in nature and they therefore have "no excuse" before God. He now begins to show that Jews also suppress the truth God has given them and that they, too, are "without excuse."

Paul's argument in these verses develops in two clear stages, marked by a shift from the second person (vv. 1−5) to the third person (vv. 6−11). In the former paragraph, he exposes as false the Jews' presumption of superiority over the Gentile. In the latter, he sets forth the theoretical basis for this exposé, arguing that God assesses all people on the same basis.

Self-Righteous Jews Are as Guilty as the Gentiles (2:1−5)

THE "THEREFORE" THAT opens this section is unexpected. How can Paul's indictment of Jews be a *conclusion* drawn from his indictment of Gentiles in chapter 1? Two considerations provide the answer. (1) As we suggested in our interpretation of 1:23, Paul's "target" in 1:21−32 may be a bit wider than Gentiles per se. What he does is demonstrate the plight of people in light of natural revelation—and Jews, of course, receive natural revelation along with all other people. Thus he may well claim that the general indictment of 1:21−32 justifies the conclusion that Jews, also, "have no excuse" before God.[3]

(2) Another consideration is even more to the point. In chapter 2, Paul is not picking up the argument in 1:21−32, but the universal indictment in 1:18−20: Jews are without excuse because they are, along with all people, guilty of suppressing the truth. We find, then, a general parallelism in Paul's argument that matches a key concern of his throughout this section: Jews, like Gentiles (see 1:20), are "without excuse" before God and are therefore, in the long run, no better off than Gentiles.

---

1. E.g., Calvin, *The Epistle of Paul the Apostle to the Romans*, 83−84; Barrett, *The Epistle to the Romans*, 42−43.

2. So most commentators; see Moo, *The Epistle to the Romans*, 128.

3. See esp. Cranfield, *The Epistle to the Romans*, 140−41.

By the time Paul writes Romans, he has been preaching the gospel for at least twenty-two years. He knows exactly how people will respond to the various points he makes. How often must Paul have condemned the Gentiles for their sin only to note Jews in the audience joining in with his criticism and priding themselves on being far superior to them. Thus, we can almost see Paul at the beginning of chapter 2 fixing his gaze on these self-satisfied Jews and blasting them in the same way he has condemned the Gentiles.

But how can Paul claim that Jews are doing "the same things" as the Gentiles (2:1)? Probably he means the same kinds of things. Jews in the first century were not idolaters, nor was homosexuality common among them. But they did commit many of the sins Paul lists in 1:29–31. Perhaps he even thinks of their preoccupation with the law as a kind of idolatry. In any case, their "judging" of other people rebounds directly onto them. For since they are doing the same things as these other people, they condemn themselves at the same time. No one can escape this judgment.

(1) God's judgment is "based on truth" (*aletheia;* v. 2). It is just and impartial, based on the facts (Paul develops this point in vv. 6–11).

(2) Relying on "the riches of [God's] kindness, tolerance and patience" to avoid judgment will not work (vv. 3–4). These words together connote God's grace and willingness to forgive. "Kindness" (*chrestotes*) occurs again in Romans in 11:22, where it is the opposite of God's "sternness," and it appears regularly in the Psalms to denote God's goodness to Israel.[4] "Tolerance" (*anoche*) occurs in only one other place in the New Testament, where it refers again to God's "forbearance" (Rom. 3:25). Paul's use of this language suggests he is thinking at this point of the Jewish people. For we must remember that the Jews' assumption of superiority over Gentiles was not a matter of ego or personal boasting. Out of all the nations of the earth, God had chosen Israel as his people. Surely, Jews may well have reasoned, as God's chosen people, they are immune from judgment—his "tolerance" and "kindness" will always cause him to overlook our sins.

In fact, we have numerous Jewish texts from about this period that display precisely this attitude (see Bridging Contexts). It is this assumption Paul attacks here. Without denying the Jews' special favor, he criticizes them for "showing contempt" (*kataphroneo*) for God's goodness to them (v. 4). How? God's kindness, Paul says, was intended to lead "you toward repentance." Instead, apparently, the Jews were regarding it as a carte blanche to sin with impunity. As a result, concludes the apostle, the Jews are "storing up wrath" against themselves, a wrath that will be inflicted on the day of God's coming righteous judgment (v. 5).

---

4. See, e.g., Ps. 25:7; 31:19; 68:10; 119:48; 145:7; note also the intertestamental book *Pss. Sol.* 5:18.

God Judges Every Human Being
Impartially on the Same Basis (2:6–11)

THIS IMPORTANT PARAGRAPH supports a point that is implicit, but vital, to Paul's indictment of self-righteous Jews in 2:1–5: God assesses Jews and Gentiles on the same basis. In effect, Paul argues, there is a level playing field when it comes to God's ultimate verdict. The Jew, therefore, simply by virtue of being a Jew cannot claim immunity from judgment. The argument of these verses is clear and logical, following a pattern we label *chiasm*. This word comes from the name for the Greek letter that looks much like our "X." It describes a structure in which the basic sequence follows an A-B-B'-A' pattern. Note how verses 6–11 fall into such a pattern:

A God will judge everyone according to his works (v. 6)
   B People who do good will attain eternal life (v. 7)
      C People who do evil will suffer wrath (v. 8)
      C' Wrath for those who do evil (v. 9)
   B' Glory for those who do good (v. 10)
A' God judges impartially (v. 11)

Sometimes in a chiasm, the main point comes at the center. In this case, however, the main point appears at the outer edges. In verse 6 Paul quotes from the Old Testament to show that "works" (NIV, "what he has done") will be the basis for God's judgment. The exact source of Paul's quotation is not certain, since several verses (esp. Prov. 24:12; cf. also Ps. 62:12; Eccl. 1:14; Hos. 12:2) make a similar point. "Works" (*erga*) is a general term denoting anything a person does. Key to Paul's argument is the word "each person"—including both Jews and Gentiles.

Paul makes a similar point in verse 11 by insisting that God "does not show favoritism." The word for "favoritism" (*prosopolempsia*, lit., "receiving the face") was apparently coined by Christians to translate a Hebrew expression that vividly conveys the sense of partiality: treating someone on the basis of outward appearance. God, Paul claims, does not do this. He will not let a person go free in the judgment simply because of some external circumstance.

The impartiality of God is not a new idea with Paul, for many Jews asserted the same thing (e.g., Sir. 35:15: "The Lord is the judge, and with him there is no partiality [lit., glory of the face]"). But Paul's apparent application of the "partiality" principle to Jews in terms of their covenant privileges and the judgment is a new and radical concept. He seems to be denying the covenant itself and, implicitly, God's own revelation in the Old Testament. Already, therefore, we see emerging the question of the continuity between the Old Testament and the gospel that becomes so central to the argument of Romans (see esp. 3:1–8; chs. 9–11).

In the middle of the chiasm Paul spells out the implications of God's impartial judgment, based on works, for two opposite kinds of people. On the one hand (v. 7), God will "render eternal life" to those "who by their persistence in a good work are seeking glory and honor and immortality" (pers. trans.). On the other hand (v. 8) are "those who are self-seeking and who reject the truth and follow evil." The NIV's rendering of "self-seeking" captures the sense of the Greek word (*eritheia*) well. The only pre-New Testament occurrence of the word is in Aristotle, who uses it to decry politicians who seek office for private gain rather than the public good.[5] Such people earn for themselves "wrath and anger." These two words do not have separate meanings here; they combine to emphasize the concept of condemnation.[6]

Just in case we missed the point, Paul goes over, more briefly, the same ground again in verses 9 and 10. His addition in each verse of the phrase "first for the Jew, then for the Gentile," however, reveals the point of application he wants us to draw from the argument. Indeed, by applying the phrase to both salvation and condemnation, Paul extends the principle of "Jew first" (cf. 1:16) in a direction that no Jew would probably have anticipated. Paul's point seems to be that, as God's chosen people, the Jews are especially the addressees of God's Word. When they respond positively, they are the first to receive blessing. But in the same way, they will also be the first to be judged for failure to respond.

TWO ISSUES, ONE hermeneutical and the other contextual, need to be tackled if we are to get the full force of Paul's teaching in this paragraph. We begin with the contextual issue.

Jewish traditions behind 1:18–2:5. Paul's indictment of the Gentiles in 1:21–32 and his shift of argument at 2:1 can only be fully appreciated when we recognize that he is adapting widespread Jewish teaching about Gentile sin and Jewish prerogatives. Many Jewish passages reflect this teaching in various degrees, but the clearest and most detailed example comes from an intertestamental book that is part of the Apocrypha. In Wisdom of Solomon 12:23–14:31, the author castigates the Gentiles for their depravity. We cannot quote this entire section, but a selection will reveal the extent of similarity with Paul's indictment of the Gentiles in Romans 1:21–32.

---

5. Gal. 5:20; Phil. 1:17; 2:3; James 3:14, 16.

6. The two terms (*thymos* and *orge*) occur together with no distinction in meaning elsewhere in both the Old Testament (Ps. 77:9; Dan. 3:13; Mic. 5:15) and New (Eph. 4:31; Col. 3:8; Rev. 19:15).

Therefore those who lived unrighteously, in a life of folly,
you tormented through their own abominations.
For they went far astray on the paths of error,
accepting as gods those animals that even their enemies despised;
they were deceived like foolish infants. (12:23–24)

For all people who were ignorant of God were foolish by nature;
and they were unable from the good things that are seen to know the
   one who exists,
nor did they recognize the artisan while paying heed to his works;
but they supposed that either fire or wind or swift air,
or the circle of the stars, or turbulent water,
or the luminaries of heaven were the gods that rule the world.
If through delight in the beauty of these things people assumed them
   to be gods,
let them know how much better than these is their Lord,
for the author of beauty created them.
And if people were amazed at their power and working,
let them perceive from them
how much more powerful is the one who formed them.
For from the greatness and beauty of created things
comes a corresponding perception of their Creator. (13:1–5)

Yet again, not even they are to be excused;
for if they had the power to know so much
that they could investigate the world,
how did they fail to find sooner the Lord of these things? (13:8–9)

For the idea of making idols was the beginning of fornication,
and the invention of them was the corruption of life. (14:12)

Then it was not enough for them to err about the knowledge of God,
but though living in great strife due to ignorance,
they call such great evils peace.
For whether they kill children in their initiations, or celebrate secret
   mysteries,
or hold frenzied revels with strange customs,
they no longer keep either their lives or their marriages pure,
but they either treacherously kill one another, or grieve one another
   by adultery,
and all is a raging riot of blood and murder, theft and deceit,
   corruption, faithlessness, tumult, perjury,
confusion over what is good, forgetfulness of favors,
defiling of souls, sexual perversion,
disorder in marriages, adultery, and debauchery.

For the worship of idols not to be named
is the beginning and cause and end of every evil. (14:22–27)

But you, our God, are kind and true,
patient, and ruling all things in mercy.
For even if we sin we are yours, knowing your power;
but we will not sin, because we know that you acknowledge us
    as yours.
For to know you is complete righteousness,
and to know your power is the root of immortality. (15:1–3)

Like Paul, the writer of this Jewish wisdom book criticizes Gentiles for idolatry, suggests that idolatry is the origin of many other sins ("the beginning of fornication," 14:12), claims that the Gentiles are "not … to be excused" (13:8) because they have ample evidence for God's existence and qualities in creation (13:1–5), and shows that the Gentiles' rejection of knowledge of God leads to all kinds of evil (14:22–27).

This close degree of correspondence in the argument may imply that Paul is depending directly on this first-century B.C. book for his own teaching. But it is also possible that both Wisdom of Solomon and Paul reflect independently a widespread Jewish tradition about the Gentile world. In either case, Paul's dependence on this teaching is obvious.

An appreciation of the background against which Paul writes here enhances the rhetorical effectiveness of his argument. What the apostle teaches about the Gentiles in 1:21–32 is probably not new to the Roman Christians. Though mainly Gentile themselves, they are undoubtedly well acquainted with both the Old Testament and Jewish traditions. As they read this part of the letter, they perhaps have a twofold reaction. While the teaching is familiar to them, they may be upset that Paul, apostle to the Gentiles, repeats this standard Jewish diatribe about Gentiles. Has not Christ broken down the barrier between Jew and Gentile, paving the way to bring both near to God through the cross (Eph. 2:11–18)? The Jewish Christians in the readership, by contrast, may be tempted to gloat a bit that Paul continues the traditional Gentile-bashing that they had been so familiar with from their days in the synagogue.

But the reaction of both groups takes a dramatic turn when they begin reading Romans 2. For the normal sequence of the tradition, reflected in Wisdom of Solomon 15, is that Gentiles are idolaters and fornicators, condemned to hell, but *we* Jews are God's people, loved by him even when we sin (15:2). It is just this assumption of Jewish superiority that Paul attacks in Romans 2:1–5. He insists that too many Jews abuse their covenant status by viewing it as a guaranteed protection from God's wrath no matter what they do.

The Old Testament prophets condemned such an attitude (see, e.g., Jer. 7), but it persisted as a widespread tendency right into the New Testament period. Yet Paul goes farther than the prophets, for he implies that the Jews have no real advantage over the Gentiles at all (see Rom. 2:6–11). This kind of argument will hearten the Gentile Christians in Rome and dismay the Jewish Christians. Is Paul denying the existence of God's covenant with Israel? How can he do that without denying the Old Testament itself?

Paul does not resolve these questions at this point, although 3:1–8 shows he is aware of them and chapters 9–11 tackle the issue head-on. At this point, Paul's purpose is to introduce a sudden and dramatic shift into a tradition that the Roman Christians are undoubtedly familiar with in order to bring home forcefully his contention, essential to the universal scope of the gospel, that all people are equal before God in the judgment.

The hermeneutical significance of the Jews. The biggest hermeneutical issue facing the interpreter of Romans who wants to make its message relevant to the church today is the role played by the Jews in the argument of the letter. Though not always fully appreciated in the past, the central role of the Jewish people in Romans is now almost universally recognized. Paul's exposition of the gospel in this letter has the Jews as its constant backdrop. He refers to them constantly, talks repeatedly about their law, the Torah, and devotes three chapters to them (chs. 9–11). He wants to show that Jews, just as much as Gentiles, are sinful and in need of the gospel, that their law cannot protect them from judgment, and that the gospel provides for the true fulfillment of the promises God made to them in the Old Testament.

But the relevance of these points for a contemporary, usually non-Jewish, congregation is not always so clear. In 2:1–5, for instance, Paul criticizes Jews for an attitude of superiority arising from their covenant relationship to God. What point can contemporary preachers make to their congregations if there are no Jews present?

The problem we have briefly sketched is a big one, and we will have to come back to it repeatedly in different contexts. But we want to suggest two general principles here that can give us some guidance as we wrestle with these different passages.

(1) We cannot simply equate the Jews in Romans with any other group (except perhaps Jews) in our own day. The very reason why Paul must spend so much time discussing the Jews in Romans is because they have, by virtue of the Old Testament covenant, a unique status. No other people has been chosen by God as Israel was. No other group can simply be substituted for the Jews in Paul's argument. This first point is the most important one to make, because it is the most neglected. In an understandable desire to make the text relevant, preachers will routinely apply to people generally, or to

Christians, what Paul says about the Jews in Romans. As we will see below, such an application is not always wrong. But the preacher, if he or she is to be faithful to the text, must at least pause to ask the question whether such application is legitimate.

(2) We have some basis to think that the Jews in Romans have a paradigmatic significance. We will note several points at which Paul seems to imply that what is true for Jews is true also of people in general (e.g., 6:14; 7:4). As people blessed above all others with access to God and his Word, the Jews represent the very best of humankind apart from Christ. Without, therefore, forgetting for one minute that many things Paul says about them in Romans refer only to them, we have, I think, some reason to apply some of the general truths about them to people more generally. Abuse of this hermeneutical "opening" is easy, so we need to be cautious about applying it and must ground our applications clearly in the text. But we will suggest some specific places where analogies of this sort can be drawn—including one in this text.

PRESUMING ON GRACE. With great caution I want now to apply the hermeneutical approach outlined above to 2:1–5. The main point of the paragraph is clear enough: Jews must not think they can sin with impunity just because they are in covenant relationship with God. Indeed, in light of verses 6–11, Paul appears to go one step farther: Jews have no right to think that the covenant, in itself, puts them in any better situation than the Gentiles before God.

This point remains, of course, entirely valid and applies to Jews today as much as it did in Paul's day. Getting Jewish people to respond to the gospel often requires that we help them first sense their need of the gospel—a need they may not sense if they are convinced their own religion takes care of any sin problem. As I write, considerable controversy has arisen over a plan of the Southern Baptist Convention to conduct an evangelistic campaign in Chicago. Especially controversial has been the preparation of material targeted to religious people such as Jews. The Southern Baptists are being accused of "proselytizing," a word that tends to have the negative nuance of forced conversion. Criticisms of this kind will grow over the next years as our culture becomes increasingly intolerant of any religion that claims to have the truth and seeks to win others over to that truth. But texts such as this one remind us that Jews need to experience God's grace in Christ.

Can any further significance be drawn from this paragraph? Can we apply its principle to groups other than Jews? Some interpreters are sure that we can, because they think Paul is addressing prideful people of any nationality in this text. But if, as I have argued, his remarks are directed to Jews, the problem remains.

I readily admit that the text gives no explicit indication of any extended application. But I do think that Paul's paradigmatic treatment of the Jews elsewhere may give us some basis to do so. For while the Jewish situation is in some respects unique, in others it is similar to people in other religions, including Christianity. We, too, can "show contempt" for God's kindness toward us by using it as a "open sesame" for sin. "God will forgive; that's his 'business,'" the French skeptic Voltaire once said; and too many believers adopt just this attitude. We grow cavalier toward our sin because we think God will simply overlook it out of his love for us in Christ.

But sin is a serious matter, whether we are in Christ or not. To be sure, I think Scripture teaches that the believer is eternally secure in Christ; and this security puts the Christian in a different position than the Jew under the old covenant. But the Scripture also teaches that a lack of concern about sin is incompatible with true faith. Thus Paul's warning in this text about "presuming on God's grace" carries a warning for the Christian as well as for the Jew.

Salvation by works? In verses 6–11 Paul "levels the playing field" for Jew and Gentile. Both, Paul affirms, will be judged impartially by God on the basis of works. Doing evil will bring wrath, but doing good will bring "eternal life" (v. 7).

But how can Paul say that doing good will lead to eternal life? Does he not make clear elsewhere that our "works" can never put us in right relationship with God (cf. 3:20; Eph. 2:11)? His apparently optimistic view of the possibility of salvation apart from explicit faith in God surfaces later in this chapter (2:13–16, 26–27). It constitutes an explosive theological issue, especially in our day of pluralism. We will have to deal with each of these other texts in turn, but interpreters take five basic approaches to the problem here.

(1) Paul may be referring to faithful Jews and moral Gentiles before the coming of Christ. Living when they did, they would have had no opportunity to respond to the gospel; thus, God regarded their persistence in doing good as a sufficient basis for their salvation.[7]

(2) Paul may be referring to Christians whose works, produced by faith, are taken into account by God in his ultimate salvific verdict.[8]

---

7. This view was especially popular in the patristic period; see, e.g., Chrysostom.

8. See, with variations, Godet, *Commentary on Romans*, 119; Cranfield, *The Epistle to the Romans*, 151–53.

(3) Paul may be referring to people generally who are saved by their works. His teaching here, then, contradicts his teaching on justification by faith alone elsewhere.[9]

(4) Paul may be referring to people who, without coming to know Christ explicitly, are enabled by God's grace to be saved and so produce works that God approves in the judgment.[10]

(5) Paul may not be referring to anyone in particular. His purpose here is to enunciate the basis on which, outside of Christ, God judges people. Whether anyone actually persists in good works adequately enough to earn salvation Paul simply does not say. His subsequent argument reveals that, in fact, no one can do so (see 3:9, 20).[11]

View (3), positing as it does a contradiction in Paul's teaching, should be set aside and only entertained as a last resort. Not only is it unlikely that Paul would contradict himself on so vital an issue within the same context, but such a contradiction also flies in the face of the truthfulness of Scripture that we think is abundantly attested. View (1) should also be set aside— nothing here suggests that Paul is looking only at the past. View (4) needs to be considered more seriously. Its advocates often insist that God will judge people on the basis of the light that they have received. But the context of Romans 1–3 reveals that only the light of the gospel truly saves. God's grace works through that gospel. So it is unlikely that Paul countenances the idea that people may be saved apart from that gospel here.

Thus we are left with view (2)—that Paul refers to Gentile Christians— and view (5)—that he simply sets forth the criterion of salvation apart from gospel without implying that anyone meets that criterion. We think the latter is better. It is true that works, produced by faith, are taken into account by God in the judgment (see 2 Cor. 5:10; James 2:14–26). But assuming faith as the basis for those works in this context is a big assumption. Paul has not been talking about faith or about Christians. What he has been talking about is the standard by which God judges all human beings. That standard is works (v. 6). People who do evil works will suffer wrath. People who persist in doing good will gain eternal life. In both cases, it is the criterion of judgment, not the people who meet that criterion, that Paul has in mind. We must remember that Paul is in the process of building a case. It can be summarized like this:

---

9. See, e.g., E. P. Sanders, *Paul, the Law and the Jewish People* (Philadelphia: Fortress, 1983), 123–35. He thinks the tension may exist because Paul has taken over in chapter 2 a Jewish synagogue homily.

10. See, e.g., Augustine, *On Grace* 7.17; Klyne R. Snodgrass, "Justification by Grace— to the Doers. An Analysis of the Place of Romans 2 in the Theology of Paul," *NTS* 32 (1986): 72–93.

11. See, e.g., Murray, *The Epistle to the Romans*, 1:78–79.

Salvation for both Jew and Gentile is available only by doing good
(2:6, 11, 13)

The power of sin prevents both Jew and Gentile from doing good
(3:9–19)

Therefore: No one can be saved by doing good (3:20)

To think that in verses 8 and 10 Paul must be thinking of specific people who gain salvation by works is to miss the point of these verses in the larger argument.

To conclude, then: We do not think these verses give any grounds for thinking that salvation can be gained apart from the gospel. Paul's argument in 1:18–3:20 is intended to establish the reason why God has unleashed his saving power in the gospel. Human beings are locked in sin and need to be rescued. For Paul to introduce at this point the possibility of salvation apart from the gospel would undercut his own argument.

What, then, do we say about people who have never had a chance to hear the gospel and either accept or reject it? Are they automatically excluded from salvation because they do not have a chance to hear? This very question was one of my key objections to the gospel when friends of mine in college first confronted me with the claims of Christ. The contemporary pluralistic environment has sharpened the question even further. Influential theologians—some within the evangelical movement—are arguing that people of genuine moral commitment can be saved apart from explicit faith in Christ. Karl Rahner, an influential Roman Catholic theologian, has coined the term "anonymous Christians" to describe such people.

While attractive for many reasons, this view simply does not square with the claims of Scripture. Paul's argument in this part of Romans is straightforward: All people are under sin's power and can escape the wrath that sin brings only by responding in faith to the gospel of God's righteousness in Christ (see 3:9, 20, 21–22). To be sure, we cannot always know just how God may reveal his gospel to people. As Paul's own example powerfully demonstrates, the preaching of the gospel by missionaries and others is God's normal means of making his gospel known to people. But we must allow that God may have other ways of revealing his gospel to people that we do not know or even understand. So, while insisting that only faith in the gospel can save, we perhaps need to be open to different ways by which people may come to know the gospel.

One final point should be made. The problem of those who have not heard takes on a slightly different complexion depending on whether one is a Calvinist or an Arminian. The Arminian, in a sense, has the bigger problem here. For Arminians believe that God's prevenient grace puts all people in the position of being able to respond to the gospel. Their response is, therefore, the crucial factor. Calvinists, by contrast, while insisting on the need for response, also claim that the ultimate cause of salvation lies in God's election, his specific choice of certain persons for salvation. The Calvinist can therefore argue that God will, in his sovereignty, see that every person he has chosen will also be exposed, in one way or another, to the gospel. Having determined the end, God will also enact the means.

I must confess that I am little closer to a compelling answer to my question about those who have not heard than I was when I was first converted. I think Scripture requires that we insist on faith in Christ as the necessary means of salvation. And I trust utterly in the absolute fairness of the God who has revealed himself to me in Jesus Christ. I am content to leave my questions in his hands and hope for clearer resolution in heaven.

Romans 2:12-16

ALL WHO SIN apart from the law will also perish apart from the law, and all who sin under the law will be judged by the law. ¹³For it is not those who hear the law who are righteous in God's sight, but it is those who obey the law who will be declared righteous. ¹⁴(Indeed, when Gentiles, who do not have the law, do by nature things required by the law, they are a law for themselves, even though they do not have the law, ¹⁵since they show that the requirements of the law are written on their hearts, their consciences also bearing witness, and their thoughts now accusing, now even defending them.) ¹⁶This will take place on the day when God will judge men's secrets through Jesus Christ, as my gospel declares.

IN THIS SHORT PARAGRAPH Paul both continues his argument from 2:1–11 and prepares the way for the subsequent discussion in 2:17–29. The issue of equitable judgment for both Jew and Gentile is carried on from 2:1–11. What is new in these verses is the introduction of the topic of the law. We can understand why the matter comes up here. For Paul has argued in 2:6–11 that Jews are in the same situation as Gentiles when it comes to God's judgment. But what Paul seems blithely to ignore is that Jews are hardly in the same situation as Gentiles. They have many privileges and blessings from God that the Gentiles do not have. Preeminent among these, especially in the eyes of first-century Jews, was the law. Paul intends to show here that the Jews' possession of the law does not give to them a decisive advantage over the Gentiles (2:12). He shows this by arguing that (1) it is doing, not possessing, the law that counts (2:13), and (2) even Gentiles have "law" in a certain sense (2:14–15).

The division in verse 12 between those "who sin apart from the law" and those "who sin under the law" corresponds to the key division in humankind that Paul deals with in the letter as a whole (1:16) and in the immediate context (2:9–10): Gentiles and Jews. "Law" (Gk. *nomos*) refers to the law of Moses—the requirements that God imposed on his people at Sinai through Moses. It was to Israel alone that this law was given, and they were made responsible for it. Therefore, when Jews sin, they sin "under" it or "in its sphere" (Gk. *en*). Gentiles, by contrast, sin "apart from" that law (Gk. *anomos*).

In either case, however, the result is the same: condemnation. The parallelism in the verse makes clear that "judge" (*krino*) in the second part of verse 12 means the same as "perish" (*apollymi*) in the first part. But why does sinning "under the law" bring condemnation? Why can the law not protect the Jews from God's wrath? Paul explains in verse 13: "It is not those who hear the law who are righteous in God's sight, but it is those who obey the law who will be declared righteous." The teaching was not new with Paul; the rabbis made the same point: "Not the expounding [of the law] is the chief thing, but the doing [of it]."[1]

Verse 13 again raises the question whether Paul teaches that people can be put right with God by what they do. Noting James 2:24, many interpreters conclude that Paul indeed means that people will be declared right by God in the judgment on the basis of their works. This does not contradict Paul's teaching elsewhere because Paul's use of "declared righteous" language describes the initial acceptance of the sinner before God—an acceptance mediated by faith alone.[2] But we think that, as in 2:8 and 10, Paul is simply asserting the standard of God's assessment (see Contemporary Significance on 2:1–11). No person ever actually meets the standard of obeying the law required for right standing with God.

Verses 14–15 are a self-contained unit that describe the Gentiles' relationship to "law." Who are these Gentiles? Three possibilities, familiar to us by now from the similar situation in 2:8 and 10 (and, to some extent, 2:13), are to be considered: Gentiles who fulfill the law and are saved apart from the gospel, Gentiles who obey parts of the law but who are not saved, and Gentile Christians. If Paul were thinking of Gentile Christians, then verses 14–15 probably explain the last part of verse 13: Those who obey the law and are declared righteous are those Gentile Christians who "do by nature the things of the law."[3] But applying the language of verses 14–15 to Gentile Christians pays too little attention to the background of Paul's teaching (see Bridging Contexts), and it also gives an unnatural interpretation to the key phrase "by nature." Christians obey God's law not by some innate ability, but by the power of the indwelling Spirit.

Thus, Paul is again apparently describing Gentiles generally. But that they might be saved by their obedience is an incorrect inference from verse 15, as we will see. If Paul is describing Gentiles generally in verses 14–15, then they are probably connected with the first part of verse 12, where Paul asserted that Gentiles sin "apart from the law." He now wants to qualify that

---

1. See *m. ʾAbot* 1:17.

2. See Godet, *Commentary on Romans*, 122; Cranfield, *The Epistle to the Romans*, 154–55; Dunn, *Romans*, 97–98.

3. See Cranfield, *The Epistle to the Romans*, 155–56.

remark by noting that Gentiles do, in a certain sense, have access to law. To be sure, they do not have *the* law—that is, the law of Moses, the Torah. But their frequent conformity to many of the requirements of that law (e.g., they do not murder, steal, or commit adultery) shows that they have a knowledge of God's basic moral requirements—God's "law" in an extended sense.

Paul's use of the word "conscience" (*syneidesis*) in verse 15 helps explain his point. God, Paul suggests, has built into all people a basic sense of right and wrong. Only the Jews have God's law in its complete written form, but all people have "law" of God.

The language of "written on their hearts" in verse 15 could again suggest that Paul is thinking of Gentile Christians, who, by virtue of the new covenant (Jer. 31:31–34) have the law written on the heart. But it is significant that Paul does *not* say that the law is written on the heart but that the "requirements of the law" (lit., "the work of the law") are. The Gentiles' innate knowledge of God's law leads them often to do what is right. When this happens, their consciences, along with their thoughts, "defend" them, convincing them that they are doing what God requires.

But they will not always obey, and when they do not, the conscience has the opposite effect: It "accuses" them. A few interpreters think that Paul is describing two classes of people: the majority who do not do the law God has given them and are condemned, and a minority who respond positively to God's law and are saved because of it. But Paul's language is much more naturally taken to refer to the same individuals. All Gentiles sometimes do the law and sometimes do not, and their consciences therefore both accuse and defend them.

Paul's reference to God's judgment in Christ in verse 16 is not easy to integrate into his argument. The NIV takes verses 14–15 as a parenthesis, suggesting that verse 16 goes with verses 12–13: "will be judged by the law [v. 12b] . . . when God will judge men's secrets." But it is better to take verse 16 with the final verbs in verse 15. The constant self-criticism of the Gentiles finds its ultimate meaning in the judgment of God at the end of history. That judgment, Paul affirms, takes place "through Jesus Christ," whom God has appointed as the arbiter (see, e.g., "the judgment seat of Christ" in 2 Cor. 5:10). This Christologically oriented judgment is fully in accord with the gospel Paul preaches.

Bridging Contexts

IN KEEPING WITH our purpose in each of these sections, we will look at two words from 2:12–16 that contemporary readers may "hear" differently than did the original audience of Romans: law and nature.

Law. We use the term *law* in a bewildering variety of ways, to describe everything from the formal stipulations that government imposes on us (e.g., "federal law") to the observed normal tendencies of the material world ("the laws of physics"). Few of us would bring these kinds of definitions of "law" to our reading of Romans, for we are obviously dealing with religious material far removed from a state code or a scientific textbook. But many of us bring to Romans a concept of God's law derived from systematic theology: the sum total of God's requirements for holy living. Luther was especially influential in using the word in this way, and it has become customary among Lutherans to divide all Scripture into the two categories: law (what God requires of us) and gospel (what God gives us).

But Paul's use of *nomos* (law) comes directly from the Old Testament and the world of Judaism in which he grew up. *Nomos* was specifically Torah— the law God gave Israel through Moses. Paul can thus claim that the law came into the world 430 years after Abraham (Gal. 3:17; see Rom. 5:13–14, 20). Moreover, as Paul's repeated references to doing (e.g., Rom. 10:5), obeying (e.g., 2:27) or observing (e.g., 2:25) the law indicate, he uses *law* to refer to the commands of the law of Moses. As he puts it in Galatians 3:12, "the law is not based on faith."

To understand Paul's argument in Romans, where he uses *nomos* over seventy times, we must realize that he is almost always referring to this specific law. The first occurrences already reveal this focus: Gentiles are those who sin "apart from the law" (2:12), for they "do not have the law" (2:14); Jews, on the other hand, are those who live "under the law" (2:12).

But Paul occasionally uses *nomos* in an extended, or broader, sense. In 2:14, for instance, he claims that Gentiles who do not have the law (Torah) nevertheless can become "a law for themselves." Here *nomos* has the more general sense of the divine demand without regard to its specific form. A passage that reveals this sense especially clearly is 1 Corinthians 9:19–21:

> Though I am free and belong to no man, I make myself a slave to everyone, to win as many as possible. To the Jews I became like a Jew, to win the Jews. To those under the law I became like one under the law (though I myself am not under the law), so as to win those under the law. To those not having the law I became like one not having the law (though I am not free from God's law but am under Christ's law), so as to win those not having the law.

Here, as in Romans 2:12, "those under the law" are the Jews and "those not having the law" are Gentiles. Paul himself claims he is "not under the law" in this sense of the word. He no longer feels bound to follow the specific law of Moses, the Torah. But, he quickly adds, this does not mean that he is "free from God's law." Clearly this last use of "law" must encompass God's moral demand generally.

Paul can also use *nomos* by synecdoche (a part standing for the whole) to refer to the Pentateuch (1 Cor. 9:8, 9; 14:21, 34; Gal. 4:21b) or even to the Old Testament as a whole (Rom. 3:19). And, though debated, we will argue that the evidence suggests he can also occasionally use the word broadly to mean rule or principle (see Rom. 3:28; 7:23; 8:2).

But such extended uses represent a small percentage (less than 10 percent) of Paul's uses of *nomos*. Most of the time his reference is to the Torah, the body of commandments that God imposed on Israel through Moses at Sinai. We must be careful not to import into the word other meanings without explicit warrant from the context.

Nature. We argued in 2:14 that we indeed have clear contextual warrant for a broader sense of the term *law*. Only by positing such a reference can we make sense of Paul's claim that Gentiles who "do not have the law" are "a law for themselves." A second indicator that helps us to understand the context of Paul's argument is his reference to "nature" (*physis*). For the Greeks, the "natural law" or "unwritten law" was an important idea, establishing the basis for universal moral norms and for the "positive" law enacted in the city-states. The Stoics, a school of philosophers influential in Paul's day, rooted this law in nature. Jews familiar with this tradition then used *physis* in a similar way, to demonstrate the universal applicability of the moral standards found in the law of Moses. Paul clearly reflects this tradition in 2:14, and first-century readers would immediately have understood that he was endorsing this widespread tradition about the unwritten universal moral law.

NATURAL LAW. Many of the points Paul touches on in this paragraph are important for our understanding of Christian truth: the reality of judgment (vv. 12, 16), the searching nature of that judgment ("men's secrets," v. 16), and the standard of judgment (obedience to the law, v. 13). But distinctive to this passage is Paul's endorsement of the idea of "natural law"—knowledge of God's basic moral demand available to all people. How people have access to this law Paul does not say. But his reference to the "conscience" and "thoughts" in verse 15 suggests the knowledge is innate, built into people through God's creation.

As was true of natural revelation in chapter 1, natural law is the subject of a lot of debate in our day. Our pluralistic environment raises pointedly the question of the basis for those fundamental moral norms by which a society governs itself. "Positive" law—that is, specific law enacted by a lawgiver or lawmaker—must have a universal basis if it is to be universally applicable or avoid being arbitrary. On what basis, for instance, can a democratic society decide to require all its citizens to refrain from stealing from other people? Granted the incredible variety of ethnic, national, and religious traditions represented in, for instance, the United States, what underlying moral code can be discovered that justifies such a law?

Under the impetus of such issues, the tendency increasingly is to base positive law on the notion of "the common good." But that idea is slippery and open to being imposed on the minority by the majority. For instance, the government of the Netherlands has recently decided that it is in the common good to allow people to put to death aged and sick relatives.

The idea of natural law that Paul endorses here helps us to establish a foundation for universal moral norms and therefore for positive law, which will not be undermined by the whims of society or the convenience of the majority. As I write, a debate that flares up periodically in the United States has again been in the public eye. A judge posted the Ten Commandments in her courtroom, and she has been ordered to take them down.

Christian theologians have long viewed the Ten Commandments as a reflection of the natural law and therefore applicable to all people. But it is increasingly difficult in our society to separate this natural law from its religious context. We are not arguing that the Ten Commandments should be adopted as natural law. But we think the debate focuses attention on the larger question of moral norms. The idea of natural law, widespread among the Greeks and Romans and taken over by both Jews and Christians, may help to bring some moral order out of the current chaos. It establishes a set of norms that is outside of and therefore "above" society.

The difficulty, of course, is to find those norms. The Ten Commandments are tied closely to the Judeo-Christian heritage, and one can then understand why people of other religious persuasions are not happy about their being posted in a classroom. Moreover, as we will suggest latter in this commentary, there is some question whether the Ten Commandments (and especially the Sabbath law) continue even to be a direct representation of Christian moral law. What we are facing in many cultures all over the world, then, is the challenge of finding some basis for natural law in a multicultural, multireligious environment. As long as a nation is not tied directly to a single religion (as some of the Islamic states continue to be), a natural law that all citizens can agree to will be hard to come by.

Romans 2:17–29

NOW YOU, IF you call yourself a Jew; if you rely on the law and brag about your relationship to God; [18]if you know his will and approve of what is superior because you are instructed by the law; [19]if you are convinced that you are a guide for the blind, a light for those who are in the dark, [20]an instructor of the foolish, a teacher of infants, because you have in the law the embodiment of knowledge and truth—[21]you, then, who teach others, do you not teach yourself? You who preach against stealing, do you steal? [22]You who say that people should not commit adultery, do you commit adultery? You who abhor idols, do you rob temples? [23]You who brag about the law, do you dishonor God by breaking the law? [24]As it is written: "God's name is blasphemed among the Gentiles because of you."

[25]Circumcision has value if you observe the law, but if you break the law, you have become as though you had not been circumcised. [26]If those who are not circumcised keep the law's requirements, will they not be regarded as though they were circumcised? [27]The one who is not circumcised physically and yet obeys the law will condemn you who, even though you have the written code and circumcision, are a lawbreaker.

[28]A man is not a Jew if he is only one outwardly, nor is circumcision merely outward and physical. [29]No, a man is a Jew if he is one inwardly; and circumcision is circumcision of the heart, by the Spirit, not by the written code. Such a man's praise is not from men, but from God.

Original Meaning

PAUL BEGAN HIS TEACHING about the Jews' spiritual status before the Lord in the diatribe style, letting the Roman Christians "overhear" his challenge to a hypothetical but representative Jew (2:1–5). The second singular form of the verbs throughout 2:17–29 reveals that he returns to that style here. In the previous passage, Paul did not explicitly mention the Jew as his target. For rhetorical effect, he allowed his readers to infer what that target was. But he now comes out in the open: "Now you, if you call yourself a Jew . . ." (v. 17). This section falls into two units, the first focusing on the law (vv. 17–24) and the second on circumcision (vv. 25–29).

Possession of the law and the covenant sign of circumcision were perhaps the two most distinguishing marks of being Jewish. Given to Israel by God himself, they signaled the fact that the Jews were a special people, elevated above all other peoples. In discussing their value in these verses, then, Paul is discussing the ultimate value of being Jewish.

Let us recall the key point the apostle has made thus far: The Jews, because they do "the same things" as the Gentiles, are, like the Gentiles, subject to God's wrath (vv. 1–5). But in putting the Gentiles and the Jews on equal footing, Paul could be accused of ignoring the special place that Jews have before God. Thus, without dismissing the Jews' privileges entirely (see 3:1), he insists that the blessings God gave his people Israel did not, in themselves, bring rescue from divine judgment. Those blessings must be responded to in obedience. As Paul has made clear already (vv. 6, 13), it is doing God's will, not knowing it or teaching it, that matters in the judgment. At precisely this point the Jews have fallen short.

The Law (2:17–24)

IN A SERIES of "if" clauses, Paul begins by enumerating many of the privileges enjoyed by the Jews (vv. 17–20). Some interpreters think Paul is engaging in a certain amount of sarcasm here, as if these privileges were ones the Jews bragged about but were not really theirs at all. But this misses the point of the text.[1] All the privileges Paul lists are legitimate, and almost every one has explicit Old Testament warrant. The problem is not that the Jews are illegitimately boasting in what is not really theirs. The problem, rather, is that they are not living up to their claim. Paul's choice of the diatribe style, with its second person address and back-and-forth dialogical character, is particularly appropriate for this kind of argument. We find the second-century writer Epictetus using the same kind of style to contest the claim of some philosophers to be "true Stoics" because they did not live out their philosophy.[2]

In verses 17–20 Paul enumerates nine privileges the Jews enjoy:

(1) They possess the name "Jew" (Gk. *Ioudaios*). This first privilege is also the most general. The term *Jew* originally referred to a person from the region occupied by the descendants of Judah, but it was applied generally to Israelite people after the Exile. By Paul's day, the term was widely used in this more general sense. The name signified that one belonged to that people, distinct

---

1. See Fitzmyer, *Romans*, 315.

2. See esp. *Diss.* 2.19–20; 3.7, 17. On the whole subject, see esp. S. Stowers, *The Diatribe and Paul's Letter to the Romans* (Chico, Calif.: Scholars, 1981), 112.

from all others, whom God had chosen to be his own. All other benefits flow from this fundamental one.

(2) They "rely on the law." The law, as we have seen, is the law of Moses, the Torah. Jews were proud that they alone had been entrusted with this record of God's character and will. They therefore tended to "rely" on it for deliverance from judgment. Paul implicitly makes the same point as Micah made six centuries earlier. After rebuking the leaders of Israel for their sin, the prophet said, "Yet they lean upon the LORD and say, 'Is not the LORD among us? No disaster will come upon us'" (Mic. 3:11).

(3) They "brag about [their] relationship to God." The NIV "brag" suggests the idea of improper pride. But the Greek word used (*kauchaomai*) is perhaps better translated "boast." Boasting is not always a bad thing. Paul's use of the word is decisively influenced by Jeremiah 9:23–24, which he quotes in 1 Corinthians 1:31 and 2 Corinthians 10:17:

> This is what the LORD says:
> "Let not the wise man boast of his wisdom
>   or the strong man boast of his strength
>   or the rich man boast of his riches,
> but let him who boasts boast about this:
>   that he understands and knows me,
> that I am the LORD, who exercises kindness,
>   justice and righteousness on earth,
>   for in these I delight,"
> declares the LORD.

Boasting, in other words, is not always wrong; it depends on what one is boasting in. It does not appear wrong for Jews to boast in their relationship to God, for God himself has established a relationship with them.

(4) They know God's will (v. 18). Paul began this section of the letter by announcing that God has given to all people knowledge about himself (1:19). Now he specifically includes the Jews.

(5) They "approve of what is superior." Although the difference is not great, this can also be translated, "distinguish the things that really matter."[3] In either case, the point is that the Jews are able to discern right from wrong. They can do so because, Paul adds, they are "instructed by the law."

The next four matters of Jewish pride flow from the prerogatives Paul has enumerated in 2:17–18. They all involve the Jews' sense of superiority with respect to other peoples.

---

3. The verb *diaphero*, used in the participial form as the object of "approve," can mean either "be worth more" (Matt. 6:26; 10:31; 12:12; Luke 12:7, 24) or "differ" (1 Cor. 15:41).

(6) and (7) They are "a guide for the blind" and "a light for those who are in the dark" (2:19). These are two ways of saying the same thing. As a natural outcome of the Jews' knowledge of God through the law, they are in a position to help others understand the truth about God. The language echoes Old Testament descriptions of the mission of Israel to the nations. Note Isaiah 42:6–7, for example:

> "I, the LORD, have called you in righteousness;
>   I will take hold of your hand.
> I will keep you and will make you
>   to be a covenant for the people
>   and *a light* for the Gentiles,
>   *to open eyes that are blind,*
>   to free captives from prison
>   and to release from the dungeon those who sit in darkness."
>   (italics added)

While Jesus gave an ironic twist to this claim, calling the Pharisees "blind guides" (Matt. 15:14), there is nothing to suggest that Paul uses similar irony here. The Jews are convinced they are the religious instructors of the world, according to God's own appointment.

(8) and (9) The Jews are also convinced that they are "instructors of the foolish" and "teachers of infants" (v. 20a)—two more claims that obviously go together. "Foolish" (*aphron*) is not as pejorative as this word group is, for instance, in Proverbs, where it denotes the person who rebels against God's standards and goes his or her own way. Here it refers to Gentiles as people who, without detailed knowledge of God and his Word, inevitably fall into wrong forms of worship and behavior (see 1:22). Similarly, from a Jewish point of view, Gentiles are "infants" in terms of their religious sensibilities. They need to be taught true knowledge of God.

Many Jewish texts from this time show this attitude was typical. We may cite two as illustrative: "In those days, he says, 'The Lord will be patient and cause the children of the earth to hear. Reveal it to them with your wisdom, for you are their guides'" (*1 Enoch* 105:1). "The people of the great God will again be strong who will be guides in life for all mortals" (*Syb. Or.* 3.194–95).

The end of verse 20 reveals again Paul's preoccupation with the law in this section. His enumeration of general Jewish blessings ended with the words "because you are instructed by the law" (v. 18); now he states: "because you have in the law the embodiment of knowledge and truth." In "natural revelation" the Gentiles have knowledge of God and are therefore "without excuse" when they sin (1:20). Jews have knowledge of God in the special revelation of God's law so that they, likewise, "have no excuse" (2:1) when they sin.

Paul breaks off his conditional sentence at the end of 2:20 (the break is marked in the NIV with a dash). He does this so that he can get the maximum rhetorical effect from the charge that he now levels against the Jews. By repeating in summary form some of the privileges he listed in verses 17–20, Paul highlights effectively the contrast between claim and reality:

> You, then, who teach others, do you not teach yourself? You who preach against stealing, do you steal? You who say that people should not commit adultery, do you commit adultery? You who abhor idols, do you rob temples? You who brag about the law, do you dishonor God by breaking the law?

Only two points in these fairly obvious charges need comment. (1) What Paul means by accusing the Jews of robbing temples (v. 22) is unclear. The obvious interpretation, of course, is that the Jews are guilty of robbing pagan temples. We have some evidence that Jews at this time were relaxing the Old Testament strictures against using precious metals melted down from idols. So Paul may be citing this practice as evidence that their horror of idolatry is insincere.[4] Other interpreters think Paul may be referring to the Jerusalem temple and that their robbery consists in holding back the taxes imposed on them for its upkeep. A third possibility is that Paul is speaking metaphorically of sacrilege committed by the Jews—as, for instance, when they elevate the law to such a position that it challenges God's own unique status.[5] The first interpretation is really the only one that fits the context, since the action of robbing temples must be the opposite of the Jews' abhorrence of idols.

(2) Note the summarizing character of verse 23. The NIV takes this verse as a question, but it may be an assertion, giving even more weight to it. Here is the essence of the matter for Paul: The Jews' legitimate boasting (NIV "brag"; see comments on v. 17) about the law means that their failure to obey it brings dishonor on God himself. By failing to demonstrate in day-to-day living the qualities that the law they profess to love, they not only fail to be the light that God wants them to be—they actually harm the reputation of God.

Paul highlights this point in verse 24 with his quotation of Isaiah 52:5. Although the blaspheming of God's name in Isaiah comes about because of

---

4. So most commentators. See, for instance, Godet, *Commentary on Romans*, 129; Murray, *The Epistle to the Romans*, 1:84; Dunn, *Romans*, 114–15.

5. See esp. D. Garlington, "IEROSULEIN and the Idolatry of Israel (Romans 2.22)," *NTS* 36 (1990): 142–51; see also Cranfield, *The Epistle to the Romans*, 169–70; Fitzmyer, *Romans*, 318.

pagan oppression of Israel, Paul creates an ironic twist by attributing this blasphemy to Israel's sinfulness in the midst of pagans. But he is still fair to the larger context from which he draws the quotation, for Israel's oppression by pagan nations is itself a result of her sin.[6]

Circumcision (2:25–29)

NEXT TO THE LAW, circumcision was the most important distinguishing mark of Jewishness (see Bridging Contexts section). It is natural, then, for Paul to discuss it along with the law (2:17–24) in his continuing attempt to erode the Jews' confidence in their inherited religious advantages.

Paul does not deny that "circumcision has value" (a point he reaffirms in 3:1). But its value is contingent on obedience: Only Jews who "observe the law" will profit from it. What does Paul mean by observing the law? Many interpreters think he is reflecting standard Old Testament and Jewish teaching that one's covenant relationship with God can be guaranteed only through a heartfelt, faith-filled practice of God's law. Perfect conformity is not required, as, of course, the sacrificial laws make clear; what God expects is a consistent, sincere attempt to live by his standards.[7]

There are two problems with this interpretation. (1) Paul consistently distinguishes between "doing," "practicing," or "observing" the law and faith; he never mixes them (cf. 3:27–28 and comments; 4:2–5, 13–16; 10:5–8; Gal. 3:12). (2) The present verse must be interpreted in light of the ultimate destination of Paul's argument, that no person can be justified "by observing the law" (3:20). For these reasons, we must see in 2:25a a negative point: Circumcision has no value to rescue Jews from God's wrath because their obedience to the law never reaches the level required for salvation. The second part of verse 25 simply states the negative corollary of this point: Failing to obey the law can annul the value of circumcision.

Verse 26 draws a natural inference from verse 25: If doing the law, not circumcision, is what saves, then Gentiles who, though uncircumcised, obey the law can be saved. Here again, as in 2:8, 10, 14–15, we face the problem of identifying these "righteous" Gentiles. Scholars give the same answers: Gentiles generally who are saved because they lead moral lives, Gentile Christians, and a hypothetical construct. We are again convinced that the third view is preferable.

To be sure, one can make a better case here than in any of the other texts that Paul has Gentile Christians in mind. For verse 27 lends a note of realism

---

6. Schreiner, *Romans,* 134–35.

7. See, e.g., Murray, *The Epistle to the Romans,* 1:85–86; Cranfield, *The Epistle to the Romans,* 171–72.

to the picture, and verses 28–29 refer to the Spirit, possessed only by Christians.[8] But the realism of verse 27 is simply part of the rhetorical effect Paul wants to produce. Having put before the Jew with whom he is debating the figure of a Gentile who has done the law and has therefore joined the people of God (v. 26), Paul brings the imagery home by talking about this Gentile standing in judgment over the disobedient Jew. All this is part of his effort to show the Jews that they cannot count on circumcision to save them at the judgment. The apostle makes clear elsewhere that there is, in fact, no person who can do the law and be saved (3:20). Thus, he must again here be speaking hypothetically, theorizing about the existence of a law-observant Gentile and what the consequences would be.

Verses 28–29 are a kind of appendix to this argument. Paul has made clear that being circumcised and possessing the law (v. 27b) do not, by themselves, qualify a person to be part of God's true, spiritual people. Such outward marks, to be sure, can show that a person belongs to the "physical" Israel. But real Jewishness can never be determined by physical birth, by cuts on our skin, or by devotion to a particular book. To be a "real Jew" is an inward matter. It is marked by the "circumcision of the heart," a circumcision that comes in the context of the Spirit, not the "written code."

Circumcision of the heart is, of course, no new requirement. Moses himself called on the people of Israel to "circumcise your hearts, therefore, and do not be stiff-necked any longer" (Deut. 10:16; see also Jer. 4:4). God's true people have always been marked by faith-filled commitment to God and not merely by external rites. But Paul does go beyond the Old Testament by insisting that this heart circumcision is accomplished "in" or "by" (Gk. *en*) the "Spirit" (*pneuma*) and not the "letter" (*gramma*).

The NIV "written code" is a good rendering of *gramma*, since Paul seems to use the term to denote the law of Moses as a law by its nature written in letters on stone tablets (see esp. 2 Cor. 3:6–7). In contrast to this law, *pneuma* must refer not to the human spirit but to God's Spirit. This is clearly what Paul intends in the other places where he contrasts *gramma* and *pneuma* (Rom. 7:6; 2 Cor. 3:6–7). What he does, then, at the end of this chapter, is to anticipate the direction of his argument. He will show that only those who, through faith in Christ, have received the Spirit of God make up God's true people. Implicit here is a radical redefinition of "Jew" that will require a lot more explanation as Paul moves forward in this letter.

---

8. Therefore, for instance, Murray, who holds our view on vv. 8, 10, and 14–15, thinks that Gentile Christians are in view here (*The Epistle to the Romans*, 1:86–87).

CIRCUMCISION. CIRCUMCISION WAS first instituted by God as a sign of his covenant with Abraham in Genesis 17:9–13:

Then God said to Abraham, "As for you, you must keep my covenant, you and your descendants after you for the generations to come. This is my covenant with you and your descendants after you, the covenant you are to keep: Every male among you shall be circumcised. You are to undergo circumcision, and it will be the sign of the covenant between me and you. For the generations to come every male among you who is eight days old must be circumcised, including those born in your household or bought with money from a foreigner—those who are not your offspring. Whether born in your household or bought with your money, they must be circumcised. My covenant in your flesh is to be an everlasting covenant.

Circumcision was routinely practiced in Israel from that time on. But the crisis during the Maccabean Revolt (166–160 B.C.) elevated it to a new level of significance. There was a growing movement among Jews to adopt Hellenistic ways of thinking and to abandon their Jewish faith. Therefore, says the historian who wrote 1 Maccabees, they "removed the marks of circumcision, and abandoned the holy covenant. They joined with the Gentiles and sold themselves to do evil" (1 Macc. 1:15).

Antiochus IV Epiphanes, the Seleucid tyrant who sought to eradicate the Jewish religion, was well aware of the immense symbolic value of the rite. He accordingly made circumcision of a child a capital offense (1 Macc. 1:48, 58–61). Pious Jews rose up in resistance, "choos[ing] to die rather than to be defiled by food or to profane the holy covenant" (1:63). Eventually successful in restoring the Jewish faith, pious Jews naturally accorded to circumcision an even greater importance than before.

At about the same time, more and more Jews living in the Diaspora mingled with Gentiles. In such a situation, physical rites like circumcision took on increasing importance as a way of keeping strict adherents of a religion separate from the pagan influence all around. One can cite the traditional hair and clothing styles maintained in our day by orthodox Jews as a similar response.

Against this background, then, we can understand why circumcision was so central and emotional an issue in the debates between Jews and Christians, and between Judaizers and other Christians, in the early days of the church (e.g., Acts 15; Galatians). Allowing Gentiles to become God's people without being circumcised was tantamount to denying the Jewish faith. At the same time, the term *circumcision* sometimes stood for the Jewish faith generally (cf. Eph. 2:11). His discussion of the rite in 2:25–29 grows out of this background.

The polemic of Romans 2. Most Christians reading Romans 2 probably accept Paul's indictment of the Jews at face value. But those who know either ancient Judaism or contemporary Jews and who read carefully what Paul is saying may have some uneasiness. Take verses 17—24. How can Paul utter so blanket a condemnation of the Jews? He seems to suggest that Jews routinely steal and commit adultery. Yet this is manifestly unfair, since most Jews in Paul's day, in fact, led moral lives and were often model citizens.

Similar problems emerge at other places in Romans 2. As we have noted in our exposition, Paul seems to discount any real value in the Mosaic covenant, arguing that it gives the Jews no real advantage vis-à-vis Gentiles (vv. 6—11, 12, 25—27). At the same time, he appears to paint a rosy picture of the Gentiles, seemingly attributing to them the ability to obey the law and to be saved (e.g., vv. 8, 10, 14—15, 26—27). In an effort to level the playing field between Jews and Gentiles, in other words, Paul appears to have both unfairly criticized the Jews and given the Gentiles far too much credit.

Is Paul then guilty of unfair exaggeration? If so, how can his argument in this paragraph possibly have any effect on people who know that things are not as Paul suggests? To bring the issue home to us: How can we give credit to a text that appears to indulge in some unfair "religion bashing?" Only if we can remove these obstacles to hearing the text will the contemporary reader be able both to understand and accept the teaching of this chapter.

Scholars have given a lot of attention to these matters in recent decades, and they have come to very different conclusions. Some have indeed decided that Paul distorts the situation in the interests of making Christianity seem as superior to Judaism as possible.[9] But we think Paul's polemic in chapter 2 can be justified in its context when we consider four factors.

(1) In vv. 21—22, Paul is not describing all Jews or even a typical Jew. Rather, he is choosing an extreme illustration of the point he wants to make, namely, that the practice of Jews does not match their talking. It is no accident that two of the activities the apostle uses as illustrations—stealing and adultery—are prohibited in the Ten Commandments and cited elsewhere in the New Testament in just this kind of exemplary manner (see Matt. 19:18; Rom. 13:9). Some scholars have further reduced the strength of these accusations by suggesting that Paul may imply in his accusation Jesus' "interiorising" interpretation of the law (Matt. 5:21—48);[10] that is, what Paul accuses the Jews of doing is not the outward acts of theft and adultery, but the inner attitude of greed and lust. What Jew—or any human being—is immune

---

9. The clearest example of this approach is H. Räisänen, *Paul and the Law* (Philadelphia: Fortress, 1983), see esp. pp. 99—108.

10. See, for instance, Barrett, *The Epistle to the Romans*, 56—57.

from such sins? We are not sure that Paul intends this kind of spiritual inter-pretation, but we are sure he does not intend to suggest that Jews generally commit such acts.

(2) As we have argued at length, many scholars are guilty of overem-phasizing Paul's teaching in this chapter on the spiritual potential of the Gentiles (see esp. Contemporary Significance section on 2:1–11; also Orig-inal Meaning notes on 2:13–15, 26–27). Paul clearly affirms that they have access to divine moral law (2:14–15) and can sometimes exhibit such ster-ling behavior so as to put Jews to shame (2:26–27). But he does not claim that they can be saved apart from the gospel, and he certainly does not suggest that, overall, they are in a better religious position than the Jews.

(3) Although he never comes out and says it in so many words, Romans 2 clearly indicates that Paul does, indeed, deny Jews can be saved through the Mosaic covenant. This, we must remember, is the view he is attacking: the widespread belief among Jews that their salvation was virtually guaranteed sim-ply because they were Jews. Moreover, Jewish identity in Paul's day was increasingly connected to the law of Moses. Even circumcision, though insti-tuted long before the law was given, was linked in Jewish thinking to obedi-ence to the law.[11] So in denying that circumcision, the mark of the covenant, is without value if the law is not obeyed, Paul is in effect denying that the Mosaic covenant can save. But if this is the case, then Jews are, at least in this respect, in the same position of the Gentiles: able to achieve salvation apart from the gospel only through personal works (an impossible task).

(4) It is vital to keep in mind that Paul says nothing about the Jews in this chapter that he does not say about the Gentiles. Paul is not "anti-Semitic"; he is "anti-natural man." Once the Mosaic covenant is rightly understood and the shift in salvation history that occurred with the coming of Messiah fully appreciated, it becomes obvious that Jews are no different from other peo-ple when it comes to salvation. Paul, to be sure, spends much more time on Jews than he does on Gentiles. But this is simply because the Jews' special place in salvation history gave them a much stronger reason to believe that they did not need the gospel than Gentiles had.

CHRISTIANITY AND JUDAISM. We have anticipated in the earlier sections many of the points of enduring importance that Paul has made in this section. His overall concern is to help the Roman

---

11. This point is implicit in Paul's claim in Gal. 5:3: "Again I declare to every man who lets himself be circumcised that he is obligated to obey the whole law."

Christians—and us!—understand why Jews need Christ just as much as Gentiles do. But we should look again at this argument in light of some strong cultural currents in our time.

The horror of the *Shoah*, or the Holocaust, has provided a powerful motive to reexamine Jewish-Christian relationships. Many Jews blame Christians for the Holocaust. Christians have rightly asked themselves whether such an accusation is justified. Some have concluded that, in fact, it is. The Holocaust is not simply the fault of Gentiles, some of whom claimed to be Christian or to stand in the Christian heritage. The Holocaust, rather, is the fault ultimately of the Christian faith itself—at least as traditionally understood. For the New Testament itself, so these people claim, is inherently anti-Semitic. It denies validity to the Jewish faith, and it is the Jewish faith that is inherent to the self-identity of the Jewish people.

According to this line of thinking, then, the Christian church can avoid anti-Semitism only by (1) abandoning its faith or (2) by radically reinterpreting the New Testament. In later sections we will look more closely at how this reinterpretation is being carried out, particularly with respect to Romans. But for now our concern is with the larger issue of anti-Semitism. Is Romans 2 really anti-Semitic because it challenges the Jews' understanding of salvation? How should Christians respond to Jewish friends and neighbors in light of Romans 2?

Don Hagner usefully distinguishes between "anti-Semitism" and "anti-Judaism."[12] The former is irrational hatred of the Jewish nation or people; the latter is opposition to the Jewish religion as ultimately a valid expression of the truth. Despite ingenious attempts to argue otherwise, the New Testament is certainly "anti-Jewish." That is, it contests the claim that the Old Testament is the final expression of God's truth and that people can find eternal salvation within the boundaries set down by Abraham, Moses, the prophets, and Torah. Romans 2 is one of those passages that makes this point clear. Neither circumcision, the sign of the covenant, nor the law, the center of that covenant, can rescue a Jew from God's wrath. Only the gospel of Christ can do that.

But we should not, therefore, allow others to label Christians as "anti-Semitic." Christians do not hate or despise Jewish people even if we are convinced that their religion does not provide for their salvation. Nor do we hate Arabs because we don't think that Islam saves, or Indians because we question the validity of Hinduism (or Buddhism), or secularists because we do not think materialism is the final answer to life.

---

12. D. A. Hagner, "Paul's Quarrel with Judaism," in *Anti-Semitism and Early Christianity: Issues of Polemic and Faith*, ed. C. A. Evans and D. A. Hagner (Minneapolis: Fortress, 1993), 128–50.

But we need also to admit that anti-Semitism lurks right around the corner—particularly when we are dealing with texts such as Romans 2. We must draw the conclusion that Paul himself draws from his discussion: that the Jewish people cannot be saved in their own religion and need to hear and respond to the gospel. Never should we compromise on this.

At the same time, we also need to avoid any hint of triumphalism when we make these points. When we understand Paul's argument correctly, we recognize that all of us are naturally in the same plight as the Jews: locked up under sin and helpless to save ourselves. Indeed, if we are faithful to Paul, we will acknowledge that, from a natural standpoint, Jews start in a position of advantage to us (3:1). But rescue from our plight, coming solely as a matter of God's grace, is nothing we can take any credit for.

As with all people, we need sympathetically to understand where Jews are coming from. Precisely because so many Jews resisted Jesus and the early church and because the first Christians had to define themselves over against the Jewish faith, we find a lot of polemic against Judaism in the New Testament. History, of course, is littered with the debris of Jewish-Christian debates and fights. With this behind us, it is easy to construct a caricature of the Jewish faith. Indeed, as recent work is revealing, Christian scholars in the past have often been guilty of misrepresenting the Jewish faith, portraying it as far more petty and legalistic than it really was. These misrepresentations have filtered down to the church at large.

What can we do about this situation? We suggest two things. (1) If we are really interested, we should find a good recent book on the Jewish faith.[13] (2) Whenever occasion arises, we should seek to understand from Jews themselves what they believe. Modern Judaism is, of course, a diverse religion. So only by trying to understand what a particular Jew believes will we be able to enter into his or her world and to share the gospel sensitively and tellingly.

---

13. See, for instance, D. S. Ariel, *What Do Jews Believe?* (New York: Schocken, 1995); N. De Lange, *An Introduction to Judaism* (Cambridge: Cambridge Univ. Press, 2000).

Romans 3:1-8

WHAT ADVANTAGE, THEN, is there in being a Jew, or what value is there in circumcision? ²Much in every way! First of all, they have been entrusted with the very words of God. ³What if some did not have faith? Will their lack of faith nullify God's faithfulness? ⁴Not at all! Let God be true, and every man a liar. As it is written:

> "So that you may be proved right when you speak
> and prevail when you judge."

⁵But if our unrighteousness brings out God's righteousness more clearly, what shall we say? That God is unjust in bringing his wrath on us? (I am using a human argument.) ⁶Certainly not! If that were so, how could God judge the world? ⁷Someone might argue, "If my falsehood enhances God's truthfulness and so increases his glory, why am I still condemned as a sinner?" ⁸Why not say—as we are being slanderously reported as saying and as some claim that we say—"Let us do evil that good may result"? Their condemnation is deserved.

IN OVER TWENTY YEARS of ministry, I have taught the same subject many times. By now I can predict with almost 100 percent accuracy what questions students will ask at what point in the lectures. Paul, similarly, has been preaching the gospel for over twenty years by the time he writes Romans. He also knows that his teaching on certain topics will inevitably raise certain questions or even spark certain wrong conclusions among his hearers. As he sets his gospel before the Roman Christians, therefore, we find him repeatedly pausing in his argument to deal with questions that he knows his readers will be asking or to dismiss false conclusions he fears they may be drawing.

Nowhere in Romans is this more evident than at 3:1. Paul has just spent a chapter arguing that Jews stand in the same position before God as Gentiles do. Thus, if we have followed Paul's argument, when he asks in 3:1, "What advantage, then, is there in being a Jew, or what value is there in circumcision?" we are ready to answer "none." But Paul surprises us: "Much in every way!" he emphatically responds (v. 2a). He knows his argument in chapter 2 may give the impression that all the Jews' privileges are now revoked. He is also aware that many Gentile Christians will be eager to draw just this conclusion. Consequently, he forestalls them. He acknowledges, of course, that the Jews' privileges give them no ultimate advantage over Gentiles in the judgment, because God will assess both Jew and Gentile on the basis of what they have done. But this does not mean that the Jews have no privileges.

"First of all" (*proton*) they have been "entrusted with the very words [*logia*] of God" (3:2b). Paul's "first" is not followed by a "second." Some think *proton* means simply "chief" or "most important."[1] But it is more likely that Paul intends to give a longer list of Jewish privileges (like those noted in 9:4–5), but he gets sidetracked by his concern to clarify the limitations on the Jews' privilege of possessing God's Word.

If this section begins on a relatively clear note, the same cannot be said of its remainder. Verses 3–8 are some of the most difficult to interpret in the entire letter. The main problem is to sort out the different "speakers" that Paul uses to make his points. Clearly he is asking questions that reflect some kind of view in opposition to his own, and he responds to these questions. But it is not at all clear which are the opponent's questions and which are Paul's answers.

Critical to our view of the paragraph as a whole is the identity of the people who ask in verse 5 about "our unrighteousness." Are they people who are generally wondering about the fairness of God in judging people when their sin enhances God's glory? Or are they Jews wondering how God can be "righteous" when he judges the sins of the Jews?

It is probably the latter. Paul seems to be grappling here with the common Jewish belief that God's "righteousness," his "covenant faithfulness," gave the Jews virtual immunity from judgment. In response, Paul affirms that the marvelous blessing of knowing God's Word (v. 2) is a double-edged sword. For God's Word promises blessing for obedience, but it also warns about the curse that will fall on disobedience. God remains faithful (v. 3) and righteous (v. 5) in all his dealings. But Jews must understand that the ultimate standard of righteousness is his own holy character, and that holy character requires him to respond to sin with wrath (v. 6).

But the Jewish objector is still not satisfied, arguing it is unfair for God to condemn Jews for acts that enhance his glory (v. 7). Paul responds with a counterquestion intended to show the absurdity of such an objection (v. 8):

---

1. Godet, *Commentary on Romans*, 132.

Should we then take the view that any act is justified so long as it brings good in the end?

With the main lines of the argument in place, we can now focus on several of the details that still require comment. In verse 3, the Jews' "lack of faith" [*apistia*] is probably, in light of the contrast with God's "faithfulness" (*pistis*), not so much their failure to believe as their failure to be true to their covenant obligations. God, through his law, had imposed on Israel requirements they needed to fulfill in order to maintain the covenant relationship. But Israel as a whole failed to keep these commands. How would God respond? Would he cease to be faithful because Israel has not been faithful? With an emphatic negation characteristic of the diatribe style and of Romans, Paul rejects any such idea— "Not at all!" (*me genoito*; see also 3:6, 31; 6:2, 15; 7:7, 13; 9:14; 11:1, 11).

The failure of Israel, Paul insists, in no way diminishes God's commitment to hold up his end of the covenant arrangement (v. 4a). God will always be "true" even if every person has become a "liar." The context shows that "true" is another way of asserting God's faithfulness. This use of the word is rooted in the Old Testament, where the Greek *aletheia* translates '*emeth*.

At the end of verse 4, Paul adds a quotation from Psalm 51:4 to explain the nature of God's faithfulness. David wrote this psalm after he had been caught in his sin with Bathsheba. His words quoted express the purpose of his confession of sin: that God might be shown to be right and just in punishing him.[2] In Psalm 51:4, God's being in the right denotes the fairness of his judgment. Paul is hinting that his concept of God's faithfulness (Rom. 3:3–4a) is broader than the usual Jewish view. Jews in Paul's day tended to think of God's faithfulness as oriented positively toward themselves: God would do good things for his people. But, Paul reminds them, God is also faithful when he punishes the sin of his people—as David himself acknowledges.

With this context in mind, we can now understand the question Paul puts on Jewish lips in verse 5. Isn't God unfair to inflict wrath on Jews when their very unfaithfulness to the covenant led to the establishment of his righteousness in an even greater way in Christ? Behind this question is a certain Jewish view of God's righteousness (see Bridging Contexts section). Paul dismisses such an objection by suggesting the inference that would have to follow from that line of reasoning: God could never then judge anyone, since in his providence he turns all sin into the praise of his name. Yet the Scriptures teach that "God [will] judge the world" (v. 6; see Gen. 18:25: "Will not the Judge of all the earth do right?").

---

2. This interpretation depends on reading the verb *krinesthai* in the second line of the psalm quotation, as the NIV does, as a middle (so most commentators; see Matt. 5:40; 1 Cor. 6:6) rather than as a passive, "when you are judged" (in favor of this reading, see, e.g., Käsemann, *Commentary on Romans*, 81).

How verse 7 fits into the development of the argument is not clear. The introductory words in the NIV translation, "Someone might argue," do not correspond to anything in the Greek text. They have been added to show that, in the opinion of the translators, Paul is here again quoting an objection. But some interpreters think that verse 7 carries on Paul's own argument from verse 6. Paul has claimed that God must judge the world. But he could not do so, Paul points out, if the excuse that "God used my sin for good" were allowed. Anyone could come up with such an excuse.[3] On the whole, however, with most commentators, the interpretation represented in the NIV is preferable. Verse 7, then, enunciates an objection to Paul's logic similar to that in verse 5: It is unfair for God to condemn people whose sin leads to his glory.

Verse 8 is difficult to translate and to understand. Some scholars think that Paul continues the objection from verse 7, only to dismiss the whole line of reasoning at the end of the verse: "Their condemnation is deserved."[4] But it makes better sense of the flow if verse 8 is Paul's own counterquestion, designed to show the absurdity of the objection in verse 7. If the objector is right, and if God should not condemn Jews when they sin because their sin enhances God's glory, then the general inference would be that sin is justified as long as it eventually brings good. "Let us do evil that good may result" is the logical conclusion from this way of looking at sin. In a ironic twist, Paul adds a parenthesis, noting that some people (probably Jews) have accused Paul of teaching this very thing! Therefore, Paul concludes, the "condemnation" of people who argue this way "is deserved." Jews cannot excuse their sin just because God uses it for good in his salvation-historical scheme.

GOD'S RIGHTEOUSNESS. One reason why modern readers find it so hard to follow the argument in this section is that Paul touches the surface of a deep and fundamental issue among the Jews of his day: the nature of God's righteousness. In the Old Testament, as we noted in the Bridging Contexts section on 1:16–17, the idea of God's righteousness (Gk. *dikaiosyne*; Heb. *sedeq* or *sᵉdaqa*) is especially often tied to his covenant with Israel. God's righteousness, then, often refers to his commitment to uphold the covenant arrangement with Israel, and, in this sense, it seems often to be virtually equivalent to his mercy or faithfulness.

Note, for instance, Psalm 36:5–6:

---

3. See, for instance, Godet, *Commentary on Romans*, 137.
4. I took this view in my earlier commentary; see Moo, *The Epistle to the Romans*, 194–95.

> Your *love*, O LORD, reaches to the heavens,
>   your *faithfulness* to the skies.
> Your *righteousness* is like the mighty mountains,
>   your *justice* like the great deep.
> O LORD, you preserve both man and beast. (italics added)

Here God's "righteousness" is parallel to his "love" (or "mercy" [Gk. *eleos*]) and "faithfulness" (Gk. *aletheia*) and is the basis for his positive work of "preserv[ing] both man and beast." It is not surprising, then, that many Jews came to believe that God's righteousness would always be "on their side," guaranteeing their deliverance from their enemies. But then blow after blow fell on Israel. Most of the people were carried into exile by victorious foreign powers, to Assyria in the eighth century B.C. and to Babylonia in the sixth. Some Jews were eventually able to return and reestablish a national presence (see Ezra and Nehemiah), but the nation remained small and insignificant for most of its existence. Finally came the Romans, who annexed Israel into their empire.

These experiences, so contrary to the Jews' expectations about God's power and faithfulness to them, brought to the forefront the issue of theodicy: the justice of God. How could God allow his people to suffer under foreign tyranny? What was he doing? What were his purposes? These questions, in one way of another, drove most of the theologizing of Jews during these centuries. A central concept in all this discussion was the nature of God's righteousness. The dominant tendency was to reaffirm the positive sense of God's righteousness and to see it as a continuing foundation for Israel's hope. God was allowing his people to experience setbacks and difficulties with the purpose of chastising and disciplining them. But he remained committed to Israel; his righteousness will endure forever. It is against this background that we must read Romans 3:3–8.

Paul grapples with the prevalent Jewish conviction that God's righteousness continued to guarantee Israel immunity from judgment. In opposition to this belief, the apostle implicitly advances an alternative understanding of that righteousness. In his view, God's *dikaiosyne* never had the covenant with Israel as its ultimate locus. Rather, his ultimate concern was always with his own name and glory.

To be sure, many scholars have argued that the Jewish view was essentially on target, that in the Old Testament God's righteousness involves his relationship with Israel and is wholly positive in its effects.[5] But especially John Piper has shown that Paul's wider interpretation of God's righteousness is, in

---

5. See, for instance, G. von Rad, *Old Testament Theology* (2 vols.; New York: Harper & Row, 1962), 1:370–77.

fact, true to the Old Testament picture.[6] God's righteousness is, most basically, his commitment always to act in accordance with his own character. With respect to Israel, this means that God will uphold his promises to them. But Jewish interpreters conveniently overlooked the fact that God, in the covenant, promised both to bless Israel *if they obeyed* but to punish them if they disobeyed.

This is made especially clear in the "curses and blessings" of Deuteronomy 28 and the offer of life versus death in 30:11−20. Later Old Testament authors confirm that God's righteousness can have a negative as well as positive effect on Israel. Note especially Nehemiah 9:32−33:

> Now therefore, O our God, the great, mighty and awesome God, who keeps his covenant of love, do not let all this hardship seem trifling in your eyes—the hardship that has come upon us, upon our kings and leaders, upon our priests and prophets, upon our fathers and all your people, from the days of the kings of Assyria until today. In all that has happened to us, you have been just; you have acted faithfully, while we did wrong.

God is just or righteous even when he punishes his people for their sin.

Paul works with this wider conception of God's righteousness in order to explicate the situation in salvation history that has come about with the coming of Christ. The gospel in no way cancels Israel's prerogatives (Rom. 3:1−2). But, Paul insists, we must rightly understand those prerogatives. Being entrusted with God's Word has never meant that Israel is immune from judgment; in fact, that very Word promises judgment for disobedience. Such a judgment, in Paul's view, has now taken place. God has brought his curses down on Israel, and, in keeping with prophetic voices within the Old Testament itself (see esp. Jer. 31:31−34), the old covenant needs to be replaced with a new one.

STANDING ON THE PROMISES. The Jews may have misunderstood the nature of God's faithfulness, but they were correct to believe that whatever he has promised he will do. Paul agrees: "Let God be true, and every man a liar!" God is utterly reliable. We can depend on his carrying out, to the letter, every promise he has made to us.

Now we must be careful to interpret those promises correctly. Many Christians make the mistake of thinking that every promise in the Bible is

---

6. Piper, *The Justification of God: An Exegetical and Theological Study of Romans 9:1−23* (Grand Rapids: Baker, 1983).

directed right to them. In fact, however, many promises are made to specific people in specific circumstances. Take, for instance, the often-quoted promise about national repentance and restoration: "If my people, who are called by my name, will humble themselves and pray and seek my face and turn from their wicked ways, then will I hear from heaven and will forgive their sin and will heal their land" (2 Chron. 7:14). I have heard Christians apply this promise to the United States, and others apply it to the church.

The latter application is certainly closer to the original meaning than the former, but both are questionable. The promise is given to the nation of Israel. It comes in the midst of Solomon's dedication of the temple to the Lord. Now one can argue that, by analogy, the principle of this verse applies to other situations. But the point is that we cannot simply go to such promises and, ignoring the context and the original recipients, always assume that they are for us.

But there remain many promises that do apply to us: promises given to the church of Jesus Christ and to believers individually. We will look at one of the most famous of these promises later in this book: "And we know that in all things God works for the good of those who love him, who have been called according to his purpose" (Rom. 8:28). Paul reminds us in the present chapter that we can have utter certainty about God's fulfilling these promises for us. In an uncertain world, here is certainty; in a world without foundations, here is a rock-solid foundation.

To be sure, our failure to believe and obey may qualify some of the promises that God makes to us. But ultimately even our failures do not diminish God's faithfulness to us. As Paul puts it in another passage (2 Tim. 2:11–13):

Here is a trustworthy saying:
If we died with him,
   we will also live with him;
if we endure,
   we will also reign with him.
If we disown him,
   he will also disown us;
if we are faithless,
   he will remain faithful,
   for he cannot disown himself.

Or, to quote the well-known hymn:

Standing on the promises that cannot fail,
When the howling storms of doubt and fear assail,
By the living Word of God I shall prevail,
Standing on the promises of God.

False security. The Jewish tendency to think that the covenant made them secure from all threat of judgment has parallels in the Christian church. I happen to believe that the genuine Christian does have security; that is, if we have truly come to know Christ, we can be absolutely certain that we will appear before him in glory.

But a belief in "eternal security," as we sometimes call it, is open to abuse. (1) Some people may think that they are secure when they are not because they have never truly come to faith. They have "walked up the aisle," raised their hand at an invitation, or been baptized—but they have never truly submitted to Christ as Lord. Such people are not "secure" in Christ. We need to help them understand what real conversion is and challenge each professed believer to make sure that his or her profession matches the spiritual reality.

(2) But even genuine Christians can err in this matter. God's Word does, I believe, promise that he will infallibly bring to eternal glory those who are truly his. But that Word also makes clear that our eternal glory is contingent on a life of obedience. To be sure, some theologians try to minimize or even dismiss this latter idea. But too many texts (e.g., 8:12–13) make this point quite clear. Bringing together in one neat package God's promise to keep us secure with the need for us to be obedient in order to enjoy that promise is not easy.

Theologians have spent much time debating over just how to do it. But our point here is a relatively simple one: Believers should not so presume on their "security" that they fail to make every effort to bring their lives into obedience to Christ. It is precisely for this reason that many contemporary theologians and preachers prefer the slogan "perseverance of the saints" to "eternal security." For the former contains the reminder that the saints need to persevere if they expect to attain glory. We believe that God gives every aid needed for us to persevere. But we must also recognize that our commitment and dedication to the cause is also required.

Romans 3:9–20

WHAT SHALL WE conclude then? Are we any better? Not at all! We have already made the charge that Jews and Gentiles alike are all under sin. ¹⁰As it is written:

"There is no one righteous, not even one;
¹¹   there is no one who understands,
    no one who seeks God.
¹²All have turned away,
    they have together become worthless;
    there is no one who does good,
    not even one."
¹³"Their throats are open graves;
    their tongues practice deceit."
"The poison of vipers is on their lips."
¹⁴   "Their mouths are full of cursing and bitterness."
¹⁵"Their feet are swift to shed blood;
¹⁶   ruin and misery mark their ways,
¹⁷and the way of peace they do not know."
¹⁸   "There is no fear of God before their eyes."

¹⁹Now we know that whatever the law says, it says to those who are under the law, so that every mouth may be silenced and the whole world held accountable to God. ²⁰Therefore no one will be declared righteous in his sight by observing the law; rather, through the law we become conscious of sin.

PAUL NOW DRAWS from his extended discussion of sin and God's wrath in 1:18–3:8 a conclusion and an implication from that conclusion, both of which are foundational to his argument in the letter as a whole. The conclusion comes in verse 9: All people, including both Jews and Gentiles, are "under sin." Paul states the implication at the end of the passage: "No one will be declared righteous in his [God's] sight by observing the law." Supporting the conclusion of verse 9 is a series of Old Testament quotations—the longest such series in the New Testament (vv. 10–18).

The question-and-answer format of verse 9 resembles the style of verses 1–8, and the questions are probably sparked by what he has taught in these verses. But to understand the exact connection, we first have to be sure about the translation and interpretation of the second question. A person reading the NIV could be pardoned for wondering what is going on in the Greek. For the text reads, "Are we any better?" while the footnote suggests precisely the opposite, "Are we any worse?" The difference has to do not with a textual variant but with the interpretation of a Greek verb (*proecho*), whose basic meaning is "surpass." The specific form of the verb used here (*proechometha*) can be either passive voice ("Are we surpassed?"[1]) or middle voice, with an active meaning ("Do we surpass?"). The subject of the verb is the Jews and the implied comparison, granted the context, is almost certainly the Gentiles.

Along with most English translations and commentaries, we think the latter meaning is probably intended here. But the point is roughly the same whatever translation we go with. In either case the question is whether there is, in the last analysis, any basic difference between Jew and Gentile. We can understand how Paul's discussion in verses 1–8 may have raised just this question. For in verses 1–2 he has asserted that Jews do have certain privileges, while in chapter 2 as a whole he has criticized the Jews to such an extent that some may conclude they are worse off than the Gentiles.

The "Not at all!" that NIV has as Paul's response to this question does not translate the same Greek expression (*me genoito*) that we find elsewhere in Romans (see comment on 3:4). Some interpreters therefore insist that Paul's negation here is weaker, having the sense of "not entirely" (the Greek is *ou pantos*). Such a nuanced negative is required, they argue, because Paul has already affirmed that Jews do have an advantage over Gentiles in a certain sense: They have been "entrusted with the very words of God" (3:2).[2]

But we do not need to nuance the negative to achieve harmony between the two texts. The context makes clear enough that the distinction Paul denies here (as throughout ch. 2) has to do with the specific issue of rescue from God's wrath. It is just this point that Paul reiterates as his explanation (*gar*, "for," not translated in NIV) of his negation at the end of v. 9: "[For] we have already made the charge that both Jews and Gentiles alike are all under sin." The exact phraseology is important: People do not just commit sin, but they are "under sin." We will explore the significance of this language in the Contemporary Significance section.

---

1. See the margin notes of the NIV, NRSV, and REB; Sanday and Headlam, *The Epistle to the Romans*, 76; Fitzmyer, *Romans*, 330–31.

2. See, e.g., Cranfield, *The Epistle to the Romans*, 190. The only other occurrence of the phrase in the New Testament has this nuanced meaning (1 Cor. 5:10).

With his typical introductory formula, "As it is written," Paul now moves to a series of Old Testament quotations that substantiate the universality of sin. Paul quotes mainly from Psalms and Isaiah. At first sight the arrangement of the quotations appears to be haphazard. But a closer look uncovers a certain structure. The phrase "there is no" (*ouk estin*) links the quotations in verses 10b–12, which establish the general point of universal human sin. In verses 13–14, Paul focuses on sins of speech, referring to a different organ of speech in each of the four lines. Verses 15–17 then enumerate sins of violence against others. Verse 18, finally, returns to where Paul began, using "there is no" (Gk. *ouk estin*) to state basic human disregard for God.

A few scholars have suggested that Paul may be quoting from an early Christian collection of Old Testament passages.[3] We have some evidence that such collections of "proof texts" from the Old Testament (called a *florilegium*) existed, either in oral or written form, in the early days of the church. But we have no way of knowing whether we have one of them here.

The quotations also raise a hermeneutical issue. Some of the words Paul quotes do, indeed, refer to human beings generally in their original contexts (e.g., verses 10b–12). But in the case of others, the original referents were wicked enemies (verses 13–14) or the unrighteous within Israel (verses 15–17). How can Paul apply all these texts to people generally? Some, indeed, deny that Paul is doing any such thing; they use these quotations as evidence that Paul is condemning in this context only unrighteous Jews.[4] But Paul's language seems pretty clear: "Jews and Gentiles alike are *all* under sin" (v. 9); "there is *no one* righteous" (v. 10, italics added). Perhaps, then, Paul is implying that all Jews must now be considered to belong to the category of the "wicked" (see Bridging Contexts).

The language in verses 10b–12 is taken from Psalm 14:1–3 (cf. also Ps. 53:1–3). The "there is no one" reverberates like a steady beat in these lines, hammering home Paul's point that all people, Jew and Greek alike, are under sin's power. The quotation, like most of Paul's, seems to be taken from the Greek Old Testament, the Septuagint (LXX). But a comparison between the Psalm text and Romans 3:10b–12 reveals one significant difference. Where the Psalmist claims that "there is no one who does good," Paul quotes "there is no one righteous" (*dikaios*). A few commentators think that the change is because Paul is also alluding to Ecclesiastes 7:20: "There is not a righteous man on earth who does what is right and never sins."[5] But the importance of "righteous" language in this part of Romans makes it more likely that Paul himself has introduced this change to tailor the quotation more closely to its context.

3. See, e.g., Käsemann, *Commentary on Romans*, 86.
4. See Davies, *Faith and Obedience*, 82–96.
5. Dunn, *Romans*, 150.

After highlighting the universality of sin, Paul goes on to illustrate this point in turn by enumerating representative sins. The first series (vv. 13–14), focusing on sins of speech, comes from three separate Psalm verses: Psalm 5:9; 140:3b; and 10:7. Paul may have arranged the verses to match the sequence of organs that people use when they speak: throat, tongue, lips, mouth. Paul uses the quotations to paint a vivid picture of the way people use their words to harm others.

The next series of representative sins concentrates generally on violence (vv. 15–17). The quotation is taken from Isaiah 59:7–8a, with possible allusion to Proverbs 1:16. The series concludes with a final general proof of the universality of human refusal to honor God: "There is no fear of God before their eyes" (Rom. 3:18, quoting Ps. 36:1b).

In verse 19 Paul announces the conclusion to be drawn from this series of quotations: "Whatever the law says, it says to those who are under the law, so that every mouth may be silenced and the whole world held accountable to God." The first occurrence of "law" must refer to the quotations that he has just finished, many of which come from the Psalms. Here, then, is one of the few times when Paul uses the word "law" (*nomos*) in a canonical sense, to denote Scripture (see Bridging Contexts section of 2:12–16). But in his second use of *nomos* in this verse, Paul reverts to his usual usage: Those "under the law" are Jews, accountable by God for the law of Moses he has imposed on them.

The conclusion Paul draws from this is interesting: "Every" mouth is "silenced"; the "whole world" is accountable to God. The imagery is judicial. We are to picture the defendant closing his or her mouth with nothing to say in defense after the prosecuting attorney (i.e., the Old Testament quotations of vv. 10b–18) has finished. That defendant recognizes that he or she is at the mercy of the judge (God), who is about to pronounce sentence.

But how can Old Testament verses that, Paul says, apply to the Jews ("those under the law") bring all of humanity under conviction? A few have thought that this universal conclusion requires that "those under the law" include all people. *Nomos*, then, would refer to divine law generally, whether Mosaic or "natural" (cf. 2:14).[6] But this broad an application of *nomos* is unusual in Paul and does not fit with the language "under the law." Thus an alternative is preferable. Paul knows full well that the most difficult case he has to prove is that Jews, who are recipients of God's revelation and covenant blessing, are sinners accountable for God. By proving from the Old Testament, then, that Jews are condemned, Paul feels it legitimate to extend that verdict to all people.

---

6. Murray, *The Epistle to the Romans*, 1:106–7.

The NIV, with its "therefore" (*dioti*) suggests that verse 20 is a conclusion to be drawn from verse 19. This makes good sense. But *dioti* can also be translated "because," and this may make even better sense. Paul is aware that Jews may well want to excuse themselves from the universal charge he has made in verse 19. They will want to appeal to their relationship to God's law as a reason why they are exempt from the verdict of condemnation. Consequently, Paul meets this objection by claiming that the law is powerless to change the Jews' basic standing before God: "No one will be declared righteous in his sight by observing the law."

Paul's language here echoes Psalm 143:2b: "No one living is righteous before you." But the significant addition, of course, is Paul's reference to the law. The NIV "observing the law" translates a phrase that has been the center of a heated debate in the last few years: *erga nomou* (lit., "works of the law"). Paul is the only New Testament author to use the phrase (see also Rom. 3:28; Gal. 2:16; 3:2, 5, 10). In each case, he denies that "righteousness" (or its equivalent) can be based on these "works of the law."

Almost all modern interpreters agree that the "law" in this phrase is the Mosaic law and that Paul is talking about some kind of Torah-observance. But scholars disagree over whether the emphasis is on "works" or on "law." If the former, then Paul's point is that even works done in obedience to the law of Moses cannot bring a person into relationship with God. A legitimate inference, then, is that no works of any kind, done in obedience to any law or moral impulse, can justify. But if the emphasis is on the word "law," Paul may be focusing not so much on the *performance* of the law as on the *possession* of the law. On this view, his point is narrowly focused on the Jews and cannot be extended beyond them. He is arguing that the Mosaic law and the covenant of which it is a part cannot justify—no more.

A powerful force in favor of this second view is a revised interpretation of Judaism that has become widespread in the last thirty years. But despite this force, we think the former view is preferable. Jewish antecedents to the phrase "works of the law" suggest that it means simply "things done in obedience to the law"; no further nuance is justified. The phrase appears to function in Paul as an equivalent to the simple word "works" (cf. 3:20, 28 with 4:2, 3–5). This interpretation makes good sense in the context of first-century Judaism (see Bridging Contexts).

Having told us what the law cannot do—bring one into relationship with God—Paul concludes by telling us what the law *does* accomplish: Through it "we become conscious of sin." "Become conscious" in the NIV translates the Greek noun *epignosis*, "knowledge." But since "knowledge" in the Bible often refers to intimate acquaintance or understanding, the NIV rendering is on target here. By setting before people a detailed record of God's will, the law makes people vividly aware of how short of God's requirements they fall. It therefore brings awareness of sinfulness.

READING OLD TESTAMENT quotations against their contexts. We have emphasized before in this commentary (see "Bridging Contexts" section on 1:1–7) how important it is to read Romans against the background of the Old Testament. This is obviously necessary in 3:10–18, where we have a series of explicit quotations. But we can sometimes miss the nuance of the quotation by neglecting to look carefully at the context from which Paul takes it. This does not mean that Paul, or other New Testament authors, always quote the Old Testament in a way that fits the original context. But the careful reader of the New Testament should always check the Old Testament context to see if that context might illuminate the New Testament application.

To illustrate, we give below the larger Old Testament contexts from which Paul's quotations in vv. 10–18 are taken (the language Paul uses [or its equivalent] is in italics).

Psalm 14:1–8 (see Rom. 3:10b–12)

> For the director of music. Of David.
> The fool says in his heart,
>   "There is no God."
> They are corrupt, their deeds are vile;
>   *there is no one who does good.*
> The LORD looks down from heaven
>   on the sons of men
> to see if *there are any who understand,*
>   *any who seek God.*
> *All have turned aside,*
>   *they have together become corrupt;*
> *there is no one who does good,*
>   *not even one.*
> Will evildoers never learn—
>   those who devour my people as men eat bread
>   and who do not call on the LORD?
> There they are, overwhelmed with dread,
>   for God is present in the company of the righteous.
> You evildoers frustrate the plans of the poor,
>   but the LORD is their refuge.

Oh, that salvation for Israel would come out of Zion!
  When the LORD restores the fortunes of his people,
  let Jacob rejoice and Israel be glad!

Psalm 5:5–10 (Rom. 3:13a)

The arrogant cannot stand in your presence;
  you hate all who do wrong.
You destroy those who tell lies;
  bloodthirsty and deceitful men
  the LORD abhors.
But I, by your great mercy,
  will come into your house;
in reverence will I bow down
  toward your holy temple.
Lead me, O LORD, in your righteousness
  because of my enemies—
  make straight your way before me.
Not a word from their mouth can be trusted;
  their heart is filled with destruction.
Their throat is an open grave
  with their tongue they speak deceit.
Declare them guilty, O God!
  Let their intrigues be their downfall.
Banish them for their many sins,
  for they have rebelled against you.

Psalm 140:1–4 (Rom. 3:13b)

For the director of music. A psalm of David.
Rescue me, O LORD, from evil men;
  protect me from men of violence,
who devise evil plans in their hearts
  and stir up war every day.
They make their tongues as sharp as a serpent's;
  the poison of vipers is on their lips.
Keep me, O LORD, from the hands of the wicked;
  protect me from men of violence
  who plan to trip my feet.

Psalm 10:4–7 (v. 14)

In his pride the wicked does not seek him;
  in all his thoughts there is no room for God.

His ways are always prosperous;
    he is haughty and your laws are far from him;
    he sneers at all his enemies.
He says to himself, "Nothing will shake me;
    I'll always be happy and never have trouble."
His mouth is full of curses and lies and threats;
    trouble and evil are under his tongue.

Isaiah 59:4—10 (Rom. 3:15—17)

No one calls for justice;
    no one pleads his case with integrity.
They rely on empty arguments and speak lies;
    they conceive trouble and give birth to evil.
They hatch the eggs of vipers
    and spin a spider's web.
Whoever eats their eggs will die,
    and when one is broken, an adder is hatched.
Their cobwebs are useless for clothing;
    they cannot cover themselves with what they make.
Their deeds are evil deeds,
    and acts of violence are in their hands.
Their feet rush into sin
    they are swift to shed innocent blood.
Their thoughts are evil thoughts;
    ruin and destruction mark their ways.
The way of peace they do not know;
    there is no justice in their paths.
They have turned them into crooked roads;
    no one who walks in them will know peace.
So justice is far from us,
    and righteousness does not reach us.
We look for light, but all is darkness;
    for brightness, but we walk in deep shadows.
Like the blind we grope along the wall,
    feeling our way like men without eyes.
At midday we stumble as if it were twilight;
    among the strong, we are like the dead.

Psalm 36:1—4 (Rom. 3:18)

For the director of music. Of David the servant of the LORD.
An oracle is within my heart
    concerning the sinfulness of the wicked:

There is no fear of God
   before his eyes.
For in his own eyes he flatters himself
   too much to detect or hate his sin.
The words of his mouth are wicked and deceitful;
   he has ceased to be wise and to do good.
Even on his bed he plots evil;
   he commits himself to a sinful course
   and does not reject what is wrong.

What immediately strikes us when we see these contexts is that every one of them (with the possible exception of the Isaiah quotation) focuses on wicked or unrighteous people, in distinction from the writer and other righteous Israelites. We would certainly never have guessed this from the quotations in Romans by themselves.

What are we to conclude from this observation? As we noted above, some scholars think this proves that Paul is referring in these quotations only to unrighteous Jews. But a more likely explanation is that Paul deliberately chose to take his words from these contexts in order to make a subtle, but important point: in light of Christ, all Jews must now be considered to be in the category of the "wicked." The original readers of Romans would be well aware that the words Paul quotes apply only to the wicked, and they may well have wondered at first about how Paul can apply them to all Jews. But then they would realize the rhetorical point that Paul is making: All Jews (along with all Gentiles) are "unrighteous."

Reading Paul in the context of first-century Judaism. Since God has revealed himself to us in space-and-time history, that history becomes an indispensable context for the accurate interpretation of the Bible. Most Christians, therefore, understand the need to investigate "backgrounds" in study of the Bible. Many excellent books that help the average Bible reader do just that have appeared in recent years.

But what some students of the Bible may not understand is how debated some of these background data really are. The potential for serious misunderstanding of the Biblical texts is therefore large. We may conclude, for instance, that a particular text must have a certain meaning because it was written against a specific background. But suppose that background is not correct? Then our interpretation will also be wrong. The answer to this problem is not to dismiss background information, but to be as certain as possible that the background is accurate, and to be cautious about forcing texts to fit a background.

Nowhere in the interpretation of the Bible is this problem of correct background more debated or more important than in passages such as

Romans 3:20. In denying that a person can be "justified by works of the law" (lit. trans.), Paul is clearly arguing against someone who thinks that a person *can* be justified in this way. But who is this person? And what exactly were they claiming?

Almost everyone today agrees that the person Paul is debating is a Jew. That means that the "law" Paul refers to is the Mosaic law, the law that Jews put so much stock in. But why does he use the phrase "works of the law"? Why not just "law"? Here is where we enter into the issue of Jewish backgrounds. In the past, most interpreters of Paul assumed, or argued, that these texts reveal a battle between Paul and legalistic Jews. Jews thought that their observing the law would save them; Paul insists that it cannot and that only the grace of Christ can save them.

But many contemporary interpreters are no longer sure that this is what Paul is talking about. One of the reasons for their hesitation is that they do not think the Jews in Paul's day believed they were saved by doing the law. Rather, Jews believed that they were saved because God had chosen them. In his covenant with Abraham and Moses, God entered into a relationship with the Jewish people. He chose them to be his people. Thus, Jews were "saved" by God's grace in the Jewish covenant. To be sure, they understood that they had to obey the law God had given them. But they did not obey it to "get saved"; they obeyed to maintain the salvation God had already given them.

This way of understanding salvation in ancient Judaism had been brought up by scholars in the past. But it has been particularly in the last twenty years that this interpretation has become popular. The view is often labeled "covenant nomism." The word "covenant," of course, reflects this view's emphasis on the centrality of the covenant for Jewish salvation, and "nomism" is deliberately chosen as a contrast to "legalism." The Jews were not "legalistic" (i.e., thinking they had to do the law to get saved) but "nomistic" (i.e., seeking to obey the law to stay saved and to honor the God who had chosen them).

The popularity of the "covenant nomism" understanding has created a revolution in the study of Paul. So much of what he writes about being justified is against the Jewish background that any change in the background changes Paul's teaching as well. It is as if one suddenly looked at a familiar object against a whole different backdrop. The object changes its shape and its size. How is Paul's teaching about being justified changed when we look at it against this different Jewish background? Not everyone agrees, but one of the most popular interpretations goes like this:

1. "Works of the law" is a phrase that refers to the Jews' covenant obligation.

2. Jews were insisting that they, and they alone, could be "justified before God" because only they had been put into covenant relationship with God.

3. Therefore, Paul denies that the Jews have any "corner" on justification because of their covenant relationship. That covenant will not put them into relationship with God, for God is determined to justify all people on the same basis—through faith in Christ.[7]

What are we to make of this new interpretation? There is much that is right about it. "Covenant nomism" is, indeed, a more accurate view of what Jews in Paul's day believed about salvation than many of the traditional views. For instance, I can remember being taught when I was first a Christian that Jews believed they could be saved only by doing more good works than bad. In the judgment, God would "weigh" their works, and only if the scales tipped in favor of the good could a Jew be saved. This is little more than a caricature of what Jews believed. It completely misses the emphasis in so many Jewish writings on the importance of God's grace in the covenant with his people.

Advocates of "covenant nomism" are also right to emphasize that Paul was deeply concerned to demonstrate that God's grace was for all people. He wrote against the Jews' assumption of exclusive rights to salvation and insisted that Gentiles had just as much right to be saved as did the Jews (see, e.g., Rom. 2; 3:28–30; 4:9–17). But I myself do not think that we can completely buy into this new view.

(1) "Covenant nomism," while a generally accurate picture of the Jews' understanding of salvation, does not tell the whole story. The Jewish material from this period of time reveals a lot of differences in what Jews believed about the basics of their faith. To be sure, advocates of covenant nomism insist that virtually all the relevant writings agree in this view. But other scholars are not so sure, and a pretty convincing case can be made that at least some Jews made "doing the law" a lot more important in salvation than "covenant nomism" allows. Indeed, one can almost expect this kind of development. In any religion that puts a lot of emphasis on "law"—Christianity included!—legalism is a persistent problem.

Moreover, "covenant nomism" itself implies that doing the law is essential for salvation. Jews viewed God's judgment as the time when a person's salvation was ultimately determined. Especially during the persecutions of the intertestamental period, a division between faithful Jews and apostate Jews became more and more apparent. Both were born as Jews, heirs of the

---

7. The best representative of this general approach in Romans is Dunn, *Romans*; see, e.g., *Romans*, 158–60.

covenant; but, many Jews taught, the faithful Jew was saved and the apostate Jew was not. Why? Because the faithful Jew followed God's law and the apostate Jew did not. In this sense, fidelity to the law *was* essential for salvation among the Jews.

If the traditional view is guilty of overemphasizing the degree of legalism in the Jewish religion, "covenant nomism" is guilty of underemphasizing it. The bottom line is this: We are not convinced that the background against which generations of scholars interpreted Paul's teaching on justification is that far off the mark. Adjustments, particularly in some of the more extreme presentations, are needed. But these adjustments are not so violent as to require a whole new interpretation of Paul's teaching.

(2) Another reason why I have reservations about the new paradigm on Paul is that I do not think that it finally offers a convincing interpretation of Paul's teaching. We will be looking at many specific passages as we work through the commentary. But let me make two quick points on verse 20. (a) Many advocates of the new paradigm insist that the key issue Paul is grappling with is the relationship between Jew and Gentile in the people of God. So they tend to interpret "justify" to mean "accept into God's people." But this does not do justice to the vertical emphasis in Paul's justification teaching. As he makes clear in verse 20, it is being justified *before God* ("in his sight") that is the ultimate issue. Justification is God's acceptance of us; belonging to the people of God is penultimate.

(b) "Works of the law," as we argued in the Original Meaning section, mean "deeds done in obedience to the law." The other nuances that advocates of the new paradigm find in the phrase are not clearly present.

We conclude, then, that Paul in verse 20 is combating what we might call a "syncretistic" view of salvation that seems to have been widespread in first-century Judaism. God, in his covenant, had provided the basis for salvation. But the individual Jew could be saved only by faithfully doing the law in response to God's covenant election. In Romans 2 Paul shows that Jews cannot depend on their covenant for salvation, so that they cannot be put right with God by doing the law. Their "works" are now in the same category as that of the Gentiles—unable to secure salvation because of the pervasive power of sin.

 COMING TO GRIPS with sin. We can easily miss the precise wording of verse 9 and its significance. Paul does not say that all people "commit sins," as if doing things contrary to God's will is just an occasional problem. Nor does he even say that all people are "sinners,"

suggesting that sin is a pervasive problem. Rather, he says that all people are "under sin." Paul uses this kind of language to speak of a situation of domination or even slavery. See, for instance, Galatians 3:22: "But the Scripture declares that the whole world is a prisoner of sin [lit., "held prisoner *under* sin"], so that what was promised, being given through faith in Jesus Christ, might be given to those who believe" (see also Rom. 6:14, 15; 7:14; 1 Cor. 9:20; Gal. 3:23, 25; 4:2–5, 9, 21; Eph. 1:22). For Paul, then, the human plight is not that people commit sins or even that they are in the habit of committing sins. The problem is that people are helpless prisoners of sin.

Why is this point important? Mainly because our understanding of someone's problem dictates the answer to that problem. Marxists, for instance, believe that the basic human problem is the unequal distribution of wealth. Their solution is, therefore, to exert state control over the economy so that there will be no more rich and poor.

By contrast, many of the great philosophers and moral teachers in the history of the world have been convinced that the basic problem of human beings is that they are ignorant. The solution? Knowledge. That is, teach people, and they will be made into better people, and the problems of the world will disappear. This almost mystical belief in knowledge pervades our society, and many politicians propose programs based on this assumption. In recent months, for example, a blizzard of advertising encouraging children not to smoke has appeared in the United States. The assumption is clear: Teach children how foolish and dangerous it is to smoke, and they will never start. But if Paul is right, the problem, to pursue the analogy, is not that children are tempted to smoke. The problem, rather, is that many children are part of an environment in which peer pressure leads them to smoke. They may acknowledge that smoking is a bad habit and not really want to start. But they do not have the ability to resist the peer pressure. They are, as it were, enslaved to that pressure.

This is Paul's, and the Bible's, analysis of the human predicament: People, by nature, are addicted to sin. They are imprisoned under it, unable to free themselves by anything they can do. Knowing this, then, God has sent to us not a teacher or a politician but a liberator—one who has the power to set us free from our sins. Teaching, of course, is a very good thing—at least it had better be, because I do it all the time! But we must understand that is can never be, by itself, the ultimate solution to any one person's problems or to the problems of the world.

The communist governments that came to power in the twentieth century illustrate vividly the problem. Built on the Marxist philosophy, these governments forced rich people to distribute their resources with the poor. But taking the place of the rich landholders was a new privileged class of bureaucrats. Communism changed the privileged class, but it could not eradicate the basic human selfishness that inevitably leads to the hoarding of wealth and the championing of class distinctions.

When we really see the people all around us—at work, in our neighborhoods, at the store—as helpless captives of sin, we will be better motivated to help them find the true liberator who alone can rescue them from their captivity. Only Jesus Christ, proclaimed in the gospel, can break through the walls of sin that imprison human beings.

The poverty of works. As a result of our analysis of verse 20, we concluded that Paul denies that Jews can gain acceptance with God by doing the law. Their "works," the things they do in obedience to Torah, cannot justify them. But can the situation of Jews and their law be applied more broadly? Most defenders of the new paradigm deny that it can be. But in our view "works of the law" is not a technical expression for an exclusively Jewish phenomenon. It is, rather, a subset of the larger category "works." What Jews "do" in obedience to the law is but one particular form of what people "do" in obedience to "natural" law or "conscience" or whatever moral authority they may recognize.

Thus, we think it is appropriate to apply what Paul says in verse 20 to human beings generally. The Reformers consistently interpreted Paul's language in just this way, finding in verses like these the bedrock on which they built their understanding of the gospel. No person can be put right with God by what a person does. Faith, and specifically faith in Jesus Christ, is the only solution (see 3:21ff.).

The basic theology of Paul's argument on this point can quickly be seen by highlighting three key claims he makes in these chapters:

> "For it is not those who hear the law who are righteous in God's sight, but it is those who obey the law who will be declared righteous." (2:13)
> "What shall we conclude then? Are we any better? Not at all! We have already made the charge that Jews and Gentiles alike are all under sin." (3:9)
> "Therefore no one will be declared righteous in his sight by observing the law; rather, through the law we become conscious of sin." (3:20)

Taken out of context, the first and the third of these verses can be seen as contradictory. But between them is 3:9, asserting the universal domination of sin. Read as a sequential argument, 2:13 states the standard by which God judges all people: works. But the power of sin makes it impossible for any person to do those works that will win God's final approval. Thus, the conclusion follows: No person, *in fact*, can be justified by what he or she does.

The idea that our efforts, however sincere, cannot get us what we want cuts against the grain of natural human pride. We tend to have a high opinion of ourselves, particularly when things are going well. Carried over into religion, this natural human impulse leads to theories of salvation that give human effort a basic role. Such a view of salvation is officially adopted by some world religions. Christians who understand that human effort will never put a person in relationship with God must help people recognize the ultimate poverty of their works.

But Christians can also bring over into our own view and practice of faith a similar overemphasis on our own efforts. To be sure, as Paul will make clear in Romans 6 and 12, Christians need to be dedicated to producing works pleasing to God. But we can never take credit for these works, nor should we ever think that these works will make us acceptable to God.

Romans 3:21–26

BUT NOW A righteousness from God, apart from law, has been made known, to which the Law and the Prophets testify. ²²This righteousness from God comes through faith in Jesus Christ to all who believe. There is no difference, ²³for all have sinned and fall short of the glory of God, ²⁴and are justified freely by his grace through the redemption that came by Christ Jesus. ²⁵God presented him as a sacrifice of atonement, through faith in his blood. He did this to demonstrate his justice, because in his forbearance he had left the sins committed beforehand unpunished—²⁶he did it to demonstrate his justice at the present time, so as to be just and the one who justifies those who have faith in Jesus.

MARTIN LUTHER CLAIMED that this section was "the chief point, and the very central place of the Epistle, and of the whole Bible."[1] Quite a claim! We will not try to defend it here, since there are so many other great paragraphs that could vie for the title "central place in the Bible." But the paragraph is extraordinarily important. Rarely does the Bible bring together in so few verses so many important theological ideas: the righteousness of God, justification, the shift in salvation history, faith, sin, redemption, grace, propitiation, forgiveness, and the justice of God. Here, more than anywhere else in Romans, Paul explains why Christ's coming means "good news" for needy, sinful people.

The gospel Paul proclaims here expands on the brief introduction to the theme of justification by faith in 1:17. As we have seen, Paul takes a detour from the main line of his argument in 1:18–3:20 to show why God's intervention in Christ was needed. Now he resumes that argument. Note the similarity between 1:17 and 3:21:

For in the gospel a righteousness from God is revealed.
But now a righteousness from God, apart from law, has been made known.

The language of "righteousness" (3:21, 22, 25, 26), "justify" (vv. 24, 26), and "just" (v. 26) dominates this paragraph. All these English words come from

---

1. Margin of the Luther Bible, on 3:23ff.

the same Greek root (*dikai-*), so they develop one basic theme. But part of the power of these verses stems from the way Paul plays several variations on this theme (see esp. comments on 3:25b–26).

The Righteousness of God by Faith (3:21–22a)

IN VERSES 21–22A, Paul reveals the very heart of the good news: God's righteousness is available to all who put their faith in Jesus Christ. This righteousness is the same as Paul already announced in 1:17. It is better translated *"the* righteousness *of* God." Paul refers to a definite "righteousness": the process by which God acts to put people in right relationship with himself. The "but now" that opens the paragraph contrasts the situation in the time period before Christ, which Paul has described in the previous chapters, with the situation that now exists after his coming (see also 1 Cor. 15:20; Eph. 2:13; Col. 1:22). In other words, Christ's coming announces a decisive shift in salvation history.

God's plan of salvation unfolds in stages—a "history"—and the coming of Jesus the Messiah inaugurates a new stage in that plan. Paul elaborates this idea in the two contrasting phrases "apart from law" and "to which the Law and the Prophets testify." Some interpreters think Paul is saying that God has made known a new kind of righteousness—one that is "apart from law," that is, a righteousness not based on the law (the NIV translation suggests this interpretation). But it fits Paul's focus on salvation history better to take the phrase with the verb "make known"; note the NAB rendering, that "the righteousness of God has been manifested apart from the law." "Law," then, as usually in Paul, refers to the Mosaic law.

Paul beautifully captures in just a few words the continuity and discontinuity in God's plan of salvation. The discontinuity? God reveals his righteousness in Christ "apart from" the law of Moses. Like the "old wineskins" of Jesus' parable (Mark 2:22), the Mosaic covenant simply cannot contain the "new wine" of the gospel. The continuity? The entire Old Testament ("the Law and the Prophets") testifies to this new work of God in Christ. The cross is no afterthought, no "Plan B"; it has been God's intention from the beginning to reveal his saving righteousness by sending his Son as a sacrifice for us.

At the beginning of verse 22, Paul reiterates another point already made in 1:17: This righteousness of God is available only "through faith." Now, however, Paul is more explicit: God's righteousness "comes through faith in Jesus Christ to all who believe." The translation "faith in Jesus Christ" appears in almost all modern translations. But another translation is possible and is being supported by a growing number of scholars: "faith *of* Jesus Christ."

The debated construction is a genitive: *pisteos Iesou Christou*. The NIV takes this genitive to be "objective"; that is, "Jesus Christ" is the *object* of the noun "faith." But it can equally well be a "subjective" genitive, with Jesus Christ being the subject of "faith" (note the identical construction in 4:16, *pisteos Abraam*, which means "the faith Abraham exercised").[2]

This alternative is particularly attractive here because it removes what otherwise seems to be a needless repetition: "faith in Jesus Christ" and "to all who believe." Paul would then be making clear that our salvation comes about both because of Christ's "faith" or "faithfulness" to the task God gave him to do as well as from our faith in him. This idea is theologically acceptable, and Paul does use the noun *pistis* to refer to God's faithfulness in 3:3.

Other considerations, however, lead me to keep the usual translation here, "faith in Jesus Christ."[3] In the present context Paul consistently uses *pistis* to denote the response of believers to God (see, e.g., 3:25, 26, 27, 28, 30, 31; also throughout ch. 4). Moreover, Paul's failure ever to make Jesus the subject of the verb *pisteuo* (believe, entrust) makes it difficult to think that *Iesou Christou* is a subjective genitive. Adding "to all who believe" is not needless repetition, because Paul continues to be especially concerned to show that God's work in Christ is for everyone. His righteousness is "activated" *only* for those who believe, but it is also for *all* those who believe.

The Backdrop of Universal Sinfulness (3:22b–23)

WHY DOES GOD'S righteousness need to be available for "all who believe"? Because "all have sinned." Paul here inserts a brief reminder of his teaching in 1:18–3:20, which we need to understand to appreciate the universal dimensions of the gospel. As Paul has argued, there is no basic "difference" or "distinction" (*diastole*; see also 10:12) between people, especially between Jew and Gentile. All are under sin's power, and all "fall short of the glory of God."

God's glory (*doxa*) in the Bible is, first of all, his own awesome presence. But the Bible teaches that God's people are destined to share in that glory; thus *doxa* also describes the eternal destiny of believers (see esp. Rom. 8:18; Phil. 3:21; 2 Thess. 2:14). Jewish texts speak of Adam's having lost the "glory" of being like God at the time of the Fall, and all human beings since him share that fate. But what the first Adam lost, the second Adam, Christ, will restore.

---

2. See esp. L. T. Johnson, "Rom 3:21–26 and the Faith of Jesus," *CBQ* 44 (1982): 77–90; R. B. Hays, "PISTIS and Pauline Christology: What Is at Stake?" in *SBL 1991 Seminar Papers* (ed. E. H. Lovering Jr.; Atlanta: Scholars, 1991), 714–29.

3. This is the view of most commentators; see esp. Murray, *The Epistle to the Romans*, 1:363–74; Dunn, *Romans*, 166–67; Schreiner, *Romans*, 181–86.

Justified Through Redeeming Grace (3:24)

THE NIV, BY putting a comma at the end of verse 23, implies that verse 24 simply continues verse 23. But it is better to follow other versions (e.g., TEV) that make verse 24 a new sentence. The verb "justify" (*dikaioo*) brings us back to the initial topic of God's "righteousness" (*dikaiosyne*) after the parenthesis of verses 22b–23. In verse 22a, Paul has emphasized that God's justifying work is available through faith. Now he adds two further points: We are justified by means of God's grace and on the basis of his redemptive work in Jesus Christ.

"Grace" (*charis*) is a key theological idea in Paul. He uses the word to stress that all God does on our behalf is done freely and without compulsion. It is God's very nature to be free from any outside "requirements" about how he acts. Nothing we can do requires him to put us right with himself. We receive what he does as a pure gift.

"Redemption" (*apolytrosis*) has the basic sense of "to liberate by paying a price." This word and words related to it (e.g., "ransom" [*lytron*]) are used widely in the New Testament to describe the significance of Christ's death (Mark 10:45; Luke 24:21; Rom. 8:23; 1 Cor. 1:30; Eph. 1:7, 14; 4:30; Col. 1:14; Titus 2:14; 1 Peter 1:18). In Paul's day the words referred to the way in which people could pay money to buy the freedom of slaves or prisoners of war. Some interpreters doubt that Paul intends this original meaning of the word, but he probably does.[4] The connotation of liberating a slave through payment of a price fits perfectly his earlier use of slavery imagery to depict the human predicament ("under sin" in 3:9).

Christ's Sacrifice Vindicates God's Justice (3:25–26)

THESE VERSES EXPLAIN just *how* God was able to redeem people in Christ (v. 25a) and *why* he did it the way he did (vv. 25b–26). The means of redemption was Christ's sacrificial death. That much is clear about the beginning of verse 25, but little else is. Especially debated is the meaning of the word translated in NIV "sacrifice of atonement" (*hilasterion*). In secular Greek, this word and its cognates often refer to various means by which the wrath of the gods could be "propitiated." A sacrifice was offered or a monument dedicated, acts that served to "turn away" the wrath of a god. Many interpreters think Paul uses the word in this sense. Many English versions accordingly translate this word as "propitiation" (e.g., KJV; NASB).[5]

---

4. See esp. L. Morris, *The Apostolic Preaching of the Cross* (Grand Rapids: Eerdmans, 1965), 9–26.

5. See, e.g., ibid., 136–56.

C. H. Dodd, true to his distaste for the idea of God's wrath (see Bridging Contexts section on 1:18–32), wanted to render *hilasterion* as "expiation" (see RSV).[6] This English word refers to wiping away or forgiving sins; no allusion to God's wrath is included. But to understand this word, we must begin at a different point and ask what *hilasterion* refers to. In its only other use in the New Testament (Heb. 9:5) and in twenty-one of its twenty-seven occurrences in the LXX, *hilasterion* refers to what NIV calls the "atonement cover" (what used to be called the "mercy seat")—the cover of the ark where sacrificial blood was sprinkled as a means of propitiating God's wrath. This atonement cover is prominent in Leviticus 16, where the Day of Atonement ritual is described. The "atonement cover," therefore, came to represent for the Jews the place where, or the means by which, God took care of his people's sin problem.

It makes perfect sense for Paul to allude to this central item in Israel's atonement ritual.[7] Christ, in his sacrifice on the cross, is now the place where God takes care of his people's sins. The meaning, then, is broad, encompassing the acts of both expiation and propitiation. The NIV's "sacrifice of atonement" (cf. also NRSV) is probably a good translation. Paul goes on to highlight the importance of faith once again, adding that the benefit of this sacrifice is attained "through faith in his blood" (or simply "through faith"; "in blood" can also be taken with "sacrifice").

In verses 25b–26a, Paul indicates why God had to redeem people by the costly giving of his own Son as a sacrifice: It was "to demonstrate his [God's] justice." "Justice" translates *dikaiosyne*, which Paul has used in verses 21–22 to refer to God's saving righteousness, the process by which he puts people right before him. Some interpreters think Paul must use the word in this sense here too, but the context points us in a different direction. It was "because in his forbearance he had left sins committed beforehand unpunished" that God sent Christ to display his *dikaiosyne*. Only if *dikaiosyne* here and in verse 26a refers to God's justice does this connection make sense.

In the Old Testament period, God did not punish sins with the full severity he should have. People who sinned should have suffered spiritual death, because they did not yet have an adequate sacrifice to atone for their sins. But in his mercy God "passed over" their sins. In doing so, however, he acted against his character, which requires that he respond to sin with wrath. So the coming of Christ "satisfied" God's justice. In giving himself as a "sacrifice

---

6. See esp. C. H. Dodd, "ἱλάσκεσθαι, Its Cognates, Derivatives, and Synonyms in the Septuagint," *JTS* 32 (1931): 352–60.

7. This interpretation, which was held by a number of older commentators (e.g., Luther, Calvin, and Bengel), is growing in popularity with modern commentators also (e.g., Barrett, *Epistle to the Romans*, 77–78; Fitzmyer, *Romans*, 349–50; Schreiner, *Romans*, 193–94).

of atonement," Christ paid the price for the sins of all people—both before his time (v. 25b) and after (v. 26a).

Consequently, Paul summarizes, we can see how God can be "just and the one who justifies those who have faith in Jesus" (v. 26b). He accepts as righteous before him sinful people who have faith, and he accepts sinners as righteous without violating his own just character because Christ has fully satisfied God's demand that all who commit sin must die. By faith in Christ, we are joined to him. He becomes our representative, and his death is accredited to us.

SPEAKING ABOUT GOD. While God comes near to us in the incarnation of his Son, our world and his "world" are far apart in many ways. As long as we are part of this material world, we will always find it difficult to comprehend the things of God. Thus, to accommodate our weakness, God speaks to us in ways we can understand from our experience. Throughout the Bible, we find analogies used to communicate spiritual realities in earthly terms. Especially obvious are what we call "anthropomorphisms": attributing to God the "form" (*morphos*) of a human being (*anthropos*) to describe his character and actions. Thus, though God has no body, we find the Bible telling us that he sees with his eyes (e.g., Ps. 11:4), hears with his ears (Ps. 130:2), and delivers with his powerful arm (e.g., Ex. 6:6).

The Bible also uses analogies to describe the eternal state that God's people will enjoy in the afterlife. While a few Christians have thought the language used in Revelation 21, describing the new Jerusalem, might actually describe the reality of heaven, most interpreters agree it is an attempt to portray in common earthly terms a state of existence that cannot be directly described.

Most readers of the Bible have no trouble identifying the use of analogy in these kinds of passages. But the Bible also uses analogies and metaphors to get across theological truth. Romans 3:21–26 furnishes a wonderful example. Paul draws in this passage on several different kinds of human experience to depict the significance of Christ's death. The language of "righteousness" and "justify" comes from the realm of the law court (see Bridging Contexts section on 1:16–17). "Justification" is what a judge does when he declares innocent the defendant in a trial. God's "righteousness" carries the legal connotation of "vindication." When he intervenes in Christ, he is vindicating his name and displaying his faithfulness to the "contract" he has entered into with the world.

The word "redemption," by contrast, comes from the world of commerce and slavery. One redeems slaves by purchasing their freedom. Paul also uses the imagery of sacrifice, as he depicts Christ in verse 25 as the one in whom God now acts to take care, once and for all, of the problem of human sin.

Some of these metaphors do not translate as well into our society as others. In the ancient world, some scholars have maintained, religion *was* sacrifice. It was central to the experiences most people had in their religion. But sacrifice is not common in our day, so that the sacrificial language of the New Testament does not speak to us as directly as it did to first-century readers. We have to do some "digging" to get a sense of what sacrifice was and what it meant so that the text can speak to us with full power. Nor is the redemption of slaves common today, though it does occur. In recent days, for instance, people in some wealthy countries have raised money to purchase freedom for slaves in some African and Middle Eastern nations. That transaction is, indeed, a redemption, and it sheds light on what God has done for us in Christ.

But whatever the analogy or metaphor, and however near or far it may be to our own experience, we face two big dangers in interpreting this language. (1) We may misunderstand what is meant by the biblical analogy by failing to recognize differences between the biblical concept and a modern one. The modern person who thinks that God "redeems" people the way we "redeem" a coupon, for instance, will miss what Paul is talking about.

(2) We may unfairly elevate one metaphor over another. To be sure, the Bible uses certain metaphors for theological truth so often that we are justified in giving them a great deal of weight. Note, for example, how often the New Testament portrays God as our "Father." But both lay people and theologians alike have sometimes made the mistake of focusing on one metaphor so much that they miss others.

For instance, Protestant theologians have often virtually equated salvation with justification. Now the law-court imagery of justification is vitally important in our understanding of what God has done for us in Christ. But it is not the only metaphor used for this reality. God also "reconciles" us (relational language), "adopts" us (familial language), "sanctifies" us (cultic language), and so on. Roman Catholic theologians have sometimes made a similar mistake by focusing too exclusively on the "body of Christ" metaphor. To comprehend fully what God does for us in Christ, we need to make use of all the biblical metaphors.

(3) A third way we can misuse the analogies Scripture uses to communicate theological truth is to take them further than the Bible does. No analogy is ever perfect. A person will use an analogy because it is parallel to the point being illustrated in some vital respect, but it will almost never be parallel in all respects. For instance, we may say that a business executive who resigned his post in the midst of an investigation of his company for fraud

"sacrificed himself" for the good of the company. The analogy exists at one key point: As a sacrifice suffers harm for the good of others, so the executive suffered harm for the good of the company. But it is foolish for us to ask what god the executive sacrificed himself to or how he could have lived through the experience. We call this illegitimate extension of an analogy, making it "walk on all fours."

The theological idea of "redemption" illustrates this tendency well. Paul and other biblical authors, as we have seen, portray Christ's sacrifice as a "ransom"—a price paid to secure the release of captives. Confronted with this imagery, people have naturally asked, "To whom did God pay the ransom?" The answer given by many theologians, especially in the patristic period, was Satan. The church fathers argued that because of sin, the devil had the right to keep people captive to himself. Human beings sinned, and the devil therefore had control of them. In order to secure their release, God had to pay the devil a ransom, the death of Christ. So popular was this interpretation that Gustaf Aulen called it the "classic" view of the atonement.[8]

But the Bible nowhere teaches any ransom paid to the devil. The biblical writers repeatedly use the concept of redemption to connote that God in Christ had to liberate people from slavery to sin and that he paid a price to accomplish this. These are the points of contact between "secular" redemption and what God had done in Christ. But biblical writers nowhere speculate on whom the ransom was paid to. Their silence here suggests that this was not part of the analogy they were using.

Sacrifice of atonement. In our exposition above, we argued that the much-debated word *hilasterion* in verse 25 "refers to" the atonement cover of the ark and "means" sacrifice of atonement. I would like to expand on this interpretation, in two ways.

(1) Note the distinction made between "refers to" and "means." People who study language insist this is an important distinction. Although we may not put it in precisely those terms, we make this distinction all the time. For instance, when a successful politician is soundly defeated in what looks to be his last race, we may say that he had met his "Waterloo." Now "Waterloo" *refers to* the battle lost by Napoleon at that place in 1815, but it *means* a decisive and perhaps final defeat. To insist that the word can only function in one way or the other is to miss the flexibility of language both to "refer" and to "mean."

It is precisely this mistake that some interpreters of Romans 3:25 make. They want—I think rightly—to keep the notion of propitiation in Paul's language here. But they think that if *hilasterion* refers to the "atonement cover," they cannot keep this theologically significant idea. Such is not the case. Since

---

8. Gustaf Aulen, *Christus Victor* (rpt.; New York: Collier, 1986).

the "atonement cover" came to stand for the central act of atonement in Israel's experience, Paul's reference to it carries with it all the significance associated with that act of atonement. A fair reading of the Old Testament makes clear that the Day of Atonement ritual included both remission of sins (expiation) and the turning away of God's wrath (propitiation). The very word "atonement" (from the Heb. root *kpr*) contains the idea of the removal of punishment due sin and includes a change in God's attitude toward the sinner.[9]

In other words, I am trying to have my cake and eat it twice. Atonement cover, expiation, and propitiation are all involved in this single word *hilasterion*. But this expansive interpretation is justified when we distinguish between "reference" and "meaning." When the Roman Christians came to the word *hilasterion*, they would immediately have thought of the Day of Atonement ritual and all that it meant. Those yearly days of atonement are now fulfilled in the one great "Day of Atonement," when Christ died on a Roman cross for the sins of the world.

"BUT NOW." Martin Lloyd-Jones, the great British preacher and expositor of Romans, once said that "there are no more wonderful words in the whole of Scripture than just these two words, 'But now.'" How could he make such an extravagant claim? He was thinking of the many occasions when New Testament writers use these two words to contrast the state of people or the world outside of Christ, with the situation in Christ (note: italics added in the following quotations):

> What benefit did you reap at that time from the things you are now ashamed of? Those things result in death! *But now* that you have been set free from sin and have become slaves to God, the benefit you reap leads to holiness, and the result is eternal life. (Rom. 6:21–22)

> For when we were controlled by the sinful nature, the sinful passions aroused by the law were at work in our bodies, so that we bore fruit for death. *But now*, by dying to what once bound us, we have been released from the law so that we serve in the new way of the Spirit, and not in the old way of the written code. (Rom. 7:5–6)

> Now to him who is able to establish you by my gospel and the proclamation of Jesus Christ, according to the revelation of the mystery hidden for long ages past, *but now* revealed and made known through the

---

9. See esp. Paul Garnet, "Atonement Constructions in the Old Testament and the Qumran Scrolls," *EvQ* 46 (1974): 131–63.

prophetic writings by the command of the eternal God, so that all nations might believe and obey him—to the only wise God be glory forever through Jesus Christ! Amen. (Rom. 16:25–27)

Formerly, when you did not know God, you were slaves to those who by nature are not gods. *But now* that you know God—or rather are known by God—how is it that you are turning back to those weak and miserable principles? Do you wish to be enslaved by them all over again? (Gal. 4:8–9)

Therefore, remember that formerly you who are Gentiles by birth and called "uncircumcised" by those who call themselves "the circumcision" (that done in the body by the hands of men)—remember that at that time you were separate from Christ, excluded from citizenship in Israel and foreigners to the covenants of the promise, without hope and without God in the world. *But now* in Christ Jesus you who once were far away have been brought near through the blood of Christ. (Eph. 2:11–13)

For you were once darkness, *but now* you are light in the Lord. Live as children of light. (Eph. 5:8)

Once you were alienated from God and were enemies in your minds because of your evil behavior. *But now* he has reconciled you by Christ's physical body through death to present you holy in his sight, without blemish and free from accusation. (Col. 1:21–22)

You used to walk in these ways, in the life you once lived. *But now* you must rid yourselves of all such things as these: anger, rage, malice, slander, and filthy language from your lips. (Col. 3:7–8)

At that time his voice shook the earth, *but now* he has promised, "Once more I will shake not only the earth but also the heavens." (Heb. 12:26)

Once you were not a people, *but now* you are the people of God; once you had not received mercy, *but now* you have received mercy. (1 Peter 2:10)

For you were like sheep going astray, *but now* you have returned to the Shepherd and Overseer of your souls. (1 Peter 2:25)

As these passages reveal, the "but now" transition can refer to what God did in Christ to bring in the new age of salvation (e.g., Rom. 3:21; 7:5–6; 16:25–27; Eph. 2:11–13), or to the personal experience of transfer from the old life of sin and death to the new life of righteousness and eternal life (e.g.,

Col. 3:7–8). By using this language as often as they do, New Testament authors suggest we will derive great spiritual benefit from contemplating the contrast between our old life and the new. "Once" we were far from God, alienated from him and his people, stumbling in darkness, and destined for hell. "But now" we have been brought near to the God of this universe. We enjoy all the benefits of belonging to God's own people. We "walk in the light," understanding God's will and seeking to follow it. We are destined for glory.

One of the striking things in these verses is that they are objective in their orientation. That is, they do not say much about a difference in the way we may *feel*. They focus on the difference of who we *are* in God's sight. A basic theme of Romans, coming to expression again and again in the letter, is the need for Christians to understand who they are. Paul will say much more on this subject in chapters 5–8. But he lays the foundation here by reminding us of the great turning point in world history: the revelation of God's righteousness in Christ, inaugurating a new age in which a restored relationship with the God of the universe is available for all.

I enjoy that restored relationship. The "but now" transition from the old life to the new is something I have personally experienced. It happened for me when I was a senior in college—emotionally messed up because of some broken relationships and insecure about who I was and where I was going. I called out in despair, "God, if you are there, help me." The amazing thing is that he did. He led me to some students who shared the gospel with me, and I responded. I have been a Christian now for almost thirty years, but it is not always easy to remember what I was like in college. Yet I will never forget how lost I felt. That helps me appreciate all the more how secure I now feel—secure because I am a child of God, experiencing daily his fatherly care. If you are reading these words, you have probably had your own "but now" experience. Take some time to remember who you were and contemplate who you now are.

Grace. As our conversion recedes further and further into the past, many of us have a hard time remembering just how joyous is the "but now" transition we have been talking about. The good news becomes old hat, and we lose the sense of wonder and awe we first had when we understood that God had adopted us into his family. Why is this? There are many reasons, but Paul touches on two of them in these chapters: We fail to remember who we are, and we fail to remember who God is.

Who are we? In ourselves, apart from Christ, we are helpless slaves of sin, held captive by a power that we can never overcome. And who is God? Among so many other things, he is a holy and just. Because he is holy, he cannot tolerate sin. Sin simply cannot exist in his presence. It is foreign to the essence of his being. God can no more exist in an atmosphere of sin that I can exist in a vacuum. Because he is just, he must punish sin. God can do anything, we sometimes think. But he cannot act in a way that violates his own nature; he would "unmake" himself if he tried. Here, then, is the dilemma God himself faces. His love reaches out to us, sinful rebels that we are; but his holiness and justice prevent him from simply sweeping sin under the carpet. It must be punished. James Denney, in a classic book on the death of Christ, puts the problem, and the answer, like this:

> There can be no gospel unless there is such a thing as a righteousness of God for the ungodly. But just as little can there be any gospel unless the integrity of God's character be maintained. The problem of the sinful world, the problem of all religion, the problem of God in dealing with a sinful race, is how to unite these two things. The Christian answer to the problem is given by Paul in the words: "Jesus Christ, whom God set forth a propitiation (or, in propitiatory power) in his blood."[10]

C. S. Lewis explores the same idea more imaginatively in the first of his children's novels, *The Lion, the Witch, and the Wardrobe.* Because of selfishness and greed, a little boy has fallen into the hands of a wicked witch. Aslan, the God character, cannot, for all his immense power, rescue the boy; for he must acknowledge the "magic," the law of nature, that has given the witch power over the boy. But there is a "deeper magic from the dawn of time" that enables one who dies willingly for someone else to take on that person's punishment and let them go free. Thus, Aslan allows the wicked witch to execute him.

Most of us are familiar with this way of understanding the death of Christ. Modern theologians, to be sure, do not like the idea. They think it is a holdover from the Middle Ages, when theologians were obsessed with legality. They think it turns God into a schizophrenic being who has to "buy off" his own holiness with his love. But the view we have sketched above is rooted solidly in this text of Romans and provides a more satisfying understanding of the cross than any other. Only such a conception does real justice to the biblical picture of sinful humanity and a holy God. Pascal has put it very well: "Grace is indeed needed to turn a man into a saint; and he who doubts it does not know what a saint or a man is."[11]

---

10. James Denney, *The Death of Christ* (London: Tyndale, 1951), 98.
11. Pascal, *Pensées,* 508.

Romans 3:27–31

❧

W HERE, THEN, IS boasting? It is excluded. On what principle? On that of observing the law? No, but on that of faith. 28For we maintain that a man is justified by faith apart from observing the law. 29Is God the God of Jews only? Is he not the God of Gentiles too? Yes, of Gentiles too, 30since there is only one God, who will justify the circumcised by faith and the uncircumcised through that same faith. 31Do we, then, nullify the law by this faith? Not at all! Rather, we uphold the law.

THE QUESTION THAT begins this paragraph suggests it is closely related to 3:21–26. Many commentators, therefore, attach verses 27–31 to verses 21–26. But we think that verses 27–31 go more with chapter 4 than with 3:21–26, for two reasons. (1) Romans 3:27–31 only develops one of the ideas from 3:21–26: faith as the only way to experience God's justification. The other significant theological concepts brought up in verses 21–26 (redemption, grace, propitiation, God's justice) are dropped. (2) The topics treated in 3:27–31 mirror those taken up in chapter 4:

Romans 3:27–31	Romans 4
Boasting is excluded (v. 27)	Abraham had no right to boast (vv. 1–2)
... because one is justified by faith, not works of the law (v. 28)	... because Abraham was justified by faith, not works (vv. 3–8)
Circumcised and uncircumcised are united under the one God through faith (vv. 29–30)	Circumcised and uncircumcised are united as children of Abraham through faith (vv. 9–17)

What Paul does in 3:27–31, then, is quickly touch on the basic points he wants to make about faith before developing them at greater length with respect to Abraham.

Paul reverts in verse 27 to the question-and-answer format so popular in the diatribe. This suggests that he is again engaged in dialogue with someone about the significance of the gospel. Who is this person? A human being in general, most commentators answer: Paul wants every person to understand that God's way of justifying people—by grace—absolutely excludes any possibility that we may take credit for our salvation. But another possible identification of this person is more specific: the Jew. Paul used this same language of "boasting" or "bragging" about Jews in 2:17, so he may be reminding Jews that they can no longer brag about their superiority to Gentiles. God justifies both Jew and Gentile on the same basis (see vv. 29–30).[1]

Paul probably does have a Jew in mind here. But, as verses 27b–28 show, it is the Jews' tendency to take pride in their obedience to the law that he particularly criticizes. As elsewhere in Romans, then, Jewish boasting in "works of the law" is representative of human boasting in accomplishments. All such boasting is nonsense in light of God's grace.

Paul explains why all such boasting is ruled out in the end of verse 27, but the translation and interpretation are debated. The Greek literally translates, "Through what law [*nomos*]? Of works? No, but through the law [*nomos*] of faith [*pistis*]." The NIV reflects a popular interpretation by translating the word *nomos* as "principle." In effect, then, *nomos* becomes something of a formal addition without any real significance.

This meaning of the word is possible. But many recent commentators protest that giving *nomos* this general meaning does not do justice to Paul's focus in this context on the Mosaic law. They therefore argue that Paul is contrasting two ways of viewing, or responding to, the law of Moses: one way that focuses only on the works it demands, and another that recognizes in the law a demand for faith as well.[2] But the NIV interpretation is probably better, since Paul generally avoids associating faith with the Mosaic law (see comments on 2:13 and 2:26–27).

If this is the case, then verse 28 unpacks this "principle . . . of faith": "For we maintain that a man is justified by faith apart from observing the law." "Observing the law" again here translates the Greek *erga nomou*, "works of the law" (see comment on 3:20); as in that earlier verse, the phrase means "works done in obedience to the law of Moses." Significantly, even in what seems so general a principle, Paul focuses on Jewish obedience to the law of Moses. His primary concern continues to be to show that Jews need the gospel, for by demonstrating this, he will have shown that all people need it.

Verse 28 is a famous statement of the doctrine of justification by faith, and, under the influence of Luther, many of us almost automatically add an "alone" after faith. The word is not, of course, found in the verse. But it legitimately

---

1. Dunn, *Romans*, 185–86.
2. See esp. Cranfield, *The Epistle to the Romans*, 219–20; Dunn, *Romans*, 185–87.

brings out the sense of what Paul is saying (long before Luther, the Roman Catholic theologian Aquinas had also added it). For in denying that even the best human works can justify us (e.g., Jewish obedience to God's holy law), Paul is, in effect, denying that anything a human being does will ever justify one before God.

Verses 29–30 bring to the surface again one of the central subthemes of the letter: the equality between Jew and Gentile before God. Paul turns the Jews' vaunted belief in monotheism against their tendency to confine salvation to themselves in exclusion from Gentiles. For if, as Jews proudly confess, there is only one God, then this God must be equally God of Gentiles as well as Jews. Rightly understood, this demolishes any ultimate difference between Jew and Gentile before the Lord. Thus, Paul concludes, God will justify both "the circumcised" (Jews) and "the uncircumcised" (Gentiles) on the same basis: through faith.

Paul's pastoral sensitivity reveals itself again in verse 31. As we have noted (see comment on 2:1), the sequence of thought in Romans is to some extent dictated by the questions and objections Paul knows people will raise about the gospel. He has just insisted that doing the law contributes nothing to justification. But he knows that some people will conclude from that teaching that the law is no good at all: It is "nullified." Thus he responds: "Not at all [*me genoito*]! Rather, we uphold the law."

In other words, the Mosaic law may not play a role in justification, but Paul does not want his readers to conclude that it plays no role at all in God's plan of salvation. But just what role does it play? Paul does not explicitly say how his preaching "upholds" the law, but we can surmise that he elaborates elsewhere in the letter. Four main possibilities should be considered:

1. We uphold the Mosaic law as a testimony to the gospel (ch. 4).[3]
2. We uphold the Mosaic law as bringing conviction of sin (3:19–20).[4]
3. We uphold the Mosaic law as a source of guidance for the Christian life (13:8–10).[5]
4. We uphold the Mosaic law as a standard of God's holiness, now fulfilled in Christ (8:4).[6]

The first possibility is popular and may seem the most obvious reading, for Paul goes on in chapter 4 to show how the story of Abraham testifies to justification by faith. But if this had been Paul's intention, it is surprising that he does not use the word *nomos* (law) in 4:2 to signify this connection. The

3. See Godet, *Commentary on Romans*, 166; Käsemann, *Commentary on Romans*, 105.
4. See Andrew J. Bandstra, *The Law and the Elements of the World* (Kampen: Kok, 1964), 99–100.
5. See Murray, *The Epistle to the Romans*, 1:124–25; Schreiner, *Romans*, 207–8.
6. See Fitzmyer, *Romans*, 367.

second is also unlikely because Paul, in this context at least, is talking about the law as a moral authority. Both the third and fourth interpretations fit this emphasis, and which Paul intends we cannot determine from this context alone.

Our understanding, in light of the way that the argument develops, is that the fourth is the more likely. Paul affirms the valid demand that God makes of people in the law, and that demand cannot simply be swept under the carpet. But one of the things Christ does is to fulfill the law on our behalf. We who are in Christ are therefore accounted as having fulfilled the law and been set free from its penalties for disobedience. It is, paradoxically, this very freedom from the law's condemnation that puts us into a relationship in which true obedience, motivated and directed by the Spirit, can come about.

THE MEANING OF "LAW." As we noted when the word *nomos* first appeared in Romans (see comment on 2:12), the contemporary reader must read this word in light of its usage in Paul's context, not in ours. We use "law" is an extraordinary number of ways, and we easily misunderstand Paul if we read one of those meanings when he intends quite another. We argued that Paul uses the word in a thoroughly Jewish context. He, of course, is a Jew himself (a fact we sometimes forget), his vocabulary is formed by long and intimate acquaintance with the Old Testament, and in Romans he writes about Jewish matters. There can be no doubt, then, that for Paul *nomos* is basically and usually the Mosaic law—the revelation of God's will for Israel mediated through Moses at Mount Sinai.

Yet we have just argued that *nomos* does not have this meaning in verse 27. Is this consistent? We earlier set down the principle that we should assume Paul uses *nomos* to refer to the Mosaic law *unless clear contextual indicators pointed in another direction*. Our case for taking *nomos* in verse 27 to mean principle, rule, or authority rests on this caveat. We think Paul provides sufficient clues in the context that he is not using the word in the normal way.

First, of course, it must be established that the alternate meaning for the word actually exists. For, except in rare circumstances, context is never a strong enough basis to justify a new meaning for a word. Some interpreters indeed deny that *nomos* ever has the general sense of rule or principle— what we might call a "formal" meaning. But enough examples exist, even from Jewish writers contemporary to Paul, to show that this meaning is possible.

Josephus, for instance, a Jewish historian who wrote just after Paul's time, speaks of the *"nomoi* of warfare," that is, the (unwritten) rules that govern military strategy (*J.W.* 5.123). Similarly, Philo, a first-century Jewish philosopher, can refer to the *nomoi* or norms of music (*On the Creation* 54, 70).[7] So this meaning of the word is available for Paul to use if he wants to.

But what is the evidence from the context that this is what he in fact means? Three items point in this direction. (1) The first is the most general and the weakest; by itself it is not compelling. The word *nomos* often has a formal meaning when it is followed by a nonpersonal word in the genitive, as it is here with "works" (*ergon*) and "faith" (*pisteos*).[8] In fact, of the four other places where Paul qualifies *nomos* in this way, three may very well have this formal meaning (Rom. 7:25; 8:2; 9:31; Eph. 2:15 is probably a reference to the Mosaic law).

(2) Paul distances faith from the Mosaic law in this particular context (v. 28). This makes the combination "law of faith" unexpected.

(3) The final argument is broader, involving the more general theological context that Paul sets up and within which he uses words like *nomos* and *pistis*. Any given occurrence of an author's words must be interpreted in light of the particular field of usage an author has himself established. Paul seems to have established a "field of discourse" in which *nomos* and *pistis* exist in separate categories. This is seen, for example, in the way he contrasts "faith" and "law" or "works of the law" (Rom. 3:20; Gal. 2:16; 3:2, 5, 10, 11–12; Phil. 3:9). Another indication is that the apostle frequently speaks of the law as something to be obeyed or done but never as something to be believed (see esp. the contrasts in Rom. 10:5–6 and Gal. 3:11–12).

What all this suggests is that Paul's own world of discourse did not allow for *pistis* and *nomos* (in the sense of Mosaic law) to be associated. They are on opposite sides of his linguistic categories. Some will, of course, reply that verses like this one as well as 8:2 and 9:31–32 show that this distinction does not always hold. Thus, the decision gets down to a matter of weighing the strength of these verses against the preponderant usage in Paul. We certainly understand how scholars can reach different decisions on the matter. But what I wanted to do here was briefly sketch the method that lies behind my decision to interpret "law of faith" in Romans 3:27 as I do. Only by taking into consideration all these factors can we accurately move from Paul's meaning to its application in our day.

---

7. The best presentation of this evidence is found in Heikki Räisänen, "Sprachliches zum Spiel des Paulus mit NOMOS," in *The Torah and Christ* (Helsinki: Kirjapaino Raamattutalu, 1986), 119–47.

8. See Michael Winger, *By What Law? The Meaning of* νόμος *in the Letters of Paul* (Atlanta: Scholars, 1992), 92.

BOASTING. ONE OF the most common and perhaps basic of all sins is illegitimate pride—what Paul calls "boasting." The tendency for finite, weak, and sinful human beings to think too much of ourselves is endemic and hard to rid ourselves of. John calls it "boasting of what [a person] has and does" (1 John 2:16). We easily bring such boasting into our relationship with God. In addition to being sinful, it carries two great dangers. (1) It stifles our worship. As long as we think, however subconsciously, that we have contributed something to our salvation, we will not put God on as high a plane as we should. We will loom too large and he will seem too small—and we will not worship with the absolute sense of humility, dependence, and thanksgiving that always marks the best worship.

(2) The other danger arises from the fact that the accomplishments in which we are tempted to boast are so inconsistent and imperfect. When things are going well and we are feeling pretty good about ourselves, it is easy to put confidence in ourselves. But the inevitable difficult times will come— and if our confidence rests in ourselves, we will find ourselves with no good foundation on which to stand.

A more subtle kind of illegitimate boasting is often only a hair's breadth from a legitimate sense of contentment from doing the will of the Lord. When we obey the Lord by avoiding a sin we were tempted to commit or by doing an act of kindness, it is entirely appropriate for us to have a sense of contentment and even of self-satisfaction. Paul, for instance, can express legitimate pride in his ministry, calling himself an "expert builder" (1 Cor. 3:10) and boasting about how he "worked harder" than all the other apostles (15:10). But, significantly, in each of these texts, Paul attributes the value of his ministry to the working of God's grace. Pride in our good deeds or works of ministry must always recognize that God, not ourselves, is the cause of whatever good we accomplish.

But this perspective is hard to maintain. I know I can hardly perform a "righteous act" without instantly marring it with pride. I recently joined some other people from my church to help paint the house of a brother who was seriously ill. In the midst of my painting comes a persistent voice that begins by saying, "You are doing a good deed. God is going to be happy with you." Perhaps there is nothing wrong with this feeling—so far. But quickly the voice moves on to say, "You should take pride in what you are doing. God is surely bound to reward you because you are being so good." The minute we think that our good works exert a claim on God, we have moved from legitimate contentment to illegitimate boasting. All our works, however good they may be—and all our works in this life are inevitably stained by sin— are the product of God's grace, as his Spirit moves in us.

Romans 4:1–8

WHAT THEN SHALL we say that Abraham, our forefather, discovered in this matter? ²If, in fact, Abraham was justified by works, he had something to boast about—but not before God. ³What does the Scripture say? "Abraham believed God, and it was credited to him as righteousness."

⁴Now when a man works, his wages are not credited to him as a gift, but as an obligation. ⁵However, to the man who does not work but trusts God who justifies the wicked, his faith is credited as righteousness. ⁶David says the same thing when he speaks of the blessedness of the man to whom God credits righteousness apart from works:

⁷"Blessed are they
    whose transgressions are forgiven,
    whose sins are covered.
⁸Blessed is the man
    whose sin the Lord will never count against him."

IN 3:27–31, PAUL BRIEFLY mentions two implications of the truth that we are justified by faith and not by "observing the law" (v. 28): We cannot boast in our own religious accomplishments (v. 27), and Jews and Gentiles have equal access to justification (vv. 29–30). In chapter 4 he develops both these points with reference to Abraham (see comments on 3:27–31).

In 4:1–8, Paul shows that Abraham himself had nothing to boast about before God because he, also, was justified by faith. Then, in 4:9–17, he argues that Abraham's justification by faith means that he is qualified to be the spiritual father of both believing Jews and believing Gentiles. Verses 18–22 expand on the nature of Abraham's faith before Paul wraps up his exposition with a final application to Christians (vv. 23–25).

Throughout the chapter, Paul grounds his exposition in the key verse, cited in 4:3, of Genesis 15:6: "Abraham believed God, and it was credited to him as righteousness." The focus is especially on the nature and meaning of Abraham's believing. Another way to look at the chapter, then, is in terms of a series of antitheses by which Paul unfolds the significance of Abraham's faith—and of ours:

1. Faith is something completely different from "works" (vv. 3–8).
2. Faith does not depend on any religious ceremony (e.g., circumcision) (vv. 9–12).
3. Faith is not related to the law (vv. 13–17).
4. Faith often rests in a promise that flies in the face of what is natural and normal (vv. 18–22).

As he does so often in Romans (see also 3:1, 9, 27; 4:9; 6:1, 15; 7:1, 7, 13; 9:14, 30; 10:14; 11:1, 11), Paul uses a question to introduce the next stage of his argument. The question he asks in 4:1 about what Abraham "discovered in this matter" relates to the argument of 3:27–31. Paul introduces Abraham here for two reasons. (1) The Jews revered Abraham as both the ancestor of God's people and as a model of faithfulness to the law. If the apostle is to convince Christians in Rome who know Jewish history and tradition to endorse the gospel of justification by faith, he must prove that Abraham, in fact, is on his side in this dispute.

(2) Abraham is a key figure in God's plan of salvation as revealed in the Old Testament. One of Paul's purposes in Romans is to demonstrate that the gospel is in continuity with the Old Testament (see, e.g., 1:2; 3:21). Proving that the story of Abraham fits into Paul's conception of salvation history is an important step toward this goal.

Having introduced Abraham in 4:1, Paul now moves directly to the attack: "If, in fact, Abraham was justified by works [as, apparently, at least some Jews believed], he has something to boast about [and our argument in 3:27–31 that boasting is excluded falls to the ground]." Paul immediately responds to his line of argument: "but not before God." Just what Paul means by this response is not clear. He may mean that Abraham's justification by works would give him a reason to boast before other people—but not before God.[1] But the logic of Paul's argument, as 4:3–8 reveals, is to reject the possibility of justification by works at all. Thus, his response probably means something like "from God's perspective, Abraham has no right at all to boast because he was not, and could not be, justified by works."[2]

Paul grounds this response in Scripture (4:3). Genesis 15:6 is a foundational Old Testament verse for Paul's characteristic emphasis on justification by faith (see also Gal. 3:6). This verse describes Abraham's response to God's

---

1. E.g., Godet, *Commentary on Romans*, 169–70; Sanday and Headlam, *The Epistle to the Romans*, 99–100.
2. See, e.g., Murray, *The Epistle to the Romans*, 1:129–30; Cranfield, *The Epistle to the Romans*, 228.

promise that he would have descendants as innumerable as the stars in the sky. But this promise, in turn, stands in a sequence of similar divine promises to Abraham about his role as the founder of a nation and mediator of world-wide blessing (see esp. Gen. 12:1–3). So Paul probably reads Genesis 15:6 as a summary of Abraham's response to God's promise to him generally.

But what does "crediting" Abraham's faith "as righteousness" mean? Some interpreters think the text equates Abraham's faith with righteousness. That is, Abraham's belief is taken by God to be a righteous act. Jewish tradition tended to take this interpretation. But the Hebrew construction in this verse (awkwardly taken over in the Greek) suggests a different interpretation. "Crediting" Abraham's faith as righteousness means "to account to him a righteousness that does not inherently belong to him."[3] When Abraham believed God, God granted him the status of "righteousness"; he considered him "right" before God.

Paul himself is concerned to unpack the significance of this "crediting" of Abraham's faith for righteousness. Thus, in 4:4–5 he explains the nature of this crediting and in verses 6–8 furnishes further scriptural support for the idea. Note, then, how Paul returns to the language of "crediting" both at the end of verse 5, in verse 6, and again in the quotation in verse 8 (the word translated "count" represents the same Greek word [*logizomai*] translated "credited").

The logic of verses 4–5 is not easy to understand at first sight because Paul does not express the major premise of his argument. Thus it may be helpful to unpack his logic in a slightly different arrangement of his argument:

> When we "work," an employer pays us wages not "as a gift" but "as an obligation" (v. 4).
> God is a God of grace, who always gives freely and without constraint; he can never be "obligated" to any person (the assumed premise in the argument).
> Therefore, God cannot "credit" human beings anything on the basis of their "works" (v. 5)

The premise we have added is implied in the language of "gift" in verse 4 and the famous assertion of verse 5 that God "justifies the wicked." Indeed, the fact that God always relates to his creatures freely and without compulsion, by grace, is a theological axiom in Paul. That is, this is a fundamental perspective on God that he never argues but assumes as self-evident. If God were to justify people on the basis of their works, this axiom would be violated: God would be giving people something they had earned. In the context

---

3. O. Palmer Robertson, "Genesis 15:6: New Covenant Exposition of an Old Covenant Text," *WTJ* 42 (1980): 265–66.

of this argument, then, Paul's description of the Christian as one who "does not work" (v. 5) is not, as Morris puts it, "canonizing laziness."[4] As the contrast shows ("but who trusts God"), Paul is referring to the fact that Christians do not base their relationship to God on their actions.

In typical Jewish fashion, Paul now confirms the truth he has found in a text from the "Law" (Gen. 15:6) with a text from the "Writings" (see Bridging Contexts section). He quotes Psalm 32:1–2a. In these verses, David joins his testimony to that of Moses, revealing that it is people "to whom God credits righteousness apart from works" that are truly blessed. Since Paul sees this verse as confirmation of his interpretation of Genesis 15:6, his careful wording shows that the view of Genesis 15:6 we defended above is on the right track.

The key point in what David says in Psalm 32 for Paul is that the people who are blessed are not those who have earned something from God; they are the ones who have received something from him. Their transgressions are forgiven, their sins "covered," and God does not hold their sin against them. That these people continue to sin is obvious, but God does not hold their sin against them. He accepts them and blesses them. These verses therefore confirm what Paul has argued in Romans 4:4–5: God "justifies the wicked." That is, he "declares innocent" people who are really not, in themselves, innocent. He grants them a status they have not earned and do not deserve.

Here we find the heart of the good news: God accepts us, through our faith, just as we are. In his grace he "covers" our sins, not counting them against us. We will elaborate this point in the Contemporary Significance section.

MODERN READERS UNACQUAINTED with Jewish methods of scriptural argument or with the way Abraham was understood in Paul's day cannot fully appreciate the argument of verses 1–8. So we will briefly survey each of these points.

Abraham. The story of Abraham in Genesis 12–22 revolves around God's promise to Abraham. The basic elements of that promise are found in Genesis 12:2–3. God promises that Abraham will become a great nation, that he will magnify and bless Abraham, and that Abraham, in turn, will be a cause of blessing for "all peoples on earth." Time passes, yet Abraham remains childless. God therefore responds to Abraham's concern by renewing his promise about descendants and emphasizing that they will possess the land of Israel. God then ratifies his promise by entering into a covenant with Abraham (ch. 15).

---

4. Morris, *The Epistle to the Romans*, 198.

A further step comes in Genesis 17. God elaborates on his promise, stressing especially the many nations that will come from Abraham (vv. 4–6) and the land that Abraham's descendants will have as an "everlasting possession" (v. 8). God then institutes circumcision as a "sign of the covenant" between God and Abraham (v. 11). He also promises that Abraham's descendants will come from his union with Sarah, even though she is past child-bearing age (vv. 15–16). Abraham laughs at the idea of Sarah having a child (vv. 17–18), as does Sarah herself when the promise is later renewed (18:10–12). Yet God fulfills the promise, and Isaac is born to Abraham and Sarah in their old age (21:1–7).

The last significant stage in the history of Abraham and the promise comes when God tests Abraham by ordering him to offer Isaac as a sacrifice, an order that is rescinded at the last minute (Gen. 22). Throughout the rest of the Old Testament, God's people refer to the covenant made with Abraham, Isaac, and Jacob as the foundation for their existence and hope for the future (e.g., Ex. 32:13; Deut. 1:8).

Jews in Paul's day continued and elaborated this tradition. They revered Abraham as their "father" (see Isa. 51:1–2; *m. Qidd.* 4.14; cf. Rom. 4:1), the ancestor to whom they could trace their own unique status as God's covenant people. His life was a model of true piety. The following representative texts give a sense of how highly Jews regarded Abraham:

Abraham was perfect in all his deeds with the Lord, and well-pleasing in righteousness all the days of his life. (*Jubilees* 23:10)

Abraham . . . did not sin against you. (Prayer of Manasseh 8)

Was not Abraham found faithful when tested, and it was reckoned to him as righteousness? (1 Macc. 2:52)

Abraham was the great father of a multitude of nations,
and no one has been found like him in glory.
He kept the law of the Most High,
and entered into a covenant with him;
he certified the covenant in his flesh,
and when he was tested he proved faithful.
Therefore the Lord assured him with an oath
that the nations would be blessed through his offspring;
that he would make him as numerous as the dust of the earth,
and exalt his offspring like the stars,
and give them an inheritance from sea to sea
and from the Euphrates to the ends of the earth.
(Sirach 44:19–21)

Especially important for what Paul says about Abraham in Romans 4 is the tendency, revealed in these sources, to attach Abraham's righteousness to the "testing" episode of Genesis 22 and to draw a connection between God's covenant with Abraham and his obedience of the law. In contrast, Paul argues that *Abraham's faith* in response to the promise of God was the basis for his righteousness (Rom. 4:3) and that the law had nothing to do with his stature or the promise made to him (4:13–16).

Methods of citing the Old Testament. The significance of Genesis 15:6 for all of chapter 4 is obvious. Paul introduces this text as the basis for his exposition (Rom. 4:3), closes his argument with another formal reference to the verse (4:22), and refers to its language throughout (vv. 5, 6, 8, 9). Romans 4, then, is an exposition of Genesis 15:6 or, at least, a theological reflection on this passage of the Pentateuch. This kind of broad elaboration of an Old Testament passage (often given the term *midrash*) was common among the Jews in Paul's day. Many scholars use this term to describe Romans 4. But considerable debate surrounds the proper meaning and application of this term, so we should probably be cautious in using it here. Yet the way Paul plays various themes on a single text was familiar to his first readers.

Another specific element in Paul's use of the Old Testament in this chapter is also familiar: the corroboration of the point he makes about Genesis 15:6 by appealing to Psalm 32:1–2a. In our day, Jews typically divide the Old Testament into three basic parts: the "Law" (*torah*, the first five books of the Old Testament, the Pentateuch), the "Prophets" (*nebi'im*, including books like Samuel and Kings), and the "Writings" (*ketubim*, Psalms, Proverbs, etc.). Indeed, a common Jewish way of denoting the Old Testament is to use the first three letters from these Hebrew names: the "Tanak." In Paul's day, Jews often collapsed together the second and third parts of the Old Testament.

The point of all this is that a common method of argumentation from Scripture was to cite passages from both the "Law" and the "Prophets and Writings"—just as Paul does. Furthermore, Paul follows a common Jewish practice by using a common word as the link between these passages: In both Genesis 15:6 and Psalm 32:1–2a we find the crucial term "credited" or "reckoned" (*logizomai*). The Jews called this technique *gezerah shewa* ("equal decision").

Whatever we call it, therefore, Paul's way of arguing from the Old Testament was thoroughly familiar to his readers in Rome, who, whatever their ethnic background, were conversant with Jewish tradition. Yet these same Jewish techniques can pose a problem for modern readers, for many do not recognize them today as legitimate methods of interpretation. The problem is a big one, and we will return to it elsewhere. Suffice to say here that the techniques Paul uses in chapter 4 should prove no stumbling block to us. The significance the apostle finds in Genesis 15:6 is fair to that text, and his association of that text with Psalm 32:1–2a is based more on a genuinely common theme than on a common word.

JUSTIFYING THE WICKED. The "God who justifies the wicked" (v. 5) is a famous, troubling, and controversial description of God. It is famous because it expresses in a compact way the essence of the traditional Protestant view of justification: that when God justifies us, he does not change us morally but rather grants us a new "legal" status before him. Most Christian theologians before the Reformation had taught that justification included *both* acceptance with God *and* a transformation of our very being. They generally believed also that people had to "prepare" themselves to receive God's gift of justification, that God declared people righteous who really were righteous because of the prior working of God's grace in a person's life.

Luther, Calvin, and the other Reformers insisted that Paul taught otherwise. They systematically separated "justification" from "regeneration" and "sanctification" and argued that a person could do nothing to prepare himself or herself for God's justifying work. One can easily understand how Romans 4:5 was an important proof text for the Reformers' view. By boldly asserting that it is "the wicked" whom God justifies, Paul makes clear that justification is his creative, "synthetic," act by which he accounts a person righteous in his sight—a person who is really not, in himself or herself, righteous. Justification, as the Reformers put it in their famous slogans, is *sola gratia*, "by grace alone," and *sola fidei*, "by faith alone."

What can be troubling about the idea that God "justifies the wicked" is that it seems to make God guilty of an injustice. He does, in fact, what he told judges in the Old Testament never to do (Prov. 17:15; Isa. 5:23) and what he himself pledges not to do: "I will not acquit [or justify] the guilty" (Ex. 23:7). The Reformers' understanding has therefore been criticized as a violation of principles of justice, a "legal fiction" that makes no sense whatsoever.

The Reformers responded to such criticisms by advancing the idea of "imputed righteousness." The people whom God justifies are not righteous in themselves. But because they are "in Christ," his perfect righteousness is "credited" to them. God's justification is ultimately "just," then, because it is based on the righteousness that every believer has *in Christ*. Even theologians who accept the general Reformation position on justification debate whether this idea is correct or not. I am not sure myself about the idea, although it makes logical sense and has some exegetical basis (see, e.g., Rom. 8:1–4; 2 Cor. 5:20).

But it is important to bring out into the open one of the main reasons why a lot of theologians find the idea of "imputed righteousness" troubling: It is perceived as letting Christians "off the hook" in their own pursuit of holiness. If Christ's righteousness is credited to us and he fulfills the law in our place, then we might conclude it is unimportant whether we actually please God or not. Has not Christ already done it for us? Or, to relate the objection to the general Reformation teaching on justification: If God justifies us while we are "wicked," why should we bother trying to lead holy lives? God has already accepted us, right?

This objection is an old one, as Romans 6 reveals. We will have a chance there to explore Paul's response to it in some detail. But what must be said here is that Paul's teaching about God's "justifying the wicked" cannot be seen in isolation. Yes, it is clear that God puts us right before him when we are still sinners and that justification in itself does not change our moral status or basic nature. But Paul insists that God does more than "justify" us when we become Christians. He also "regenerates" us, "sanctifies" us, and causes his Spirit to indwell us. These acts of God change us "from within." Paul is one with James in insisting that a genuine Christian *must* always reveal the transforming work of God in a new life of obedience. But what the Reformers saw so clearly—and I think so accurately—was that becoming a Christian is first and foremost a change in our status before God. Sentenced to eternal death because of sin, God intervenes in a sheer act of grace and declares us innocent before him.

What difference to us does it make when we truly appreciate that we are justified "by grace alone," "by faith alone"? Perhaps the most important thing is an overwhelming sense of amazement at what God has done for us, an amazement that immediately spills over into worship. It is not by accident that some of our greatest hymns focus on just this sense of awe at the grace of God. We sing of "amazing grace," "amazing love"—and truly it is amazing that the almighty and all-holy God would give us, people who live sinfully in rebellion against him, a new status of righteousness, completely free of charge.

Once we truly understand this, worship follows as a matter of course. This is why it is so important that our worship singing focuses on God and not on ourselves. Well-crafted, theologically accurate lyrics set to effective music is one of the greatest stimulants to worship that God has given his people. May we use that gift well!

Romans 4:9-12

IS THIS BLESSEDNESS only for the circumcised, or also for the uncircumcised? We have been saying that Abraham's faith was credited to him as righteousness. ¹⁰Under what circumstances was it credited? Was it after he was circumcised, or before? It was not after, but before! ¹¹And he received the sign of circumcision, a seal of the righteousness that he had by faith while he was still uncircumcised. So then, he is the father of all who believe but have not been circumcised, in order that righteousness might be credited to them. ¹²And he is also the father of the circumcised who not only are circumcised but who also walk in the footsteps of the faith that our father Abraham had before he was circumcised.

IN THIS BRIEF PARAGRAPH, Paul moves from the vertical significance of Abraham's faith (its meaning for our relationship to God) to its horizontal significance (its meaning for the relationship of Jew and Gentile in the people of God). Paul introduced Abraham at the beginning of the chapter in a typically Jewish way: "our forefather," with the "our" referring to Paul and other Jewish Christians (4:1). Even there, however, Paul added a significant qualification (not translated in the NIV): "according to the flesh." He now makes clear why that qualification was needed. For from the standpoint of faith, Abraham is far more than the ancestor of the Jewish people; he is the father of all who believe as he himself did. God's people are determined not by biological descent from Abraham but by spiritual descent from him.

The "blessedness" Paul mentions in 4:9 refers to the blessing David pronounced on those "whose sin the Lord will never count against [them]" (4:7–8). That blessing is therefore acceptance before God. Is this acceptance, Paul asks, available only to "the circumcised," that is, Jews—as most Jews believed? Or is it also available to the "uncircumcised," that is, Gentiles? Before answering his question, Paul reminds us of the key text he is using to answer this question, namely, Genesis 15:6 (cf. Rom. 4:3), which he paraphrases in 4:9b.

In verse 10, Paul finds an answer to that question by noting the chronological relationship between God's pronouncement of Abraham's righteousness (Gen. 15:6) and the institution of circumcision (Gen. 17). The righteousness, Paul points out, came first—according to one rabbinic tradition, twenty-nine years before the circumcision.

But simple chronology is not a conclusive point. Paul goes on in 4:11 to explain the true significance of circumcision. Alluding to Genesis 17:11, Paul calls circumcision a "sign," a "seal of the righteousness that he [Abraham] had by faith." Circumcision, in Abraham's case, was not the basis or even the condition for his righteous status before God. The rite simply put a seal on what was already true.

In verses 11b–12 Paul draws out the significance of what he has said in verse 11a. (1) Abraham is the "father of all who believe but have not been circumcised." Gentiles who have faith can claim Abraham as their father. They believe as he did, and they receive, as he did, righteousness as a gift from God. They do not need to be circumcised to receive this gift. At this point, Paul's argument moves well beyond the Old Testament. For in making circumcision a requirement for all males descended from Abraham, the Old Testament certainly implies that one can belong to the people of God only by accepting circumcision. But, as we will see in 4:16–17, there is another strand of teaching about Abraham in Genesis, a strand that emphasizes his role as the "father of many nations." With insight gained through God's revelation in Christ, Paul can now identify these other nations with Gentiles who believe and who can belong to Abraham's spiritual family without being circumcised.

(2) Abraham is also "the father of the circumcised who not only are circumcised but who also walk in the footsteps of the faith that our father Abraham had before he was circumcised." As the NIV translates, Paul makes Abraham also the father of Jewish Christians—people who are circumcised *and who also* believe as Abraham did.

The Greek is capable of another interpretation. On this view, "the circumcised" is an initial broad category that Paul then breaks down into two components: those who are circumcised and those who believe as Abraham did. Paul would then be referring both to Jews generally and to Jewish-Christians particularly. Scholars who advocate this interpretation note that Paul will later affirm that God's promise to the patriarchs continues to have relevance for the Jewish people as well as for the church (Rom. 9:5; 11:28).[1] But Paul is not yet to this point in his argument. The structure of the sentence, taken overall, points to one group only in 4:12: those who are both circumcised and believe as Abraham did (i.e., Jewish Christians).

---

1. Käsemann, *Commentary on Romans*, 116–17; Fitzmyer, *Romans*, 381–82.

Bridging Contexts

CIRCUMCISION AND JUDAISM. In the Bridging Contexts section on 2:17–29, we sketched briefly the significance that circumcision came to have for Jews during the intertestamental period. The Jews, following strictly God's command in Genesis 17, insisted on circumcision as an essential mark (for males, of course) of belonging to the Jewish people. Even Philo, who gave allegorical interpretations of most Jewish rituals, including circumcision, still insisted that the physical act was required. It is for this reason that Paul can use the word "circumcision" to refer to Jews and "uncircumcision" to Gentiles (Rom. 3:30; 4:9, 11–12).

But how about a Gentile who wanted to become a Jew? A few scholars think that some Jews in Paul's day were relaxing the requirement that Gentiles undergo circumcision in order to convert to Judaism. They base this conclusion on an intriguing passage in the Jewish historian Josephus about the conversion of a pagan king named Izates (*Ant.* 20.17–48). But there is no doubt that the prevalent view was that only circumcised Gentiles could be considered genuine converts.[2]

As a result of this requirement, few Gentile men, however attracted to Judaism they may have been, became converts. Circumcision was a physical, even painful, barrier to Gentiles who wanted to identify with God's people. They were excluded and undoubtedly felt that exclusion. No matter how much they identified with Jewish teaching and morals, they were still outside. Paul speaks directly of this kind of alienation in Ephesians 2:11–12:

> Therefore, remember that formerly you who are Gentiles by birth and called "uncircumcised" by those who call themselves "the circumcision" (that done in the body by the hands of men)—remember that at that time you were separate from Christ, excluded from citizenship in Israel and foreigners to the covenants of the promise, without hope and without God in the world.

When we read Romans 4:9–12 today, we might not appreciate what it meant for Gentiles to be offered the opportunity to become full members in God's people, with equal rights with those who were Jewish by birth. By faith they, along with Jews, can call Abraham their "father" and enjoy the privileges and blessings promised to his descendants.

---

2. See the discussion in George Foot Moore, *Judaism in the First Centuries of the Christian Era* (rpt.; 2 vols.; New York: Schocken, 1971), 1:323–35.

CIRCUMCISION AND BAPTISM? Finding relevance in a text like this one is a challenge for the modern Christian reader or preacher. The focus is on what happened long ago, and the topic—the religious value of circumcision—is one that seems to have no significance for the church today. Faced with this problem, the usual approach is to find analogies in the text to contemporary situations or practices.

A few commentators have taken just such an approach with circumcision. Their starting point is the contention that several texts in Paul suggest that he viewed baptism and circumcision as similar rites. Circumcision, after all, was a sign that a person belonged to God's old covenant people, while baptism seems to be the equivalent new covenant sign. Note, for instance, the connection between baptism and circumcision implied by Colossians 2:11–13:

> In him you were also *circumcised*, in the putting off of the sinful nature, not with a *circumcision* done by the hands of men but with the *circumcision* done by Christ, having been buried with him in *baptism* and raised with him through your faith in the power of God, who raised him from the dead. When you were dead in your sins and in the uncircumcision of your sinful nature, God made you alive with Christ. He forgave us all our sins. (italics added)

Further reason to think our text may have an allusion to baptism is found in the word "seal." Second-century Christians applied this word to baptism (see *Hermas, Similitudes* 8.6.3; *1 Clement* 7:6; 8:6), and Paul may himself be alluding to baptism in several other places where he uses the word (2 Cor. 1:22; Eph. 1:13; 4:30). Perhaps, then, we can get some relevance out of Romans 4:9–12 by applying some of what Paul says here to baptism.[3]

But our desire to be relevant should never outrun the evidence from the text. I warn my exegesis students about what I call "homiletical expediency": the tendency to determine the meaning of a text based on how it will preach. But we cannot (or at least we should not!) preach what is not there. It is unlikely that there is anything about baptism in Romans 4:9–12.[4] Colossians 2 is not a good basis to argue that Paul thinks baptism corresponds to circumcision. In that text, Paul uses circumcision as a metaphor for conversion and then associates baptism with that conversion. The connection between seal and baptism in Paul is so tenuous that we can base nothing on that argument either.

---

3. See, e.g., Käsemann, *Commentary on Romans*, 117.
4. See, e.g., Dunn, *Romans*, 209–10.

What relevance, then, does this passage have? Paul's main concern is clearly to show how faith enables both Jew and Gentile to become descendants of Abraham, to belong on the same footing, in other words, to the people of God. Taken with many other passages in Romans on the same theme (e.g., 3:29–30; 4:16–17; 10:9–13), these verses embody the principle of a single people of God that embraces all kinds of individuals. If Gentiles can be granted admission to God's people, the way is open for anyone to have that same access. No longer is God the God of Jews in an ethnically restricted way. Paul himself draws out the implications of the inclusion of Gentiles in a text similar to Romans 4, concluding with the words:

> You are all sons of God through faith in Christ Jesus, for all of you who were baptized into Christ have clothed yourselves with Christ. There is neither Jew nor Greek, slave nor free, male nor female, for you are all one in Christ Jesus. If you belong to Christ, then you are Abraham's seed, and heirs according to the promise. (Gal. 3:26–29)

What we find, therefore, is that the inclusion of Gentiles into God's people becomes the leading edge of a broader principle: the removal of all outward distinctions in the face of God's grace and the universal offer of the gospel. The implications for the church are far-reaching. The church is called to be a genuinely "countercultural" institution, in which the usual barriers to association—race, national background, economic status, etc.—have no relevance at all.

Yet while the church broadly defined may look like this, individual churches rarely do. For what appear to be good reasons, our churches tend to be monochromatic: suburban, middle- and upper-class white, inner city black, Hispanic, Korean, etc. One understands the natural tendency to feel comfortable worshiping with people who are like us. But one of the purposes of the church is to force us out of our comfort zones so that we can benefit from association with people who are like us in their faith in Christ but different from us in every other way. By breaking down the barrier separating Jew and Gentile, Christ shows that he wants to build a real "rainbow coalition" among his people. Unfortunately, we can stifle that intention by insisting on building local churches that target only one kind of person.

Romans 4:13–22

❦

IT WAS NOT through law that Abraham and his offspring received the promise that he would be heir of the world, but through the righteousness that comes by faith. ¹⁴For if those who live by law are heirs, faith has no value and the promise is worthless, ¹⁵because law brings wrath. And where there is no law there is no transgression.

¹⁶Therefore, the promise comes by faith, so that it may be by grace and may be guaranteed to all Abraham's offspring— not only to those who are of the law but also to those who are of the faith of Abraham. He is the father of us all. ¹⁷As it is written: "I have made you a father of many nations." He is our father in the sight of God, in whom he believed—the God who gives life to the dead and calls things that are not as though they were.

¹⁸Against all hope, Abraham in hope believed and so became the father of many nations, just as it had been said to him, "So shall your offspring be." ¹⁹Without weakening in his faith, he faced the fact that his body was as good as dead— since he was about a hundred years old—and that Sarah's womb was also dead. ²⁰Yet he did not waver through unbelief regarding the promise of God, but was strengthened in his faith and gave glory to God, ²¹being fully persuaded that God had power to do what he had promised. ²²This is why "it was credited to him as righteousness."

THIS SECTION IS often broken into two parts. There is some basis for this division, since Paul's focus moves from a contrast between law and faith in verses 13–16 or 17 to a positive description of faith in verses 17 or 18–22. But the theme of "promise" binds this entire section together in a unity.[1] Used for the first time in Romans here, the noun "promise" (*epangelia*) occurs four times (vv. 13, 14, 16, 20) and the verb "promise" (*epangello*) once (v. 21).[2]

---

1. See esp. Halvor Moxnes, *Theology in Conflict: Studies in Paul's Understanding of God in Romans* (Leiden: Brill, 1980), 113.

2. The verb "promise beforehand" (one word in Greek) occurs in 1:2.

As we noted in our survey of Abraham's significance in the Bridging Contexts section on 4:1–8, the concept of promise is central to the story of Abraham. Paul makes three points about that "promise" to Abraham here. (1) The promise is based on faith, not the law (vv. 13–15). (2) The promise, because it is based on faith, unites Jews and Gentiles together into one people of God (vv. 16–17). (3) The faith with which Abraham responded to God's promise was firm and unwavering (vv. 18–22). Then, lest we forget the starting point of this whole discussion, in verse 22 Paul brings it back to Genesis 15:6.

Faith, Not Law, Secures the Promise (4:13–15)

THE STORY OF God's promise to Abraham, first issued when God called him to leave his home in Haran (Gen. 12:1–3) and renewed and elaborated on several occasions, was certainly familiar to the Roman Christians. What is interesting here, however, is how Paul defines that promise: that Abraham should be the "heir of the world." Genesis repeatedly mentions the fact that Abraham will be a blessing to all the world, but the focus tends to be on his biological descendants and the land God promised them. Jewish interpreters highlighted this ethnic element in the promise. Thus Paul's focus on "the world" may have a polemical intent, carrying on his insistence that Abraham is the father of all who believe (Rom. 4:11–12).

The introduction of "law" (v. 13) also has a polemical purpose. As we have noted, many of Paul's Jewish contemporaries taught that Abraham's stature and role had much to do with his obedience to the law of Moses. Paul wants to make clear that this is not the case. In Galatians 3, where he engages in a similar argument, he focuses on chronology: the promise to Abraham could have nothing to do with the law of Moses, because that law was given 430 years after Abraham (Gal. 3:17). Here Paul says nothing about timing; rather, he speaks more principially: The promise did not come because people obeyed the law, but "through the righteousness that comes by faith."

Verses 14–15 explain why Abraham and those who came after him could never have inherited God's promised blessings through the law. The phrase "those who live by law" describes people who might try to base their hope of blessing on doing what the Mosaic law demanded. Were such people to inherit the blessing, Paul points out, "faith has no value and the promise is worthless." Paul may mean that bringing law into this matter eviscerates the very meaning of "faith" and "promise." How can the blessing truly be, from God's side, a matter of his sheer promise and, from the human side, a matter of faith if people can earn it through their obedience to the law (cf. the distinction between faith and works in 4:4–5)?[3] However, Paul is more likely making a simpler

---

3. See, e.g., Barrett, *The Epistle to the Romans*, 94–95.

point: If the fulfillment of the promise depends on obedience to the law, it will never happen, for people can never obey the law adequately.[4]

In the first part of verse 15, Paul substantiates the point he made in verse 14 by showing what the law *does* as opposed to what it cannot do: The law "brings wrath." This assertion is part of an important motif developed in the earlier chapters of Romans (see esp. 3:20; 5:20; 7:5). It is a startling assertion when we remember that Jews typically viewed the Mosaic law as one of the greatest blessings they possessed. How can Paul claim that the law has produced wrath? The end of verse 15 implicitly provides the answer: "Where there is no law there is no transgression."

A few commentators think Paul is formulating a general statement about law here: Only where God has revealed his will to people can he accuse them of committing sins.[5] But this interpretation does not do justice to the meaning of a key word that Paul uses here: "transgression" (*parabasis*). Paul only uses this word to depict the disobedience to a law or a commandment that a person has directly been made responsible for (see also 2:23; 5:14; Gal. 3:19; 1 Tim. 2:14). Transgression, therefore, is a sin. But not all sin is transgression. Anytime we fall short of conformity to God's image, we sin; but only when we directly violate a commandment God has given us do we commit a transgression. For this reason, then, transgression is also a more serious form of sin, meriting greater judgment.

If my teenage children stay out later than they generally are supposed to, they will be punished. But if they stay out past the time that I have clearly established with them before they leave home, the punishment will probably be more severe. So it is that God's law, paradoxically, can "bring wrath." By setting down in detail his expectations of Israel, God has heightened the degree of accountability. Then when Israel sinned, the punishment was greater than it would have been otherwise.

Because Faith Secures the Promise, Both Jew and Gentile Can Benefit from It (4:16–17)

PAUL HAS INTRODUCED a ruling antithesis in verse 13: The promise comes "not through law" but "through the righteousness that comes by faith." Verses 14–15 explain "not through law"; verses 16–17 now elaborate the significance of "through the righteousness that comes by faith." But, reflecting a key emphasis throughout this section (see also 3:29–30; 4:11–12), Paul focuses on one consequence in particular, that the promised blessing can be guaranteed to *all* Abraham's "offspring."

---

4. See, e.g., Godet, *Commentary on Romans*, 176–77; Cranfield, *The Epistle to the Romans*, 240.
5. E.g., Murray, *The Epistle to the Romans*, 1:143.

"Offspring" translates the Greek *sperma* (lit., seed), a word important in both the Genesis promise passages (Gen. 12:7; 13:15—16; 15:5, 18; 16:10; 17:7—12, 19; 21:12) and in Paul (Rom. 9:7, 8; Gal. 3:16, 19, 29). It is a collective word, usually referring to one's physical descendants. But Paul has given that notion a spiritual significance in Romans 4:11—12, where Abraham has been cited as the father of believers. At the end of 4:16, Paul specifies the two groups that make up this spiritual seed of Abraham: "those who are of the law" and "those who are of the faith of Abraham."

By putting it this way, Paul might be indicating that he is thinking of both Jews generally (i.e., "those of the law") and of Gentile believers.[6] It is true that in Romans 9—11, Paul considers Israel as a whole still a beneficiary of God's promise. But in the present context, his concern is to show that the promise to Abraham is valid for all believers. Almost certainly, then, he is referring to Jewish Christians and Gentile Christians. At the end of 4:16, Paul affirms that Abraham "is the father of us all," and he follows this claim up with scriptural attestation in verse 17a: "I have made you a father of many nations." This quotation comes from Genesis 17:5, which brings to expression a key part of the promise. It is not clear in the Genesis text whether the reference is physical or spiritual, but Paul interprets it spiritually.

The end of verse 17 consists of a rather awkward addition that characterizes the God in whom Abraham believed as "the God who gives life to the dead." In light of 4:18—20, this phrase almost certainly alludes to the miracle by which God brought life out of the "dead" womb (v. 19) of Sarah. But what Paul means by describing God as the one who "calls things that are not as though they were" is not so clear. Since the verb "call" (*kaleo*) can be used to depict God's creative activity (Isa. 41:4; 48:13), Paul may be referring to God's ability to create something out of nothing—as he has done in creating faith among the Gentiles.[7] But the verb more likely means here simply "to name, address." Paul is describing from another angle the miracle that God wrought in bringing children to Abraham and Sarah. Even before they had children, God spoke of the "many nations" that would come from them as if they already existed.

The Character of Abraham's Faith (4:18—22)

PAUL MOVES FROM a description of the God in whom Abraham believed to a description of that belief itself. What Paul says about Abraham's faith rests on a widespread tradition, which surfaces also in Hebrews 11:11—12. The emphasis is on Abraham's (and Sarah's) conviction that God would do what

---

6. E.g., Fitzmyer, *Romans*, 385.
7. See, e.g., Cranfield, *The Epistle to the Romans*, 244—45.

he had promised, even when all the "physical" evidence pointed in the other direction.

The opening antithesis in 4:18 neatly captures this tension: Abraham believed "against all hope . . . in hope." From a human standpoint, there was no hope that he and Sarah would ever have children. He was a hundred years old and Sarah's womb was "dead" (4:19). Abraham did not ignore this evidence. Rather, he faced these facts and took them fully into account. But they did not cause Abraham's faith to weaken. Why not? Because his faith was also "in hope"—the hope that springs from God's word of promise (4:18b). Therefore, Paul concludes, Abraham did not "waver through unbelief regarding the promise of God" (v. 20a).

The alert reader of Genesis may ask whether this is really true. For Genesis 17:17 tells us that Abraham "laughed" at one point when he was told of God's promise about having a son. Jewish interpreters—and some Christians—have tried to get around this apparent failure by insisting that Abraham's laughter was one of joy. But this is not the case. What Paul is claiming is that Abraham, overall, maintained a firm conviction in God's promise and acted on it. He had his momentary doubts, it is true, but they were momentary and always overcome by his faith in the God who had promised. By doing so, Abraham glorified God, because he took him at his word (4:20b–21). This is why, Paul concludes, "it [faith] was credited to him as righteousness." Here, at the end of Paul's exposition of Abraham's faith and its consequences, he cites again the key verse with which he began (Gen. 15:6; cf. Rom. 4:3).

JEWISH TRADITIONS BEHIND 4:13–22. In my Bridging Contexts sections, I usually describe texts, traditions, or customs that existed in the first century and that provide the context in which we must read Paul's teaching. I hope I have not given the impression that we cannot understand the basic message of the Bible unless we know these contexts. Not at all. The Reformers wanted to put the Bible into the hands of every believer because they were firmly convinced of its "perspicuity"—through the ministry of the Spirit, every believer can understand the essential message of Scripture. What Paul says about faith, promise, and Abraham in 4:13–22 should be obvious to the person who knows nothing at all about Jewish tradition or first-century Christianity.

Nevertheless, I maintain that acquaintance with the world of the first century can heighten our appreciation of what Scripture means and introduce nuances into it that we may otherwise miss. Such, I think, is the case with

4:13—22. By knowing about some of the traditions behind this passage, we will be able to hear the text more like the first readers would have.

As Paul exposits the meaning of God's promise to Abraham, he interacts in virtually every verse with another viewpoint with which his readers were familiar. Paul's insistence on faith rather than the law as the basis for inheriting what God had promised (4:13—17) shows he is anxious to contradict the tendency of Jewish interpreters to focus on Abraham's obedience to the law as the foundation for the promise (see Bridging Contexts section on 4:1—8). Paul's original readers were probably accustomed to thinking of Abraham in terms of faith, obedience, and law—all jumbled together. Paul's reading of the Genesis narrative in light of Christ, however, has convinced him that distinctions among these aspects of Abraham's relationship to God are fundamental to an appreciation of the gospel. Thus, he goes to some lengths to make these distinctions clear.

One verse that takes on added significance in light of the background is Romans 4:17. Here Paul quotes Genesis 17:5: "I have made you a father of many nations." In context, "nations" clearly is interchangeable with "offspring" (or "seed") in Romans 4:16. We would probably pass over this point without noting anything interesting about it. But when read against the Old Testament and Jewish background, we suddenly realize Paul is making a significant theological point. For Jewish interpreters of the Old Testament tended to restrict Abraham's "seed" to Israel and "the nations" to physical descendants of Abraham.[8]

To be sure, the covenant with Abraham always included ultimate blessing, in some form, for the nations (e.g., Gen. 12:3; 18:18; 22:18; 26:4). But a distinction between Abraham's seed or descendants, who become participants in the covenant, and the nations, who receive benefits through Abraham in some unspecified way, seems strictly to be maintained.[9] Paul now breaks down that distinction: Gentiles are included along with Jews in Abraham's "offspring." They are now equal recipients with the Jews of God's covenant blessings.

Another verse in which we find a particularly rich allusion to specific Jewish traditions is 4:17, where Paul characterizes the God in whom Abraham believed as "the God who gives life to the dead and calls things that are not as though they were."[10] Particularly relevant to this verse is 1 Samuel 2:5—6:

---

8. Some commentators, however, do include spiritual as well as physical descendants of Abraham in the "nations" of ch. 17 (see, e.g., G. C. Aalders, *Genesis* [2 vols; Grand Rapids: Zondervan, 1981], 1:305).

9. See, e.g., Terrence L. Donaldson, *Paul and the Gentiles: Remapping the Apostle's Convictional World* (Minneapolis: Fortress, 1997), 98.

10. God's life-giving power is featured in a liturgy that all first-century Jews were familiar with: the *Shemoneh Esreh*, or "The Eighteen Benedictions."

Those who were full hire themselves out for food,
> but those who were hungry hunger no more.
She who was barren has borne seven children,
> but she who has had many sons pines away.
The LORD brings death and *makes alive;*
> he brings down to the grave and raises up. (italics added)

Here the Lord's life-giving power is linked to the removal of a woman's barrenness. Those knowledgeable about the Old Testament knew that the speaker of these words is Hannah, who herself was barren but was given a son (Samuel) destined to play a significant role in salvation history. So this description of God sets off a series of associations in the minds of Paul's readers that places God's "giving life" to Abraham and Sarah in a wider context.

We commented above on the possible meaning of the description of God as one "who calls things that are not as though they were." We eventually decided that the phrase probably refers in this context to God's "address" of descendants of Abraham who were not yet born. But Paul's readers would still detect in the phrase overtones of the common use of this phrase to refer to God's creative power—specifically, his ability to create something "out of nothing" (creation *ex nihilo*). The Jewish philosopher Philo was especially fond of this idea and speaks of God in these terms throughout his writings. *Special Laws* 4.187 is particularly close to Paul's wording: "For this is to follow God since He too can do both but wills the good only. This was shown both in the creation and in the ordering of the world. He called the non-existent into existence and produced order from disorder...."

This same kind of language was also applied to the conversion of Gentiles. A book written at about the time of Paul, *Joseph and Aseneth*, describes how Joseph converted Aseneth, his Egyptian wife, to Judaism. Note the language of 8:9, where Joseph prays for Aseneth: "Lord God of my father Israel, the Most High, the Powerful One of Jacob, who gave life to all things and called them from the darkness to the light ... make her alive again by your life...." While we do not think Paul is using the language just this way, he may well have been alluding to this idea. God is one who can create something out of nothing. He can create faith in the heart of a Gentile. The relevance of this idea to Paul's discussion of Gentiles who are joined to the people of God by faith is obvious.

FAITH. FEW WORDS are more important to Christians than the term *faith*. This is as it should be. For, as Paul explains the gospel in Romans, faith is at the heart of the matter. But faith can be something we talk about without really understanding. Some Christians seem to equate "faith" with agreeing to a set of doctrinal statements. Others think that allowing themselves to be baptized and participating regularly in communion is faith. Still others view faith as an emotion that they can stir up as a way of getting what they want from God. We cannot give here a full biblical view of faith or deal with all the current perversions of the word. But Paul says three things about faith in 4:13—22 that go a long way toward filling out for us its meaning.

(1) Faith is distinct from the law (4:13—14). Paul here reiterates a point he has already made several times in the letter (see 3:20, 27—28; 4:4—5). The law is something that must be "done," commandments that are to be obeyed. Faith, by contrast, is an attitude, a willingness to receive. Calvin likens faith to "open hands." Believing means that we stretch out our arms and open our hands to receive the gift God wants to give us. We can take no credit for accepting a gift, nor can we take any credit for our faith. For faith is not exactly something that we "do." Some extreme Lutheran theologians were so anxious to distinguish faith from what we do that they spoke of God believing *through* us. But God calls on *us* to believe. *We* believe, even if God creates the situation in which our faith is possible. But our faith is a response to God, not a "work" that puts him in our debt.

In our achievement-oriented world, giving faith its necessary central place in our lives is not always easy to do. We are tempted to ground our relationship to God in what we do and to begin to think that our "doing" is so impressive that God will be forced to bless us for it. Such an attitude toward God breeds serious problems. One of my former students is a counselor in a church located in a part of North America where hard work and human achievement are greatly admired. He is constantly counseling believers who are in despair about their ability to "live up to God's expectations of them." His message to them can be summed up in one word: faith. God accepts us not because of what we do but because we have humbled ourselves before him and have received from him the gift of salvation. Doing God's will is a necessary result of faith, but it must never be put in its place as the mainstay of our relationship to God.

(2) Faith has power not in itself but because of the one in whom we place our faith. One of the most famous lines in all sports history is Al Michaels's rhetorical question toward the end of the 1980 Olympic hockey match between the United States and the USSR: "Do you believe in miracles?" Believing in miracles has become a common way of speaking. Its popularity owes much to the current fad in religion: a belief in some kind of supernatural power that has a positive influence in people's lives. Preoccupation with angels, as witnessed by at least one popular television program, is another indicator of this fad. But the Bible does not talk about belief in miracles; it talks about belief in the God who works miracles.

This is just the way Paul speaks about God in the midst of describing Abraham's faith in 4:17–21. Abraham recognized in God the One who can give life to things that are dead and can speak about things that do not exist as if they did. These points had specific application to Abraham's own situation. He needed to believe that God could bring life, a son, out of the deadness of Sarah's womb and his own impotence. He had to believe that the things God promised him were so sure that God could address them as if they already existed. God's character and person guides our faith and channels its expectations.

(3) Faith is based on God's Word, not on the evidence of our senses. Abraham fully confronted the physical impossibility that he and Sarah would ever have children, but this did not keep him from believing God would do exactly as he promised. Even when a son had been born to him and he had been ordered to kill the child, Abraham did not doubt God would fulfill his promise to create for him a great people through that child. For, Hebrews tells us, Abraham believed that "God could raise the dead" (Heb. 11:19).

The key to a full-bodied Christian experience is the ability to keep believing, day in and day out, that the ultimate reality is not what we see around us but what we cannot see—the spiritual realm. Paul calls this spiritual realm "the heavenly realms," a key idea in his letter to the Ephesians, for just this reason. Like Abraham, therefore, we need to believe "against all hope": trusting in God and his promises even when the evidence goes against it.

But Paul also says that Abraham believed "in hope." By this he means that Abraham's faith was based on the hope that God had given him through a specific promise. In order to highlight the fact that faith often goes against the evidence of our senses, some theologians have called faith "a leap in the dark." But this is not accurate. Abraham did not arbitrarily and without any basis put his faith in the God of Israel or think that he would have a son with Sarah. God had spoken to him, and his word was the basis of Abraham's faith.

Similarly, we must also realize that our faith is based on the solid reality of God's written Word to us in the Scripture and of his living Word, Jesus Christ, active to capture our hearts for himself. We must carefully read Scripture and seek to understand the working of God's Spirit in the world so that our faith is not misdirected. I think here of the many Christians who are convinced that God has promised them health, or wealth, or a particular job, or a particular man or woman to marry, and so on. Their faith, while often noble, probably has no basis in God's Word. As our faith must be directed to the God in whom we believe, so also it must be directed by what he revealed to us.

Romans 4:23–25

THE WORDS "IT was credited to him" were written not for him alone, ²⁴but also for us, to whom God will credit righteousness—for us who believe in him who raised Jesus our Lord from the dead. ²⁵He was delivered over to death for our sins and was raised to life for our justification.

VERSES 23–24 FOLLOW directly from verse 22, where Paul quoted the last words of Genesis 15:6: "It was credited to him as righteousness." As Paul draws his exposition of this Old Testament text, with what it says about Abraham's faith, to an end, he makes explicit what has been implicit throughout, that it has direct application to Christians. As God "credited" Abraham's faith "for righteousness," so he does the same for us. And as Abraham believed in the "God who gives life to the dead" (v. 17), so do we. In Abraham's case, God revealed this power in creating life in the dead womb of Sarah. For us, this power of God is manifested in his raising from the dead Jesus our Lord. Paul often describes God as the One who raised Jesus from the dead (Rom. 8:11; 10:9; 1 Cor. 6:14; 15:15; 2 Cor. 4:14), but he rarely makes God the object of our belief. He does so here to make Christian faith as similar to Abraham's faith as possible.

In verse 25, Paul adds a description of this Jesus whom God raised from the dead. The description falls into two parallel lines:

| who | was delivered over to death | for our sins |
| and | was raised to life | for our justification |

This parallelism, along with some language that is unusual in Paul, suggests the apostle may be quoting a brief confessional formula circulating in the early church. He probably adds it here because it continues the emphasis on Jesus' resurrection. The first line reflects the language about the Suffering Servant in the Greek translation (LXX) of Isaiah 53, particularly verse 12: "Because of their sins he was delivered over." This language from Isaiah 53 was applied by Jesus himself to his death (e.g., Mark 9:31; 10:33). "Delivered over" is probably a "divine passive," that is, the implied subject is God (see Rom. 8:32: God "gave him up for us all").

In the first line of this confession, the preposition "for" (Gk. *dia* followed by accusative) probably means "because of." In the second line, however, it is difficult to give the same word this meaning. For Christ's resurrection was not based on, or caused by, our justification. Probably, then, the word "for" in the second line has the sense "in order to accomplish." The parallelism between the two lines is rhetorical and does not extend to the meaning of the word.

ONLY ONE BRIEF matter calls for comment: the significance of the confessional statement in verse 25. We have detected such traditional statements elsewhere in Romans (see comments on 1:3–4). It makes sense for Paul to include such common early Christian formulations in his letter as a way of creating rapport with a church he has never visited. By using language familiar to his readers, he both assures them that he can be trusted and creates a more personal response to his teaching. At the same time, identifying the verse as part of a tradition makes it easier to think that the same pronoun might have a different meaning in the two lines.

This brief Christological statement was probably part of a hymn, written to be remembered and perhaps even sung in worship. This kind of poetic genre usually features parallel constructions and words in order to achieve a rhetorical effect. Often, the parallels will not have the same function or meaning.

THE STRONG CURRENT of pluralism in our culture has forced Christians to reexamine all kinds of issues in order to defend more ably the uniqueness of the Christian faith as the only way to God. One perennial issue, of course, is the fate of those who have never heard the gospel of Christ. One argument often used to support the idea that one can be saved without explicit faith in Christ is that the Old Testament saints were saved in just this way. Abraham, for instance, was "justified" through his faith in God—not through faith in Christ, who had not yet come. Why, then, cannot people in our day who, like Abraham, have not heard about Christ, likewise be saved by faith in God?

Some deny this line of reasoning by insisting that Abraham did in fact believe in Christ. But we have no good textual evidence to support this idea. What we can say is that Abraham believed in the God *who had made certain promises.* His faith, as Paul makes clear, was oriented not just vaguely to "God," but to the specific promises God had made to him. In other words, Abraham believed in God and in what God had revealed about himself and about his plan. Those who argue that people in our day believe in God the same way Abraham did miss the vital point that "God" must be given content. He is a person, not a mere verbalization or abstract concept. Thus, one should first insist that a person in our day who wants to be saved by believing in God as Abraham did must also believe in the same God in whom Abraham believed.

But we can go further. God reveals more and more of himself as his plan of salvation unfolds. Each of those further revelations becomes part of the "content" of God. One cannot claim to believe in the God of the Bible without including that content. In our day, God has definitively revealed himself in Jesus Christ. Were Abraham alive today, he could not be saved apart from faith in God-as-revealed-in-Christ. Thus, we must also conclude that only people who believe in this particular God-as-revealed-in-Christ have hope for salvation.

Romans 5:1–11

THEREFORE, SINCE WE have been justified through faith, we have peace with God through our Lord Jesus Christ, ²through whom we have gained access by faith into this grace in which we now stand. And we rejoice in the hope of the glory of God. ³Not only so, but we also rejoice in our sufferings, because we know that suffering produces perseverance; ⁴perseverance, character; and character, hope. ⁵And hope does not disappoint us, because God has poured out his love into our hearts by the Holy Spirit, whom he has given us.

⁶You see, at just the right time, when we were still powerless, Christ died for the ungodly. ⁷Very rarely will anyone die for a righteous man, though for a good man someone might possibly dare to die. ⁸But God demonstrates his own love for us in this: While we were still sinners, Christ died for us.

⁹Since we have now been justified by his blood, how much more shall we be saved from God's wrath through him! ¹⁰For if, when we were God's enemies, we were reconciled to him through the death of his Son, how much more, having been reconciled, shall we be saved through his life! ¹¹Not only is this so, but we also rejoice in God through our Lord Jesus Christ, through whom we have now received reconciliation.

PAUL'S EXPOSITION OF the gospel of Jesus Christ takes a decisive turn at 5:1. Up to this point, his focus has been on the power of the gospel to put people who are locked up in sin and under sentence of God's wrath into a right relationship with God. Through the preaching of the good news, God invites all people—Jew and Gentile alike—to believe in Christ and enter into this new relationship. Now Paul turns his attention to what comes after one's justification by faith. Chapters 5–8 focus on two matters in particular: the certainty we can have that our justification will lead to final salvation, and the new power God gives us in our continuing struggle against sin and the law.

The first theme—what theologians call "assurance"—dominates the first (5:1–11) and last (8:18–39) paragraphs in these chapters. These two sections frame the argument of Romans 5–8, forming what we call an *inclusio*. The famous argument about Adam and Christ (5:12–21) grounds the claim for assurance in 5:1–11. Then, in chapters 6–7, Paul deals with two continuing threats to our assurance: sin and the law. In 8:1–17 he shows how the work of God's Spirit overcomes these threats. As we hope to show in the sections that follow, this way of reading the argument of Romans makes better sense than the traditional division of the first part of the letter into sections about "justification" (chs. 1–5) and "sanctification" (chs. 5–8).[1]

The theme of 5:1–11 is not easy to label because Paul mentions so many different topics: "peace with God"/"reconciliation" (vv. 1, 10, 11), "access to grace" (v. 2), hope in the glory of God and for final salvation (vv. 2, 5, 9, 10), joy in suffering (vv. 3–4), and God's love for us (vv. 5–8). We can understand why Murray, for instance, uses the broad caption "The Blessings of Justification."[2] But one particular topic emerges as the unifying focal point of the paragraph: *hope for final salvation*. The key verses are:

v. 2b: "we rejoice in the hope of the glory of God"

v. 5a: "And hope does not disappoint us"

v. 9: "Since we have now been justified by his blood, how much more shall we be saved from God's wrath through him!"

v. 10: "For if, when we were God's enemies, we were reconciled to him through the death of his Son, how much more, having been reconciled, shall we be saved through his life!"

The parallel "how much more" arguments of verses 9–10 reiterate the hope that Paul has introduced earlier in this passage. All the other elements revolve around this theme of hope. The peace and grace of verses 1–2a create the transition from the argument of chapters 1–4 to the proclamation of hope in 5:2b. Suffering (5:3–4), rather than a threat to hope, can actually be a spur to hope. And our hope is certain not only because it is based in God's work for us (5:9–10) but also because it is rooted in God's love for us (5:5–8).

Being Justified Means We Have Peace and Hope (5:1–4)

WITH THE WORDS "Therefore, since we have been justified through faith," Paul signals an important transition in his argument. He has established the truth of justification by faith in chapters 1–4. Now he will elaborate the results of the new status God has given us in Christ.

---

1. For the traditional view, see, e.g., Godet, *Commentary on Romans*, 231; Murray, *The Epistle to the Romans*, 1:211–12. Several modern commentators, while not necessarily subscribing to the "justification" and "sanctification" labels, also argue for a major break between chs. 5 and 6 (e.g., Dunn, *Romans*, 242–44). For putting the major break between chs. 4 and 5, see esp. Nygren, *Commentary on Romans*, 187–89; Cranfield, *The Epistle to the Romans*, 252–54.

2. Murray, *The Epistle to the Romans*, 1:158.

(1) One of those results is "peace with God." "Peace" is a rich biblical word. Our English word "peace," in keeping with the secular Greek use of *eirene*, often has a negative sense: the absence of hostility. But the Old Testament and Jewish conception of peace, *shalom*, was much more positive, connoting a general sense of harmonious well-being. Note Isaiah 32:17–18:

> The fruit of righteousness will be peace;
> > the effect of righteousness will be quietness and confidence forever.
> My people will live in peaceful dwelling places,
> > in secure homes,
> > in undisturbed places of rest.

This peace is the objective state of harmony with God that believers who have been justified enjoy. As the marginal reading in the NIV here suggests, it is hard to be certain about precisely what Paul is saying concerning this peace. The problem is a textual variant in the Greek text. Most manuscripts have the word *echomen*, an indicative verb meaning "we have peace." The NIV, along with most other translations, assumes this reading. But some very good manuscripts have the subjunctive form of this same verb, *echōmen*, which means "Let us have peace" or "Let us enjoy peace." A good argument can be made for this latter reading as the *lectio difficilior* (the more difficult reading),[3] but we think context finally decides the issue in favor of the usual rendering.[4] As 5:2 suggests, Paul is in an "indicative" mode, detailing for us the benefits that our new justified status brings.

(2) Another wonderful result of our justification is "access by faith into this grace in which we now stand" (v. 2). The Greek word behind "access" (*prosagoge*) suggests the same idea as the English word, as when, for instance, we say a person has "access" to the President. But Paul surprises us by claiming not, as we would expect, that we now have constant access to God, but that we have access "into this grace." He therefore implies again how fundamental the notion of grace is to him. But grace here does not, as in these earlier verses, refer to the freedom with which God acts toward his creatures. Rather, it is a state in which the believer lives. God's free giving to us does not stop when we become Christians. It continues to be poured out on us so much that we can be said to live in a constant state of grace (cf. 5:21; 6:14, 15).

(3) The third result of our new justified state is that "we rejoice in the hope of the glory of God." The verb for "rejoice" (*kauchaomai*) suggests both the idea of taking confidence in and of rejoicing in; some versions translate "boast" (see

---

3. See esp. Sanday and Headlam, *The Epistle to the Romans*, 120; Murray, *The Epistle to the Romans*, 1:158–59. In textual criticism, the *lectio difficilior* is often the preferred reading since in manuscript transition, scribes tended to make grammar easier rather than more obscure.

4. Most modern commentators agree.

comments on 2:17; 3:27). Paul introduces what becomes the theme of this paragraph: the hope we have as Christians to share in God's glory.

But Paul quickly adds in a surprising development, "we also rejoice [or boast, *kauchaomai* again] in our sufferings" (5:3). Having ministered with people for so many years, Paul knows that many will react to this enumeration of blessings in one of two ways. Some will think he is promising believers a trouble-free existence, suggesting life will be a "bed of roses" now that they belong to God. Others, who have been Christians long enough to know that suffering does not come to an end with conversion, may dismiss Paul as an unrealistic dreamer. Thus Paul takes the offensive. Yes, he says in effect, I know Christians will continue to suffer. But life's difficulties do not contradict what I have been saying about the wonderful blessings of being a Christian; in fact, God actually uses them to bring us even greater blessing.

The key is the way we respond to the difficult trials that come our way. What we must do is to recognize that God uses them to build into our lives "perseverance" (*hypomone*; cf. 2:7; 15:4–5), which, in turn, leads to "character" (*dokime*, the quality that comes from having been "proved"; cf. 2 Cor. 2:9; 8:2; 9:13; 13:3; Phil. 2:22). Then we can truly "rejoice" in the midst of suffering, knowing that God is at work even in these evil things to bring us blessing. Paradoxically, Paul claims at the end of verse 4, suffering can actually lead to "hope." Just as resistance to a muscle strengthens it, so challenges to our hope can strengthen it.

We Hope Because God Loves Us in Christ (5:5–8)

HAVING RETURNED TO the subject of "hope" at the end of verse 4, Paul introduces in verse 5 the aspect of hope that will dominate the rest of this paragraph: the certainty that believers will indeed receive what they hope for. While the NIV renders the verb here as a present, it is better to take it as a future: "Hope *will* not disappoint us" (the Greek verb, *kataischynei*, can be either). This is because Paul is alluding to Old Testament passages that speak of people who hope in God not being disappointed or ashamed at the time of judgment (see Ps. 22:5; 25:3, 20; Isa. 28:16 [quoted by Paul in Rom. 9:33 and 10:11]). Our claim that Christ will rescue us from God's wrath will some day be vindicated. God will do what he promised.

How can we be sure? In Romans 5:5b–10, Paul gives two basic reasons: God's love for us in Christ (vv. 5b–8) and God's work for us in Christ (vv. 9–10). God does not mete out his love for us in tiny measures; he "has poured" (*ekcheo*) it into our hearts. This verb is used to describe the "pouring out" of the Spirit on the day of Pentecost (Acts 2:17–18). Paul therefore cleverly alludes to the Spirit here. It is the Spirit, dwelling in the heart of believers, who communicates God's love to us (cf. Rom. 5:5). Paul says much more about this ministry of the Holy Spirit and about God's love for us in chapter 8.

Alongside this subjective evidence of God's love, we also have objective proof of that love in the cross of Christ. At the time God determined, at just the right point in salvation history, "Christ died for the ungodly" (v. 6; cf. also, for this sense of time, 3:26; 8:18; 13:11).[5] Sending his Son to die for people who refused to worship him (the basic connotation of "ungodly") reveals the magnitude of God's love for us.

To make sure we do not miss this point, Paul reinforces it in verse 7 with an analogy: "Very rarely will anyone die for a righteous man, though for a good man someone might possibly dare to die." Though the issue is disputed, a difference between "a good man" and "a righteous man" seems to be the key to the interpretation. A "righteous" person is one we might respect, but a "good" person is one we might love.[6] Rarely will a person give his or her life for someone they merely respect; but occasionally a person dies for the sake of someone they love—a soldier for his buddies, a parent for her children. The awesome quality of God's love for us is seen in that Christ died for us while we were "still sinners"—hating God, in rebellion against him (v. 8).

We Hope Because God Has Acted for Us in Christ (5:9–11)

AS WE NOTED above in the introduction to 5:1–11, verses 9–10 are parallel. Paul begins each by reminding us what God has already done for us through the death of Christ: He "justified" us (v. 9) and "reconciled" us to him (v. 10). "How much more," then, Paul reasons, can we be sure that God will complete his work by saving us from his wrath in the last day. Bringing rebellious sinners into relationship with God is an act of amazing love (vv. 5–8). Now that he has done that, Paul suggests, we can be absolutely confident he will do what, in this sense, is the "easier" thing: deliver from wrath people whom God has already brought to himself.

Two specific points in these verses require comment. (1) Paul interchanges "justify" and "reconcile" in his argument. Does this suggest that they mean the same thing? Not at all. Rather, they are two ways of describing what happens when God first accepts us. He declares us innocent and absolves us from punishment for our sins ("justify"), and he removes the hostility that existed

---

5. See, e.g., Murray, *The Epistle to the Romans*, 1:167. Other interpreters think the phrase could suggest that it was the "right time" in world history for God to bring salvation (cf. Gal. 4:4; note, e.g., Sanday and Headlam, *The Epistle to the Romans*, 127).

6. The church father Irenaeus, for instance, said that the Gnostics characterized the God of the Old Testament as "righteous" and the God of the New Testament as "good" (*Adv. Haer.* 1.27.1).

between us and him because of that sin ("reconcile"). The former is a judicial idea, the latter a relational one.

(2) Paul claims that being "saved" (the verb is *sozo*) comes *after* we are justified and reconciled. This may seem unusual, since we often use the word "save" to refer to our initial acceptance with the Lord ("I was saved in 1971"). Paul does use the word this way (see, e.g., 8:34), but he more often uses it to depict the believer's final deliverance from death and the wrath of God in the last day. Later in Romans, Paul claims that "our salvation is nearer now than when we first believed" (13:11; see also 1 Cor. 3:15; 5:5; Phil. 2:12). The gospel, Paul has announced in his statement of the letter's theme, is the "power of God for ... salvation" (Rom. 1:16). But that salvation is not completed until we have put sin and death behind us and been vindicated in the judgment. Being justified and reconciled to God is the critical step on the way to salvation; if these are in place, eventual salvation is certain.

In verse 11, Paul returns to the theme of rejoicing (see vv. 2–3) as he rounds off his teaching in this paragraph. Joy and confidence (the verb is again *kauchaomai*) should be our response to the blessings we have already received and to the wonderful and certain promises about the blessings God has yet to give us. We have already "received reconciliation," and that means salvation is certain. "Hope will not disappoint us," because God is working on our behalf "through our Lord Jesus Christ."

Bridging Contexts

PEACE. *Peace* is an elastic term. Like the waxed nose in Luther's famous analogy, it can be stretched to mean many different things. I am old enough to have been in college during the years when everyone was talking about "peace." Long-haired strangers greeted one another with the single word "Peace." "Give peace a chance" was the cry of the day. It even had its own symbol. At my present advanced age, I find myself beginning to long for the "peace" of retirement. Each of us, therefore, brings some baggage from our culture and personal experience to the phrase "peace with God" in verse 1. Some of that baggage may help us understand the true sense of the phrase, but much of it will simply lead us astray. As always, we need first to establish what the phrase meant to a first-century Jewish-Christian like Paul.

We begin where we usually do when we try to learn how Paul used a word: with the Greek Old Testament. The translators of the LXX used *eirene* (peace) for the common and wide-ranging Hebrew word *shalom*. This word could be applied, like our word "peace," to a cessation of hostilities between peoples, as when Joshua entered into a "treaty of peace" with the Gibeonites

(Josh. 9:15). But the word more often has a religious sense, referring to the well-being and prosperity of people who have been blessed by God.

Shalom occurs especially often as a blessing, as when Eli responds to Hannah, "Go in peace, and may the God of Israel grant you what you have asked of him" (1 Sam. 1:17; see also, e.g., Gen. 26:29; 44:17). As this blessing suggests, God is viewed as the One who gives the gift of peace. Note too the well-known benediction, "the LORD turn his face toward you and give you peace" (Num. 6:26).

Especially significant for Paul is the prophets' use of *shalom* to depict the salvation that God will bring to his people in the last days. Isaiah 52:7, for example, brings together three terms that are theologically important in Paul (quoted in Rom. 10:15): "How beautiful on the mountains are the feet of those who bring good news, who proclaim *peace*, who bring *good tidings*, who proclaim *salvation*, who say to Zion, 'Your God reigns!'" (italics added; see also Isa. 54:10; Ezek. 34:25; 37:26). When God intervenes in the last days to deliver Israel from her enemies and establish her securely in the land, she enjoys ultimate peace. In keeping with the typical New Testament perspective on the fulfillment of these prophecies in Christ, Paul transfers the term *peace* from the national blessing of Israel to the personal experience of every believer.

The peace God gives us in Christ has two closely related, but distinguishable, aspects. First is the "peace of God," an inner sense of security and serenity that wells up in our hearts when we appreciate the blessings we enjoy in Christ (see, e.g., Phil. 4:7). But it is the second aspect that Paul refers to in Romans 5:1: "peace *with* God," the objective position we find ourselves in because God has ceased to be hostile toward us and has reconciled us to himself (see 5:10–11). Paul often uses peace in this sense (see esp. Eph. 2:14, 15, 17; also Rom. 2:10; 8:6; 14:17).

Justification and judgment. For Paul, as we have seen, God's verdict of justification marks the entrance into the Christian life. When we respond to the gospel in faith, God declares us innocent and our relationship with him begins. To be sure, some verses in Paul (see esp. Gal. 5:6) may suggest justification is more than a past event for the believer.[7] But, on the whole, as Romans 5:1 suggests, justification is the entry point into our Christian experience.

In Jewish theology, however, justification and its opposite, condemnation, were verdicts that would be delivered only on the Day of Judgment. Jesus uses the language in typical Jewish fashion: "By your words you will be acquitted [justified], and by your words you will be condemned" (Matt. 12:37). Paul's

---

7. See on this point esp. James D. G. Dunn, *The Theology of Paul the Apostle* (Grand Rapids: Eerdmans, 1998), 386.

claim that a person can be justified in this life is a radical departure from Jewish thinking. In a way characteristic of the New Testament perspective, he proclaims that believers in Christ can experience an eschatological event.

This does not mean, however, that Paul does away with the typical Jewish teaching about a future day of judgment. He affirms that some day Christians as well as non-Christians will have to stand before God to be judged. To be sure, some theologians think Christians will come to that Day only to have the degree of reward to which they are entitled determined. But I think the New Testament teaches that the eternal destiny of *all* people, believers or not, will be determined on that day (see Matt. 25:31–46; Rom. 14:10; 2 Cor. 5:10).

With this background in view, we begin to understand better why Paul must focus on the issue of assurance in these verses. Christians, he has asserted, are "justified." But we have not yet appeared before God on the Judgment Day. How can we know that this verdict of justification will do us any good when that Day comes? It is this underlying question that sparks his teaching here and throughout these chapters. The apostle's answer is clear: In justifying us, God has already pronounced his verdict over us. It can be neither rescinded nor changed. True, we must still appear before God to have our "case" disposed of. But we can face that day with utter confidence, since God in Christ has already decided the case in our favor. Justification releases us from any uncertainty or fear about that judgment.

LIVING OUT OF GRACE. As we commented above, Paul's claim that we have continuing "access" to grace and that we "stand" in it reveals the importance of the term *grace* for him. Grace reminds us that God intervenes on behalf of his rebellious creation out of his own free will and without any obligation (see 4:4–5). While God always acts in grace, so radical and so far-reaching is his intervention on our behalf in Christ that the word can be especially applied to the event of justification and its consequences. But what we sometimes forget, and what Paul's words in 5:2 remind us of, is that grace stands over the entire Christian experience. We not only get into relationship with God by grace; we live out that relationship day-by-day by grace. Thus, we must never fall into the trap of thinking that we can put grace behind us.

The daily provision I enjoy comes not from my hard work but from God, who has chosen in his grace to bless me. Whatever good I accomplish in ministry comes because God graciously works through me. I "stand in grace"; I live out my life, in all its dimensions, within the sphere of blessing that Christ has won for me. The famous hymn "Amazing Grace" puts it well. Yes, as the first stanza reminds us, God's amazing grace has "saved a wretch like me." But that same amazing grace undergirds all my life. We go on to sing in the fourth stanza, " 'Tis grace hath brought me safe thus far, And grace will lead me home."

Peace and suffering. People give many different meanings to the word "peace" (see Bridging Contexts section), but almost everyone wants it. People want to be "at peace" with themselves, and they hope to "rest in peace." Yet no ultimate peace is possible without coming to terms with God. People who search for peace will never find it until they find peace with God. Lack of such peace is the basic human predicament. Indeed, people are in a state of hostility with him. Paul refers to this state in verse 10, calling us "God's enemies."

Scholars debate about whether this means that we are hostile to God[8] or that God is hostile to us.[9] But we do not need to choose between these alternatives.[10] As Paul has made clear, we all have a natural, built-in hostility toward God. Despite the revelation of his existence and power in the world around us (cf. 1:19–22), we turn away from him, refusing to worship him or to give thanks to him (1:20–21). In turn, God must stand in judgment over us, sentencing us to experience his wrath (1:18; 2:5).

Disruption in our relationship with our Creator effects all areas of our existence. No one can experience true "peace" until he or she has "peace with God," available in Jesus Christ, who is, indeed, "our peace" (Eph. 2:14). Only if the hostility between God and ourselves is ended can we ever have the comfort of true serenity and well-being that all people crave. We can enjoy the "peace *of* God" only by first establishing "peace *with* God." If you are reading this book, you are probably a believer in Jesus Christ and you have the "peace with God" that the gospel offers. But some of you may not have made this commitment. God invites you to accept his offer of peace and so enjoy the comfort that comes only from knowing you are in harmony with your Creator.

But let us not misunderstand what the peace that God wants to give us really means. True peace, we are tempted to think, should mean that we have no more worries and no more problems. Some Christians, indeed, argue for this definition of "peace with God." They teach that the Christian, if exhibiting "real faith," will enjoy material prosperity and physical well-being. These are the purveyors of the "health-and-wealth" gospel, who spread their

---

8. See, e.g., Käsemann, *Commentary on Romans*, 139.

9. E.g., Ralph Martin, *Reconciliation: A Study of Paul's Theology* (rev. ed.; Grand Rapids: Zondervan, 1989), 144.

10. Most commentators agree that both are included here.

ideas through radio, television, and websites. But even if we do not buy into the extreme of the health-and-wealth gospel, most of us, I suspect, particularly in North America, are prone to the tendency to dismiss suffering as a rather remote possibility and perhaps to regard it as something basically out of keeping with the "victorious Christian life."

Thus, it is important to take to heart what Paul says about suffering in verses 3–4. These verses make four points, implicitly or explicitly, that can give us a better perspective on suffering. (1) Suffering is a normal part of a consistent Christian life. Just after he planted churches on the first missionary journey, Paul warned his new converts, "We must go through many hardships to enter the kingdom of God" (Acts 14:22). Jesus himself promised that "in this world you will have trouble" (John 16:33). Paul can even call suffering a gracious gift from the Lord: "For it has been granted to you on behalf of Christ not only to believe on him, but also to suffer for him" (Phil. 1:29).

Everywhere the New Testament assumes that believers will suffer. God has adopted us as his children, but we still live in a world hostile to God and his values. Precisely because we are God's children, and to the degree that we live out his values, people hostile to God will be hostile toward us. Paul assumes this perspective by introducing the fact of suffering in verse 3 without any preamble or explanation.

(2) God uses suffering to accomplish his purposes. What Paul says about suffering in verses 3–4 is echoed in James 1:2–4 and 1 Peter 1:6: The trials of life are a means of testing our faith and giving substance and strength to our Christian commitment. I wish this were not so. I do not take any perverse pleasure in going through hard times. I certainly do not look forward to painful experiences that will undoubtedly yet come. But if I am honest, I must also admit that I too easily settle down in this world. I am prone to lose my fervor for God and his work and to seek security and comfort in this life at the expense of my Christian values.

I know from experience that the difficult times I go through loosen my tie to this world and bring me closer to the Lord. A young pastor in our area, a man with three children still at home, was dying of cancer. He said that he would not have wanted to avoid this trial because of the wonderful spiritual benefit it brought to him. I sometimes wish I could mature in Christ the way I should without having to suffer. But I know in my heart that I am just not built that way and that only suffering will pry me from this world and its pleasures.

(3) We are to rejoice *in the midst of*, but not *in*, suffering. The pastor whom I just referred to was sincere in what he said about the spiritual benefit of his suffering. But this does not mean that he did not grieve to be leaving his family behind or groan from the pain. He did not think the cancer was a good thing or something to rejoice in. Yet some Christians almost go this far in

their application of verses like Romans 5:3—as if we are to praise God *for* cancer, the loss of a job, or the death of a loved one. We must never praise God *for*, or rejoice in, evil things. God hates these things. They are no part of his original creation, and he will someday eradicate them. Paul calls on us to rejoice *in the midst* of afflictions, and even to rejoice *because of* afflictions (knowing what God will accomplish with them). But he does not ask us to be joyful *about* the affliction itself.

(4) The suffering Paul speaks of here includes all the difficulties of this life. The word Paul uses for "sufferings" in verse 3 is the plural of *thlipsis* (tribulations). He sometimes uses this word to refer to persecution in the narrow sense—that is, difficulties experienced because of one's witness for Christ (e.g., 1 Thess. 1:6). Some interpreters think that most New Testament passages about suffering, including this one, have this more restrictive meaning. They are certainly right to claim that suffering "for the sake of Christ" is often the focus (see, e.g., 1 Peter). But even in texts such as these, I am not sure that we can confine the reference to persecution.

In a certain sense, everything that a Christian suffers is "on behalf of Christ." The evil things we face reflect the conflict between "this age," dominated by Satan and sin, and "the age to come," to which the believer has been transferred by faith. All suffering betrays the presence of the enemy and attacks our relationship with Christ. Furthermore, as we have argued, the end of chapter 8 and the beginning of chapter 5 are closely related. This means that the suffering Paul mentions in 5:3 is likely related to the trials he lists in 8:35: "trouble or hardship or persecution or famine or nakedness or danger or sword." More than persecution per se is included.

Romans 5:12–21

THEREFORE, JUST AS sin entered the world through one man, and death through sin, and in this way death came to all men, because all sinned—[13]for before the law was given, sin was in the world. But sin is not taken into account when there is no law. [14]Nevertheless, death reigned from the time of Adam to the time of Moses, even over those who did not sin by breaking a command, as did Adam, who was a pattern of the one to come.

[15]But the gift is not like the trespass. For if the many died by the trespass of the one man, how much more did God's grace and the gift that came by the grace of the one man, Jesus Christ, overflow to the many! [16]Again, the gift of God is not like the result of the one man's sin: The judgment followed one sin and brought condemnation, but the gift followed many trespasses and brought justification. [17]For if, by the trespass of the one man, death reigned through that one man, how much more will those who receive God's abundant provision of grace and of the gift of righteousness reign in life through the one man, Jesus Christ.

[18]Consequently, just as the result of one trespass was condemnation for all men, so also the result of one act of righteousness was justification that brings life for all men. [19]For just as through the disobedience of the one man the many were made sinners, so also through the obedience of the one man the many will be made righteous.

[20]The law was added so that the trespass might increase. But where sin increased, grace increased all the more, [21]so that, just as sin reigned in death, so also grace might reign through righteousness to bring eternal life through Jesus Christ our Lord.

THE "THEREFORE" AT the beginning of this paragraph suggests that Paul is now going to draw a conclusion from what he has been saying before this. If this is so, then the connection may be with the argument just concluded in 5:1–11: The certainty of salvation results in the contrasting "headships" of Adam and Christ.[1] But the "therefore" can also gather up the argument of the letter up to this point. In other words, Paul may be beginning a new section of the letter at 5:12.[2]

But 5:12–21 does not read like a conclusion from anything Paul has been arguing earlier. These verses highlight Christ's power as the "second Adam," who more than reverses the dire consequences of the first Adam's sin, to ensure that those in him will have eternal life (vv. 20–21). This argument functions naturally as the *basis* for what Paul has said in verses 1–11: Our hope of sharing God's glory is certain because we are in Christ, who has guaranteed life for us. This appears to be the best reading of the sequence of thought in chapter 5. We can therefore paraphrase the opening words of verse 12: "in order to accomplish what I have just taught [e.g., the certainty of salvation]...."[3]

Many Christians generally familiar with the Bible immediately think "original sin" when they hear Romans 5:12–21. To be sure, this section is probably the most important passage in the Bible on this controversial doctrine. But a careful look at its structure reveals that Adam and his sin are not Paul's focus here. The basic building block of the paragraph is a "just as ... so also" comparison. Paul introduces this comparison in verse 12 ("just as"), but he never completes it (most English versions, like the NIV, signal the break with a dash at the end of the verse). He later resumes the comparison and finally completes it in verses 18–19. The point is this: In each place, Adam and the sin and death he brought into the world are in the "just as" clause; Christ and the righteousness and life he provides are in the "so also" clause.

If we think about it for a moment, it is obvious that the "so also" clause makes the main point. If I say, for example, "just as the Chicago Cubs disappointed their fans this year, so also they will again next year," I am arguing from what everyone knows—the Cubs are a model of futility—to the point I am trying to make—they will continue on the same course. Paul seems to assume his readers know all about Adam and how his sin brought sin and death to the entire human race. He can use that well-known fact to argue for what he really wants to get across to his readers: Christ is like Adam in that what he did affects all people. But, unlike Adam, who brought death, Christ brings life. Therefore, all who belong to Christ can be confident that they are under the "reign" of grace, which brings eternal life (v. 21).

As already noted, the heart of this paragraph lies in the comparisons between Adam and Christ in verses 12, 18–19. Paul interrupts the compar-

---

1. E.g., Cranfield, *The Epistle to the Romans*, 269; Morris, *The Epistle to the Romans*, 228.

2. Melanchthon took this approach.

3. The Greek construction is *dia touto*. We are taking *dia* to indicate a "final cause" and *touto* to refer to the promise of final salvation in vv. 9–10. See, for more detail, Moo, *The Epistle to the Romans*, 316–18.

ison to make a point about sin and the law (vv. 13–14) and about the differences between Adam and Christ (vv. 15–17). Verses 20–21 bring the argument of the paragraph home to the reader.

Adam, Sin, and Universal Death (5:12)

IN A VERSE where every word—indeed, every punctuation mark!—is the object of intense controversy, we must put aside some issues and just try to get a good sense of what Paul is teaching. A first step toward this end is to note what seems to be a chiastic relationship among the four clauses in the verse:

A *Sin* came into the world through Adam
  B With sin came *death*
  B' *Death* spread to all people
A' Because all people *sinned*

The first two clauses set the stage by making a general point: Adam's fall introduced sin into the world, and death came as a result of sin. The Genesis narrative, of course, makes this point crystal clear, as God warns the first human couple, "When you eat of it [the tree of the knowledge of good and evil] you will surely die" (Gen. 2:17).

What is this death? Theologians have debated the issue for centuries. But Paul seems to think of death as both physical and spiritual: separation from the body and estrangement from God. Both are the result of sin.[4] That a physical element is present in death is evident from verses 13–14. But verses 18–19, where Paul replaces the death of verse 12 with "condemnation" and being "made sinners," shows that his focus is on spiritual death. The sin Adam introduced into the world spelled spiritual disaster for the human race.

The second two clauses of verse 12 emphasize the universal extent of this nexus of sin and death. Death, Paul affirms, affects all people because all people have "sinned." That all human beings stand under God's sentence of wrath because of sin is a point the apostle has already made in Romans (see esp. 1:18–19; 3:9, 23). He may be saying here again no more than that every person is estranged from God because every person has, at some time or another in his or her life, sinned.[5] But in verses 18–19, where, as we have seen, Paul repeats and completes the comparison we have in this verse, he suggests

---

4. Beker calls this idea in Paul "total death" (*Paul the Apostle*, 224). Most of the commentators agree with this idea. But commentators who think the death here is physical only include Godet (*Commentary on Romans*, 205) and Murray (*The Epistle to the Romans*, 1:181–82).

5. We are assuming, with most scholars, that the Greek construction *eph' ho* means "because" (see, for detail and argument, Moo, *The Epistle to the Romans*, 321–22).

a close relationship between Adam's sin and the condemnation that all people stand under: "The result of one [man's] trespass was condemnation for all men" (v. 18a).

Because of this, and also because of the need to explain why every single person sins, many scholars think there is more to Paul's "because all sinned" than meets the eye. Some argue that the phrase means "because every human being, personally, sinned as a result of inheriting a sinful nature from Adam."[6] Others go further: Since Paul claims that we die both because *we* sin (v. 12) and because *Adam* sinned (v. 18), we must blend these two together: We all sinned when Adam sinned. As the representative of the human race, Adam's sin is at the same time the sin of every other human being who ever lives.[7]

This is not the place to argue all these points (see Bridging Contexts and Contemporary Significance sections). Here I want to make two quick points. (1) Exegetical evidence is not clear-cut in favor of one of these views or the other; we must, therefore, be cautious about drawing conclusions. (2) I think the context and the background (see Bridging Contexts section) favor a third option: "All sinned" means "all people sinned in and with Adam." But whatever our decision on this contested point, we should be clear about one matter: Sin and the spiritual death that results from sin are universal.

Sin and Death Even Apart from the Law (5:13–14)

ALREADY IN VERSE 12, Paul has begun to lose control of his syntax as he lapses into a series of run-on clauses. At the end of the verse he abandons it altogether. Apparently, he is convinced that something he has said in this verse requires elaboration before he can move on to finish the comparison that is at the heart of this paragraph. As a result, as he has done throughout chapters 1–4, he brings the Mosaic law into the picture.

But why does he do so here? There are two possibilities. (1) Paul may be *explaining* the universal reign of death. If, indeed, "sin is not taken into account" when there is no law (v. 13b), and if, nevertheless, people still died during the time between Adam and Moses when there was not law (v. 14), then the only possible explanation for the death of these people is the sin of Adam

---

6. Luther and Calvin both defend this view (although Calvin appears to go further in his *Institutes* [2.1.5–8]). Many others who do not think the phrase means this nevertheless think a "missing connection" must be added in Paul's argument: All people sin (individually) *because all people inherit a sinful nature from Adam* as a result of his sin (see, e.g., Sanday and Headlam, *The Epistle to the Romans*, 134; Cranfield, *The Epistle to the Romans*, 274–81).

7. Perhaps the best defense of this view is John Murray, *The Imputation of Adam's Sin* (Grand Rapids: Eerdmans, 1959).

himself. They died because they had sinned "in" Adam, and Adam did, indeed, break a "law": the commandment not to eat of fruit of the tree of good and evil in the Garden of Eden.[8]

(2) However, while this interpretation explains the logic of these two verses and fits in well with our understanding of verse 12d, it faces an insuperable objection: Paul affirms that people before Moses died for their own sins (see, e.g., 1:32; note also Gen. 6). For this reason, we think the second interpretation of these verses is preferable: Paul is *reinforcing* his teaching about the universality of death. Many Jews believed that there could be no sin or death apart from the law. They may have thought that Paul's claim in verse 12 that all people had sinned and died does not make sense. Thus, Paul affirms that, indeed, sin existed before the Mosaic law was given, and that people were condemned for their sin. The presence of positive law turns sin into "transgression" (*parabasis*, the word Paul uses in v. 14 and which NIV translates "by breaking a command"; see notes on 4:15). Sin may not be charged to one's individual account (v. 13b) apart from law. But sin is still sin and brings God's condemnation and wrath.

The Contrast Between Adam and Christ (5:15–17)

AT THE END of verse 14, almost as an aside, Paul expresses the premise on which the whole argument of verses 12–21 is built: Adam was a "pattern [or type, *typos*] of the one to come," that is, of Christ. But before he pursues the similarity between these two as a result of this relationship, the apostle notes some of the differences. These differences boil down to one great fact: In Christ God deals with people on the basis of grace.

The word "grace" and the related word "gift" occur seven times in these three verses. What happened as a result of Adam's sin is entirely a matter of "just deserts." "Death" (vv. 15, 17), "judgment," and "condemnation" (v. 16) inevitably and justly follow sin. But what has happened as a result of Christ is quite different. In place of condemnation, Christ brings "justification" (v. 16). Condemnation came as a result of "one sin," but justification "followed many trespasses" (v. 16). We see in this circumstance, Paul concludes, evidence of the overwhelming grace of God. As Cranfield puts it, "That one single misdeed should be answered by judgment, this is perfectly understandable: that the accumulated sins and guilt of all the ages should be answered by God's free gift, this is the miracle of miracles, utterly beyond human comprehension."[9]

---

8. See, e.g., Godet, *Commentary on Romans*, 209–10 (he thinks the death, however, is physical only).

9. Cranfield, *The Epistle to the Romans*, 286.

The power of God's grace operating through the work of Christ means there is a "how much more" in the quality of what Christ accomplishes in comparison with what Adam has done (v. 17). Christ more than cancels the effects of Adam's sin—he enables those who have received the "abundant provision of grace" and "the gift of righteousness" not just to experience life but to "reign in life."

The Comparison Between Adam and Christ (5:18–19)

LIKE MANY OF us, Paul sometimes gets tangled up in his syntax and does not finish sentences be begins (see introductory comments on this section regarding v. 12). But, unlike some of us, Paul knows when he has left a sentence or an idea hanging. Thus, in verses 18–19 he returns to the idea of verse 12 and completes it.

Verses 18–19 are similar in structure. Each features Adam in the first ("just as") clause and Christ in the second ("so also") clause. Each contrasts what Adam did with what Christ did. Adam committed a "trespass" (v. 18); he disobeyed (v. 19). Christ, by contrast, committed an "act of righteousness" (v. 18); he obeyed (v. 19). Where Adam turned away from God and violated his commandment, Christ turned toward God and continually did the will of his Father. The singular "act of righteousness" suggests Paul is thinking of a single manifestation of Christ's obedience to his Father—probably in submitting to the Father's will to die on a Roman cross.

Finally, and most important, each verse also contrasts the results of Adam's sin with the results of Christ's obedience. Elaborating on the death he mentioned in verse 12, Paul asserts that Adam's disobedience led to "condemnation for all men" (v. 18) and that "the many were made sinners" as a result of what Adam did (v. 19). The NIV translation "made sinners" and "made righteous" in verse 19 suggests that Paul's point here is that Adam's sin led people to become sinners while Christ enabled people to become good and law-abiding. But the Greek verb used in both places (*kathistemi*) suggests rather a forensic idea: Because of Adam's sin, "the many" were "appointed to" or "inaugurated into" a state of sinfulness; and because of Christ's obedience, the many "were appointed to" a status of righteousness (i.e., they were justified).

But why does Paul speak of "the many"? Its identical function to the word "all" in verse 18 suggests that "many" in verse 19 is a Semitism that means "everyone" (see also v. 15).[10] But is Paul then asserting that all people will experience justification—that salvation is universal? We don't think so (see Contemporary Significance section for explanation).

---

10. See esp. J. Jeremias, *TNDT*, 6:536–41. However, he exaggerates the frequency of this usage.

The Conclusion:
Grace Reigns! (5:20–21)

PAUL REVEALS THE degree to which he is concerned with the place of the Mosaic law in the plan of God by bringing it up again at the end of this paragraph. We can understand why he does so. He has sketched the religious history of the world in the broadest of strokes. Adam sealed the fate of all people; Christ, the second Adam, enables people to escape that fate and to come nearer to God than was ever possible before.

But Jews or any student of the Old Testament might object: How about all the things God did for Israel? How can all that revelatory history be left out of account? Paul, of course, believes firmly in the enduring value of the Old Testament. But he is equally convinced that its law does not fundamentally alter the situation described in these verses. In an "offensive" move typical of his argument in Romans, he claims that God intended the Mosaic law to have a *negative* role in salvation history: It was added "so that the trespass might increase." The law did not bring relief from the Adamic condition of sin and death; instead, it made it worse.

But how did that happen? Paul may be thinking of the way a command can stimulate rebellion in people. There is something in all of us that rebels against an order, making what is prohibited more attractive than ever before. This idea of "forbidden fruits" is found in other ancient literature.[11] But the singular "trespass" (*paraptoma*) is against this understanding (a word Paul uses in vv. 15, 16, and 18 to refer to Adam's sin). What he probably means in verse 20, then, is that the law has made the situation of sin that Adam introduced even worse. As we commented on 4:15, Paul believes that the Mosaic law, by making people accountable to a specific and detailed series of commandments, brings greater judgment on those sins.[12]

But no matter how much sin may have "increased" or become worse, God's grace has more than compensated. Under the law, sins were "taken into account," that is, charged against us (v. 13), and so "sin reigned in death." In the dominion of death introduced by Adam, sin holds sway over us. But "through righteousness," that is, as a result of being justified, "grace ... reigns." Its benevolent rule leads each of us who has experienced the righteousness made available in Christ to "eternal life." If we are confident that sin has brought death and untold devastation into the world, we can be even more confident that the grace of God that justifies us will also save us from his wrath in the judgment (see 5:9–10).

---

11. See, e.g., Augustine, *Spirit and Letter* 4.6.
12. See esp. Cranfield, *The Epistle to the Romans*, 292–93.

Bridging Contexts

ADAM IN PAUL'S DAY. The idea that something Adam did thousands of years ago can determine our eternal destiny is one that most modern people find difficult or even abhorrent. Yet, as we have seen, Paul appears to assume his readers are acquainted with the significance of Adam's sin. But what would they have understood about it? If we can give a definite answer to this question, we will be in a much better position to decide what Paul is teaching about the relationship between Adam's sin and the sin and death of all other people. Unfortunately, we cannot be sure what Paul or his readers may have assumed about these matters, because our sources do not agree.

The account of the Fall in Genesis 3 is not clear about the effects of Adam's sin on his posterity. But the modern reader probably misses one overwhelmingly important fact about the account: The name "Adam" means "man" or "human being." Indeed, translators of the Bible have a difficult time deciding what occurrences of the relevant Hebrew word (*ʾadam*) in Genesis 2–5 to translate "man" or "human being" and which to translate with the personal name "Adam." The modern English reader can get a better sense of how the Hebrew must have sounded to readers in Paul day by substituting "man" for every place "Adam" appears in these chapters.

The point, then, is this: Woven into the very fabric of the Genesis narrative is the idea that Adam is more than just an isolated individual; in some, sense, he is "man." When, therefore, the Lord warns the "man" that if he eats from the tree of the knowledge of good and evil, "you will surely die" (Gen. 2:17), a warning of *universal* death may also be intended.

What is somewhat surprising is that the Old Testament says almost nothing about Adam after these first chapters of Genesis.[13] But Jewish writers indulged in much speculation about him. Some of this speculation was fanciful, eventually leading to esoteric Gnostic-type ideas. But some of the Jewish teaching focused on the question of the origin of sin and death and is directly relevant for our purposes.

We find some evidence of at least four different traditions.

(1) Eve brought sin into the world and caused all people to die. See Sirach 25:24: "From a woman sin had its beginning, and because of her we all die."

(2) Satan brought death into the world. See Wisdom 2:24: "Through the devil's envy death entered into the world."

---

13. The only relevant text is the intriguing reference to Adam's breaking of the "covenant" in Hos. 6:7.

(3) Adam's sin brought death to all people. See especially *Syriac Apocalypse of Baruch* 23:4: "When Adam sinned a death was decreed against those who were to be born"; also from the same book, 48:2: "What did you [Adam] do to all who were born after you?"

(4) Every person dies because of his or her own sin. It is interesting that this point is explicit in the same book that also attributes universal death to Adam. *Syriac Apocalypse of Baruch* 54:19: "Adam is, therefore, not the cause, except only for himself, but each of us has become our own Adam"; see also 54:15: "Although Adam sinned first and has brought death upon all who were not in his own time, yet each of them who has been born from him has prepared for himself the coming torments."

In Romans 5, Paul makes no mention of the role of Eve (though see 2 Cor. 11:3; 1 Tim. 2:14) or Satan. But, as we have seen, he appears to attribute responsibility for universal death both to Adam (Rom. 5:18–19) and to every individual (5:12). The Jewish tradition, as *Syriac Apocalypse of Baruch* so clearly reveals, was ambivalent on just this point. Jews acknowledged the determinative role of Adam in bringing sin and death to all the world, but wanted also to insist that every person was responsible for his or her own death.

Paul reflects this same ambivalence.[14] Whether he resolves it by suggesting a particular relationship between Adam's sin and the sin of all other people is debated (see Original Meaning and Contemporary Significance sections). But at least we can say this much: Paul's first readers probably assumed without argument that Adam had some kind of representative significance and that his sin therefore brought death to all people.

A corporate way of thinking. One of the reasons we sometimes have difficulty understanding what the Bible teaches is that many of us live in cultures with assumptions about "the way the world works" that are very different from those of the Bible writers. The teaching of Scripture is sometimes like an iceberg: What is taught at the surface of the text rests on huge assumptions that lie beneath that level. Paul's teaching about the corporate significance of Adam and Christ is a classic instance of this culture clash. Those of us who have been raised in the Western world are heirs of an individualistic tradition. As one who has grown up in the United States, I have had drilled into me since birth the "rugged individualism" of my culture. My choices, I have been taught both explicitly and implicitly, determine who I will be, what I will do, and how successful I will be.

---

14. See esp. A. J. M. Wedderburn, "The Theological Structure of Romans V.12," *NTS* 19 (1972–73): 338–39.

The Bible certainly does not deny individual responsibility. But it also has a much stronger sense of how people are related to one another in ways that mean the decision of one can affect many others. The classic example in the Old Testament is the sin of Achan (Josh. 7). Contrary to God's command, Achan kept for himself some of the spoils from the battle of Jericho. When the Israelites then tried to take the city of Ai, they were defeated. Why? Because Achan had sinned (7:20)! Note Joshua 7:11: Not only did all Israel suffer because of his sin, but the Lord even said, *"Israel* has sinned; they have violated my covenant" (italics added).

This notion of *corporate solidarity* is an important part of the way both Old and New Testament authors looked at the world. Even in the West, we are beginning to understand this better than we used to. Modern psychology has revealed ways in which our apparently "free" choices are, in fact, directed by our background and environment. But we still have difficulty with the idea that someone else's decision or act might decisively affect us. Yet Paul's argument here and in several other places in Romans assumes this truth. To appreciate and apply his argument, we must sympathetically identify with the corporate perspective his teaching assumes.

DEATH. WE SOMETIMES do not realize the implications of decisions we make about certain texts or issues. I myself was blissfully unaware of the minefield I was straying into when I began to study the meaning of "death" in Romans 5:12. I knew, of course, that a decision on whether death here is physical or spiritual would have significance for this text, and I could sense some of the theological issues involved (e.g., does Adam's sin bring to me only physical death or condemnation as well?). But I had no idea that my interpretation would have a bearing on some of the intense debates about the time and length of creation until my son pointed it out to me.

As a biologist and a committed Christian, my son has struggled to make sense out of both Scripture and science on this matter. As a result of his study of biology, he was strongly inclined to think that God created the world over a long period of time and that Genesis 1 allows for such an interpretation. But he had a problem reconciling this interpretation with the apparent teaching of Scripture that death entered the world only with Adam and Eve. For basic to the existence and development of plants and animals as we know them is death. The whole grand process of life cannot exist without death. How, then, can plants and animals have existed for thousands of years if death only entered the picture with Adam?

A brief, "seven-literal-day" creation might solve this problem. But does the connection between death and human sin rule out a longer creative process? Only if Adam introduced into the world for the first time physical death. But this is not clear. Old Testament scholars debate the meaning of "death" in Genesis 2; New Testament scholars debate its meaning in Romans 5:12 and elsewhere; and theologians try to decide if God's "good creation" is compatible with the existence of physical death.

My own inclination, as I have suggested in the Original Meaning section above, is to interpret the death that Adam introduced as spiritual but as including also physical death as a penalty. In other words, I think it possible that physical death did indeed exist in the world before Adam, but that Adam's sin turned a natural process into a fearful penalty for all his posterity. But I am not so much concerned here with deciding this issue, but with pointing out the sometimes unexpected consequences of the interpretive decisions we make.

Original sin. While Romans 5:12–21 does not have "original sin" as its focus, it still remains the most important text in the Bible on this vexing theological doctrine. In the following paragraphs, I want briefly to sketch some of the main explanations and then to draw out some consequences of our belief on this matter.

We generally use the expression *original sin* to refer to the biblical teaching about the relationship between the first or original sin of Adam and the sin and death of all other people. At the risk of a gross simplification, I think we can summarize the views that Christians hold on this matter into three general categories.

(1) *Imitation.* The early church father Pelagius is the most famous exponent of this view. He did not think there was any *real* connection between our sin and Adam's. What Adam did was to set a bad example for us that the rest of us have all followed. This view is generally considered to be suborthodox, if not heretical. Why? (a) Pelagius's view cannot explain the data of Romans 5. Paul clearly teaches some kind of real relationship between Adam's sin and ours. (b) Nor can it explain the universality of sin. I have five children; they do not all imitate me in the same way. How could it be that every single person who has ever lived—the vast majority of whom have never even heard of Adam—would imitate his turn away from God? Clearly some other factor must be involved if we are to explain Paul's insistence that "all sinned" (v. 12).

(2) *Infection.* Almost all Christians agree, then, that Adam's sin introduced a stain into the human race itself, a stain on human nature that inevitably leads people to turn away from God rather than toward him. This fatal "bent" is the result of Adam's sin, and all people descended from Adam possess it.

Many passages in the Old and New Testaments teach this basic truth about humanity, but it is not explicitly taught in Romans 5:12–21.

Nevertheless, as we noted above, many interpreters think it is implicit in the logic of 5:18–19. Paul affirms, for instance, that "the result of one trespass was condemnation for all men" (v. 18). What we find here, many argue in light of biblical teaching elsewhere, is a compressed statement giving only the original cause and the ultimate end. Missing is the process that connects them. "One trespass" contaminated human nature; this "infection" has been passed down to all Adam's posterity. Everyone therefore sins, and as a result everyone is condemned.

(3) *Inclusion*. Many other interpreters, however, are not convinced that we can assume so much in verse 18. The relationship between the sin of Adam and the sin of all people is closer. How can Paul say in the same passage that all die because all sin (v. 12) and all die because Adam sinned (v. 18)? Because Adam's sin is, at the same time, the sin of everyone else as well. I think Paul does infer this idea of inclusion here in Romans 5:12–21. I lean this way for three basic reasons: (a) the repeated emphasis on the determinative significance of the "one" act of the "one" man Adam (vv. 15, 16, 17, 18, 19); (b) the corporate background of Paul's thinking as sketched above; and (c) the more natural parallel it creates between Christ and Adam.

But I do not want to spend a lot of space here defending a particular view of original sin. I would rather draw three implications from our discussion, two pertaining to the inclusive idea I hold and one pertaining more generally to the issue of sin and death as a whole.

(1) The inclusive interpretation suffers from a credibility problem, well stated by theologian Wolfhart Pannenberg: "It is impossible for me to be held jointly responsible as though I were a joint cause for an act that another did many generations ago and in a situation radically different from mine."[15] C. W. Carter makes the same point in a different way: "Guilt stems from a culpable act traceable to the unethical conduct of a morally responsible person."[16] To put it bluntly: It is not fair for God to condemn me to eternal death for a sin Adam committed thousands of years ago.

We must not minimize this objection. But two things can be said. (a) Any orthodox view of sin creates a similar problem. To explain the universality of sin, we must assume at least that Adam's sin has predisposed every person to sin. So, either way, people end up condemned because of something that

---

15. Wolfhart Pannenberg, *Anthropology in Theological Perspective* (Philadelphia: Westminster, 1985), 124.

16. C. W. Carter, "Hamartiology: Evil, the Marrer of God's Creative Purpose and Work," in *A Contemporary Wesleyan Theology* (ed. C. W. Carter; 2 vols.; Grand Rapids: Zondervan, 1983), 1:267.

Adam did. (b) While theologians who hold the inclusive view argue about just what our relationship to Adam might be, they all insist that it is a genuine relationship and that, in a way we cannot understand, we really did sin when Adam did. We do not die for a sin someone else commits; we die for a sin we committed.[17]

(2) The inclusive interpretation has potentially great importance for one of the most difficult of all theological and pastoral issues: the fate of infants and other people without the mental capacity ever to commit a sin or to respond to the gospel. While there is a lot of debate over the details, theologians who think that Adam has infected us all with sin but that we each ultimately die only when we sin personally usually teach that deceased infants go to heaven. After all, they have never committed a personal act of sin.

But if one holds the inclusive view, the situation is quite different. Since all people have sinned in Adam, all people, including children of any age, have already been condemned. Does this mean that any child who is not old enough to understand and respond to the gospel is automatically lost? No. Theologians who hold the inclusive view take three different positions. Some think that God, in an act of grace, accepts into heaven all those who never had a chance to commit a sin in their own persons. Others think that the children of believing parents will be saved. Still others think that God's election will determine the matter: Infants chosen by God for salvation from eternity past will be saved, while those not been chosen will not be.

I have personally wrestled with this emotive question especially since my niece was born with such severe handicaps that she is not expected to live long. What am I to say to her parents when she dies? What do I respond when they ask me, the "family theologian," where their daughter will spend eternity? All that is within me wants to be able to assure them that their daughter is in heaven. But I am not yet convinced Scripture gives me the right to do so. And I don't want to be a purveyor of "cheap comfort," giving hope based on my emotions rather than on Scripture.

I do not yet have an answer I am comfortable with. But two things I can say. (a) God is just and loving; we can leave such questions in his hands. (b) Whatever position we take will be decisively influenced by our theology of sin and salvation. This, after all, is the ultimate purpose of theology. We put together what God says on issues to come to a conclusion about truths we can use to comfort, rebuke, and exhort ourselves and others. All theology is finally pastoral theology.

(3) Our final remark about the teaching on sin in this chapter is this: After all the dust of debate settles, we need to have a deep appreciation of

---

17. A good discussion of the whole matter of original sin is Anthony Hoekema, *Created in God's Image* (Grand Rapids: Eerdmans, 1986), 154—67.

the reality of sin and death. Basic to the Christian worldview is a view of humanity as inherently bent away from God, with all the tragedy that comes from this sinful condition. Indeed, Christianity offers at this point a succinct and convincing explanation for the human misery and hatred we see in the world around us. Original sin may not make sense to many people; they may find it irrational or even unjust. But what better explanation for the extent and persistence of "crimes against humanity"? When will we come to realize that genocide in Africa or in Yugoslavia is not abnormal but, in reality, just another manifestation of the kind of hatred that has marked human beings throughout the centuries? Pascal put the point well:

> Original sin is foolishness to men, but it is admitted to be such. You must not then reproach me for the want of reason in this doctrine, since I admit it to be without reason. But this foolishness is wiser than all the wisdom of men. For without this, what can we say that man is? His whole state depends on this imperceptible point. And how should it be perceived by his reason, since it is a thing against reason, and since reason, far from finding it out by her own ways, is averse to it when it is presented to her?[18]

Universalism. As we have noted repeatedly in this commentary, one of the strongest winds blowing in the present theological climate consists of the twin currents of tolerance and pluralism. As our world grows smaller, we become better acquainted with people of other religions. Human charity, fanned by the emphasis on tolerance in our multicultural environment, makes it more and more difficult to assert that Christ is the only way to salvation. In such a climate, it is not surprising that a belief in universalism is growing among Christians.

Universalism is the belief that all people will eventually be saved. It comes in a variety of forms, some of its adherents asserting that all religions can offer a way to God, others that God will bring to himself any people who have not come to know Christ during this life after their death. Romans 5:18—19 is a text often cited by adherents of universalism. For does not Paul here assert that just as "all people" were condemned as a result of Adam's trespass, so "all people" will be made alive in Christ? If we want to pound the pulpit and denounce all people as sinners, don't we need also to admit that all people will also find life in Christ?

The problem with this view, of course, is that flies in the face of plain biblical teaching that some people will not, in fact, be saved; that hell will never be unpopulated (see, e.g., Rom. 2:12; 2 Thess. 1:8—9; cf. also the whole argu-

---

18. Pascal, *Pensées* 445.

ment of Rom. 1:18–3:20). Even in the present passage, Paul signals an important distinction just at this point between the work of Adam and the work of Christ. Throughout 5:12–21, Paul strains to make Adam and Christ as parallel as possible. All the more striking, then, is his breaking of that parallelism by adding the word "receive" in verse 17: It is, Paul says, only those "who *receive* God's abundant provision of grace" who will "reign in life." What must a person do to experience the death that Adam brought? Simply be born. What must a person do to experience the life that Christ brings? Receive God's gift—that is, respond to the gospel through faith in Christ (see 3:21–26).

What, then, do we do with the apparent universalism in verses 18–19? Two alternatives are popular. (1) Paul may be claiming only that Christ makes life *possible* for every person. In his work on the cross, Christ sets people free from sin and lays the foundation for their new life. But to become real, a person must accept the offer of freedom from sin's penalty. (2) Paul may be saying that as "all who are in Adam" die, so "all who are in Christ" will live (cf. 1 Cor. 15:22). All people are in Adam, and so all people die. But only those who "receive the gift" are in Christ, and so only they will live. Either explanation makes sense of the passage and fits Paul's teaching elsewhere. But we think the second fits the context a bit better.

Universalism certainly has both a strong emotional and a theological attraction. Most of us would like to think that neighbors, friends, and work associates are going to heaven. A belief that all people will one day be reconciled to God seems to honor his lordship over all creation. But the doctrine simply does not have biblical support.

Many of you reading this commentary undoubtedly agree with these sentiments. But many of us tend to be "unconscious" universalists anyway, not really believing in our hearts that the nice people we know might be headed for hell. Thus, our zeal to share the gospel with them is sapped. Evangelistic zeal should be rooted in a love for people and a desire to glorify God by bringing people into relationship with him. But a deep sense of the fact that people without the Lord are, indeed, lost is also a potent motivation.

Romans 6:1–14

WHAT SHALL WE say, then? Shall we go on sinning so that grace may increase? ²By no means! We died to sin; how can we live in it any longer? ³Or don't you know that all of us who were baptized into Christ Jesus were baptized into his death? ⁴We were therefore buried with him through baptism into death in order that, just as Christ was raised from the dead through the glory of the Father, we too may live a new life.

⁵If we have been united with him like this in his death, we will certainly also be united with him in his resurrection. ⁶For we know that our old self was crucified with him so that the body of sin might be done away with, that we should no longer be slaves to sin—⁷because anyone who has died has been freed from sin.

⁸Now if we died with Christ, we believe that we will also live with him. ⁹For we know that since Christ was raised from the dead, he cannot die again; death no longer has mastery over him. ¹⁰The death he died, he died to sin once for all; but the life he lives, he lives to God.

¹¹In the same way, count yourselves dead to sin but alive to God in Christ Jesus. ¹²Therefore do not let sin reign in your mortal body so that you obey its evil desires. ¹³Do not offer the parts of your body to sin, as instruments of wickedness, but rather offer yourselves to God, as those who have been brought from death to life; and offer the parts of your body to him as instruments of righteousness. ¹⁴For sin shall not be your master, because you are not under law, but under grace.

IN CHAPTER 5, Paul has assured us that our new relationship with God will result in salvation from God's wrath in the judgment. Because we are in Christ, we can be confident of the eternal life he has secured for us. But what does this new relationship mean for our lives in the present? Are we simply "in limbo," waiting for the day of final salvation? Not at all, Paul now makes clear. For Christ has set us free not only from the *penalty* of sin, but also from the *power* of sin. The Westminster Larger Catechism makes the same point in more theological terms:

Question: Wherein do justification and sanctification differ?

Answer: Although sanctification be inseparably joined with justification, yet they differ, in that God in justification imputeth the righteousness of Christ; in sanctification his Spirit infuseth grace, and enableth to the exercise thereof; in the former, sin is pardoned; in the other, it is subdued.

God gives us hope for the future, but he also wants to transform the way we live until we attain that hope.

The immediate occasion for Paul's teaching in chapter 6 is 5:20b: "But where sin increased, grace increased all the more." As he has often done in Romans, Paul anticipates how his point may be misunderstood. He therefore asks in 6:1, "What shall we say, then? Shall we go on sinning so that grace may increase?" But his discussion in chapter 6 is probably prompted also by a broader and more theological concern. The good news that a person can be put right with God by faith alone can easily lead to the conclusion that such people no longer need to try to live in obedience to God. Paul wants to head off any notion that his gospel countenances such a lackadaisical attitude toward morality.

Believers not only *should not* think that God's grace in Christ condones sin; true believers *cannot* think in such a way. For God has decisively changed the believer's position in relationship to sin. As he began to do in chapter 5, Paul portrays sin as a power or master that exercises control over people (see also 3:9). Paul now uses the imagery of slavery, mastery, and freedom to make his point. We should no longer "be slaves to sin" (6:6) because we have been "set free" from sin and become "slaves" to God and righteousness (6:17—22); sin is no longer our "master" (6:14a).

United with Christ in Death and Resurrection (6:1–5)

WITH THE QUESTION-AND-ANSWER format, Paul uses again the diatribe style so common in Romans (6:1–2; see esp. 3:1–9, 27–31; 4:1–12). In this case, however, the person he is dialoging with is not a Jew but a Christian. Paul's purpose is to show that being a believer makes a decisive difference in one's relationship to sin.

Specifically, Paul says, "we died to sin" (v. 2). What does he mean by this? Clearly he does not mean that Christians are not tempted by sin or that we are incapable of sinning—as his commands in verses 11–14 make clear. He uses the imagery of "death" for two reasons. (1) It creates an obvious point of contact with the death of Christ, an important step in Paul's argument (vv. 3–4). (2) It is a powerful image of a decisive shift in state. When someone becomes a Christian, Paul implies, their change of state in relationship

to sin is as dramatic as a change from life to death. He spells out the implication of this change in a rhetorical question: "How can we live in it any
longer?" This question may be turned into a statement: We who are Christians no longer live under the domination of sin. We cannot, therefore, go
on living in sin the way we used to.

In verses 3–5, Paul shows how the transfer from the state of sin to new
life in Christ has taken place. In baptism, we are joined to Christ and to his
death and resurrection. As Paul will make clear later in this passage, Christ's
own death was a death "to sin" and his resurrection meant living "to God"
(v. 10). Therefore, those who participate in Christ's death and resurrection also
have "died to sin" and now "live to God."

Paul's use of the language of "baptism" in verses 3–4 is somewhat surprising. In light of the prominence he gives to faith in chapters 1–4, we
would have expected him to say that "those of us who have believed in Christ
Jesus have been united with his death" (v. 3) and that "we were buried with
him through our faith into death" (v. 4). Why "baptism" here?

Some interpreters think that Paul uses the language here in a metaphorical way. *Baptizo*, the Greek verb, means basically "immerse in" (see, e.g.,
Mark 10:38–39 and parallels; 1 Cor. 10:2), so Paul may simply be saying, in
a vivid way, that believers have been "immersed" in Christ.[1] Other interpreters think Paul may be referring to "baptism in the Spirit."[2] But Paul usually uses the verb *baptizo* to refer to Christian water baptism (1 Cor. 1:13–17;
12:13 [though debated]; 15:29; Gal. 3:27). Moreover, the noun "baptism"
(Gk. *baptisma*) in verse 4 almost always has this meaning.

With the great majority of commentators, then, we think Paul here refers
to water baptism as the point in time at which people become joined with
Christ (see Bridging Contexts and Contemporary Significance sections for
further discussion). When we were baptized "into" Christ (i.e., so as to be
joined with him), we were baptized "into his death."

Verse 4 then elaborates that "we were buried with Christ into death."
Paul may mention burial here because he is thinking of the physical actions
of baptism as symbolic of the believer's transfer from death to life. As Christ
was buried in his grave, so the believer goes down into the water to symbolize
his or her death to the old life.[3] But while this interpretation is popular, it is
probably not correct. Nothing here or elsewhere in the New Testament suggests that the actions of baptism (going down into water and coming up out

---

1. See Morris, *The Epistle to the Romans*, 246 (although he does not exclude reference to
water baptism as well).
2. E.g., Martin Lloyd-Jones, *Romans: An Exposition of Chapter 6*.
3. See, e.g., Bruce, *The Letter of Paul to the Romans*, 129.

of it) have symbolic significance. Note too that Paul does not say we were buried "like" Christ; rather, we were buried "with him."

Most likely, then, Paul uses the verb "buried" because he is thinking of the way the Christian is identified with Christ in all of the major events of his redemptive work. In 1 Corinthians 15:3–4, Paul rehearses these basic redemptive events: "Christ died for our sins according to the Scriptures . . . he was buried . . . he was raised on the third day according to the Scriptures." We who believe have participated with Christ in each of these events: We died "with him" (Rom. 6:3, 5, 6, 8); we were buried "with him" (6:4); we will be raised "with him" (6:5, 8).[4] Baptism stands for our whole conversion experience. By it, we have been brought into union with Christ and the powerful events of his redemptive work. The effects of these events are therefore at work in us. That means we now have the ability to "live a new life" (6:4b).

Verse 5 states what Paul has implied in verse 4: Believers not only participate in Christ's death (so that we have died to sin), but also in his resurrection (so that we can live a new life). The NIV does not clearly bring out an interesting element in the Greek here: Paul speaks of the "likeness" or "form" (*homoioma*) of Christ's death and resurrection. Paul's purpose in using this word is debated, but probably he wants to suggest that Christ's death and resurrection have a certain nature that enables other people to participate in them.[5]

Paul uses a future tense to describe our participation in the resurrection: "We will . . . be united" (6:5). Since he here suggests that believers even now experience new life in Christ (vv. 4, 13), this future may be "logical"—that is, Paul may be saying that participation in Christ's resurrection always follows participation in his death (see Eph. 2:6; Col. 2:12).[6] But we prefer to think that the future is a genuine temporal future: While we do indeed now enjoy new life, our "being raised with Christ" awaits his Parousia.[7] Philippians 3:20–21 is particularly close to Paul's idea here: "But our citizenship is in heaven. And we eagerly await a Savior from there, the Lord Jesus Christ, who, by the power that enables him to bring everything under his control, will transform our lowly bodies so that they will be like his glorious body."

The Results of Dying with Christ (6:6–7)

ALTHOUGH MANY COMMENTATORS attach verse 6 to verse 5 (note in the NIV that verses 5–6 are set in the same paragraph break), we think a minor break

---

4. G. R. Beasley-Murray, *Baptism in the New Testament* (Grand Rapids: Eerdmans, 1962), 133.

5. The other uses of this word in Paul are equally contested; see Rom. 1:23; 5:14; 8:3; Phil. 2:7.

6. E.g., Godet, *Commentary on Romans*, 243–44; Cranfield, *The Epistle to the Romans*, 308.

7. Most commentators agree that the verb is true future.

occurs after verse 5. In verses 3—5 Paul has established the fact that believers participate in Jesus' death and resurrection. Now he elaborates each of these facts, the "death" side in verses 6—7 and the "life" side in verses 8—10.

In verse 6, Paul replaces the "we" of verses 3—5 with "the old self" or "old man" (Gk. *anthropos*) and death by crucifixion. Paul, of course, refers to crucifixion to emphasize our participation in Jesus' death itself (see also Gal. 2:20). Why he uses the phrase the "old self" is not clear. Many interpreters think that the "old self" refers to the old, sinful nature that believers get rid of when they come to Christ. But this is probably not accurate (see Contemporary Significance section). In light of Romans 5, the phrase is likely Paul's way of referring to what we were in Adam. As John R. W. Stott puts is, "what was crucified with Christ was not a part of me called my old nature, but the whole of me as I was before I was converted."[8]

Paul is especially concerned that we understand what follows from this action. The result is that the "body of sin [i.e., our bodies as dominated by sin] might be done away with." This NIV translation is a bit strong; the alternate reading, "rendered powerless," better suits this verb.[9] What Paul is saying is that our identification with Christ means we are no longer dominated by sin. The purpose is that "we should no longer be slaves to sin." Since sin's power over us has been broken, we should reflect that new freedom in the way we live. Sin should no longer characterize us. Verse 7 backs up what Paul claims in verse 6 by reminding his readers of a fairly widespread ancient proverb to the effect that "death severs the hold of sin on a person."

The Results of Being Raised with Christ (6:8—10)

IN VERSE 8, Paul shows that living with Christ automatically follows dying with him. The one always includes the other. As in verse 5, many interpreters think that living with Christ is something a believer has already experienced. But the future tense again more likely refers to that coming Day when believers will be bodily raised with Christ. But while our bodily resurrection lies in the future, we enjoy even now the benefits of Christ's resurrection.

In verse 9 Paul explains just what Christ's own resurrection means: He now lives in a state in which death is no longer possible and has no power over him. He has conquered death and, Paul implies, we who belong to him also have the assurance of conquering death.

---

8. John R. W. Stott, *Men Made New: An Exposition of Romans 5—8* (London: Inter-Varsity, 1966), 45.

9. The verb is *katargeo*, which is distinctly Pauline in the New Testament (25 of its 26 New Testament occurrences are in Paul). For parallels to his usage here, see esp. Rom. 3:31; 4:14; 7:2, 6; Gal. 3:17; 5:4; Eph. 2:15.

Paul returns to his main point in verse 10, which functions as kind of a "bottom line" for much of what he has argued in this paragraph. When Christ himself died, he "died to sin"; in his having come to life, he now lives "to God." The claim that Christ "died to sin" is difficult, for Paul has used this language in verse 2 of sinful people who need to be rescued from sin's domination. Why would Christ, the sinless one, have to "die to sin"? Thus, some interpreters think that death to sin in this verse refers to his atoning work: He "affected sin" by dying, bearing the penalty of sin for us all.[10]

But it is better to refer the striking language of "death to sin" to the same thing throughout this passage if we can. True, Jesus was not held under sin's power in a way that turned him into a sinner. But as a result of his real identification with human beings, he was subject to the power of sin. He was therefore tempted as we are (Heb. 2:14–17). In this sense, he, too, needed to "die" to sin's power. We can, therefore, maintain the general parallelism between Christ's death and ours with him. Similarly, Paul does not imply that Christ ever lived without seeking God's good and glory. But his resurrection gave him new power to carry out God's will and purposes.

Putting Our New Status into Action (6:11–14)

THE GENERAL STRUCTURE of 6:1–14 reflects a common pattern in Paul: What God has done for us is the basis and stimulus for what we need to do for God. The "indicative" mode, in which Paul tells us of the wonderful redemptive events, leads to the "imperative," telling us how we are to respond to those events. But verse 11 suggests an intermediate step between these two: coming to grips with the truth of what Paul has been teaching. Only by constantly (the Greek verb is in the present tense) looking at ourselves as people who really have died to sin and been made alive in Christ will we be able to live out the new status God has given us. Since Paul himself uses the imagery of the slave, we may use the analogy of a newly freed slave after the Civil War in America. That slave would know in a certain sense that he or she was liberated, but it might take some time for this truth to penetrate the consciousness in a way that led to changes in behavior.

In verses 12–13, Paul moves into the realm of action. He begins with the negative: We must not let sin "reign" in our lives. Some interpreters think the Greek construction Paul uses means "*stop* letting sin reign,"[11] but this is probably not the case.[12] The command is simply, "Don't let sin reign."

---

10. See, e.g., Cranfield, *The Epistle to the Romans*, 313–14.

11. E.g., Godet, *Commentary on Romans*, 250; Cranfield, *The Epistle to the Romans*, 316.

12. The construction of *me* with the present tense that we find here does not always, or even normally, connote the idea of ceasing an action already engaged in (see esp. J. Louw, "On Greek Prohibitions," *Acta Classica* 2 [1959]: 43–57).

Here we are faced with the tension between the indicative and the imperative. Paul claims in verse 14 that sin is no longer our master—in effect, sin does not reign. Yet this does not prevent him from commanding us not to let sin reign. Sorting out the exact relationship of these ideas is not easy. But this much can be said: The victory over sin that God has won for us in Christ is a victory that must be appropriated. Putting away those sins that plague us will be no automatic process, something that will happen without our cooperation. No, Paul insists, a determination of our own will is called for to turn what has happened in principle into actuality.

Verse 13 makes the same point in a different way. With the words "instruments" and "parts of your body," Paul brings before us a picture of all our varied capacities and abilities, which we are to withdraw from the use of our master sin and place at the disposal of our new master, God. It is "righteousness," that standard of right behavior God reveals to us, that we are now to serve.

Just in case we become overbalanced toward the imperative side, Paul concludes with one more reminder of the "indicative": "Sin shall not be your master." The verb here is *kyrieuo*, from the same root as the word *kyrios*, "Lord." By putting the basic point he has made earlier (v. 6) in the form of a promise, Paul emphasizes that our freedom from sin's power is a continuing state we can look forward to enjoying forever. Why is this? "Because you are not under law, but under grace."

These words are often quoted as almost a slogan apart from their context, but we must determine what Paul intends them to mean here. One popular view can be eliminated immediately: Paul is not saying that Christians have no commandments for which they are responsible. This view depends on taking "law" in a broad sense to mean any law, or "law" in general. But, as is usually the case in Paul, "law" (*nomos*) refers to the Mosaic law. Other interpreters think that "under law" means under the condemnation pronounced by the law, and "under grace" means the freedom from condemnation experienced by those who enjoy God's grace.[13] But there seems to be no good reason for adding the nuance "condemnation" here.

Most likely Paul refers generally to the fact that believers no longer live under the domination of the Mosaic law. Because we stand under the new covenant, the law of the old covenant no longer has direct control over us. The contrast between "law" and "grace," then, is a salvation-historical contrast: The Mosaic law dominates the old regime from which we have been set free in Christ; grace dominates the new regime inaugurated by Jesus.[14]

---

13. See, e.g., Calvin, *Epistle of Paul to the Romans*, 233; Murray, *The Epistle to the Romans*, 1:229; Cranfield, *The Epistle to the Romans*, 319–20.

14. So also Schreiner, *Romans*, 326–27.

We find the same basic contrast in the famous John 1:17 passage: "For the law was given through Moses; grace and truth came through Jesus Christ." Paul has presented the Mosaic law as a power that leads to sinning (recall Rom. 5:20: "The law was added so that the trespass might increase"). In other words, for believers to be set free from the dominion of sin (6:14a), they need also to be set free from the dominion of the law.[15]

THOUGHTS ON BAPTISM. Romans 6:1–14 is rich in theology and practical insight. Our understanding of the Christian life owes much to this text. Yet one of the most controversial elements in this passage is mentioned only in passing: baptism (vv. 3–4). The debate surrounding the significance of baptism in these verses affords a classic example of the way our reading of the New Testament is affected by our own background and theology. In the Bridging Contexts sections in this commentary we have often focused on the first-century context. But, as the word "bridging" and the plural "contexts" indicates, this section must tackle not only the context of the writers but also the context of the readers of the New Testament.

As postmodernism has emphasized (to an extreme and unnecessary degree at times), every reader brings his or her own context to a text. Each of us reads the New Testament out of our own situation—children of certain parents, members of a certain church, adherents of a particular theology. We cannot, of course, escape our context, but we can recognize what it is and allow for it as we read the New Testament so that we do not simply read our own biases into the text. The significance of baptism in 6:3–4 is a classic case in point. Establishing the first-century context by getting some idea of the general New Testament teaching on baptism is necessary if we are to interpret these verses accurately. Yet even before we turn to the first-century context, we need to consider briefly the "contexts" each of us brings to our reading of the passage.

Baptism has been, and still is, a controversial issue among Christians. Many of us have strongly held beliefs on baptism, often established in deliberate distinction to the views of other Christians. My own spiritual pilgrimage reflects a common pattern in the understanding of baptism. I was baptized as an infant in the Lutheran church in which I was raised. My later confirmation class presented the truth of the gospel clearly, but it did not really

---

15. We discuss the whole matter of the Christian and the law in more detail in conjunction with 7:1–6.

come home to me. I was confirmed anyway and assumed that the spiritual side of my life was taken care of. But almost a decade later I realized that this was not the case. Through campus friends, the Spirit made clear that I did not really have a relationship with God and that I could only find such a relationship by committing myself personally to Jesus Christ.

My own spiritual obduracy was no doubt much at fault for my failure to understand this personal dimension of Christian faith as I was growing up. But I also blamed the Lutheran church for failing to make this as clear as it might have been. A key focus of my blame was the impression I was given that the rites of baptism, confirmation, and Communion provided for all my spiritual needs. Thus, when I truly came to know Christ in college, I was baptized, convinced that my infant baptism had no value at all. In getting to know thousands of students at my seminary over the last twenty-five years and in interviewing applicants for membership in my local church, I have heard this kind of story again and again.

The point, then, is this: There exists among evangelical Christians a strong bias against any hint of sacramentalism. Too much emphasis on rites such as baptism and the Lord's Supper can undercut the paramount need for a personal and meaningful engagement with God in Christ. Baptism is to be administered only to people who have come to faith, and it is only a symbol. What happens, then, when we bring this kind of background to our reading of Romans 6? We tend to do all we can to minimize baptism. We desperately try to keep water out of the passage. We interpret "baptism" as a metaphor for an overwhelming experience or as shorthand for "baptism in the Spirit."

If water cannot absolutely be excluded, we make sure to confine its significance to the realm of the symbolic. Baptism, so the popular teaching goes, is a picture of our conversion. As we go down under the water, we symbolize our death to the old life; when we emerge again from the water, we symbolize our entrance into the new life of Christ. In baptism, therefore, we act out experiences that Christ went through: As he died, was buried, and was raised, so we, in baptism, do the same things.

But there is another side to our current context we must consider. While the dominant move among evangelicals has been away from sacramental ideas, the opposite current, growing recently, is also evident: Evangelicals who grew up in nonsacramental traditions have come to think that baptism and the Lord's Supper are far more important than they used to think. Such Christians, who may attend Lutheran or Episcopal churches, have a vested interest in finding as much water as possible in Romans 6 and in general giving to baptism an important role in Christian experience. I am not myself among their number. But I now think that I overreacted against my sacramental upbringing in the enthusiasm of my postconversion joy.

Thus, along with every other reader of Romans 6, I bring certain baggage to this text. We need to recognize that baggage and not to let it determine our interpretation. The more radical postmodern thinkers are convinced that we cannot do it; as a result, what we get out of Romans 6 will be exactly what we bring to it ("reader-response"). I am more optimistic about our ability to be objective about the meaning of texts—particularly when we engage in discussion with people from other perspectives and when we ask the Holy Spirit to keep us from error. Whether I have succeeded in being objective is a question you all will have to answer as you consider what I say regarding this text. But let me reiterate briefly why I do not think we can keep water out of the passage or confine baptism to a symbol only.

Consider carefully the wording of verse 4a: "We were therefore buried with him through baptism into death. . . ." Note these three points. (1) *Baptisma,* the word used here, almost always denotes water baptism (see Matt. 3:7; 21:25; Mark 1:4; 10:38, 39; 11:30; Luke 3:3; 7:29; 12:50; 20:4; Acts 1:22; 10:37; 13:24; 18:25; 19:3, 4; Rom. 6:4; Eph. 4:5; 1 Peter 3:21).[16] (2) Baptism does not *symbolize* our being buried with Christ; it is the *means* "through" which we were identified with him. (3) We are not buried *as* Christ was buried; we are buried *with* Christ. It seems to me, therefore, that we cannot escape the conclusion that Paul presents water baptism here as the means by which we are brought into relationship with Christ. My sense that baptism in Romans 6 is more important than many evangelicals have recognized is confirmed by other texts that move in the same direction (see esp. Acts 2:38; 8:36, 38; Col. 2:12; 1 Peter 3:21).

Does Romans 6, then, teach a full-blown sacramental view of baptism? Many interpreters think so: In baptism, God acts by grace to bring people into relationship with himself. But two things make me wary of going that far. (1) Paul himself does not make baptism a prominent part of his own ministry: "Christ did not send me to baptize, but to preach the gospel—not with words of human wisdom, lest the cross of Christ be emptied of its power" (1 Cor. 1:17). (2) Paul has to this point in Romans highlighted the personal decision of faith as the critical means by which we get into relationship with God. Baptism is mentioned, in passing, in only these two verses.

At this point, then, we need to look carefully at the other "context": the New Testament teaching on baptism. Although the issue is debated, the

---

16. Only in Mark 10:38—39 (parallel Luke 12:50) does *baptisma* not refer to immersion in water. Even here, however, Jesus' application of this term to his death rests on his own water baptism as his point of identification with sinful people (see Douglas J. Moo, *The Old Testament in the Gospel Passion Narratives* [Sheffield: Almond, 1983], 116–20). On *baptisma,* see esp. J. Ysebart, *Greek Baptismal Terminology: Its Origin and Early Development* (Nijmegen: Dekker & van de Vegt, 1962), 51–53.

studies of James Dunn have convinced me of one critical point: The New Testament presents water baptism as one component of a larger experience, which Dunn calls "conversion-initiation."[17] Faith, repentance, water baptism, and the gift of the Holy Spirit are the four key elements of this "coming to Christ" experience.

What is especially important for our understanding of Romans 6 is that New Testament authors can refer to one of these elements and presume the others. We can therefore explain why Luke uses such a variety of expressions to describe people who come to Christ in the book of Acts: faith (Acts 14:1; 15:11; 16:1), repentance (3:19; 17:30; 26:20), repentance, water baptism, and the gift of the Spirit (2:38), and the gift of the Spirit and water baptism (10:45–48; 19:2–7). This broader New Testament context gives us the right to presume that when Paul refers to baptism in Romans 6:3–4, he intends to include faith, repentance, and the gift of the Spirit.

Baptism for Paul and the other New Testament writers had significance only as one part of a larger experience. It set the seal on one's conversion. Therefore, baptism in Romans 6 stands, by synecdoche, for the entire conversion experience. One gets into relationship with God not by baptism in itself but by conversion, of which baptism is one key element.

 THE SIGNIFICANCE OF BAPTISM. Thus far, we have given only superficial consideration to a complex subject. Clearly, we are in no position to draw sweeping conclusions about the meaning of baptism. But at the risk of outrunning our exegetical data, let me venture three suggestions.

(1) Many evangelicals must give more attention to a theology of baptism. For reasons outlined above, many of us are suspicious of baptism. We worry that people will think they can become Christians (or make their children into Christians) simply by going through an external rite. I can appreciate the concern. Many churches present baptism in such a light, and we are right to fear the deadening influence of an external sacramentalism on evangelism, Christian experience, and the life of the church.

But a concern about an excess in one direction does not justify an excess in the other. I have attended churches in which baptism is rarely mentioned.

---

17. James D. G. Dunn, *Baptism in the Holy Spirit* (London: SCM, 1970), 145, etc. See also D. A. Tappeiner, "Hermeneutics, the Analogy of Faith and New Testament Sacramental Realism," *EvQ* 49 (1977): 40–52. My own view on baptism has also been influenced strongly by the fine study of G. R. Beasley-Murray, *Baptism in the New Testament* (New York: Macmillan, 1962).

More often, churches practice or even emphasize baptism but give no explanation for why it is done. Christ commanded us to do it, so we do it. But we really have no idea—or so we imply—why we are doing it. The evangelical church as a whole is marked by a poverty of any kind of theology of baptism and the Lord's Supper. To be sure, there is some reason for this. The New Testament says little explicitly about baptism; its significance has to be teased out from indirect references and broad theological perspectives. But we who are Christian theologians, pastors, and leaders owe it to the church to develop a biblical and coherent explanation of baptism.

(2) If I am right about Romans 6, baptism is an important part of the conversion experience. To use biblical imagery, it sets a seal on that experience. Thus, baptism in water should probably be administered to a person as shortly after that person's coming to faith in Christ as possible. Acts 8 is instructive in this regard. After bringing the Ethiopian court official to faith, Philip does not enroll him in a series of baptismal classes; he baptizes him, out in the middle of the desert, right on the spot (Acts 8:36–38).

Of course, we often have good reason to delay baptism after conversion. In the modern church, logistics can play a role: We have to wait for the baptismal tank to be filled. There are theological concerns as well: New converts, we think, need to understand their baptism before experiencing it. What we practice will be the reflection of our theology. The more we emphasize the symbolic value of baptism, the more its efficacy will depend on the ability of the person being baptized to understand it. Thus, we feel some degree of instruction is important.

But if we think that baptism focuses on something God is doing for us, then our ability to understand what is happening is not as crucial. God will work however little or much we understand. Of course, we do not want simply to go through the rite without any concern at all about whether people understand it. But instruction is less important.

(3) Another vexing issue arises here: How about children? Should very young children be baptized if we think they are genuinely converted? A blanket conclusion is out of order. Too many specific factors make every situation different. For instance, many children will want to be baptized because their parents are pressuring them to do so or because they want to do what other children their age are doing. Careful and wise evaluation of each child's spiritual condition and motivations is obviously needed. But my own belief is that, where circumstances permit, children who are genuinely converted should be baptized.

In sketching briefly my own spiritual pilgrimage in the Bridging Contexts section, I mentioned I was baptized shortly after being converted in college. This was no accident: I became involved after my conversion in a church that insisted a person had to be baptized in order to be saved. I have often dialogued with pastors and theologians who hold this perspective over the years (hearing my views, they apparently think I am a "kindred spirit"!). I respect their view and understand their logic. But I think they have gone beyond the evidence.

To be sure, I have argued that water baptism is part of the conversion experience. But "experience" is an important word. When one asks Paul what a person must do to be a Christian, his answer is clear: believe in the Lord Jesus. God responds to our faith (which, rightly understood, includes repentance) with the gift of his Spirit. A person is a Christian, destined for salvation (see Rom. 5:9–10) from that point on. Water baptism should then follow. It is always dangerous to put words into the mouth of a scriptural author, but I think if Paul had ever been asked about an "unbaptized believer," he would have responded: "Well, yes, such a person is saved; but why in the world isn't she baptized?"

"Old self"/"new self." In verse 6 Paul proclaims that "our old self [has been] crucified with [Christ]." This verse, along with several others in which Paul uses similar imagery (Eph. 4:22–24; Col. 3:9–11), has been the basis for some popular views of the Christian life. I want briefly to sketch two popular options and then comment on them in light of Romans 6.

A particularly widespread view, taught by some theologians and by one of the most effective campus ministries, is the "two-nature" approach. What Paul teaches here is that the believer's old "sin nature" is dealt a deathblow at conversion. That nature still exists but is no longer dominant, for the believer also possesses a new nature. Progress in the Christian life comes as one uses spiritual disciplines to foster the growth of the new nature and the gradual diminution of the old.

At the other extreme is what we might call the "new creation" view. This language comes from 2 Corinthians 5:17, one of the key texts used to support this view: "Therefore, if anyone is in Christ, he is a new creation; the old has gone, the new has come!" Adherents of this approach claim that the first view does not do justice to Romans 6:6. For Paul claims here that the "old self" has been crucified—not just reduced in power, but actually put to death. When a person comes to Christ, that "old self" is done away with; what is left is the "new self." Progress in the Christian life comes, then, not by way of struggle (as adherents of this view think the first view teaches) but by "letting go and letting God" do the work. Since we are a "new creation," all we need to do is let our new, "natural" person take over. We will automatically do what pleases God.

In trying to present the differences in these two views, I am no doubt guilty of some caricature. Many thoughtful adherents of each of these perspectives will protest that their own position is far more nuanced than I have suggested. Nevertheless, I have certainly read books and heard sermons and lectures that presented these views pretty much as I have described them. The question to ask here is which of these views does justice to Romans 6:6 and other passages about "old self"/"new self." My answer? Neither. For what both views assume is that "old self" has a kind of "ontological" meaning: Either it refers to one part of ourselves or our whole being.

What I suggest is that "old self" is a relational and corporate concept. It does not refer to a part of us or to a nature within us. Rather, it is Paul's way of describing our sinful condition as children of Adam. What is crucified, then, is that relationship. Our tie to Adam is dissolved; he and the sin and death he represents no longer dictate terms to us. Moreover, if the "old self" is Adam as corporate head of the human race, then the "new self" is Christ, corporate head of the church.

That this thinking is on the right track is suggested by the way Paul can use "new self" language to describe Christ (Eph. 4:13) and the Christian community (Eph. 2:15; Col. 3:10—11). Progress in the Christian life will come as we learn to live out the new relationship God has put us in. We belong to a new corporate structure or regime, dominated by Christ and not by Adam. That new relationship provides, in principle, for all the power we need to stop sinning and to live to God's glory.

What some of the traditional options have missed, then, is the corporate and relational nature of Paul's concept of salvation and the Christian life. In Romans 5—8 especially Paul uses a contrast in two eras or regimes to picture the difference between life outside of Christ and life in Christ. God, to be sure, is at work to change us from within, as Paul will show in chapter 8 in talking about the work of the Holy Spirit. But at this point the governing idea is not that God changes us inside, but that he moves us from one regime to another. In dying to sin, we have a new position with respect to sin. It no longer rules over us and dictates our conduct. Our "old self," in other words, has been crucified; our Adamic servitude has been decisively and irreversibly ended.

I know of no better illustration for the overall idea Paul presents in Romans 6 than Martin Lloyd-Jones's analogy of the two fields. He asks us to consider a typical British country scene, with two fields enclosed by high rock walls. Every person begins life in one of those fields—a field ruled over by Satan and sin. We have no chance of scaling the walls and escaping the field on our own. But God, in his grace, reaches down and takes us out of that Satan-dominated field and sets us down in the adjacent field—a field ruled by Christ and by righteousness. A decisive change in our position has taken place— we are in whole new relationship to sin.

However, as Lloyd-Jones points out, we can still hear Satan calling across the wall from that old field where we used to live. Out of long habit, we sometimes still obey his voice, even though we don't have to. This captures well the combination of decisive change in status along with continuing openness to sin that marks Paul's teaching in Romans 6. If I may extend the illustration, we overcome sin by moving further and further away from the wall dividing the fields so that the voice of Satan grows fainter.

Romans 6:15–23

WHAT THEN? SHALL we sin because we are not under law but under grace? By no means! ¹⁶Don't you know that when you offer yourselves to someone to obey him as slaves, you are slaves to the one whom you obey—whether you are slaves to sin, which leads to death, or to obedience, which leads to righteousness? ¹⁷But thanks be to God that, though you used to be slaves to sin, you whole-heartedly obeyed the form of teaching to which you were entrusted. ¹⁸You have been set free from sin and have become slaves to righteousness.

¹⁹I put this in human terms because you are weak in your natural selves. Just as you used to offer the parts of your body in slavery to impurity and to ever-increasing wickedness, so now offer them in slavery to righteousness leading to holiness. ²⁰When you were slaves to sin, you were free from the control of righteousness. ²¹What benefit did you reap at that time from the things you are now ashamed of? Those things result in death! ²²But now that you have been set free from sin and have become slaves to God, the benefit you reap leads to holiness, and the result is eternal life. ²³For the wages of sin is death, but the gift of God is eternal life in Christ Jesus our Lord.

PAUL CARRIES FORTH the theme of 6:1–14 in this section. He continues to proclaim that believers are set free from sin (vv. 18, 22). But the emphasis shifts slightly. Whereas freedom was the dominant motif in verses 1–14, slavery now takes center stage. Paul uses this imagery both to remind us of what our state used to be ("slaves to sin," vv. 17, 20) and to encourage us to recognize what we have now become in Christ ("slaves to righteousness," v. 18; "slaves to God," v. 22). This paragraph focuses, therefore, on the transfer from one state of slavery to another and the implications that ensue from that transfer.

As he did in 6:1, Paul asks and responds to a rhetorical question about the continuing state of sinfulness to set up the argument of the paragraph (vv. 15–16). Dominating the paragraph structurally are two of his beloved "once"/"but now" contrasts: verses 17–18 and 20–23. In verse 19 the apostle turns to the imperative mode to set out the response that believers should make to the transfer of power he describes in these two contrasts. God has given us a new master, and we must now obey that master.

The questions that open the two main sections in Romans 6 reveal the common theme Paul pursues: "Shall we go on sinning so that grace may increase?" (v. 1); "Shall we sin because we are not under law but under grace?" (v. 15). As the former question is sparked by what Paul said in 5:20 about the power of grace, so the question in 6:15 is stimulated by what he has just said at the end of verse 14. Proclaiming that believers have been transferred from the regime of the Mosaic law to the regime of grace may lead some Christians to think that sin does not matter. Indeed, the danger that believers will "presume on grace" and not pursue a life of obedience to the Lord is an ever-present danger in the Christian church.

Paul usually uses the introductory phrase "don't you know" (v. 16) to cite a fact that his readers already know. In this case, they will recognize what Paul says as a proverbial truth: When we habitually "offer" ourselves to someone, we become a slave of that to which we offer ourselves. Sin, then, is a serious matter. Though set free from it, we can in effect become its slaves again if we give ourselves to it.

Paul heightens the seriousness of the issue at the end of verse 16 by making it clear that we are ultimately confronted with a choice of only two masters to serve: sin and obedience. We would expect the contrast with sin to be righteousness or God (see vv. 18, 20–21). But Paul obviously wants to hammer home the importance of obedience, so he uses this word in a positive sense to denote the Christian moral demand. Serving sin leads to death, but serving obedience "leads to righteousness." Some interpreters think that "righteousness" here has forensic flavor and refers to vindication at the judgment (see "life" in vv. 22, 23).[1] But Paul is obviously using *dikaio-* language in a different nuance here from what he did in chapters 1–4. In keeping with Old Testament and Jewish usage, righteousness has a moral sense: conduct pleasing to God.[2]

From what Paul has said so far, we may assume that we stand in a state of neutrality with respect to the choice of serving "sin" or "obedience." So, elaborating the theme of 6:1–10, Paul now reminds us that this is certainly not the case. "Thanks ... to God," believers have left slavery to sin and have "wholeheartedly obeyed the form of teaching to which [they] were entrusted."

---

1. E.g., Cranfield, *The Epistle to the Romans,* 322.
2. See, e.g., Godet, *Commentary on Romans,* 255.

Two elements in this assertion require comment. (1) Why does Paul say *"form* of teaching"? It is unlikely that he is thinking of a certain form of Christian teaching as opposed to another form since he speaks so generally here. More likely he is contrasting the Christian pattern of teaching with the Jewish pattern (see 2:20).[3] Believers are not "under" the law of Moses (6:14–15), but they do have a pattern of teaching for which they are responsible.

(2) The other noteworthy feature of this sentence is the passive form of the verb: Believers have "been entrusted" or "been handed over" (*paradidomi,* the verb used in the Gospels of Jesus' being "handed over" to the Roman authorities [e.g., Matt. 26:15–16; 27:2]). Believers do not choose whether they will serve Christ as Lord or obey the teaching he has given us. God has already given us over to it.

Verse 18 goes on to summarize the "indicative" of the believer's transfer from one realm to another: from "sin" to "righteousness." The necessary moral implications of conversion to Christ are again made clear: We have been made "slaves" of that moral conduct God expects of his people (see comments on "righteousness" in v. 16).

Verse 19a is something of an aside, as Paul explains why he is using the imagery of slavery: "because you are weak in your natural selves." "Natural selves" translates *sarx* (lit., flesh), the word Paul customarily uses to describe the human condition apart from God. What he suggests, therefore, is that the limitations of our human understanding make it necessary for him to use imprecise, but still appropriate analogies.

Verse 19b is the center of this paragraph. A reminder of the new situation God has put us in comes just before it (vv. 17–18), and a further reminder of that same status comes immediately after it (vv. 20–23). But, as in 6:1–14, Paul does not want us to think that the "indicative" of God's act undermines or cancels the need for the "imperative" or our response. Using the same verb as he did in 6:13, Paul again appeals to us to "offer" (*paristemi*) all our capacities and abilities "in slavery to righteousness leading to holiness."

"Holiness" (*hagiasmos*) denotes either the *state* of holiness or the *process* of sanctification.[4] In either case, Paul sees our commitment to righteousness as resulting in God-likeness. In an interesting comparison, Paul suggests that our commitment to serve righteousness should be just as strong as our previous commitment to "impurity" and "wickedness." One thinks of the single-minded pursuit with which some people seek fame, money, or power. Our pursuit of righteousness and holiness should be just as dedicated.

---

3. Käsemann, *Commentary on Romans,* 181.

4. See, e.g., Murray, *The Epistle to the Romans,* 1:234–35, for the former, and Sanday and Headlam, *The Epistle to the Romans,* 169, for the latter.

The transfer from the realm of sin and death to the realm of righteousness and life (vv. 20–23) is the ground for the command in verse 19. (Verse 20 begins with a *gar* ["for"], not translated in the NIV.) Paul again contrasts the "when" of our pre-Christian past (vv. 20–21) with the "now" of our Christian present (vv. 22–23). Non-Christians often pride themselves on being free, in contrast to Christians, who in their estimation have lost their human autonomy by bowing the knee to Christ. Paul notes that non-Christians do, indeed, have a freedom—the freedom not to be able to lead righteous lives. Genuine autonomy is not an option. If one is not serving God, then, whether knowingly or not, one is serving sin.

To bring to our minds even more forcibly the negative side of our pre-Christian past, Paul reminds us of the shame we feel for what we used to do. Just how he makes this point in verse 21 is debated. The NIV suggests that Paul asks a rhetorical question implying the answer "none."[5] But it is preferable to follow here the punctuation adopted in, for instance, the NJB: "What did you gain from living like that? Experiences of which you are now ashamed, for that sort of behaviour ends in death."[6] The verse then matches the structure of verse 22 almost exactly:

	Status	*Result*	*Outcome*
Before we were Christians (v. 21):	slaves of sin, free from righteousness	fruit bringing shame	death
Now that we are Christians (v. 22):	free from sin, slaves of God	fruit bringing sanctification	life

Verse 23 not only explains the contrasting "outcomes" of death and life, but also brings the chapter to a fitting conclusion. That sin leads to death has been a background motif since 5:12. Only by remembering the dark side of life outside of Christ can we truly appreciate God's "gift" to us, the gift of his grace that brings "eternal life in Christ Jesus our Lord." As Lloyd-Jones points out, this verse makes three contrasts basic to Paul's teaching in this part of the letter:

the master that is served—sin versus God
the outcome of that service—death versus eternal life
how that outcome is reached—a "wage" earned versus
     a "gift" received.

---

5. For a defense, see, e.g., Murray, *The Epistle to the Romans*, 1:235–36.

6. The latest editions of the Greek New Testament adopt this punctuation; see esp. Cranfield, *The Epistle to the Romans*, 328.

Bridging Contexts

A TWO-REGIME FRAMEWORK. As we have been demonstrating, in Romans 5–8 Paul tries to make sense of Christian existence by using an overarching framework: the contrast between two regimes. Since this framework is basic to most of what Paul says in these chapters, we will easily misunderstand the specifics of what he says if we do not keep this framework in view.

Paul adapted his two-regime contrast from Jewish apocalyptic thinking. In this stream of Judaism, history was divided into two ages: "the present age," dominated by sin, Gentiles, and Satan; and "the age to come," when God will vindicate himself and his people, banish evil, and establish his eternal kingdom. We find remnants of this widespread Jewish conception throughout Paul's writings, as when he contrasts "the present age" and "the one to come" (Eph. 1:21) and speaks of "the rulers of this age" (1 Cor. 2:6, 8), "the god of this age" (2 Cor. 4:4), or "the present evil age" (Gal. 1:4).

But the apostle is forced by the circumstances of God's work in Christ to modify this scheme. For through Christ's death and resurrection, the "new age" has been inaugurated. Yet the present evil age does not come to an end, nor is the new age yet present in its full and final form. Evil and sin still exist, and believers are themselves not yet perfected. So Paul applies the scheme not only to salvation history but also to the individual experience of believers. In one sense, the change of ages took place when the redemptive work of Christ was finished. In another sense, the change of ages takes place only as individuals come to faith and appropriate the benefits of Christ's redemptive work. In other words, Paul applies his "two-age" contrast to both salvation history and individual history, and occasionally confusion can result from their overlap.

We find the evidence of this scheme throughout Romans 5–8, as Paul repeatedly contrasts the powers of the old age with those of the new age. But since Paul uses the motif of "rule" or "authority" more than the temporal category, we may speak more accurately of two "regimes":

The Old Regime	The New Regime
Adam	Christ
Sin	Righteousness; obedience
Death	Life
Law	Grace
Flesh	Spirit

Paul pictures the believer as one who has been transferred from the one regime to the other. We have been placed in a new situation, dominated by a new set of powers. But in keeping with New Testament eschatology, our domination by the new powers does not yet mean that we are rescued from any possible contamination from the old regime. That regime still exists, and through our continuing participation in this world, it can still affect us.

WHAT GOD GIVES versus what we do. Running as a constant motif through Romans 6 is the interplay between what we have several times called the "indicative" and the "imperative." In the former mode, Paul insists that God has himself accomplished our decisive break with sin: "We died to sin" (v. 2); "our old self was crucified with him" (v. 6); we are "dead to sin but alive to God" (v. 11); we "have been brought from death to life" (v. 13); "sin shall not be your master" (v. 14); "you have been set free from sin and have become slaves of righteousness" (v. 18); "you have been set free from sin and have become slaves to God" (v. 22).

But Paul regularly intersperses his indicatives with imperatives that make us responsible for winning the battle against sin: "Do not let sin reign" (v. 12); "do not offer the parts of your body to sin . . . but . . . offer yourselves to God" (v. 13); "offer [the parts of your body] in slavery to righteousness leading to holiness" (v. 19). The combination of these emphases presents both a theological and a practical problem.

The theological problem is to combine these two so that we can achieve a coherent picture and at the same time do justice to Paul's teachings on related topics. No theologian completely ignores one of these emphases or the other, but many focus on one side or the other. One popular option has been to isolate the two into separate compartments. This is the approach of the "liberal" theologians in the late 1800s and early 1900s, who emphasized the ethical teaching of the Bible at the expense of its "religious" teaching. What people did was severed from what they believed. At the other extreme are those who virtually subsume the imperative under the indicative. What God has done is so overwhelmingly powerful that Christian obedience becomes a kind of automatic response. It is almost as if God acts through us.

Most scholars recognize these two views as extreme and seek some way to integrate the indicative and imperative without dismissing either one. One thing is clear in Paul: The imperative grows out of the indicative. In Romans 6, for instance, Paul does not call on people to wage a war against sin with the hope that God will take their side and win the war for them. Throughout his teaching—and, indeed, throughout the Bible—God takes the initiative. In grace, he acts to help his people, and he asks them to respond. As the title of one of the most influential essays on this subject says, "Being Precedes Act."[7] Or, to use the phrase found throughout the literature: Christians are called to "become what they are."

At the same time, God's acts on our behalf are not finished. He has more things to give us and to accomplish in us. This means that we can also speak of "becoming what we will be." What God will one day make us should be a spur to getting as close to that ideal as possible.

While, then, it is clear that the imperative is based on this indicative, we must be careful not to separate the two, as if our obedience is the product of our own unaided effort. "Justification by faith and sanctification by struggle" is the slogan that has been coined to describe this kind of view of the Christian life. We must recognize that the grace and power of God that justified us continue to be at work to sanctify us. God expects us to obey him, but our very obedience is the product of his grace. The Puritan Jeremiah Bourroughs put it like this: "From him [Christ] as from a fountain, sanctification flows into the souls of the Saints: their sanctification comes not so much from their struggling, and endeavors, and vows, and resolutions, as it comes flowing to them from their union with him."[8] Or, to use the imagery of theologian Helmut Thielicke, believers are responsible to open their mouths so that they may drink from the river of sanctifying grace.

In the practical experience of living the Christian life, we find both extremes as well. The one extreme we call *moralism* or *legalism*. In its strict sense, legalism is the effort to gain salvation by our own efforts. While some religions tend toward legalism, it is seldom found, at least in its pure form, among Christians. But common is a softer "legalism": the belief, perhaps not even clearly articulated, that we can obey God by our own efforts or through our own program. Many well-intentioned believers fall into this trap, implicitly separating the indicative of God's grace from the moral effort of Christians so that the two are virtually unrelated. Self-help programs are a fad these days, and believers easily bring this human-centered perspective into their life of faith.

To guard against moralism we must root all of our obedience in those disciplines of the Christian life that put us in touch with God's own power: reading Scripture, worship, prayer. It is through these means that God has promised to communicate his grace to us. We must always evaluate our own personal as well as the church's programs of Christian living against this test:

---

7. Michael Parsons, "Being Precedes Act: Indicative and Imperative in Paul's Writing," *EvQ* 88 (1988): 99–127. This essay has been reprinted, along with an excellent selection of other essays on Paul's ethics, in *Understanding Paul's Ethics: Twentieth-Century Approaches*, ed. Brian S. Rosner (Grand Rapids: Eerdmans, 1995).

8. *Saints' Treasury* 46, quoted in E. F. Kevan, *The Grace of Law: A Study of Puritan Theology* (rpt.; Grand Rapids: Baker, 1976), 236.

Are they effective channels of God's grace? No program that does not pass this test will make any real or long-lasting change in the lives of believers.

At the opposite extreme from moralism is what we might call the *magical view* of the Christian life. Again, we find sincere and dedicated believers who fall into this trap. They write books and present seminars, all with the basic thrust that the key to the victorious Christian life is simply letting our new redeemed natures take their course. "Let go and let God" is the slogan. The indicative is given pride of place in this approach, and it is often attractively presented as an alternative to legalism or moralism.

But the magical view gives insufficient emphasis to the reality of the imperative. God commands us to act, and the very fact that Paul's letters are peppered with commands shows that obedience is not automatic. True, Jesus compared the believer to the tree that automatically produces good fruit. But, as one theologian has astutely noted, "people are not trees." Trees do not refuse the water that trickles down to their roots; they do not remove themselves from fertile soil to plant themselves in bad soil. People, yes even Christians, do these kinds of things.

Thus, we need to listen to and respond to the commands of Scripture. Particularly troublesome is the tendency of Christians to think that the indicative is all they need. If God has already given me "all things" in Christ (see Rom. 8:32), why do I need to bother to obey him? As we noted, Paul has already suggested (6:2) that no genuine Christian should ever think this way, for we no longer live in the realm of sin. But Paul goes on to make clear that our enjoyment of eternal life is contingent on our obedience (see 8:12–13). Paul agrees with James: Faith without works is dead; it cannot save (James 2:14–26).

Romans 7:1–6

D O YOU NOT know, brothers—for I am speaking to
men who know the law—that the law has authority
over a man only as long as he lives? [2]For example, by
law a married woman is bound to her husband as long as he is
alive, but if her husband dies, she is released from the law of
marriage. [3]So then, if she marries another man while her husband is still alive, she is called an adulteress. But if her husband dies, she is released from that law and is not an
adulteress, even though she marries another man.

[4]So, my brothers, you also died to the law through the
body of Christ, that you might belong to another, to him who
was raised from the dead, in order that we might bear fruit to
God. [5]For when we were controlled by the sinful nature, the
sinful passions aroused by the law were at work in our bodies,
so that we bore fruit for death. [6]But now, by dying to what
once bound us, we have been released from the law so that we
serve in the new way of the Spirit, and not in the old way of
the written code.

THE NEGATIVE EFFECT of the Mosaic law has been
a recurring motif in Romans. Paul has argued that
possession of the law did not improve Israel's situation before the Lord. For it is not possession
of the law but obedience that counts, and Israel failed to fulfill the law (2:12–
13, 17–24). As a result, the law is unable to justify a person (3:20, 28). In fact,
the overall impact of the law on Israel has been negative: It stirs up consciousness of sin (3:20), brings wrath (4:15), and increases trespass (5:20). If
Christians are to be free from sin, they must therefore also be taken out from
under the law's binding authority (6:14–15).

In 7:1–6 Paul gathers up these points into a section that directly addresses
the negative effects of the Mosaic law and its relationship to believers. Arising directly from the "not under law, but under grace" contrast of 6:14–15,
these verses assert that Christians have been set free from the binding authority of the Mosaic law (7:4, the center of the paragraph). Verses 1–3 lead up
to this central point with a general principle and illustration; verses 5–6 provide further explanation and elaboration.

Much of what Paul says in this paragraph parallels chapter 6: As believers "die to sin" (6:2) and are set free from it (6:6), so they "die to the law" (7:4) and are set free from it (7:6). As freedom from sin leads to serving God and producing fruit pleasing to him (6:18–22), so freedom from the law leads to serving "in the new way of the Spirit" (7:6) and producing "fruit to God" (7:4). These parallels may suggest that 6:15–7:6 is a single, two-staged, exposition of the new life that freedom from sin and the law produces.[1] But it is better to view chapters 6 and 7 as somewhat parallel arguments about the believer's relationship to two of the key powers of the old regime: sin and the Mosaic law.

This section begins with a general principle: "The law [*nomos*] has authority over a man only as long as he lives." Paul's "do you not know" formula suggests that this principle is one his readers are familiar with (see comments on 6:16).[2] Indeed, he claims to be speaking to "men who know the law." Some interpreters think Paul signals a shift in audience here. He has focused on all Christians in Rome in the letter thus far (see 1:7), but now turns to Jewish Christians, the ones who have intimate acquaintance with the Mosaic law.[3] Others suggest that *nomos* here refers to secular, Roman law, or to law as a general principle.[4]

But *nomos* refers to the Mosaic law throughout this context. This does not mean, however, that Paul addresses only Jewish Christians. Many of the Gentile Christians in Rome had probably been "God-fearers," that is, Gentiles sympathetic to Judaism but without becoming converts. They would have known the Mosaic law as well as Jewish Christians. Paul may well then be alluding to a maxim of the rabbis: "If a person is dead, he is free from the Torah and the fulfilling of the commandments."[5]

Verses 2–3 are sometimes taken as an allegorical illustration of verse 4. The woman whose husband dies, freeing her from the "law of marriage," is like the Christian who "dies to the law." As the death of her husband allows her to marry another man, so the Christian's death to the law allows him or her to "belong to another," Jesus Christ. But to make the allegory work, some juggling with the parallels has to be done. In the illustration it is the death of the husband that brings freedom, but in the application the believer, not the law (= the first husband), dies. Various more or less ingenious attempts to make the allegory work have been proposed, but it is simpler to think of

---

1. E.g., Morris, *The Epistle to the Romans*, 260.

2. The Greek is a bit different: a literal translation in 6:16 is "do you not know" (*ouk oidate*); here in 7:1 it is "or are you ignorant" (*e agnoeite*). This latter construction occurs only here and in 6:3 in Paul's letters (another minor agreement between the chapters).

3. See especially Minear, *The Obedience of Faith*, 62, 64.

4. E.g., Sanday and Headlam, *The Epistle to the Romans*, 172; Käsemann, *Commentary on Romans*, 187.

5. *b. Shabb.* 30a; *bar. Shabb.* 151.

verses 2–3 not as an allegory but as an illustration of the point of verse 1 with some application to verse 4. Paul simply wants to show that a death can indeed bring freedom from the law; at the same time, he hints that such freedom can also lead to a new relationship.

In verse 4, the heart of the paragraph, Paul draws an inference from verses 1–3: Believers have suffered a death in relationship to the law, a death that frees them from the law and enables them to enter into a new relationship. The imagery of dying to something means the same thing it did in 6:2, 10, namely, release from bondage. Believers have not only been released from bondage to sin, they have also been released from bondage to the Mosaic law. This release was accomplished through "the body of Christ"—probably a reference to Jesus' death on the cross.

Picking up imagery from the illustration in verses 2–3, Paul notes an important result of being released from the law: Believers are able to be joined to Christ. Paul assumes a person cannot be bound to the law and to Christ at the same time. As in 6:14–15, he is thinking of the Mosaic law as a power that rules over the old regime. If one lives under its absolute authority, one cannot at the same time belong to Christ. One must first be released from the law's authority and then one can be related to Christ.

What lies in the background of Paul's teaching is his salvation-historical conception. The era of the law has come to an end with the redemptive work of Christ. To be "under the law," then, means to be in that old era and to effectively deny that Christ, "the end of the law," has come (see the Contemporary Significance section for elaboration and application of this). Last in verse 4, but by no means least, is the purpose for which we are freed from the law and joined to Christ: so that we can "bear fruit to God." Practical works of service should flow from our new relationship.

In verses 5–6 Paul elaborates the salvation-historical background he has assumed in verse 4. We find here another of Paul's "when"/"but now" contrasts. He describes life in the old era or old regime in verse 5. Basic to that life was the fact that we were "controlled by the sinful nature." "Sinful nature" is the way the NIV translates Paul's use of the word *sarx* (lit., flesh) in a negative, ethical sense. This word is hard to bring over accurately into English (see Bridging Contexts section on 8:1–13). The apostle uses *sarx* in these contexts to denote human existence apart from God—it has almost the same sense as the "world" in John's writings. To be "in the flesh," then, is to live in a world bounded by this life and its concerns: to make decisions and behave without any regard for God or for the spiritual realm.

The results of this kind of life are obvious: "sinful passions" and "death." But, as Paul has insisted again and again in the letter, the law of Moses did not bring relief from the matrix of sin and death; instead, it made it worse. Those sinful passions, Paul claims, were "aroused by the law." As he will explain in verses 7–12, God's law arouses sin by stimulating rebellion. Thus, we can see why a person must be released from that law (v. 4) if he or she is to serve God.

This is precisely the situation in the new regime (v. 6): We have "died to what once bound us," and we have been "released from the law so that we serve in the new way of the Spirit, and not in the old way of the written code." "Written code" translates *gramma* (lit., letter). Paul has used the "letter"/"Spirit" contrast earlier in Romans (2:29), where, as we argued, *gramma* refers to the Mosaic law in contrast to the Holy Spirit. A few commentators want to give *gramma* a more nuanced meaning here, referring to the misuse of the law.[6] But the context shows that it must refer to the same thing that *nomos* refers to. Paul shifts to *gramma* because it more clearly connotes the "outward" nature of the Mosaic law. Written on stone tablets, the law of God cannot change the human heart; only God's Spirit can do that. Paul will develop this ministry of the Spirit in chapter 8.

INTERPRETING THE ILLUSTRATION **in verses 2–3.** In our comments on 3:21–26, we noted the danger of abusing analogies by squeezing more meaning out of them than the author intends. Paul's marriage analogy in verses 2–3 is a good illustration of this point. Readers of Romans have found more significance than Paul probably intended in two different ways.

(1) Some scholars, as we noted above, assume this illustration is an allegory. That is, Paul intends every detail to correspond with one of the theological points he makes in verse 4. As we also noted, this approach does not seem to work because the details of the illustration and its application do not correspond. But this difficulty has not dissuaded some interpreters from pursuing the allegorical approach. They are persuaded that a more nuanced understanding of verses 2–3 can maintain a close parallel with verse 4.

Many specific suggestions have been made. The most popular and certainly the most attractive is the one put forth by Godet. He considers the woman to stand for the "true self," the first husband for the "old man," and the second husband for "Christ." What dies, therefore, is our "old man," and because of its death the law no longer keeps us from entering a new relationship with Christ.[7] The problems with this interpretation are apparent. Nothing in the

---

6. See esp. Cranfield, *The Epistle to the Romans*, 339–40; Dunn, *Romans*, 366–67.

7. Godet, *Commentary on Romans*, 265. See also Sanday and Headlam, *The Epistle to the Romans*, 172–73.

text suggests that we should interpret the first husband as the "old man." In fact, this interpretation of verses 2–3 does not really match up well with verse 4, the text that verses 2–3 are designed to interpret. These interpretations, and others like them, are the product of a blind insistence that every detail in the illustration must have a theological counterpart. But illustrations and analogies rarely "walk on all fours" (see Bridging Contexts section of 3:21–26). To insist they must is to add to the text what the author has not put there.

(2) Another overinterpretation of this illustration is found more among laypeople than among scholars. In teaching Romans, I have found most people are not overly concerned with what Paul is teaching about the Mosaic law (which does not seem to be relevant to them). What they are interested in knowing is what verses 2–3 contribute to a biblical view of divorce and remarriage. Many insist that these verses prove that a remarriage on any other basis than the death of a spouse is adulterous. Whatever we think of the broader biblical teaching on this issue, these verses probably cannot be applied in this way. Paul is not concerned here to teach about marriage or divorce but is citing an example to prove a theological point.

With such a purpose, people often generalize about a situation in order to keep the analogy straightforward and simple. For instance, I have illustrated the internal basis of Paul's ethics by likening the Christian to an airliner, which is guided to its destination by an on-board computer. All of us recognize that many airplanes are not, in fact, computer-guided, because they are too old or too small, or because the electronic system has failed. But these many exceptions do not detract from the force of the analogy. So Paul may well recognize circumstances in which a woman might not be an "adulteress" if she were to marry while her husband is still alive. Certainly both Roman and Jewish law (which Paul refers to in v. 1) allowed for remarriage after a legitimate divorce.

Letter and Spirit. Though obscured by the NIV, the end of verse 6 contrasts "the letter" (*gramma*) and "the Spirit" (*pneuma*). The sense Paul gives this contrast—the Old Testament law versus the new covenant gift of the Spirit— can be difficult to perceive because of the history and contemporary use of this contrast. Christian theologians in the Middle Ages applied the contrast to different ways of reading the Old Testament. The *gramma* referred to the literal, surface meaning, the *pneuma* to the deeper or allegorical meaning. We use this pair of terms in a similar way in modern parlance, when we speak, for instance, of someone who may have disobeyed "the letter of the law" but respected its "spirit." It should be obvious that Paul gives little or no support to this application of the language in any of his uses of it (Rom. 2:29; 7:6; 2 Cor. 3:6–7). We need to put our modern use of the terminology to the side so that we can accurately understand what Paul means by it.

CHRISTIANS AND LAW. The central claim of 7:1–6 is that believers have been released from the law. What does this mean in practice?

(1) Paul is *not* teaching that Christians are no longer responsible to obey a set of commandments. Note that the law Paul refers to is the Mosaic law, the Torah. He consistently uses *nomos* with this reference throughout Romans; in 7:7 he even quotes one of the Ten Commandments to illustrate the law he is talking about. When Paul says that we are "not under law" (6:14–15) or that we have been "released from the law" (7:6), what he means is that we are no longer under a specific form of God's law, not that we are not under God's law at all.

According to 1 Corinthians 9:19–21, Paul views the law of Moses as a subset of the law of God generally. Believers may not be subject to the law of Moses; but, Paul implies in that text, we are subject to "the law of Christ." Most of us have heard of or seen these texts abused in the way we are warning about. Shortly after I became a Christian, I was involved in an extremist charismatic group on my college campus. Among other things, just about everyone in the group spoke in tongues at the same time in our public meetings—creating quite a Babel of sound! As a rather naive young believer, I questioned this practice at a meeting, citing Paul's command to the Corinthians that only one person should speak in a tongue at a time and someone should interpret. I was firmly put in my place and told that we are "not under the law but under the Spirit."

(2) Paul teaches that believers are still obliged to obey the commandments God has given them. He reminds the Corinthians that "keeping God's commands is what counts" (1 Cor. 7:19). He also says that he himself is "under Christ's law" (9:21). After proclaiming throughout Galatians that Christians are no longer under the Mosaic law, Paul warns them not to draw the wrong conclusions. God still expects believers to follow the command of love (Gal. 5:13–15) and to fulfill "the law of Christ" (6:2).

Just what this "law of Christ" might be is not clear from Paul's teaching. Some interpreters think it consists only in the example of Christ. Others think it is simply the command that we love our neighbors as ourselves. But the many commandments in Paul's own letters, along with the plural "commands" in 1 Corinthians 7:19, suggest a broader interpretation: the example of Jesus and the commands he and his apostles issue as a guide to the Spirit-filled life. As we will see in chapters 8 and 12, Paul stresses that Christian obedience is the reflection of the Spirit's work in transforming our minds and hearts. But commandments are needed to guide that transforming work. God has therefore given us in the New Testament specific commands to direct our conduct and to show us when we are straying from his moral will.

(3) A third matter arises inevitably from the first two points: What role does the Old Testament law have in this "law of Christ" that governs Christians? Perhaps the most popular answer among evangelical Christians stems from the Puritan tradition. Puritan theologians made a basic distinction between two different functions of the Mosaic law. On the one hand, it was a "covenant of works" that God established between himself and Israel. God gave Israel his law and demanded that they obey it; if they did not, they would die. On the other hand, the law functioned as a revelation of God's moral will.

Applying this distinction to Paul, the Puritans concluded that when Paul said that believers are no longer "under the law" or that we are released from it, he means that we are no longer under the law *as a covenant of works*. That is, the law no longer has power to condemn us for our sins. But we are still under the law as a revelation of God's moral will. To be sure, we need no longer obey the civil and ceremonial law, for those parts of the law have been fulfilled in Christ. But an important, indeed a basic, component of the "law of Christ" is the moral law of the Old Testament, manifested especially in the Ten Commandments.

A large swath of contemporary evangelicalism is the heir to this Puritan tradition. We may not use the same terminology they did, but the view of the Mosaic law is similar. This position, however, rests on two distinctions that are not as clear in Paul as we may think they are. The first is the distinction between the law as revelation of God's will and law as covenant of works, or, to phrase it another way, between the commanding function of the law and the condemning function of the law. Paul does not clearly distinguish these. In fact, in texts like 1 Corinthians 9:19–21, it is clear that not being "under the Mosaic law" means "not being under its commands," for the issue there has to do with the way Paul behaves. In other words, it is hard to maintain that being "under the law" in Romans 6:14–15 and being "released from the law" in 7:6 do not include the commanding element of the law.

Equally questionable is the time-honored distinction among the civil, ceremonial, and moral law. Some interpreters use these distinctions to argue, for instance, that Paul is claiming in 6:14–15 and 7:4, 6 only that believers are no longer obliged to obey the civil and/or ceremonial parts of the law. But Jews certainly did not divide up the law in this way, and evidence from the New Testament that early Christians did is slim.

We conclude, then, that we cannot restrict Paul's claim that believers have been "released from the law" to a certain function of the law or to certain parts of the law. The believer has been set free from the commanding authority of the Mosaic law—period. What this means in practice is that no part of the Old Testament law stands any longer as a direct and unmediated guide to Christian living. Like a person who is free from the laws of the state of Indiana because she has moved to Illinois, so Christians are free from the law of the old covenant because we now belong to the new covenant.

Does our freedom from the Old Testament law include even the Ten Commandments? Yes and no. Yes in the sense that those commandments as part of the Mosaic law no longer stand over us. But no in the sense that the teaching of nine of the ten commandments is explicitly taken up by New Testament authors and made part of the "law of Christ." (The one commandment that is not taken over is, of course, the Sabbath command.) What all this means in practice, then, is that we should look to the New Testament for those commandments that express God's moral will for us as new covenant Christians. Its teachings, properly interpreted, are to be obeyed. But this does not mean that we should no longer read the Old Testament law. It remains God's Word, given, as all Scripture, for our enlightenment (2 Tim. 3:16).

Moreover, although the new covenant believer does not stand directly under Old Testament law, that law itself serves an important function in helping us understand our obligations. New Testament teachings are informed by the Old Testament law. For instance, the New Testament prohibits *porneia*—unlawful sexual conduct. But what is included in such illegitimate sexual conduct? The New Testament writers never spell it out because the scope of this conduct has been defined clearly in the Old Testament law. Thus, we continue to read the Old Testament law as a guide to our interpretation of New Testament law.[8]

---

8. For elaboration of this view, with response from scholars holding different views, see *The Law, the Gospel, and the Modern Christian: Five Views*, ed. Wayne Strickland (Grand Rapids: Zondervan, 1993).

Romans 7:7–12

W HAT SHALL WE say, then? Is the law sin? Certainly not! Indeed I would not have known what sin was except through the law. For I would not have known what coveting really was if the law had not said, "Do not covet." ⁸But sin, seizing the opportunity afforded by the commandment, produced in me every kind of covetous desire. For apart from law, sin is dead. ⁹Once I was alive apart from law; but when the commandment came, sin sprang to life and I died. ¹⁰I found that the very commandment that was intended to bring life actually brought death. ¹¹For sin, seizing the opportunity afforded by the commandment, deceived me, and through the commandment put me to death. ¹²So then, the law is holy, and the commandment is holy, righteous and good.

PAUL'S NEGATIVE EVALUATION of the effect of the Mosaic law reaches its crescendo in 7:1–6. He accuses the law of arousing sin (v. 5) and of keeping those who are under its authority from coming to know Christ (v. 4) or experiencing the new life of the Spirit (v. 6). The believer's release from the power of the law is just as much good news as her release from the power of sin (ch. 6). No wonder, then, that Paul asks, "Is the law sin?"

Paul again anticipates the direction that readers of Romans will take his argument and seeks to head them off from drawing what might seem the logical conclusion. "Certainly not!" he responds; rather, "the law is holy, and the commandment is holy, righteous and good" (v. 12). The law may have had a disastrous effect, but the fault is not the law's. The fault, as Paul explains in 7:7b–11, is sin, which uses God's good law to bring death.

"What shall we say, then?" resumes the dialogical style of chapter 6 (cf. 6:1, 15). As he did there, Paul anticipates a key objection to his presentation of the gospel. For he seems to imply in verses like 5:20 and 7:5 that the law is an evil thing. But if this were really his view, he would forfeit any claim that the gospel is the fulfillment of the Old Testament. As some of the later Gnostics did, the Old Testament would be severed from the New and the God of Israel from the God of Jesus Christ; the gospel would replace, not fulfill, the Old Testament.

Thus, Paul resolutely denies any such idea, restating the point positively in 7:12. This does not mean, however, that he is retreating from what he said about the negative effects of the law. The word translated "indeed" in the NIV in verse 7 is *alla*—an adversative conjunction with the sense "though indeed": "No, the law is not sin, although it is indeed true that the law and sin are related." What is this relationship?

Paul claims he came to "know" sin through the law and uses the tenth commandment to illustrate: "I would not have known what coveting really was if the law had not said, 'Do not covet.'" Paul's coming to know sin might mean that he came to know what sin was—the law *defined* it for him. But Paul usually uses the verb "know" (both *ginosko* and *oida* are used here) with a simple direct object to mean "come to understand" or even "experience." The latter meaning is illustrated in 2 Corinthians 5:21, where he says that Jesus did not *know* sin, while Romans 11:34, "Who has *known* the mind of the Lord?" illustrates the former. This "come to understand" meaning is the more common in Paul and is probably intended here. The Mosaic law helped him come to understand clearly the extent and seriousness of his sin.

Why does Paul quote this particular prohibition? The verb he uses is *epithymeo*, the Greek word for "desire." Some interpreters think it has a sexual connotation here and that Paul is referring to his own personal experience of awakening to sinfulness at the time of puberty.[1] But Paul rarely confines "desire" to the sexual sphere. Rather, in keeping with Jewish tradition, he gives an abbreviated citation of the tenth commandment (Ex. 20:17; Deut. 5:21) as a fit summary of the Mosaic law as a whole.[2]

In the first sentence in verse 8, Paul takes the argument one step further. Not only did he come to understand sin through the law; he also was led into greater sinning through that same law. Just how this happened Paul does not explain. But he probably has in mind the power of a definite prohibition to stimulate in sinful people a rebellious reaction. Told not to do something, we desire all the more to do it. Thus, paradoxically, the very prohibition of a sin leads to even more of that same sin. In this way, Paul says, sin uses the law as an "opportunity" or bridgehead (*aphorme*; cf. also 7:11; 2 Cor. 5:12; 11:12; Gal. 5:13; 1 Tim. 5:14) to accomplish its purposes in people. Note how Paul continues to picture sin as a power.

---

1. See esp. Robert H. Gundry, "The Moral Frustration of Paul before His Conversion: Sexual Lust in Romans 7:7–25," in *Pauline Studies: Essays Presented to Professor F. F. Bruce on His 70th Bithday*, ed. Donald A. Hagner and Murray J. Harris (Grand Rapids: Eerdmans, 1980), 232–33.

2. Both Philo (*Decalogue* 142–43, 173) and the author of 4 Maccabees (2:6) use the tenth commandment to summarize the Mosaic law.

Until now, we have avoided identifying the experience Paul is describing. But what he describes in verses 8b–10a requires us to deal with this controversial question. The law became a bridgehead for sin by portraying the contrasting fates of "I" and "sin":

"apart from law"	*"when the commandment came"*
"sin is *dead*" (v. 8c)	"sin sprang to *life*" (v. 9b)
"I was *alive*" (v. 9a)	"I *died*" (v. 10a)

The seemingly obvious explanation is that Paul is referring to an experience in his own life. He understood that he was, indeed, "dead in his sins" when the true meaning of God's law came home to him—perhaps at puberty,[3] perhaps just before, or as part of, his conversion.[4] But this interpretation has a serious snag: We must interpret the key verbs subjectively. Paul "thought he was alive" before he understood the law; he "came to realize that he was dead" afterward.

This problem is neatly avoided if we were to use a different interpretation, namely, that Paul is describing the experience of Adam in the Garden of Eden. Adam and Eve are the only human beings who ever truly passed from "life" to "death" "when the commandment came." When they disobeyed the command not to eat of the tree of the knowledge of good and evil, they passed from spiritual life to spiritual death. Paul has already emphasized the corporate significance of Adam's actions in this context (ch. 5). So he may be continuing that line of thought, showing how he, and all people, came to experience spiritual death.[5] But this view also has a problem: Paul is not speaking here about "law" in general, but about the Mosaic law—a law that came long after the time of Adam and Eve.

The best explanation, then, finds Paul in these verses to be describing the experience that he and all Jews have gone through as part of the people of Israel.[6] Jews in Paul's day had a lively sense of their involvement with the great acts in the history of Israel (see Bridging Contexts section). It would be natural for Paul to merge his own experience relative to sin and the law with the experience of his people Israel. As he has made clear throughout Romans, the coming of the commandment (= the giving of the law of Moses) meant for Israel not "life" but "death." Their sin was exposed and magnified, and greater wrath came on them (4:15; 5:20).

---

3. See again Gundry, "Moral Frustration."

4. Augustine, *Against Two Letters of the Pelagians* 1.9; Calvin, *The Epistle of Paul to the Romans*, 255; Murray, *The Epistle to the Romans*, 1:251.

5. Käsemann, *Commentary on Romans*, 196–97; Dunn, *Romans*, 378–86.

6. See Moo, *The Epistle to the Romans*, 423–31.

To be sure, the law held out within it the promise of life (7:10). As Leviticus 18:5 (quoted by Paul in Rom. 10:5 and Gal. 3:12) teaches, "Keep my decrees and laws, for the man who obeys them will live by them." But the power of sin already at loose in the world through Adam kept this good intention from being realized. People were unable to obey the law (see Rom. 3:9). Thus, the law imprisoned Israel in their state of sin (see Gal. 3:23) and led, in fact, to her "death."

Verse 11 reiterates the same point about sin, using the law as a "bridgehead" that Paul made already in verse 8a; the two then act as a kind of "frame" around the narrative of verses 8b–10. With the "so then" of verse 12 Paul comes back to his main point. Sin has indeed used the law to bring death to Israel. But the law is innocent; it provides the "opportunity" only. Thus, it can be concluded that the law is not sin (v. 7); it is "holy, righteous and good."

"KNOWING" SIN AND **Greek vocabulary**. Anyone who has read books or commentaries on the Bible has run into arguments that go something like this: "Although the same English word occurs in both verses, the Greek (or Hebrew) words are different. The one means 'x' while the other means 'y.' Therefore the verses have different meanings." Such arguments are often valid. There are words in Greek and Hebrew with slightly different meanings that we render in English with the same word. I have pointed out a number of these in this commentary.

The problem, however, is that there has been a long history of overemphasizing these kinds of distinctions. Some interpreters wrongly assume that two Greek words with similar meanings in English always have a different nuance. Especially, then, when a biblical writer shifts from one of these words to another, it is automatically assumed that he intends a difference in meaning. Verse 7 is a case in point. When Paul says, "I would not have known what sin was," the English verb "know" translates the Greek *ginosko*. But when he goes on to say, "I would not have known what coveting really was," the word "know" translates *oida*. Commentators therefore argue that Paul has a different nuance in mind in the two statements. The first, Sanday and Headlam claim, refers to "an intimate, experiential acquaintance," while the second connotes "simple knowledge that there was such a thing as lust."[7]

As contemporary linguistic studies have shown, however, words with a similar meaning (i.e., synonyms) may have distinct nuances but are sometimes used with exactly the same connotation. A moment's reflection on how we

---

7. Sanday and Headlam, *The Epistle to the Romans*, 179.

actually use English will make this point clear. For instance, I refer throughout this commentary to "interpreters," "scholars," and "commentators." At times I deliberately choose one word instead of another because of a difference in meaning. I may, for instance, choose "interpreter" rather than "commentator" because I refer to people who have written on Romans but not in the form of a commentary. Or I may choose "interpreter" over "scholar" because I am referring to a writer whose "scholarship" I am uncertain about! But in the majority of cases, I intend no distinction in meaning. I may, for example, be aware that I have used "scholar" in the previous two sentences and so I should vary my language by choosing a synonym.

The point, then, is this: Speakers and writers often vary their vocabulary for reasons of style and not just for reasons of meaning. In an article on the two Greek verbs for "know" (*ginosko* and *oida*) Moises Silva has noted that the two do seem to have different connotations at times. But he also points out that the one verb was used far more often in certain kinds of constructions than the other verb, suggesting that authors sometimes used one or the other simply because of the syntactical situation.[8] What is ultimately decisive, therefore, is context: Does it make sense in a particular context to think that the author intends a difference in the words? In verse 7 we, along with most other modern interpreters, doubt that Paul intends to use these two Greek verbs to connote two different kinds of "knowing."

"I" in Paul's world. Modern readers of Romans 7 can be excused for wondering what all the fuss is about. Why do scholars debate the reference of the word "I" in verses 7–25? Is this not another example of the way scholars waste their energies working on problems that do not exist? The text says "I"; Paul wrote Romans; "I" refers to Paul. What could be clearer?

Of course, we are familiar with situations in which we use the first person singular pronoun in a rhetorical sense to refer to a person in general. Paul himself uses the pronoun this way earlier in the letter: "Someone might argue, 'If my falsehood enhances God's truthfulness and so increases his glory, why am I still condemned as a sinner?'" (see also 1 Cor. 13:1–3). But we usually signal this use of "I" clearly, often with a conditional construction (note the "if" in Rom. 3:7 and 1 Cor. 13:1–3). Paul does not use that kind of construction in Romans 7; he speaks directly of this "I" in the past tense in 7:7–12 and in the present tense in 7:13–25. What possible basis could there be for any reference except to his own experience? In fact, there are two.

(1) The former may be quickly mentioned because we have dealt with it in the Original Meaning section above: In verses 8–10 Paul describes an

---

8. Moises Silva, "The Pauline Style as Lexical Choice: ΓΙΝΩΣΚΕΙΝ and Related Verbs," in *Pauline Studies*, 184–207.

experience that he could not have had. He had never been "alive" (in a spiritual sense) apart from the law because he was born a sinner condemned because of Adam's sin (5:12–21) and as a Jew "under the law." Nor, for the same reason, had he "died" "when the commandment came." So we have at this point impetus from the text itself to ponder just what Paul might mean by "I" in Romans 7.

(2) The second basis for a broader use of "I" is the context of Paul's world. As we argued in commenting on 5:12–21, Paul's culture was far more alive to the corporate dimension of life than we are. People were viewed less in isolation and more as parts of units—family, tribe, nation, and so on. One's own nature and destiny were often seen to be a product more of participation in these corporate structures than of one's own personal decisions. Jews in particular emphasized the importance of solidarity with the nation. In the Passover ritual, recited each year, every Jew confesses that he or she was a slave in Egypt and was redeemed through God's mighty deeds.[9] The individual Jew is in solidarity with the nation as a whole; what the nation has experienced, the individual Jew has experienced.

Several Old Testament passages suggest that "I" can be used to denote the nation of Israel. Note, for instance, Micah's description of the judgment of Israel in Micah 7:7–10 (see also Jer. 10:19–22; Lam. 1:9–22; 2:20–22):

> But as for me, I watch in hope for the LORD,
> I wait for God my Savior;
> my God will hear me.
> Do not gloat over me, my enemy!
> Though I have fallen, I will rise.
> Though I sit in darkness,
> the LORD will be my light.
> Because I have sinned against him,
> I will bear the LORD's wrath,
> until he pleads my case
> and establishes my right.
> He will bring me out into the light;
> I will see his righteousness.
> Then my enemy will see it
> and will be covered with shame,
> she who said to me,
> "Where is the LORD your God?"

---

9. See, e.g., *m. Pesaḥ* 10, and the discussion in W. D. Davies, *Paul and Rabbinic Judaism* (London: SPCK, 1948), 102–4.

My eyes will see her downfall;
> even now she will be trampled underfoot
> like mire in the streets.

I am not suggesting that Paul uses "I" here to refer to the nation of Israel per se. As most scholars today recognize, the style of Romans 7 requires that "I" include reference to Paul himself. But I do think the corporate way of thinking so typical of Paul's world opens the way for us to take seriously the possibility that in this chapter he is not always referring to experiences from his own personal life but to experiences he has had in solidarity with his people Israel.

DEATH, THE LAW of Moses, and us. Our interpretation of 7:7—12 in terms of the experience of the Jewish people with the law of Moses poses a challenge to contemporary application. Here is another text in which "homiletical expediency" may well push us to adopt a view more easily applied in our day. If Paul, for instance, were describing the experience of human beings in general with law or command, we could apply what he says to the situation of every person.[10] But how can Paul's narration of the way sin used the Mosaic law to bring death to the Jewish people help the contemporary reader in Romans? In two ways.

(1) This paragraph, considered overall, is "an apology for the law." What Paul has said about the baneful effects of the law in the life of Israel may give the impression that the law was itself an evil thing or, at best, a wrong turn in salvation history. A Bible widely used during much of the twentieth century was the *Scofield Reference Bible*. The notes in this Bible, representing a strongly dispensational slant, suggested that Israel's acceptance of God's law was a mistake. Most dispensationalists today disavow this interpretation of God's law in the life of Israel. But this negative view of the law is still alive and well in some parts of the church.

This present passage reminds us, however, that the law comes from God and bears his own character of goodness, holiness, and righteousness. Because of the particular place he found himself in salvation history and the specific problems he had to deal with, Paul tends to focus on the negative side of the law. But he would never doubt the value of the law as a revelation of God's holiness and character. Nor would he ever suggest that the law cannot still

---

10. This is, in fact, the direction taken in one of the most influential books ever written on Romans 7, Werner Georg Kümmel, *Römer 7 und die Bekehrung des Paulus* (Leipzig: J. C. Hinrichs, 1929).

be read with profit. We may not be "under" its direct authority any more, but we must continue to meditate on his law both as a means of better appreciating just who our God is and what he values and as a means of understanding our own place in the plan that God unfolds in Scripture.

(2) A second application of this paragraph stems from a hermeneutical point we made in the Bridging Contexts section on 2:1–16. Paul presents the experience of Israel with the law of Moses as a paradigm for the experience of all people with "law" of any kind. Israel, in a sense, stands as a test case. God acts in history to create Israel as a nation and to give the Israelites their own land. He displays his power on their behalf and constantly showers them with blessing. In response to his merciful acts, he asks Israel to obey the law he gave them.

Yet, though faced with the undeniable evidence of God's reality and power and the promise of blessing for obedience, the people do not keep that law. Rather, Israel keeps turning away from God, ignoring his laws and spurning his grace. Thus, eventually God sends his people into exile in judgment and promises a new arrangement for his people in which he will enable obedience to his law. What the history of Israel with the law reveals is the inability of human beings to obey God. If Israel, with all her blessings, could not obey the law God gave directly to her, no person can hope to obey whatever law they put themselves under.

Most people have their own code of morality they try to live up to. Sometimes that code, via God's grace in natural law, reflects his own standards; sometimes it is far from divine law. But whatever the law may be, this text suggests, the sinful condition of all people renders it impossible to obey. We always fall short of the law, and the law therefore reveals the power of sin, our own helplessness, and the need for someone to liberate us from our miserable state. Truly law, in whatever form, brings death. By realizing this, we can appreciate the good news of Jesus Christ all the more. Some churches have the practice in every worship service of reading a portion from the law followed by a text from the gospel. The practice in many ways reflects the place of law in Paul's own teaching.

Romans 7:13–25

DID THAT WHICH is good, then, become death to me? By no means! But in order that sin might be recognized as sin, it produced death in me through what was good, so that through the commandment sin might become utterly sinful.

¹⁴We know that the law is spiritual; but I am unspiritual, sold as a slave to sin. ¹⁵I do not understand what I do. For what I want to do I do not do, but what I hate I do. ¹⁶And if I do what I do not want to do, I agree that the law is good. ¹⁷As it is, it is no longer I myself who do it, but it is sin living in me. ¹⁸I know that nothing good lives in me, that is, in my sinful nature. For I have the desire to do what is good, but I cannot carry it out. ¹⁹For what I do is not the good I want to do; no, the evil I do not want to do—this I keep on doing. ²⁰Now if I do what I do not want to do, it is no longer I who do it, but it is sin living in me that does it.

²¹So I find this law at work: When I want to do good, evil is right there with me. ²²For in my inner being I delight in God's law; ²³but I see another law at work in the members of my body, waging war against the law of my mind and making me a prisoner of the law of sin at work within my members. ²⁴What a wretched man I am! Who will rescue me from this body of death? ²⁵Thanks be to God—through Jesus Christ our Lord!

So then, I myself in my mind am a slave to God's law, but in the sinful nature a slave to the law of sin.

THIS PASSAGE IS one of the most controversial in all of Romans. Since early in the history of the church scholars and laypeople alike have debated just what experience Paul refers to. The debate is an important one, for it influences our understanding and practice of the Christian life.

If we are to have any hope of accurately understanding these verses, we must start where Paul does: with the Mosaic law. His main concern is not anthropology, the Christian life, or theories of sanctification. These come in along the way, but the apostle's purpose here is to explain why the Mosaic law has brought death to Israel. The way sin has used the law to bring death to God's Old Testament people was the burden of 7:7–12. But one large question remains unanswered: How could sin do this? The answer comes in 7:14: "I am unspiritual, sold as a slave to sin." Sin, after all, is no independent entity. It exists only as human beings miss the mark of God's holiness, and people are bound to sin because they are "sold as slaves" to it. We agree with God's law in our minds, but we cannot obey it (7:15–20).

Paul summarizes the struggle in 7:21–25: The good law of God is at war with the "law of sin." Because people are held captive under that law of sin, they can never escape the penalty for disobedience, death—at least, not on their own. But Christ does rescue us from "this body of death" (vv. 24–25). What Paul explains in these verses is that the law comes to people already held captive under sin; thus, of course, they are incapable of obeying it. It is human incapacity that explains the failure of the law. As Paul summarizes the point in 8:3: The law was "powerless . . . in that it was weakened by the sinful nature."

What Paul says about the "weakness" of the law is valid no matter whose experience he might be describing in these verses. The central claim of this text is undebatable: The law cannot free us from spiritual death. But the subsidiary issue of the identity of the "I" here is still important. The debate over this matter has been long and intense, and the various viewpoints have been taken. But three main directions in interpretation have emerged. Before plunging into the details of the text, I want to explain each one briefly and alert the reader to my own approach.

(1) Most lay Christians think that Paul is describing his own experience as a normal, mature believer.[1] Having described how he first came to know the law in 7:7–12 (past tense), he now shares with us his continuing struggle (present tense), even as a Christian, to fulfill the law of God. For while God has redeemed him from sin, he is still in the body, subject to temptation and the continuing struggle with the "sinful nature." Thus, his obedience is not perfect. But he joyfully looks forward to the day when God will transform his body (7:24–25a). In the meantime, he continues to find himself divided between service to the law of God and service to "the law of sin" (7:25b). In other words, Paul reflects in this passage the "already–not yet" tension of Christian existence. The new regime has come, and believers belong to it by faith. But the old regime still exists and exerts its influence on believers. Struggle with sin inevitably marks our life in this world.

---

1. Many commentators agree. See esp. Murray, *The Epistle to the Romans*, 1:256–59; Nygren, *Commentary on Romans*, 284–97; Barrett, *The Epistle to the Romans*, 151–53; Cranfield, *The Epistle to the Romans*, 344–47; Dunn, *Romans*, 387–89, 403–12; Morris, *The Epistle to the Romans*, 284–88.

(2) Most Pauline scholars think that Paul describes his life as a Jew under the law.[2] Having shown how he and other Jews became captive to the law of sin when the law was given (7:7–12), Paul now describes what life under the law was like. While delighting in the law of God and seeking earnestly to obey it, Jews were unable to do so. They were held captive like prisoners under the power of sin (7:14, 23). Only Jesus Christ, Paul recognizes, can save Jews from the spiritual death that holds sway over them (7:24b–25a). But until they come to that realization, they will remain captives to the "law of sin" (7:25b).

(3) Finding something to like and something to dislike in each of these views, a compromise interpretation is also popular: Paul describes the experience of an immature Christian.[3] Advocates of this approach argue that it does justice to two key elements in the text. (a) The person Paul describes seems to be a believer, for he or she "delights in God's law" in the "inner being," as only the regenerate can do. (b) But this person is clearly not gaining victory over sin. Why not? Here a notable silence in the text needs to be noted: Never does the person seek to please God through the Holy Spirit. Paul seems to be describing a new believer who is still trying to lead the Christian life by doing the law rather than by the power of the Spirit.

Therefore, according to this last view, chapters 7–8 together carry a hidden command: The believer must "get out of Romans 7 and into Romans 8." Advocates of the first view would argue that the believer is always in both Romans 7 and Romans 8. According to the second view, it is God in Christ who offers to transfer the Jew from Romans 7 into Romans 8.

We adopt the second view, that Paul is describing his life as a Jew under the law, before he came to Christ. We freely acknowledge that each view can marshal solid arguments in its favor. But the balance tilts toward the "unregenerate" interpretation. In the Bridging Contexts and Contemporary Significance sections, as well as in the exposition that immediately follows, we deal with many of the specific arguments. What ultimately is decisive for me is the fact that Paul's description of the person in 7:13–25 is contradictory to his description of the Christian in chapters 6 and 8. Note the following contrasts:

---

2. We cannot here give the evidence for this assertion. But, among the commentators, see esp. Godet, *Commentary on Romans*, 292–93; Käsemann, *Commentary on Romans*, 199–212.

3. This view is found more among popular expositions than in the scholarly literature; see, for a good defense, Lloyd-Jones, *Romans: An Exposition of Chapters 7:1–8:4*, 229–57. Another compromise view holds that Paul is describing the sin-prone nature found in every person, Christian or not (Richard N. Longenecker, *Paul, Apostle of Liberty* [rpt.; Grand Rapids: Baker, 1976], 109–16; Bandstra, *The Law and the Elements of the World*, 134–49; David Wenham, "The Christian Life: A Life of Tension? A Consideration of the Nature of Christian Experience in Paul," in *Pauline Studies*, 80–94).

"I am unspiritual, sold as a slave to sin" (7:14)	"you have been set free from sin" (6:18, 22; cf. 6:2, 6, 14)
"making me a prisoner of the law of sin" (7:23)	"through Christ Jesus the law of the Spirit of life set me free from the law of sin and death" (8:2)

Advocates of the other views, of course, have answers for these apparent contradictions. But I don't find them persuasive. In what follows, therefore, we will assume that Paul is describing his experience as a Jew under the law.

A Summary and Transition (7:13)

THIS VERSE SUMMARIZES what Paul has taught in 7:7–12, so that we can consider it the conclusion to the previous paragraph. He again notes that God's law has been the occasion that enables us to see sin for what it really is: "that sin might be recognized as sin," that "sin might become utterly sinful." In other words, the law becomes an instrument that sin uses to bring death. The form of the verse, however, similar to 7:7 with its question and emphatic response ("By no means!"), suggests that it introduces what follows. This verse, therefore, is transitional, gathering up the argument so far and launching the new focus: the problem with "me."

The Divided "I" (7:14–20)

IN VERSE 14, Paul characterizes the two chief "actors" in the drama that follows. The law of Moses, as Paul has made clear in verse 12, is "spiritual"; that is, it has a divine origin (see, for this use of "spiritual," 1 Cor. 10:3–4). But "I am unspiritual, sold as a slave to sin." "Unspiritual" translates *sarkinos*, which means "composed of flesh." Paul can use this word to describe "carnal" Christians (1 Cor. 3:1–3), so it does not necessarily mean that the "I" is unregenerate. But the following description seems to tilt the scales in this direction. "Sold as a slave to sin" (lit., "sold under sin") may mean simply that the believer continues to be exposed to the influence of sin.[4] But "sold," as the NIV suggests, often refers to being sold into slavery (see Matt. 18:25), and Paul has used "under sin" to describe the condition of all people apart from Christ (3:9).

In verses 15–20, Paul graphically portrays the struggle he finds within himself to follow through on his conviction that "the law is spiritual." As he looks at this struggle, he is in consternation; he does not "understand" what he does. He finds himself unable to do what he wants to do. He is torn between willing and doing, and this tension reveals two truths. (1) The fact

---

4. E.g., Cranfield, *The Epistle to the Romans*, 357–58.

that he wills what is good shows that he acknowledges the goodness of the law (v. 16). He knows it is God's law, his revealed will for his life, and he is trying to do it as best he can.

(2) But he finds that he cannot do the law. This reveals that "it is no longer I myself who do it, but it is sin living in me" (v. 17). Paul is not disclaiming responsibility for his actions. Rather, he is trying to explain his actions by revealing the force within himself that leads him to act as he does. That force is "sin," a power he has been describing throughout Romans 5–7.

The beginning of verse 18 continues this analysis of "indwelling" sin: "I know that nothing good lives in me, that is, in my sinful nature [*sarx*; lit., flesh]." Two very different interpretations of this verse exist, each lining up with one of the major views of the identity of the "I" in these verses. Those who think the "I" is regenerate usually insist that the "that is" qualification is restrictive: Paul, the Christian, has a certain part of himself—a sinful nature—that disposes him to sin. Those who think the "I" is unregenerate usually take the "that is" clause as a definition: Paul, the Jew under the law, is still "flesh"; that is, he is still "in the flesh," in a condition in which sinful passions are aroused by the law (see 7:5). We incline toward this second interpretation because it better fits the way Paul uses *sarx* in this context. But the other is certainly possible.

In verses 18b–20, Paul once more rehearses the struggle between willing and doing that reveals his sinful condition and makes it impossible for him to obey the law.

The Conclusion: The Law of God Versus the "Law of Sin" (7:21–25)

PAUL DRAWS THE conclusion from the struggle between his will and his act, using the word "law" (*nomos*). This word occurs seven times in these verses. Throughout the chapter thus far he has used *nomos* in its usual sense to denote the body of legislation given by God through Moses to the people of Israel. But several occurrences of the word in these verses do not fit this sense: "this law" (v. 21), "another law" (v. 23), and "the law of sin" (v. 25).

Most interpreters agree that *nomos* in verse 21 means "principle" or "rule." Here is a principle Paul derives from his struggle: "When I want to do good, evil is right there with me." He goes on to explain this struggle in verses 22–23. "God's law," in which Paul delights in his "inner being," is the Mosaic law. His use of "inner being" (lit., "inner person") is one reason why many interpreters think Paul must be writing here as a Christian, for Paul only uses this phrase elsewhere of a Christian (2 Cor. 4:16; Eph. 3:16). But the phrase does not have a technical Christian application. It was used widely in secular

Greek to refer to "man . . . according to his Godward, immortal side."[5] Paul continues to emphasize the two "sides" of people: willing versus doing (vv. 15–20), "inner being" versus "members" (vv. 22–23), "mind" versus "flesh" (NIV "sinful nature") (v. 25).

Since "God's law" in verse 22 refers to the Mosaic law, we would expect "another law" in verse 23 to denote a different law entirely. This has been the traditional interpretation.[6] In a rhetorical *tour de force*, Paul contrasts God's law with another "law," "the law of sin." For just as God in his law makes a claim on our lives, so sin, acting through our members, exerts its own claim on us. These two claims battle for our allegiance. The upshot, Paul says, is that we are "prisoners of the law of sin." God's law simply does not have the power to deliver us from the power of sin.

While I think this interpretation is correct, we should note that a different interpretation has become popular. According to this view, Paul contrasts two sides of the Mosaic law. On its one side, it is the revelation of God's will for us, the law with which our minds agree. But on its other side, that same law also has been coopted by sin and used to bring death to us.[7] The problem with this view is twofold. (1) It is not the most natural way to read "another"—we expect a reference to a different "law" entirely. (2) It gives the Mosaic law a function that it has not had in this context. In verses 15–20, the struggle is between Paul's will to do God's law and sin that dwells within him. The law, which is "spiritual" (v. 14), is always ranged on the "good" side of this battle. It would be unusual for Paul to shift that perspective here.

In verse 24 Paul finally reacts to the situation he has described: "What a wretched man I am! Who will rescue me from this body of death?" What rescue does Paul anticipate here? Some, particularly those who think Paul is writing as a Christian, take "body of death" to refer to the mortal body—doomed to die because of sin. The deliverance therefore comes with resurrection.[8] Others think that "death" refers to the state of spiritual frustration and condemnation that Paul has described throughout this chapter. Paul's assertion in 8:10 that the "body is dead because of sin" could certainly favor the former view. But he has consistently used "death" in chapter 7 to refer to the state of spiritual frustration and condemnation.[9] So the rescue he hopes

---

5. J. Jeremias, "ἄνθρωπος," *TDNT* 1:365.

6. See most of the commentators; note esp. the argument in Winger, *By What Law?* 186–88.

7. See, e.g., Dunn, *Romans,* 395; Snodgrass, "Spheres of Influence: A Possible Solution for the Problem of Paul and the Law," *JSNT* 32 (1988): 106–7.

8. See esp. Murray, *The Epistle to the Romans,* 1:268; Dunn, *Romans,* 397.

9. E.g., Godet, *Commentary on Romans,* 289–90; Gundry, "Moral Frustration," 239.

---

for is probably deliverance from the sin-dominated body, spiritually dead because of sin (see 6:6).

In verse 25a Paul gives thanks for the rescue, provided through "Jesus Christ our Lord." Here is one of the most important arguments in favor of applying verses 14–25 to Christian experience. For only a Christian knows to thank God for deliverance in Christ. Significantly, the person who gives thanks for deliverance immediately goes on to reiterate his divided state. Surely this shows that Paul writes as a Christian, confident about ultimate victory in Christ (v. 25a), but also keenly aware of the struggle between the power of sin and the law of God that marks his existence in this life, caught between the "two eras."

We admit the force of the argument, but we think the sequence can be explained on the view we are arguing. Having expressed the desire for rescue from the frustration of not being able to do God's law that he felt as a Jew under the law, Paul the Christian cannot refrain from interjecting a thanksgiving for the source of the deliverance he has experienced. In other words, he sums up the struggle he has been describing throughout verses 14–25 in verse 25b.

Bridging Contexts

ISSUES IN THE **larger perspective.** The debate over the meaning of this text affords a classic example of a certain kind of interpretive problem. I think most expositors would admit that the exegetical evidence (i.e., lexicography, grammar, etc.) does not all point in the same direction. Each basic interpretation of this passage can cite evidence in its favor and a long and distinguished list of advocates. Anyone who thinks the matter is clear-cut lacks either objectivity or charity—or both!

What becomes decisive, then, in the interpretation of a text like this one is the larger perspective we bring to it. My own experience with this passage is a good illustration. In my early years of teaching, I held pretty strongly the view that Paul was speaking as a mature Christian. But one term I was teaching through a series of texts about the law. As I worked through text after text, I developed a perspective on the law different from what I had previously held. When I came to Romans 7 with this perspective, the text looked different than it had before. Within this new framework, I suddenly saw how the text made better sense as a description of Paul's pre-Christian experience. I experienced what we commonly call today (following Thomas Kuhn) a "paradigm shift."

Three issues are especially critical to this larger perspective that we bring to the text: context, teaching elsewhere, and especially the assumptions we bring to our interpretation. I will look at each of these in turn in order to help the modern reader grapple with this vexing passage.

(1) *Context*. (a) Arguments for the regenerate view. Almost all interpreters agree that we must interpret 7:14–25 within the "two regime" framework that is fundamental to all of Paul's teaching (and, indeed, to all of the New Testament) but which is especially prominent in chapters 5–8. We have briefly described this framework in the Bridging Contexts section on 6:15–23. According to it, the "new era" of messianic redemption has broken into history, and believers become a part of that new era through Christ. They are no longer "in Adam" (5:12–21), sin's power over them is broken (ch. 6), the Mosaic law has no final authority over them (7:1–6), and they are indwelt by the Spirit, adopted into God's family, and destined for eternal life and glory (ch. 8).

But the "old era" has not been eradicated. It still exists, and believers continue to be subject to its power. They must therefore battle against sin's continuing influence (6:11–14, 19) and long for the day when they will be delivered from frustration and from the mortal body (8:10–11, 19–23). The "already–not yet" tension is how scholars often describe the implications of this framework for the outlook of the believer. We are "already" justified and reconciled, indwelt by the Spirit, but we are "not yet" glorified and resurrected, still subject to sin's lure.

How does 7:14–25 fit into this framework? The struggle Paul depicts in these verses makes excellent sense as a description of this eschatological tension in which the believer is caught, as James Dunn has especially emphasized.[10] On this view Paul cautions against an overinterpretation of his claim that believers are "freed from sin" (6:6, 18, 22). He does not want us to think that sin's power is entirely done away with and that the Christian life will be a cake walk. No, the reality is that sin and death are still powerful forces with which the believer must reckon. In 7:14–25, therefore, Paul goes out of his way to depict the seriousness of the struggle that we still have before us. As he has done throughout Romans, Paul responds to his teaching in 6:1–7:6 with another perspective that gives balance to his conclusion. Context, then, can favor the "regenerate" interpretation.

(b) Arguments for the unregenerate view. But, looked at from another angle, context can also favor the "unregenerate" viewpoint. For 7:14–25 is not a response to the teaching of chapter 6; rather, it carries on the discussion of the Mosaic law from 7:1–6 and 7:7–12. Paul's purpose is to vindicate the law; he wants to keep people from concluding on the basis of 7:1–6 that the law

---

10. See his commentary, esp. pp. 411–12; also his article, "Rom. 7,14–25 in the Theology of Paul," *TZ* 31 (1975): 257–73.

is a bad thing. Thus, he shows that sin, not the law, is at fault in the death that has come to those who are "bound to the law" (cf. v. 6). But those who struggle to do the law and are frustrated when they do not are Jews. They are the ones who are "under the law" (see 2:12; 3:19).

Paul cannot, then, be describing Christian experience in 7:14–25, for Christians no longer struggle to do the Mosaic law; they are not under it (6:14, 15; cf. 7:4, 6). To put the matter in a different way, Paul is certainly continuing to describe the two different regimes of salvation history. But he has consistently placed law in the old regime. Thus 7:14–25, which speaks about the struggle to obey the law, must be about the old regime. Romans 7:5–6 provides a kind of "heading" for the argument that follows. In 7:7–25, Paul elaborates on the situation described in verse 5: "When we were controlled by the sinful nature, the sinful passions aroused by the law were at work in our bodies, so that we bore fruit for death." Chapter 8 then picks up on 7:6: "Now, by dying to what once bound us, we have been released from the law so that we serve in the new way of the Spirit, and not in the old way of the written code."

My purpose here is not necessarily to choose between these contextual scenarios (although I, of course, incline to the second). Rather, I want to point out that the choice we make here will have significant, even decisive, effect on our final interpretation.

(2) *Teaching elsewhere.* Scholars agree that Paul teaches two things about the believer and sin: We are no longer slaves to sin's power, and we will continue to struggle with sin and to commit sins. The difficulty is knowing just how to fit 7:14–25 into this twofold observation. One of the marks of Luther's theology is the recognition that the believer is, as the famous Latin phrase has it, *simul justus et peccator,* "at the same time just and a sinner." This is another way of expressing the eschatological tension described in the last section.

A verse that brings this perspective to classic expression is Galatians 5:17: "For the sinful nature desires what is contrary to the Spirit, and the Spirit what is contrary to the sinful nature. They are in conflict with each other, so that you do not do what you want." We may well decide that the long exposition of struggle in Romans 7:14–25 is simply an expansion of this verse. This reading of Paul's teaching tends to emphasize the continuing struggle with sin that Paul expects the Christian to have. The more we emphasize this side of Paul's teaching, the more natural it will be to fit 7:14–25 into it.

The other side is put well by David Wenham in his article on this passage.[11] He freely acknowledges that Paul teaches the reality of continuing struggle with sin in the Christian life. But he wonders whether the struggle

---

11. See his "The Christian Life: A Life of Tension?"

depicted in 7:14–25 goes a bit too far. For Paul not only describes a struggle in these verses; he seems to suggest that this struggle ends in defeat: I am "a prisoner of the law of sin" (v. 23). By contrast, Paul proclaims loudly that the believer has been put in an entirely new position with respect to sin. We have a new power over sin (ch. 6), and that power must reveal itself in a life of righteousness and holiness (6:21–23). Thus, the more we emphasize the victory over sin that Paul proclaims and expects of the Christian, the more difficult we will find it to fit 7:14–25 into Paul's description of the Christian life.

(3) *Our own assumptions.* This may be the most powerful factor of all, tilting our reading of 7:14–25 in one direction or the other. We have noted before in these sections that our reading of the New Testament is always affected by our situation, background, and culture. We bring "baggage" to the text we read, which can seriously affect the conclusions we reach. I doubt that any text in the Bible illustrates this better than 7:14–25.

I have taught Romans now for over fifteen years in all kinds of contexts: seminary classrooms, extension classes, high school and adult Sunday school classes, retreats, and so on. Invariably, when I come to 7:14–25 and ask people what the passage means and why, I will get from a good number of students this kind of response: "This passage must be about the normal, or mature Christian because Paul describes the same kind of struggle with sin that I am having." I usually respond, first, by gently pointing out two key assumptions in this argument: that the speaker is a "mature Christian" and that the struggle is only one that a Christian could have. Both are necessary assumptions if this argument is to work.

Can we make these assumptions? Do I not run the risk of forcing the New Testament to conform to my own level of spirituality rather than letting the New Testament stand in judgment over my spiritual condition? Perhaps my struggle is not a struggle that mature Christians should be having. Now I don't want to suggest that mature Christians do not struggle with sin. They do, and I believe that struggle is one we will always have in this life (see Contemporary Significance section). But I think we also need to do justice to the New Testament insistence that genuine believers will produce fruit exemplifying their new life in Christ and that such fruit is necessary if we are to go free in the judgment. It is dangerous to assume that I am a mature Christian and then conclude that any passage that fits my situation must also be describing a mature Christian.

But the other assumption also needs scrutiny. If pushed to the wall, I will usually admit to my classes that verses 15–20 could, indeed, be describing the struggle of a mature believer to fulfill God's will in his or her life. But those verses are part of an argument, the conclusion of which is that the struggle ends in defeat (vv. 21–25). Verses 15–20, in other words, may be describing the struggle any sincere religious devotee has in doing what his or her god is demanding. It may, indeed, fit Christian experience; but unless it fits *only* Christian experience, the point at issue is not proven.

I have selected an example from one side of the argument to illustrate the danger of bringing our assumptions to the text without realizing we are doing it or allowing for them. And I chose this example because it is the one I have most often been faced with. But let me hasten to add that the assumptions can be just as pernicious on the other side. I think of the Christian who is a strong devotee of the "victorious Christian life" philosophy. In fact, I can mention one particular devotee of that viewpoint as a good case in point.

In my early years at Trinity (before I had "seen the light"), I taught that 7:14–25 described the experience of a mature Christian. In the midst of my teaching on this point one day in class, a student rose from the back of the classroom, walked calmly to the front, and in the surprised silence that ensued said, "Anyone who believes that this passage is describing the Christian life has never experienced the life of the Spirit." She then took her seat again. I don't remember how I responded, although I expect it was not very profound. But the incident illustrates the point I am making. Each of us brings a certain view of what the Christian life "must be like" to this text. If we do not subject that view itself to the scrutiny of Scripture, we can be guilty of forcing Romans 7:14–25 into a mold of our own making. We cannot rid ourselves of the baggage we bring to the text. But we must acknowledge the baggage is there and try to stay balanced by compensating for the direction in which it is making us lean.

 WHEN MY CHILDREN were young, they liked reading "Choose Your Own Adventure" books. The book would begin by establishing a basic direction for the plot, but would then offer the reader choices about the development of the plot as the book went along. I am tempted to entitle this section "Choose Your Own Application." I have argued a certain view of verses 14–25 in the sections above: Paul describes the defeat he experienced trying to obey the Mosaic law as a Jew before he became a Christian. But I recognize that a good case can be made for other views of the text. I therefore hesitate to apply the text as if my own view were the only possible one.

Nevertheless, I am also reluctant to open the door to a relativism in which each reader gets to choose what the biblical text means. So I will compromise. I will base my application on my interpretation of the text but, along the way, make clear where the other interpretations offer valid insights about this text and the Christian life.

The Jew, the Christian, and the law. Application of the text should begin with the main point in the passage: the human weakness that makes it impossible for the Mosaic law to rescue us from the power of sin and death. The law was given to people already locked up under sin's power. They could not obey it; by making people accountable to a definite and clear standard of conduct, the law revealed their sinful state and plunged them even deeper into despair and death.

A number of commentators think we can expand the horizons of application by taking "law" in this passage to refer not to the Mosaic law, but to the law of God in any form: Torah for Israel, natural law and conscience for Gentiles, perhaps even the law of Christ for Christians. But it seems most likely that Paul continues throughout this passage to refer to the law of Moses. Even so, we must remember that he views the experience of the Jews with the Mosaic law as paradigmatic. In describing his own situation under the law of Moses, the apostle is implicitly describing the situation of every human being confronted with "law." Therefore, even if Paul is not recounting his own failure as a Christian to obey God's law, a principle emerges from the passage that is applicable to anyone, including the Christian: Law can never rescue us from our predicament. Romans 7 stands as a warning never to think we can please God by our own efforts. We can never fulfill his law; we will always have to confess that we are "debtors to grace."

On the view of the passage we have argued, the primary application for these verses belongs to the unbeliever. Advocates of the "mature Christian" interpretation often argue that only the regenerate person "delights" in God's law (v. 22). There is a sense, certainly, in which the believer, because of the indwelling Spirit, has a deeper appreciation of God's revealed will. But pious Jews also delighted in God's law. They studied it, revered it, and sought to obey it. As Paul says in 10:2, Jews are "zealous for God." As we have noted, the Jew stands as an example of a certain kind of person.

While I think his existential approach to Romans 7 is off track, Rudolf Bultmann is ultimately right about this: Romans 7 is about the "religious person." Paul is looking at the very best of human beings outside of Christ. We can then think of people in our day who fit this profile, people who have a deep and sincere desire to do good and find approval with their god. Indeed, in the pluralistic environment of our day, people completely dedicated to various religions and beliefs are all around us. But the experience of Paul and other Jews under the law proves the point: Sincerity is not enough. As long as people are "sold as slaves to sin," sincerity by itself can never lead to genuine fulfillment of God's law.

Some interpreters claim that Paul cannot be describing his experience under the law in these verses because the struggle he reveals here does not fit his own claim that he was, as far as "legalistic righteousness" goes, "faultless" (Phil. 3:6). But Paul is talking about two different things in these texts. In Philippians he is describing his "official" *status*: born as a Jew and seeking to follow God's law, he was "righteous" according to Jewish definitions. But in Romans he is describing his *experience*.

A parallel often cited here is Luther's description of his life as a monk. Looking back at that time of his life from the perspective of his Christian experience, he could claim to have been a faithful, obedient monk—"righteous" by the standards of that time—yet filled with doubt and despair. Indeed, Luther, and Paul before him, undoubtedly recognize a degree of frustration and failure in their pre-Christian experience that they did not fully realize at the time.

Many of us can relate to this. It is not a matter of retrojecting into our past a problem that did not exist in order to "justify" our conversion (as some sociologists of religion would argue). It is, rather, that our new understanding of spiritual reality helps us to understand the nature of the insecurity, doubt, and frustration we often suppressed or ignored in those years.

From this backward look arises another clear application of this text. With Paul, we should break out in thanksgiving to God when we recognize the state from which he has rescued us. I can well remember the terrible insecurity I felt before coming to Christ. I did not then recognize the source of that insecurity, but in hindsight it is clear. I had no foundation in a relationship to God and was seeking foundations everywhere else—only to have them crumble sooner or later. All of us who read Romans 7 as Christians can identify, to some degree, with the struggle and frustration Paul depicts here. Looking back at that time is good for us, for it moves us all the more to praise God for his rescue of us in Jesus Christ.

Advocates of the "mature Christian" interpretation, as noted above, think this text provides warrant for thinking that the Christian life will be marked by continuing struggle with sin. Let me make clear that while I do not agree with their interpretation of Romans 7, I certainly agree with the larger point. Paul makes abundantly clear elsewhere (e.g., Rom. 6:11–13; Gal. 5:17; Eph. 6:10–17) that believers have a never-ending fight on their hands to put into practice the victory over sin we experience in Christ. My problem with taking Romans 7 as a description of this struggle, as I indicated above, is that Paul does not just describe a struggle here (e.g., 7:15–20); he describes a struggle that ends in frustration and defeat (7:21–25).

This is not true to Paul's understanding of the Christian life. Our "death to sin" (ch. 6), the indwelling power of the Holy Spirit (ch. 8), and the renewal of our minds (12:1–2) will inevitably mean that we sin less and less. Yes, we will never become sinless, but we will certainly *sin less*. Paul does not seem to reflect this in Romans 7, however, nor do the negative tones of verses 21–25 fit the eventual victory that is ours in Christ.

Whatever our view of Romans 7 might be, then, we need to avoid what I think all interpreters would agree is a misuse of the text: using it to justify sin or stagnation in the Christian life. I have all too often encountered believers with just this attitude: "I am really struggling with a sin, and it keeps getting the best of me. But that's alright—Paul had the same problem [Rom. 7]." Paul may indeed have had that problem. But this does not make it appropriate—for Paul or for us. We should never regard the sins we commit with complacency. They are not supposed to be there. God hates them, and he has given us the power to get rid of them.

Romans 8:1–13

THEREFORE, THERE IS now no condemnation for those who are in Christ Jesus, ²because through Christ Jesus the law of the Spirit of life set me free from the law of sin and death. ³For what the law was powerless to do in that it was weakened by the sinful nature, God did by sending his own Son in the likeness of sinful man to be a sin offering. And so he condemned sin in sinful man, ⁴in order that the righteous requirements of the law might be fully met in us, who do not live according to the sinful nature but according to the Spirit.

⁵Those who live according to the sinful nature have their minds set on what that nature desires; but those who live in accordance with the Spirit have their minds set on what the Spirit desires. ⁶The mind of sinful man is death, but the mind controlled by the Spirit is life and peace; ⁷the sinful mind is hostile to God. It does not submit to God's law, nor can it do so. ⁸Those controlled by the sinful nature cannot please God.

⁹You, however, are controlled not by the sinful nature but by the Spirit, if the Spirit of God lives in you. And if anyone does not have the Spirit of Christ, he does not belong to Christ. ¹⁰But if Christ is in you, your body is dead because of sin, yet your spirit is alive because of righteousness. ¹¹And if the Spirit of him who raised Jesus from the dead is living in you, he who raised Christ from the dead will also give life to your mortal bodies through his Spirit, who lives in you.

¹²Therefore, brothers, we have an obligation—but it is not to the sinful nature, to live according to it. ¹³For if you live according to the sinful nature, you will die; but if by the Spirit you put to death the misdeeds of the body, you will live.

Original Meaning

ROMANS 8 HAS been called the "inner sanctuary within the cathedral of Christian faith." It sets before us some of the most wonderful blessings we enjoy as believers: being free from God's condemnation, indwelt by God's own Spirit, adopted into his family, destined for resurrection and glory, and full of hope because of God's love for us and because of his promise to bring good to us in every circumstance of life.

How does this rehearsal of the glorious benefits of being "in Christ" fit into Paul's argument in these chapters? The first part of the chapter (8:1–13) has two purposes. (1) It elaborates the reference to the "new way of the Spirit" in 7:6 after the "interruption" in which Paul deals with questions about the law (7:7–25). Reference to the Holy Spirit is long overdue in Paul's discussion of the believer's existence. Possessing the Spirit is *the* mark of being a new covenant believer, and his ministry must be basic to any description of what it means to be a Christian. While the Holy Spirit is not really the topic of Romans 8, Paul gives the Spirit the key role in mediating to us the blessings of our new life. Twenty-one times Paul uses the word *pneuma* (S/spirit) in Romans 8, and all but two (vv. 15a, 16b) refer to the Holy Spirit.

(2) Verses 1–13 have another, more fundamental purpose. Chapters 6 and 7 are slight detours from the main line of Paul's argument, in which he deals with sin and the law, two key threats to the security of our new life. Now he is in a position to return to the main road by continuing his exposition of the believer's security in Christ. So in this section he reaffirms our new life in Christ (vv. 1–4) and draws out its consequences for the moral life (vv. 5–8), the future, "resurrection" life (vv. 9–11), and the responsibility of the believer (vv. 12–13).

New Life Through the Spirit's Liberating Work (8:1–4)

"THERE IS NOW no condemnation for those who are in Christ Jesus" takes us back to 5:12–21, where Paul showed how those who belong to Christ escape the "condemnation" (*katakrima*) that came to all people through Adam's sin (note that *katakrima* occurs only in 5:16, 18; 8:1 in the New Testament). Paul continues to use the forensic imagery that is so important to his conception of the gospel. Because we are justified by faith in conjunction with our union with Christ, we escape the sentence of spiritual death that our sins have justly earned. Transferred into the new regime of life, we no longer fear that our sins will ever condemn us.

In verse 2 Paul explains why we need no longer worry about condemnation: "because through Christ Jesus the law of the Spirit of life set me free from the law of sin and death." We have encountered two other places in Romans in which Paul opposes one law (*nomos*) to another law: 3:27 and 7:22–23. In each case scholars are divided over whether Paul intends to oppose one function of the Mosaic law to another function of that same law or whether one or both occurrences of "law" might refer to something besides the Mosaic law (e.g., a principle or authority). In both texts we argued the latter (see comments on 3:27; 7:22–23).

The same is true in this verse. "Law of sin and death" could, considering the argument of Romans 7, refer to the Mosaic law, used by sin to bring death.

But Paul has used a similar expression in 7:23 to refer to the authority or power of sin. This is probably what he means here as well. "The law of the Spirit," then, denotes the authority or power exercised by the Holy Spirit.[1] The Spirit exerts a liberating power through the work of Christ that takes us out of the realm of sin and the spiritual death to which sin inevitably leads.

As verse 2 grounds verse 1 ("because"), so verses 3–4 ground verse 2 ("for"). The liberating work of the Spirit takes place "through Christ Jesus." Paul now elaborates. As he has shown in chapter 7, the Mosaic law was powerless to rescue human beings from the authority of sin and death. It was "weakened by the sinful nature"; that is, its demands could not be met because the people to whom the law was given were in the realm of "flesh" (*sarx*; NIV "sinful nature").[2] But God in Christ has intervened to do what the law could not.

Paul indulges in a play on the word "flesh" that is obscured in the NIV. The law was weakened "by the flesh"; yet God also "condemned sin in the flesh." He won the victory over sin in the very realm where it seemed to rule unchallenged: in the "flesh." In claiming that Christ came "in the likeness of flesh" to offer himself as a sacrifice for our sins, Paul carefully balances Jesus' full humanity with his sinlessness. Christ did indeed become fully human by taking on "flesh." But calling that flesh "sinful" might suggest that Christ took on *fallen* human nature. If so, he would not have been qualified to be our sinless Redeemer. So Paul clarifies by adding the important word "likeness."

In other words, Christ did not, like every other person since Adam, succumb to the tyranny of flesh. He did not himself sin, nor did he inherit the penalty of sin, namely, death. Paul uses the language of "interchange": Christ became what we are so that we could become what he is. By "condemning" sin in Christ as our sacrifice, he can now justly avoid "condemning" us who are in Christ.

The purpose of this work of God in Christ is spelled out in verse 4. The NIV translation is misleading. Paul does not claim that the "righteous *requirements* of the law" are fulfilled in us; he says that "the righteous *requirement* of the law was fulfilled in us" (the Greek word *dikaioma* is singular). The difference

---

1. This is the interpretation in most of the commentaries (e.g., Godet, *Commentary on Romans*, 297; Cranfield, *The Epistle to the Romans*, 375–76; Fitzmyer, *Romans*, 482–83). And see esp. the article of Leander E. Keck, "The Law and 'The Law of Sin and Death' (Rom 8:1–4): Reflections on the Spirit and Ethics in Paul," in *The Divine Helmsman: Studies on God's Control of Human Events, Presented to Lou H. Silberman*, ed. J. L. Crenshaw and S. Sandmel (New York: KTAV, 1980), 41–57. The view that the "law of Spirit" is the Mosaic law operating in the context of the Spirit is not yet well represented in the commentaries. See, however, Dunn, *Romans*, 416–18; note also Snodgrass, "Spheres of Influence," 99.

2. Note that throughout this chapter, I will frequently be using "flesh" as a translation for *sarx*, but will not note it each time. The NIV rarely uses this translation.

may not be great if Paul is thinking of the way that the Spirit enables Christians to obey the commandments of the law (note v. 7).[3] But the singular word, along with the passive form of "fulfill," suggests a different idea: God in Christ has fulfilled the entirety of the law's demand on our behalf.[4]

Note that Paul's purpose here is to show how we are no longer condemned. The reason is that we have, in Christ, effectively fulfilled God's demand expressed in the law. This happens as we "walk in the Spirit." If Paul is referring here to the way Christians do the law in their own lives, then this expression will be instrumental: We fulfill the law *by* living in the power of the Spirit. But the expression can, on our view, be a simple definition: The people in whom the law is fulfilled are those who live in the realm of the Spirit.

Life in the Spirit Versus Death in the Flesh (8:5–8)

AT THE END of verse 4, Paul introduces a contrast that governs these next four verses: "the sinful nature" versus the Spirit. "Sinful nature" is the NIV rendering of the Greek word *sarx* (flesh), when this word refers to the sinful tendencies of human beings. But the variety of constructions in which *sarx* occurs in these verses forces translators to use several different paraphrases. We prefer, for the sake of continuity of argument, to use the more literal "flesh" throughout (see footnote 2; also Bridging Contexts section).

In verses 5–8, then, Paul presents a series of contrasts between flesh and Spirit. His overall intention is clear: to show that *sarx* brings death while the Spirit brings life (v. 6). Paul leads up to this key claim by tracing people's manner of life to their underlying way of thinking. In verse 4, he has used the antithesis of "living" (lit., "walking") by the flesh/Spirit. The beginning of verse 5 picks up this same idea with a slightly different Greek construction (simply "according to the flesh/Spirit"). The lifestyle of the flesh flows from a mind oriented to the flesh, whereas the lifestyle of the Spirit comes from a mind oriented to the Spirit. And "the mind of the flesh is death" whereas the "mind of the Spirit [brings] life and peace."

"Mind" translates *phronema*, which can be rendered "mind-set"; it denotes the basic direction of a person's will (this noun occurs only in Romans 8 in the New Testament [vv. 6, 7, 27], though note the use of the cognate verb in Phil. 1:7; 2:2, 5; 3:15, 19; 4:5). Romans 8:7–8 explains why "the mind of the flesh" brings death. The orientation of the will reflects the values of this world as "hostile to God," revealed in the fact that people who have that

---

3. See, e.g., Schreiner, *Romans*, 404–8.

4. See, e.g., Nygren, *Commentary on Romans*, 316–20; Fitzmyer, *Romans*, 487–88; see esp. the excellent discussion of Paul's ethics in Deidun, *New Covenant Morality in Paul*, 72–75.

will cannot obey God's law (v. 7). Thus, people who are "in the flesh [NIV controlled by the sinful nature] cannot please God" (v. 8).

Assurance of Future, Resurrection Life (8:9–11)

PAUL SIGNALS A shift in direction by turning directly to his readers: "*You*, however, are controlled not by the flesh but by the Spirit." Paul's "two-regime" theological framework is evident here. What he says, literally, is that "you are not in the flesh, but in the Spirit." *Flesh* and *Spirit* are two of the main powers belonging, respectively, to the old regime and the new (see 7:5–6). By God's grace in Christ, Christians have been taken out of the realm dominated by "flesh"—the narrowly human outlook that leads to sin—and placed in the realm dominated by God's Holy Spirit. It is clear, then, that the "in flesh"/"in Spirit" language is metaphorical—a way of indicating that people are dominated by one or the other of these forces.

This becomes even clearer at the end of verse 9, where Paul shifts to the opposite metaphorical concept: We are "in the Spirit" if the Spirit "lives in" us. In whom does the Spirit live? In every person who is genuinely a Christian. Not to have the Spirit of Christ is not to belong to Christ at all. The New Testament teaches that the gift of the Holy Spirit is an automatic benefit for anyone who knows Christ (see comments on 6:1–14). We must, then, give full force to the indicative mode of verse 9: Every Christian really is "in the Spirit"—under his domination and control. We may not always reflect that domination (see 8:12–13), but it is a fundamental fact of our Christian existence and the basis for a life of confidence and obedience to the Lord.

In an effort to maintain balance that is typical of Romans, Paul goes on to comment about a situation in which the Spirit's dominance might not be so obvious: the believer's continued existence in a physical body that is doomed to die and is still all too susceptible to the influence of sin. Yes, Paul says, even with Christ in us, our bodies are still "dead because of sin." Physical death is a penalty for sin that must still be carried out. Yet the Christian can take confidence because "your spirit is alive because of righteousness."

According to the NIV translation in verse 10, it is the human "spirit" (small "s") that has been given new spiritual life. The contrast between *pneuma* ("spirit") and *soma* ("body") might favor this rendering.[5] But *pneuma* consistently refers to the Holy Spirit in this chapter, and the Greek word behind "alive" is not an adjective, but a noun: *zoe*, "life." Furthermore, the word "your" in "your spirit" does not occur in the Greek. Probably, then, Paul refers here to

---

5. See, e.g., Godet, *Commentary on Romans*, 305; Fitzmyer, *Romans*, 491.

the Holy Spirit, the power of "life" that has come to reside in every believer.[6] It is because of this power of life within us that we can be certain of future resurrection. Our bodies may be doomed to die, but the Spirit, the Spirit of life, the Spirit of the God who raised our Lord Jesus from the dead, dwells within us and guarantees that our bodies will not end in the grave. God, through the Spirit, will give life to those bodies again.[7]

Our Obligation (8:12–13)

MOST COMMENTARIES AND translations put a major break between verses 11 and 12 and put verses 12–13 in a paragraph with verses 14–17. But verses 12–13 are not the introduction to the "children of God" theme of verses 14–17; they are the conclusion to Paul's teaching about life in Christ through the Spirit (8:1–11). The "Spirit of life" (v. 2) sets us free from condemnation so that we can now enjoy new life, and because "the Spirit is life" (cf. v. 10) we are also assured of eternal life in a resurrected body. But God's gift of new life through his Spirit carries with it an obligation. That obligation is not to "the flesh" (*sarx*; NIV sinful nature), that power of the old regime from which we have been delivered. It is to the Spirit, the power of the new regime.

To be sure, Paul does not state this positive side of our obligation. He breaks off his sentence at the end of verse 12 to emphasize the importance of our obligation in verse 13. We will ultimately inherit the new eternal life God has promised us only if we actively use the Spirit to "put to death the misdeeds of the body." Continuing to live "according to the flesh" means that we will suffer spiritual death. The tension between the "indicative" of what God gives us and the "imperative" of what we must do comes to a head here. We will say more about this tension in the Contemporary Significance section.

Three points can be made briefly here. (1) Paul is serious about the need for us to put into effect the new life God gives us. Our response is not optional; it is necessary. (2) However, this response is itself empowered by the Spirit. We cannot stop committing sins in our own power; it can only be done "by the Spirit." (3) Paul never suggests that the inheritance of future life requires that we stop sinning altogether. What he demands in this verse is clear, long-term, progress in becoming less like the world (i.e., "the flesh") and more like Christ.

---

6. So most contemporary commentators; see, e.g., Cranfield, *The Epistle to the Romans*, 390; Dunn, *Romans*, 431–32. See also the discussion in Fee, *God's Empowering Presence*, 550–51.

7. "Through his Spirit, who lives in you" rests on a disputed variant reading (*dia* plus the genitive); the alternative, strongly advocated by, e.g., Fee (*God's Empowering Presence*, 543, 553) would be translated "because of his Spirit, who lives in you" (*dia* plus the accusative).

Bridging Contexts

UNDERSTANDING FLESH (SARX). Sometimes there is justice in life. Whenever I taught Romans over the last couple of decades, I always criticized the NIV translators' decision to translate *sarx* (flesh) when Paul uses in it in a negative way as "sinful nature." I argued that by introducing the word "nature" in these contexts, the translators were setting up a potentially serious misrepresentation of Paul's understanding of Christian existence.

Three years ago, however, I was appointed to the committee charged with reviewing the NIV translation. One of my first tasks was to suggest a better rendering of *sarx*. But it wasn't long before I realized the difficulty faced by the translator here. I thought it might simply be best to use the English word "flesh" in each place where Paul uses *sarx*. But, as some of my colleagues rightly noted, most English readers think of the term *flesh* either as the meat on our bones or as sexual sin. Neither is anywhere close to what Paul intends. I tried various other alternatives but could come up with nothing better than "sinful nature." So the decision came down to this: Should we continue to use "sinful nature," even though that phrase may give a wrong impression? Or should we stick with "flesh," even though many English readers may not understand it? The committee elected to stay with "sinful nature," at least in most places.

This story illustrates and introduces two points relating to this word *sarx*: the complexity of this word in Paul and the hazards of translation. Both points need brief treatment as we seek to bridge Paul's context and ours.

(1) Paul's use of *sarx* is one of the most debated points in his theology.[8] He sometimes uses the word to refer to the physical body as a whole (1 Cor. 6:16; 2 Cor. 7:1; 12:7; Gal. 5:13, 16; Eph. 5:31), as in secular Greek. But the physical element is often lost in Paul when he uses the word to refer to the person generally (see lit. trans. of Rom. 3:20: "No flesh will be justified by works of the law"). The Greeks used *sarx* in this way, but Paul's usage is probably strongly influenced by the Old Testament. For *sarx* translates the Hebrew *basar*, which often refers to humankind in general (see lit. trans. of Gen. 6:12b: "All flesh has corrupted their ways").

Particularly important for Paul's special use of *sarx* is the way it sometimes connotes in the LXX what is human in distinction from God and the spiritual realm: "All flesh is [NIV all men are] like grass. . . . The grass withers and the flowers fall . . . but the word of our God stands forever" (Isa. 40:6–8). Paul often implies this notion of the "narrowly human" when he uses the word *sarx*.

---

8. See, e.g., the history of research in Robert Jewett, *Paul's Anthropological Terms: A Study of Their Use in Conflict Settings* (Leiden: Brill, 1971), 49–95.

Many scholars divide Paul's use of the word into two categories: the neutral and the ethical. But the two categories are rather at different points in a single continuous spectrum.

Even, therefore, when Paul speaks of Abraham as "our forefather according to the flesh" (Rom. 4:1) or of Jesus as being "a descendant of David according to the flesh" (1:3, both lit. trans.), Paul implies that what he has said is not the whole story. Abraham is the physical father of the Jews, and that is not in itself negative. But it is ultimately, as he argues in Romans 4, too limited a view of Abraham, for he is also the father of all who believe. Similarly, it is obviously the case that Jesus' existence in the flesh does not mean he was sinful or that this was a bad state. But, again, more must be said. For Jesus is not only Messiah from a physical, human perspective; he is also "Son of God in power according to the Spirit of holiness" (1:4, lit. trans.).

We have to try to bring this broad, Old Testament-based background into our understanding of Paul's use of *sarx* to describe the situation outside of Christ. What the apostle seems to mean is a condition, natural to people, in which God and the spiritual realm are left out of account. To be "in the flesh" (7:5; 8:8—9) is to be helplessly trapped in this situation. Thus, people naturally think in a "narrowly human" way ("the mind of the flesh"—8:5–6) and live in a "narrowly human" way ("live [or walk] according to the flesh"—8:4–5). In contrast, Christians, who no longer are in this condition, must not act as if they were. They must cease living "according to the flesh" (8:13).

Paul is again thinking in salvation-historical terms, helping us understand who we are by contrasting the old regime of the flesh from which we have been rescued with the new regime of the Spirit to which we now belong. Only by carefully reading the relevant passages and comparing Paul's uses of *sarx* across his writings can we bridge the context from his day to ours.

(2) But bridging the contexts in translation is more difficult. The Italians have a famous saying about translation: *Traddutore, traditore:* "Translators, traitors." What they mean is that any attempt to translate a book into another language inevitably fails to capture all the meaning and nuances of the original. Languages differ significantly. What one language expresses elegantly in a single word may not have a single word equivalent in other languages; a wordplay in one language does not work in another because the range of meanings of the words involved is different. Anyone who has tried to translate from one language to another knows just how hard the task can sometimes be and that the translator must always make difficult choices.

The rendering of Paul's *sarx* into English is an excellent case in point. One could, of course, argue that the "literal" meaning of the word ("flesh") should be preserved. But what do we mean by "literal"? Lurking behind this word is a false assumption about the way languages work, namely, that every word has a simple equivalent in another language that the translator can simply plug in. A lot of people who ask me what is the "most literal" translation of the Bible seem to have this impression of language.

But things are not that simple. Words have different meanings, and other languages often use different words to translate those meanings. I can use "bit" to refer to the implement I put in a horse's mouth and to describe how powerful my computer is. Other languages undoubtedly have different words for these two meanings of a single English word. Imagine the confusion if I insisted on translating the English word "bit" with a single word in these other languages!

But let's return to *flesh*. When one looks in an English dictionary, the meanings given for this word are: (1) "the soft parts of the body of an animal ..."; (2) "edible parts of an animal ..."; (3) (a) "the physical being of man"; (b) "human nature."[9] None of these is quite what Paul means by *sarx*. The last is the closest, but would the normal English reader know a meaning that comes so far down the list of definitions? Moreover, if the translator chooses to use "flesh" for every occurrence of *sarx* in Paul, the English reader might think that Christ came "in the flesh" in just the way that people apart from Christ are "in the flesh," thereby eliminating either the sinlessness of Christ or the sinfulness of people.

I think it fair to say, then, that no good solution to the problem of translating *sarx* into English exists. The translator has to decide which of the alternatives has fewest problems, which gets closest to what Paul seems to intend. English readers of the Bible should not despair: Good translation gets the message of the Bible over clearly enough. But English readers should also understand that even the best translation will often not quite get the meaning of the original. Comparing other translations and the use of commentaries and other reference materials can do a lot to overcome the inevitable deficiency of an English translation.

THE TRINITY IN ROMANS 8:1–13. Most students of the Bible know that one of the great distinguishing doctrines of the Christian church—the Trinity—is never explicitly taught in the Bible. The famous formulation about God as the "three in one," three persons within a single Godhead, is not found in the Scripture. The closest we get are formulations such as Matthew 28:19, where Jesus commands his disciples to baptize "in the name of the Father and of the Son and of the Holy Spirit."

---

9. *Webster's New Collegiate Dictionary* (Springfield, Mass.: G. & C. Merriam, 1980).

Why, then, does the Christian church hold this doctrine? Because we are convinced that the Trinitarian formulation is the only way to do justice to what the entire Bible teaches about God: Father, Christ, and the Holy Spirit. "There is one God" is clearly taught in the New Testament as well as the Old (e.g., Rom. 3:30; 1 Cor. 8:4–6; James 2:19). But equally clear is the teaching that Jesus is God (e.g., John 20:28; Rom. 9:5; Titus 2:13; Heb. 1:8) and that the Holy Spirit is God (Acts 5:3–4). Only the doctrine of the Trinity can account for the claims made in all these texts.

Another, less direct, witness to the Trinity are the many passages that fall into a Trinitarian pattern. The New Testament writers, perhaps before they had even formally worked out the conception of the Trinity, were writing about God in ways that showed they were assuming such a view. Romans 8:1–13 affords two of the clearest examples of this consciousness. (1) Note how Paul involves Father, Son, and Spirit in the work of redemption (vv. 2–3). God the Father sends his Son to condemn sin (v. 3), and the Holy Spirit applies the benefits of that action to release us from sin and death. Salvation is the work of the Triune God. All three persons are active in rescuing us from sin and bringing us into the new life. Our thanksgiving and worship, therefore, are appropriately directed to all three persons. Many of the great hymns of the faith reflect this Trinitarian structure.

(2) Note also how Paul varies the way he talks about God's work in our hearts in verses 9–10: "You, however, are controlled not by the sinful nature but by the Spirit, if the Spirit of God lives in you. And if anyone does not have the Spirit of Christ, he does not belong to Christ. But if Christ is in you, your body is dead because of sin, yet your spirit is alive because of righteousness." What takes up his dwelling in us is first the "Spirit of God," then the "Spirit of Christ," then, finally, "Christ." Paul does not mean that the Spirit and Christ are two names for the same person or that they are interchangeable. Rather, both are involved so intimately in the work of God in our lives that he can shift virtually unconsciously from one to the other.

Theological metaphors once again. In the Bridging Contexts section of 3:21–26, we noted how biblical writers use various metaphors to capture theological truth. Romans 8:9 illustrates the point once more, though the NIV obscures this fact somewhat. Let us therefore start with a literal rendering: "You are not in the flesh but in the Spirit, if the Spirit of God dwells in you. And if someone does not have the Spirit of Christ, that person does not belong to him." Note how Paul can shift within these two verses from the metaphor of our being "in" the Spirit to the metaphor of the Spirit being "in" us. Neither, of course, is ontologically true. But both are pictures of a theological truth: The believer is under the dominance of God's Spirit.

How easily we can use the metaphors of Scripture and not always understand them was brought home to me forcefully one day when I got home from work to find my son David, then about five years old, rushing up to me, exclaiming excitedly, "Daddy, Daddy, I just asked Jesus into my tummy!" A metaphor such as "asking Jesus into the heart" can become such a cliché that it ceases to have significance. We miss the truth that the metaphor is designed to point to.

The importance of our mind-set. In discussing verse 6, we suggested that the Greek word *phronema* that Paul uses there might best be rendered "mind-set." Note how the NIV translates the cognate verb (*phroneo*) in verse 5: "have their minds set on." These two Greek words are distinctively Pauline. Twenty-three of the twenty-six New Testament occurrences of *phroneo* are found in Paul (Rom. 8:5; 11:20; 12:3, 16; 14:6; 15:5; 1 Cor. 13:11; 2 Cor. 13:11; Gal. 5:10; Phil. 1:7; 2:2, 5; 3:15, 19; 4:2, 10; Col. 3:2; see also Matt. 16:23; Mark 8:33; Acts 28:22), and all four New Testament occurrences of *phronema* come in this chapter (vv. 6 [2x], 7, 27). These words include intellectual activity ("thinking" in the narrow sense), but go beyond it to involve the will also. The *phronema* is our fundamental orientation, the convictions and heart attitude that steers the course of our life.

As such, having the "mind-set" of the Spirit is the crucial "middle" step between existence in the sphere of the Spirit (v. 9) and living according to the Spirit (v. 4b). Cultivating a Spirit-led, Spirit-filled disposition of heart and mind is necessary if we are to live in a way that pleases God.

These verses, therefore, raise a fundamental question: How are we forming our "minds"? What are we putting in them? What are we exposing them to? Christians who read nothing but the latest novels, watch nothing but network television, and talk to nobody but unbelievers are never going to form the mind-set of the Spirit. All the input comes from one direction, reflecting the value system of the "flesh." No wonder we so often think and act in "fleshly" ways!

If we are serious about progressing in the Christian life, we must seek every day to feed our minds with spiritual food. Too easily our "quiet times" can degenerate into routine exercises in which the mind is hardly involved. We read Scripture, but we don't really seek to engage it by asking what it means or how it applies to us. We pray, but we follow the same pattern every day. Our daily times with the Lord can be one way in which we develop the mind-set of the Spirit, but only if the mind is really involved.

God's gift and our obligation. The juxtaposition of verses 1 and 13 is jarring. In the former, Paul boldly proclaims that "there is now no condemnation for those who are in Christ Jesus." But in the latter he warns, "If you live according to the flesh, you will die; but if by the Spirit you put to death the

---

257

misdeeds of the body, you will live." How can both be true? If there truly is "no condemnation" for believers, then how can we warn believers that they may die if they live the wrong way? Has God secured our eternal life once for all? Or is it still up to us to earn that eternal life?

Theologians have answered these questions in very different ways, and their views have filtered down to Christians. The result is that people have very different ideas about the Christian life and how to lead it. What is important is to maintain a careful balance between what God gives us in Christ and what we must do in response to that gift.

A few interpreters have tried to avoid the tension between these verses altogether by particular readings of verse 13. Some think that the people Paul addresses ("you") may be church attenders who do not really know the Lord. But how can Paul then urge them to use the Spirit to fight sin? Others think that "death" and "life" in the verse are physical only. But it is nonsense for Paul to suggest that physical death, the fate all who do not live until the Lord returns, will be the penalty only for Christians who live according to the flesh. The "death" Paul warns about and the "life" he promises are spiritual, not physical. Paul affirms that his Christian readers will be damned if they continue to follow the dictates of the flesh.

But how then does the need to put sin away from us relate to the promise of verse 1? Here two basic theological traditions part company. Calvinists and Arminians are agreed that the believer must progress in the battle against sin if he or she is to attain eternal life. But the Arminian believes that a regenerate person might, indeed, be so lured by the flesh that he or she fails to progress in the Christian life. At some point, then, that person might cease to be "in Christ." Thus, the promise of verse 1 no longer applies to that person. The Calvinist, by contrast, believes that the influence of the Spirit in a believer's life is so dominant that he or she can never reach the point of falling permanently into a lifestyle of sin and so forfeit the promise of "no condemnation."

Each of these theological traditions, in other words, focuses on different sides of the truth Paul presents in these verses. The Calvinist does full justice to verse 1 with its ringing promise of "no condemnation"; the Arminian does full justice to the warning of verse 13. Both words need to be heard if we are to maintain a balance in our Christian walk. Security without responsibility breeds passivity, but responsibility without security leads to anxiety.

I have counseled both types of Christians. During an interim pastorate, I got to know an elder in the church. He proclaimed himself a strong Calvinist and delighted to discuss Reformed theology. I eventually discovered that he was having sex outside his marriage. But he was not worried about it; he was eternally secure in Christ. I also remember counseling a young woman who was extremely performance oriented. She brought this attitude into her

Christianity and was eternally in despair because she had not lived up to the Lord's expectations of her. She could not grasp her security in Christ—that Christ had taken her sins so that her performance was no longer the basis for her acceptance.

The truth question cannot be evaded. We need to preserve security and responsibility in balance. But how do we combine them in a way that is both coherent and true to Scripture? When push comes to shove, I myself think the strength of the assurances Paul gives to justified believers in this part of Romans (see esp. 5:9–10, 21; 8:1–4, 10–11, 28–30, 31–39) favors the Calvinist interpretation. No true believer can ever suffer condemnation. The verdict of innocence has already been proclaimed in the divine court, and it cannot be changed. But precisely because I take this view, I bend over backwards to do justice to the responsibility side of biblical teaching. As John Murray, a Calvinist himself, says, "The believer's once-for-all death to the law of sin does not free him from the necessity of mortifying sin in his members; it makes it *necessary* and *possible* for him to do so."[10]

The Spirit's presence in our lives inevitably produces fruit pleasing to God. Thus, we are secure. But the Spirit does not do his work apart from our response. I like the careful balance Paul achieves in verse 13: "By the *Spirit you* put to death the misdeeds of the body" (italics added). Paul puts the responsibility squarely on our shoulders: *You* need to put sin to death. But at the same time, he makes it clear that we can only do it *through the Spirit.*

---

10. Murray, *The Epistle to the Romans*, 1:294.

Romans 8:14–17

BECAUSE THOSE WHO are led by the Spirit of God are sons of God. ¹⁵For you did not receive a spirit that makes you a slave again to fear, but you received the Spirit of sonship. And by him we cry, "Abba, Father." ¹⁶The Spirit himself testifies with our spirit that we are God's children. ¹⁷Now if we are children, then we are heirs—heirs of God and co-heirs with Christ, if indeed we share in his sufferings in order that we may also share in his glory.

Original Meaning

IF 8:1–13 IS ABOUT "the Spirit of life," then 8:14–17 are about "the Spirit of adoption." God has made us his children through the work of his Spirit. As a result, we rejoice now in being able to call God "Father." But we also rejoice in knowing that God, having adopted us, has also made us his heirs. We can therefore look forward to the future with confidence.

Paul attaches verses 14–17 to verse 13; note the way the NIV continues the same sentence from verse 13 into verse 14. It is "because" the Spirit leads us that we can be confident we "will live." The recognition that we are God's own children is yet another basis for our assurance that, indeed, "there is now no condemnation for those who are in Christ Jesus" (8:1).

In popular speech, Christians often use language such as "led by the Spirit" to refer to guidance: "I was led by the Spirit to witness to her." But this is probably not what Paul means here.[1] As in Galatians 5:18, where the same construction occurs, "being led by the Spirit" means "having the basic orientation of your life determined by the Spirit."[2] The phrase is a way of summing up the various descriptions of the life of the Spirit in 8:4–9.

Paul's effort to balance the indicative and the imperative is again noticeable. Because of the Spirit's work, we have life (8:1–11). In order to attain eternal life, we must use the Spirit to put away sin (8:12–13). And we know we will live because the Spirit has taken possession of us (8:14). The "middle

---

1. Although most early Christian interpreters understood guidance to be the topic here.

2. The Greek uses the passive of the verb *ago*, "lead," with the dative *pneumati*, "by the Spirit." On its meanings, see Brendan Byrne, *"Sons of God"—"Seed of Abraham": A Study of the Idea of Sonship of God of All Christians in Paul Against the Jewish Background* (Rome: Pontifical Biblical Institute, 1979), 98.

term" in Paul's argument from Spirit to life is being "the sons of God." The imagery is drawn from the Old Testament, where God is pictured as the "father" of Israel (e.g., Deut. 32:6; Isa. 64:8; cf. *Jubilees* 1:25) and Israel as his "son" (Ex. 4:22; Jer. 3:19; 31:9; Hos. 11:1) or the people of Israel as his "sons" (Deut. 14:1; Isa. 43:6; Hos. 1:10 [quoted in Rom. 9:26]).

In 8:15—16, Paul pauses in his argument to elaborate the link between the Spirit and being God's sons. Verse 15 centers on a contrast between two different spirits: "a spirit that makes you a slave again to fear" and "the Spirit of sonship." Commentators have suggested various identifications for this "spirit of fear,"[3] but this is the wrong tack to take. Paul is using a rhetorical device to explain the nature of the Spirit we have received. He is saying, in effect, that the Spirit of God we have received is not a spirit of fear but the Spirit who makes us God's sons.

As the NIV note indicates, the word "sonship" (*huiothesia*) can also be translated "adoption" (the word does not occur in the LXX; in the New Testament see also Rom. 8:23; 9:4; Gal. 4:5; Eph. 1:5). The legal act of adoption was not practiced by the Jews, so almost certainly Paul uses the image of the Greco-Roman practice whereby a man could formally confer on a child all the legal rights of a birth child.[4] This, Paul suggests, is what God's Spirit confers on every believer—the rights and privileges of God's own children.

Naturally, then, we are moved to cry out in a spontaneous outburst, "*Abba, Father!*" It is sometimes claimed that Jews never called God "*Abba*." This is not strictly true, although it was an unusual way to speak of God. What is most important is that the Spirit enables us to experience the same kind of intimate relationship to the Father that Jesus did, who also called God "*Abba*" (Mark 14:36). Not only does the Spirit confer on us this status; he also is the one who, testifying with our own spirits, gives us the inner certainty of knowing that we truly are God's dearly loved children.

Verse 17 resumes the main course of Paul's argument in this paragraph, which runs from "Spirit" to "sonship" to "heir." The transition is a natural one. The adopted child is guaranteed legally all the benefits of the natural child, including being the heir of his new father. But precisely because the adopted child is an heir, there is still something incomplete in his status. Though legally part of a new family, adopted children do not yet possess all the benefits of their new status. Thus, Paul reminds us, we Christians must still await the consummation of that new status. One day we will enter into the

---

3. E.g., the Holy Spirit in the Old Testament, who created a sense of slavery and fear in people through the law (so many Puritans; cf. Kevan, *Grace of Law*, 88—89).

4. See esp. Francis Lyall, *Slaves, Citizens, Sons: Legal Metaphors in the Epistles* (Grand Rapids: Zondervan, 1984), 67—99.

inheritance, following the Son who has gone ahead of us. We will share in his own glorious state. In the meantime, however, we must follow him in the road he himself walked on the way to glory—the road of suffering.

FROM SLAVES TO SONS. Understanding Romans 8:14—17 is easier when we recognize in the text a pattern of argument that Paul uses elsewhere in greater detail. Note the parallels between Romans 8:1—17 and Galatians 4:3b—7:

Galatians 4:3b—7	*Romans 8:1—17*
we were in slavery under the basic principles of the world (v. 3b)	set me free from the law of sin and death (v. 2b)
But when the time had fully come, God sent his Son, born of a woman, born under law (v. 4)	God did by sending his own Son in the likeness of sinful man (v. 3b)
to redeem those under law (v. 5a)	to be a sin offering. And so he condemned sin in the flesh (v. 3b)
that we might receive the full rights of sons [*huiothesia*] (v. 6)	you received the Spirit of sonship [*huiothesia*] (v. 15b)
Because you are sons, God sent the Spirit of his Son into our hearts, the Spirit who calls out, "*Abba*, Father" (v. 6)	And by him we cry, "*Abba*, Father" (v. 15c) Cf. the Spirit of God lives in you (v. 9b)
So you are no longer a slave, but a son (v. 7a)	For you did not receive a spirit that makes you a slave again to fear (v. 15a)
and since you are a son, God has made you also an heir (v. 7b)	Now if we are children, then we are heirs (v. 17a)

In both passages, Paul affirms that believers are transformed from slaves to sons through the sacrificial death of Christ, "sent" as one like us. This new status is called "adoption" (*huiothesia*) and is tied to the indwelling Spirit, the Spirit who makes us aware that we now belong to God as his dearly loved children. In both, being God's children leads to our being his heirs. Of course, Paul loosens the tight argument of Galatians 4:1—7 by weaving elements from that text into a larger context in Romans 8. As the context of Galatians suggests, Paul may have used the imagery of the slave-become-a-son to depict the new status of Israel in Christ. If so, he adapts the imagery and broadens its scope to include all believers. We see once again here, then, the way Paul can view Israel's experience as paradigmatic for the situation of all people.

One other element of this conceptual scheme requires comment: the focus on "sons" (8:14) and "sonship" (8:15). As Paul's shift to "children" in verses 16–17 suggests, his use of "sons" is not meant to exclude women from the status he describes. He uses the male terminology because in his culture it was usual for males both to be adopted and to stand as representative of both genders. In other words, to bring this message from Paul's culture to ours, it seems appropriate, as the NRSV does, to translate *uioi* in verse 14 as "children." This may be the best alternative, but one important point may be lost. For our status as "sons" is closely tied, Paul suggests, to Jesus' status as *the* Son (8:3, 29; cf. Gal. 4:4). We are "sons of God" because we identify with Jesus, *the* Son. This echo is muted if we drop the terminology of *son* here.

SECURITY. THE FEELING of being rejected is all too common in our world. Husbands reject wives and wives husbands as the divorce rate soars. Parents reject children and children parents. High school students reject other students because they do not fit with the "in group." Every reader can fill in the blank with his or her own experience of rejection. The sad fact is that it is increasingly difficult to find a secure and permanent relationship. As a result, people feel uneasy and uncertain. I know wives married twenty-five years to loving husbands who find it hard to trust their husbands because of the broken marriages they see all around them.

Of course, no human relationship can ever provide ultimate security. The best-intentioned spouse can die at any time. But what our fellow humans can never supply, God does. In the midst of our disillusionment and doubt, he offers the most secure relationship imaginable: adoption into his own eternal family. Through our faith in Christ, the Son of God, we become his "brothers and sisters" (see Heb. 2:10–13), children of God and co-heirs with Christ of all that God has promised those who love him. We belong to the ultimate "in group," those who are the dearly loved children of the God of the universe. Nor do we have to worry about being rejected from this relationship. As Paul has been teaching throughout these chapters and will do again in 8:18–39, our adoption is permanent. Nothing can change that; nothing and nobody can keep us from enjoying God's favor and blessing forever.

No wonder we spontaneously cry out, "*Abba,* Father!" How could anyone who really understands that they have been adopted into God's family and been given all the privileges his children enjoy *not* break out in amazed thanksgiving and praise? Some believers, bothered by the excesses of extreme charismatic groups, sometimes recoil against any expression of emotion. They worry that people will base their faith on their emotions rather than on the solid rock of God's work in Christ on our behalf. They are right to worry. Some Christians do indeed seem to be all emotion, constantly on a roller-coaster ride of faith that lacks the stability that comes from a thorough appropriation of God's Word.

But emotion should be part of any real experience of the living God. We will express our emotions differently. Some of us are naturally egregious and raise our hands in public worship without even thinking about it. Others of us may be less inclined to public display, though moved just as much as our more outgoing brothers and sisters. But, however we express them, the joy and praise that well up within us when we appreciate anew our status in Christ are inevitable.

But do we rightly appreciate that status? Probably never to the degree we should. Meditation on Scripture can help. Singing great lyrics about God's gift to us in Christ can wonderfully bring home to us afresh the marvels of God's grace in our lives. One of my own favorite hymns is "And Can It Be?" One stanza in particular from that hymn seems a fitting note on which to end this section and to awaken our emotions:

No condemnation now I dread,
Jesus, and all in Him, is mine!
Alive in Him, my living Head,
And clothed in righteousness divine,
Bold I approach th' eternal throne,
And claim the crown, thru Christ my own.
Amazing love! how can it be
That Thou, my God, shouldst die for me?

Romans 8:18–30

ICONSIDER THAT our present sufferings are not worth comparing with the glory that will be revealed in us. ¹⁹The creation waits in eager expectation for the sons of God to be
revealed. ²⁰For the creation was subjected to frustration, not
by its own choice, but by the will of the one who subjected it,
in hope ²¹that the creation itself will be liberated from its
bondage to decay and brought into the glorious freedom of
the children of God.

²²We know that the whole creation has been groaning as in
the pains of childbirth right up to the present time. ²³Not only
so, but we ourselves, who have the firstfruits of the Spirit,
groan inwardly as we wait eagerly for our adoption as sons,
the redemption of our bodies. ²⁴For in this hope we were
saved. But hope that is seen is no hope at all. Who hopes for
what he already has? ²⁵But if we hope for what we do not yet
have, we wait for it patiently.

²⁶In the same way, the Spirit helps us in our weakness. We
do not know what we ought to pray for, but the Spirit himself
intercedes for us with groans that words cannot express. ²⁷And
he who searches our hearts knows the mind of the Spirit,
because the Spirit intercedes for the saints in accordance with
God's will.

²⁸And we know that in all things God works for the good
of those who love him, who have been called according to his
purpose. ²⁹For those God foreknew he also predestined to be
conformed to the likeness of his Son, that he might be the
firstborn among many brothers. ³⁰And those he predestined,
he also called; those he called, he also justified; those he justified, he also glorified.

PAUL BEGAN THE great second section of his exposition of the gospel by assuring believers of their
sure hope for salvation in the judgment (5:1–11).
He now returns to where he started, setting
before us the wonderful fact and the solid basis for our hope as Christians.
The immediate stimulus is the end of 8:17, where he reminded us that we

need to share in Christ's sufferings if we expect to share in his glory. The theme of 8:18–30 is the believer's future glory. This passage begins ("the glory that will be revealed in us," v. 18) and ends ("those he justified, he also glorified," v. 30) on this note.

In between, Paul makes two basic points about this glory. (1) It is the climax in God's plan both for his people and for his creation generally. Since we have not reached that climax, we must eagerly and patiently wait for it (vv. 18–25). (2) God himself provides what we need in order to wait eagerly and patiently. The Spirit helps us pray (vv. 26–27), and God promises to oversee everything for our good (v. 28) according to his unbreakable plan for us (vv. 29–30). The Holy Spirit is not as prominent as in 8:1–17. But he still plays a critical role as the "bridge" between our present experience as God's children and our final adoption into his family (v. 23).

Anticipation of Future Glory (8:19–25)

AS IN CHAPTER 5 (see 5:3–4), Paul does not try to hide the fact that believers suffer. Indeed, he highlights it. As people who identify with one who came to overturn the values of this world, Christians will inevitably share in the rejection and trials Christ himself experienced. Committed Christian living will always rub the world the wrong way at some point, and friction is inevitable.

But those sufferings aren't worth comparing to the glory that will be "revealed in us" (v. 18). This last phrase is hard to translate. The preposition Paul uses (*eis*) means neither "in" nor "to" (e.g., NRSV) exactly. What Paul is implying is that the glory he speaks of already exists; as Peter puts it, our final salvation is "kept in heaven . . . ready to be revealed in the last time" (1 Peter 1:4–5). So what now exists will one day be given "to" us so that it can come to reside "in" us, transforming us into Christ's own image (see Rom. 8:29).

In verses 19–21, Paul accentuates the importance of this revelation of glory by tying the liberation of the whole of creation to it. Interpreters debate just what this "creation" (*ktisis*) might refer to. Because he speaks so personally (e.g., in v. 22, it groans), many think he is referring only to human beings, or perhaps to unbelievers. Paul can use the word to refer to human "creatures" (Gal. 6:15; Col. 1:23), but he usually applies it to God's entire creation (Rom. 1:20, 25; 8:39; 2 Cor. 5:17; Col. 1:15). The key to its meaning here is the fact that Paul insists that the frustration "creation" is experiencing is not its own fault. We must, therefore, exclude all human beings, since they all had a part in the Fall. With most modern commentators, we conclude that Paul refers to all of subhuman creation: plants, animals, rocks, and so on.[1]

---

1. See esp. Cranfield, *The Epistle to the Romans*, 410–13.

Following the lead of the psalmists, Paul personifies the created world, using vivid poetic language to speak of its "frustration" (v. 20) and its eventual "liberation" (v. 21). The entire created world has failed to attain its purpose. Because of human sin, it is not what God intended it to be. "The one who subjected it," then, might be Adam, Satan, or God.[2] But only God truly "subjected" creation—in his decree after the Fall—and only God did it "in hope that the entire creation itself will be liberated." God will one day set the created world free from the decay that mars everything after the fall of human beings into sin. The fate of creation is bound up with that of humanity. As it was through them that creation was marred, so it is through the glorified children of God that it will be restored again.

Creation, then, groans "as in the pains of childbirth." The pain a woman about to deliver a child experiences is a vivid metaphor of suffering that has a joyous outcome. Biblical writers use this imagery to put a Christian "spin" on the difficulties of this life (see Matt. 24:8; Mark 13:8; John 16:20–22). From a Christian perspective, suffering is but a momentary thing that eventuates in eternal joy (see Rom. 8:18). Thus, Christians join creation in this kind of groaning (8:23).

Many interpreters take the phrase "who have the firstfruits of the Spirit" concessively: We groan *despite* the fact that we have the Spirit.[3] But it makes better sense to give it a causal interpretation: We groan *because* we have the Spirit.[4] Once the Spirit, with his demand for holiness, enters our lives, we sense as never before just what God wants us to be. As a result, the Spirit increases our frustration at not meeting God's standard and our yearning to be what he wants us to be. What do we wait for? "The redemption of the body" refers to the rescue of the body from sin and death that will happen when it is raised from the dead (see 8:10–11).

But how can Paul suggest that we yearn also for "our adoption as sons"? Has he not said that we have already been adopted (8:16)? Here we find a classic New Testament example of the "already-not yet" tension that pervades its teaching about the Christian life. Yes, we are God's children already—justified, reconciled, and brought into his family. But we are not yet God's children in the way we one day will be—possessing the full inheritance, enjoying perfect holiness in resurrected bodies, and glorified.

In light of this tension, therefore, it becomes clear that "hope" is an inevitable part of Christian living. We were "saved" in this hope; that is, hope

---

2. In favor of Adam, cf., e.g., G. W. H. Lampe, "The New Testament Doctrine of *Ktisis*," *SJT* 17 (1964): 458; in favor of Satan, see, e.g., Godet, *Commentary on Romans*, 314–15; in favor of God are almost all modern commentators.

3. E.g., Godet, *Commentary on Romans*, 318.

4. E.g., Dunn, *Romans*, 473–74.

has been a part of our salvation since the time of our conversion. The very nature of hope means that we await something we cannot now see. God has promised us glory, a glory already existing in heaven for us. But we cannot see it, hear it, or taste it; we must simply hope.

Nevertheless, Paul assures us, this hope is not of the normal human kind— "I hope I win the lottery." No, Christian hope is solidly founded in God himself. Thus, we can "wait for it patiently [*hypomones*]" or, perhaps better, "with endurance." This word suggests the ability to bear up under the trials that come our way (cf. Rom. 5:3–4; Heb. 10:36; 12:1; James 1:3–4; 5:11). "Wait for," the same word Paul used of creation in Romans 8:19, connotes a person craning his or her neck to spot someone or something coming. In the next few verses (8:26–30), Paul will explain why believers can look so eagerly and hopefully for what is coming.

God's Provision for Our Time of Waiting (8:26–30)

THE PHRASE "IN the same way" that connects these verses to their context is often thought to relate to the "groaning" language Paul uses in this passage: creation groans (v. 22), Christians groan (v. 23), and "in the same way," the Spirit groans.[5] But a closer connection is with the immediately preceding verse: As hope sustains us in our time of suffering (vv. 24–25), so also the Spirit sustains us in our time of weakness.[6] "Weakness," then, refers to the limitations of our human condition. Because of these limitations, "we do not know what we ought to pray for."

Our insight into God's will is far short of perfect, and so in many situations we are puzzled to know what exactly to pray for. But the Spirit comes to our aid, interceding on our behalf with "groans that words cannot express." A few interpreters think Paul may be referring to speaking in tongues here.[7] But the gift of tongues is given only to some Christians (1 Cor. 12:30). Others suggest Paul is using vivid imagery to refer to the Spirit's prayer in our hearts to the Lord.[8] Still other commentators think Paul refers to the Christian's own audible but wordless groanings as he or she struggles before the Lord in prayer.[9]

A decision between these last two alternatives is difficult. "Groaning" has been used metaphorically in the context (v. 22), so the former is certainly possible. Moreover, the word translated "that words that cannot express" in NIV

---

5. E.g., Godet, *Commentary on Romans*, 320; Dunn, *Romans*, 476.

6. See esp. Murray, *The Epistle to the Romans*, 1:310–11.

7. E.g., Käsemann, *Commentary on Romans*, 239–42; Fee, *God's Empowering Presence*, 577–86.

8. E.g., Cranfield, *The Epistle to the Romans*, 422.

9. E.g., Morris, *The Epistle to the Romans*, 326–28.

can mean either "unspoken" (not expressed at all) or "ineffable" (not expressed in *words*). Whichever it is, Paul's main point is clear enough: These groanings of the Spirit are perfectly in accord with God's will (v. 27). Thus God, who knows the heart, hears and answers those prayers. Our inability to pray as precisely as we would like is no hindrance to the working out of God's perfect will in our lives. We may not know what to ask for in a given situation, but the Spirit does. His requests are in perfect harmony with the will of the Lord for us. As Jesus intercedes for us before the Father (cf. 8:34), guaranteeing our salvation, so the Spirit intercedes for us in our hearts, preparing us for that salvation.

In this time of expectant suffering, the Spirit's intercession is one great support. Another is the providence of God. "Providence" is the word we use to describe God's beneficial rule over all the events of life. The famous promise of 8:28 is one of the great biblical descriptions of providence. Translations, affected by a textual variant, differ considerably. Three questions must be answered. (1) What is the subject of "work"? The Spirit (the subject in vv. 26–27; see REB)?[10] God (the subject of the last clause of v. 27; see NIV; NASB)?[11] Or "all things" (NRSV)?[12] The most natural way to read the verse is with "all things" as the subject. In the last analysis, however, the identity of the grammatical subject does not make much difference, for it is only God, through his Spirit, who can cause "all things" to work for our good.

(2) Another question is whether the verb (*synergeo*) should be translated "works together" (most translations) or simply "works" (NIV). The NIV is probably correct here. So we would translate, "We know that all things work toward the good of those who love God and are called according to his purpose." In this context, the "good" is especially the final glory to which God has destined us. But it also includes the benefits of being a child of God in this life (see Contemporary Significance section).

(3) Finally, for whom is this promise valid? All believers. Paul defines Christians from a human direction ("those who love [God]") and from the divine direction ("who have been called according to his purpose"). "Those who love God" is simply a way of describing God's people (see 1 Cor. 2:9;

---

10. See, e.g., Fee, *God's Empowering Presence*, 588–90.

11. This would be the required reading if the textual variant that adds *ho theos* ("God") were correct. It has support in some good manuscripts (the early papyrus P46, and the two early Alexandrian uncials A and B). But most modern interpreters dismiss it as an early scribal attempt to clarify the verse (see, e.g., Bruce M. Metzger, *A Textual Commentary on the Greek New Testament* [New York: United Bible Societies, 1971], 518). But "God" could still be the understood subject of the verse (see, e.g., Sanday and Headlam, *The Epistle to the Romans*, 215; Byrne, *Sons of God*, 113–14).

12. See esp. Cranfield, *The Epistle to the Romans*, 424–29.

8:3; Eph. 6:24); it is not a qualification of the promise, as if Paul means that God only works good if believers love God enough.

The "purpose" of God is outlined in 8:29–30. God has instituted a series of actions that create, sustain, and bring his people to glory. The first action is the most controversial. The Greek verb "to foreknow" (*proginosko*) generally means to know something ahead of time. Some interpreters insist it must therefore mean that here as well. God "knew something" about us ahead of time, and on that basis, he "predestined" us. Usually what God is thought to have known is that a certain person will respond positively to the gospel and believe.[13]

But the biblical use of "know" and "foreknow" creates a different picture. In Scripture God's knowing often refers to his entering into relationship with someone. "You only have I known [NIV chosen] of all the families of the earth," God claims (Amos 3:2). God knows everything *about* every family on earth, but Israel alone has he entered into relationship with. In four of its six New Testament occurrences, "foreknow" and its cognate noun, "foreknowledge," has this sense (Acts 2:23; Rom. 11:2; 1 Peter 1:2; 3:17; cf. also Acts 26:5; 2 Peter 3:17). This is probably the meaning the verb has here. Adding to the probability of this interpretation is the fact that the verb has a personal object ("those").

What Paul is saying, then, is that God's plan for us began in a decision to enter into relationship with us. This led, in turn, to his decision to "predestine" us. As the English verb suggests, this word (*proorizo*) simply means to direct a person to a particular goal (the verb also occurs in v. 30; cf. Acts 4:28; 1 Cor. 2:7; Eph. 1:5, 11). Paul spells out the goal: "to be conformed to the likeness of his Son." The last stage of Christian existence is to be "conformed" to Christ's own glorious body (see Phil. 3:21). God enters into relationship with us so that we may attain that goal.

Paul's reference to conformity to Christ as the goal of predestination interrupts his sequence of verbs. In verse 30 he continues the sequence, beginning where he left off, with predestination. "Calling" is not a general gospel invitation. It is God's effective summoning of us into relationship with himself through Christ (see 1:7). After setting us on the road to the goal of conformity to Christ, God in his grace and by his Spirit reaches out and brings us into his own people. He then "justifies" us, that is, declares us innocent before him (see chs. 1–4).

Finally, as the capstone to this series, he "glorifies" that person. This verb is in the same tense (aorist) as all the other verbs in this sequence, a tense that often (though not always) refers to action in the past. Why Paul

---

13. E.g., Godet, *Commentary on Romans*, 324–25.

uses that tense here for a verb whose action is yet future is not clear. Probably the best explanation is that he is viewing matters from God's perspective. God has already made the decision to glorify all those whom he has justified.

This sequence of verbs is a famous debating ground over issues of soteriology—election, predestination, eternal security (see Contemporary Significance section). But we must not lose sight of Paul's main point, namely, to assure believers that God has a plan he is unfolding, one that provides fully for our future glory. He wants us to come away from this text not with theological questions but with a renewed sense of assurance: that the God who began a good work in us will indeed bring it to completion in the day of Christ Jesus (Phil. 1:6).

FOLLOWING THE ARGUMENT. One of the biggest mistakes we can make in reading the Bible is to read paragraphs in isolation from one another. Certain devotional books, by selecting daily readings from all over the Bible, unfortunately encourage this practice. But the biblical authors meant their books to be read as books. Reading a paragraph chosen at random from the middle of, say, 2 Kings is something like reading a paragraph in isolation from the middle of the latest John Grisham novel. To be sure, the various biblical genres are not really comparable to a modern novel, and some of the genres require far less sequential reading than others (e.g., the Psalms). But the point is still valid. We can get the full meaning from any text of Scripture only as we appreciate the way the author intended it to function in the context of his whole book.

The principle of contextual reading is particularly important in Romans. For in this letter Paul is mounting an argument. He is trying to convince the Roman Christians of the power and truth of the gospel as he preaches it. Once we understand the overall argument, we will have a much better appreciation for the meaning of its particular parts. Conversely, relating the parts accurately to one another will help us determine the overall argument.

Modern Western readers miss the nuances of Paul's argument because we are used to reading in a linear fashion. That is, we are trained by our culture to assume an author will develop his argument in a straightforward sequence:

Consider A
and consider B
and C
and thus, the conclusion, D

But the culture of the biblical writers was much more accustomed to cyclical styles of argument. Especially common was what is called the "chiastic" form of argument:

Consider A
  thus B
  B' again
Because of A'

In this particular example, the conclusion the author is driving at comes in the middle of his argument. But it can also work the other way, with the main point appearing at the opposite ends of the sequence. We have suggested in our exposition of both 5:1–11 and 8:18–39 that these two paragraphs function as the "bookends" to Paul's argument in chapters 5–8. A comparison of vocabulary in these two sections provides further support for the relationship:

	5:1–11	(5:12–8:17)	8:18–39
love (of God/Christ)	5:5, 8	–	8:35, 39
justify	5:1, 9	6:7	8:30 [2x], 33
peace	5:1	8:6	–
glory	5:2	6:4	8:18, 21, 30 (glorify)
hope	5:2, 4, 5	–	8:20, 24 [4x], 25
tribulation/suffering	5:3 [2x]	–	8:18, 35
save	5:9, 10	–	8:24
endurance/perseverance	5:3, 4	–	8:25

One can, of course, prove anything by means of selective statistics. But the words above are the key words in both paragraphs. While emphases differ, Paul makes the same basic point in each section: The justified believer can be confident that he or she will experience final salvation because of God's love for him or her, the work of Christ, and the ministry of the Holy Spirit.

Recognizing the relation between these sections has three important consequences for our reading of this part of Romans. (1) It reinforces our belief that chapters 5–8 form an integral section within Romans. Without breaking these chapters off from their surroundings and recognizing that we need to appreciate the continuity between chapters 4 and 5 on the one hand and chapters 8 and 9 on the other, we must nevertheless understand these chapters in special relationship to each other.

(2) This will lead to a more accurate interpretation of the argument as a whole. Scholars have argued for centuries over the exact contribution of these chapters to Paul's argument in Romans. Once we recognize the inclusio that frames these chapters, we can conclude with some confidence that

their overall purpose is to convince justified believers that they have assurance for the last judgment.

(3) Having isolated the main point, we can then understand better the contribution of each individual section. As we have seen, we will be less inclined to think that 5:12–21 is about original sin when we recognize its connection to 5:1–11 and the unfolding defense of Christian assurance.

Creation and restoration. Paul's interesting allusions to the subhuman creation in 8:19–22 have sparked considerable interest. Nowhere else in the New Testament do we have a text quite like this, dealing with the fall and the restoration not just of human beings, but of the world in general. As a first step toward the goal of applying this passage, we will consider here some of the teaching in Paul's day that may have influenced him.

Particularly important were certain Jewish apocalyptic traditions. *Apocalyptic* is the term applied to a broad movement within the Jewish world of Paul's day. Having its origins in the crises that the Jewish people experienced in the two centuries before Christ, the apocalyptic movement found comfort for God's suffering people in the ultimate realities of the spiritual realm. On earth, God's people were having a difficult time. But from heaven's perspective, a plan of God was unfolding that would inevitably bring redemption to those loyal to God. The term *apocalyptic* comes from the Greek word meaning "revelation" (*apokalypsis*), and writers in the apocalyptic movement insisted that they possessed a revelation of just what God was up to in history. While it differs in some important respects from Jewish apocalypses, the book of Revelation is an example of a New Testament apocalyptic book.

What does all this have to do with Romans 8? In trying to make sense of the world, apocalyptic writers often sharply contrasted the new world of God's redemptive work with the old world of sin and death. God's vindication of his saints would not take place gradually through the processes of history, but would happen suddenly in a spectacular display of God's power. So sharp was the move from this world to the next that the redemptive work of God was often pictured as a new creation that would affect the entire universe. As a reflex of this development, attention was also directed to the way human sin affected the cosmos. Note the following sample of texts:

> For I made the world for their sake, and when Adam transgressed my statutes, what had been made was judged. (4 Ezra 7:11)

> In those days, mountains shall dance like rams; and the hills shall leap like kids satiated with milk. And the faces of all the angels in heaven shall glow with joy, because on that day the Elect One has arisen. And the earth shall rejoice; and the righteous ones shall dwell upon her and the elect ones shall walk upon her. (*1 Enoch* 51:4–5)

That which will happen at that time bears upon the whole earth. Therefore, all who live will notice it.... The earth will also yield fruits ten thousandfold. And on one vine will be a thousand branches, and one branch will produce a thousand clusters, and one cluster will produce a thousand grapes, and one grape will produce a cor of wine. And those who are hungry will enjoy themselves and they will, moreover, see marvels every day. For winds will go out in front of me every morning to bring the fragrance of aromatic fruits and clouds at the end of the day to distill the dew of health. And it will happen at that time that the treasury of manna will come down again from on high, and they will eat of it in those years because these are they who will have arrived at the consummation of time. (*2 Apocalypse of Baruch* 29:1–2, 5–8)

We should not, therefore, be so sad regarding the evil which has come now, but much more (distressed) regarding that which is in the future. For greater than the two evils will be the trial when the Mighty One will renew his creation. (*2 Apocalypse of Baruch* 32:5–6)

One can easily see the similarities between the tradition reflected in these texts and Romans 8:19–22. Scholars generally agree that Paul was influenced by this apocalyptic movement in his understanding of and presentation of God's work in Christ.

But we should not neglect a potentially more significant source for Paul's idea of the fall and restoration of creation, namely, the latter chapters of Isaiah. No Old Testament passage had a greater influence on Paul's theology. These chapters present the coming salvation of God as an event involving the entire universe. See, for instance, Isaiah 65:17–21, where the Lord promises:

"Behold, I will create
   new heavens and a new earth.
The former things will not be remembered,
   nor will they come to mind.
But be glad and rejoice forever
   in what I will create,
for I will create Jerusalem to be a delight
   and its people a joy.
I will rejoice over Jerusalem
   and take delight in my people;
the sound of weeping and of crying
   will be heard in it no more.
Never again will there be in it
   an infant who lives but a few days,
   or an old man who does not live out his years;

he who dies at a hundred
will be thought a mere youth;
he who fails to reach a hundred
will be considered accursed.
They will build houses and dwell in them;
they will plant vineyards and eat their fruit.
No longer will they build houses and others live in them,
or plant and others eat.
For as the days of a tree,
so will be the days of my people;
my chosen ones will long enjoy
the works of their hands.
They will not toil in vain
or bear children doomed to misfortune;
for they will be a people blessed by the LORD,
they and their descendants with them.
Before they call I will answer;
while they are still speaking I will hear.
The wolf and the lamb will feed together,
and the lion will eat straw like the ox,
but dust will be the serpent's food.
They will neither harm nor destroy
on all my holy mountain,"

says the LORD.

The apocalyptic tradition itself builds on these new creation motifs from Isaiah. Thus, as is usually the case in the history of ideas, we find a trajectory of teaching on this matter beginning in the Old Testament and extending to Paul. Just what part of that tradition Paul himself draws on is difficult to say, and perhaps he himself would not have known his exact sources. The concept of a renewal of the world was "in the air" of Paul's Jewish worldview.

CONCERN FOR THE ENVIRONMENT. Concern for the health and future of the world of nature is one of the most powerful forces in our culture. In twenty years, the environmental movement has moved from the fringe to the mainstream of contemporary life. It affects our lives in countless ways, influencing everything from the way we take out our garbage to the way we vote. Yet evangelical Christians in general have been slow to reckon with the movement, and what little many evangelicals know about the movement tends to be negative. Many believers, I find, view the environmental movement with suspicion, if not downright hostility.

I would argue, however, that passages such as Romans 8:19–22 should lead believers to be environmentalists. These verses make clear that God intends to liberate, or redeem, the created world along with his own children. Creation now is not what God intended it to be; it has been "subjected to frustration" (v. 20). But God will free the created world from this bondage one day, bringing it into the glorious freedom of his own children (v. 21). To be sure, human beings continue even in this passage to be the focus of God's plan. But Paul reveals that God is also concerned about the entire world he has made. Simply understood, this leads to environmentalism, that is, concern for the environment in which we live.

Of course, everything depends on what we mean by environmentalism. Reason for Christian hostility is easy to understand if we brand environmentalism by some of its more extreme advocates. Indeed, an anti-Christian bias is evident in some early environmental thinking. Some theorists in the movement argued that the Christian worldview enshrined an anthropocentric view of the universe that justified unconcern for and, indeed, the exploitation of, the natural world.[14] In its place, some environmentalists advocate a biocentric view that values all life equally. Edward Abbey, the most famous of the "eco-warriors," signaled the logical extreme of such thinking when he said that he would rather kill a man than a snake. Believers who read such statements and hear about the worship of "Mother Earth" in pagan and New Age religions naturally conclude that Christianity and environmentalism are incompatible.

But such a conclusion is short-sighted and unfortunate. Properly understood, concern for the environment is a natural product of the Christian worldview, as some scholars have been pointing out for many years.[15] God created the world, pronounced it good, and entrusted its care to human beings. True, God gave human beings the right to use its resources for our good. But in making us "rulers" (Gen. 1:26) of the created world, he does not give us the right to do anything we want with it. Rather, we are appointed as stewards of creation. We are to manage it not only for ourselves but for itself, for, as passages like Romans 8:19–21 make clear, it has value in itself, apart from what human beings may gain from it.

Indeed, I find that some Christian reaction against environmentalism is profoundly un-Christian, compounded of equal mixtures of selfishness and

---

14. See, e.g., Roderick Nash, *Wilderness and the American Mind* (3d ed.; New Haven, Conn.: Yale Univ. Press, 1982).

15. See, on this text, Fred van Dyke, et al., *Redeeming Creation: The Biblical Basis for Environmental Stewardship* (Downers Grove, Ill.: InterVarsity, 1996), 85–88.

materialism. Catering to our pleasure and maintaining our present, often luxurious standard of living become more important than tending the world God has made and ensuring that its wonderful resources will be available for generations yet to come. Believers will naturally continue to debate what actions may be needed in order to fulfill the stewardship mandate God has given us. But we owe it to that mandate to become informed, from the best and most neutral sources we can find, about what the problems really are, and to be willing to make sacrifices to maintain the world he has entrusted to us.[16]

All things work toward the good. Christians in every generation have found inestimable comfort in the wonderful promise of Romans 8:28, and rightly so. This is surely one of the greatest promises of God to his people anywhere in the Bible. But it is also one of the most misunderstood. To appreciate what God promises here, we must first clear away two misconceptions about the meaning of the verse.

(1) As we briefly noted in the Original Meaning section, this verse may not be promising that all things will work *together* for good. I have heard the verse preached with just this point as the central emphasis. God, so the preacher argued, does not promise to bring good to us in every situation. Rather, as a cook combines ingredients to make a tasty dish of food, so God mixes together the circumstances of life in such a way as ultimately to bring good to us.

There are two reasons for hesitating to embrace this "mixing" idea. (a) The verb used here (*synergeo*) may not mean "work *together.*" To be sure, in its three other New Testament occurrences, it does seem to have this meaning (see 1 Cor. 16:16; 2 Cor. 6:1; James 2:22). But the verb often lost the "with" idea in the period when Paul was writing.[17] Unlike the other places where the verb occurs in the New Testament, the context here does not readily supply an object for the "with" idea. (b) Even if we do translate "work together," it is by no means clear that "all things" are working with each other. It is equally plausible that Paul means that all things work together with the Spirit, with God, or with believers to produce good.[18] On the whole, then, an application of 8:28 that focuses on the "with" idea is built on an uncertain foundation.

(2) A second common misunderstanding of this promise is more serious. Most of us have probably heard someone (perhaps ourselves!) applying Romans 8:28 something like this: "Yes, you may have lost your job, but you can be sure of getting an even better one; because 'all things are working for

---

16. For an excellent taxonomy of Christian views on the environment, see Raymond E. Grizzle, Paul E. Rothrock, and Christopher B. Barrett, "Evangelicals and Environmentalism: Past, Present, and Future," *TrinJ* 19 (1998): 3–27. See also other articles on environmentalism in that volume and also in *TrinJ* 18 (1997).

17. See the standard lexicons.

18. Godet, *Commentary on Romans*, 322–23.

good.'" Or, "Don't be upset about your fiancé breaking off your engagement, because God must have an even better life partner for you; Romans 8:28 promises. . . ." The difficulty with this application is that it interprets "good" from a narrow and often materialistic perspective. From God's perspective, "good" must be defined in spiritual terms. The ultimate good is God's glory, and he is glorified when his children live as Christ did (v. 29) and attain the glory he has destined them for (v. 30; cf. vv. 31–39).

As we have seen in 5:3–4, God uses suffering to build Christian character in us, conform us to Christ, and prepare us for final glory. What he promises us in 8:28, then, is not that every difficult experience will lead to something good in this life. The "good" God may have in mind may involve the next life entirely. He may take us out of a secure, well-paying job in order to shake us out of a materialistic lifestyle that does not honor biblical priorities, and we may never have as good a job again. He may want to set us free from an engagement to be married because he wants to use us in a ministry that would be difficult or impossible for a married person. Remember that it is by sharing in Christ's sufferings that we eventually will be able to share in his glory as well (8:17).

This is not to say that material blessings *cannot* be included in the "good" of Romans 8:28. As the Old Testament especially makes clear, God delights to give his people good things in this life as well as in the next. In an effort to avoid a materialistic interpretation of 8:28, we must not succumb to the opposite extreme of denying God's interest in the material world. This would be to fall into a dualism far removed from the biblical perspective of a God who is both Creator of this world and Redeemer. Rather, the point I am making is that we tend to apply the promise of this verse in a purely materialistic way. This clearly fails to take into account the spiritual realm that is ultimately more important than the material.

We have suggested a couple of things that Romans 8:28 does *not* mean. But I do not want to leave this magnificent promise on a negative note. So let me conclude by reflecting again on what it *does* mean. Essentially, it promises that nothing will touch our lives that is not under the control and direction of our loving heavenly Father. Everything we do and say, everything people do to us or say about us, every experience we will ever have—all are sovereignly used by God for our good. We will not always understand how the things we experience work to good, and we certainly will not always enjoy them. But we do know that nothing comes into our lives that God does not allow and use for his own beneficent purposes. Paul's overarching purpose in Romans 5–8 is to give us assurance for the life to come. But verses like 8:28 show that he also wants to give us assurance for the present life as well. God has ordained not only the ends but the means.

The great plan of God. If, then 8:28 gives assurance for the present life, verses 29–30 focus again on the future. God has a plan, Paul says. That plan begins with his foreknowing us, and then leads to his predestining, calling, justifying, and finally glorifying us. This series has been the focus of a lot of theological debate over the years. We cannot really apply the verses until we understand just what the theology is here.

Calvinist theologians think these verses provide evidence for two characteristic teachings in that view of salvation: that becoming a Christian is ultimately rooted in God's free choice, and that those whom God chooses and then become his people will always be saved in the last day. We usually call these doctrines, respectively, unconditional election and eternal security. Calvinists insist that the verb "foreknow" means "choose beforehand." Thus, the whole process by which God brings people into relationship with himself starts with him. He chooses, and because he does so, we believe and thus are justified. They also argue that the series of verbs in verses 29–30 is an unbreakable chain. All whom God chooses and then justifies he will also glorify. There can be no change or variation: Every justified believer will be saved in the end.

One can easily see how Calvinists can use these verses to support their distinctive view of salvation. But how would Arminians respond? First of all, the Arminian theologian insists on viewing these verses in light of the whole picture. Throughout Romans, Paul has proclaimed that believing in Jesus Christ is the way to be saved, and believing is a real choice that human beings must make. Thus, the whole process cannot simply be predetermined.

Arminians also note that the Calvinist interpretation of 8:29–30 rests on three key decisions. (1) First is the decision to interpret "foreknow" in terms of choosing. As we saw above in the Original Meaning section, this verb can also mean "know ahead of time." What Paul may be saying, then, is that God knows about every person's decision to believe or not believe ahead of time; and it is those who choose to believe whom he predestines, calls, and justifies. We do not believe because God has chosen us (the Calvinist view); we are chosen because we believe.

(2) Many (though not all) Arminians also contest the decision of Calvinists to interpret verses 28–29 in individual terms. What Paul teaches here, they allege, is that God has chosen the church. It is the body of Christ as a whole that God has elected by his grace, and individuals become members of that elect body through their faith.[19]

---

19. A good overview of this approach is found in R. Shank, *Elect in the Son: A Study of the Doctrine of Election* (Springfield, Mass.: Westcott, 1970), see esp. 45–55, 154–55. See also Karl Barth, *Church Dogmatics* 2.2.

(3) Arminians also question whether it is fair to view the series of verbs in these verses as an unbreakable chain. What Paul describes, they claim, are the decisions God has made on our behalf. He is determined to glorify everyone whom he has justified. But Scripture teaches that believers have the freedom to refuse the gift God offers us, to opt out of the sequence of decisions he has made. A truly justified person may, indeed, fail to attain glory—not because God did not will it (for he did), but because that person chose to reject what God had willed.

The issue we raise here is massive, and we will have to return to it again when we comment on 9:6–29. As my interpretation above has revealed, I come down on the Calvinist side. I think that "foreknow" means "chose beforehand," that Paul is talking about individual people, and that God's will to glorify the believer cannot be thwarted—even by us. Naturally, this decision about the meaning of the verses affects my application. The idea that we can be "Calminians," combining Calvinism and Arminianism in one system, is attractive but irrational. I can logically be a Calvinist in one doctrine and Arminian in another; but I cannot be both with respect to the same doctrine. I cannot both believe my faith is based ultimately on God's choice *and* that God's choice is ultimately based on my faith. Or, at least, I cannot believe it and remain rational. I may as well believe that black is white.

Thus, I want to include in my application of these verses some specific points stemming from my Calvinistic exegesis. For instance, the knowledge that God has chosen me on the basis of his own free will alone should stimulate awe and wonder at what he has done and a deeper sense of thanksgiving for his unmerited gift.

But I would like to leave this great passage on a practical application that both Calvinist and Arminian can agree on: God has done all that is needed to secure our eternal glory. He has already made the decision: "Those whom he justified he glorified." We may disagree about whether believers can refuse to accept that decision. But from God's side at least, the matter has already been determined. That means that no genuine believer need ever wonder whether he or she "has what it takes" to get to heaven. None of us does. But that doesn't matter in the end. God himself has supplied all we need. As we have seen repeatedly in Romans 5–8, Paul is anxious to preserve a balance in which God's gift to us does not cancel our need to respond to that gift. This passage is about that gift, and that is what we must emphasize in our application.

Romans 8:31–39

W HAT, THEN, SHALL we say in response to this? If God is for us, who can be against us? [32]He who did not spare his own Son, but gave him up for us all—how will he not also, along with him, graciously give us all things? [33]Who will bring any charge against those whom God has chosen? It is God who justifies. [34]Who is he that condemns? Christ Jesus, who died—more than that, who was raised to life—is at the right hand of God and is also interceding for us. [35]Who shall separate us from the love of Christ? Shall trouble or hardship or persecution or famine or nakedness or danger or sword? [36]As it is written:

"For your sake we face death all day long;
    we are considered as sheep to be slaughtered."

[37]No, in all these things we are more than conquerors through him who loved us. [38]For I am convinced that neither death nor life, neither angels nor demons, neither the present nor the future, nor any powers, [39]neither height nor depth, nor anything else in all creation, will be able to separate us from the love of God that is in Christ Jesus our Lord.

THIS MAGNIFICENT CELEBRATION of God's eternal commitment to his people is well known to most Christians. But most of us know it as a passage torn from its context, a text read, for instance, at funerals. Such a passage is, of course, appropriate at funerals, but we should remember that Paul has a specific purpose for these verses within his argument in Romans. He uses every rhetorical device in his arsenal to move his readers. He wants us to internalize the truth he has been teaching to move us to a new level of confidence in God's provision for us.

How much of the letter do verses 31–39 bring to a climax? Since 9:1 initiates a new stage in the argument, the paragraph may conclude all of chapters 1–8.[1] At the other extreme, some think these verses belong only to the immediately preceding argument in 8:29–30.[2] The best option is to view this

---

1. See, e.g., Godet, *Commentary on Romans,* 329; Cranfield, *The Epistle to the Romans,* 434.
2. E.g., E. H. Gifford, *The Epistle of St. Paul to the Romans* (London: John Murray, 1886), 161.

section as the conclusion to chapters 5–8. As we have pointed out (see comments on 8:18–30), verses 31–39 share several key words and themes with the beginning of chapter 5. A call to celebrate our security in Christ makes for a natural conclusion to what Paul has been teaching in these chapters. He adduces two reasons for us to celebrate our security: the *work* of God for us in Christ (vv. 31–34) and the *love* of God for us in Christ (vv. 35–39).

The Work of God for Us in Christ (8:31–34)

AS HE HAS done so often in Romans, Paul launches a new direction with a question: "What, then, shall we say in response to this?" "This" is actually plural in the Greek (*tauta*, "these things"); it refers to the many reasons for our confidence that Paul has rehearsed in chapters 5–8. All those reasons can be neatly summed up in one statement: God is "for us." Who, then, Paul rightly asks, can be "against us?" Of course, we know (and Paul recognizes [see 5:3–4; 8:17–18]) that many people and things still oppose us: people who hate Christians, the trials of life, Satan himself. But Paul's point is that with God on our side, none of this opposition ultimately matters. As Chrysostom has written:

> Yet those that be against us, so far are they from thwarting us at all, that even without their will they become to us the causes of crowns, and procurers of countless blessings, so that God's wisdom turneth their plots unto our salvation and glory. See how really no one is against us![3]

Verse 32 is not explicitly connected to verse 31, but it reinforces Paul's point. God's being "for us" is seen climactically in his giving of his beloved Son. If he has done that, we can be certain he will also give us "all things"— or, to put it in the terms of verse 31, nothing can ultimately oppose us. The gift of God in the death of his Son as a basis for our hope harks back to 5:5–8. But the way Paul puts it here suggests a comparison between Christ and Isaac. As Abraham did not spare his beloved son Isaac, so God does not spare his beloved Son (see Gen. 22). The "all things" we are guaranteed as a result of Christ's death for us includes both our final glory and all that God provides to bring us to that glory (see the "good" of Rom. 8:28).

The punctuation of verse 33–34 is difficult to sort out. Older Greek manuscripts of the New Testament contain no punctuation at all, so editors of modern Bibles have to decide how to do it. At least six different possibilities exist here. The NIV reflects probably the best of the options, with each verse featuring a question and answer.

---

3. Chrysostom, from his homily on this passage of Romans.

"Bring [a] charge" (v. 33) is the first of several judicial terms in this context. Again, Paul's point is not that nothing will ever try to prosecute us in the court of God's justice. Satan, "the accuser," will certainly do so, and he will bring our sins as evidence of our guilt. But the prosecution will be unsuccessful, for God has chosen us to be his and has justified us already—pronounced over us the verdict of "innocent" that can never be reversed. Paul alludes at this point to Isaiah 50:8—9a:

> He who vindicates me is near.
>   Who then will bring charges against me?
>   Let us face each other!
> Who is my accuser?
>   Let him confront me!
> It is the sovereign LORD who helps me.
>   Who is he that will condemn me?

Verse 34 provides more evidence for the same point. No one can successfully condemn us because Christ has died for us and has been raised to life to be our intercessor before the Father. With such a defense attorney, it is no wonder the prosecution loses it case!

The Love of God for Us in Christ (8:35–39)

THE QUESTION AT the beginning of verse 35 shifts the focus of the paragraph. It is parallel to the one in verse 31, but sets the tone for verses 35–39 by introducing Christ's love into the picture. Knowing we are declared innocent of all charges against us is a wonderful assurance. But Christ not only defends us; he loves us and enters into relationship with us, and nothing will ever separate us from that love. To make sure we get the point, Paul specifies some threats at the end of verse 35. As a comparison with 2 Corinthians 11:26–27 and 12:10 reveals, Paul himself has gone through most of these. He has learned by experience that they cannot disrupt his relationship with Christ.

The quotation of Psalm 44:22 in verse 36 is a bit of a detour in the logic of Paul's argument. But the detour reveals two of his key concerns: to remind us that suffering is a natural and expected part of the Christian life (cf. 5:3–4; 8:17), and to root the experiences of Christians in the experience of God's old covenant people.

With verse 37, Paul returns to the main line of his teaching in verse 35. In all the varied difficulties of life, we are "more than conquerors." This felicitous rendering of the Greek verb *hypernikao* (to more than triumph over) goes all the way back to the sixteenth-century Geneva Bible. Paul may have chosen this rare intensive form of the verb simply to emphasize the certainty of our triumph. But he may also be suggesting that we more than triumph over adversity; in God's good hand, it even leads to our "good" (v. 28).

Paul concludes his celebration of God's love for us in Christ with his own personal testimony: "*I am persuaded....*" The list following is arranged in four pairs, with "powers" thrown in between the third and fourth pair. We can easily "overinterpret" such a list, insisting on a precision of definitions that misses the point of Paul's rhetoric. In general, however, "death" and "life" refer to the two basic states of human existence. "Angels" and "demons" (*archai*, i.e., "rulers," which Paul uses to denote evil spiritual beings [see Eph. 6:12; Col. 2:15]) summarize the entirety of the spiritual world.

A few interpreters take "present things" and "coming things" (lit. trans.) as spiritual beings too, but evidence is lacking for these as such titles. Probably Paul chooses to summarize all of history, along with the people and events it contains, in a temporal perspective. It is not clear why Paul disrupts his neat parallelism with the word "powers" at this point, but the word refers again to spiritual beings (1 Cor. 15:24; Eph. 1:21).

"Height" and "depth" are the most difficult of the pairs of terms to identify. Since these words were applied to the space above and below the horizon, and since ancient people often invested celestial phenomena with spiritual significance, Paul may be referring to spiritual beings again.[4] Yet Paul uses similar language in Ephesians 3:18 in a simple spatial sense. Thus, perhaps, he chooses yet another way of trying to help us understand that there is nothing in all the world—whether we are dead or alive, whether they are things we now face or things we will face in the future, whether they are above us or below us—that can separate us from the "love of God that is in Christ Jesus our Lord." As the chapter began with "no condemnation" (Rom. 8:1), so it ends with the bookends of "no separation" (8:35, 39).

RHETORICAL LANGUAGE. We have used the term *rhetorical* in this commentary to refer to Paul's language or argument. Rhetoric was important in the ancient Greco-Roman world, where it referred to the science of persuasion. The *rhetor*, a person skilled in methods of swaying and convincing an audience, was much in demand. Various methods of persuasion were developed, and scholars have often identified these forms in the New Testament.

The modern use of the term *rhetorical* is broader, but clearly rooted in this ancient usage. We speak, for instance, of a "rhetorical question"—meaning

---

4. E.g., Käsemann, *Commentary on Romans*, 251.

a question that does not seek information but which seeks to advance an argument. We have used "rhetorical" in this commentary in this broader sense. It refers to language Paul has chosen not just because of its content but because of its ability to move the reader to a certain reaction.

A modern example may help. In Norman Maclean's wonderful short novel based on his early life in rural Montana, *A River Runs Through It*, he reflects on the joys of those growing-up years. "What a beautiful world it was once," he writes.[5] When I was reading that book, this sentence brought me up short. The picture of a time and place simpler, closer to nature, and uncomplicated by the cares and ambitions of adult life flashed before me. Why did that sentence have such power? Partly because of the way Maclean framed it. He could have communicated the same information by saying, for example, "It was a beautiful world then"; or "The world was a beautiful place then." But neither has the rhetorical power of the phraseology Maclean actually uses. The difference is hard to put into words, but I think it is clear that Maclean's way of putting it forces us to savor the idea in a way that other ways of putting it would not.

Paul does the same sort of thing. Failing to recognize this important aspect to Paul's language will mean failing to let his language accomplish the purposes for which he wrote it. The apostle is not just conveying information to us; he is trying to persuade us to accept what he says as true and to allow it to transform the way we think and live.

Nowhere in Romans is the rhetorical force of language more evident than in 8:31–39. The full force of the language cannot be reproduced in English, but much of it comes through in translation. Consider, for instance, the many questions that Paul uses in these verses. He is not asking his readers for information; he is trying to draw us into the discussion in a way that a flat assertion will not. He could simply have said, "No one can separate us from the love of Christ" (see v. 35). But by asking the question "Who shall separate us from the love of Christ," he forces us to pause and consider the matter. Who, indeed? My persecutors? My unbelieving family members? Satan? We are involved; and we therefore "own" Paul's ultimate response, "No ... we are more than conquerors."

Another rhetorical device Paul uses is the omission of connecting words between sentences. This device is less obvious in English because modern versions often leave Greek particles and conjunctions untranslated; thus, their absence in verses 31–39 does not stick out so much. Paul's questions and answers follow upon one another almost without pause. The result is that the paragraph has more the flavor of solemn proclamation than of logical

---

5. N. Maclean, *A River Runs Through It* (Chicago: Univ. of Chicago Press, 1976), 56.

argument. We are encouraged to pause and savor each wonderful reminder of God's grace to us in Christ.

A third element of the text with rhetorical function is Paul's list of things that might separate us from Christ's love in verse 35 and in verses 38–39. Such lists are common in the New Testament, particularly in passages that urge believers to avoid certain behavior and adopt another kind of behavior. An author often illustrates each kind of behavior by citing examples. Scholars recognize in these lists a typical form of speaking used widely in the ancient world. They call them (not surprisingly!) "vice lists" and "virtue lists." The lists we find in verses 35 and 38–39 are not, of course, vice or virtue lists. But they function in a similar way, as Paul tries to bring home to us a general point by illustrating with specifics.

Like a good preacher, Paul realizes his readers will tend to keep what he says at the level of the abstract unless they have specific, concrete examples to get their hands on. Paul could make the point he wants to make by answering his question "Who shall separate us from the love of Christ" with a simple "Nothing." But by going into specifics about just what is included in that "nothing," he makes his point far more effectively.

Another feature of these lists is also important to understand: They are often composed rather haphazardly. The author does not usually sit down and carefully craft the list. Rather, he casually mentions examples of the sort of thing that comes to mind. What this means for the reader is that we must avoid the temptation to think these lists are either comprehensive or that the individual items are carefully distinguished from one another.

When Paul, for example, follows up his question about who can separate us from Christ's love by asking, "Shall trouble or hardship or persecution or famine or nakedness or danger or sword?" we should not insist that "trouble" (Gk. *thlipsis*) and "hardship" (Gk. *stenochoria*) are two distinct ideas. In fact, a quick search of a concordance reveals that the two are often used together as a pair to connote the general idea of suffering (see, e.g., Deut. 28:53, 55, 57; Isa. 8:22; 30:6; Rom. 2:9; 2 Cor. 6:4). To insist that each word must have a distinct meaning fails to recognize the rhetorical effect of the pair. It functions something like our common expression "sick and tired." If I say that I am "sick and tired" of the hot weather, I am not expecting someone to think I am *both* "sick" *and* "tired." The two work together to convey a single idea.

Nor should I think that Paul intends this list to include every possible thing that might separate me from Christ's love. Moreover, the very wording of these lists will often have more to do with rhetoric than with content. Consider some of the "pairs" in Paul's additional list of threats to our security in Christ in verses 38–39. When Paul speaks of "neither height nor depth," he may not have in mind specific spiritual powers (as some interpreters think) or even any clear conception of the makeup of the universe (a realm above the world and one below it). He may simply be trying to communicate the idea of "everything" by using spatial imagery.

The reader of the Bible, then, needs to be alert to rhetorical devices. In a laudable effort to understand every detail of the Word that God has given us, we are prone to overinterpret single words and phrases, often missing the bigger picture. Even more tragically, we can forget that the biblical writers are trying to get us to respond to what they are saying. They choose language and phraseology designed to stir our emotions and move our wills. A preoccupation with the minutia of the text can keep us from appreciating its ultimate purpose and power.

SPIRITUAL FORCES. Three of the nine potential threats to our security in Christ that Paul lists in verses 38–39 refer to spiritual beings: "angels," "rulers" (NIV "demons"), and "powers." Two others—"height" and "depth"—may have such a reference (see Original Meaning section). We might think this to be a disproportionate amount of attention being paid to the spiritual realm. But it fits both Paul's own day—and, increasingly, our own. In the first century, people were paying less and less attention to the official gods of Greece and Rome and getting involved in various Eastern religions, mystery religions, and astrology. Most people believed that the world of nature and the world of humankind were controlled by spiritual beings and influences, including the stars. In such an atmosphere, it is no wonder that Paul offers as much attention as he does on spiritual beings. His readers need assurance that Christ's love is powerful enough to overcome any spiritual force they may ever have heard of.

People in our culture are also turning away from the official gods of the Judeo-Christian tradition to embrace all kinds of Eastern, New Age, and spiritualist religions. Belief in spiritual beings and their influence on human affairs is increasing, replacing the rationalism of the scientific age. Christians are not immune from the trend. We, too, have seen a reawakening of interest in the spiritual realm, as the novels of Frank Perretti both testify to and contribute to. Demons, we have been reminded, exist and continue to exercise power. Some believers have become almost paralyzed in fear at the prospect.

As C. S. Lewis wisely remarked, we tend either to ignore Satan and his minions or to give them far too much credit. The church seems to be in the latter phase at the present. Therefore Paul's emphatic assertion that no spiritual being can separate us from Christ is needed in the church today. We need to recognize and proclaim that God in Christ has won a victory over the "powers and authorities" (Col. 2:15), and that they have no power to keep us from inheriting the salvation God has promised all who love him. Nothing on earth can separate us from God's love for us in Christ, and neither can anything in heaven.

Angels. One aspect of this matter perhaps remains puzzling: Why does Paul include "angels" among potential threats to our security? Are not angels "ministering spirits sent to serve those who will inherit salvation" (Heb. 1:14)? How can they possibly "separate us from the love of God"? A few interpreters have tried to solve the problem by suggesting that Paul may have in mind fallen angels (cf. 2 Peter 2:4; Jude 6) or spiritual beings of all kinds (cf. 1 Cor. 4:9; 6:3 [?]; 13:1). But Paul usually uses the word *angelos* to refer to the "good angels"; when paired with "rulers" (NIV "demons"), this would seem especially clear.[6] Why, then, does he include them in this list of powers that might hinder the believer's security in Christ?

Recall that the items in lists such as this one do not always have a specific, independent significance. They are often chosen for rhetorical effect and without regard to precise meaning. Thus the phrase "angels nor demons" may simply be Paul's way of summing up the entirety of the spiritual realm. He may not have thought much about the specific role of angels in the matter.

Yet it is significant that Paul chooses to include the entire spiritual realm, not just its evil side, in this list. He seems to suggest that even good spiritual beings can somehow be a threat to our relationship with Christ. We can understand this perhaps by glancing quickly at Colossians and by considering the role of angels in our modern culture.

Paul writes to the Christians in Colosse in order to counter false teaching that had invaded the community. One of the elements of that false teaching was a preoccupation with angels. The false teachers were apparently making so much of these angels that the uniqueness of Christ was being threatened. So Paul insists that Christ is superior to any spiritual being: "For by him all things were created: things in heaven and on earth, visible and invisible, whether thrones or powers or rulers or authorities; all things were created by him and for him" (1:16); "you have been given fullness in Christ, who is the head over every power and authority" (2:10).

The false teachers were so involved with angels that they were apparently worshiping them (Col. 2:18).[7] What Paul counters in his letter to the Colossians is, in fact, a persistent tendency in the history of Christianity. Believers

---

6. See, e.g., Murray, *The Epistle to the Romans*, 1:332–33.

7. The Greek phrase here, *threskeia ton angelon*, is debated. Some commentators think it means "the worship done by angels"; but it probably refers to the worship given by Christians to angels. See Murray J. Harris, *Colossians and Philemon* (Grand Rapids: Eerdmans, 1991), 120–21.

in almost every age have succumbed to a fascination of the spiritual realm, speculating about angels, their makeup, and their significance. Sometimes the interest in angels has become so intense that it has become virtually a cult.

Our own day has seen a renewed interest in angels. The popular Frank Perretti novels have focused the attention of many Christians on the significance of the spiritual realm in general and on the role of ministering angels in particular. In the wider culture, television shows about angels, such as *Touched by an Angel*, have become popular. This interest in angels has, of course, had positive results. Non-Christians have been shaken out of their narrow materialism by a presentation of the reality of angelic intervention in the affairs of humans. Believers have had their convictions about the ultimate significance of the spiritual realm strengthened.

But interest in angels can also deflect both Christians and non-Christians alike from the real spiritual issue. Belief in angels is perfect for people who want their religion to offer them hope and comfort without any obligations. Angels do good things for us but don't demand anything from us. For non-Christians, then, interest in angels can provide a warm, fuzzy feeling of being religious or spiritual while inoculating them against coming to grips with the source of the only true spiritual experience, the God who has revealed himself in Jesus Christ.

For Christians, an overemphasis on angels can lead to the kind of problem Paul denounces at Colosse. Believers can become so interested in these spiritual beings that they fail to give Christ the supreme spiritual position he alone should have. Thus, angels can threaten a believer's security in Christ. If Satan cannot deflect our worship of the Lord by getting us involved in sin, he will seek to accomplish the same end by getting us to give too much of our attention to good, but subsidiary, persons or things.

Romans 9:1–5

I SPEAK THE truth in Christ—I am not lying, my conscience
confirms it in the Holy Spirit—²I have great sorrow and
unceasing anguish in my heart. ³For I could wish that I
myself were cursed and cut off from Christ for the sake of my
brothers, those of my own race, ⁴the people of Israel. Theirs is
the adoption as sons; theirs the divine glory, the covenants, the
receiving of the law, the temple worship and the promises.
⁵Theirs are the patriarchs, and from them is traced the human
ancestry of Christ, who is God over all, forever praised! Amen.

AFTER PAUL'S GRAND CELEBRATION of God's faithfulness to us in Christ (8:31–39), we would expect
the theological part of Romans to be over. He
can now go on to spell out the implications of
that theology for Christian living, which he does beginning in chapter 12.
But what about chapters 9–11? What is their place in this letter?

Some commentators have thought that Paul's discussion of Israel in these
chapters is a kind of digression or even excursus—a section that does not fit
into the letter.[1] Others have found a place for this section only by attaching it
to Paul's teaching about soteriology in 8:29–30; that is, chapters 9–11 is really
about predestination.[2] But neither view does justice to what the apostle is really
about in Romans. From the beginning of the letter, he has wanted to prove that
the gospel, the theme of the letter, is "the gospel of God"—good news sent by
the God of the Old Testament, and thus good news that was "promised beforehand through his prophets in the Holy Scriptures" (1:2). Indeed, for Paul there
can be no good news in Christ unless what God has done in him is part of the
one master plan that the Old Testament reveals to us.

It is just for this reason that Paul must talk about Israel's role in light of the
good news of Christ. For by his day it has become clear that most Jews have
not responded to the good news. Again and again Paul preached to Jews, only
to see minimal response. When he turned to the Gentiles, however, the

---

1. See, e.g., Dodd, *Epistle to the Romans*, 149–50; Sanday and Headlam, *The Epistle to the
Romans*, 225.

2. Augustine took this approach (see the analysis in P. Gorday, *Principles of Patristic Exegesis: Romans 9–11 in Origen, John Chrysostom, and Augustine* [New York: Edwin Mellen, 1983],
esp. 1–3, 190–91, 232–33).

response was much greater. So he now confronts a church that is largely Gentile. How does such a situation fit with God's promises in the Old Testament? Did not he promise to send his Messiah to *Israel*, to glorify his people *Israel*, and to bless *Israel* in the kingdom that was coming? How can that promise be fulfilled in a church that is largely Gentile? God seems to have promised "A" and then done "B." Can "B" then really be tied to "A" as the fulfillment of what was promised?

These are the issues Paul is trying to answer in chapters 9–11 (he hinted at them in 3:1–8). He wants his readers to understand how, indeed, God's work in the gospel of Christ is perfectly in accord with what he promised in the Old Testament. Jews, of course, needed this message. If they are to embrace the gospel, they must see how it is truly the fulfillment of the Old Testament. Jewish-Christians also need to be assured that their faith in Christ does not mean they have ceased to believe in the God of the Old Testament and of their Jewish heritage. But Gentile-Christians must also see a connection between Old and New Testaments in the plan of salvation. They must see that their own faith has its roots sunk deeply into Old Testament soil.

Moreover, as Paul makes explicit in chapter 11 (vv. 13, 17–24, 25), there is a practical reason why the Gentiles need to take this message to heart. They have become the majority in the early Christian church—in Rome as elsewhere. They have a tendency to brag about their status and to look down on Jewish Christians. So Paul wants to undercut their arrogance by showing that their spiritual blessings are all the result of what God has done through his people Israel.

Ultimately, then, Romans 9–11 is not about Israel—it is about God. The theme of the section is found in 9:6: "It is not as though God's word had failed." God, Paul argues, is consistent and utterly faithful to his promises. In order to prove this thesis, he makes three basic points about Israel in these chapters, relating to Israel's past, present, and future. (1) God's promises to Israel in the past are consistent with what he is now doing in saving only some Jews and Gentiles as well (9:6–29). In 9:30–10:21, Paul leaves the main path of his argument to analyze in more detail the surprising turn of events, as so many Jews have refused to believe in Jesus the Messiah while so many Gentiles do. (2) In 11:1–10, Paul turns to Israel's present, showing that God is even now fulfilling his promise by saving many Jews. (3) The climax comes in the future (11:11–32), when "all Israel will be saved" (v. 26). Paul concludes the section with a hymn praising the marvelous plan of God (11:33–36).

The present section (9:1–5) sets the stage for this grand argument. Speaking personally, Paul contrasts Israel's prerogatives with her plight. Promised so much (vv. 4–5), Israel stands accursed and cut off from God as a result of the gospel. The tension created by this situation drives the argument of these chapters.

The first five verses of chapter 9 reveal that Paul was deeply concerned about the matters he writes about in these chapters. These verses also reveal a fact about Paul that is easy for us to forget: He was a Jew and never lost his sense of Jewish identity or his love for his fellow Jews. In verse 1, he goes out of his way to stress the sincerity of this concern. He makes the point both positively—"I speak the truth in Christ"—and negatively—"I am not lying"—and adds the witness of his conscience as led by the Holy Spirit.

Why such a strong assertion of truthfulness? Probably because Paul well knows that many of his fellow Jews are suspicious of his loyalty and patriotism. Because he was used by God to bring so many Gentiles into the people of God, Paul was viewed by a good number of Jews as a traitor and as one who had lost any natural affection for his own people. This Paul denies. In fact, he has "great sorrow and unceasing anguish in [his] heart" (v. 2). Paul never explicitly says what has led to such deep sorrow. A few modern interpreters, convinced that Paul believes Israel is saved through her own covenant with God, think that Paul's sorrow is motivated by Israel's failure to extend her privileges to the Gentiles (see Contemporary Significance for more details). But what Paul says in verse 3 shows that the problem is more basic: Israel is not saved!

In offering to become himself "cursed and cut off from Christ" for the sake of his fellow Jews, Paul implies that Israel herself stands under this judgment. By refusing to accept Jesus as the Messiah and the fulfillment of God's plan of redemption for them, most Jews have cut themselves off from God's people and from the salvation he promises to his people. The Greek word for "cursed" is *anathema*, a word transliterated into English that describes someone who is excommunicated. In the New Testament, it refers to a person excluded from God's people and under sentence of damnation (see 1 Cor. 12:3; 16:22; Gal. 1:8−9).

Many interpreters are disturbed at the idea that Paul would really wish to be damned for the sake of his people. Some therefore seize on the fact that the Greek verb used at the beginning of verse 3 is in the imperfect tense to suggest that Paul means only that he used to pray that way, or that he would pray that way if he could (the NIV translation "I could wish" suggests this notion).[3] But these interpretations are too subtle. We should simply let Paul's wish stand as a way of indicating his deep love for his fellow people. Whether he thought the request could be granted is simply not in view.

While obscured in the NIV translation, Paul describes Jews in the last part of verse 3 as his (lit.) "kinspeople according to the flesh [*sarx*]." As so often in Paul, *sarx* connotes a worldly or human point of view (see comments on 8:1−13). By contrast, Paul now will describe his fellow Jews from the stand-

---

3. Cranfield, *The Epistle to the Romans*, 454−57; Moo, *Epistle to the Romans*, 558.

point of the divine promise. They are, first, "Israelites" (NIV "the people of Israel"). The name is important. In many Jewish intertestamental books, foreigners use the word "Jew" as a simple national designation, but when Jews speak about themselves and their special position in salvation history, they call themselves "Israelites."[4]

As Israelites, Jews have been blessed with "the adoption of sons ... the divine glory, the covenants, the receiving of the law, the temple worship and the promises." Most of these prerogatives are clear enough, but a couple deserve fuller treatment. Paul's claim that the Jews enjoy "adoption" (*huiothesia*) is striking in light of 8:16, 23, where he has applied that blessing to Christians. Probably he thinks of Israel's "adoption" as a national blessing that does not confer salvation on individual Jews (see, e.g., Ex. 4:22; Deut. 14:1; Isa. 63:16; Hos. 11:1).[5] But Paul's application of the same word to regenerate believers and to Israel "according to the flesh" within the space of twenty verses summarizes the tension between Israel's promises and the church's blessing that infuses these chapters.

We find a parallel situation with the next blessing, the "divine glory" (or simply "glory"; Gk. *doxa*). In its context here, Paul is undoubtedly referring to God's presence with the people of Israel (see, e.g., Ex. 16:7; 24:16; 40:34–35). But the reader of Romans will not have forgotten that Paul has just attributed this characteristic to Christians (8:18, 30).

After breaking his syntax, Paul concludes in verse 5 with two final blessings enjoyed by Israel: "the patriarchs" and the Messiah. The patriarchs—Abraham, Isaac, and Jacob especially—are significant not so much in themselves but because God entered into a solemn covenant with them. This covenant was to be valid between God and their descendants forever. Paul returns to this same point in 11:28, which forms then something of an inclusio with this mention of the patriarchs here in the opening verses of Paul's argument about Israel.

The greatest blessing promised to Israel was the Messiah, that is, the Christ. From a strictly human point of view ("according to the flesh" here again; NIV "the human ancestry"), the Messiah was to arise from the people of Israel. But from the divine point of view, he is more; indeed, he is God. At least, this is the reading found in several English translations (NIV; KJV; NASB; JB; NRSV). Note, for instance, the NRSV: "From them, according to the flesh, comes the Messiah, who is over all, God blessed forever. Amen." Here the Messiah is identified as "God."

Other English translations do not make this identification. Note, for instance, the RSV: "Of their race, according to the flesh, is the Christ. God

---

4. This pattern is esp. clear in 1 Maccabees; see Moo, *The Epistle to the Romans*, 561.
5. See esp. Murray, *The Epistle to the Romans*, 2:4–5.

who is over all be blessed for ever. Amen" (see also NEB; TEV). As may be obvious from these conflicting renderings, the issue is how to punctuate the verse. Since most ancient manuscripts do not have punctuation, modern interpreters have to decide whether to put a comma or a period after "Messiah." The issue is complicated, but both the syntax and the context favor the comma.[6] This verse, therefore, deserves to be numbered among those few in the New Testament that explicitly call Jesus "God."

PAUL AS MOSES AND MARTYR. The reader of Romans who knows his or her Bible well will immediately spot in verse 3 one of those allusions to the Old Testament that we have underscored as especially important in Romans. In Exodus 32, the people of God fall into idolatry by fashioning a golden calf and worshiping it. When Moses discovers the sin of the people, he earnestly pleads with God not to destroy the people:

> The next day Moses said to the people, "You have committed a great sin. But now I will go up to the LORD; perhaps I can make atonement for your sin."
> So Moses went back to the LORD and said, "Oh, what a great sin these people have committed! They have made themselves gods of gold. But now, please forgive their sin—but if not, then blot me out of the book you have written." (Ex. 32:30–32)

Moses' identification with the people is so strong that he is willing to suffer damnation with them, if that should be God's will for him. Paul likewise identifies with Israel to the point of offering to become "cursed" for them. The many direct references and allusions to the Moses story throughout these chapters (e.g., Rom. 9:14–18; 10:19; 11:13–14) make it almost certain that Paul sees Moses as a model for his own intercessory position between God and Israel. This suggests, in turn, that Paul saw himself, like Moses, as a critical figure in salvation history.[7]

---

6. See esp. Bruce M. Metzger, "The Punctuation of Rom. 9:5," in *Christ and Spirit in the New Testament: In Honour of Charles Francis Digby Moule* (ed. B. Lindars and S. Smalley; Cambridge: Cambridge Univ. Press, 1973), 95–112; Murray J. Harris, *Jesus as "God": Theos as a Christological Title in the New Testament* (Grand Rapids: Baker, 1992), 144–72.

7. This same perspective will emerge again in Romans 11, when Paul talks about his own ministry to Gentiles and, indirectly, to Jews (11:13–14). The salvation-historical significance of Paul has been highlighted esp. by Johannes Munck (e.g., *Paul and the Salvation of Mankind* [London: SCM, 1959]), although Munck takes the idea too far.

But the careful reader will also note that Paul goes one step further than Moses: He offers to suffer God's curse on behalf of Israel. In the context, it is clear that this "for the sake of" (Gk. *hyper*) means "in place of." Paul offers himself as a substitute for the people of Israel. Feeding into this idea may well be traditions from the intertestamental period. The severe persecution that came on the Jews at the time of Antiochus IV Epiphanes in 168 B.C. resulted in many martyrdoms among the Jews. To find meaning in these terrible deaths, some Jewish authors speculated that the suffering of these martyrs had an atoning value for Israel. By their suffering, the martyrs were blotting out the sins of Israel and bringing salvation and blessing to the people. Perhaps the most famous passage is 4 Maccabees 17:17–22:

> The tyrant himself and all his council marveled at their [the martyrs'] endurance, because of which they now stand before the divine throne and live the life of eternal blessedness. For Moses says, "All who are consecrated are under your hands." These, then, who have been consecrated for the sake of God, are honored, not only with this honor, but also by the fact that because of them our enemies did not rule over our nation, the tyrant was punished, and the homeland purified—they having become, as it were, a ransom for the sin of our nation. And through the blood of those devout ones and their death as an atoning sacrifice, divine Providence preserved Israel that previously had been mistreated.

By reflecting these Old Testament and Jewish traditions in his prayer, Paul suggests that he also faces a time of crisis in the life of God's people. The threat does not come from a secular tyrant, as in the Maccabean period, but from the people's own sin, as in the days of Moses. Yet these stories, the reader knows, both had happy endings: The people of God were preserved and God's plan went forward. So also, perhaps, Paul foreshadows the positive end of his own struggle over the salvation of God's people.

IN THESE VERSES, Paul sets up the tension that will generate the argument of the following chapters: God has blessed Israel and promised them many more blessings (vv. 4–5), yet Israel stands accursed before God (v. 3). This is not the place to anticipate the ins and outs of the argument that unfolds in these chapters. But it is the place to introduce one issue that we will touch on repeatedly as we follow Paul's logic: the status of Israel in light of the gospel.

Interpreters have traditionally assumed that the plight of Israel that drives Paul's theologizing is her failure to accept God's gift of salvation in Christ. Many Jews, of course, did accept that gift, and Paul wants us to remember them (see 11:1–10). But the majority have not, so Paul laments the situation of Israel as a whole throughout chapters 9–11.

But a strong revisionist movement today has challenged this traditional view of Israel's plight. Nothing Paul says in these chapters, its advocates argue, suggests that Israel is no longer the people of God, destined for judgment. To be sure, Israel has sinned. But her sin has not separated her from God, for God's love for his people is unbreakable and his covenant promise irrevocable. Rather, Israel's sin is the sin of selfishness. Seeking to keep God's grace all to themselves, Jews have refused to acknowledge that God had sent Jesus to offer salvation to Gentiles. It is this failure on the part of Jews to recognize what God has done in Christ for the Gentiles and through Paul in preaching to the Gentiles that brings him sorrow.[8]

Integral to this interpretation of Israel in Romans 9–11 is the assumption that God's covenant with the people of Israel is salvific and eternal. The Jewish people are saved through their own "Torah covenant," while Gentiles are saved through the "Christ covenant." This so-called "bi-covenantal" view arose toward the end of the 1800s but has become especially popular in the last decades of the twentieth century.

Two factors external to the text have propelled the popularity of this alternative interpretation. (1) The first is the Holocaust. Here, many Jews and Christians agree, is the shocking logical conclusion of the church's insistence that salvation can be found only in Christ. By excluding Jews from salvation, Christians in effect deny the value of Judaism and open the door to persecution. To be truly "Christian," then, the church needs to repudiate her exclusivistic views. (2) Also involved is the pluralism of our age. Every religion, so we are taught, is but a different way to the same God. Judaism must be seen as valid as Christianity.

We have discussed both these trends elsewhere in the commentary, and we will deal with their specifics in light of the exegetical evidence elsewhere in chapters 9–11. But I want to get this broad concern out on the table as we begin working through these chapters. Our interpretation of Scripture is always affected by factors external to the text—from the specifics of our own personalities and backgrounds to the generalities of cultural movements

---

8. See esp. Lloyd Gaston, *Paul and the Torah* (Vancouver: Univ. of British Columbia Press, 1987), 135–50; John Gager, *The Origins of Anti-Semitism: Attitudes Toward Judaism in Pagan and Christian Antiquity* (New York: Oxford Univ. Press, 1983), 197–212; S. G. Hall III, *Christian Anti-Semitism and Paul's Theology* (Minneapolis: Fortress, 1993), 88–93, 113–27.

and influences. The contemporary significance of Romans 9–11 will depend considerably on our recognizing these influences and on our ability, by the Spirit's help, to let the text speak to and through them.

As I have argued earlier in this commentary, I am confident that God can enable us to hear him speak in the midst of all our personal and cultural prejudices. But we must actively seek to let him do so—by humility, by a willingness to listen, and, most of all, by seeking the Spirit's help and guidance.

Romans 9:6–13

I T IS NOT as though God's word had failed. For not all who are descended from Israel are Israel. ⁷Nor because they are his descendants are they all Abraham's children. On the contrary, "It is through Isaac that your offspring will be reckoned." ⁸In other words, it is not the natural children who are God's children, but it is the children of the promise who are regarded as Abraham's offspring. ⁹For this was how the promise was stated: "At the appointed time I will return, and Sarah will have a son."

¹⁰Not only that, but Rebekah's children had one and the same father, our father Isaac. ¹¹Yet, before the twins were born or had done anything good or bad—in order that God's purpose in election might stand: ¹²not by works but by him who calls—she was told, "The older will serve the younger." ¹³Just as it is written: "Jacob I loved, but Esau I hated."

PAUL STATES THE THESIS of chapters 9–11 in 9:6a. Then, in 9:6b–29 he presents his first response to the problem of God's faithfulness to his word of promise to Israel. It focuses on Israel's past and explores the exact meaning and scope of that promise. Essentially, Paul wants to show that God never promised salvation to all of Israel. He has always chosen some from within national Israel to be his true people—what the prophets called a "remnant" (see v. 27). If, then, only a minority of Jews has responded to the gospel and joined God's eschatological people, no contradiction with the Old Testament can be found.

But Paul goes a step further. God has always reserved for himself the right to determine who his people will be; he is that kind of God, free and sovereign. That means that he can also invite Gentiles to join his eschatological people. Indeed, the Old Testament itself predicts this would happen.

The argument we have just sketched unfolds in three stages. Romans 9:6b–13 and 24–29 carry on the main line of development. The former paragraph begins with (v. 7), and the latter paragraph ends with (vv. 27–29), a focus on God's "call"—an inclusio that reveals the key idea of the section. In both paragraphs, Paul shows how God is free to call whom he wants into his people. The paragraph between these two (9:14–23) takes up the question inevitably sparked by this teaching: the fairness of God.

Verses 6–13 begin by looking at the call of God in the patriarchal era, when God was first forming his people. It features two parallel sections, each of which looks at how God's call affected a set of brothers: Isaac and Ishmael in verses 7–9, and Jacob and Esau in verses 10–13. In each Paul quotes the Old Testament twice to substantiate his argument.

The Thesis of Chapters 9–11: The Reliability of God (9:6a)

IN VERSE 6A we hear the thesis that Paul defends in these three chapters: "It is not as though God's word had failed." This issue arises because Israel's cursed status (9:3) appears to contradict the blessings and promises God had bestowed on her (9:4–5). To defend the gospel, Paul must defend God's faithfulness to his promises to Israel. For if God has gone back on his word to Israel, then a deep chasm between the Old and New Testament opens up, and the good news can no longer claim the God of Israel as its author. The whole plan of salvation crashes.

The Thesis of 9:7–29: The "Israel" within Israel (9:6b)

VERSE 6B SETS forth the thesis for verses 7–29: "Not all who are descended from Israel are Israel." Clearly, Paul differentiates two "Israels": what we might call a "physical" Israel, based on descent, and a "spiritual" Israel. What is the "spiritual" Israel Paul has in view? While the point is debated, we think it likely that in Galatians 6:16, Paul refers to the entire church as "Israel," as the NIV translates: "Peace and mercy to all who follow this rule, even to the Israel of God." With this translation and punctuation, "Israel of God," is identical to "all who follow the rule"—in the context including both Jewish and Gentile Christians.[1] This, then, may be what Paul means here: Not all Jews by birth belong to the "Israel of God," the church.[2]

But this use of the word "Israel" is quite out of keeping in Romans 9–11, where Paul is so concerned to guard the continuing privileges of Israel. Nor does it fit the development of the argument in 9:7–13, which focuses on God's choice of a spiritual people *from within* physical Israel. Almost certainly, then, the "Israel" at the end of verse 6 is the spiritual Israel that is to be found within physical Israel. All Jews belong to the larger Israel by birth, but only those Jews called by God belong to the true Israel.

---

1. For the arguments about this text and a defense of the conclusion we adopt here, see Richard N. Longenecker, *Galatians* (Waco, Tex.: Word, 1990), 297–99. For an alternate view, taking "Israel of God" to refer only to Jewish Christians, see esp. Peter Richardson, *Israel in the Apostolic Church* (Cambridge: Cambridge Univ. Press, 1969), 74–84.

2. See, e.g., N. T. Wright, *The Climax of the Covenant: Christ and the Law in Pauline Theology* (Edinburgh: T. & T. Clark, 1991), 238.

God's Choice of Isaac over Ishmael (9:7–9)

THAT PAUL SHOULD first turn to Abraham to substantiate this point is not surprising. Abraham was, after all, the ancestor of the Jewish people as a whole (see Gen. 12:1–3; Rom. 4:1). Yet Jews belong to Abraham in different ways, Paul affirms. All who can claim him as their physical ancestor are his "children," but only those who have him as their spiritual father as well are his "offspring." The reader of the NIV may be puzzled at this point, because I am not using the words in the same way it does. My way of putting it reflects an exegetical decision and translation decision crucial in following Paul's argument.

The NIV translates the same Greek word, *sperma* (seed), as "descendants" in verse 7 and as "offspring" in verses 8–9. To follow Paul's argument more accurately, I will use "offspring" throughout. Exegetically, the NIV suggests in its translation of verse 7 that "descendants"/"offspring" is the larger category while "children" is the narrow, spiritual category. But the sequel in verses 8–9 uses "offspring" of the narrower group. Since the Greek allows it, therefore, I prefer to take "offspring" in verse 7 also as the reference to the spiritual descendants of Abraham: "It is not the case that all of Abraham's children are his offspring."[3]

A quotation from Genesis 21:12 grounds this assertion. God determined that Abraham's offspring would be "called" (*kaleo*; NIV "reckoned"). The word *kaleo* is a key word in Paul's argument. God spoke these words to Abraham when the latter expressed reluctance to banish his other son, Ishmael. Thus it is clear, Paul concludes in verse 8, that it is only the "children of the promise" who are "regarded as Abraham's offspring." That is, only those descendants of Abraham from the line of Isaac can be considered "Israel" in the narrower sense.

Paul wraps up this argument from the sons of Abraham with a final scriptural quotation (v. 9), a loose rendering of Genesis 18:10 or 18:14 (or perhaps both). The quotation reminds us of God's gracious and miraculous intervention to enable Sarah, who was infertile, to bear the child of the promise (see Rom. 4:18–20). The initiative, Paul makes clear again, is with God. Inheriting the promise is not based on birth alone; it depends on God's gracious intervention.

God's Choice of Jacob Over Esau (9:10–13)

THIS SAME POINT becomes even clearer in 9:10–13. For one can argue that Isaac and Ishmael are distinguished by a key physical difference: The former was born to Sarah and the latter to Hagar. Thus, to dispel any idea that phys-

---

3. See, further, Moo, *The Epistle to the Romans*, 575.

ical descent plays a role in the promise, Paul brings us down one generation, to two children born to the same parents and at the same time. "Rebekah's children," Paul reminds us, were born in one single act of conception. This way of rendering the Greek of verse 10 is natural and provides the necessary advance on the argument of verses 7–9. For what makes Jacob and Esau different from Ishmael and Isaac is not only that they had the same mother as well as the same father, but that they were conceived at the same time.

The syntax of verses 11–12 is quite muddled, but the NIV does the best job we can with it. The main clause comes only at the end of the long complex sentence: "She was told, 'The older will serve the younger.'" This quotation (from Gen. 25:23) neatly expresses Paul's key point, that God's choice reversed the natural order of birth. But to make the matter clear, Paul precedes the main clause, with its quotation, with two subordinate clauses: one reminding us of the circumstances in which God's words came to Rebekah, and the second expressing the purpose of that situation.

God appointed Jacob over Esau to carry on the line of promise before the two boys had been born and before they had "done anything good or bad" (v. 11a). In this way, "God's purpose in election might stand" (v. 11b). The Greek word for "election" (*ekloge*) comes from the root *kaleo* (to call) and means calling out, choosing.

The phrase at the beginning of verse 12, "not by works but by him who calls," can express the purpose of election (so NIV) or, more likely, continue the circumstances of God's word to Rebekah from verse 11a: Since God chose Jacob over Esau before they were born or had done anything, it is clear that Jacob's status was based not on works but on the God who calls. When God is the subject of the verb "call" in Paul, it always refers to an effective summons. God does not just invite Jacob, or other people, to a certain privilege or position; he brings them into it. So God was able to tell Rebekah before the twins were ever born just what role each of her sons would have. It was not a matter of chance but of determination by God's own call.

Paul concludes his discussion of Jacob and Esau with yet another quotation: "Jacob I loved, but Esau I hated." This quotation (from Mal. 1:2−3) is a lightning rod in the debate over this passage and its theological implications. The first matter to decide is the meaning of the word "hate." Some think "hate" may mean simply, in Semitic fashion, "love less."[4] But the Old Testament context points in a different direction. That context is clearly covenantal, so that "love" means, in effect, "choose," while "hate" means "reject."[5]

---

4. E.g., Fitzmyer, *Romans*, 563.
5. See R. L. Smith, *Micah-Malachi* (Waco, Tex.: Word, 1984), 305; Cranfield, *The Epistle to the Romans*, 480.

The other issue is the question of the significance of the names "Jacob" and "Esau." Many modern interpreters, noting that these names in Malachi represent, respectively, the nations of Israel and Edom, insist that this is Paul's meaning also. He is reflecting on the way God has acted in history to choose as his covenant people Israel while rejecting other nations, such as Edom.[6] Such a conclusion will affect our interpretation of this entire passage. But the conclusion that Paul is thinking of Jacob and Esau here as individuals is hard to resist. He has specifically rehearsed their personal histories in verses 11–12, referring to their birth and their "works." It is difficult to think that Paul switches from this personal reference to a corporate one, without warning, in verse 13.[7] We explore the significance of this exegetical decision in the Contemporary Significance section.

PAUL'S QUOTATIONS of the Old Testament. Granted Paul's purpose in Romans 9–11, we should not be surprised to find these chapters filled with quotations of the Old Testament. An exact count is difficult because it is not always clear what should count as a quotation (as opposed to an allusion) and because it is hard to know how to count composite quotations. But a rough count finds twenty-four quotations in Romans 9–11. When we consider that there are about eighty quotations in all Paul's letters, this figure is remarkable. In other words, 30 percent of Paul's Old Testament quotations are in these three chapters.[8] Thus, an accurate interpretation demands a careful look at how Paul uses the Old Testament to buttress and illustrate his argument. We will set the stage here by looking at the function of the four quotations in verses 6–13.

All four of these quotations are taken from Old Testament passages that describe the way God has acted in history to create the "line of promise." Through Abraham God brought into being a people who would be blessed by him and, in turn, be a blessing to the nations (Gen. 12:1–3). Knowing this promise and recognizing that his wife, Sarah, was infertile, Abraham had a child, Ishmael, through Sarah's maidservant, Hagar (Gen. 16). But God insisted that it would be through a son of Sarah that the people of promise

---

6. See, e.g., Cranfield, *The Epistle to the Romans*, 480–81; Fitzmyer, *Romans*, 562–63; and the useful broader discussion in William W. Klein, *The New Chosen People: A Corporate View of Election* (Grand Rapids: Zondervan, 1990), 173.

7. See esp. Schreiner, *Romans*, 497–503; Piper, *The Justification of God*, 45–54.

8. For the statistics, with analysis, see Christopher D. Stanley, *Paul and the Language of Scripture: Citation Technique in the Pauline Epistles and Contemporary Literature* (Cambridge: Cambridge University Press, 1992).

would be created (17:15–16), and Paul quotes from these assurances in Romans 9:9 (Gen. 18:10, 14).

Once Sarah had given birth to her son, Isaac, she wanted to drive away Hagar and Ishmael so that they would not compete for the inheritance. Abraham was reluctant, but God assured him by promising to make Ishmael into a nation and by assuring him that through Isaac he would "reckon" Abraham's offspring. Paul quotes this promise (from Gen. 21:12) in Romans 9:7. In their Old Testament context, then, these texts emphasize that God selected Isaac to be the one through whom he would create a special people of blessing and through whom his promise would be fulfilled.

The texts about Jacob and Esau (in vv. 12–13) are similar. Again we find God selecting one individual over another to carry on the line of promise. God's determinative role in elevating Jacob over Esau is seen in his prediction to Rebekah, their mother, that the older twin would serve the younger (Gen. 25:23, quoted in Rom. 9:12). Then hundreds of years later, speaking to the tension between the nations of Israel and Edom in his day, the prophet Malachi reminds the people how God determined to bless "Jacob" (= Israel) and to reject and condemn "Esau" (= Edom) (Mal. 1:2–3, quoted in Rom. 9:13).

What seems clear is that none of these texts says anything directly about the spiritual fate of the individuals Isaac, Ishmael, Jacob, and Esau. The Old Testament does not—at least in these texts—reflect on whether they were saved or not; it is concerned solely with the roles they would play in salvation history. God's election of them is not election to salvation but election to play a certain role in the unfolding plan of God. If Paul is using these texts in accordance with their original intent, he, too, must be reflecting on the way God has chosen certain people, or nations, to play positive and negative roles in salvation history. Isaac, Jacob, and Israel contributed to God's plan by carrying on his promise. Ishmael, Esau, and Edom contributed also to that plan by opposing God and his people and giving God the opportunity to display his glory.

As most Bible students know, this conclusion has important ramifications for the theology of Romans 9. For this passage has been a basic source of support for a Calvinist view of election. But if Paul applies Old Testament texts according to their original intent, the Calvinists' appeal to Romans 9 is undercut and perhaps excluded altogether. Calvinist interpreters have then made the mistake of reading election to salvation into a text that is not about that at all.[9]

In the Contemporary Significance section, we will evaluate this claim. But here, as a step toward that end, we want to consider the significance of the Old Testament quotations. The difficulty with the line of argument that we

---

9. For this approach in general, see esp. Klein, *The New Chosen People*; H. L. Ellison, *The Mystery of Israel: An Exposition of Romans 9–11* (Grand Rapids: Eerdmans, 1966).

have outlined in the last paragraph is simply this: Paul does not always apply his Old Testament quotations in accordance with their original intent. The whole matter of "the use of the Old Testament in the New" is complicated and debated. But most scholars agree that Paul, as well as other New Testament authors, find significance in Old Testament passages they quote that goes beyond the meaning of the original.

We have an outstanding example of this "shift of application" in Paul's quotation of Hosea 2:23 and 1:10 in Romans 9:25–26. Paul applies an Old Testament passage about the northern tribes of Israel to the Gentiles. This same kind of shift occurs frequently in Paul. We do not think Paul quotes the Old Testament arbitrarily or that he is unfair to the meaning of the original. Rather, he finds a deeper significance in the Old Testament text by reading it in light of the climax of salvation history in Jesus Christ.[10] But the upshot is that we cannot assume that Paul will apply the texts he quotes with exactly the same sense they have in their own context.

This, of course, does not mean that Paul does not often do so. Interpreters who deny that Paul can be speaking about individual salvation in 9:6–13 because of the Old Testament texts he cites may have a legitimate argument. But that is not a decisive argument. We cannot be sure that Paul applies these texts to the historical origins of the line of promise. Paul may be treating Isaac and Jacob on the one hand and Ishmael and Esau on the other ahistorically, as types of salvation and damnation.[11] Or he may be citing the history of the promise in order to isolate a principle of God's sovereign calling that he applies to the salvation of individuals in his own day.[12] Only a careful appraisal of verses 6–13 in their context can decide this issue.

GOD'S RELIABILITY. Can God be trusted to do what he says? This is the ultimate question Paul seeks to answer in chapters 9–11. God's dealings with Israel raise the question, but its implications go much further. If God indeed promised he would bless Israel and then turned around and blessed the church instead, he might do the same again. His promises to the church might in turn be fulfilled, for instance, in a completely different entity. His promises to me personally as a believer might not be reliable either. Absolute trust in God to accomplish what he has promised is fundamental to our security as believers.

---

10. See, on this, my essay "The Problem of Sensus Plenior," in *Hermeneutics, Authority, Canon,* ed. D. A. Carson and J. D. Woodbridge (Grand Rapids: Zondervan, 1986).

11. Käsemann, *Commentary on Romans,* 261–66.

12. Piper, *The Justification of God,* 45–54.

In Romans 8, Paul has mentioned some of those wonderful promises: God works all things touching our lives for good (8:28); our present sufferings are as nothing compared to the glory God will give us (8:18); nothing will keep us from enjoying that glory in the end (8:29–30; cf. vv. 31–39). Will God keep those promises to us? Absolutely! For God is utterly trustworthy and all-powerful. Nothing can keep him from doing what he said he will do. Our human parents usually want the very best for us, but they do not have the power always to make it happen. Other people in our lives have the power to fulfill their promises to us (my boss can give me the raise he promised; the government can provide for my failing years), but they are not always trustworthy. God combines both in his fatherly concern for us, his dearly loved children.

God's election. Throughout this commentary, the contemporary significance we have derived has often been theological in nature. I make no apology for this, for the text often demands such application. Paul is trying to help us understand the gospel, and he wants us to think the right things about it. It is the mind of the Christian he is seeking to shape.

Of course, the shaping of our minds has important practical ramifications. The theology Paul teaches is always practical theology: Truth about God that must change our perspective and, ultimately, our behavior. Thus, we have sought to show where Paul's theology might lead in terms of contemporary issues and of Christian lifestyle. But we deliberately seek to avoid the impression that what a believer *thinks* is somehow not worthy to be significant in its own right.

Verses 6–13 are a case in point. Paul's purpose is not to set forth Abraham, Isaac, or Jacob as people whose behavior we are to imitate. Any application of this passage along such lines betrays its integrity. What Paul is doing is trying to convince us of a theological truth by reminding us of how God has acted in the past. The significance of the passage will lie in determining just what that truth is.

As we noted above, Romans 9:6–23 has long been used to support what we generally know as a Calvinistic view of election. We briefly described the basics of this view in our comments on 8:29–30. To recapitulate: Calvinists think that God chooses individuals to be saved based on nothing but his own free decision. Nothing a person has done or will do—not even faith—has any bearing on God's choice. As Augustine, in some ways a forerunner of Calvinism, put it, "God does not choose us because we believe, but that we may believe."[13] But does Romans 9:6–23 teach this? In our discussion of verses 14–23 we will tackle the volatile issue of "double predestination." Here we will focus on the issue of election to salvation.

---

13. *Predestination of the Saints* 17.34.

One can understand why Calvinists think that verses 6–13 support their understanding of election. Paul explicitly says he is talking about "election" (v. 11), and he uses the related language of "calling" twice (vv. 7, 12). Throughout the passage, he makes clear that God's calling had nothing to do with one's natural descent (v. 8) or one's works (vv. 11–12). The initiative is clearly with God as the "[one] who calls" (v. 12), not with what a person does.

Arminians, of course, who believe that God chooses people on the basis of his seeing ahead of time who will believe and who will not, do not think the passage teaches the "unconditional election" of Calvinist soteriology. They tend to fall into two camps in their interpretation of these verses. (1) Some think Paul is indeed teaching about individual salvation, but that nothing in the passage excludes the idea that God's choice of people to be saved is based on foreseen faith. Paul is at pains to deny that works have any role in God's choice, but Paul says nothing about faith. In light of the vital role that Paul gives to human believing in chapters 1–4, we are surely justified in assuming it in this passage.[14]

(2) But most contemporary Arminian interpreters take the tack that we have already described in the previous section: The text is simply not about individual salvation. Paul is writing about how God has acted in history to create his own people and to further his plan of salvation. He is ultimately concerned not about individuals but about nations: Israel and the Gentiles. Where individuals may come into play, they either represent nations or the focus is on their role in history, not their eternal destiny.

Arminian interpreters are right to protest against the tendency of many interpreters to import the issues of later Christian theology into Paul's first-century text. Too easily we read Paul against our own individualistic heritage and miss the corporate concerns of the first century (see comments on 5:12–21). As we noted above, the Old Testament texts Paul cites may suggest he is thinking about the destiny of nations in history, not about that of individuals in the afterlife. Nevertheless, when all allowance is made for these points, I think that 9:6–13 does support a Calvinist view of election. Two points are particularly important.

(1) The words Paul uses throughout these verses are words that he elsewhere applies to the salvation of individuals:

> Being "the offspring" (*sperma*) of Abraham (9:7–8)—cf. 4:13, 16, 18; Gal. 3:16, 19, 29 (the only exception is 2 Cor. 11:22)
>
> "Regarded [or reckoned] as" (*logizomai eis*) (9:8)—cf. 2:26; 4:3, 5, 9, 22 (Gen. 15:6); cf. also Rom. 4:4, 6, 8, 10, 11, 23, 24; Gal. 3:6 (Gen. 15:6)

---

14. See esp. Sanday and Headlam, *The Epistle to the Romans*, 248–50; Godet, *Commentary on Romans*, 348–49; Jack W. Cottrell, "Conditional Election," in *Grace Unlimited* (ed. Clark Pinnock; Minneapolis: Bethany, 1975), 51–73.

Being "the children of the promise" (9:8)—cf. Gal. 4:28

"Call" (*kaleo*), when God is the subject (9:12; cf. v. 7)—cf. 8:30; 9:24–26;
    1 Cor. 1:9; 7:15, 17–18, 20–22, 24; Gal. 1:6, 15; 5:8, 13; Eph. 4:1, 4; Col.
    3:15; 1 Thess. 2:12; 4:7; 5:24; 2 Thess. 2:14; 1 Tim. 6:12; 2 Tim. 1:9

"Not by [or apart from] works" (9:12)—cf. 4:6; 9:32; 11:6; Eph. 2:9

Taken together, this complex of vocabulary points unmistakably to the issue of salvation. Contact with Romans 4, where Paul shows how Abraham and his descendants were credited righteousness by their faith and not by their works, is particularly obvious.

(2) A reference to the way God saves individuals suits the context best. Paul is trying to show why there exists a spiritual Israel *within* physical Israel (v. 6b). Reference to God's election of Israel as a nation does not serve this argument, nor does an analysis of the way God has used people in salvation history. What he seeks to show is that God's promise to Israel never guaranteed salvation for all Jews. Verses 6–13 advance this argument only if Paul is applying what he says there to the status of individual Jews. We agree, then, with the basic thesis of John Piper in his careful analysis of this passage: Paul uses the Old Testament story of God's sovereign selection of Isaac and Jacob to establish a basic principle about the way God selects people.[15] The language Paul uses and the context of the verses make it clear that he applies this principle to God's election of individuals to salvation.

But, we rightly ask, how about my faith? Is it of no importance then? A meaningless, robotic response that God forces me to make? The Arminian has a legitimate protest at this point. Nevertheless, I don't think we can smuggle faith into verses 6–13 as the *basis* on which God chooses. Paul makes not just the negative point, that God does *not* choose on the basis of works, but the positive point also: He chooses based on his decision to choose (v. 12a).

Nevertheless, faith cannot be omitted from the salvation equation. However much we may want to claim that salvation is based on God's choice, we must also insist that the human decision to believe is also both real and critical. We are not puppets in God's hands, passively moving as he directs. We are responsible human beings, called by God to exercise faith in his Son. The evidence of Scripture compels us to maintain a fine balance at this point. The Bible teaches in passages such as 9:6–13 that God is the one who ultimately determines, by his own free decision, who is to be saved. But it also teaches that every human being is called upon to respond to God's offer of salvation in faith.

Paul himself seeks to keep this balance in these chapters. In 9:6–29, he maintains that Israel is set aside because of God's decision. But in 9:30–10:21,

---

15. Piper, *The Justification of God*, 45–54.

he argues that Israel is set aside because she has willfully refused to believe. Divine sovereignty and human responsibility in salvation stand in some tension with one another, but they are not logically contradictory.[16] To be truly biblical, we must carefully maintain a balance in which both are given full weight.

What difference, we may finally ask, does it finally make whether I believe in the Calvinist view of unconditional election or not? I need to write carefully here. On the one hand, both Calvinism and Arminianism are fully orthodox views. Each can marshal impressive biblical support in its favor. I am thankful to teach in a school and worship in a church where each view is strongly represented and where proponents of each view accept and honor those who hold the opposite view. On the other hand, I do not want to suggest that it makes no difference which view we believe or that each one has equal support from the Bible.

I am generally (though not consistently) Calvinistic in my soteriology. I think the Bible supports my view, and it does make a difference. How? Primarily in doing full justice to the biblical presentation of a God who is both all-powerful and completely free in his actions. In a text closely related to Romans 9, Paul makes the point that God's election cannot be "by works," for, if it were, "grace would no longer be grace" (11:5–6). Now my Arminian brothers and sisters will insist that foreseen faith, as the product of "prevenient grace," need be no threat to God's freedom and grace. But by making the human decision to believe the crucial point of distinction between those who are saved and those who are not, and thus making God's election a response to human choice, this perspective seems to me to minimize the power and wonder of grace.

---

16. On the larger theological and philosophical issues involved here, see esp. John Feinberg, "God Ordains All Things," in *Predestination and Free Will* (ed. D. and R. Basinger; Downers Grove, Ill.: InterVarsity, 1986), 17–43; D. A. Carson, *Divine Sovereignty and Human Responsibility* (Atlanta: Knox, 1981), 201–22.

Romans 9:14–23

WHAT THEN SHALL we say? Is God unjust? Not at all! [15]For he says to Moses,

> "I will have mercy on whom I have mercy,
>   and I will have compassion on whom I have
>   compassion."

[16]It does not, therefore, depend on man's desire or effort, but on God's mercy. [17]For the Scripture says to Pharaoh: "I raised you up for this very purpose, that I might display my power in you and that my name might be proclaimed in all the earth." [18]Therefore God has mercy on whom he wants to have mercy, and he hardens whom he wants to harden.

[19]One of you will say to me: "Then why does God still blame us? For who resists his will?" [20]But who are you, O man, to talk back to God? "Shall what is formed say to him who formed it, 'Why did you make me like this?'" [21]Does not the potter have the right to make out of the same lump of clay some pottery for noble purposes and some for common use?

[22]What if God, choosing to show his wrath and make his power known, bore with great patience the objects of his wrath—prepared for destruction? [23]What if he did this to make the riches of his glory known to the objects of his mercy, whom he prepared in advance for glory.

AS WE HAVE NOTED elsewhere in Romans, Paul writes this letter as a seasoned teacher. He knows the questions people will have about his teaching and raises them himself in order to head off misunderstandings. He knows his teaching about the sovereignty of God in election will stir questions and objections. Indeed, the questions are easy to anticipate; they are the same ones we ask when confronted with the unconditional election of God: "Isn't it unfair for God to act this way?" (cf. v. 14); and "How can God hold us responsible if he is the one who determines what happens?" (cf. v. 19). So before he goes on with his teaching about how God has selected only some Jews to be saved along with many Gentiles (vv. 24–29), he pauses to deal with them.

God Is Just Because He Acts for His Glory (9:14–18)

THE RHETORICAL QUESTIONS and emphatic negative response in verse 14 show that Paul reverts, appropriately, to the diatribe style in order to clear away objections to his teaching. He has taught that God chose Jacob and rejected Esau simply because it was his will to do so; nothing about them led God to act toward them as he did (9:10–13). The question "Is God unjust?" is a natural one to ask in response to this teaching.

Readers of Romans are sometimes puzzled that Paul does not appear to answer this question in verses 15–18. But if we properly understand the question, we will be able to see that he does, indeed, answer it. The key is to put the issue of God's justice or righteousness in its biblical context. Determining right or wrong, what is just or unjust, demands a standard for measurement. That standard is ultimately nothing less than God's own character (see comments on 3:25–26). God, therefore, acts justly when he acts in accordance with his own person and plan. This is precisely the point Paul makes in 9:15–18. The argument falls into two parallel parts, each with a quotation from the Old Testament (vv. 15 and 17) and a conclusion drawn from the quotation ("therefore," vv. 16, 18).

(1) Paul first quotes Exodus 33:19, where God reveals to Moses a fundamental aspect of his character: He is free to bestow mercy on whomever he wishes. This means, Paul points out, that "it does not . . . depend on man's desire or effort, but on God's mercy" (Rom. 9:16). What is the "it"? Probably, in light of verse 15, God's bestowal of mercy on people.[1] Receiving favor from God does not depend on anything a person can will or do, but only on God's own will to show mercy. Note that Paul's inclusion of both "willing" and "doing" supports our conclusion that he excludes faith as well as works as sources of election (see v. 12).

(2) A second quotation reinforces the freedom of God to act as he wishes, but now from a negative side (v. 17). God's deliverance of his people from slavery in Egypt is a basic part of the story line of the Bible. God's message about his mercy was originally spoken to Moses, the man God used to deliver his people (v. 15). Perhaps because of this reference, Paul now turns to Moses' antagonist in the story, Pharaoh, and cites a word that God spoke to him (Ex. 9:16). The essence of the message is that God brought Pharaoh onto the stage of history ("raised [him] up") to accomplish his own purposes, namely, to display his power and broadcast his name. By resisting God's determination to release his people from captivity, Pharaoh forced Moses to work a series of miracles, culminating in the parting of the "Sea of Reeds," to bring Israel out of Egypt. This display of God's power became known throughout that part of the world (cf. Josh. 2:10).

---

1. See, e.g., Cranfield, *The Epistle to the Romans*, 484–85.

Verse 18 draws the conclusion not only from verse 17 but from verses 15–16 as well. It summarizes the freedom of God as it has an impact on human beings in both a positive and negative way. As God's message to Moses shows that he is free to show mercy to whomever he wants, so his word to Pharaoh shows that he is free to "harden" whomever he wants. Anyone familiar with the Exodus story recognizes the importance of the word "harden" in the Exodus account. It is because Pharaoh's heart was "hardened" that he continued to resist God's will in the face of increasingly spectacular miraculous displays.

The word "harden" (Gk. *skleryno*) refers to being in a state of insensitivity to God, his Word, and his work. The book of Exodus is not clear about the relationship between God's decision to harden Pharaoh's heart and Pharaoh's own hardening of his heart. But the point is not all that important, since Paul clearly gives the initiative to God. But to what do God's "having mercy" and "hardening" refer? The same options are available here as for the similar issue of God's election in 9:7–13. Many think Paul refers to the roles of Moses (and Israel) and Pharaoh (and Egypt) in salvation history. But again, we think that what he says here has direct relevance to the issue of personal salvation. It is God who determines who is to be saved and who is to be kept in a state of spiritual blindness.

God Is Free to Use His Creatures as He Wills (9:19–23)

PAUL'S REASSERTION OF God's sovereignty in salvation (v. 18) sparks another round of question and answer (the diatribe style again). Paul's fictional sparring partner asks: "Then why does God still blame us? For who resists his will?" Paul again does not answer as we might expect. He offers no logical explanation of how God's determinative will and human responsibility cohere. Still less does he suggest that God's will is but his response to human decisions—as we would have expected him to say if, indeed, God's will to save were based on foreseen faith. No, rather than taking the defensive, Paul goes full speed ahead with yet further assertions of the freedom of God to do as he wants with his creatures.

In addressing his sparring partner as "Man" (*anthropos;* lit., human being), Paul reminds him of his creaturely status. What right, Paul asks, does this created being have to question God's ways and complain about how God has made him (v. 20)? Alluding to a rich Old Testament and Jewish tradition (see Bridging Contexts section), Paul uses the imagery of the potter with his clay to depict God's relationship to human beings. As is the case with any analogy, the parallel is by no means perfect. Human beings, created in God's own image, have the power to think and make decisions; they are far more than inert clay. But the analogy works well at the one vital point the apostle wants to make here: God's right to fashion from the clay the kinds of vessels he wants. Some will be vessels of "honor" (*time;* NIV "for noble purposes"), others vessels of "dishonor" (*atimia;* NIV "common use").

Paul uses similar language to describe the different roles believers have in the "household of God" (see 2 Tim. 2:20). So, again, he may be depicting the different roles people have played in salvation history.[2] But the parallel with "objects of his wrath" and "objects of his mercy, whom he prepared in advance for glory" (Rom. 9:22–23) suggest rather that he is thinking of God's freedom to choose some people to be saved and leave others in their spiritual deadness.[3]

Paul concludes his excursus about God's freedom to bestow and withhold salvation as he chooses with a final complicated question. We will forego here a survey of the many suggestions for untangling the complex web of Paul's syntax.[4] The NIV translation reflects the best option. It makes the following decisions. (1) Verses 22–23 form a question that has no direct answer (the NIV indicates the lack of sequel with the dash). The "What if" at the beginning suggests that Paul is saying, in effect: "What if God has acted in this way? Who will question God's authority?"

(2) The word "choosing" (or "willing") has a causal rather than a concessive function. Paul is not saying that God has been patient with sinful people *even though* he wanted "to show his wrath and make his power known" by subjecting them to punishment instantly (see NASB). Rather it is *because* God wants publicly to display that wrath and power that he has done so. By reserving the outward display of his wrath against sinners until the end of history, God is able to make his judgment all the more obvious.

(3) The third decision reflected in the NIV is to make verse 23 the larger purpose of God's bearing with sinful people. God has tolerated sinners not only so he can display his wrath and power all the more clearly; he has done so especially in order to "make the riches of his glory known to the objects of this mercy, whom he prepared in advance for glory" (v. 23).

Behind verses 22–23 is a Jewish tradition that questioned why God was waiting so long to judge sinners and establish justice in the world. The cry of the martyrs in Revelation 6:10 reflects the same basic question: "How long, Sovereign Lord, holy and true, until you judge the inhabitants of the earth and avenge our blood?" Paul answers this question by showing how God is using this time before the end to prepare for an even greater display of his

---

2. See, e.g., Morris, *The Epistle to the Romans,* 366; Cranfield, *The Epistle to the Romans,* 491–92; H. H. Rowley, *The Biblical Doctrine of Election* (London: Lutterworth, 1950), 40–42.

3. See Murray, *The Epistle to the Romans,* 2:32–33; Piper, *The Justification of God,* 174–83.

4. See Moo, *The Epistle to the Romans,* 604–5, for a full discussion.

powerful judgment and to bring glory to his chosen people. We find in these verses, then, one final contrast, echoing those that Paul has used throughout this passage:

"Jacob I loved, but Esau I hated" (v. 13)
"God has mercy on whom he wants to have mercy, and he hardens whom
   he wants to harden" (v. 18)
"pottery for noble purposes and some for common use" (v. 21)
"objects of his mercy, whom he prepared in advance for glory"/"objects
   of his wrath—prepared for destruction" (vv. 22–23)

The contrast between wrath and glory shows that Paul is writing about individuals destined for judgment on the one hand and individuals destined for glory on the other. Salvation is the issue. What becomes explicit in this last contrast is implicit in the others as well.

THE HARDENING OF **Pharaoh's heart**. God "hardens whom he wants to harden" (v. 18b) is arguably one of the most controversial claims in Scripture. Before we can discuss its theological significance, we must consider the Old Testament background that informs Paul's assertion. The verb "harden" appears suddenly on the scene in verse 18. But the reader knowledgeable about Scripture will recognize that the Old Testament quotation about God's purpose with Pharaoh in verse 17 is what sparks his use of the word. "Hardening" is, after all, a basic theme in the story of Pharaoh and the Exodus.

The author of the Pentateuch refers to the hardening of Pharaoh's heart twenty times in Exodus 4–14. Three different Hebrew verbs are used (from the roots *ḥzq*, *qsh*, and *kbd*), translated by three different Greek verbs in the LXX (*skleryno*, which Paul uses in Rom. 9:18, *katischyo*, and *baryno*). What is particularly important for our assessment of the significance of Paul's hardening theology is the interaction of God and Pharaoh in his hardening.

The first reference to Pharaoh's hardening is a prediction God makes to Moses in Exodus 4:21: 'The LORD said to Moses, 'When you return to Egypt, see that you perform before Pharaoh all the wonders I have given you the power to do. But I will harden his heart so that he will not let the people go'" (see also 7:3). In the narrative that follows, the hardening of the hearts of Pharaoh and his officials is put in three different ways. (1) Following the pattern of 4:21 and 7:3, God hardens the hearts of Pharaoh and his officials (9:12; 10:1, 20, 27; 11:10; 14:4, 8, 17). (2) Pharaoh hardens his own heart (8:15, 32; 9:34; 13:15). (3) Hardening is put in the passive, leaving it open who the initiator of the action might be (e.g., 7:13: "Yet Pharaoh's heart became hard and he would not listen to them, just as the LORD had said"; see also 7:22; 8:19; 9:7, 35).

What are we to make of this evidence? Many interpreters argue that God's hardening is but his judicial reaction to Pharaoh's prior decision to harden his own heart. They note that God does not harden Pharaoh's heart (9:12) until Pharaoh has first hardened his own heart (8:15, 32). This view is the critical assumption in the explanation of Romans 9:18 that I have frequently read in popular books on "Bible difficulties" and heard in sermons and lectures. God's hardening of people is explained simply as his reaction to the decision of people to harden their own hearts.[5]

But apart from the problem of Paul's "whom he wants to harden" for this view, it is not clearly supported in Exodus. For before Pharaoh hardens his own heart, we have two predictions that God will harden Pharaoh (4:21; 7:3) and three references to the hardening in the passive voice (7:13, 14, 22). As so often in Scripture, the implied subject of the passive verb may well be God.[6] I think it safe to say, then, that the text of Exodus does not make clear the relationship between God's hardening and Pharaoh's own hardening. Both are clearly taught, but which preceded the other cannot be determined. What this means, then, is that we cannot assume a particular relationship between divine and human initiatives in hardening when we come to Romans 9:18. We will have to let that text speak for itself.

The imagery of God as potter. As we mentioned in the Original Meaning section, Paul's allusion to God as the potter and human beings as the clay in verses 20–21 taps into a widespread Old Testament and Jewish tradition. This tradition may shed light on Paul's purpose in using the imagery. The texts closest to 9:21 are Isaiah 29:16 and 45:9:

> You turn things upside down,
>   as if the potter were thought to be like the clay!
> Shall what is formed say to him who formed it,
>   "He did not make me"?
> Can the pot say of the potter,
>   "He knows nothing"?

> Woe to him who quarrels with his Maker,
>   to him who is but a potsherd among the potsherds on the ground.

---

5. See, e.g., Godet, *Commentary on Romans*, 355; Morris, *The Epistle to the Romans*, 361–62. See also Klein, *New Chosen People*, 166–67.

6. See esp., for this line of interpretation, Greg K. Beale, "An Exegetical and Theological Consideration of the Hardening of Pharaoh's Heart in Exodus 4–14 and Romans 9," *TrinJ* 5 (1984): 129–54.

Does the clay say to the potter,
  "What are you making?"
Does your work say,
  "He has no hands"?

But closest to Romans 9:22 are Jeremiah 18:6—10 and especially Wisdom of Solomon 15:7:

> "O house of Israel, can I not do with you as this potter does?" declares the LORD. "Like clay in the hand of the potter, so are you in my hand, O house of Israel. If at any time I announce that a nation or kingdom is to be uprooted, torn down and destroyed, and if that nation I warned repents of its evil, then I will relent and not inflict on it the disaster I had planned. And if at another time I announce that a nation or kingdom is to be built up and planted, and if it does evil in my sight and does not obey me, then I will reconsider the good I had intended to do for it."

A potter kneads the soft earth
and laboriously molds each vessel for our service,
fashioning out of the same clay
both the vessels that serve clean uses
and those for contrary uses, making all alike;
but which shall be the use of each of them
the worker in clay decides.

Interpreters evaluate the significance of these parallels in different ways. Some stress that at least two of the passages (Isa. 45:9 and Jer. 18:6—10) use the imagery to describe God's right to use and to reshape *nations* as he chooses, which would provide yet more evidence that Paul is writing throughout this passage about God's use of nations in salvation history rather than the salvation of individuals. But other texts (esp. Isa. 29:16) denounce the *hybris* of individual people who dare to question the ways of God. Paul may have been familiar with this passage from his knowledge (in oral form, of course) of the teaching of Jesus. For the Lord used a verse from this same context (29:13) to scold the scribes and the Pharisees (see Matt. 15:8—9; Mark 7:6—7). The fact is that the imagery of God as potter was so common that it is impossible to be sure which text or texts Paul may have had in mind (see also, e.g., Job 10:9; 38:14; Isa. 64:8; Sir. 33:13; *T. Naph.* 2.2, 4; 1QS 11:22). We must again, then, avoid reading into Romans ideas drawn from specific Old Testament or Jewish texts.

THE DARK SIDE of election. I have argued that Romans 9:6–23 teaches that individuals become Christians only because God, by a free act of his will, chooses them and predestines them to faith and glory. Our turning to Christ in faith is a real decision we make and is essential if we are to be saved, but we only turn to Christ because God has elected us. Many good exegetes and theologians dispute this conclusion, finding it incompatible with the biblical teaching about the freedom of human beings and the call for all to respond in faith to the gospel. Many laypeople likewise react against the doctrine out of a sometimes vague sense that it is just not fair.

But if the idea of God's unconditional election to salvation stirs controversy, imagine the level of reaction against the idea that God might also choose to send people to hell on the basis of his own sovereign decision. Yet we cannot avoid considering whether, indeed, Paul teaches this "dark side" of election, for three key texts in Romans 9:6–23 seem to suggest this idea:

"Jacob I loved, but Esau I hated." (9:13)

Therefore God has mercy on whom he wants to have mercy, and he hardens whom he wants to harden. (9:18)

What if God, choosing to show his wrath and make his power known, bore with great patience the objects of his wrath—prepared for destruction? What if he did this to make the riches of his glory known to the objects of his mercy, whom he prepared in advance for glory. (9:22–23)

In each of these, Paul seems to suggest that God chooses people to be damned just as he chooses people to be saved. Hence theologians, particularly of a Calvinist persuasion, speak of "double predestination."

Is the idea really taught in this passage? I cautiously conclude that it is—although in a different form from what many Calvinists hold. As I have argued, the texts cited above all refer to or are applied to God's work in the lives of individuals. God chooses certain individuals and rejects others on the basis of his own will (vv. 15, 18)—not on the basis of physical descent (vv. 8, 10), anything they do or will do (vv. 12, 16), or what they will (v. 16). It is "the God who calls" that determines the issue. But if God has unconditionally chosen some to be saved, the parallelism suggests that he also unconditionally destines others to wrath.

To be sure, interpreters argue that Paul disrupts the parallelism in significant ways. They claim that the hardening of 9:18, given the background of Exodus, is based on one's prior self-hardening—a claim we have found to be dubious. More to the point is the difference in 9:22–23 between "objects of his wrath—prepared for destruction" and "objects of his mercy, whom he prepared in advance for glory." The latter text is clear: God himself "prepared in advance" those people who receive his mercy and attain glory. But Paul's description of the "objects of wrath" is significantly different: He uses a participle that is middle or passive in form (*katertismena*). If middle, it could mean that these people "prepared themselves" for destruction;[7] if passive, that they were "prepared" by their own sins[8] or by God.[9]

Certainty is impossible here, but the change in construction may suggest that Paul views God's election to salvation and predestination to wrath as different in some way (see below). This consideration is not sufficient, however, to overturn the overall impression that both human salvation and damnation are sovereign acts of God.

But before we conclude that the two acts are completely parallel, one other factor must be considered. Paul teaches that all people are involved in Adam's sin and are therefore under a sentence of death because of their sin (Rom. 5:12–21). God's decision to destine some people to wrath comes, we believe, *after* (in a logical sense) that sin.[10] God's "hardening," then, does not cause spiritual insensitivity; it maintains people in the state of sin that they have already chosen. When God chooses people to be saved, he acts out of pure grace, granting a blessing to people who in no way deserve it. But when he destines people to wrath, he sentences them to the fate they have already chosen for themselves. It is perhaps for just this reason that we find the shift in construction in 9:22–23 and that Paul never uses the words "call" or "election" to refer to God's decision to leave people in their sins and the wrath they deserve. For this same reason, I prefer not to use the expression *double predestination*, as if both God's acts of predestination are of the same kind.

As we reflect on the contemporary significance of this doctrine, two points must be made. (1) As we noted above, the idea that God destines people to hell sparks strong reaction—and understandably. Most of us instinctively feel there is something unfair about God's choosing to rescue some from sin and destining others to their fate. But at some point, we must look carefully at that reaction and decide whether it is justified. I was teaching a seminar some years ago in which I brought up this doctrine. As is always the case, the idea met a lot of resistance. One student in particular was very vocal, insisting that "God just couldn't be like that."

---

7. E.g., F. Prat, *The Theology of Saint Paul* (2 vols.; Westminster, Md.: Newman, 1952), 1:257.

8. E.g., Godet, *Commentary on Romans*, 361–62; Morris, *The Epistle to the Romans*, 368.

9. E.g., Käsemann, *Commentary on Romans*, 271–72; Piper, *The Justification of God*, 194.

10. The logical sequence of God's decision to create people, the fall, and his decision to damn people is a matter of controversy among Calvinist theologians. I don't think it serves our purposes to go into this issue here.

Now such a response may or may not be justified. If one is saying, in effect, "My years of study of the Bible have led me to a view of God that is simply incompatible with this doctrine," I can understand and even sympathize. We can then enter into a dialog in which we seek to come to a mutual understanding about the relationship between Paul's teaching about God in Romans 9 and the broader biblical perspective. The student may have to adjust his or her view in light of Romans 9, or I may have to adjust my interpretation of Romans 9 in light of the teaching of Scripture elsewhere.

But the student in that seminar was not reflecting that kind of objection. Rather, she was saying, in effect, "That doctrine just doesn't fit my idea of what God must be like." At that point a critical question must be asked: Where did her idea of God come from? She failed to cite biblical evidence, so I could only conclude that she was reflecting a picture of God drawn from her general culture and perhaps her own church tradition. But surely such ideas should not be allowed to stand in judgment over Scripture. If our belief in the authority of the Bible means anything, it means that we must submit to what the Bible teaches and bring our own perceptions and ideas into line with Scripture.

(2) This leads to my second point. While I have some of the same problems and questions with this doctrine that most believers have, I also think that it ultimately fits well into the biblical picture of God. *Your God Is Too Small*, the title of the popular book by J. B. Phillips some years ago, is a criticism that might be rightly made to many Christians and many churches. Out of pride in ourselves and our achievements and a culturally influenced belief in ourselves as "masters of our fate," we have a hard time giving God his due.

Yet the Bible presents God as the one who plants and uproots nations (e.g., Isa. 40:12–31; Daniel), whose very word determines the fate of battles. He determines the outcome of every event in human history, from great to small. Particularly relevant to the issue we are considering is God's sovereignty over even evil events. God, Scripture teaches, sent his Son to be crucified by sinful people (Acts 2:23); God determined that Judas would sinfully betray Jesus (e.g., Luke 22:22). Suffusing all of what Paul says in these verses about God's sovereignty in election, and coming to the surface explicitly in Romans 9:20–21, is this biblical view of a God who acts with absolute freedom toward his creatures.

Paul's emphasis at this point receives a lot of criticism from certain scholars. J. C. O'Neill, for example, calls Paul's argument here "thoroughly immoral."[11] We hear in those words the reaction of arrogant humanity, protesting against any encroachment on our "rights" from God or anyone else.

---

11. J. C. O'Neill, *Paul's Letter to the Romans* (Baltimore: Penguin, 1975), 158.

The same reaction easily invades the church, rendering our worship less than what it should be because our picture of God is not as high as it should be. Perhaps we can turn what can seem to be a problem into a virtue by allowing Paul's presentation of the sovereignty of God in election and perdition to stimulate in us a new appreciation for the greatness and incomprehensible purposes of God.

Romans 9:24–29

EVEN US, WHOM he also called, not only from the Jews but also from the Gentiles? ²⁵As he says in Hosea:

"I will call them 'my people' who are not my people;
and I will call her 'my loved one' who is not my
loved one,"

²⁶and,

"It will happen that in the very place where it was
said to them,
'You are not my people,'
they will be called 'sons of the living God.'"

²⁷Isaiah cries out concerning Israel:

"Though the number of the Israelites be like the sand
by the sea,
only the remnant will be saved.
²⁸For the Lord will carry out
his sentence on earth with speed and finality."

²⁹It is just as Isaiah said previously:

"Unless the Lord Almighty
had left us descendants,
we would have become like Sodom,
we would have been like Gomorrah."

PUTTING A PARAGRAPH break between 9:23 and 9:24 may seem strange, since the sentence Paul began in verse 22 continues into verse 24: The "even us" picks up the reference to "objects of his mercy" in verse 23. But the loose syntactical continuity masks the fact that Paul in verse 24 is returning to the main course of his argument. We now hear again the theme that dominated 9:6–13: God's call is the sole basis for inclusion in the true people of God. "What counts is grace, not race," as N. T. Wright puts it.[1]

---

1. Wright, *The Climax of the Covenant,* 238.

Paul now takes a step further by taking this principle to its logical conclusion. Since God's grace is what matters, then he is free to call Gentiles into his kingdom as well as Jews. The apostle makes this point in verse 24, the "heading" for the paragraph. He then grounds his assertion with quotations from Scripture. The structure of the paragraph is chiastic, the verses falling into an A B B' A' pattern:

A God calls (some) Jews (v. 24a)
  B God calls Gentiles (v. 24b)
  B' Old Testament confirms God's call of Gentiles (vv. 25–26)
A' Old Testament confirms God's call of (some) Jews (vv. 27–29)

The verb "call" (*kaleo*) has its usual sense when God is its subject: his effective summons to enter into relationship with himself. It is another way of describing what Paul has said in 9:23, that the people to whom God shows mercy are "prepared [beforehand]" by him for that blessing and for eventual glory. In Paul's day, those people included both Jews and Gentiles. In fact, in Rome and elsewhere on the mission field, it was increasingly becoming the case that Gentiles outnumbered Jews. It is just this unexpected circumstance that Paul is trying to reconcile with the Old Testament here. Thus, he quotes Scripture to substantiate both sides of the situation.

Since he has mentioned the Gentiles last, Paul begins with them. His quotes in verses 25 and 26 are from the book of Hosea. He quotes freely from Hosea 2:23 in verse 25 and then verbatim from the LXX of Hosea 1:10a in verse 26. Although the promise of inclusion into God's people in Hosea is directed to the northern tribes of Israel, Paul applies it to the Gentiles. By God's gracious call, they have been transferred from the status of "not my people" and "not my loved one" to the status of "my people," "my loved one," and "sons of the living God."

Under the old covenant, as Paul puts it in Ephesians 2, the Gentiles were "excluded from citizenship in Israel and foreigners to the covenants of the promise, without hope and without God in the world" (Eph. 2:12). While God graciously extended his covenant grace to some Gentiles (e.g., Rahab, Ruth; see also the book of Jonah), his people were largely identified with, or drawn from, Israel. Under the new covenant, however, all that has changed. God shows no distinction, giving his grace to both Jew and Gentile alike. This, Paul insists, was predicted in the Old Testament itself (see Bridging Contexts section for more on Paul's use of Hosea).

If the Old Testament and Jewish tradition make it important for Paul to justify the inclusion of Gentiles, it also requires him to show why not all Jews are being included. Thus the quotations he uses about Israel in verses 27–29 focus not on God's call of Jews per se but on his call of only a minority of Jews. Isaiah 10:22–23, quoted in part in Romans 9:27–28, is one of the great "remnant" texts in the Old Testament. The remnant conception emerged in the prophets as a message of both judgment and hope—judgment, because the continuing sinfulness of Israel brought God's judgment on the people as a whole, resulting in the salvation of only some of the people; hope, because despite Israel's sinfulness, God maintained his commitment to his covenant and pledged to save at least some of the people.

We hear both notes in the Isaiah 10 quotation. On the one hand, though the people of Israel are numerous, God will save *only* the remnant. (The word "only" has nothing corresponding to it in the Greek text, but is a legitimate contextual gloss.) On the other hand, this remnant *will be saved*. Verse 28, which quotes from Isaiah 10:23, is difficult to interpret. But probably it reinforces the note of judgment from Romans 9:27: God will carry out the judgment he has decreed against Israel with certainty and with dispatch.

Paul ends his series of quotations with another one from Isaiah (Isa. 1:9, quoted in Rom. 9:29). What probably drew his attention to Isaiah 1:9 is the word "descendants" (Gk. *sperma*), which is the key word at the beginning of this section (see comments on Rom. 9:7–8). This word is much more positive, holding out hope to Israel because God is determined to preserve "descendants" for Israel—people who will inherit this promise to Abraham. The verse thus anticipates Paul's word of hope about Israel in chapter 11.

HOSEA, ISAIAH, AND PAUL. As we have repeatedly said in this commentary, we must pay careful attention to Paul's use of the Old Testament if we expect to get the full meaning out of Romans. The series of four quotations in 9:25–29 affords a fascinating example of this "deeper" reading of the letter.

What first strikes the alert reader is that Paul seems to have misapplied his quotations of Hosea 2:23 and 1:10 in Romans 9:25–26. Hosea prophecies about the mercy God will show to the rejected northern tribes of Israel; Paul applies the prophecies to the inclusion of Gentiles. We can avoid the conflict if we interpret Hosea to be referring to Gentiles[2] or Paul to be referring to Jews.[3] But neither alternative does justice to the respective texts. Others think that Paul quotes by analogy: God's calling of Gentiles operates on

---

2. See T. Laetsch: "Very clearly God here prophesies the admission of the heathen into covenant relations with God" (*Bible Commentary on the Minor Prophets* [St. Louis: Concordia, 1956], 75).

3. J. A. Battle Jr., "Paul's Use of the Old Testament in Romans 9:25–26," *GTJ* 2 (1981): 115–29.

the same principle as God's promised renewal of the ten northern tribes.[4] But Paul requires more than an analogy to establish from Scripture justification for God's calling of Gentiles to be his people. How then do we explain what Paul does here? Is he guilty of taking words out of context to suit his own argument?

We think not. True, Paul is not quoting Hosea in strict accordance with the "original meaning" of the prophecies. But set against the larger picture of salvation history, the prophecies assume a broader significance in accord with the way Paul applies them. The key is the Abraham story. Especially the divine promises that are basic to that story provide Paul with the key to salvation history and therefore to his hermeneutics of Old Testament interpretation. Indeed, at the risk of exaggeration, we may almost say that continuity with Abraham is the key to Paul's argument about the Gentiles in Romans.

Abraham is, of course, the basis for Romans 4. But Abraham is also central to the argument about the nature and extent of the people of God in Romans 9–11. The chapters begin with a reminder that Israel possesses the promises and the patriarchs (9:4–5), and all the rest of the discussion is, in a sense, an elaboration of what these promises, connected with the patriarchs, really mean. Thus, the way in which Abraham's "descendants" are "reckoned" is central in Romans 9. The point, then, about the Hosea prophecies is this: They echo the Abrahamic promise of Genesis.

The opening words of Hosea 1:10 (which Paul does not quote) predict that the "Israelites will be like the sand on the seashore, which cannot be measured or counted." This theme of innumerable descendants is a constant refrain in the Abrahamic promise texts of Genesis, and the analogy with the "dust of the earth" or "the sand on the seashore" is used four times (Gen. 13:16; 22:17; 28:14; 32:12). As Douglas Stuart reconstructs the logic, then, Paul can quote Hosea to refer to Gentiles because "those who are in Christ constitute Abraham's seed, of whom this prediction of great growth was made...."[5]

That our explanation of Paul's use of Hosea is on the right track is confirmed by the fact that Abrahamic allusions surface in the two other quotations in these verses as well. Isaiah 10:22, quoted in Romans 9:27, uses "the sand by the sea" language from Genesis. And Isaiah 1:9, quoted in Romans 9:29, picks up the key word "descendants" (*sperma*) from the Abraham story (see 4:13, 16, 18; 9:7–8). Paul began this section (see comments on 9:7–9)

---

4. See, e.g., S. Lewis Johnson, "Evidence from Romans 9–11," in *A Case for Premillennialism: A New Consensus* (ed. D. K. Campbell and J. L. Townsend; Chicago: Moody, 1992), 207–10; J. Ridderbos, *Isaiah* (Grand Rapids: Zondervan, 1985), 565–66.

5. Douglas Stuart, *Hosea-Jonah* (WBC; Waco, Tex.: Word, 1987), 41.

by affirming that Abraham's true "descendants" are selected by God from among all his "children." He ends it by affirming that Abraham's descendants also number people who are not biologically related to him at all. All who have faith are ultimately Abraham's children (4:10–12).

READING THE SCRIPTURE STORY. Paul's reading of the Old Testament against a broad theological background says something to us about our own reading of the Scriptures. Scholars debate about whether modern Christians should interpret and apply the Old Testament with the same degree of creativity that the New Testament writers did. But surely we should follow their lead in reading the Old Testament as a single integral story about God's plan of redemption that finds its fulfillment in Christ. Yet too many of us do not know the story well enough to do that. We read bits and pieces of the Old Testament over time, but often have little idea about how the whole thing fits together. Would we read a novel of Dickens like that—opening up a chapter or a page at random and seeing what "we can get out of it"?

Admittedly, the Bible cannot ultimately be compared to a novel, and we can learn a great deal by reading a single psalm, proverb, or book. But we will not appreciate the significance of specific texts until we have an idea of where they fit into the story line. Years ago preachers and teachers could assume that most of their listeners knew that story line. They were addressing people who had grown up with the biblical story, whether in church or in the culture. But we cannot assume that any more in our post-Christian society. At the seminary where I teach, we have had to revamp our curriculum, installing some basic Bible survey requirements for graduate students because we have learned we cannot assume they are familiar with the Bible's story.

Those of us who preach and teach, therefore, need to take more seriously the importance of helping the people to whom we minister to see the big picture of the Bible's wonderful narrative of God's redemptive plan. We need to offer classes that expose people to the breadth of the Scripture story. We need to make sure to show how specific texts inform, and are informed by, the Scriptures as a whole. And all of us—preachers, teachers, and laypeople alike—need to learn the "old, old story" so well that we can revel in the marvelous interrelationship between all the parts of Scripture.

WHAT THEN SHALL we say? That the Gentiles, who did not pursue righteousness, have obtained it, a righteousness that is by faith; ³¹but Israel, who pursued a law of righteousness, has not attained it. ³²Why not? Because they pursued it not by faith but as if it were by works. They stumbled over the "stumbling stone." ³³As it is written:

> "See, I lay in Zion a stone that causes men to stumble
>   and a rock that makes them fall,
> and the one who trusts in him will never be put to shame."

¹⁰:¹Brothers, my heart's desire and prayer to God for the Israelites is that they may be saved. ²For I can testify about them that they are zealous for God, but their zeal is not based on knowledge. ³Since they did not know the righteousness that comes from God and sought to establish their own, they did not submit to God's righteousness. ⁴Christ is the end of the law so that there may be righteousness for everyone who believes.

⁵Moses describes in this way the righteousness that is by the law: "The man who does these things will live by them." ⁶But the righteousness that is by faith says: "Do not say in your heart, 'Who will ascend into heaven?'" (that is, to bring Christ down) ⁷"or 'Who will descend into the deep?'" (that is, to bring Christ up from the dead). ⁸But what does it say? "The word is near you; it is in your mouth and in your heart," that is, the word of faith we are proclaiming: ⁹That if you confess with your mouth, "Jesus is Lord," and believe in your heart that God raised him from the dead, you will be saved. ¹⁰For it is with your heart that you believe and are justified, and it is with your mouth that you confess and are saved. ¹¹As the Scripture says, "Anyone who trusts in him will never be put to shame." ¹²For there is no difference between Jew and Gentile—the same Lord is Lord of all and richly blesses all who call on him, ¹³for, "Everyone who calls on the name of the Lord will be saved."

WITH 9:30, WE COME to a major break in Paul's argument. At first glance, it might seem to make better sense to put that break at the chapter division, where Paul's address "brothers" occurs.[1] But a closer look shows that 9:30 is, indeed, the place to make the break.[2] This is seen, first, in the "what then shall we say?" question, which often indicates a shift of argument in Romans (see 4:1; 6:1; 7:7; 8:31; 9:14). It is confirmed by a shift in characteristic vocabulary. Beginning in verse 30, the words "righteousness" and "faith"/"believe" become dominant. These words are at the heart of Paul's argument in 9:30–10:13. Three times Paul contrasts two kinds of righteousness:

> "Righteousness that is by faith" versus "a law of righteousness" (9:30–31)
> "God's righteousness" versus "their own [righteousness]" (10:3)
> "The righteousness that is by faith" (10:6) versus "the righteousness that is by the law" (10:5)

These contrasts are at the center of the three different paragraphs into which this section divides: 9:30–33; 10:1–4; and 10:5–13. In each of them Paul explains that Israel has failed to enjoy the blessings of messianic salvation because she has been preoccupied with a righteousness based on the law. Gentiles, on the other hand, are streaming into the kingdom because they have embraced a righteousness based on faith. Paul pauses in this section to reflect on the puzzling turn in salvation history he has described in 9:6–29: Only a remnant of Jews are being saved, while Gentiles, once "not [a] people," are being called "sons of the living God." He uses the critical heart of the gospel—righteousness by faith—to explain this turn of events. All of 9:30–10:21, then, is something of an excursus within the argument of chapters 9–11.

Israel's False Pursuit (9:30–33)

IN 9:6–29, PAUL explained the ethnic composition of God's people in his day as a result of divine election. God "calls" both Jews and Gentiles into his messianic kingdom. Now he explains the same circumstance from the opposite side: the decision of human beings to believe. Gentiles have been able to enjoy God's blessings just for this reason. They had not been pursuing their own righteousness; ignorant of God's promises and excluded from the covenant, they had no concept of right standing with God. But when God

---

1. E.g., Gifford, *Epistle of St. Paul to the Romans,* 182.
2. So almost all modern commentaries.

offered it to them in his grace and through the preaching of the gospel, they responded in faith and so obtained it.

In contrast to the Gentiles, however, is the situation of Israel (9:31). Paul can speak of Israel generally because the great majority of Jews have refused to respond to the gospel. Of course, many have, and Paul will highlight them in the next stage of his argument (11:1–10). But the contrast between the wonderful promises made to Israel and the few number who have recognized their fulfillment in Christ is so great that Paul feels it is fair to speak of the failure of "Israel" as a whole.

We would expect Paul to create a neat contrast with the Gentiles by asserting that Israel pursued, but failed to obtain, righteousness. Instead, however, he claims that they were pursuing "a law of righteousness" and that they failed to attain "it" (i.e., this "law"). Why does Paul disrupt his parallelism to bring "law" to the forefront? Answers vary. A few commentators think that "law" (*nomos*) has a formal meaning here: principle or authority. Israel, Paul would be saying, sought the principle of righteousness but did not attain it.[3] On this view, we can almost omit the word "law" without losing any of Paul's meaning.

While this is attractive and does justice to the prominence of righteousness in this part of the letter, we must reject this view. When Paul uses *nomos* in a formal sense elsewhere, it always comes as a rhetorical contrast to "law" in its specific reference to the law of Moses (see 3:27; 7:21–25; 8:2). We do not find such a contrast here. Probably, then, *nomos* refers to the law of Moses, as it usually does in Paul. Moreover, Paul goes on in 9:32 to claim that Israel failed to attain that law because she pursued it "as if it were by works" rather than through faith.

Paul may be suggesting, then, that the law of Moses, when rightly interpreted, calls for faith and not just for works. Israel's problem was that she was so preoccupied with the latter that she missed the former.[4] But, as we have noted earlier (see comments on 2:25–29), Paul consistently confines *nomos* to the *commands* God gave Israel through Moses. The Pentateuch as a whole, of course, calls for faith, but not the commandments. They demand works. So Paul's formulation "law of righteousness" is probably an attempt to make two points at once: Israel pursued righteousness, but she did not obtain it because she elevated *nomos* to the central position of concern. The people of Israel, therefore, focused narrowly on the works the law demanded and

---

3. E.g., Sanday and Headlam, *The Epistle to the Romans,* 279; Murray, *The Epistle to the Romans,* 2:43.

4. Cranfield, *The Epistle to the Romans,* 507–10; Daniel P. Fuller, *Gospel and Law: Contrast or Continuum? The Hermeneutics of Dispensationalism and Covenant Theology* (Grand Rapids: Eerdmans, 1980), 71–79.

missed the larger demand of God to submit to him in faith. Thus they failed to obtain righteousness.[5]

Paul explains this basic problem again in 9:32b—33, but in different terms. He draws the picture of a walker so intent on pursuing a certain goal that she stumbles and falls over a rock lying right in her path. So Israel, myopically concentrating on the law and its demands, missed Christ, "the stone" that God placed in her path. This imagery comes from Isaiah 8:14 and 28:16, which Paul quotes in Romans 9:33. These texts, along with another "stone" text (Ps. 118:22), are quoted together in 1 Peter 2:6—8, suggesting that they may have been brought together via the key word "stone" by Christians before Paul's day.[6]

Israel's Lack of Knowledge (10:1–4)

THE FOUR VERSES in this paragraph unfold in "staircase" sequence, as Paul justifies each of his assertions in the verse immediately following it. (Though not obvious from the NIV, each verse begins with a *gar*, "for.") Filling in the logical connections that Paul leaves implicit, the argument runs as follows:

I long for Israel's salvation (v. 1);
and I must do so for they have zeal for God but lack knowledge (v. 2);
as is seen in the fact that they seek their own righteousness while ignoring God's (v. 3);
and seeking their own righteousness, through the law, is wrong, because Christ is the culmination of the law (v. 4)

Central to the paragraph, as in the others in this section (9:30—33; 10:5—13) is a contrast between two kinds of righteousness: "their own" and "God's" (v. 3).

As he did in 9:1—2, Paul makes clear how deeply he feels about the failure of Israel to embrace the salvation God offers in Jesus (10:1). Verse 2 explains why Paul continues to pray for Israel's salvation: The Jews have zeal for God but they do not have knowledge. "Zeal" for the Lord finds its outstanding Old Testament example in Phinehas, who killed an Israelite and his pagan lover for flaunting the laws of God (Num. 25). But zeal became an especially prominent and important virtue during the intertestamental period, when the very existence of Israel was threatened by persecution.

In Paul's day the spirit of violent resistance to foreign oppression coalesced in the Zealot movement. Jesus himself displayed zeal for the Lord

---

5. For this general approach see, e.g., Schreiner, *Romans*, 536—38; Westerholm, *Israel's Law*, 127.

6. See, e.g., Barnabas Lindars, *New Testament Apologetic: The Doctrinal Significance of the Old Testament Quotations* (London: SCM, 1961), 177—79.

when he cleared the temple (John 2:17). There can therefore be no doubt that Paul regards the zeal of his fellow Israelites as a good thing. The problem, however, is that—like the pre-Christian Paul (Acts 22:3; Phil. 3:6)—their zeal was not directed by knowledge. As Paul makes clear in Romans 10:3–4, what the Jews did not understand was that God now is offering a right relationship with himself through faith in Jesus Christ, the culmination of salvation history.

Thus, instead of submitting to God's righteousness, the Jews sought to "establish their own." "God's righteousness" refers to that act by which God declares sinful people to be just in his sight (see also 1:17; 3:21, 22; see comments on 1:17). But what does its opposite in this verse ("their own righteousness") mean? James Dunn takes it to mean the right standing with God that Israel as a whole tried to keep to themselves and not share with the Gentiles. His interpretation of this phrase reflects his understanding of the critique Paul directs at Jews throughout Romans. Paul does not fault Jews, Dunn argues, because they tried to become righteous by doing the law. Rather, he faults them for refusing to see that God is now extending his offer of righteousness to Gentiles.[7]

Dunn certainly puts his finger on one element in Paul's criticism of the Jews (see, e.g., 3:29–30). But he errs in making this issue so central to Paul's concern. Paul's ultimate criticism of Israel is not just salvation-historical—Jews failed to see that God was doing something new with the Gentiles. It is also anthropological—Jews failed to seek a relationship with God in the right way. Both criticisms are found in this context. Jews are faulted for failing to recognize Christ as the culmination of God's plan (10:4) and the rock on which the new people of God is to be built (9:33). But Paul also faults them for being overly concerned with works and neglecting faith (9:32).

Romans 10:3 refers to both these problems. In failing to submit to God's righteousness, the Jews were guilty of missing the decisive turn in salvation history that had come with Christ, for God's righteousness in Paul is clearly bound up with Christ (see 1:17; 3:21–22). But in seeking to establish their own righteousness, they were also guilty of relying on their own works.

Paul refers to the idea of one's own righteousness in only one other passage: Philippians 3:9. Here he describes his own former life as a Jew, claiming to have possessed "a righteousness of my own that comes from the law." As a Jew, Paul is implying, he was convinced that his obedience to the law was necessary to confirm God's gift of righteousness through the covenant. He was guilty of thinking that his own works were necessary to maintain his covenant relationship. "Their own [righteousness]" in Romans 10:3 must

---

7. Dunn, *Romans,* 587–88. Many others, of course, hold Dunn's view on this matter.

mean the same thing. Paul faults Israel for trying to find a relationship with God through the law.[8]

Verse 4 explains why it is wrong of Israel to do this. Israel's pursuit of a righteousness based on the law completely misses the point that the era of the law has ended. For "Christ is the culmination of the law, so that righteousness might be available to everyone who believes" (pers. trans.). This, at least, is how I understand this controversial verse.

Two exegetical decisions lead to this interpretation. (1) I am taking the prepositional phrase that ends the verse (*eis dikaiosynen* . . .) as stating the purpose of the first clause rather than as a restriction on the word "law." Those who take it in the latter sense think that Paul is announcing the "end" of the law as a means of attaining righteousness.[9] But the syntax favors my rendering.[10]

(2) I am interpreting the word *telos* as a combination of the ideas of "end" and "goal." Many scholars opt for one or the other meaning. Paul often uses *telos* to mean "end," in the sense of termination (see, e.g., 1 Cor. 15:24: "Then the *telos* will come, when he [Christ] hands over the kingdom to God the Father"). This meaning would fit Paul's purpose in the context: Jews are wrong to seek their own righteousness, based on the law (v. 3) because the law has been terminated (v. 4).[11] Others, however, point to the fact that *telos* outside the New Testament usually means "goal," and that Paul also uses the word with this meaning (see, e.g., 1 Tim. 1:5: "The *telos* of this command is love, which comes from a pure heart and a good conscience and a sincere faith"). They insist that the translation "end" implies that Christ does away with the law, and that Paul does not teach this.

Interpreters who translate "goal" divide over just how it should be taken here. A few think Paul is referring to Christ as the "inner meaning" of the law, the goal to which all the law points.[12] But most think he is looking at the matter from a salvation-historical perspective.[13] With the coming of Christ, the goal toward which the law was pointing has been reached. I think this latter idea is close to Paul's point. But if we think about it a minute, we will see that the idea of "end" is bound up with this meaning also. Paul may well here

---

8. See esp. Schreiner, *Romans*, 843–44; see also Westerholm, *Israel's Law*, 114–16.

9. See, e.g., Murray, *The Epistle to the Romans*, 2:49–51; Morris, *The Epistle to the Romans*, 379–81. Most who hold this view think Paul is viewing the law from a Jewish perspective: Christ ends the false understanding of the law as a means of salvation.

10. See esp. Mark A. Seifrid, "Paul's Approach to the Old Testament in Rom. 10:6–8," *TrinJ* 6 (1985): 8–9, who does a thorough survey of the construction we find in verse 4.

11. For this view, see, e.g., Godet, *Commentary on Romans*, 376; Käsemann, *Commentary on Romans*, 282–83; Nygren, *Commentary on Romans*, 379–80.

12. See esp. Cranfield, *The Epistle to the Romans*, 516–19.

13. See esp. Robert Badenas, *Christ, the End of the Law: Romans 10:4 in Pauline Perspective* (Sheffield: JSOT, 1985); cf. also Fitzmyer, *Romans*, 584–85.

be thinking of the race course imagery he has used in 9:30–32 ("pursuing" and "obtaining"). Let's picture Israel as the runner, the law as the race, and Christ as the finish line. What Israel has failed to understand, Paul is saying, is that the finish line has been reached. The Messiah and the salvation he brings have come. Thus, the "race" has attained its end and goal—or, to use the best English equivalents, its "culmination" or "climax."[14]

As a result of Christ's coming and bringing the law to its culmination, righteousness is now available for everyone who believes. Christ opens a new phase in salvation history, in which God extends his offer of a right relationship with himself to Gentiles as well as to Jews. Faith, apart from ethnic origin or works, is the sole basis for experiencing this gift he offers to the world.

Righteousness for Everyone Who Believes (10:5–13)

VERSES 5–13 ELABORATE on the two key points Paul has made in verse 4: Christ ends the era of the law, making available a righteousness that can be attained through faith (vv. 5–10); and this righteousness is now available to anyone who believes (vv. 11–13).

In verses 5–6 we find the third contrast between two kinds of righteousness. The "law of righteousness" of 9:31 and "their own [righteousness]" of 10:3 is now described as "the righteousness that is by the law"; while, as in 9:30, "God's righteousness" (10:3) is defined as the "righteousness that is by faith." Paul then identifies each righteousness by means of the Old Testament.

The apostle cites Leviticus 18:5 in Romans 10:5 to describe legal righteousness: "The man who does these things will live by them." Paul is not suggesting here that Moses taught that one could be saved by doing the law. "Living" in the Old Testament context refers to the enjoyment of covenant privilege and not necessarily to eternal life.[15] Rather, Paul's point is that any righteousness based on the law is, by definition, something one can get only by "doing." For "doing" is what the law is all about, as Leviticus 18:5 makes clear (see also Gal. 3:12, where Paul quotes Lev. 18:5 with a similar application).[16]

In contrast to this legal righteousness, then, is the "righteousness that is by faith." Paul uses a figure of speech, putting words from Deuteronomy 9:4 and 30:10–14 on the lips of this righteousness. The general point he wants

---

14. For this general approach, see esp. Barrett, *The Epistle to the Romans,* 197–98; Dunn, *Romans,* 589–90. For more detail, see Moo, *The Epistle to the Romans,* 638–41.

15. See, e.g., Walter J. Kaiser Jr., "Leviticus and Paul: 'Do This and You Shall Live' (Eternally?)," *JETS* 14 (1971): 19–28; cf. also Gordon Wenham, *A Commentary on Leviticus* (Grand Rapids: Eerdmans, 1979), 253.

16. See, for this general approach, Murray, *The Epistle to the Romans,* 2:249–51; Bryce L. Martin, *Christ and the Law in Paul* (Leiden: Brill, 1989), 139–40.

to make about the righteousness by faith is clear enough: Through Christ's being brought down to earth (i.e., his incarnation, Rom. 10:6) and his being brought up from the dead (10:7), God has made righteousness readily available (10:8). One does not have to ascend into heaven or plumb the depths of the sea to discover it. All one needs to do to attain righteousness is to respond in faith to the gospel as it is preached.

However, Paul's choice of words from Deuteronomy 30:10–14 to express this point is provocative, for that passage is about the law, not the gospel. Paul betrays here again his hermeneutical boldness in reading the Old Testament in light of Christ. He seems to be implying that the grace of God offered to Israel in the old covenant is now available to all people through the new covenant (see, for more detail, the Bridging Contexts section).[17]

Verses 9–10 draw conclusions from what Paul has said about "the righteousness that is by faith" in verses 6–8. Deuteronomy 30:14, which Paul cites in Romans 10:8, refers to the "mouth" and the "heart." In verse 9 he elaborates each of these. With the mouth one confesses "Jesus is Lord." The confession that Jesus is Lord is one of the most basic distinguishing marks of being a Christian (see esp. Phil. 2:11; cf. 1 Cor. 12:3). With the heart one believes that God raised Jesus from the dead. The fulfillment of these two conditions brings salvation. Verse 10 elaborates further, only now in reverse order (chiasm), with the heart coming first and then the mouth. Heart belief leads to justification, confession with the mouth to salvation.

Verse 11 is transitional. It grounds verse 10 by showing from the Old Testament that putting one's trust in Christ will bring vindication in the judgment. The quotation is from Isaiah 28:16, which Paul has already quoted in Romans 9:33. The "him" in the quotation is actually the "stone," as a quotation of the full verse reveals: "So this is what the Sovereign LORD says: 'See, I lay a stone in Zion, a tested stone, a precious cornerstone for a sure foundation; the one who trusts will never be dismayed.'" But Paul has implicitly identified that "stone" with Christ in 9:32–33 (see also 1 Peter 2:6–8). "Trusts" in verse 11 translates the Greek verb *pisteuo* (to believe), so the tie with believing in Romans 10:10a is clear. "Put to shame" is often in the Bible a metaphor for condemnation at the judgment. Note, for example, Isaiah 50:7–8:

> Because the Sovereign LORD helps me,
>   I will not be disgraced.
> Therefore have I set my face like flint,
>   and I know I will not be put to shame.

---

17. For similar views, see esp. Seifrid, "Paul's Approach," 35–37; Godet, *Commentary on Romans*, 378–83; Murray, *The Epistle to the Romans*, 2:52–53; Cranfield, *The Epistle to the Romans*, 524–26.

He who vindicates me is near.
> Who then will bring charges against me?
> Let us face each other!
Who is my accuser?
> Let him confront me![18]

In addition to looking back to verse 10, the quotation in verse 11 also anticipates what is to come. For it stresses that the faith that leads to vindication in the judgment is open to "anyone." Paul elaborates this in verse 12, returning to his central claim that the gospel opens the doors to salvation to all people on the same basis. As he does elsewhere in Romans, the "no difference" principle among people is to be applied especially to the key divide created by the Old Testament between Jew and Gentile (1:16; 2:9, 10, 11; cf. 3:22–23). The confession "Jesus is Lord" unites both in the same faith and the same hope, for Jesus is "Lord of all and richly blesses all who call on him."

The verb "call on" (*epikaleo*) is apparently the trigger that leads Paul to yet another Old Testament text that underscores the universality of God's offer in the gospel (Joel 2:32): "Everyone who calls on the name of the LORD will be saved." The "LORD" in Joel is Yahweh, the covenant name of God. But Paul identifies this "Lord" with Jesus (see Rom. 10:9, 12), the "stone" of Isaiah 28:16 (Rom. 10:11). Verse 13, then, is important evidence that the early Christians identified Jesus with God.

Bridging Contexts

GOD'S OLD TESTAMENT "word" and his New Testament "word." Bringing Paul's message about "the righteousness that is by faith" in 10:6–8 into our own time requires us to investigate just why he uses wording from Deuteronomy 9:4 and 30:10–14 to make his points. Particularly we need to look at this matter because the texts at first sight seem so inappropriately applied. As we noted above, the Deuteronomy 30 passage is about the Mosaic law, yet Paul uses the wording of that passage to characterize the righteousness by faith *in contrast to* the righteousness that is by the law (v. 5). Such a *tour de force* certainly catches our attention! And it has caught the attention of innumerable scholars as well. Richard Hays's provocative and stimulating book on Paul's use of the Old Testament opens with this passage as a kind of "test case."[19] Let's first get an idea of the situation by setting out side by side the Old Testament texts and Romans 10:6–8:

---

18. Note also the parallels between this text and 8:33–34.
19. Hays, *Echoes of Scripture*.

Deuteronomy	*Romans 10*
9:4After the LORD your God has driven them out before you, *do not say in your heart* [NIV to yourself], "The LORD has brought me here to take possession of this land because of my righteousness." No, it is on account of the wickedness of these nations that the LORD is going to drive them out before you. 30:10. . . if you obey the LORD your God and keep his commands and decrees that are written in this Book of the Law and turn to the LORD your God with all your heart and with all your soul. 11Now what I am commanding you today is not too difficult for you or beyond your reach. 12It is not up in heaven, so that you have to ask, *"Who will ascend into heaven* to get it and proclaim it to us so we may obey it?" 13Nor is it beyond the sea, so that you have to ask, *"Who will cross the sea* to get it and proclaim it to us so we may obey it?" [note the translation in the Aramaic targum: "Neither is the law beyond the great sea that one may say: would that we had one like the prophet Jonah who would descend into the depths of the Great Sea and bring it up for us"; cf. also Ps. 107:26: "They mounted up to the heavens and went down to the depths; in their peril their courage melted away.] 14No, *the word is very near you; it is in your mouth and in your heart* so you may obey it.	v. 6a: Do not say in your heart
	v. 6b: "Who will ascend into heaven?" (that is, to bring Christ down)
	v. 7: or "Who will descend into the deep?" (that is, to bring Christ up from the dead)
	v. 8: But what does it say? "The word is near you; it is in your mouth and in your heart," that is, the word of faith we are proclaiming.

Paul is selective in the portions of Deuteronomy he quotes—so selective that some scholars don't think he is quoting at all but simply borrowing a bit of wording from these texts.[20] But Paul signals his intention to quote with his

---

20. E.g., Sanday and Headlam, *The Epistle to the Romans*, 287–88; Fitzmyer, *Romans*, 589–91.

three "that is" phrases, each introducing his application of the text. This kind of phrase is found elsewhere in Jewish literature to introduce interpretations of Old Testament texts.

The first reference (Deut. 9:4) is straightforward. We may think that the words are few enough as to leave doubt about whether Paul intended "Do not say in your heart" to be a quotation from the Deuteronomy text. But these words occur only here in the Old Testament, so they are distinctive.[21] Moreover, they are most appropriate to Paul's application. Moses warns the Israelites about presuming to think that the Lord has blessed them because of their own righteousness, just as Paul has scolded the Jews for seeking to establish "their own [righteousness]" in Romans 10:3.

The situation regarding the Deuteronomy 30 references is much more complicated. Paul quotes three phrases from this passage and then applies the words to the events of the gospel. The second phrase, however, is obviously different: In place of "crossing the sea" in Deuteronomy 30:13, Paul speaks of "descending into the deeps." Some scholars therefore think that Paul may be jumping to a quotation of Psalm 107:26 (see above).[22] But Old Testament and Jewish writers frequently interchanged the imagery of the "sea" and the "deep" (*abyssos*, the "abyss"); note the Aramaic paraphrase of Deuteronomy 30:13 we cite above. Probably, then, Paul is adapting the language of the Deuteronomy text, abetted by the easy interchange between "sea" and "the deep," to his application to the resurrection of Christ.

The bigger question—and one harder to answer—is *why* Paul has applied language about "commanding" to "the righteousness that is by faith." What conceivable hermeneutical principle can justify him in making such an application? Many allege Paul is arbitrary: He wrests the language from its context to make it mean something quite different. But we have seen again and again in Romans how the apostle bases his application of the Old Testament on solid theological reading. Some interpreters think Paul is working with an implicit identification of Christ with the law, so what the Old Testament says about the law, Paul can apply to Christ.

But we think a more likely explanation emerges when we consider the real purpose of Paul's use of this language from Deuteronomy. This becomes clear in verse 8: The message about righteousness by faith, preached by Paul and the other apostles, is both accessible and understandable. The notion of God's "word" is the key bridging concept. In Deuteronomy the word takes the form of a command; here in Romans, that word is the message of faith. As God made available his will to his old covenant people, so now he makes available his will for the new covenant. Yet the new covenant word has an added element

---

21. At least, they occur only here in the LXX that Paul generally seems to have quoted from.
22. E.g., Fitzmyer, *Romans*, 589.

of "nearness." Christ, as the One who brings the law to its culmination (v. 4), also writes that law on the hearts of God's people, as was predicted by Jeremiah in his famous "new covenant" prophecy (Jer. 31:31–34). So in Christ, the law has come near to God's people in a way that it never had before. All that is now required of human beings is that they accept God's word in faith.

Penetrating behind Paul's appropriation of Deuteronomy 30 to its underlying rationale sheds rich light on Paul's purposes in this passage. He wants us to see that God's word in the gospel stands in continuity with God's word in the Old Testament. Looked at from one perspective, that Old Testament word, as "law," demanded an obedience that was impossible (v. 5). But, from another perspective, God's Old Testament word was a demonstration of God's grace, as he revealed himself and his will to a sinful and rebellious people. Now, in Christ, God has brought that word of grace to its climax—and all people need to do is accept the gift of righteousness he offers by believing.

Confessing with the mouth? When my wife and I were living in St. Andrews, Scotland, we frequently encountered a passionate, though over-enthusiastic evangelist. She roamed the streets all day and much of the night, accosting people and loudly proclaiming to them her own faith and the need for them to "turn" before they "burned." In conversation with her one day, I asked why she had such zeal for evangelism. She quoted Romans 10:10b: "It is with your mouth that you confess and are saved." Confession with the mouth, she argued, was clearly set forth as a requirement for salvation, and she was determined to make sure that she fulfilled the condition.

Her use of this text, I think, was a classic instance of overinterpretation as a result of missing the rhetorical purposes of the text. "Heart" and "mouth" are found in the quotation of Deuteronomy 30:14 in Romans 10:8. Paul then plays on both these terms in verses 9–10 to show how the Deuteronomy text finds specific fulfillment in the preaching of the gospel. Nothing that he says elsewhere in his letters suggests that verbal profession is required to be saved. Obviously, Paul expects his converts to be active in sharing the gospel, and the St. Andrews evangelist puts most of us to shame on that score. But Paul also makes clear that belief in the heart is all that is needed to bring one into the kingdom of God. Insisting on verbal confession is a misreading of Paul's rhetoric in Romans 10:10.

THE IMPORTANCE OF **the whole Bible.** One of the reasons for the enduring power of Romans is its constant attention to one of the great issues in Christian theology: the relationship between the Old Testament and the New. No issue was so important in establishing the identity of the early Christian movement. Was it to be a sect of Judaism, as some of the former Pharisees apparently wanted (Acts 15:1, 5)? Or, at the opposite extreme, was it to be a new religion, with little or no relationship to the Old Testament and Judaism, as the second-century heretic Marcion wanted?

Paul takes the opportunity in Romans to face this issue head-on, for the church in Rome was in need of direction on this matter. Jewish Christians were apparently insisting on the continuing importance of law-observance; Gentile Christians saw no need to burden themselves with these require- ments. Jewish Christians thought that the Old Testament guaranteed them the inside track to salvation; Gentile Christians, basking in their majority in the church, thought that they were the ones in the driver's seat. Thus, as Paul presents his gospel to this church he has never visited, he refers again and again to its relationship to the Old Testament. Over the course of the letter, he builds a balanced view, in which both the continuity and disconti- nuity between Old Testament and New, law and gospel, emerge.

We have had occasion to refer to specific points of continuity and discon- tinuity throughout the commentary as we have encountered them in the text. Now is a good time to survey the whole picture. Basic, of course, is our under- standing of the theology Paul is teaching. But, as for the Roman Christians, so it is true for us that the theology of the relation of the Old and New Testaments carries innumerable practical implications. In what follows, then, I will focus on these practical implications, keeping the theology in the background.

(1) We must continue to read, study, and meditate on the Old Testament. Christ may have fulfilled the Old Testament and brought the law to its intended goal (Rom. 10:4). But Paul is clear about its enduring value for believers. The Law and the Prophets bear witness to the revelation of God's righteousness in Christ. If we do not understand them, we will be unable to understand the gospel. For the gospel is presented in terms that can be under- stood only through thorough acquaintance with the Old Testament.

Consider, for instance, the great summary of the gospel in Romans 3:21– 26. The key words are "righteousness from God" (vv. 21, 22), "faith" (vv. 22, 26), "sin" (v. 23), "the glory of God" (v. 23), "redemption" (v. 24), "grace" (v. 24), "sacrifice of atonement" (v. 25), and "[God's] justice" (vv. 25, 26). We cannot hope to understand any of these words apart from the Old Testament, and more than a cursory concordance search is needed.

- Appreciating the real meaning of sin can come only as we soak our- selves in the story of the Fall and of Israel's constant failures.
- Comprehending what it means for God to be "just" and the consequent problem that human sin causes is possible only if we have reflected on the God who is revealed as "the Holy One" and if we have absorbed the lessons of the many outbreaks of his fierce wrath against human sin.

- Cherishing "the old rugged cross" reaches new depths of emotion when we comprehend how Christ was appointed by God to be the one in whom the great and final "Day of Atonement" was celebrated.
- Appreciating what Paul is saying about the "righteousness that is by faith" in Romans 10:6–8 is impossible without being familiar with Deuteronomy and its teaching about the grace of God in the covenant with Israel.

In Romans 15:4, Paul puts what we are saying this way: "For everything that was written in the past was written to teach us, so that through endurance and the encouragement of the Scriptures we might have hope." His reference is to the Old Testament. "Everything" in it, Paul claims, was written to teach us, and its purpose is that we "might have hope." Scripture accomplishes this purpose by engendering in us the ability to bear up in difficult times ("endurance") and the joy that comes from knowing God's enduring commitment to his people ("encouragement").

Nowhere in the Old Testament do I find such endurance and encouragement as in the Psalms. Luther once expressed amazement that any Christian would not know the book of Psalms by heart. I confess I don't, even though I spend more time there (in comparison with other Old Testament books) than I should. But "overhearing" the psalmists express their complaints about injustice, their laments about God's apparent unconcern for them, and their thanksgiving for his assuring presence and activity extraordinarily stimulates my own devotion.

In different ways, all the Old Testament accomplishes the same purpose. Yet I find that many believers in our day are abysmally ignorant of the Old Testament. To the degree that they read the Bible at all, they focus all too often on the New Testament alone. I remember suggesting in our midweek Bible study some years ago that we study Micah for a few weeks. One would have thought that I proposed studying the Code of Hammurabi in its original language. I was amazed at the reaction: What in the world would an Old Testament prophet with a strange name have to say to us today? Paul would certainly deplore this attitude. For by neglecting the Old Testament, we neglect the only source we have to fill out the meaning of the gospel and make it more than mere words for us.

(2) We are no longer obliged to obey the commandments of the Old Testament law. Many Christians generally agree here, but the exact relationship of the Old Testament law to the Christian believer has been a dividing point between systems of Protestant theology. Lutherans and dispensationalists, to differing degrees and with some nuancing, tend to include all Old Testament laws in the assertion above. Those in the Reformed camp, following the lead of Calvin, Zwingli, the Westminster divines, and most of the Puritans, usually

insist that at least the Ten Commandments remain directly applicable to the Christian believer. They argue that in these commandments we are given God's eternal moral law, and it can no more be revoked than God can change his eternal moral standards.

We would need an entire volume adequately to deal with these issues.[23] I have already sketched my own view and some of the exegetical evidence to support it in the Contemporary Significance section on 7:1–6. So I will concentrate here on the practical implications of my view.

Lest you dismiss me too quickly as a wild-eyed fanatic, two factors that lessen the practical impact of the view I am arguing should be mentioned. What I am doing is simply applying to a small part of the Old Testament law what almost all Christians do with most of it already. We agree that Christ's fulfilling of the law means that we need no longer obey the "ritual law" and the "civil" law. We do not have to slaughter lambs at church, nor do we stone adulterers.[24] Most of the laws in Exodus, Leviticus, Numbers, and Deuteronomy fall into these categories. With my view, the principle is simply extended to what is sometimes called the "moral" law.

As I have argued before, the New Testament writers treat the law of Moses as a unity. If it is fulfilled (Matt. 5:17), all of it is fulfilled. Christ is the "culmination" of the law—not just a part of it. So when Paul claims that we have "died" to the law (Rom. 7:4) and are no longer "under" it (6:14–15), we must accept that, as new covenant believers, we are freed from obligation to the old covenant law *in toto*. But the effect of this view is that we read all the Old Testament law just as we already read most of it.

Another important mitigating factor is the fact that the moral law of the Old Testament law is taken up into and repeated in "the law of Christ." Nine of the Ten Commandments are explicitly repeated in the New Testament as binding on believers. The exception is the Sabbath command, and this is partly why Christians have disagreed so much about the new covenant day of worship (e.g., Seventh Day Adventists) and what behavior is appropriate for that day.[25] When students ask what practical difference it would make were they to adopt my view as opposed to the typical "moral law" view, I answer, "Not much. The differences lie more in how we put together the Testaments than in what we would actually do or avoid doing."

---

23. For a useful survey of the main views, see *Five Views on Law and Gospel*, ed. Wayne Strickland (Grand Rapids: Zondervan, 1996).

24. I am, of course, aware of some Christians, usually called "theonomists," who maintain the relevance of the civil law (see the article by Greg Bahnsen in *Five Views on Law and Gospel*). But the view is confined to a small minority of believers.

25. We will discuss the Sabbath issue further in the Contemporary Significance section on 14:1–12.

At the risk of extreme generalization, we may therefore conclude that Paul in Romans says an emphatic "yes" to the Old Testament but a qualified "no" to the law. I say "qualified" because Paul certainly gives Jews, "born under the law," the right to continue to obey the law as means of expressing their piety. Obeying God's law is not a bad thing; one just cannot insist that Gentiles do it. And the law, along with the rest of the Old Testament, must continue to be read and studied for the light it sheds on God's character and the moral requirements of the gospel.

Good news for everyone. Another of the great themes of Romans is the universality of the gospel. From the opening statement of the letter's theme (1:16), Paul has made clear that the gospel he preaches is for Jew and Gentile alike. In the verses we have just interpreted, Paul restates this theme in no uncertain terms:

> "*Anyone* who trusts in him will never be put to shame" (v. 11; cf. Isa. 28:16)
> "There is no difference between Jew and Gentile—the same Lord is Lord of *all* and richly blesses *all* who call on him" (v. 12)
> "*Everyone* who calls on the name of the Lord will be saved" (v. 13; cf. Joel 2:32)

Paul focuses on Jew and Gentile because of the Old Testament background and because of the specific situation in the Roman church. But clearly the "no difference" principle, while applied specifically to Jew and Gentile, is all encompassing. In the Contemporary Significance section on 4:9–12, we applied the principle to the life of the church. Here, because of the context, we might apply the point to the missionary work of the church.

Offering the gospel to all nations and ethnic groups is the logical conclusion from the principle we see in these verses. The church of Christ in general has committed itself to this great and yet unfinished task. But we are easily deflected from that goal. Ironically, one of the causes of the problem in recent years has been a theology that has emerged from within the Christian missionary movement itself. Some of its theoreticians have put forth what is sometimes called the "church growth" approach to missions. Quite pragmatic, this approach argues—with understandable logic—that the church should concentrate its resources on people groups who are receptive to the gospel. The result, of course, is a lack of attention to those people groups that are not now receptive—the Islamic world being a prime example.

Church growth strategists are sincere in their concern to win as many to Christ as possible, and they stress that the day for these other ethnic groups will come. But I wonder whether the pragmatic allocation of missionary resources that these missiologists advocate does justice to the principle of universality that Paul enunciates in passages such as this one. Decisions about where to send missionaries are not easy, but we cannot predict where God will call his people to minister. Nor should we direct or deflect that call on the basis of pragmatics.

Romans 10:14–21

HOW, THEN, CAN they call on the one they have not believed in? And how can they believe in the one of whom they have not heard? And how can they hear without someone preaching to them? ¹⁵And how can they preach unless they are sent? As it is written, "How beautiful are the feet of those who bring good news!"

¹⁶But not all the Israelites accepted the good news. For Isaiah says, "Lord, who has believed our message?" ¹⁷Consequently, faith comes from hearing the message, and the message is heard through the word of Christ. ¹⁸But I ask: Did they not hear? Of course they did:

> "Their voice has gone out into all the earth,
> their words to the ends of the world."

¹⁹Again I ask: Did Israel not understand? First, Moses says,

> "I will make you envious by those who are not a nation;
> I will make you angry by a nation that has no
> understanding."

²⁰And Isaiah boldly says,

> "I was found by those who did not seek me;
> I revealed myself to those who did not ask for me."

²¹But concerning Israel he says,

> "All day long I have held out my hands
> to a disobedient and obstinate people."

THE IMMEDIATE JUMPING-OFF point for this paragraph is the quotation of Joel 2:32 in Romans 10:13. This prophecy promises salvation for "everyone who calls on the name of the Lord." In verses 14–21, Paul works back from this "calling on the Lord" to the steps that come before it: belief → preaching of the gospel → being sent to preach the gospel (vv. 14b–15).

Paul then turns explicitly to the situation of Israel in verses 16–21. He reiterates again the need for the message to be proclaimed if people are to believe (vv. 16–17). Then, with two Old Testament quotations, he shows that Israel has indeed both heard the message (v. 18) and understood it (v. 19). Two more Old Testament quotations finish off this paragraph, so that all of 9:30–10:21 ends on the same note at which the section began: Gentiles, who did not seek God, are finding him (10:20; cf. 9:30), while Israel, though offered God's grace, continues stubbornly to reject it (10:21; cf. 9:31–32). Although 10:13, then, is the immediate trigger for these verses, the paragraph ultimately picks up Paul's indictment of Israel from 10:2–3. Despite her zeal, Paul has charged, Israel is guilty of not understanding and submitting to God's righteousness in Christ, but Israel has no excuse for not responding.

In 10:14–15a, Paul uses four rhetorical questions to outline the sequence if a person is to be "saved" (cf. v. 13). The steps are, in reverse order to what Paul cites: the sending of preachers, preaching, hearing the message about Christ, believing in Christ, and calling on "the name of the Lord." The questions are put in the third person plural ("they"), but it is not clear who Paul has in mind. Since much of the paragraph is directed against Israel, many think that the implied subject in 10:14–15 is Israelites.[1] But more likely Paul sets up his indictment of Israel in 10:16ff. by first speaking generally about what is required for *any* person (see "everyone" in v. 13) to be saved.[2]

The quotation from Isaiah 52:7 at the end of verse 15 serves two functions. (1) It confirms that preaching the good news is needed if people are to hear and to be saved. (2) It also suggests, however, that the last condition for salvation Paul lists in verses 14–15a has been met: Preachers have been sent. Paul was no doubt attracted to the Isaiah text both because of its context (see Bridging Contexts) and because of its use of "gospel" language (*euangelizomenon agatha*, lit., "those who preach good news of good things"). The text would have even greater eschatological significance if Paul understood the word *horaioi* to mean "timely" rather than "beautiful," but it is not clear that he did.[3]

In translating "Israelites" in verse 16, the NIV makes an exegetical decision, for the underlying Greek simply has vague third person verbs ("they"). Paul could, then, simply be continuing his discussion from verses 14–15 of what people generally must do to be saved. But the quotation of Isaiah 53:1, which is applied to Jews in John 12:38, suggests that the NIV interpretation is correct:

---

1. E.g., Sanday and Headlam, *The Epistle to the Romans*, 295; Cranfield, *The Epistle to the Romans*, 533.

2. See, e.g., Käsemann, *Commentary on Romans*, 294; Murray, *The Epistle to the Romans*, 2:60; Dunn, *Romans*, 620.

3. In Greek outside the New Testament, *horaios* usually means "timely" (BAGD), and the relevant Hebrew word in Isa. 52:7 can also have this meaning (*nawu*; cf. BDB). But the other three occurrences of *horaios* in the New Testament all mean "beautiful" (Matt. 23:27; Acts 3:2, 10).

Paul now turns to Israel. The mention of the "good news" leads him to the central issue: While Israel has heard the good news (vv. 17ff.), she has not "believed."

The expression "not all" in verse 16 is a literary device called "litotes"; it means "only a few." But Paul probably uses this specific language in order to echo the "remnant" theology he introduced in 9:6b: "*Not all* who are descended from Israel are Israel" (see also 9:27). After his somewhat premature condemnation of Israel in 10:16, Paul resumes the logical unfolding of the steps necessary for salvation in 10:17. He begins by restating the second step mentioned in 10:14: Faith comes from hearing. Since the Greek word for "hearing" is the same as the word for "message" in the Isaiah quotation (*akoe*), this statement also builds on that quotation (NIV "hearing the messge" tries to capture this connection). The last part of verse 17, then, restates the third step in the salvation sequence (v. 14c): Hearing, the kind that can lead to faith, can only happen when a definite salvific word from God is proclaimed. That word is "the word of Christ," the message about his lordship and resurrection (vv. 8−9).

Since Paul has focused in verse 17 on hearing, it is natural that he should focus on this critical step in verse 18. His question "Did they not hear?" as the NIV rendering indicates, expects a positive answer (the particle *ouk* in Greek indicates this). Paul explicitly supplies this response—"Of course they did"—and then quotes Psalm 19:4 to substantiate his affirmative: "Their voice has gone out into all the earth, their words to the ends of the world." Paul again demonstrates the freedom with which he treats the Old Testament, for Psalm 19 is about God's revelation of his character in nature. Yet Paul applies it to the preaching of the gospel (see Bridging Contexts for further discussion).

Also puzzling is Paul's apparent claim that the message has gone "into all the earth." Since the second line of Psalm 19:4 in the LXX uses *oikoumene*, "inhabited earth," he may implicitly confine the reference to the Roman empire of his day. And he is undoubtedly thinking corporately rather than individually, in terms of the gospel being proclaimed to every ethnic group or region within the empire.[4] But we have little reason to think that gospel preaching had spread even to this extent in A.D. 57. Thus, we should probably view Paul's application of this verse as hyperbole. He simply uses the language given to him in the quotation to assert that the gospel had been proclaimed so widely that Jews have no excuse for not responding (see also the similar Col. 1:23).

---

4. E.g., Johannes Munck, *Christ and Israel: An Interpretation of Romans 9−11* (Philadelphia: Fortress, 1967), 95−99.

"Again I ask" (v. 19) matches the "But I ask" at the beginning of verse 18. Having demonstrated that Israel has heard, Paul now wants to probe more deeply into the nature of this "hearing." Was it superficial? Not at all. Israel, Paul affirms, understood. What they understood is that God could very well act in such a way as to include Gentiles in his people and to bring judgment on his own people Israel (vv. 19–21). Moses, Paul suggests, was the "first" in a long line of prophets to suggest that God would eventually extend his grace beyond the confines of Israel. Those who are "not a nation" (cf. "not my people" in 9:26) will stir up Israel's jealousy, predicts Moses in Deuteronomy 32:21. Paul announces a theme he will take up later to explain the oscillation in salvation history between Jew and Gentiles (11:11–14).

Isaiah is another prophet who predicted the inclusion of Gentiles: "I was found by those who did not seek me; I revealed myself to those who did not ask for me" (Isa. 65:1). This prophecy refers to God's offer of grace to a rebellious Israel. But, as Paul did with Hosea 1:10 and 2:23 in Romans 9:25–26, he applies the verse to the Gentiles. He probably intentionally returns to the note on which this section began: Gentiles who were not seeking righteousness have found it (9:30); Gentiles who did ask for God have found him (10:20).

In 10:21 Paul finally turns back to the failure of Israel, the issue that has dominated this section. He quotes Isaiah 65:2 to make two points: God continues to extend his grace to Israel (he "holds out his hands" to them), and Israel continues to rebel (they are "disobedient and obstinate").

Bridging Contexts

MORE ON PAUL and the Old Testament. Turning again to Paul's use of the Old Testament may seem like overkill, since we have dealt with this issue in the last two units. But the extent to which Paul argues in this paragraph from the Old Testament—six quotations in eight verses—demands that we pay attention to this matter, and each new quotation offers additional insight into Paul's methods and purposes in forging connections between Old Testament and New.

The quotations in 10:14–21 reveal three important assumptions about Paul's use of the Old Testament. He expects us to recognize and share these assumptions so that we can understand what he wants to teach about the relationship of the gospel to the Old Testament. We can formulate these three assumptions as reading strategies that we need to employ when we come to quotations.

(1) We need to pay careful attention to the Old Testament context from which Paul's quotations come. Often that context will explain and/or elucidate his use of the words we find in the text. Those words are sometimes but the

tip of the iceberg, with the Old Testament context supplying important information about what Paul is teaching. Three of the quotations in 10:14–21 illustrate this first strategy.

Isaiah 52:7, quoted in Romans 10:15b, comes in a passage rich in theological implications for New Testament fulfillment (see Isa. 52:4–10):

> For this is what the Sovereign LORD says:
> "At first my people went down to Egypt to live;
>   lately, Assyria has oppressed them.
> "And now what do I have here?" declares the LORD.
> "For my people have been taken away for nothing,
>   and those who rule them mock,"
>   declares the LORD.
> "And all day long
>   my name is constantly blasphemed.
> Therefore my people will know my name;
>   therefore in that day they will know
> that it is I who foretold it.
>   Yes, it is I."
> How beautiful on the mountains
>   are the feet of those who bring good news,
> who proclaim peace,
>   who bring good tidings,
>   who proclaim salvation,
> who say to Zion,
>   "Your God reigns!"
> Listen! Your watchmen lift up their voices;
>   together they shout for joy.
> When the LORD returns to Zion,
>   they will see it with their own eyes.
> Burst into songs of joy together,
>   you ruins of Jerusalem,
> for the LORD has comforted his people,
>   he has redeemed Jerusalem.
> The LORD will lay bare his holy arm
>   in the sight of all the nations,
> and all the ends of the earth
>   will see the salvation of our God.

Note that Isaiah 52:5 has already been quoted by Paul in Romans 2:24. It is probably no mere chance that led Paul to quote twice from this text in the same letter. For this passage contains the basic scheme of salvation history as Paul presents it in Romans: sin and disobedience of Israel at the present (Isa. 52:4–5), to be changed when God sends the good news of "salvation" to Zion (52:7), and both Israel (52:9) and the Gentiles ("the ends of the earth," 52:10) are saved. The alert reader of Romans should be led by the explicit quotations back to this great Isaiah prophecy and allow Isaiah and Paul mutually to interpret one another.

A second example of the importance of context is the quotation from Isaiah 53:1 in Romans 10:16. Paul's application of the text is straightforward. But the reader will recognize that Paul is led to this text because all of Isaiah 53, the fourth Servant Song, was applied to Jesus in the early church (see Paul's quotation from this same song in Rom. 15:21).

We see the same approach in Paul's use of Deuteronomy 32:21 in Romans 10:19. In its original context, this verse states God's "equivalent" response to Israel's idolatry: Because Israel has made God jealous with "what is no god" (Deut. 32:21a), God will make Israel "jealous" with what is "no people." The phrase "no people" is probably the catchphrase that draws Paul's attention to this text, since he quotes the Hosea prophecy about those who are "not my people" becoming the people of God in Romans 9:25–26.[5]

But Deuteronomy 32, which rehearses the history of God's gracious acts on Israel's behalf and Israel's stubborn and sinful response to those acts, is one that Paul also seems to have valued in its own right as an important confirmation of his own view of salvation history. He accordingly sees in the words a prophecy of the mission to the Gentiles: The inclusion of Gentiles in the new people of God stimulates the Jews to jealousy and causes Israel to respond in wrath against this movement in salvation history. Old Testament scholars debate about whether the "not a people" in Deuteronomy 32:21 refers to an uncivilized nation unworthy of the name "people"[6] or whether it has the more theological sense of a people whom God has not chosen.[7] If it is the latter, Paul's use of the text is not far from its original meaning.

(2) We must realize that Paul does not always quote the Old Testament to "prove" a point. People quote texts with much broader purposes than this in mind, as I illustrated with the example of my son's *Dirty Harry* quote (see Bridging Contexts section on 1:1–7). Paul is no exception. When we find him quoting an Old Testament passage about God's universal natural revelation and applying it to the gospel (Ps. 19:4 in Rom. 10:18), we should not rush

---

5. Bruce, *The Letter of Paul to the Romans*, 198.

6. See, e.g., S. R. Driver, *A Critical and Exegetical Commentary on Deuteronomy* (Edinburgh: T. & T. Clark, 1895), 365–66.

7. See, e.g., C. F. Keil and F. Delitszch, *Commentary on the Old Testament*, vol. 1: *The Pentateuch* (reprint; 3 vols. in one; Grand Rapids: Eerdmans, n.d.), 3:477–78.

to wonder whether his use of the psalm is valid. This may be the wrong issue entirely. Paul may simply be using the language of the psalm, with the "echoes" of God's universal revelation that it awakes, to suggest that what God did in natural revelation he now does in the gospel.[8] He may also have been attracted to Psalm 19:4 because the "ends of the world" is similar to the language Isaiah uses to describe the extension of God's grace to the Gentiles (see Isa. 45:22; 49:6; 52:10; 62:11).

(3) We often have to look below the surface to discover the basis for Paul's application of Old Testament quotations. His use of Isaiah 65:1 in Romans 10:20 illustrates the principle. Paul, of course, applies the passage to the Gentiles: Those who did not seek God or ask for him have found him. A few scholars think Paul's use of the passage is straightforward because, they argue, Isaiah 65:1 is about Gentile inclusion in the people of God.[9] But the majority of Old Testament scholars claim that the verse is about Israel, and they seem to be right.[10]

As he did in 9:25−26, then, Paul again applies an Old Testament prophecy about Israel to the Gentiles. Has he misread the Old Testament, or does he just not care about the original meaning? No. Paul has too much respect for the Old Testament, and knows it too well, to proceed in so arbitrary a manner. If we look more carefully below the surface of the quotation to Paul's underlying theological structures, we can understand better how he can apply the text in the way that he does.

When we discussed Paul's surprising application of Hosea 1:10 and 2:23 to the Gentiles (see Bridging Contexts section of 9:25−26), we found that the story of God's promise to Abraham was at the root of the matter. But having brought these Hosea texts into the orbit of the Abrahamic promise of Gentile inclusion, we can understand how Isaiah 65:1 could have been swept into the same hermeneutical approach. For the "not my people" and "not my loved one" language of Hosea is similar to the "did not seek me" and "did not

---

8. See esp. Hays, *Echoes of Scripture*, 175. The lack of an introductory formula, in contrast to the clear introductions in vv. 16, 19, 20, and 21, may suggest that Paul intends less than a "proof" from Scripture. This is the view of many of the Greek Fathers; and see also Godet, *Commentary on Romans*, 388; Dunn, *Romans*, 624; Fitzmyer, *Romans*, 599.

9. See, most recently, J. A. Motyer, *The Prophecy of Isaiah* (Downers Grove, Ill.: Inter-Varsity, 1993), 523. Such scholars argue that the second part of v. 1 should be translated "a nation not called by my name" (the reading of the Masoretic text) and that the verse therefore refers to Gentiles (cf. KJV).

10. This is the majority view among Old Testament commentators. See, recently, John Oswalt, *The Book of Isaiah: Chapters 40−66* (NICOT; Grand Rapids: Eerdmans, 1998), 636. This majority thinks that the last phrase in the verse should be translated "a nation that did not call on my name," as the editors of the basic modern Hebrew text (BHS) suggest and LXX seems to follow (cf., e.g., NIV, NRSV).

ask for me" language of Isaiah. While proof is impossible, we think it is probable that Paul uses a universalistic interpretation of the Abrahamic promises as a key lens through which he reads Isaiah 65:1.

EXPANDING OUR HORIZONS **in reading the New Testament.** An obvious point of contemporary significance emerges from the discussion we have just concluded: Many of us need to broaden the way we look for connections between the Old and New Testaments. We can begin by reading the New Testament more like an ordinary piece of literature.

I do not want you to misunderstand what I am saying here. I am not for a minute suggesting that we take anything from the Bible's unique status as an inspired and inerrant Word from God. No other book has its authority. But I think our insistence on the Bible's unique role in the life of the church can blind us to the fact that it has been written, and thus must be read, like any other book. Good interpreters recognize this, and so they use those methods appropriate to the study of any book in studying the Bible: defining its words, putting together its syntax, paying attention to context, and so on.

Most of us also recognize that the Bible uses literary techniques that are found in almost any of the world's literature. The Bible exaggerates for effect (hyperbole), uses similes and metaphors, and employs various genres (poetry, narrative, parable, etc.). Like other literature, the Bible also uses language and ideas from earlier pieces of literature. Especially does the Bible like to quote itself: Old Testament writers refer to earlier Old Testament passages and New Testament writers refer to the Old Testament and earlier New Testament texts. When they do so, they are not always quoting as a "proof text." That is, they are not always claiming that what they are saying is true *because* such and such a text teaches the same thing.

To be sure, the New Testament authors often use the Old Testament in this way. But I think many of us assume, wrongly, that this is the only purpose they have in citing the Old Testament. This is shortsighted. Like any work of literature, the New Testament sometimes quotes or alludes to the Old Testament to evoke a style or tradition. Consider the way T. S. Eliot wove classical allusions into his 1922 poem *The Waste Land*. Or consider the way someone who knows Scripture well will use scriptural language when praying. Or, yet again, consider one of my favorite hymns, which I have mentioned before in the commentary, *And Can it Be?* In the third stanza, Charles Wesley, the lyricist, describes conversion in these terms:

> Long my imprisoned spirit lay
> Fast bound in sin and nature's night.
> Thine eye diffused a quick'ning ray:
> I woke—the dungeon flamed with light!
> My chains fell off, my heart was free,
> I rose, went forth, and followed Thee.

Many years ago a former colleague of mine, David Dunbar, brought to my attention the fact that Wesley used language in this stanza drawn from the account of Peter's imprisonment and escape in Acts 12 (see esp. verses 6—9, and note the words italicized):

> And when Herod would have brought him forth, the same night Peter was sleeping between two soldiers, *bound with two chains*: and the keepers before the door kept the prison. And, behold, the angel of the Lord came upon him, and *a light shined* in the prison: and he smote Peter on the side, and raised him up, saying, Arise up quickly. And *his chains fell off* from his hands. And the angel said unto him, Gird thyself, and bind on thy sandals. And so he did. And he saith unto him, Cast thy garment about thee, and *follow me.* And he went out, and followed him; and wist not that it was true which was done by the angel; but thought he saw a vision. (KJV)

Did Wesley think that Acts 12 describes a Christian conversion? Almost certainly not. He did not allude to this text to prove anything about Christian conversion but to set off a series of reverberations in our minds that enrich the hymn for us. I know I cannot sing this verse without thinking of some of the biblical allusions it awakens, and my appreciation for what I am singing is greatly enhanced.

Paul may be using the language of Psalm 19 in Romans 10:18 in a similar way. We misunderstand him if we think he is claiming that the psalmist was predicting the preaching of Christian evangelists. As Richard Hays argues, "The citation of Ps. 19:4 does not prove that Jews have had the opportunity to hear the gospel; rather, it gives Paul a 'vocabulary of a second and higher power' with which to *assert* that they have heard it."[11] Paul uses the language of Psalm 19, instead of his own wording, because it carries with it the flavor of that text, with its emphasis on God's marvelous, universal display of his nature. Our reading of the New Testament will be immensely deepened if we open our ears to these kinds of allusions. They have great power to shape our emotions and reactions to the text.

---

11. Hays, *Echoes of Scripture,* 175. Italics are original, and he quotes from Thomas M. Greene, *The Light in Troy: Imitation and Discovery in Renaissance Poetry* (New Haven: Yale Univ. Press, 1982), 39.

Missions and the Word of God. Before I studied or taught Romans, I had often heard 10:14−15 quoted in missionary sermons to prove the need to "send out" missionaries. Like many who listened to such sermons, I did not have a good sense of the context from which the verses were taken. When I studied that context, I realized that the usual application of the verses was not on target. That text is not encouraging us to send out missionaries. Rather, it is asserting that God has already done so. He has sent out people like Paul and the other apostles to preach the good news. Israel has heard that good news but failed to believe it. This is the issue in Romans 10.

But this text still has important things to teach us about missions—and the message is one the church must pay close attention to in the new millennium. For, while Paul is not calling on the church to send out missionaries with the message of the gospel, he is nevertheless clearly assuming it needs to be done. People can only believe in Jesus when they hear about him, and they can hear about him only when someone presents the good news. "Faith comes from hearing the message, and the message is heard through the word of Christ" (v. 17).

The absolute need for people to hear the gospel preached if they are to be saved was one of the greatest forces impelling the modern missionary enterprise, begun in the early 1800s and flourishing yet today. Yet the tie between preaching the gospel and being saved is being severed in many churches and denominations. Caving in to the flood of postmodern malaise and afraid of seeming intolerant, many churches have lost missionary zeal. Reasons vary, of course. But some teach that other religions are also ways to God, so why bother sending missionaries if people can be saved within their own religion? Others teach that God reveals himself to all people in various ways, so that an oral or written presentation of the gospel is unnecessary.

But the text before us shows such viewpoints as the false teachings or easy generalizations they really are. Paul links salvation to belief, which he in turn ties to hearing the message about Christ. People must be "sent out" so that the message can be proclaimed to all people. Paul himself, of course, was among those whom God had sent out. In his own life of difficult travel, he illustrates the theology he teaches: People need to hear the gospel so that they can be saved.

I do not want to minimize the problems inherent in a theology that ties salvation to response to God's Word. I, too, struggle with the question of fairness, wondering about those many people who never had a chance to respond to the Word of God. And I do not want to dogmatize beyond the text about the ways in which God may bring his message to people.

But I do think Romans 10:14−21, in the context of Paul's life and theology, teaches that response to God's Word is the only way to salvation and that sending out people to proclaim that word is God's chosen way to bring that Word "to the ends of the earth." The twenty-first century church needs to embrace this theology and staunchly defend it against the many attacks that are sure to increase. We need also to translate that theology into practice so that the sending of missionaries can again take top priority in the life of the church. Too many churches spend far too much on themselves and far too little on missions. We so easily turn inward and become preoccupied with our problems and potential, neglecting the millions who have never heard the Word and the wonderful potential to bring God glory by showing them the way into the kingdom.

Romans 11:1–10

I ASK THEN: Did God reject his people? By no means! I am an Israelite myself, a descendant of Abraham, from the tribe of Benjamin. ²God did not reject his people, whom he foreknew. Don't you know what the Scripture says in the passage about Elijah—how he appealed to God against Israel: ³"Lord, they have killed your prophets and torn down your altars; I am the only one left, and they are trying to kill me"? ⁴And what was God's answer to him? "I have reserved for myself seven thousand who have not bowed the knee to Baal." ⁵So too, at the present time there is a remnant chosen by grace. ⁶And if by grace, then it is no longer by works; if it were, grace would no longer be grace.

⁷What then? What Israel sought so earnestly it did not obtain, but the elect did. The others were hardened, ⁸as it is written:

> "God gave them a spirit of stupor,
>> eyes so that they could not see
>> and ears so that they could not hear,
> to this very day."

⁹And David says:

> "May their table become a snare and a trap,
>> a stumbling block and a retribution for them.
> ¹⁰May their eyes be darkened so they cannot see,
>> and their backs be bent forever."

Original Meaning

IN HIS FIRST RESPONSE to the question of God's faithfulness to his promises to Israel (9:6a), Paul explained what those promises did *not* mean. Specifically, they do not guarantee salvation for all the physical descendants of Israel. God has not so bound himself. He is free to choose only some Jews to be saved and is free also to save Gentiles. Now, however, after his excursus in 9:30–10:21 to explain the exclusion of Jews and inclusion of Gentiles, Paul is ready to explore what God's promise to Israel *does* mean.

Romans 11:1–32 is bracketed by assertions of God's continuing commitment to Israel: "God did not reject his people, whom he foreknew" (v. 2a); "as far as election is concerned, they [Israelites] are loved on account of the patriarchs" (v. 28b). In this sense, the whole chapter pursues one broad theme. But a significant break occurs between verses 10 and 11. As he has done in every major section in this part of this letter (see also 9:25–29; 10:18–21), Paul marks the end of a unit with a composite quotation from the Old Testament (vv. 8–10) and the beginning of another section with a rhetorical question (9:30; 11:1, 11). Paul therefore unfolds his teaching about God's enduring faithfulness to Israel in two stages.[1] If 9:6–29 have surveyed the history of God's promise in the past, 11:1–10 focus on the present and 11:11–32 on the future. At the present time, God is demonstrating his continuing concern for Israel by bringing a remnant to salvation (v. 5), but in the future "all Israel will be saved" (v. 26).

Thus, the center of the first paragraph is verse 5: "So too, at the present time there is a remnant chosen by grace." Paul leads up to this assertion by citing the evidence of his own Christian commitment (v. 1b) and the Old Testament (vv. 2b–4) for God's preservation of a remnant. He follows up his central claim by elaborating on grace (v. 6) and then, reiterating his argument from 9:6–29, concludes by showing how Israel's present condition is the result of God's sovereign choice (vv. 7–10).

God's Faithfulness to Israel Seen in the Remnant (11:1–6)

THE TRIGGER FOR Paul's question in verse 1, "Did God reject his people?" is his condemnation of Israel in 9:30–10:21. He has claimed that Israel stumbled over the rock of Christ (9:33), willfully turning away from God's righteousness in Christ (10:3). Does this mean, Paul asks, that Israel has now forfeited any claim on God's promises? Paul emphatically rejects any such conclusion—"By no means!"—and follows it up with a solemn assertion in 11:2a: "God did not reject his people, whom he foreknew."

As in 8:29, the verb "foreknow" (*proginosko*) means "choose ahead of time" (see comments there). The placement of the comma in this statement is critical. Some commentators remove the comma and so treat "whom he foreknew" as a "restrictive" clause—that is, a clause that restricts the word it modifies by identifying it. On this view, Paul is asserting that God has not rejected *the people whom he chose*. Such a statement would build on the "remnant" idea of 9:6–29, claiming that God remains faithful to that "Israel within an Israel" whom he has chosen for salvation.[2] But almost all modern versions,

---

1. See esp. Scott Hafemann, "The Salvation of Israel in Romans 11:25–32: A Response to Krister Stendahl," *Ex Auditu* 4 (1988): 45–46.
2. See, e.g., Calvin, *The Epistle of Paul the Apostle to the Romans*, 410–11.

following most of the commentaries, rightly add the comma, making the clause nonrestrictive. "Whom he foreknew" does not identify the "people" Paul is talking about; rather, it explains why God remains faithful to that people.

Paul, in other words, has all of (physical) Israel in view here, and he is reasserting the common Old Testament teaching that God chose Israel as his very own people (see, e.g., Amos 3:2a: "You only have I chosen [lit. known] of all the families of the earth"). What the apostle does in chapter 11 is show what that corporate election of Israel as a whole means for the salvation of Jews in his own day and in the future.

The evidence Paul offers for God's faithfulness to that election of Israel in his own day is the existence of a "remnant" (vv. 5–6). But he leads up to that claim with two preliminary points. (1) He begins with himself (v. 1b). Paul's reminder to his readers of his Jewish descent may have three different purposes. (a) He may be explaining why he so strongly rejects the notion that God has rejected Israel: As an Israelite himself, he simply cannot accept any such idea.[3] (b) He may be reminding his readers that the very fact God chose a Jew to be apostle to the Gentiles indicates his continuing concern for Israel.[4] (c) Or he may simply want to remind us that he himself is both a Jew and a Christian—evidence that God has not abandoned his people.[5] The last fits the context best, as Paul hints already at the remnant theme of verses 5–6.

(2) In verses 2b–4, Paul lays further groundwork for his assertion about the remnant by illustrating from an Old Testament "passage about Elijah." The reference is to the story of King Ahab's attack on the prophets of Yahweh in 1 Kings 19:1–18. After learning of Ahab's slaughter of the prophets, his pagan wife, Jezebel, threatens her nemesis with the same fate (vv. 1–2). Elijah flees to the desert, where he bemoans his fate (vv. 3–14) and where God comforts him by assuring him that he is still at work, working out his plan for Israel and the nations (vv. 15–18).

From that Old Testament passage, Paul quotes Elijah's lament about being left alone after the slaughter of the prophets (Rom. 11:3; cf. 1 Kings 19:10, 14) and the Lord's concluding reassurance to Elijah that he has preserved a remnant of seven thousand who have not given their allegiance to Baal (Rom. 11:4; cf. 1 Kings 19:18b). We saw evidence earlier in Romans 9–11 that Paul may have identified himself with Moses (9:2–3). Perhaps he now implicitly identifies himself also with Elijah. For, like Elijah, Paul is confronted with the

---

3. Sanday and Headlam, *The Epistle to the Romans*, 309; Dunn, *Romans*, 635.

4. Cranfield, *The Epistle to the Romans*, 544–45.

5. So most commentators; see, e.g., Godet, *Commentary on Romans*, 391–92; Käsemann, *Commentary on Romans*, 299.

apparent downfall of spiritual Israel, but finds new hope in God's preservation of a remnant of true believers.[6]

Paul now draws a conclusion: "So too, at the present time there is a remnant chosen by grace" (11:5). He preserves the careful balance he has maintained throughout these chapters as he discusses Israel. God's Word affirms
a continuing role for Israel in salvation history. But Israel cannot claim this
role as a matter of right, for it is due solely to the working of God's grace. This
polemical thrust becomes explicit in verse 6. "Grace" means that "works"
have no role to play, that God is entirely free to bestow his blessing on
whomever he chooses. If those blessings were in fact dependent on our
works, God would not be free in his granting of blessing, and "grace would
no longer be grace."

Israel's Present Situation: A Summary (11:7–10)

WITH THE RHETORICAL question "What then?" Paul signals the conclusion
he wants to draw from his discussion about the remnant. But his conclusion
is also a fair summary of the situation of Israel in Paul's day as he developed
it in chapters 9–10. (1) What Israel as a whole "sought so earnestly it did not
obtain" (11:7). This language reflects 9:31: "Israel, who pursued a law of
righteousness, has not attained it." This parallel allows us to supply the missing referent for the word "it" in 11:7a: It is a right standing with God that Israel
sought but did not obtain.

(2) Paul then breaks the situation of Israel in general down into two specific entities. (a) One is the "remnant." Despite the rejection of Israel as a
whole, many individual Jews have responded to the gospel. They are the
Israel within Israel (9:6), the "remnant chosen by grace" (11:5). These Jews,
"the elect" (11:7), have obtained the right standing with God that Israel as a
whole was seeking. (b) The other, larger division of Jews consists of those
who have not attained this right standing. They have been "hardened."

The Greek verb for "hardened" is *poroo,* which in secular Greek often
refers to a callous or to the hardening of a bone when it heals after being broken. But in the New Testament, the word always has a metaphorical significance, referring to spiritual obduracy (Mark 6:52; 8:17; John 12:40; 2 Cor.
3:14; cf. the noun form in Mark 3:5; Rom. 11:25; Eph. 4:18). While the
Greek verb in 9:18 is different (*skleryno*), the idea conveyed here is the same.
God confirms the spiritual insensitivity that people are locked up under by
virtue of their sin in Adam.

The Old Testament quotations in 11:8–10 provide biblical support for the
idea that it is God who hardens people. Paul, following Jewish precedent,

---

6. See, e.g., Munck, *Christ and Israel,* 109.

quotes from every part of the Hebrew canon: the Law, the Prophets, and the Writings. The quotation in verse 8 is a composite. Most of it comes from Deuteronomy 29:4, but the phrase "spirit of stupor" is from Isaiah 29:10. It is probably also the influence of Isaiah 29:10 that leads Paul to change the negative formulation of the Deuteronomy text ("the Lord has not given . . .") into a positive one: "God gave. . . ." This change, of course, also suits Paul's application better, since he is documenting the initiative of God in hardening his people.

In 11:9–10, Paul supports this idea further by quoting from one of the famous imprecatory psalms. In Psalm 69, David laments the unjust persecution he is experiencing and asks God to bring disaster on his enemies (69:22–23). These are the verses Paul quotes. What David prayed that his persecutors would experience God has brought on the majority of Jews in his own day. Paul's attention may have been drawn to this passage because Psalm 69 seems to have been widely alluded to and explicitly used in the New Testament church (see Mark 3:21; 15:23 and par.; Luke 13:35; John 2:17; 15:25; Acts 1:20; Rom. 15:3; Phil. 4:3; Rev. 3:5; 16:1).

Commentators debate over the precise application Paul intends when he mentions "their table" becoming "a snare and a trap." The most popular suggestions are that Paul alludes to the sacrificial cult of the Jews[7] or to Jewish dependence on the law.[8] But it is not clear that Paul intends either of these— or any other specific application for that matter. The language is in the Psalm text, and Paul may not have given thought to any application in his own day.

ELECTION AND REMNANT. As is true throughout Romans 9–11, Paul assumes that his readers are well acquainted with the Old Testament and its teachings as he writes 11:1–10. Yet few of us in the contemporary church know our Old Testaments as well as we should. We certainly do not have the kind of everyday, intimate experience with the Old Testament that Paul's first readers had. The Jewish Christians in Rome were, of course, raised on the Old Testament. But many, perhaps even most, of the Gentile Christians probably also had long acquaintance with the Old Testament as regular attenders of the synagogue. If we are to grasp fully what Paul teaches in verses 1–10, two Old Testament concepts are especially important to understand: election and the remnant. Since these two themes are closely intertwined in the Old Testament and in Paul's argument, we may look at them together.

---

7. E.g., Käsemann, *Commentary on Romans*, 302; Dunn, *Romans*, 643.
8. Sanday and Headlam, *The Epistle to the Romans*, 315; Morris, *The Epistle to the Romans*, 404.

Paul specifically refers to the election of Israel in verse 2 by speaking of God's foreknowing of the people. We have argued that Paul here applies God's election to the people of Israel as a whole (see also 11:28). Careful readers of Romans (or of this commentary!) may wonder how God's election of Israel as a people relates to Paul's claim in chapter 9 that God's "purpose in election" refers only to some Jews, to "the Israel within Israel" (cf. 9:6), the remnant (9:27; cf. 9:24). Paul seems to be trying to have it both ways. In order to vindicate God's faithfulness, he reaffirms God's election of the nation of Israel (ch. 11). But in order to explain the meager response of Jews in his own day, he insists that God only elects some Jews (ch. 9).

But Paul is not the muddled thinker some of his critics have accused him of being. Rather, he is building on a tradition that goes back into the Old Testament and that was developed extensively in the intertestamental period. Central to this tradition is a distinction between corporate and individual election. Some traditional explanations of Romans 9–11 have overemphasized the individual perspective, viewing the chapters as an exposition on predestination. But some contemporary approaches err in the opposite direction. The situation Paul confronts requires him to integrate the two perspectives, or, better, to interpret one in the light of the other.

Paul inherited from the Scriptures and his Jewish heritage the teaching of a corporate election of all Israel. This is the dominant note about election per se in the Old Testament. References are far too numerous to quote, but Deuteronomy 7:6 is representative: "For you are a people holy to the LORD your God. The LORD your God has chosen you out of all the peoples on the face of the earth to be his people, his treasured possession."[9] This strand of Old Testament teaching focuses on the way in which God graciously entered into relationship with the nation of Israel. This relationship is called the covenant, a binding agreement between God and Israel. God, on his part, creates Israel as a people by choosing Abraham, giving him descendants, bringing the Israelites out of Egypt, and settling them in the Promised Land. Israel, on her part, is to honor God by keeping the law he has given her. God promises to bless Israel if she obeys, but to punish her if she does not.

However, almost from the beginning (as Paul points out in ch. 9), another strand in the teaching about election is also clear. God's election of Israel as a nation provides temporal blessings and an opportunity to enter into genuine spiritual fellowship through a heart commitment to the Lord. But it does not provide for salvation in and of itself. As Israel's history proceeds, this becomes increasingly clear. More and more Jews, though elect as members of Israel,

---

9. For a full discussion, see H. H. Rowley, *The Biblical Doctrine of Election* (London: Lutterworth, 1950), and Klein, *The New Chosen People.*

rebelled against God, breaking his law and serving other gods. Thus there came into greater prominence the idea of the "remnant": those Israelites who remained committed in their hearts to the God of Abraham, Isaac, and Jacob.

Paul himself cites two of the key Old Testament remnant texts, Isaiah 10:22–23 (in Rom. 9:27–28) and 1 Kings 19:18 (in Rom. 11:4; see also Ezra 9:8, 13–15; Isa. 37:31, 32; Jer. 23:3; 31:7; 42:2; Micah 2:12; 4:7; 5:7, 8).[10] Election language, to be sure, is not usually applied to this remnant. Strictly speaking, election in the Old Testament is a corporate phenomenon. But the idea of an individual election taking place within this corporate election is present at least in germ form.

The tribulations of Israel in the intertestamental period forced many Jews to develop the notion of a true, faithful Israel within national Israel much more extensively. Under the stress of persecution, many Jews renounced their faith, and many more compromised their faith in a way unacceptable to their pious brothers and sisters. As a result, the Jewish "parties" of this period individualized election by insisting that membership in the true people of God was reserved for certain people rather than for a nation. In the Qumran community, for instance, covenantal membership was reserved for the "sons of light" and in *Psalms of Solomon* for the "pious."[11]

Paul responds to the crisis of Israel in his own day by formulating a similar idea. Only those whom God has chosen by an act of his grace are true members of God's people. God is in fact freely choosing only some Jews to be saved but many Gentiles. Paul sees this in accord with what the Old Testament teaches about God's purpose to create an "Israel within Israel." But, unlike some of his Jewish contemporaries, Paul also continues to affirm God's election of Israel as a whole. God has not completely abandoned the nation in order to concentrate only on some within it. The promises he made to the patriarchs continue to be valid (11:28). Indeed, chapter 11 is basically about what the continuing implications of that corporate election are for Israel.

IN AN EARLIER PART of this commentary, we suggested that the Jewish people in Romans (and, indeed, in the Bible as a whole) have a paradigmatic role (see Bridging Contexts section of 2:1–11). What the Jewish people do or experience represents, at certain points, a universal condition. To be sure, the principle is easily abused if we ignore

---

10. On the remnant see esp. Gerhard F. Hasel, *The Remnant: The History and Theology of the Remnant Idea from Genesis to Isaiah* (Berrien Springs, Mich.: Andrews Univ. Press, 1972).

11. See esp. Mark Seifrid, *Justification by Faith: The Origin and Development of a Central Pauline Theme* (Leiden: Brill, 1992), 81–133.

those ways in which Israel has a unique position in Romans. But the biblical story of God's election and the way it has been understood by people contain lessons for the contemporary church.

As we have just seen, the Bible teaches both an election of Israel as a nation to privilege and service and an election of individuals from within Israel (and from outside Israel as well) to salvation. In Israel's history, we find people who overemphasized one of these elections at the expense of the other. With some hesitation, I suggest we find the same sort of imbalance in the church today.

Some Jews made the mistake of assuming that God's election of Israel virtually guaranteed spiritual benefits to every member of the nation. Birth into that nation, circumcision (for males), and a reasonable faithfulness in observing the law were all that were needed to ensure one's salvation. Some segments of the church have much the same kind of attitude. People assume that they will go to heaven as long as they can claim such external credits as baptism, confirmation, church attendance, participation in the mass, and acts of service.

Churches that emphasize the sacraments and use a liturgy are more open to this problem than others. I myself grew up in such a church. Despite my baptism as an infant, the faithfulness of my parents in exposing me to the gospel through confirmation, and my regular church attendance, I had no genuine heart commitment to Christ. Faith had not been awakened in me. The fault is, of course, my own. But the church contributed to the problem by failing to bring home to me personally the need to respond to God's Word and to the sacraments to which I was regularly exposed. I was presuming on a kind of corporate election—that members of my church or my family were "in" automatically.

In Jewish history, a sectarian view developed that taught that only those who met the strict requirements of a given sect had any hope of salvation. Similarly, some churches today teach that only by conforming to certain expectations can people be saved. While they usually do not come out and say so, many of these churches implicitly teach that you can be saved only if you have had a certain kind of conversion experience. A gradual growth in faith with the moment of conversion impossible to identify is not enough; one must have had a definite, preferably emotional, experience of God's grace.

I have also known churches that looked askance at anyone who used anything but a King James Version Bible. The elect would surely know the "authorized" Bible! At the other end of a certain spectrum, the official teaching of the Roman Catholic Church continues to be that "outside the Church there is no salvation." Post-Vatican II theology has loosened these parameters to include "unconscious" participants in the church, but the principle is still there.

What is needed in the face of these contradictory impulses is a fresh commitment to the teaching of election we find in these chapters. God chooses those who are truly his. His choice is not based on anything we have done or could do. It is not determined by the nation we live in, the family we were born to, or the church we attend. It has nothing to do with how often we go to mass or how many times we have "come forward" at a Billy Graham crusade. We can put no restrictions on God's election, nor can we predict whom he will elect. Those who are elect exercise faith in Christ as the single requirement for salvation. (We can skip for now the vexing question of which comes first, election or faith.) Faith must be defined in biblical terms, and we must always remember that many things necessarily flow from faith. But we must resist any attempt to minimize faith in Christ as the central mark of the elect of God.

To borrow a metaphor from the political arena, then, Christians should make the tent of election no larger and no smaller than the extent of genuine faith in Christ. Our culture tugs us toward the former extreme, the "big tent" view of Christianity. The emphasis on tolerance for other views and a postmodern lack of concern with specifics pressures us to enlarge the tent of salvation to include people who give no indication that they are elect. But it is also easy to overreact against our culture and to confine salvation to a very small tent, covered by the canvas of our own particular hobbyhorse.

Romans 11:11–24

AGAIN I ASK: Did they stumble so as to fall beyond recovery? Not at all! Rather, because of their transgression, salvation has come to the Gentiles to make Israel envious. ¹²But if their transgression means riches for the world, and their loss means riches for the Gentiles, how much greater riches will their fullness bring!

¹³I am talking to you Gentiles. Inasmuch as I am the apostle to the Gentiles, I make much of my ministry ¹⁴in the hope that I may somehow arouse my own people to envy and save some of them. ¹⁵For if their rejection is the reconciliation of the world, what will their acceptance be but life from the dead? ¹⁶If the part of the dough offered as firstfruits is holy, then the whole batch is holy; if the root is holy, so are the branches.

¹⁷If some of the branches have been broken off, and you, though a wild olive shoot, have been grafted in among the others and now share in the nourishing sap from the olive root, ¹⁸do not boast over those branches. If you do, consider this: You do not support the root, but the root supports you. ¹⁹You will say then, "Branches were broken off so that I could be grafted in." ²⁰Granted. But they were broken off because of unbelief, and you stand by faith. Do not be arrogant, but be afraid. ²¹For if God did not spare the natural branches, he will not spare you either.

²²Consider therefore the kindness and sternness of God: sternness to those who fell, but kindness to you, provided that you continue in his kindness. Otherwise, you also will be cut off. ²³And if they do not persist in unbelief, they will be grafted in, for God is able to graft them in again. ²⁴After all, if you were cut out of an olive tree that is wild by nature, and contrary to nature were grafted into a cultivated olive tree, how much more readily will these, the natural branches, be grafted into their own olive tree!

Original Meaning AS PAUL HAS NEATLY summarized the situation in 11:7, the preaching of the gospel has divided Israel into two groups: a minority (the "remnant"), who have obtained salvation, and the majority, who have been hardened. Paul now asks whether this situation is permanent. His basic answer? No, it is not. God's rejection of Israel is not his last word. He has brought about that rejection in order to further his plan for salvation history. This plan initially is bringing salvation to the Gentiles, but it ultimately is intended to "bounce back" and benefit Israel as well. This sequence of Jewish rejection → Gentile blessing → Jewish blessing again is at the heart of these verses. Paul goes through the sequence three times (and twice again in verses 25–32), adding in two places yet a fourth stage:

verse 11	their transgression	salvation has come to the Gentiles	to make Israel envious	
verse 12a	their transgression	riches for the world		
verse 12b	their loss	riches for the Gentiles	their fullness	greater riches
verse 15	their rejection	reconciliation of the world	their acceptance	life from the dead
verses 17–23	some of the branches broken off	you, though a wild olive shoot, have been grafted in	God is able to graft them in again	

Considerable debate surrounds this sequence. Does Paul think of it as a continuing oscillation, which repeats itself many times over the course of history as Jews and Gentiles interact with one another? Or does he view it as a single, linear sequence, which leads from the Jewish rejection and Gentile acceptance of his own day to a climax of greater Jewish response to the gospel in the last days? We prefer the latter, and we will show why as the exegesis proceeds.

Paul makes clear that the argument in these verses has a practical purpose. He scolds Gentile Christians in Rome for their arrogant boasting over the Jews (vv. 13, 18–22). Here surfaces what was probably one of the basic purposes of the letter to the Romans. Gentiles have become the majority in the church at Rome as well as in the church at large. They are tempted to take undue pride in their new position, even to the extent of thinking they have now replaced the Jews in God's plans. Paul disabuses them of this notion, showing that, by an act of sheer grace, they have been added to Israel. Boasting is out of the question, then, because their own salvation is part of God's plan to offer his mercy to all people.

God's Purpose in Israel's Rejection (11:11–15)

ROMANS 11:11–32 BEGINS exactly the same way as verses 1–10: "Therefore I say" (lit. trans.), followed by a rhetorical question expecting a negative answer and concluding with Paul's favorite emphatic rejection, *me genoito* ("By no means!" in 11:1; "Not at all!" in 11:11). In verse 1, Paul asked, in effect, whether Israel's rejection was total. Now he asks whether their rejection is final: "Did they stumble so as to fall beyond recovery?" The nearest antecedent for "they" is "the others [who] were hardened" (vv. 7b–10).[1] But Paul makes a new start in verse 11, and in verse 12 "their" refers to Israel as whole. Probably, then, Paul's "they" here individualizes the reference to Israel in verse 7a.[2] While Israel at present has not obtained the righteousness they were seeking, Israelites have not for that reason fallen into irretrievable spiritual ruin.

Paul's purpose in verses 11–32 is to explain why that is not so. Their "transgression" (v. 11) of rejecting God's grace in Christ has led to salvation for the Gentiles. Paul's own ministry as portrayed in the book of Acts reveals how this happened historically. Again and again he preached the gospel in a synagogue, meeting with only moderate response and eventually being dismissed. He and his companions then turned to the Gentiles, who generally welcomed their message (see 13:44–47; 14:1–3; 18:4–7; 19:8–10; 28:23–29).

But this pattern was more than a historical accident. As Paul makes clear in Acts by citing Scripture in support and now demonstrates in Romans by revealing God's purpose behind what has happened, Jewish rejection and Gentile acceptance was God's plan for the salvation of all the world. In specific answer to his question in verse 11, Paul makes clear that Gentile salvation is not the end of the matter. Borrowing the language of Deuteronomy 32:21 (quoted in Rom. 10:19), Paul affirms that the salvation of Gentiles has the purpose of making Israel "envious" (or "jealous").

In verse 12, Paul elaborates on the sequence introduced in verse 11. In the first part of the verse, he again refers to widespread Jewish refusal to believe in Christ as "their transgression," but in the second part he calls it "their loss." The Greek word for "loss" (*hettema*) may have a quantitative meaning ("diminution" in numbers), but probably has a qualitative nuance: "defeat" or "loss."[3] In the same way, "riches for the world"/"riches for the Gentiles" replaces the "salvation" that has come to the Gentiles. But the key elaboration is in the last

---

1. See Sanday and Headlam, *The Epistle to the Romans*, 320; Cranfield, *The Epistle to the Romans*, 544–45.

2. Barrett, *The Epistle to the Romans*, 212; Hafemann, "Salvation of Israel," 50.

3. The only other known occurrences of the word have this meaning (Isa. 31:8; 1 Cor. 6:7); see BAGD.

step. Paul spoke vaguely of Israel being made "envious" (v. 11); now he speaks of "their fullness."

The Greek word for "fullness" is *pleroma*, and, like *hettema*, may have either a quantitative or qualitative meaning. With the former, *pleroma* would refer to a great number of Jews (TEV "the complete number of Jews")[4]; with the latter, to Israel's restoration to kingdom blessing.[5] The latter is the more likely meaning, but the context also suggests that the blessing Israel is to experience comes by way of an increase in the number of Jews who are saved (v. 25).

In verses 13–14, Paul interrupts his sketch of God's plan for salvation history in order to hint at the practical purpose for what he is saying. He addresses directly the Gentile Christians in the church at Rome to make them realize that God has not abandoned Israel (vv. 17–22, 25), and thus they as Gentiles have no business boasting over their fellow Jewish Christians. What he says about his own ministry in verses 13b–14 serves this same purpose. While God's original call to him included ministry to both Jews and Gentiles, Paul as "the apostle to the Gentiles" became God's "point man" in opening up the Gentile world to the gospel. One can therefore imagine Gentile Christians citing Paul's own focus on Gentiles as further evidence that God has turned his back on Israel. Thus, Paul makes clear that his ministry to Gentiles does *not* mean that he is unconcerned about his own people. His ultimate purpose in bringing the gospel to Gentiles is to arouse Israel to envy and so "save some of them."

Verse 15 returns to the main line of argument, as Paul reiterates one more time the salvation-historical sequence that dominates this passage. Israel's "rejection" is an ambiguous construction: It could refer to Israel's rejection or "throwing away" (*apobole*) of God,[6] or to God's rejection of Israel.[7] The latter is probably intended, for it makes a better contrast with God's "acceptance" of Israel later in the verse and fits Paul's concern to track Israel's present plight to God's own purpose. In a structure similar to verse 12, Paul argues from the lesser to the greater. If God's rejection of Israel has brought "the reconciliation of the world" (see 5:10–11), then "what will their acceptance be but life from the dead?" Far greater blessing than the offer of a new relationship with God for the Gentiles will come when God "accepts" Israel once again.

But what will this blessing be? "Life from the dead" has two possible meanings. It may be a metaphor for renewed spiritual life.[8] When the father in the

---

4. Godet, *Commentary on Romans*, 401; Cranfield, *The Epistle to the Romans*, 557–58.

5. E.g., Murray, *The Epistle to the Romans*, 2:79.

6. Fitzmyer, *Romans*, 612.

7. So most commentators; see, e.g., Godet, *Commentary on Romans*, 403; Dunn, *Romans*, 657.

8. So many commentators (e.g., Godet, *Commentary on Romans*, 404; Murray, *The Epistle to the Romans*, 2:82–84; Morris, *The Epistle to the Romans*, 411).

parable of the prodigal son welcomes home his repentant son, he exclaims, "This son of mine was dead and is alive again" (Luke 15:24). Paul refers to believers as people who have been brought "from death to life." But "life from the dead" probably has a more literal reference. The phrase "from the dead" (*ek nekron*) refers to the resurrection of the body in forty-six of its forty-seven occurrences in the New Testament (the only exception is Rom. 6:13). Underlying Paul's sketch of salvation history here is an apocalyptic world-view that focuses on the resurrection of the dead as the last and climactic stage in God's plan for history.

Thus, Paul suggests that the return of Israel to favor with God will occur at the climax of history, when the dead are raised.[9] This likely reference of "life from the dead" constitutes one important reason to think that Paul is describing a linear sequence of acts in salvation history that climax with the return of Christ in glory.

God's Purpose and Gentile Arrogance (11:16–24)

IN THIS PARAGRAPH, dominated by the olive tree metaphor, Paul makes more explicit his concern to stifle Gentile arrogance. The salvation-historical sequence we have seen already in verses 11, 12, and 15 is the backbone of the passage.

Verse 16 is transitional. It supports the hope Paul has expressed in verse 15 by arguing that the blessings Israel has already received will lead to even greater blessing in the future. Paul uses two metaphors to make his point, each of which uses the logic of "if the part, then the whole" to anchor Paul's confidence about a great future for Israel. The first one is drawn from Numbers 15:17–21. The "whole batch" refers to Israel as a whole, but to what does "the part of the dough offered as firstfruits" refer? Since Paul uses the word "first-fruits" (*aparche*) for the first converts in a region (Rom. 16:5; 1 Cor. 16:15; 2 Thess. 2:13), he may have in mind the remnant of Jewish Christians of his own day (cf. Rom. 11:7).[10] The salvation of the remnant shows that God still considers Israel "holy," with all the hope that this holiness implies.

In the second image, the "root" almost certainly represents the patriarchs. Jewish authors referred to the patriarchs as the "root" (e.g., *1 Enoch* 93:5, 8; Philo, *Heir* 279), and Paul himself in this context bases Israel's future hope on God's promise to the patriarchs (11:28; cf. 9:5). This being the case, it is

---

9. At least as many interpreters advocate this view, including most of the early Greek fathers, many Puritans (see Ian Murray, *The Puritan Hope: A Study in Revival and the Interpretation of Prophecy* [London: Banner of Truth, 1971], 66–72), and many contemporary commentators (e.g., Käsemann, *Commentary on Romans*, 307; Cranfield, *The Epistle to the Romans*, 562–63; Dunn, *Romans*, 658).

10. See, e.g., Cranfield, *The Epistle to the Romans*, 564; Fitzmyer, *Romans*, 614.

more likely that "firstfruits" also refers to the patriarchs.[11] God's promise to the patriarchs has not been revoked; their descendants remain "holy." By this Paul does not mean that all their descendants will be saved. Rather, "holy" (*hagios*), as in the Old Testament and 1 Corinthians 7:14, means that the people continue to be "set apart" by God for special attention.

This continuing special relationship between God and Israel gives reason to hope for a future spiritual renewal of the people—a hope Paul spells out in verses 23–24. First, however, he exploits the metaphor of root and branches he has just introduced to chastise Gentile Christians.

Paul opens with a conditional sentence (vv. 17–18a) that gets to the heart of his concern. The "if" clause rehearses the sequence of Jewish rejection and Gentile salvation that we have seen so often in this passage. The "natural branches" are, of course, Jews, while the "wild olive shoot" refers to Gentiles. Gentiles were not originally included in the people of God formed via God's promise to the patriarchs—they do not "naturally" belong to the olive tree. But now that they have been included, they have, Paul affirms in the "then" clause (v. 18a), no reason to boast over Jews. "Those branches" (v. 18) refers to the branches cut off in verse 17, that is, to those Jews in Paul's day who have not responded to the gospel.

The context reveals that the Gentiles were guilty of an arrogance toward Jews in general that extended to both Old Testament Israel and to Jewish Christians as well. Paul shows why such arrogance is wrong in verses 18b–23. He makes two basic points. (1) Gentile Christians receive the spiritual benefits they enjoy only through the Jews. They have been grafted into the olive tree, the people of God. But the roots of that tree are the Jewish patriarchs. The Gentiles have not "replaced" the Jews in God's plan. Indeed, only through the Jews do Gentiles have any hope for experiencing the blessings of belonging to God's people.

(2) Gentile Christians have not earned the right to be grafted into the olive tree. Their arrogance takes the form not only of bragging over Jews but also of boasting in their own accomplishment. Their attitude, so it seems, is that they felt so important and deserving that God removed Jews in order to include them (v. 19). Paul admits that there is some truth in what they say ("granted" in v. 20). As he has himself shown, the rejection of Jews has led to salvation for Gentiles (vv. 11–15). But he also insists that was not because of any merit in the Gentiles themselves that God did what he did. It was, rather, entirely a matter of "faith."

Jews forfeited their place because they failed to believe, while Gentile Christians have been included because they believed the message (v. 20b).

---

11. See, e.g., Godet, *Commentary on Romans*, 404–5; Murray, *The Epistle to the Romans*, 2:85.

Faith, as Paul has shown earlier in Romans, gives a person no basis for pride, for it is a matter simply of accepting the gracious gift God offers (3:27; 4:3–5). The Gentile Christians, therefore, need to replace their arrogance with fear (11:20b). For while God shows "kindness" to those who stand in faith, he shows "sternness" to those who fall (v. 22a).

Continuing in God's kindness, then, is not something one can simply take for granted. It is necessary to renew one's faith every day. Failure to do so means that one will be "cut off": removed from God's people and the salvation found only through that relationship (v. 22b). For if God did not scruple to cut off the "natural branches" when they failed to believe the good news, he certainly will not hesitate to cut off the wild olive shoots he has grafted into the tree.

All in all, then, verses 19–22 constitute one of the most serious warnings about continuing in the faith that we have anywhere in the New Testament. We will explore the theological and practical significance of the verses below. But for now we need to stress how they function to counter the egotism that the Gentile Christians in Rome are displaying, not only toward Jews but also to God himself.

After the warning to Gentile Christians, Paul concludes the olive tree imagery with a word of hope for the Jews. Just as Gentile Christians run the risk of being "cut off" if they should stop believing, so Jews can be grafted back in if they turn from unbelief to faith (v. 23). For it is surely easier to graft natural branches back in than to do what God has already done, that is, graft in, "contrary to nature," wild olive shoots (v. 24). Paul stops short here of predicting that God will graft unbelieving Israel back into the people of God again—but only just short. They prepare the way for the explicit prediction of verse 26.

Bridging Contexts

PAUL'S REVERSAL OF an Old Testament eschatological pattern. Paul is depicting in this section the sequence of events that will culminate in the last day, when the dead are raised (v. 15). His focus is eschatological. He wants to help us understand that the current state of affairs in salvation history will change one day. That state of affairs is the same for us as it was for Paul, for we stand with him in the same phase of salvation history.

To be sure, that phase has now lasted for almost two thousand years. But the amount of time between events is not the concern of Scripture. What is critical is the sequence of events. With the first coming of Christ and pouring out of the Spirit accomplished, the next event on the eschatological timetable is the return of Christ in glory and all the events that will accompany that return. That was as true for Paul as it is for us. So we, like him, still await that day when Israel's unbelief and rejection will be replaced by faith and acceptance. The "natural branches," Paul confidently expects, will be grafted in once again.

Paul does not, of course, describe this eschatological climax in a vacuum. The Old Testament prophets wrote much about what God would do for both Gentiles and Jews when Messiah came. Jewish writers built on and elaborated these predictions. One prediction that may have particularly influenced Paul's scheme in verses 11–24 is the so-called "eschatological pilgrimage tradition." According to this tradition, Israel's restoration to glory in the end times would stimulate Gentiles to offer themselves and their gifts in the service of Yahweh. The tradition is rooted firmly in the Old Testament (especially Isaiah) but is expressed most clearly in the intertestamental Jewish book *Psalms of Solomon* (esp. 17:26–46).

> He will gather a holy people. . . . He will have Gentile nations serving him under his yoke, and he will glorify the Lord in (a place) prominent (above) the whole earth. And he will purge Jerusalem (and make it) holy as it was even from the beginning, (for) nations to come from the ends of the earth to see his glory, to bring as gifts her children who had been driven out, and to see the glory of the Lord with which God has glorified her. (*Pss. Sol.* 17:26, 30–31)[12]

Paul, in light of his new understanding of events from the gospel, reverses the order of events and spiritualizes the process: Instead of Gentiles coming to worship Yahweh in Jerusalem as a result of Israel's restoration, Israel is saved in response to the extension of salvation to the Gentiles. To be sure, some scholars question whether the tradition has had much impact on Paul, since he does not quote from the key Old Testament pilgrimage texts.[13] But, while not a key text in this tradition, Isaiah 59:20–21, which Paul applies to Israel's final salvation in 11:26b–27, does contribute to it. So we have, I think, sufficient evidence that the tradition plays some role in Paul's conception of the end events.

What role does Paul himself play in this eschatological climax? Some scholars think he saw himself as the key instrument in bringing about this climax. His untiring efforts to convert Gentiles and to bring their "riches" to Jerusalem through the collection he was taking on his third missionary journey were to be the events that triggered the final salvation of Israel and

---

12. See also Isa. 2:2–3a; 56:6–7; 60:1–7; Tob. 13:11–13; 14:6–7; *T. Zeb.* 9.8; *T. Benj.* 9.2; *Sib. Or.* 3.767–95.

13. See esp. Terrence L. Donaldson, *Paul and the Gentiles: Remapping the Apostle's Convictional World* (Minneapolis: Fortress, 1997), 187–97.

the end of history.[14] Suffice it to say here that Paul in this passage appears to give himself a much more modest role in these events. His goal is to "arouse my own people to envy and save *some* of them" (v. 14, italics added). We should not minimize Paul's role in salvation history, but this verse indicates that he does not think of himself as the agent through whom God would accomplish the "eschatological pilgrimage."[15]

The olive tree. Had we been living in the first century, we would have not been surprised for Paul to choose an olive tree as an illustration. The olive tree was the "most widely cultivated fruit tree in the Mediterranean area."[16] But just as significant was the fact that the Old Testament and Jewish writings sometimes compare Israel to an olive tree (e.g., Jer. 11:16; Hos. 14:5–6) and, even more often, to a planting of some kind. The most famous of these is the comparison of Israel to a vineyard in Isaiah 5, which Jesus alludes to in his parable (Matt. 21:33–44 and par.). There is even some evidence that a Jewish synagogue in Rome had the name "of the olive."[17]

Thus, Paul's reference to an olive tree is natural. But what he says about the behavior of the olive tree is anything but natural, and scholars have devoted some energy to figuring out just what he may be trying to communicate by his description of an unusual horticultural procedure. For the practice of grafting branches from a wild, or uncultivated, olive tree into a cultivated one is just the opposite of what farmers were in the habit of doing.

Some interpreters think that Paul here betrays his urban roots—he simply was unacquainted with agriculture.[18] Others have come to Paul's defense, citing obscure ancient sources to prove that farmers did occasionally graft a wild olive shoot into a cultivated tree.[19] Still others argue that the whole debate is pointless, since it assumes, wrongly, that the analogy Paul uses must perfectly fit the circumstances of life from which it is drawn.[20] But we tentatively suggest that Paul may be deliberately describing a process that is "contrary to nature" (v. 24) in order to hint at the grace of God in bringing the Gentiles to salvation.[21] As little as a wild olive shoot would have any

---

14. This is the main theme of Johannes Munck, *Paul and the Salvation of Mankind*. We will explore this view more when we come to the collection passage in 15:23–29.

15. See, e.g., Cranfield, *The Epistle to the Romans*, 561.

16. Dunn, *Romans*, 660–61.

17. W. D. Davies, "Paul and the Gentiles: A Suggestion Concerning Romans 11.13–24," in *Jewish and Pauline Studies* (Philadelphia: Fortress, 1984), 137–44.

18. See Dodd, *Epistle to the Romans*, 118: "Paul had the limitations of a town-bred man."

19. See esp. William M. Ramsay, "The Olive-Tree and the Wild Olive," in *Paul and Other Studies in Early Christian History* (London: Hodder and Stoughton, 1908), 219–50; A. G. Baxter and J. A. Ziesler, "Paul and Arboriculture: Romans 11:17–24," *JSNT* 24 (1985): 25–32.

20. Godet, *Commentary on Romans*, 405–6; Cranfield, *The Epistle to the Romans*, 565–66.

21. Sanday and Headlam, *The Epistle to the Romans*, 327.

right to be grafted into a cultivated tree, so little right do Gentiles have to be given a place in the people of God. This is a procedure "against nature," one that overturns expectations. But such is precisely the effect of God's grace!

 THE OLIVE TREE imagery that Paul uses in this section teaches two theological truths that have considerable practical significance. We learn something about the nature of the people of God and about the doctrine of eternal security.

The olive tree imagery and the elect people of God. We learn something important about the nature of God's people. We must be cautious about finding more theology in an analogy than is justified—a practice all too common among interpreters of the Bible. But this much is clear: There is only one olive tree.

What does that olive tree represent? Many claim that it represents Israel—and, as we have seen, the Old Testament used the olive tree to stand for Israel on occasion. But Paul's "grafting in" and "cutting off" language in this paragraph seems to be referring to salvation. This suggests that we must modify the identification a bit: The olive tree stands for the "true Israel," the "Israel within an Israel" described in 9:6. In a move anticipated in 9:24–26, where Paul claims that Gentiles as well as Jews have been "called" by God and so become his people, he shows that Gentiles who are saved also belong to this "true Israel."

Ultimately, therefore, the olive tree imagery shows that there is one people of God. The roots of the tree are planted in Old Testament soil. They are the patriarchs, through whom God acted to call out a people for his own name. The Old Testament people of God was drawn almost entirely from the nation of Israel—although with notable exceptions (e.g., Rahab, Ruth, Uriah). But now, at the turn of the ages, God extends his grace and invites Gentiles to join his people on an equal footing with Jews. At the same time, this new era in salvation history also brings into clearer relief the object of faith for this people: not just God, but God "the three in one." Faith in Christ, the bringer of salvation, is now necessary. Yet Paul's imagery makes clear that the turn of the ages did not bring into existence a new people of God. Rather, Gentiles join the already existing people of God, "true Israel."

From this perspective, then, we see how wrong is the common idea that the church has "replaced" Israel. As a name for the New Testament community of faith, the church *is* "Israel." But that people include in its number both Gentiles and Jews. Clearly, therefore, the church cannot replace believing

Israel. But neither can it replace unbelieving Israel, for the two belong in different categories. Jewish unbelievers belong by birth to national Israel, and nothing can change that. But the church is a spiritual entity, made up of people from all nations, including Israel.

Moreover, Romans 11 teaches that God still regards with favor national Israel (vv. 2, 28). So we cannot even argue that national Israel has been replaced by the church as the sole place where God is now working out his plan for history. To be sure, the church, not national Israel, is the locus of God's saving work in history, and to that limited extent, we can speak of the church "replacing" Israel. But as an overall description of the relationship between the church and Israel, a "replacement" theme is not accurate.

How should we react to this theology of the church and Israel? We who are Gentile Christians need to avoid an ethnocentric view of the church that effectively puts Jewish believers on the sidelines. Like the Gentile Christians in Rome, many Christians in our day seem to operate under the assumption that the "church" is equivalent to the Gentiles. It is this equation that often lurks behind the "replacement" model we have just rejected. So many of us have grown up in churches that are overwhelmingly Gentile and think of "Jewish" entirely as a religious category that we have a hard time coming to grips with the Jewish roots and flavor of God's people.

Our culture fosters the same tendency. The Israeli Supreme Court recently ruled that one cannot be both a citizen of Israel and a Christian. For them, being "Jewish" is incompatible with being a Christian. But we must resist any such dichotomy as foreign to the New Testament. To become a Christian is not to cease to be Jewish; it is, as many messianic Jews emphasize, to become a "completed" Jew. Those of us who are Gentile Christians need to avoid the arrogance that Paul warns about in this paragraph.

While Paul does not address the matter here, Jewish Christians also need to come to grips with the oneness of God's people. While I recognize the reasons why many Jewish Christians want to form their own worship assemblies, I cannot help but think that it has an unfortunate effect on the unity and richness of the Christian community. To be sure, Paul himself recognized that Jews who became Christians had the right to continue to observe Torah. The Roman Christian community itself may have been divided into Jewish and Gentile house churches. But Paul's greater concern is that Jewish and Gentile Christians "accept one another" (15:7).

This acceptance means not just to recognize one another's legitimate claim to be Christian, but to welcome one another in a worship that praises God. The New Testament holds out to us a vision of a community in which matters such as gender, social status, and national origin do not count (Gal. 3:28; Col. 3:11). By separating into churches on the basis of national origin, we seem to be running counter to this vision. Thus, just as Gentile Christians need to repent of their own ethnocentrism, so, perhaps, do Jewish Christians.

Ultimately, of course, Paul's warning to Gentile Christians about their boasting over Jews has implications for anti-Semitism. The idea that God has now "replaced" Israel with the church, coupled with the belief that the Jews were responsible for the death of Christ, has contributed enormously to the anti-Semitism that has had so long and terrible a history. We have already seen that the New Testament does not really countenance the "replacement" idea. But we should also note, in passing, that it offers as little support for the idea that the Jewish people were responsible for the death of Christ.

For one thing, as modern English translations are beginning to recognize, there are many places in the Gospels and Acts where references to "the Jews" clearly refer only to Jewish leaders, or even certain Jewish leaders. More important, we need also to remember that the Jews' involvement in Jesus' death was representative of all humanity. The Jewish leaders were the people historically used by God to bring his Son to the cross. But it was the sin of the entire human race that ultimately required that sacrifice. We are all guilty of the blood of Christ's death, and all of us equally are offered the opportunity to have our sins cleansed by it.

Whatever its causes, anti-Semitism continues to be a problem in the church. We often treat it lightly, making Jewish jokes and calling people who are tight with their money "Jews." When pressed, we will say that we don't mean anything by it. But we do. Whether we admit it or not, such ways of speaking foster prejudice in ourselves and pass it on to others. It has no place in a community with Jewish roots and in which all nations are to be welcomed and honored.

The olive tree imagery and eternal security. The olive tree metaphor also touches on the doctrine of eternal security—the doctrine that all genuine Christians will infallibly be saved on the final day of judgment. We have defended this view earlier in this book, arguing that verses such as 5:9–10, 8:29–30, and 8:31–39 teach it. But what are we to make of the warnings of 11:19–22? Paul writes to people who have been "grafted in" to the olive tree, the true people of God. Yet he warns them that they will be "cut off," taken out of his people, if they do not "continue in his kindness." Thus, in one and the same letter we have apparently absolute promises of salvation for those who have been justified and reconciled (5:9–10), and a warning to people who have been justified and reconciled that their salvation is not certain.

The tension between these two kinds of text is found throughout the New Testament. Indeed, it is part of the larger interplay of God's sovereignty and human responsibility that is so difficult to untangle in Scripture. Earlier in chapter 11, for instance, Paul plainly attributed the hardening and rejection of Israel to God (11:7−8). Yet in verse 20, he claims that the Jews were rejected because of their own refusal to believe (cf. also chs. 9−10 for this same tension).

Faced with these two perspectives, we have essentially three options. (1) We can give full credit to both perspectives without resolving the tension. (2) We can acknowledge that God has limited his sovereignty to allow for genuine human decisions (essentially, the Arminian view). (3) We can maintain God's absolute sovereignty while limiting the freedom of human actions (essentially the Calvinist view).

How do these options work out in the matter of ultimate salvation? If we were to take the first option, we would regard both the promises and the warnings as serving different rhetorical functions. When Paul wants to encourage believers, he assures them that their salvation is certain; when he wants to prod them into action, he warns them they might lose their salvation.[22] This view, however, comes perilously close to turning Paul into a contradictory, ad hoc, writer. If we are to preserve the tension while giving Paul credit as a consistent and systematic thinker, we can only resort, I think, to the idea of mystery. Paul teaches both that salvation for the believer is assured and that a believer can lose his or her salvation, and we must leave the reconciliation of the two in the hands of God.

Yet this approach also has its problems, for it comes close to believing an out-and-out contradiction. We surely must acknowledge that God's thoughts are far beyond ours and that many mysteries will remain in our understanding of the faith. But there is a difference between believing two things we cannot reconcile and believing two things that are contradictory.

Granted the evidence we have, then, I think it is finally impossible to avoid the decision between the traditional Calvinist and Arminian viewpoints on the security of the believer. The Arminian naturally appeals to the kind of warning text we are looking at here, and there are many like this in the New Testament (in Romans, see also 14:15). The warnings in these texts appear to assume that a truly regenerate believer can turn against God and so be lost forever. The Calvinist, by contrast, cites God's promises to preserve the believer to the end and the eschatological nature of justification. That is, passages such as 5:9−10 appear to teach that God's justifying verdict is his final and therefore unchangeable verdict.

As I have mentioned before in this commentary, I teach in an institution and attend a church in which both these views are found. I am happy about that situation. Not only does it rightly acknowledge the difficulty of the

---

22. See, essentially, Nigel M. Watson, "Justified by Faith, Judged by Works—An Antinomy?" *NTS* 29 (1983): 209−21.

biblical teaching on the issue; it also means that I will not have to change jobs or churches if I change my view on the subject. For I must say that I think each side can muster some pretty solid arguments.

Nevertheless, at this point at least, I am still in the Calvinist camp. What do I do, then, with the warning in 11:19−22? Some Calvinists argue that Paul is speaking phenomenologically here. Gentile believers who fall away forever were never *really* grafted into the olive tree to begin with but only appeared to be.[23] Others argue that Paul's warning is directed not to individuals but to Gentiles as a corporate entity.[24] Still other Calvinist interpreters suggest that the cutting off of Gentile Christians who turn from God need not be final; like the Jews, they can be grafted back in again and ultimately saved.[25]

I am not entirely happy with any of these alternatives, though the first has, I think, the most promise. Another way of looking at the warning is to assume that Paul means exactly what he says—that Christians who stop believing will be lost forever—but to question whether Paul thinks that a genuine Christian will, in fact, ever stop believing.[26] Such an approach is often criticized because it makes the whole matter "hypothetical": How can there be a genuine warning if the outcome can never, in fact, happen? I acknowledge this difficulty but suggest that it is part and parcel of the need to maintain both God's sovereignty and genuine human responsibility in the process of salvation. God infallibly saves, but we are fully responsible to respond to his grace in such a way that that infallible salvation does finally transpire.

Whatever we finally make of the theology of this warning, we must come to grips with the seriousness of Paul's warning here. Whether Calvinist or Arminian, we all recognize that our response to God's grace is necessary if we are to be saved. The arrogance and complacency of the Gentile Christians in Rome is all too easy an attitude to fall into—especially for those of us who are Calvinists!

---

23. See Calvin, *The Epistle of Paul to the Romans*, 432−33.
24. See Godet, *Commentary on Romans*, 408.
25. Judith M. Gundry Volf, *Paul and Perseverance: Staying in and Falling Away* (Louisville: Westminster/John Knox, 1990), 198−99.
26. Schreiner, *Romans*, 608−9.

Romans 11:25-32

I DO NOT want you to be ignorant of this mystery, brothers, so that you may not be conceited: Israel has experienced a hardening in part until the full number of the Gentiles has come in. ²⁶And so all Israel will be saved, as it is written:

"The deliverer will come from Zion;
        he will turn godlessness away from Jacob.
²⁷And this is my covenant with them
        when I take away their sins."

²⁸As far as the gospel is concerned, they are enemies on your account; but as far as election is concerned, they are loved on account of the patriarchs, ²⁹for God's gifts and his call are irrevocable. ³⁰Just as you who were at one time disobedient to God have now received mercy as a result of their disobedience, ³¹so they too have now become disobedient in order that they too may now receive mercy as a result of God's mercy to you. ³²For God has bound all men over to disobedience so that he may have mercy on them all.

Original Meaning

IN VERSES 25–32, Paul brings the argument of this section, and indeed of all of chapters 9–11, to its climax. He divulges a "mystery," the heart of which is found in 11:26a: "And so all Israel will be saved." However, while the emphasis on "mystery" may suggest that Paul is saying something entirely new here, this is not really the case. For the salvation of all Israel is simply one of the stages in the sequence familiar to us: Jewish rejection ➔ Gentile inclusion ➔ Jewish inclusion (see comments on 11:11–24).

Now it is this last stage that receives the emphasis. Paul supports his climactic prediction about the salvation of "all Israel" by showing that it is confirmed by Scripture (vv. 26b–27), is rooted in God's promise to Israel (vv. 28–29), and manifests God's impartiality to all people, as the capstone of salvation history (vv. 30–32). All this splendid theology has, however, a down-to-earth purpose: to keep the Gentile Christians from becoming conceited (11:25a).

"All Israel Will Be Saved" (11:25–27)

THOUGH NOT TRANSLATED in the NIV, verse 25 begins with *gar*, "for," which links this new paragraph with verse 24: Paul is hopeful that Israel will be grafted back into the olive tree again, *because* a mystery has been revealed to him. But since verse 24 itself restates a key idea in verses 11–24, verses 25–32 ultimately connect to all of the previous section.

Mystery (Gk. *mysterion*) is a technical term in Paul's vocabulary (see also Rom. 16:25; 1 Cor. 2:1, 7; 4:1; 15:51; Eph. 1:9; 3:3, 4, 9; 6:19; Col. 1:26, 27; 2:2; 4:3; 1 Tim. 3:9, 16). It refers to a truth that has been "hidden" from God's people in the past but has now been disclosed in the gospel.[1] What is the mystery disclosed to Paul here? He unfolds it in three clauses:

Israel has experienced a hardening in part
until the full number of the Gentiles has come in.
And so all Israel will be saved.

Scholars debate about which part of this sequence is the focal point of the mystery. Israel's hardening? The partial and temporary nature of Israel's hardening?[2] The salvation of all Israel?[3] Each of these is part of the picture, of course. But what stands out at the real emphasis in these clauses is the manner, or sequence, in which God consummates his plan to save his people.[4] The Old Testament predicted that Gentiles would join Jews in worshiping the Lord in the last days. But wholly novel was the idea that the bulk of Israel would have to wait to enjoy the blessings of the kingdom until the set number of Gentiles had come in.

Paul has described Israel's "hardening" (*porosis*) earlier (11:7; cf. 9:18). As the existence of a remnant has already implied, this hardening is only "in part"; that is, it affects only part of Israel. But not only is the hardening partial, it is also temporary. It lasts, Paul implies, only "until the full number of Gentiles has come in." The object we must supply for "come in" is clearly the "kingdom" or some such concept (see Matt. 7:13; Luke 13:24; 23:13). "Full number" (*pleroma*), as most commentators recognize, has a numerical reference (see comments on 11:12). In other words, God has determined the number of Gentiles to be saved. Once that number is reached, Israel's hardening comes to an end (see Luke 21:23–24 for a partial parallel).

---

1. See esp. Raymond E. Brown, *The Semitic Background of the Term "Mystery" in the New Testament* (Philadelphia: Fortress, 1968).
2. E.g., Murray, *The Epistle to the Romans*, 2:92–93.
3. E.g., Cranfield, *The Epistle to the Romans*, 573–74.
4. See Beker, *Paul the Apostle*, 333–35.

The first clause of verse 26 is the storm center in the interpretation of Romans 9–11 and of the New Testament teaching about Israel in general. Four exegetical issues need to be decided.

(1) What does the transitional phrase *kai houtos* at the beginning of the verse mean? The NIV translates "and so," suggesting the idea of consequence or conclusion.[5] Others think the word may link up with the Old Testament quotation at the end of the verse: "It is in this way that all Israel will be saved, namely, just as it is written. . . ."[6] Some interpreters and many casual readers of Romans take the phrase as temporal: "and then all Israel will be saved."[7] But the normal nuance of *houtos* is to express manner, and this works well here: "and in this manner all Israel will be saved."[8] Nevertheless, the temporal idea comes sneaking in the back door, for the manner in which all Israel is saved involves a process that unfolds in temporal stages.

(2) What does Paul mean by "all Israel"? The heat of the debate over this verse has resulted in many options, but three stand out as worthy of consideration. (a) An interpretation popular among many of the Reformers and revived by several scholars recently is to take "all Israel" as referring to the entire church. As we have argued, there is precedent in Paul for using "Israel" to refer to the church (Gal. 6:16; see comments on 9:6), and the addition of "all" may suggest that Paul is now speaking not of national Israel or a part of Israel but of "the whole" of spiritual Israel.[9] It is through the removal of the hardening on Israel and the coming in of Gentiles that all the elect of God, the entire Israel, will be saved.

This option is attractive in many ways, but it founders on two points. First, Paul has used "Israel" ten times in Romans 9–11 so far, each one referring to ethnic Israel. There is no hint here of a shift to a religious category. Moreover, Paul's purpose throughout this section is to stifle Gentile pride. For him suddenly to include Gentiles in "Israel" would fuel their pride by encouraging them to assume that they have "replaced" Israel.

(b) Another possibility is that "all Israel" refers to "spiritual" Israel, the elect Jews from within national Israel. Some interpreters who understand the phrase this way argue that Paul is referring to the way that all the elect Jews will come to salvation over the course of salvation history. There is precedent for this meaning of "Israel" in Romans 9–11, since 9:6 speaks of the "Israel within

---

5. E.g., Fitzmyer, *Romans*, 622–23.

6. Peter Stuhlmacher, "Zur Interpretation von Römer 11:25–32," in *Probleme biblischer Theologie: Gerhard von Rad zum 70. Geburtstag*, ed. H. H. Wolff (Munich: Kaiser, 1971), 559–60.

7. Käsemann, *Commentary on Romans*, 313.

8. Most commentators agree; see Moo, *The Epistle to the Romans*, 720.

9. See, e.g., Calvin, *The Epistle of Paul the Apostle to the Romans*, 436; Wright, *Climax of the Covenant*, 249–50.

Israel."[10] But this is not the way Paul has used the word in the immediate context, and it is something of a truism to say that the elect will be saved.

(c) Therefore, in agreement with most commentators, we think "all Israel" refers to the totality of national Israel. This does not mean that every single Jew will be saved. The phrase "all Israel" occurs over a hundred times in the Old Testament, with a range of meanings. But often it refers to some Israelites as a representative whole. Note, for instance, 2 Samuel 16:22: "So they pitched a tent for Absalom on the roof, and he lay with his father's concubines in the sight of all Israel."[11] Furthermore, the phrase almost always refers to Israelites living at a certain point in time rather than to Israelites in every generation of the nation's history.

(3) The third exegetical issue has already been decided by our conclusions about "all Israel." If the reference is to a single generation of Israel, Paul can hardly mean anything but the Israel as it exists in the end times. This conclusion is borne out by 11:15, where, we argued, Paul connects Israel's "acceptance" by God to the resurrection of the dead. The Old Testament quotation that follows in the present passage (11:26b–27) points in the same direction, for "the deliverer" is almost certainly Christ, and his coming refers to his second coming in glory.

We conclude, then, that Paul here predicts the salvation of a significant number of Jews at the time of Christ's return in glory. The present "remnant" of Israel will be expanded to include a much larger number of Jews who will enter the eternal kingdom along with converted Gentiles.

(4) The last exegetical issue is the *means* of Israel's salvation. We need to raise the matter because some recent interpreters have suggested that Paul attributes this future salvation of Israel not to faith in Christ but to fidelity to the Torah. Paul says nothing here about Christ, so they argue. Israel is saved, Paul hints in verse 28, through the covenant God established with Israel. If this is so, then Paul ultimately teaches two ways of salvation: through the "Christ covenant" for Gentiles and through the "Torah covenant" for Jews.[12]

We have mentioned this approach earlier in the commentary (see Contemporary Significance section on 9:1–5) and will say more about it in the

---

10. See, e.g., C. M. Horne, "The Meaning of the Phrase 'And Thus All Israel Will Be Saved,'" *JETS* 21 (1978): 331–34.

11. See also Num. 16:34; Josh. 7:25; 1 Sam. 7:5; 25:1; 1 Kings 12:1; 2 Chron. 12:1; Dan. 9:11. Also frequently cited in this regard is the rabbinic text, *m. Sanh.* 10:1, which first affirms, "All Israelites have a share in the world to come," and then gives list of exceptions.

12. Important proponents of this view are Krister Stendahl, "Paul Among Jews and Gentiles," in *Paul Among Jews and Gentiles and Other Essays* (Philadelphia: Fortress, 1976); Gager, *Origins of Anti-Semitism*, 261–62; P. Lapide (with Peter Stuhlmacher), *Paul, Rabbi and Apostle* (Minneapolis: Augsburg, 1984), 47–54.

Contemporary Significance section that follows. Here we note that Paul gives no indication whatsoever that he has revoked the understanding of salvation clearly enunciated in 10:13: "Everyone [in the context both Jew and Gentile] who calls on the name of the Lord will be saved."

Paul backs up his prediction of a significant turning to Christ for salvation among Jews in the last day by citing Isaiah 59:20–21 along with a phrase from Isaiah 27:9 (Rom. 11:26b–27). As we already suggested, Paul most likely identifies "the deliverer" in this text with Christ (see the parallel in 1 Thess. 1:10). When Christ comes back, he will "turn godlessness away from Jacob" and confirm his covenantal promises to Israel by taking away their sins.

For those who have checked Paul's quotation against the original text of Isaiah (as I hope my pleas earlier in this commentary have encouraged many to do!), one striking difference is immediately apparent. Isaiah predicts that the deliverer will come "to" Zion, while Paul quotes the text as saying that the deliverer will come "from" Zion. Numerous explanations for Paul's change of wording have surfaced over the years, but none is really convincing. Perhaps best is the suggestion that Paul alludes to the tradition of the risen Christ resident in "heavenly Zion" (see Heb. 12:22). His change therefore draws attention to the Parousia of Christ.[13]

The Wrap-Up (11:28–32)

IN VERSES 28–32, Paul both provides further evidence for his claim that "all Israel will be saved" (11:26a) and wraps up chapters 9–11 by reminding us once more of some of the basic points of his argument. Verse 28 reiterates the key tension that has driven the entire discussion: "As far as the gospel is concerned, they are enemies on your account; but as far as election is concerned, they are loved on account of the patriarchs." "They," as the context makes clear, are Israelites generally. As Paul makes clear in the opening verses of chapter 9, Israel's failure to respond to the gospel has cut her off from God's salvation. From this standpoint, therefore, they are "enemies" of God. The enmity referred to may be from Israel toward God[14] or from God toward Israel.[15] It is best to take it both ways: hostility exists between God and his people Israel because of their refusal to submit to God's righteousness in Christ (see 10:3).[16]

---

13. See Bruce W. Longenecker, "Different Answers to Different Issues: Israel, the Gentiles and Salvation History in Romans 9–11," *JSNT* 36 (1989): 117; Stuhlmacher, "Interpretation," 561.

14. E.g., Dunn, *Romans*, 685.

15. E.g., Godet, *Commentary on Romans*, 412; Murray, *The Epistle to the Romans*, 2:100.

16. Käsemann, *Commentary on Romans*, 315.

Nevertheless, as Paul has hinted in 9:4–5 by listing the blessings God bestowed on Israel, the refusal of Israel to believe does not mean God has relegated Israel to the rubbish heap of history. How could he do so, since he has elected Israel (cf. 11:2), and "God's gifts and his call are irrevocable" (v. 29)? Not then for their own sake, but because of God's pledged word to the patriarchs, he will not annul Israel's election. In chapter 11, Paul has explained the significance of that continuing election: God is now saving some Jews (the remnant, vv. 1–10), and he will save a significant number of Jews at the time of Christ's return (vv. 11–27, esp. v. 26).

Paul explains just how God will manifest his grace to Israel in verses 30–31. One last time we hear again the salvation-historical sequence that dominates the latter part of chapter 11. Paul is especially concerned to emphasize the "equal treatment" that both Israel and the Gentiles receive. Note the formal parallelism:

verse 30	*verse 31*
Just as	so . . . too
you	they
at one time	now
were . . . disobedient to God	have . . . become disobedient
now	now
have . . . received mercy	in order that they too may . . . receive mercy
as a result of their disobedience	as a result of God's mercy to you

As in verse 28, the "they" of verse 31 refers to Israelites, while, in keeping with Paul's focus throughout this paragraph, "you" denotes Gentile Christians. Verse 30 is clear enough as a summary of the sequence we have seen so often in the chapter: Jewish disobedience has resulted in the Gentiles receiving God's mercy. Verse 31, then, describes the third step in the process, Jewish inclusion.

But two points in verse 31 are not so clear. (1) Why does Paul say that the Jews have "now" received mercy? Has he not just predicted that God's bestowal of mercy on Israel will come at the time of the Parousia? Some early scribes took care of the difficulty by omitting the "now" (cf. NIV note), but the word should probably be included as the "more difficult reading."[17] The best explanation is that Paul wants to emphasize the imminence of Israel's salvation. As the next item on the agenda of God's plan, the return of Christ and conversion of Israel can take place at any time.

(2) The other problem is the phrase translated in NIV "as a result of God's mercy to you." The NIV takes this phrase to express the cause of God's mercy

---

17. See the discussion in, e.g., Cranfield, *The Epistle to the Romans*, 585.

to the Jews. This translation is one possible rendering of the Greek and makes good sense, expressing Paul's teaching that the extension of God's grace to the Gentiles makes Israel "envious" and spurs their final salvation (see vv. 11, 14).[18] But the phrase in the Greek text comes immediately after the verb "have become disobedient" earlier in the verse. Moreover, the form of the phrase (a dative) may express the idea of "advantage" rather than cause.

Another way of rendering verse 31, therefore, is "so they too have now become disobedient for the sake of God's mercy to you in order that they too may now receive mercy." This way of putting the matter also fits well with what Paul teaches earlier in the chapter about God's using Israel's hardening to bring salvation to the Gentiles. Since it follows the more natural word order of the Greek, it should probably be adopted.[19]

Paul's concern to put Jew and Gentile on equal footing is reinforced by the solemn conclusion in verse 32: "God has bound all men over to disobedience so that he may have mercy on them all." God's act of "enclosing" people (Paul includes women and men) reminds us of his handing people over to the consequences of the sin they have chosen (1:24, 26, 28). God has sentenced all people to condemnation. But his purpose is ultimately a positive one: He wants to "have mercy on all." Interpreters of this verse err when they wrest it from its context and use it to prove universalism, that all people will eventually be saved. The Greek allows and the context strongly suggests that Paul has a different purpose: to show that God has both "shut up under sin" and shown mercy to all "kinds" of people[20]—especially, in this context, Jews and Gentiles.

 THE DELIVERER FROM ZION. Paul's use of the Old Testament to buttress his interpretation of salvation history is a matter of controversy again in this text. He quotes selectively from two different passages in Isaiah and makes a significant change to one of them. We should be particularly interested in such differences between the Old Testament text and the form in which it is quoted in the New. These differences can sometimes furnish an important clue to the New Testament author's exact purpose. A side-by-side comparison will give us a good basis to analyze the situation and see what we can learn from it:

---

18. It is supported by most commentators; see again esp. ibid., 583—85.

19. See also Käsemann, *Commentary on Romans*, 316; Dunn, *Romans*, 688.

20. See, e.g., Sanday and Headlam, *The Epistle to the Romans*, 338—39; Murray, *The Epistle to the Romans*, 2:102—3.

Isaiah 59:20–21

"The Redeemer will come to Zion,
to those in Jacob who repent of
their sins," declares the LORD.

"As for me, this is my covenant with
them," says the LORD. "My Spirit,
who is on you, and my words that
I have put in your mouth will not
depart from your mouth, or from the
mouths of your children, or from
the mouths of their descendants
from this time on and forever,"
says the LORD.

Isaiah 27:9

By this, then, will Jacob's guilt be
atoned for, and this will be the
full fruitage of the removal of his sin
[LXX: when I take away his sin]:
When he makes all the altar stones
to be like chalk stones crushed to
pieces, no Asherah poles or incense
altars will be left standing.

Romans 11:26b–27

The deliverer will come from Zion;
he will turn godlessness away
from Jacob.

And this is my covenant with them

when I take away their sins.

We first note that Paul here, as he usually does, is probably dependent on the LXX for his wording. This is particularly clear in the reference to Isaiah 27:9, since Paul's wording is almost identical to the LXX, which in turn differs from the Hebrew text. Paul's only change is the substitution of "their" for "his" in order to match the third person plural "them" in the previous line. The reader of the English text will often not be aware of these textual issues in the background. But many of the differences between the wording of the Old Testament text and its citation in the New Testament can be accounted for by these different text forms.

But by no means are all the differences a matter of text. Paul and the other New Testament authors also adapt the wording of the text to suit their application. Most of these changes are minor and do not affect the sense in any significant way. A good example is the change just noted of the third person singular "his" of Isaiah 27:9 to the third person plural "their." But other changes carry more significance. Note, for instance, that in the second line of the quotation Paul changes the focus from Israel's repentance to God's forgiveness. This change obviously suits his emphasis on God's sovereignty in bringing salvation history to its climax.

But the most striking change, as noted in the Original Meaning section, is the "from Zion" wording in Paul. The Hebrew text here uses the preposition *le*, probably in a local sense: "The deliverer will come *to* Zion." The LXX translates with *heneken*, "on behalf of." But neither of these readings explains how Paul can quote the text as saying that the deliverer will come "from" (*ek*) Zion.

Some scholars speculate that Paul may be quoting from a Greek text we no longer have.[21] This is always possible, since we know there were texts of the Old Testament in the first century that have not survived to our day. Another possibility is that Paul has assimilated the wording of this text to others in the Old Testament that claim Israel's deliverance will come "from Zion" (e.g., Ps. 14:7; 53:6; 110:2; Isa. 2:3).[22] Since Paul has already stitched together language from two different places in Isaiah, we must consider this a real possibility.

But the question still remains: Why has Paul introduced language from these other texts into Isaiah 59:20? Scholars speculate that he may have wanted to emphasize to conceited Gentile Christians (see Rom. 11:25) that the Redeemer will come from the Jewish people (see 9:5).[23] Or perhaps he is claiming that the final salvation of Israel will come by means of the return of Christ from heaven at his Parousia.[24] This latter interpretation makes the best sense. The New Testament suggests that "Zion" can refer to the "heavenly Jerusalem" (Heb. 12:22; note also "the Jerusalem that is above" in Gal. 4:26). Paul does not deny what Isaiah predicts: The deliverer is indeed coming "to" Zion, that is, to the Jewish people. But he wants to expand the idea by emphasizing that Israel's final redemption comes from heaven, not from earth.

Such an emphasis was needed because so many Jews in Paul's day were looking to political movements or military force as the means of their deliverance from Gentile oppression. The kingdom of God would be established, they thought, through violence (see Matt. 11:12). But Paul, in light of God's revelation of the "mystery" of salvation history in Christ, now understands that Israel's redemption will come through the intervention of Christ himself when he returns in glory. If this is correct, Paul adds the phrase "from Zion" in order to stress that it is God's intervention from heaven at the end of history that brings final salvation to his people Israel.

---

21. See esp. B. Schaller, ΗΞΕΙ ΕΚ ΣΙΩΝ Ο ΡΥΟΜΕΝΟΣ: Zur Textgestalt von Jes. 59:20f. in Röm 11:26f.," in *De Septuaginta: Studies in Honour of John William Wevers on his Sixty-Fifth Birthday*, ed. A. Pietersma and C. Cox (Toronto: Benben, 1984), 201–6.

22. See, e.g., Cranfield, *The Epistle to the Romans*, 577–78.

23. E.g., Murray, *The Epistle to the Romans*, 2:99; Fitzmyer, *Romans*, 624–25.

24. See, e.g., Käsemann, *Commentary on Romans*, 314; Dunn, *Romans*, 682.

ISRAEL AND ESCHATOLOGY. What does the Bible teach about the future of Israel? How should that teaching affect our view of the present-day nation of Israel? Our text obviously has something to say about these matters. It is precisely for this reason that there has been so much debate about the passage. Evangelical Christians are divided over eschatology, and the future of Israel is one of the key sticking points.

The Reformed tradition in theology, with its roots in the teaching of Calvin, Zwingli, and Bucer, has generally emphasized the idea of a single covenant in Scripture, spanning Old and New Testaments. There has always been only one way of salvation (faith in God) and one people of God. That means that Old Testament prophecies about "Israel" must find their fulfillment in the church, for the church is the name of the people of God in the New Testament era. That in turn means that there is little or no room for any real future for Israel as a nation or ethnic group. All people are now on the same footing; Jews as well as Gentiles can be saved, and on the same basis. Any national privileges for Israel have been revoked.

Contemporary theologians who work within this tradition usually interpret Romans 11:11–32 in terms of a continuing historical process. God hardens part of Israel so that Gentiles stream into the kingdom; and the Gentiles stimulate Jews to envy, causing some of them to embrace Christ. This process continues right up until the last day, whereupon "all Israel [has been] saved"— that is, all the Jews elect by God will have been brought to salvation. Christ will then return and the era of salvation will be ended. No special future for Israel is envisaged.

Challenging this reading of Israel in the Bible were, interestingly, a number of Puritan thinkers, who insisted that there would be a future for national Israel. But particularly well known for advocating a future for Israel is dispensationalism. This movement arose in the nineteenth century and became popular in evangelical circles through the *Scofield Reference Bible*, prophecy conferences, and the influence of Dallas Theological Seminary. A hallmark of dispensationalism (some would say *the* hallmark) is a distinction between Israel and the church. The people of God in this era form the church, and, of course, Jews can join, becoming part of the church. But the church has not replaced Israel in God's plan. He still has a distinctive future for Israel as an ethnic group. The Old Testament prophecies about Israel must be fulfilled in Israel, and Romans 11 teaches that God has a plan for Israel in distinction from the church.

The theological climate of the last few decades has made for some strange bedfellows. The emphasis on a future for the nation of Israel, a view that might be considered typical of conservative evangelicals, is now embraced by a wide spectrum of liberal theologians as well. The horror of the Holocaust has awakened many Christian thinkers to what they consider "anti-Semitic" thinking in the church; as a reaction, a concerted effort is being made to grant Israel a continuing role in God's salvation plan. Quite apart from these influences, it is fair to say that the vast majority of interpreters of Romans, from every conceivable theological perspective, now agree that Paul predicts a future salvation of Israel in chapter 11. Exactly how and when it will happen and what other events this salvation may entail continue to be debated. But let me sketch the situation as I see it and draw some conclusions.

My colleague Paul Feinberg claims that I am a dispensationalist because I maintain a future for ethnic Israel. I am flattered that he wants to include me, but I am not so sure I deserve the honor. For while I believe that Romans 11 does teach that a significant number of Jews will come to salvation in the last day, I do not draw the inferences that many dispensationalists do. I think the conversion of these Jews will take place as they believe the gospel, not through some kind of "special way," or *Sonderweg* (as German theologians call it). I think that those Jews who are converted will, like any other believers, become integrated into the church—although perhaps a church on its way to heaven, if the conversion happens at the time of Jesus' Parousia.

Nor do I think that Romans 11 entails any kind of geographic or political future for Israel. What Paul predicts in this chapter is a spiritual revivification of the Jewish people. He says nothing here, or anywhere else in his teaching, about the return of Israel to Palestine or about its political reconstitution. Any belief that God has promised Israel a political presence in the end times must come from other passages in Scripture. The key will be our hermeneutics of Old Testament prophetic interpretation: Can those prophecies be fulfilled "spiritually" in the church, or must they find a literal fulfillment in a reconstituted Israelite nation?

However we answer this specific question, we can draw a couple of practical conclusions from the theology of Israel in Romans 11. As we have already made clear, Paul's overriding concern is to stifle undue Gentile pride. In our day, as in Paul's, the church is largely a Gentile institution. Our natural tendency to prefer people like us and to think ourselves superior to people different from us is exacerbated by a "replacement" theology that often teaches that Gentiles have now taken the place of Jews in God's plan (see Contemporary Significance section of 11:11–24). A deprecatory and even hostile attitude toward Jewish Christians and Jews alike is the result.

Anti-Semitism is a powerful force in society. As I write this section, I am horrified by the news that a white supremacist walked into a Jewish daycare center and shot both adults and children. There is no room for any such hostility in the church, where Jew and Gentile have been reconciled together in Christ. We must welcome Jewish Christians into our worship and, indeed, honor them as representatives of that "root" from which we all are spiritually nourished (11:17−18). But a respect for Jewish people does not entail undue deference to Israel as a nation.

I taught for some years with a colleague who was Arab in background. He could never understand why American evangelicals consistently took the side of Israel in every Middle East dispute. The Arab side was never considered; Israel, whatever it did, was always in the right. Even if we believe that God has promised to give Israel their land again and make them a nation, we have no right to accord Israel such blind allegiance. For one thing, we have no way of knowing if the present Israel is the Israel in which God will fulfill his promises. More important, God calls us to love all people and to treat all people with respect. We have no right to overlook injustice when it occurs, whether in Israel or anywhere else. Moreover, we certainly have no right to ignore the legitimate rights and aspirations of the Arab people.

A "special way" for Israel and universalism. Our text brings together two tenets that we have already touched on in this commentary: salvation for Israel apart from Christ, and the belief that all people will be saved. Both, as we have noted, are views amenable to our culture. The Holocaust has created an environment in which people are sensitive to any hint of anti-Semitism. Many think it is anti-Semitic to insist that Christ is the only means of salvation. In addition, our pluralistic culture tends to break down the distinctions between the world's religions, fostering the idea that any religion can be a means of salvation. What does Romans 11:25−32 say to these issues?

Some interpreters insist that 11:26 stands as a watershed in New Testament soteriology. Other authors (Matthew, John) and even the early Paul (see 1 Thess. 2:16) take a hostile view toward Israel. But now, through the revelation of a mystery, Paul comes to understand that Israel will be saved—apart from Christ. Israel has a "special way" (German *Sonderweg*) to salvation, based on God's unbreakable covenant with Israel as a people. As we argued above, this view cannot be supported in the text. Paul has spent most of Romans describing his gospel, through which salvation is offered to both Jew and Gentile (e.g., 1:16; 10:10−13). But the heart of that gospel is Christ (1:3−4), and especially his death on the cross for all human beings (3:21−26). No one can be saved apart from the good news and apart from faith in Christ.[25]

---

25. For criticism of the *Sonderweg* interpretation, see esp. R. Hvalvik, "A 'Sonderweg' for Israel: A Critical Examination of a Current Interpretation of Romans 11:25−27," *JSNT* 38 (1990): 87−107.

Indeed, as a number of interpreters have pointed out, the *Sonderweg* approach is itself anti-Semitic. It effectively denies that the good news needs to be preached to Jews. Jews are then singled out from among all people as the only ones not given the opportunity to hear and respond to the offer of salvation in Christ.[26] Moreover, as N. T. Wright points out, the *Sonderweg* view is but an ultimately unstable "halfway house" on the road to full-blown religious pluralism.[27] For once we accord Jews a special position, it will be difficult to refrain from treating Moslems, Buddhists, Hindus, and so forth in the same way. Many today, it is true, have no problem with such pluralism. Indeed, they think Paul teaches it in verse 32—that the scope of God's mercy is as wide as the scope of sin. As God has shut all up under sin, so he has mercy on all as well.

Universalism has a long history in the church. The third-century theologian Origen taught it, and it has been sporadically advocated ever since. But the pluralism of our day has given it new momentum, and many people in our churches harbor such views. Some are forthright, raising objections to the idea that sincere adherents of other religions cannot be saved. They are sympathetic to the line of thinking represented in the last of C. S. Lewis's Narnia books, *The Last Battle*, in which a sincere worshiper of the god "Tash" is saved because his conduct showed he must have been unconsciously worshiping the true God, Aslan, all along. This idea of the "unconscious" believer is becoming popular in both Roman Catholic and Protestant circles.

But even Christians who reject this line of thinking as unbiblical—as we must—can fall prey to insidious universalism. What happens is that the tolerance preached everywhere in our culture subtly breaks down our conviction about the exclusivity of the gospel. We don't *say* that our neighbor or work associate can be saved because he or she is a sincere Jew or Moslem. But there is part of us that is, indeed, thinking this way. Thus, we do not have the passion to share the gospel that we should have. Implicit universalism, I think, is one of great challenges that Christians will face in the next years. The only solution is to commit ourselves to a program of indoctrination— to let our minds be so formed by the biblical worldview that we are protected from the inroads of the culture into our thinking.

---

26. See Richard H. Bell, *Provoked to Jealousy: The Origin and Purpose of the Jealousy Motif in Romans 9–11* (Tübingen: J. C. B. Mohr, 1994), 354–55.

27. *Climax of the Covenant*, 254.

Romans 11:33–36

³³ OH, THE DEPTH of the riches of the wisdom and
knowledge of God!
How unsearchable his judgments,
and his paths beyond tracing out!
³⁴ "Who has known the mind of the Lord?
Or who has been his counselor?"
³⁵ "Who has ever given to God,
that God should repay him?"
³⁶ For from him and through him and to him are all things.
To him be the glory forever! Amen.

Original Meaning

EVERY GOOD SERMON has a conclusion that should stimulate its hearers to respond to the message. In 8:31–39 Paul concludes his "sermon" on Christian assurance in chapters 5–8 by calling on his readers to exult in their security in Christ. Now in 11:33–36 he caps off his survey of salvation history by leading his readers in an expression of awe at God's extraordinary plan for the world. As in 8:31–39, the apostle uses questions to encourage us to identify with him in this outburst of amazement.

The praise to God Paul offers here falls into three strophes. In verse 33, we find three exclamations about God's wise plan. In verses 34–35, the apostle uses three rhetorical questions to remind us how far above are the thoughts and ways of God. Finally, verse 36 reminds us that God is ultimate in all things and that he is therefore deserving of our praise.

The particle "Oh" (Gk. ō) shows that the first sentence of verse 33 is an exclamation—a reaction triggered by what Paul has been saying of God's purposes in the preceding verses. The exact wording of the exclamation is not certain. According to the NIV translation, "riches" governs both "wisdom" and "knowledge."[1] But "riches" (ploutos) can also stand on its own as a third attribute of God alongside his wisdom and knowledge (see, e.g., the NRSV: "O the depth of the riches and wisdom and knowledge of God!"[2]). If we take this latter interpretation, "riches" refers to the infinite kindness of God displayed in his plan of salvation (see v. 12). This plan also displays God's "wisdom" and his

---

1. E.g., Fitzmyer, *Romans*, 634.

2. E.g., Cranfield, *The Epistle to the Romans*, 589. While Paul normally adds a genitive modifier to *ploutos* (e.g., in 2:4; 9:23), he twice uses the word absolutely in 11:12.

"knowledge"—the latter word referring perhaps to God's relational "knowing" expressed in his election (see comments on "foreknow" in 11:2).

Paul displays rhetorical care in his wording of the second two exclamations in verse 33 (the NIV merges them into one for English stylistic reasons). They have the same syntactical structure, and each begins with a similar-sounding adjective: *anexerauneta* ("unsearchable") and *anexichniastoi* ("beyond tracing out"). "Judgments" does not refer to God's judicial decisions but to his "executive" decisions for the direction of salvation history (see Ps. 19:9; 36:6; 119:75).

The three questions in verses 34–35 are taken from the Old Testament, the first two from Isaiah 40:13 and the third from (probably) Job 41:3. The questions may correspond, in reverse (chiastic) order, to the three attributes in verse 33:

"Who has known the mind of the Lord?"—knowledge
"Who has been his counselor?"—wisdom
"Who has ever given to God, that God should repay him?"—riches

These questions are obviously rhetorical and expect the answer "no one." But the wisdom tradition Paul reflects taught that wisdom was able to do what no person was able to do: understand and interpret the mind of God. As the embodiment of wisdom, then, Christ, through his work of salvation, reveals God's plan to us. If the first two questions remind us how far we are from fully understanding God, the final question reminds us of God's grace, a great theme of these chapters. What God does in his plan of salvation he does not do because anyone has earned his favor or deserves his kindness, but solely out of his own great love for us.

The affirmation of God's ultimacy in creation (v. 36a) may respond directly to verse 35—no one can demand anything from God, for he is supreme in creation—but probably reflects all of verses 33–35. The concept of God as source (*ek*), sustainer (*dia*), and goal (*eis*) of all things may reflect Greek Stoic philosophy (see Bridging Contexts). Whatever its origins, the saying expresses well the biblical teaching of God's "ultimacy": that he is far more important than his creation and must be therefore given the honor and glory due him. Paul therefore appropriately responds by ascribing glory to this wondrous and all-consuming God.

STOICISM. We have repeatedly focused on the way the Old Testament and Jewish traditions illumine Paul's teaching in Romans—and rightly so. Paul's own roots are sunk deeply in the soil of Judaism, his understanding of the gospel is worked out in conjunction with the Old Testament, and his topic in Romans requires extensive interaction with these backgrounds. But Paul was also well acquainted with the religious, philosophical, and cultural currents of the Greco-Roman world in which he lived. Though raised in a strict Jewish household (see Phil. 3:5) and taught in a rabbinical school (Acts 22:3), he also grew up in the cosmopolitan city of Tarsus. His letters reveal a man well-read in the wider culture of his time. God therefore prepared Paul for just the kind of ministry to which he called him: apostle to the Gentiles.

This means also that Paul feels free to borrow from the Greco-Roman culture whatever he thinks will help to communicate the truth of the gospel. One of the most influential philosophical movements of his day was Stoicism. Stoicism had its origins in third-century B.C. Athens, where Zeno taught in the *stoa* (the porch) in the *agora* (marketplace). Rooted in a pantheistic worldview, Stoicism in the first century was preoccupied almost exclusively with ethics. It sought to answer the question, "How can the wise man live in accordance with nature?"[3] Partly for that reason, it became popular with the Romans.

The saying we find in verse 36a sounds much like typical Stoic pronouncements about God. The second-century A.D. Stoic philosopher (and Roman emperor) Marcus Aurelius, for instance, said of God, "From you are all things, in you are all things, for you are all things" (*Meditations* 4.23). Thus, we might be tempted to conclude that Paul applies a Stoic teaching here to God, and we should not be upset if he does so. Paul obviously does not intend to bring over the entire Stoic worldview. He simply thinks that, at this point, the Stoics have said something about God that is true, understood within the biblical worldview.

But Paul may not be quoting a Stoic saying directly. Jews before Paul had taken over some of these same Stoic ideas about God (see, e.g., Philo, *Special Laws* 1.208; see also 1 Cor. 8:6). So Paul's relationship to Stoic teaching may be indirect, mediated by his Jewish background. In any case, we can appreciate this assertion about God as an example of contextualizing the gospel. Paul borrows language that his first-century readers would be familiar with in order to help them understand the absolute supremacy of God.

THEOLOGICAL HUMILITY. To my mortification and my family's delight, I received in the mail just this week an invitation to join the American Association of Retired Persons (AARP). I have reached a point of life in which I find myself prefacing many things I say with "at my

---

3. T. Paige, "Philosophy," in *Dictionary of Paul and His Letters*, ed. Gerald F. Hawthorne and Ralph P. Martin (Downers Grove, Ill.: InterVarsity, 1993), 715.

age." Undoubtedly, as my children insist, some of the sentences that follow reflect hardening of the arteries or irrational fear of anything new. But a few of these statements, I trust, reflect some wisdom that the perspective of age has inculcated.

One of the most common sentiments I express these days is a greater humility about certain theological positions I hold. Like many young people, I felt confident of my positions in the first years of my career. I sometimes propagated views orally or in print that I had not thought through as thoroughly as I should have. While I have not changed many of these views, I am much more inclined now to notice evidence that might not fit my view. Therefore, I feel much more keenly the need to nuance what I teach by calling attention to this evidence and by admitting that my own view may not be correct. Increasing age should certainly not turn us into theological milquetoasts—uncertain about what we believe and swayed by the latest wind of doctrine. And I am as passionately committed to the essence of the Christian faith as I have ever been. But I would describe my current approach in theological study and teaching as "humble."

What does all this have to do with Romans 11:33–36? Just this: Paul's reminder that God's thoughts are far beyond anything we could ever approximate and his plan more intricate and marvelous than we could even imagine certainly calls on each of us to exercise great humility in seeking to understand God and his Word. On this side of glory, all our theologizing is uncertain and tentative. Humility, willingness to listen, and respect for others are the appropriate attitudes for us finite creatures as we seek to plumb the depths of God's character and truth.

To be sure, God has graciously given us in his Word a revelation of himself and his plan that everyone can understand. The essence of what that Word says is clear and undebatable. But the details are not always as clear as our theological traditions or denominational loyalties suggest. People holding views with more tenacity than Scripture justifies have done untold damage to the church and to the cause of Christ in the world. So even as we praise God for his amazing and gracious plan of redemption, we must also bow our knees in humility before him and keep a good perspective on our own limitations in understanding the specifics of that plan.

Romans 12:1–2

THEREFORE, I URGE YOU, brothers, in view of God's mercy, to offer your bodies as living sacrifices, holy and pleasing to God—this is your spiritual act of worship. ²Do not conform any longer to the pattern of this world, but be transformed by the renewing of your mind. Then you will be able to test and approve what God's will is—his good, pleasing and perfect will.

ROMANS HAS THE REPUTATION—well deserved—of being one of the most theological books in the Bible. Unfortunately, this reputation has led many Christians and even some commentators to wonder why Paul bothers with all the practical stuff at the end of the letter. He has finished the theology section at the end of chapter 11. Why say any more?

Such an attitude betrays a basic misunderstanding of theology and its significance. All theology is practical, and all practice, if it is truly Christian, is theological. Paul's gospel is deeply theological, but it is also eminently practical. The good news of Jesus Christ is intended to transform a person's life. Until individual Christians own and live out the theology, the gospel has not accomplished its purpose.

Paul has briefly touched on the practical significance of what he writes throughout Romans 1–11 (see, e.g., 6:11–13, 19; 11:18, 20). But beginning in chapter 12 Paul turns his full attention to the ethical implications of the gospel. The "therefore" at the beginning of the chapter gathers up all the teaching of chapters 1–11 and confronts us with the all-important question: "So what?" Granted the manifold mercy of God as set it forth in the letter, what are we to do? Paul answers that question in 12:1–15:13 by touching on several key areas where Christians need to display the reality of God in a new way of living. This larger section divides into two smaller ones, with 12:1–13:14 going over several general areas of Christian obedience and 14:1–15:13 concentrating on the dispute between the "strong" and the "weak."

Why does Paul include the subjects he does in these chapters? Some interpreters think he is writing quite generally, providing a brief summary of the key areas of Christian obedience. The many parallels between Romans 12:1–15:13 and the ethical sections of Paul's other letters might suggest there is something to this idea.[1] But Paul's rebuke of the strong and the weak in 14:1–15:13 is almost certainly directed to a real dispute in the Roman community. Moreover, as we will see, several of the topics Paul takes up in 12:1–13:14 have particular relevance to Rome. Therefore we should probably take a mediating view on Paul's purpose in these chapters. He wants to give a general outline of what commitment to the gospel looks like in real life, but he fashions that outline in such a way that it relates especially well to the problems facing the Christian community in Rome.

Romans 12:1–2 is one of the best-known passages in the Bible—and deservedly so, for we find here a succinct description of the essence of the believer's response to God's grace in the gospel of Jesus Christ. It functions as the heading for all the specifics Paul will unpack in the subsequent chapters. Our response is rooted in God's grace. The NIV's "God's mercy" conceals the fact that the Greek word for "mercy" is in the plural ("mercies"). Paul is reminding us of the many displays of God's mercy he has touched on in chapters 1–11. "In view of" probably modifies "urge"; Paul exhorts us in light of the manifold mercy of God. Our obedience is the product of what God has done in our lives, not something we can manufacture on our own.

The command to "offer" ourselves to God reminds us of Romans 6, where Paul used this same verb (*paristemi*) to express the basic response of believers to God's grace to us in Christ (see 6:13, 16, 19). Indeed, all of Romans 12:1–15:13 is an explication of this basic demand in chapter 6. As new covenant Christians, we no longer offer animal sacrifices; we now offer ourselves as "living sacrifices." "Living" perhaps has a theological meaning: We offer ourselves as people who have been brought from death to life (see 6:13).[2] This may, however, be reading more into the word than we should. Paul probably wants us simply to contrast ourselves with the dead animal sacrifices of the Old Testament (see also John 6:51).[3] But God demands sacrifices that are "holy," that is, apart from profane matters and dedicated to his service.

This offering of ourselves to God constitutes, Paul concludes, our "spiritual act of worship." "Spiritual" translates a word (*logikos*) over which there is much debate, as the varied renderings in English translations suggest: "spiritual" (NIV; NRSV; NASB); "reasonable" (KJV); "true" (TEV); "offered by mind and heart" (REB); "intelligent" (Phillips).[4] But when the background is considered

---

1. For this view, see esp. Robert J. Karris, "Romans 14:1–15:13 and the Occasion of Romans," in *The Romans Debate*, 81–84.

2. See, e.g., Murray, *The Epistle to the Romans*, 2:111; Cranfield, *The Epistle to the Romans*, 600.

3. E.g., Dunn, *Romans*, 710.

4. The only other New Testament occurrence is in 1 Peter 2:2, where its meaning is also debated.

(see Bridging Contexts), we think "informed" or "understanding" is the best single equivalent in English. We give ourselves to God as his sacrifices when we understand his grace and its place in our lives. We offer ourselves not ignorantly, like animals brought to slaughter, but intelligently and willingly. This is the worship that pleases God.[5]

Verse 2 tells us how we can carry out the sweeping demand to give ourselves as sacrifices to the Lord. Building on his "two-era" concept of salvation history (see Bridging Contexts), Paul demands that we "not conform" to "this age" (lit. trans.). The NIV's rendition as "the pattern of this world" captures the general sense well enough. The old age to which we belonged in our pre-Christian past still exerts influence on us, enticing us to follow its "pattern" of sinful and ungodly behavior. Rather than "conforming" our conduct to that age, we must be "transformed" in our behavior. The neat contrast of these two words in English is not found in the Greek, which uses two different verb roots (*syschematizo* and *metamorphoo*). But the English rendering is true to the sense of the Greek and certainly makes the verse easy to remember.

The means by which we accomplish this transformation in conduct is the "renewing of your mind" (for a close parallel see Eph. 4:23; cf. also 2 Cor. 4:16; Col. 3:10; Titus 3:5). A new orientation in our thinking leads to a new orientation in behavior. Here Paul touches on the heart of New Testament ethics (see Contemporary Significance section), for the result of this transformation is that we will be able to please God by doing his will.

AN INFORMED SACRIFICE. With pardonable exaggeration, some scholars claim that, in the ancient world, religion was sacrifice. In the modern world, especially in the West, we tend to think of religion in terms of a system of belief or a way of living. But ancient people were obsessed with sacrifice. The killing and offering of animals (and even occasionally humans) to their gods was the focal point of their worship. Thus, when Paul uses the metaphor of sacrifice in Romans 12:1, he is picking up an idea that all his readers understood, not only from the Old Testament but from their everyday lives as well.

The popularity of sacrifice in ancient religion, however, could lead to abuses. People could think that all they had to do to please their god was to offer the sacrifice, without regard to their own attitude or sincerity in doing

---

5. See esp. David Peterson, *Engaging with God: A Biblical Theology of Worship* (Grand Rapids: Eerdmans, 1992), 173–76.

so. The Old Testament prophets, of course, railed at the people of Israel for just this offense, insisting that God would only honor sacrifices that came from a pure heart (e.g., Hos. 6:6; Mic. 1:6–14). Both Jewish and pagan authors in Paul's day also warned about the same kind of attitude.

These warnings probably lie behind Paul's use of the word *logikos* to describe worship pleasing to God in verse 1. Arguing that God and human beings have *logos* ("reason") in common, some Stoic philosophers insisted that only *logikos* worship is truly acceptable to God. They contrasted this "rational" worship with what they considered to be the rank superstition of so many people. This general tendency is captured well in the comment of Epictetus: "If I were a nightingale, I should be singing as a nightingale; if a swan, as a swan. But as it is, I am a rational being [*logikos*]; therefore I must be singing hymns of praise to God" (*Dis.* 1.16.20–21).

The Jewish philosopher Philo made a similar point, arguing that "that which is precious in the sight of God is not the number of victims immolated but the true purity of a rational spirit [*pneuma logikon*] in him who makes the sacrifice" (*Special Laws* 1.277; see also 1.272; cf. *T. Levi* 3:6). Paul, then, is making a similar point. Worship that pleases God is "informed"; that is, it is offered by the Christian who understands who God is, what he has given us in the gospel, and what he demands from us.

The theological framework for 12:2. Earlier in the commentary, we sketched the salvation-historical "two-age" structure that informs so much of Paul's teaching in Romans (see Bridging Contexts section on 6:15–23). A modification of the worldview prevalent in Jewish apocalyptic theology, Paul's scheme divides all of history into two eras, the one "before Christ" and the one "after Christ." The "B.C." world is dominated by sin and death, set loose in the world through Adam; the "A.C." (or, to Latinize, "A.D.") world is dominated by righteousness and life, secured by Christ.

When a person comes to Christ, that person is "transferred" into the new age or new realm. He or she is no longer under sin's dominion (see ch. 6). Yet sin still affects the believer. Although we belong to the new era introduced by Christ, the old era is still with us. We still live in a world strongly influenced by sin and ungodly ways of thinking and behaving. We are not magically set apart from that world when we believe. Indeed, God wants us to stay in that world so that, as "salt and light," we may redeem it for him.

It is this grand salvation-historical scheme that informs Paul's passing reference to "this world [age]" in verse 2. Though ever-present, pressing in on us from every side, that age must not "press us into its mold" (to adapt J. B. Phillips' famous paraphrase). Remembering that we belong to the new age Christ inaugurated, we must seek to live out the values of that new age, allowing the Spirit to transform our innermost thoughts and attitudes.

"INFORMED" WORSHIP. The contemporary church is in a ferment over worship. Musical styles have been the lightning rod for the debate: organ versus guitars, traditional hymns versus contemporary choruses, hymnals versus overhead transparencies. Some churches have maintained a traditional style of worship, but many more have adopted, to a greater or lesser degree, a contemporary approach. A few others have thrown up their hands in despair and decided to try to please everyone, with both a traditional and a contemporary service.

Sometimes missing in the heat of this battle has been attention to a more fundamental issue: What *is* worship? Fortunately, more and more people are recognizing the need to address this basic question. Several excellent books have been written, seminaries are adding courses in this area, and pastors and laypeople alike are having to think through issues that might otherwise never have surfaced.

I am no expert in worship. I have not seriously studied the issue, I do not lead worship, and I probably have as many uninformed prejudices as anyone (give me an organ, every time). But I do think that Romans 12:1 sets out two fundamental values that should inform all our discussion about worship.

(1) Worship is the way we live, not what we do on Sunday morning. The title of Ernst Käsemann's essay on this passage says it well: "Worship in Everyday Life."[6] We worship God, says Paul, by giving ourselves in sacrificial service to our Lord. We are to serve him every day, every hour, every minute.

Paul deliberately uses the word "body" (*soma*) to describe what we are to offer to God. This word focuses on the "embodied" nature of our persons, reminding us that we are physical beings, interacting with a material world. By using this word, the apostle emphasizes the degree to which our worship should involve even the very prosaic parts of life. As we eat our food, we worship God by thanking him for what he has given us, honoring him with our conversation, and providing for the bodies he has given us. As we sweat on the treadmill, we worship God by seeking to be good stewards of the body he has given us. As we seek (speaking for myself, sometimes in vain) to avoid driving with the same egotistic aggressiveness as others, we worship God by displaying the fruit of his Spirit. We do our work to the best of our ability, worshiping God by giving our best to our employers.

One of the greatest temptations in the Christian life is to bifurcate the "spiritual" world from the material, to begin thinking that only certain parts

---

6. "Worship in Everyday Life: A Note on Romans 12," in *New Testament Questions of Today* (London: SCM, 1969).

of our lives have eternal significance. All of our life is to be a continuous worship of the God who created and redeemed us.

(2) The worship we offer corporately in a worship *service* must be "informed." Nothing we said in the last paragraph takes away from the importance, indeed, the requirement, for believers to meet together regularly to worship God. What happens during that time will vary enormously, depending on our location in the world, our cultural and social context, and our denominational heritage. But verse 1 makes clear that God-pleasing worship, however expressed, must engage the mind. It must be *logikos* worship, worship appropriate for rational creatures, worship that arises from understanding something about God and his truth.

I do not think that God ultimately cares *how* we sing, but he does care about *what* we sing. The words we sing must be true, expressing something about what he has told us about himself. By reminding ourselves of such truth in our singing we are moved to the praise and worship that pleases God.

I am afraid that what passes for worship in some churches goes little beyond an emotional reaction to a certain form of music. Some writers of music and certain kinds of worship leaders know how to get people excited, but I am not always clear that they are getting people to worship. Emotions must, of course, play a role in worship. But it is both easy and tempting to focus too much on an emotional reaction to music, bypassing the mind entirely. Yet if I read Romans 12:1 rightly, this is not the kind of worship that truly pleases God. Worship that pleases him and that truly leaves its mark on a believer always engages the mind.

Renewing the mind. While we are on the subject of the mind, we should note a similar emphasis emerging from verse 2: By the "renewing of [the] mind" we transform ourselves and prove in practice God's "good, pleasing and perfect will." When we change the way we think, we change the way we live. Two elements here deserve comment and application.

(1) It is a *process.* The fact that Paul calls on believers to engage in this renewing of the mind shows that it does not automatically happen to us when we believe. God's Spirit comes to reside in us, and he provides a whole new orientation to our thinking. But our thinking itself is not instantaneously changed. The ruts of the old life are not always easy to get out of. Some of our ways of thinking are deeply ingrained, and they will not disappear overnight.

I came to Christ as a twenty-year-old college student, and, almost thirty years later, I am still fighting against the mental habits I developed in my first twenty years. Through his Spirit, God wants to reprogram my thinking. But I must respond to the Spirit's work and actively engage in the process if it is to happen.

The key question then becomes: What are we feeding into our minds? Most Christians have little choice but to spend forty or fifty hours of every week in "the world," making a living. It is hoped that most Christians also seek to spend time with unbelievers as a means of ministry and evangelism. But if we spend all our discretionary time watching network television, reading secular books, and listening to secular music, it will be a wonder if our minds are not fundamentally secular. Our job is to cooperate with God's Spirit by seeking to feed into our minds information that will reprogram our thinking in line with the values of the kingdom.

(2) Renewing the mind is, by definition, an *internal* process. In a certain sense, this concept is Paul's response to a possible criticism of his gospel. If, as he has taught, Christians are no longer "under the law," that is, bound to the law of Moses (cf. 6:14, 15; 7:4, 6), then what basis can there be for morality? What will direct Christians to live in a way pleasing to God? Paul's answer is that God is at work in us, changing from within the very way that we think. This is a far better alternative than any law, for no law can conceivably cover all the issues we face in life. No matter how detailed, "law" will always fail to cover some situations. We need to face squarely this limitation and its consequences.

Many preachers, intent on getting their people to obey God, fall into a legal approach to Christian ethics. They focus on commandments, sometimes drawn from the Old Testament, sometimes from the New, and sometimes from contemporary Christianity. By doing so, they give the impression that Christian ethics consists in conformity to those commands. As a result, Christians tend to lead a double life: "Christian" in that behavior for which they have been taught laws, but essentially secular in those areas of life not touched by those laws. A Christian may not abort her baby, because she has been taught not to do that. But she may harbor racist attitudes or cheat on her taxes without batting an eye. If renewing the mind is as important as Paul says, then the goal of ministry should be to form Christian minds in people. This will require preaching that goes beyond teaching people what is right and wrong and that inculcates a worldview in people.

Is law then wrong? Are commandments of any kind to be dispensed with by believers? No. In Galatians, Paul makes some of the same points we have been making here. He tells believers that they are no longer "under the law" (e.g., Gal. 3:25). He insists that God is at work, transforming people from within by his Spirit, who produces "fruit" pleasing to God (5:16–26). But he also insists that Christians are still bound to "the law of Christ" (6:2). Scholars debate the reference of this phrase, but I think it is Paul's shorthand for the new covenant standard of conduct. That standard is exemplified by Christ, focused on the demand of love (see 5:13–15), and illustrated in the teaching of Christ and the apostles.

The point I wish to make here is that this "law of Christ" includes commandments that are still obligatory for Christians. When New Testament writers deal with believers who are behaving in ways contrary to God's will, they are prepared to emphasize the need to obey commandments (see, e.g., 1 Cor. 7:17; 1 John [much of letter]). Thus, our emphasis on internal transformation must not exclude the continuing role of commandments in the life of the Christian.

We need to understand the roles God wants internal transformation and commandments to have in our sanctification. The heart of the matter is clearly the work of God's Spirit changing the way we think from within. But because we still live in a world hostile to God and are still prone to interpret God's Spirit for our own selfish advantage, we need commandments to indicate when we misunderstood the Spirit or failed to internalize his values.

Perhaps an illustration will help. Modern airliners are guided by their onboard computers. Pilots are told where they are and where they are to go by those computers. But airports still have runway lights. Pilots check the accuracy of the computer by visually watching those lights. So also the Christian. We are guided by our minds, in the process of being renewed so that they perfectly reflect God's will. But because that process will never be complete in this life, we still need the external guidance of God's commands. Put the commands at the heart of ethics and we end up with a superficial and incomplete obedience. But exclude the commands entirely and we end up with self-centered and erratic obedience.

Romans 12:3–8

OR BY THE GRACE given me I say to every one of you:
Do not think of yourself more highly than you ought,
but rather think of yourself with sober judgment, in
accordance with the measure of faith God has given you. ⁴Just
as each of us has one body with many members, and these
members do not all have the same function, ⁵so in Christ we
who are many form one body, and each member belongs to all
the others. ⁶We have different gifts, according to the grace
given us. If a man's gift is prophesying, let him use it in proportion to his faith. ⁷If it is serving, let him serve; if it is teaching, let him teach; ⁸if it is encouraging, let him encourage; if it
is contributing to the needs of others, let him give generously;
if it is leadership, let him govern diligently; if it is showing
mercy, let him do it cheerfully.

Original Meaning

IN 12:1–2, PAUL has encapsulated the gospel
imperative: honoring God at all times through a
transformed life that is in keeping with his will. In
12:3–15:13, Paul unpacks some of the specific
components of that will. He begins in 12:3–8 by reminding us that we live
out our transformed existence in community. Central to our community life
is a fair and sober estimate of ourselves in line with the Christian faith and
with the gifts God has given us.

Why Paul includes this particular focus in his letter to the Romans is not
clear. Since we find similar teaching in his other letters (see esp. 1 Cor. 12;
also Phil. 2:1–4), he is probably simply mentioning what he considers is a
key element in Christian obedience. But he may also have one eye on the
Roman church itself, where both "strong" and "weak" believers were thinking more of themselves than was healthy for the community.[1]

Paul underlines the importance of what he is about to say by reminding
the Roman Christians of his own authority. The "grace" given Paul is his apostolic calling, a specific manifestation of God's grace (see 1 Cor. 3:10; Gal.
2:9; Eph. 3:7–8). Paul's exhortation plays on a Greek word (*phroneo*) that means
to think, have a particular mind-set (see 8:5; see comments on 8:6, 7, 27). A

---

1. See, e.g., Wedderburn, *The Reasons for Romans*, 78–81.

paraphrase that tries to preserve this wordplay in English is "Don't think more highly of yourselves than it is right for you to think, but think with sober and accurate thinking about who you are in Christ." We should regard ourselves, Paul is saying, with "renewed minds" (cf. 12:2) that deliver us from the self-centeredness typical of the non-Christian and enable us to look at ourselves objectively and realistically.

The standard of that measurement is "the measure of faith God has given you." What is this standard? In light of the following verses, Paul may mean the specific amount of faith that God has distributed to each person. He is then encouraging us to look at ourselves in light of the gifts we have and to estimate ourselves accordingly. One person may have a great deal of faith and giftedness, while another has less. Each believer should recognize where he or she stands and pursue those ministries appropriate to them.[2] But another possibility is that the Christian faith in general is the standard of measurement—a standard that is the same for all believers. On this view, Paul is asking us to look carefully to the gospel faith and its requirements as we assess ourselves.[3] The decision between these two options is not easy, but we incline slightly to the second alternative.

Paul backs up and illustrates his call to assess our place in the Christian community accurately and in accordance with our common faith by reminding us that that community, while diverse, is at bottom a unity. Paul uses the imagery of the human body to get this point across, imagery widespread in the ancient world and familiar to us especially from 1 Corinthians 12. The church, Paul says, is like our individual bodies (Rom. 12:4–5). It has many different parts, each with its own function. But all the parts form "one body," and each part is needed if the body is to function as it should. If we are "in Christ" (v. 5), we are in his body, inescapably joined to the other members of our local Christian community. We can no more separate from each other than an arm can decide it does not want anything to do with the torso or legs.

In verses 6–8 Paul develops this notion further by listing a number of "gifts" God has given the members of the body of Christ. Paul uses this word "gift" (*charisma*) elsewhere to denote a God-given ability to serve the community of Christ in a particular way (see esp. 1 Cor. 1:7; 12:4, 9, 28, 30, 31; 1 Tim. 4:14; 2 Tim. 1:6). Paul lists gifts in 1 Corinthians 12:7–10, 28 and gifted individuals in Ephesians 4:11. None of these lists is comprehensive; rather, Paul chooses in each place to illustrate his argument by mentioning certain gifts that come to mind. In Romans 12:6–8, in contrast to the other

2. See, e.g., Barrett, *Epistle to the Romans*, 235; Bruce, *The Letter of Paul to the Romans*, 215.
3. See esp. Cranfield, *The Epistle to the Romans*, 613–16.

lists, Paul not only cites gifts but also encourages those who possess them to be active in using them for the edification of the community.

Thus, those who have the gift of prophesying should prophesy "in proportion to [their] faith." The gift of prophecy in the New Testament involves aiding the church by relaying to it truth gained from a "revelation" (see 1 Cor. 14:26, 30). That truth might be something in the future (e.g., Acts 11:27–28; 21:10–11), but more often denotes an insight into present circumstances.[4] Such prophesying can be dangerous if it is uncontrolled, so Paul urges that it be according to the *analogia* of faith. *Analogia*, from which we get the word "analogy," denotes a right "proportion" or relationship. Prophesying must be in right proportion to faith.

As with "measure of faith" in verse 3, just what "faith" (*pistis*) denotes here in verse 6 is not clear. It might be equivalent to "gift,"[5] though Paul does not elsewhere use *pistis* is this sense. Most commentators think it refers to *the* faith, the body of Christian truth.[6] It is true that Paul does use "faith" in this sense (Gal. 1:23; 1 Tim. 1:4, 19; 3:9; 4:1, 6; 6:21), but it is rare. So perhaps it is best to give the word the same meaning as in verse 3: one's own faith in Christ. Christian prophets should always speak in accordance with the standard set by their faith in Christ.[7] They need to be careful not to interject their own opinions into their prophecy, for those opinions would not be according to "the analogy of faith."

The gift of "serving" (*diakoneo*) in verse 7 can refer to a gift that all Christians share. Following the example of Christ, the "servant of the Lord," all believers are called on to serve Christ and one another (e.g., Mark 10:43–45; Rom. 15:25; Eph. 4:12). But the word *diakoneo* also has a more limited sense, referring to the ministry performed specifically by the deacon (*diakonos*, lit., "servant"; see Rom. 16:1; Phil. 1:1; 1 Tim. 3:8, 10, 12, 13). Since all the other gifts in Romans 12:6–8 refer to distinct activities, "serving" here probably refers to the special activities of the deacon: ministering to the church by organizing and providing for the material needs of the community (see, perhaps, Acts 6:1–6).[8]

"Teaching" (mentioned as a gift also in 1 Cor. 12:28; Eph. 4:11) involves passing on the truth of the gospel. The teacher must study God's Word and

---

4. On prophecy, see esp. Wayne Grudem, *The Gift of Prophecy in the New Testament and in the World Today* (Westchester, Ill.: Crossway, 1988).

5. E.g., Murray, *The Epistle to the Romans*, 2:122–23; Dunn, *Romans*, 727–28; Fee, *God's Empowering Presence*, 608–9.

6. E.g., Käsemann, *Commentary on Romans*, 341–42; Fitzmyer, *Romans*, 647–48.

7. Cranfield, *The Epistle to the Romans*, 619–21.

8. See, e.g., Godet, *Commentary on Romans*, 431–32; Murray, *The Epistle to the Romans*, 2:123–25.

be rooted in the tradition of the church so that he or she can guide the community into truth and preserve it from error.

Closely related to teaching is "encouraging" (v. 8). The Greek word (*parakaleo*) can mean to comfort or to exhort, but in this context probably denotes the activity of encouraging Christians to live out the truth of the gospel.

"Contributing to the needs of others" might take place out of one's own resources or out of the church's giving as a whole. In either case, one must contribute, Paul insists, "generously" or "with sincerity"—the word used here (*haplotes*) suggests a "single" attitude, a consistency of intent and absence of any ulterior motive (2 Cor. 8:2; 9:11, 13; 11:3; Eph. 6:5; Col. 3:22).

Since the next listed gift comes just after the one who "contributes to the needs of others" and just before one who "shows mercy," some commentators think that *ho proïstamenos* in verse 8 refers to one who "gives aid" to others.[9] But this meaning for the verb (*proïstemi*) is not well-attested, while Paul does use this same verb twice elsewhere to refer to the "leaders" of the church (1 Thess. 5:12; 1 Tim. 5:17). With most English versions, then, we think he is referring to the person who has the gift of leading the church (e.g., the elders).

Paul concludes his list by mentioning those who have the gift of "showing mercy"—probably those who are particularly sensitive to the needs of others and who give themselves to visiting the sick and other suffering people.

BODY LANGUAGE. Paul's analogy between the church and the human body is one of the most familiar in the Bible. It has had a big influence on the way we think about the church, since we use the term *body* often to refer to (especially) the local church. But what does calling the church the "body" actually communicate? Probably many different things, depending on our own personal filter through which we run the word. But if we want it to communicate what Paul wanted to communicate, we must anchor the imagery in Paul's own world. What does *he* want us to understand by his application of the term *body* to the church?

Paul was not the first to compare a group of people to the human body. A number of ancient writers used that metaphor to argue that the political state, while comprising many very different kinds of people, was still a single entity. A few writers even called the state the "body" of the emperor.[10] The

---

9. Dunn, *Romans*, 731.
10. See *TDNT*, 7:1038–39.

comparison is widespread enough to justify our thinking that it played some role in Paul's decision to use the imagery of the body. We may even consider this an adequate explanation. In this case, the church as a body is no more than a simple analogy, and it is wrong to search for any further significance in the equation.

But Paul's own use of "body" language surely suggests that the metaphor also had roots in his own theology. In our text, Paul speaks simply of people "in Christ" making up a single "body." In passages parallel to this one, he uses the expression "the body of Christ" (1 Cor. 12:27; Eph. 4:12). This language invites us to probe a bit further into the connections between Christ's own body and the use of body language for the church. Probably what pops into many of our minds at this point, because of its familiarity to us in our own worship, is the intriguing body language in Paul's account of the Lord's Supper in 1 Corinthians 11:23–29:

> For I received from the Lord what I also passed on to you: The Lord Jesus, on the night he was betrayed, took bread, and when he had given thanks, he broke it and said, "This is *my body*, which is for you; do this in remembrance of me." In the same way, after supper he took the cup, saying, "This cup is the new covenant in my blood; do this, whenever you drink it, in remembrance of me." For whenever you eat this bread and drink this cup, you proclaim the Lord's death until he comes.
>
> Therefore, whoever eats the bread or drinks the cup of the Lord in an unworthy manner will be guilty of sinning against the *body* and blood of the Lord. A man ought to examine himself before he eats of the bread and drinks of the cup. For anyone who eats and drinks without recognizing the *body* of the Lord eats and drinks judgment on himself. (italics added)

Paul follows Jesus himself in this word of institution, equating the bread with the Lord's body, broken in death. But Paul has mentioned the details of the Corinthians' celebration of the Supper for a particular reason: to rebuke them for their selfishness in the way that they were eating it (and probably also an associated fellowship meal). Therefore, while "body" in 1 Corinthians 11:27 still refers to Christ's own (physical) body, "body" in verse 29 almost certainly refers to the church. The community abuses the Lord's own body and blood (v. 27) by not "recognizing," that is, by not discerning the corporate nature of, the body of believers whom Christ through his death created and whom the church models in communion (v. 29).[11]

---

11. See Gordon D. Fee, *The First Epistle to the Corinthians* (Grand Rapids: Eerdmans, 1987), 562–64.

Here, then, Paul uses "body" to refer both to Christ's physical body and to the church, and he brings them together in a context that focuses on the corporate identity of the church. What this suggests is that when Paul uses body terminology for the church, he is thinking of Christ's death on the cross as the means by which that community was brought into being. "Each member belongs to all the others," as Paul puts it in verse 5, because each of us participates equally in the benefits of Christ's redemptive work. The unity of the church rests in the oneness of Christ as the only means of salvation (see Eph. 2:16).

But we can go one step further. Ultimately, Paul claims, the church *is* Christ's body (Eph. 1:23; 5:23, 30; Col. 1:24). This identification is a natural development from a key idea in Paul, one that comes to expression in our text: believers are "in Christ." As we saw in commenting on Romans 5:12−21, Paul thinks of Christ, like Adam, as a corporate person, one who includes within himself many others. Everyone who believes in Christ becomes a part of him. Scholars have sometimes gone far beyond the text in suggesting various philosophical and religious backgrounds for this idea. But this is unnecessary. It was the experience of Paul and the other believers, interpreted in light of the Old Testament and God's revelation in Christ, that convinced them that they were in intimate union with Christ. To be "in Christ" is to be joined to "his body."

THE LOCAL AND THE **universal church.** What should not be missed is the way Paul moves immediately from the general commands of verses 1−2 into a passage dealing with the corporate life of the church. Offering ourselves as a "living sacrifice" (singular in the Greek), transforming ourselves, developing the mind of Christ—all these take place in community: "Each member belongs to all the others" (v. 5b). And note not just in any kind of community; to be "in Christ," that is, to be a Christian, is to be part of Christ's body, the church. We can formalize church membership as a step one takes in identifying with a particular local church. But from the point of belief on, the Christian in inescapably a member of the universal church.

While the distinction between the local and universal church is helpful in some ways, Paul's letters forbid us from separating them. Every individual church is simply the universal church in its local expression. We must seriously question, then, whether Paul would even entertain the idea that a person could be a member of the universal church without being a member of a local church. Our modern proliferation of local churches creates difficulties at this point, but Paul would never imagine any believer seeking to grow in his or her faith apart from the Christian community.

The Western individualistic tradition can create problems for us at this point. A "Lone Ranger" mentality in our faith can easily set in. I am perhaps as prone to such an attitude as anyone. Naturally shy, loving books more than people, I tend to withdraw from society in general. My status as a seminary professor makes it easy for me to find excuses not to be involved in my local church. I can always claim that I am too busy ministering to others in my writings and in various speaking forums to commit to local church involvement. Yet I do not think I have good biblical grounds for such an attitude. I believe that I, like all believers, am called to live my faith in the context of a local church. Thus, I have always identified with a local church, tried to keep up my participation in it, and served it in a variety of ways.

The same principle holds true for any one of us. Television "church" is not church; just because thousands of people watch the same service and listen to the same sermon does not make it so. Why not? In verses 3–8 Paul suggests two reasons. (1) As we have seen, the implication of the relationship between verses 1–2 and verses 3–8 is that I cannot fully "renew my mind" without the active help of other believers. I cannot understand what Scripture teaches apart from dialog with others who are reading that same Scripture. I cannot live the life of a disciple of Christ apart from the nurturing context of a community of believers who encourage me, pray for me, and set an example for me. I cannot discern the blind spots in my obedience to Christ without other believers to point them out to me. Here is where the attitude of arrogance that Paul rebukes in verse 3 can get in the way. We think of ourselves "more highly than [we] ought" and so conclude that we do not need the help of others.

(2) More directly taught in the text, I must participate in the local church to help others grow. Whatever gift I have been given, I am under obligation to my Lord to use it to serve his people. That gift need not always, of course, be expressed only in a local church. The writing I am doing right now is, I hope, an expression of one of my gifts that serves the church at large. Most of the teaching that I do is apart from the local church context. Moreover, how the seminary, certainly a ministry of the church in general, relates to the local church in Pauline terms is not easy to sort out. But this much can certainly be said: The gifts God has given us are generally to be exercised in local churches. Other Christians need what each of us has to offer. As the human body is at a disadvantage without a foot, or an eye, or a kidney, so the local church is harmed when the full panoply of gifts are not being exercised within it.

Romans 12:9–21

LOVE MUST BE sincere. Hate what is evil; cling to what is good. ¹⁰Be devoted to one another in brotherly love. Honor one another above yourselves. ¹¹Never be lacking in zeal, but keep your spiritual fervor, serving the Lord. ¹²Be joyful in hope, patient in affliction, faithful in prayer. ¹³Share with God's people who are in need. Practice hospitality.

¹⁴Bless those who persecute you; bless and do not curse. ¹⁵Rejoice with those who rejoice; mourn with those who mourn. ¹⁶Live in harmony with one another. Do not be proud, but be willing to associate with people of low position. Do not be conceited.

¹⁷Do not repay anyone evil for evil. Be careful to do what is right in the eyes of everybody. ¹⁸If it is possible, as far as it depends on you, live at peace with everyone. ¹⁹Do not take revenge, my friends, but leave room for God's wrath, for it is written: "It is mine to avenge; I will repay," says the Lord. ²⁰On the contrary:

"If your enemy is hungry, feed him;
    if he is thirsty, give him something to drink.
In doing this, you will heap burning coals on his head."

²¹Do not be overcome by evil, but overcome evil with good.

Original Meaning

EVEN THE CASUAL READER of Romans senses quite a change in style at 12:9. The sentences are suddenly much shorter. Almost all contain a command, with hardly an indicative verb to be found. The subject seems to change with every verse, sometimes with every sentence. This whole section, therefore, gives the impression of a random series of commands with little structure or unity of theme.

This first impression is not far wrong. Paul does move rapidly and with little clear continuity of subject matter through a list of basic Christian moral imperatives. However, we should note also that the Greek text displays some well-thought out patterns that cannot be duplicated in English (see Bridging Contexts). Moreover, even though these verses cannot be unified around a governing theme, they do feature a persistent motif: the call for a humble and peaceable attitude toward others, both fellow Christians (vv. 10, 13, 16) and non-Christians (vv. 14, 17–21). Here, Paul suggests, is a key test of the sincerity of love, the heading for the passage as a whole (v. 9a). The humility and deference toward others is, in turn, a key ingredient in that good and perfect will of God (12:2) that Paul illustrates in these chapters.

The Heading: Sincere Love (12:9a)

JESUS HIMSELF PUT love for God and love for others at the heart of his "new covenant ethics" (Mark 12:28–34 and par.; John 13:31–35). The apostles only rarely call on their converts to love God, preferring to speak of faith and obedience instead. But they follow Jesus almost to the letter in making love for other people the central focus of their exhortations (e.g., Rom. 13:8–10; 1 Cor. 13; Gal. 5:13–15; Col. 3:14; James 2:8; 1 John 2:9–11). But "love" can be a vague idea. One of Paul's purposes here is to specify some types of behavior that manifest "sincere" love.

The Greek behind the NIV's "Love must be sincere" has no verb; a very literal rendering would be "the love sincere." Supplying an imperative verb (as almost all the translations do) is not necessarily wrong, but it obscures the fact that these words seem to be a heading for the rest of the passage. It is as if Paul gives a definition: "Love that is sincere will be. . . ." The Greek for "sincere" is *anypokritos* (lit., not hypocritical). The underlying word was often applied to the actor who "played a part" on the stage. Christians can avoid love that is mere "play-acting" if they put into practice the commands that follow.

The Many Facets of Sincere Love (12:9b–13)

PAUL MARKS OUT four sections of this paragraph by varying the Greek style.

(1) At the end of verse 9, he briefly unpacks the basic moral dimension of sincere love in two parallel clauses (using a participle in Greek). Christian love is more than a feeling; it leads to a violent hatred of evil and a tenacious attachment to what is good (the verb for "cling," *kollaomai*, refers to sexual relations in 1 Cor. 6:16, 17). With John, Paul would argue that no one truly loves who does not obey God's command (see, e.g., 2 John 6).

(2) Verse 10 features two commands that focus on the "one another" relationship among believers. The first exhortation uses two words from the *phil-* root in Greek: "Be devoted" (*philostorgoi*) to one another in "brotherly love" (*philadelphia*). This root was generally applied to loving relations among family members. As a spiritual family, the church is to exhibit the intimacy and tenderness toward one another that mark the best earthly families.

The translation of the second command in verse 10 varies. The NRSV, taking the verb used here to mean surpass, translates "outdo one another in showing honor."[1] The NIV's "honor one another above yourselves" assumes an unusual meaning for the verb, "consider better."[2] But the difference in meaning in slight. In either case, Paul exhorts believers to put other believers first as an expression of genuine love.

(3) The six commands in verses 11—12 are not similar in content, but they all have the same structure in Greek (article plus noun in the dative case followed by an adjective or participle). "Never be lacking in zeal" (lit., "in zeal, don't be lazy") is left without a referent (zealous about what?), but perhaps Paul is thinking of the "informed worship" to which every believer is called (12:1; see comments on 12:1–2).[3]

The NIV's "keep your spiritual fervor" reveals one interpretation of a difficult clause (v. 11b). Paul urges us to be "set on fire" (*zeontes*) "in" or "by" the S/spirit (*pneumati*). "Spirit" can refer to the human spirit (NIV),[4] but, in light of the reference to "the Lord" in the next clause, it probably refers to the Holy Spirit, the agent who inflames our passion for the Lord and his work.[5] Passion for the cause of Christ is exemplary, but it can be misguided and even harmful. Thus, Paul concludes the verse with a reminder that our spiritual passion must always be put in obedient service of the Lord.[6]

If the three exhortations in verse 11 all relate to zealous service, the three in verse 12 combine to encourage believers to "stay the course" in their fight with the world. We need to rejoice in the hope of a glory that is secure and certain (see 8:18–30), exhibit patience and endurance when tribulations come (see 5:3–4), and give ourselves to prayer that both of these may come to pass.

(4) Paul concludes the first series of commands by returning to the theme of verse 10a. We exhibit the familial love of true brothers and sisters in Christ by sharing with other believers who are in need. According to a literal translation Paul is saying, "Enter into fellowship with the needs of the saints." These needs are material ones: food, clothing, and housing (see also Acts 6:3;

---

1. See, e.g., Dunn, *Romans*, 741.
2. See also KJV; NASB; see, e.g., Cranfield, *The Epistle to the Romans*, 632.
3. Cranfield, *The Epistle to the Romans*, 633.
4. See, e.g., Godet, *Commentary on Romans*, 435; Murray, *The Epistle to the Romans*, 2:130–31.
5. E.g., Käsemann, *Commentary on Romans*, 346; Dunn, *Romans*, 742.
6. An interesting textual variant reads "time" (*kairo*) in place of "Lord" (*kyrio*); and several commentators support it as the "harder" reading (e.g., Godet, *Commentary on Romans*, 435; Käsemann, *Commentary on Romans*, 346). If so, then Paul is be urging believers to "serve" (i.e., to use advantageously) the time (cf. Eph. 5:16; Col. 4:5). But "serving the time" in the ancient world usually had the nuance of selfish opportunism, and it is doubtful whether Paul would have used the expression.

20:34; 28:10; Titus 3:14). "Hospitality" was badly needed in a day without motels and restaurants. Traveling missionaries and ordinary believers depended on the kindness of other Christians. While the NIV does not make this clear, the Greek calls on believers not just to show (perhaps grudgingly) hospitality to others, but to "pursue" (NIV "practice") it.

Living in Harmony with Other People (12:14−16)

A BREAK BETWEEN verses 13 and 14 is marked by a shift in style and subject matter. In verses 9−13 Paul has used mainly participles to convey his commands; in verse 14 he switches to the more typical imperative mood. He also suddenly shifts his focus from relationships with other believers to the way that same love can be shown to non-Christians. Paul's commands in verse 14 remind us of Jesus' famous teaching from the Sermon on the Mount (italics added below):

Matt. 5:44   But I tell you: Love your enemies and pray for those *who persecute you.*

Luke 6:27−28   But I tell you who hear me: Love your enemies, do good to those who hate you, *bless* those who curse you, pray for those who mistreat you.

These similarities suggest that Paul is quoting Jesus' teaching here. In fact, Paul shows more dependence on Jesus' teaching in this part of Romans than he does anywhere else in his letters. The way he weaves references to that teaching into his own exhortations without specifically citing Jesus is typical of the way the early Christians absorbed Jesus' words into their own ethical tradition. Like Jesus, Paul calls on us to turn the other cheek, displaying a love for others that goes far beyond the normal boundaries of human love.

Verse 15 may continue the theme of verse 14, calling on believers to identify with unbelievers in both their joys and their sorrows.[7] But the sentiment of this verse is close to that of 1 Corinthians 12:26: "If one part suffers, every part suffers with it; if one part is honored, every part rejoices with it" (cf. also that Rom. 12:3−8 is closely parallel to 1 Cor. 12). Probably, then, Paul turns back here again to relationships within the Christian community.

As we noted at the outset, the commands in verses 9−21 do not follow any strict logical order. In keeping with the style he uses, Paul moves rapidly from one subject to another. But we can discern a single underlying concern in verses 14−16: the need to live in harmony with other people, both unbelievers (v. 14) and believers (vv. 15−16). We pursue this goal with unbelievers by meeting their scorn and hatred with love; we display the deep-seated harmony

---

7. See, e.g., Cranfield, *The Epistle to the Romans,* 641; Dunn, *Romans,* 745−46.

that the Spirit creates among believers by making other believers' joys and sorrows our own.

The command to "live in harmony with one another" (v. 16a) summarizes the overall thrust of these verses with specific reference to the believing community. Perhaps the greatest obstacle to this unity of mind and spirit is pride. As a result, as he does in Philippians 2:1–4, Paul urges Christians to avoid pride and to humble themselves as the key step toward genuine unity. We are not to "be proud" (cf. Rom. 11:20) but to "associate with people of low position" (NIV). "People of low position" translates a single Greek word that refers either to "humble people" or to "humble things." Paul is either exhorting believers to identify with "down and outers" in the community or to give themselves to "menial work" (see NIV note; cf. TEV: "accept humble duties").

In an echo of both 11:25 and 12:3, Paul concludes the brief paragraph by warning us not to think we are wiser than we really are (cf. Prov. 3:7: "Do not be wise in your own eyes").

Overcoming Evil with Good by Refusing to Retaliate (12:17–21)

AT THE END of his brief outline of the shape of sincere love, Paul returns to a key ingredient of that love he mentioned in verse 14: responding to the persecution of unbelievers with kindness rather than with hatred. Paul introduces the point negatively: "Do not repay anyone evil for evil." Dependence on Jesus' teaching is again likely, since in the same context in which Jesus urges us to "bless those who persecute" us, he also prohibits us from exacting "eye for eye, and tooth for tooth" (Matt. 5:38). Jesus calls his disciples to a kingdom ethic of non-retaliation, and Paul renews that same call here.

But the followers of Jesus are to do more than avoid retaliation. They must also, positively, "do what is right in the eyes of everybody." Some interpreters think Paul could not possibly imply that unbelievers have the right to define "what is right" for Christians to do, so they prefer to translate "do good things *to* all people."[8] But verse 18 qualifies the extent to which believers are to conform their behavior to the expectations of unbelievers. "If it is possible" means, in effect, "if God's good and perfect will allows you to do it." Christians are to do what they can to find approval with non-Christians and to live at peace with them (v. 18c). But they must never seek approval with the world at the expense of God's moral demands; this means that harmonious relationships with unbelievers will not always lie in our power to achieve.

With verse 19, Paul returns to the theme of non-retaliation: Believers are not to seek revenge. One reason why they should not do so is that God him-

---

8. See, e.g., Käsemann, *Commentary on Romans*, 348.

self is the one who avenges wrong. "It is mine to avenge; I will repay," says God in Deuteronomy 32:35. God knows all things, sees all things, and has all power. He is a perfectly just God, who will not ultimately allow evil to go unpunished. We can therefore trust him to avenge any evil that people may do to us. We are to "leave room for God's wrath." If we try to exact revenge ourselves, we transgress onto territory that God has reserved for himself.

As Paul did in verses 17–18, he follows up the prohibition of verse 19 about not taking revenge with a positive exhortation to do good to those who may be doing evil to us (v. 20). Paul quotes Proverbs 25:21–22a to make his point. He is probably drawn to this text because of the word "enemy," the same word Jesus used in the tradition that Paul is using here (see Matt. 5:43; Luke 6:27). Providing for an enemy's hunger and thirst is similar to the actions Jesus requires of us in response to an enemy: turning the other cheek, giving our shirts to those who ask for our coats, and giving to those who beg from us (Luke 6:29–30).

In responding to our enemies in this way, the text from Proverbs goes on to say, we will "heap burning coals on his head." Most of us are familiar with this language. It has passed into Christian parlance as a way of encouraging believers to do good to those who are nasty to us. What is usually implied is that our responding to evil with good will cause people to become ashamed of their actions and perhaps seek reconciliation with the Lord.

Whether this idea of contrition is what is communicated by the imagery in Proverbs is less certain. "Coals" and "fire" in the Old Testament usually connote divine judgment. Thus, Proverbs (and Paul) may be saying that kindness toward enemies will result in further judgment on them from the Lord.[9] But this interpretation does not fit the context. With almost all modern commentators, then, we think the popular Christian interpretation of the clause is probably right: Paul urges us to show kindness to our enemies with the hope that they will become ashamed of their actions and seek the underlying reason why we can respond with such love.[10]

Verse 21 wraps up this paragraph with an appropriate bottom line: "Do not be overcome by evil, but overcome evil with good." Though redeemed and citizens of heaven, we believers still live in a world soaked in evil. We must battle constantly against the tendency to conform our behavior to this world (see 12:2). But more than the purely negative quality of resistance to

---

9. This interpretation was quite popular in the early church, but not so much recently. See, however, John Piper, *Love Your Enemies: Jesus' Love Command in the Synoptic Gospels and in the Early Christian Paraenesis* (Cambridge: Cambridge Univ. Press, 1979), 115–18.

10. Some Old Testament commentators think that the Proverbs text may refer to a Egyptian ritual in which a penitent carried a tray of burning coals over his head to symbolize his sorrow for sin. See S. Morenz, "Feurige Kohlen auf dem Haupt," in *Religion und Geschichte der alten Agypten: Gesammelte Aufsätze* (Weimar: Hermann Böhlaus, 1975), 433–44.

evil is needed. God calls us to be active in using the grace of the gospel and the power of the Spirit to win victories over the evil of this world.

THE STYLE OF PARAENESIS. A passage such as 12:9–21 carries a strong temptation for the modern Western commentator. We tend to be quite enamored of our abilities to find structure and movement in the biblical text—that is, to point out to our readers relationships that they may never have seen. How tempting it is, then, to seek structure where it doesn't exist. Indeed, we sometimes think it is beneath the New Testament writers to write without careful structure.

But the temptation to impose structure on a text is not limited to commentators. In teaching biblical texts over the years, I have seen the same assumption that a biblical text must be carefully and logical organized operating among laypeople. I think, however, that this assumption must be challenged. We seem to assume that the special inspired quality of Scripture demands that it always be logically organized. If God is organized and he inspired every text of the Bible, must not those texts likewise be organized?

Of course, a lot depends on what we mean by *organized*. Every biblical text is *deliberate*, in the sense that it was written with a particular purpose; and it is *logical*, in that, when we rightly interpret it, it makes sense. But not all biblical texts are organized in the kind of neat, logical arrangement we can display in an outline. In fact, I suspect that our tendency to use traditional outlining schemes (A., A.1., A.1.a., etc.) in summarizing biblical texts is a large part of the problem. We are not quite sure how to take a "bird's-eye" view of a text if we do not impose an outline on it. But communication is much broader than those types that are susceptible of being summarized in such an outline, and such types of communication are no less effective in accomplishing their purposes.

In 12:9–21, Paul writes in an ancient style called *paraenesis*. Scholars debate about whether we should call *paraenesis* a style or a genre and how sharply defined it was. But almost everyone agrees that such a style existed and is found widely in the ancient world.

Paraenesis has three main characteristics. (1) It was usually used for moral exhortation—to urge people to adopt certain attitudes or behaviors. (2) It usually depended heavily on tradition. That is, the writer freely borrowed from many sources. Recognizing such allusions, the readers or listeners accorded greater authority to the *paraenesis*, since they incorporated elements these people already respected. (3) It was loosely structured. The writer or speaker deliberately moved quickly from one topic to another without attempting to pursue a definite line of development. The letter of James is often thought to display a paraenetic style, as are specific parts of other New Testament letters.

Romans 12:9–21 obviously fits the parameters of *paraenesis* we have just sketched. In no obvious order of logical sequence, Paul exhorts Christians to adopt certain attitudes and forms of behavior, freely citing the Old Testament, Jewish tradition, and the teachings of Jesus to communicate his points.

One of the mistakes we make in looking at possible backgrounds to the New Testament is to assume, as one scholar has put it, that ideas in the ancient world flowed in pipelines. That is, we wrongly expect that a given teaching always remained in a pure and unadulterated form, unaffected by other teachings. Of course, we all understand that the world is not like that. Ideas jostle with each other, and rarely do we encounter one in complete isolation from others like it. So it is also with literary genres and styles. Paul uses the paraenetic style popular in the Greco-Roman world as he writes these verses. But he is also influenced by the Old Testament and Jewish wisdom style that we find, for instance, in Proverbs. The two styles—and perhaps others we have not considered—have merged to some extent, and Paul probably could not have identified just what parts of 12:9–21 come from one and what parts from the other.

For our purposes, however, the important point is that Paul writes in a style well known in the ancient world, which was effective in communicating what he wanted to get across to his readers. We need to respect the style he has used and not try to impose on the verses modern assumptions about "correct" structure or logical organization. The style he has chosen to use keeps us on our toes. The commands come rapidly, one after the other, and we have no way of predicting what is going to come next. The very changes of topic that perplex us at one level force us to grapple with each exhortation in its own right.

We are, of course, supposed to think about what Paul is saying. But he is more interested in getting us to react. The rapid-fire style of the text is effective in accomplishing this. If the medium is not entirely the message, as Marshall McLuhan would have us believe, it is vitally related to the message. Paul has arguably chosen here to use a medium that suits what he wants us to hear better than a logical style of arguing would have done.

LOVE IN ACTION. Few terms are as popular among Christians as the term *love*. And rightly so, for along with *faith* and *hope*, love is one of most important ways of expressing what Christianity is all about. The New Testament puts love at the heart of what it means to live as a Christian in relationship to other people. To be sure, we must never allow this horizontal dimension of Christianity to push out or diminish the more basic vertical dimension of our faith. Relationship with God is first and primary; our relationship to others flows from it. The problem with love, however, is that it can be a vague term. People fill it with almost any meaning they want. Particularly in a culture that thinks of love primarily as something that a person can "fall" in and out of, the biblical meaning and significance of love needs careful attention.

Biblical love, as we are constantly reminded, is not an emotion. It is an attitude, a mind-set. This distinction is one that older writers, and a few contemporary ones, try to get at by using the word "charity" to describe what the Bible is talking about. We are commanded to love; it is therefore a choice we make, a matter of the will.

To be sure, I do not think any of us can love in the way the Bible asks us to without the enabling grace of God. Love is not something that can ever be entirely the product of the human will. But our wills are involved. The Spirit may foster love within us. But it is our job to cooperate with the Spirit in developing a consistent mind-set of love toward others and to work actively at putting love into effect in the various relationships we find ourselves involved in. This is precisely the point Paul seems to be making here. "Sincere love," as we have argued, is the theme of 12:9–21. Paul wants to show what biblical love looks like in practice. The Christian who harbors an attitude of love will act in the ways that he describes here.

"Situation ethics" is no longer a popular movement. But the idea that appropriate ethical behavior takes the form of whatever is "loving" in a given situation is still with us—both in the church as well as outside it. Believers refuse to confront other believers about a sin because it would not be a "loving" thing to do. Sex even outside of marriage cannot possibly be wrong, so we rationalize, because it is the natural outcome of a "loving" relationship. We tacitly begin to define right and wrong by the standard of what is loving— defined, of course, in our terms.

But love must be defined in God's terms. He makes clear, in passages such as Romans 12:9–21, that the mind-set of love will always result in actions that are in full accord with his good and perfect will (12:2). God establishes the standards of right behavior, revealed to us in Scripture. God inspires love for others within us; the two cannot ultimately be in conflict.

We will all face times when it looks, however, as if they are in conflict. What do we do then? Suppose, for instance, that I can attain life-saving medicine for my child only by stealing it; I cannot afford to buy it, and I have exhausted all means of getting it in any other way. Am I justified in stealing if it saves the life of my child? Should love take precedence over the command of God that I not steal? Christian ethicists have debated questions such as this for years, and no general agreement has been reached, nor is it likely to be reached soon. Some insist that love takes precedence over the law in such cases, and they cite Scripture in support (e.g., Matt. 12:1–8). Others argue that God so providentially disposes of all things that he will never allow a believer to be placed in such an intolerable bind, but will always make it possible for him or her to avoid transgressing the commandments of Scripture (cf. 1 Cor. 10:13).

My own inclination is to adopt the second of these alternatives. But whichever view on this matter we take, we must recognize that such ethical dilemmas are, at the least, rare. Usually the conflict we experience is between what God has commanded in Scripture and what *we think* the "loving" thing to do is. In such situations—where, of course, we are sure of our scriptural basis—we must follow the command of God. For he ultimately determines what is loving and what is not. We are all too capable of modifying the application of love to suit our own desires.

Love and violence. Of the various manifestations of love that Paul touches on in 12:9–21, none receives more attention than non-retaliation. Building on Jesus' teaching in the Sermon on the Mount, Paul calls us to "bless those who persecute you" (v. 14). In verses 17–21, he returns to the same point and elaborates. Believers are to be people who do not adopt the world's "tit-for-tat" approach to relationships. Recognizing that God will ultimately right all wrongs and avenge all evil, we are not to avenge wrongdoing ourselves but to respond to evil with kindness and love.

Here we find one of the most distinctive of all the characteristics that are to mark Christians. The desire to avenge ourselves on those who harm us is deeply rooted in human nature. It is celebrated in books and in movies (movie theaters erupt in cheers when "the bad guy" gets his due) and is displayed in antagonistic driving on our highways every day. But God calls us, as his children, to be different. We are to imitate Christ, who, when "they hurled their insults at him," "did not retaliate; when he suffered, he made no threats" (1 Peter 2:23). As Paul makes clear, we are to go beyond refraining from doing evil to those who harm us; we are, positively, to do them good.

Seeking peace—to the extent that it lies with us—is a primary value in the kingdom of God. Imagine the transformation in society that the consistent application of such a philosophy of human relationships would bring! When my wife and I sit in two lines of traffic having to merge into one because of construction, we often remark on how much more pleasant (and safe!) the experience would be if every driver was willing to take his or her own turn.

But how far is the principle to be extended? In a chapter in his outstanding book on Christian ethics, Richard Hays argues that the New Testament calls on believers to renounce "violence in defense of justice."[11] He cites Jesus' strong condemnation of retaliation in the Sermon on the Mount and then notes passages like Romans 12:9–21 that endorse the same principle. Harming or killing enemies is no longer a justifiable option in the light of Jesus' kingdom demand. Believers must renounce violence in their personal relationships and avoid governmental positions that might force them to use violence (i.e., serving in the military, as police officers, etc.).

This pacifist understanding of New Testament teaching has a long and respected history. It has a solid basis in the teaching of Jesus (esp. Matt. 5:38–48) and in other New Testament writers. Few, if any, convincing counterexamples from the New Testament can be found (Jesus' temple cleansing did not clearly involve violence). Moreover, far too many Christians dismiss the pacifist option too quickly and for all the wrong reasons. We protest that we must defend ourselves, for, if we did not, evil would go unchecked: Our wives would be raped, murderers would run rampant, and dictators would impose their evil empires on a helpless world. But God does not always call his people to do what seems prudent, and he reminds us forcibly that he is in control of history. Our job is to obey what he tells us and not to worry overmuch about the results. They are in God's good hands.

As I have learned well over many years of argument with a former pacifist colleague, the wholesale renunciation of violence on the part of Christians can be persuasively argued. But is it finally a persuasive *biblical* position? I am not sure. As we will see in Romans 13:4, Paul clearly recognizes the right of the state to punish wrongdoers. To argue that this job must be left to non-Christians comes perilously close to a kind of "two kingdom" ethic in which what is immoral for Christians is allowed to non-Christians. If the state is God's instrument to accomplish his purposes among them the punishment of wrongdoers, how can Christians be wrong to participate in that service?

An even greater problem for the pacifist view is the Old Testament, where God commands his people to use violence against his enemies. Hays, for instance, admits that the Old Testament legitimizes violence for God's people on some occasions, but that the New Testament witness is normative. But any view that plays one Testament off against the other is suspect.

When the entire biblical witness is considered, it seems that Christians are tacitly allowed to use violence in the service of the state. But is violence allowed to the Christian in everyday personal relationships? Am I justified in defending myself or others if unjustly attacked? Here the biblical evidence is less clear. Both Jesus in Matthew 5 and Paul in Romans 12 seem to be

---

11. *The Moral Vision of the New Testament,* 317–46.

speaking about such personal relationships, and they do not appear to allow exceptions.

In any case, what they both seem clearly to prohibit is vengeance, that is, taking revenge by exacting justice from those who have done wrong to us. Paul, at least, does not seem to be speaking directly to the matter of violence in defense of the innocent. Jesus seems to suggest a much broader principle: "Do not resist an evil person" (Matt. 5:39). Furthermore, both Jesus and Paul enjoin believers, positively, to bless people who do wrong to us, to seek peace with everyone, and to respond to evil with good.

Whether defense of the innocent in our personal lives is justified biblically is unclear. But what is clear is that believers are to cultivate an attitude of love that puts the focus on the good of the other person and not on the defense of our own rights, dignity, or even, perhaps, our very lives. Lived out consistently, the Christian community can become a genuine counterculture that serves as a witness to a world increasingly caught up in the spiral of violence.

Americans demand the right to carry guns and use them because other people are. Poverty-stricken nations spend billions of dollars on weapons so that they can keep up with their neighbors. Our children are taught to defend themselves, to "fight for their rights," and so on. Jesus suggests a better way. While it would be utopian for us to think we can transform society by our attitudes, what the church is ultimately called to do is to be a witness.

Romans 13:1–7

E VERYONE MUST SUBMIT himself to the governing authorities, for there is no authority except that which God
has established. The authorities that exist have been
established by God. ²Consequently, he who rebels against the
authority is rebelling against what God has instituted, and
those who do so will bring judgment on themselves. ³For
rulers hold no terror for those who do right, but for those
who do wrong. Do you want to be free from fear of the one in
authority? Then do what is right and he will commend you.
⁴For he is God's servant to do you good. But if you do wrong,
be afraid, for he does not bear the sword for nothing. He is
God's servant, an agent of wrath to bring punishment on the
wrongdoer. ⁵Therefore, it is necessary to submit to the
authorities, not only because of possible punishment but also
because of conscience.

⁶This is also why you pay taxes, for the authorities are
God's servants, who give their full time to governing. ⁷Give
everyone what you owe him: If you owe taxes, pay taxes; if
revenue, then revenue; if respect, then respect; if honor, then
honor.

IN CONTRAST TO the series of loosely connected
exhortations in 12:9–21, this paragraph focuses
on a single point: the need for Christians to "submit" themselves to governmental authorities. Paul
issues this demand at the beginning of the paragraph. Then, in verses 1b–4,
he gives two reasons why believers must do so: because God has appointed
the authorities (vv. 1b–2), and because the authorities, with God's blessing,
will punish people who do not obey them (vv. 3–4). Verse 5 summarizes: Paul
repeats the demand to submit to authorities and then briefly mentions again
the two reasons for submission (in reverse order). "Because of possible punishment" alludes to verses 3–4, while "because of conscience" sums up the
argument of verses 1b–2. Paul concludes the paragraph on a practical note,
urging the Roman Christians to continue to pay their taxes (vv. 6–7).

Paul's sweeping and apparently unqualified demand that believers obey
whatever governing authorities tell them to do has generated a lot of dis-

cussion and debate. We will explore the key issues in the sections that follow, but one preliminary matter needs to be settled first: Why does Paul include this teaching at this point in his letter to the Romans? To some scholars, the paragraph seems to be a "strange body" in the midst of Romans 12–13, interrupting Paul's discussion of Christian love (12:9–21 and 13:8–10). They therefore argue that this paragraph must have been written and inserted by someone else after Paul wrote the letter.[1]

But we have no evidence that the letter of Romans was ever without this paragraph. In fact, it contributes to Paul's delineation of the transformed living expected of believers in the new age of redemption in an important way. From the beginning of the church the radical demands of the gospel to avoid conformity to this world were taken too far by some overly enthusiastic believers. They thought that the coming of the new age meant that everything in the world was under judgment and to be avoided by truly "spiritual" Christians. They included in "the world" such institutions as marriage (see 1 Cor. 7; 1 Tim. 4:3), sex (1 Cor. 7 again), and the government (see, e.g., 1 Tim. 2:2; Titus 3:1; 1 Peter 2:13–14).

Thus, the apostles had to combat this kind of extremism, pointing out that such activities were, in fact, appointed by God for the good of human beings. Christians should not think their faith requires them to consider these institutions as evil. This helps us understand why Paul felt it necessary to balance his demand that believers not "conform [to] this world" (12:2) with a reminder that governmental authorities were not of the world in this sense, but were, in fact, servants of God, doing his will.

There are additional reasons why 13:1–7 comes where it does here in Romans. In 12:17–21, Paul urged believers not to take vengeance but to allow God to judge. One reason why we can do that is that God has ordained government as the institution to carry out his judgment in this world. Moreover, Paul may have been aware of affairs in Rome during this period that made an exhortation to obey the government especially apropos (see Bridging Contexts).

The basic point of the paragraph is summed up in its opening words: "Everyone must submit himself to the governing authorities." Two words in this command need special attention. First, "governing authorities," as the translation suggests, refers to any person who represents the power of the state: from the local bureaucrat right up to the emperor, president, or prime minister. In the past, a few scholars argued that Paul intended the word "authorities" (Gk. *exousiai*) to refer both to human beings who exercised

---

1. See, e.g., W. Munro, *Authority in Paul and Peter: The Identification of a Pastoral Stratum in the Pauline Corpus and 1 Peter* (Cambridge: Cambridge Univ. Press, 1983), 56–67.

authority and to spiritual powers, who, according to ancient ideas, stood behind those human authorities.[2] But this view is now rightly rejected.[3]

The second key word is "submit" (*hypotasso*). What is important to understand (see Contemporary Significance section) is that this word is broader in its scope than "obey." It calls on believers to recognize that they "stand under" government in the scheme that God has instituted for ruling the world.

With the "for" in the middle of verse 1, Paul introduces his first reason why believers should recognize government's authority over them. Playing on the root of the verb "submit" (*tag-*), he reminds us that God himself has "established" or appointed (*tetagmenoi*) every authority that exists. This point is not a new one. Throughout the Bible, God's providential rule over everything is specifically applied to the rise and fall of political leaders. As Daniel tells King Nebuchadnezzar, "the Most High is sovereign over the kingdoms of men and gives them to anyone he wishes and sets over them the lowliest of men" (Dan. 4:17; see Bridging Contexts).

In verse 2, Paul draws the consequence from God's involvement in the appointment of all political authorities. When we rebel against what they tell us to do, we are rebelling against God himself, and judgment will result. Paul uses a Semitic expression, "receive judgment," to denote this judgment (see also Mark 12:40; Luke 20:47; James 3:1). But is the judgment Paul threatens us with judgment that secular authorities carry out under God's power (see v. 3)[4] or a judgment God himself will mete out at the end of history?[5] A decision between the two is difficult, but perhaps the latter fits the sequence of argument better.

Whatever we decide about the end of verse 2, it is clear that in verses 3—4 Paul specifies that one of the purposes of secular government is to act as "God's servant" in rewarding good and punishing evil. The word "servant" (*diakonos*) in the New Testament usually refers to someone who ministers consciously on God's behalf (e.g., 15:8; 16:1). But *diakonos* is also used to denote a civic official (cf. Est. 1:10; 2:2; 6:13; Jer. 25:9; Wis. Sol. 6:4).[6] This is probably what the word means here. Political official are servants *of God*. Unconsciously, they serve God's purposes in the world. They have the right,

---

2. See esp. Karl Barth, *Church and State* (London: SCM, 1939), 23—36; Oscar Cullmann, *The State in the New Testament* (New York: Harper & Row, 1956), 55—70.

3. See the esp. good discussion in Cranfield, *The Epistle to the Romans*, 656—59, all the more significant because he had earlier held this view ("Some Observations on Romans 13," *NTS* 6 [1959—60]: 241—49).

4. E.g., Godet, *Commentary on Romans*, 442; Murray, *The Epistle to the Romans*, 2:149; Cranfield, *The Epistle to the Romans*, 663—64.

5. E.g., Dunn, *Romans*, 762—63.

6. See the discussion in Moulton-Milligan, *Greek Vocabulary*.

under God, to punish wrongdoers. As Paul puts it, the authorities do not "bear the sword for nothing" (see Contemporary Significance for more on the meaning and importance of this phrase).

Since the state has a God-given responsibility to punish those who do evil, if believers want to be "free from fear of the one in authority," they should do good. They will then be commended by the government. But how can Paul claim that governments punish evil and reward good when he (and we) know of so many counterexamples—of states, such as Nazi Germany, that punished good people and rewarded evil? Is Paul describing the state as it is supposed to function under God, not necessarily how it always does? This has implications for the significance of the text, as we will show below.

With verse 5 Paul summarizes the argument of the paragraph thus far. He reiterates the command to submit and then, in chiastic order, touches on the two reasons for submission:

God ordains governing authorities (vv. 1b–2), "because of possible punishment"
The authorities punish wrongdoers (vv. 3–4), "because of conscience"

The word "conscience" (*syneidesis*) usually refers to that faculty within human beings that informs us of the morality of our actions after they have taken place.[7] But the word can be used more broadly, and this seems to be the case here.[8] *Syneidesis* here refers to our consciousness of God and of his will for us. Because we understand that God has appointed secular rulers, we must submit to them.

"This" at the beginning of verse 6 probably points to this truth. Because we are aware of God's ordaining of governing authorities, we pay taxes. The verb form Paul uses here can also be imperative—"you should pay taxes" (NJB)—but the indicative is more likely, since Paul is explaining (note the *gar*, for, in the Greek) why the Roman Christians act as they do. And just in case we have missed it, Paul reminds us of the key theological point one more time at the end of verse 6. We must respect governmental authorities because they are God's "servants." The point is even stronger here, because the word for "servant" now is *leitourgos*, which is used in the LXX for people who served in the temple and in the New Testament of "ministers" of the Lord (Rom. 15:16; cf. Phil. 2:25; Heb. 1:7; 8:2; 10:11). Paul could not more strongly have shown that civic leaders are, in fact, serving God's own purposes.

Paul concludes (v. 7) on a practical note. He first issues a general command, "Give everyone what you owe him." But the context makes clear that

---

7. See esp. C. A. Pierce, *Conscience in the New Testament* (Chicago: Allenson, 1955), 65–71.
8. Se, e.g., Cranfield, *The Epistle to the Romans*, 668.

"everyone" means especially every civic authority. This becomes even clearer as he gets down to specifics: We are to pay "taxes" (i.e., direct payments to the government, like our income tax) and "revenue" (indirect governmental assessments, e.g., customs duties).

God asks for more than a grudging outward recognition of the government's authority; we are also to accord to the rulers "respect" and "honor." "Respect" translates the Greek word *phobos* (fear), and a few commentators think that Paul may be following Jesus' lead (see Matt. 22:21) in combining honor to "Caesar" with "fear" or obedience to God.[9] But the context has not prepared us for such a shift in focus. Romans 13:7 simply brings to a practical conclusion the teaching of the paragraph. Because they are ordained by God, believers are to respect and honor governing authorities, manifesting that submission in the paying of taxes.

FEW PASSAGES OF SCRIPTURE have been studied and analyzed over the years more than Romans 13:1–7. This history of interpretation has largely been the history of attempts to avoid what the passage at first sight plainly seems to be saying. Paul appears to be demanding that every person always obey whatever any governmental authority tells that person to do, for God has appointed every authority that exists; to obey God, we must obey his appointed representatives. Yet believers in every generation have quailed before the prospect of obeying orders from what appear to be evil, even demonic, rulers—Hitler, of course, is the classic modern example.

Moreover, Scripture itself seems to present *disobedience* of secular rulers as, at least in some cases, a virtue. The classic instance is Peter and John, whom Luke apparently commends for responding to the Sanhedrin's command not to preach about Jesus with these words: "Judge for yourselves whether it is right in God's sight to obey you rather than God. For we cannot help speaking about what we have seen and heard" (Acts 4:19–20; cf. 5:29). Moreover, resistance to the beast's demands for worship in Revelation is a mark of commitment to the Lord. We will explore in the next section just how we can bring Scripture into harmony on this matter of obedience to governmental authorities. But we need first to look at both some ancient and modern issues that will help us to bridge the contexts.

Old Testament and Jewish teaching. As we noted above, what Paul says about governing authorities here stands squarely in line with typical Old

---

9. Cranfield, *The Epistle to the Romans*, 672 (as possible). Note that 1 Peter 2:17 distinguishes between "fearing" (*phobeomai*) God and "honoring" (*timao*) the emperor.

Testament and Jewish teaching. As ruler of all the universe, God controls all the affairs of human history—including especially the governments of the world. God's people therefore never need to worry about whether secular states might thwart God's will, for, as Isaiah reminds us in Isaiah 40:23–24:

> [God] brings princes to naught
>> and reduces the rulers of this world to nothing.
> No sooner are they planted,
>> no sooner are they sown,
>> no sooner do they take root in the ground,
> than he blows on them and they wither,
>> and a whirlwind sweeps them away like chaff.

The Persian monarch Cyrus exemplifies this power of God over human rulers. While apparently coming to power through his own ability and the usual political and military machinations, he was, in reality, God's "anointed," raised up to further God's plan in history (Isa. 45:1–7). We quoted above from Daniel, written when the crisis predicted by Isaiah had come to pass. God used Daniel to humble the proud and arrogant King Nebuchadnezzar, so that he would realize that "the Most High is sovereign over the kingdoms of men and gives them to anyone he wishes" (Dan. 4:17; see also 5:21).

Jewish intertestamental teaching was similar, as Wisdom 6:1–3 makes clear:

> Listen therefore, O kings, and understand;
> learn, O judges of the ends of the earth.
> Give ear, you that rule over multitudes,
> and boast of many nations.
> For your dominion was given you from the Lord,
> and your sovereignty from the Most High;
> he will search out your works and inquire into your plans.

However, alongside the belief that God stands behind secular rulers, there is also the realization that secular rulers must sometimes be resisted in the name of God. The persecution inaugurated by the Seleucid ruler Antiochus IV in the early second century B.C. is the classic Jewish example. He sought to eradicate the Jewish faith by outlawing Torah, forbidding circumcision, and halting the temple sacrifices. True devotion to God, the Jews believed, was displayed by those pious freedom fighters, the Maccabees, who initiated a guerilla war against the Seleucids (see 1 and 2 Maccabees). So Paul's Old Testament and Jewish heritage supplied him with both a robust belief that God himself appointed secular rulers for his purposes and a proud heritage of resistance to evil rulers.

Rome in Paul's day. Another context we must take into consideration in assessing the significance of this text is the Roman empire in Paul's day. Three elements are important here. (1) Paul himself had had a generally positive experience with Roman governmental officials. As a citizen of Rome, he had certain privileges, which aided him in Phillipi (Acts 16) and later in Jerusalem (21:39; 22:23–29; 25:10–11). The Roman governor of Achaia declined to forbid the preaching of the gospel when the Jews asked him to (18:12–17).

(2) Some interpreters think these good experiences led Paul to be naive about Rome and to encourage Christians blindly to obey the emperor and his minions. But this interpretation ignores a second set of data. Paul believed that the Lord of his life was unjustly killed by the Roman empire. Surely the fact of the crucified Jesus, basic to Paul's own faith and his preaching alike, would have kept him from any naiveté about government. In addition, the history of God's people, so important in forming Paul's own belief system, was filled with examples of men and women who earned great heavenly reward precisely for disobeying evil rulers (e.g., Dan. 3; 6).

(3) A final element of the first-century Roman empire may also play a role in Romans 13:1–7: a growing discontent with the power of the government. The Roman historian Tacitus tells us that there was considerable resistance in the middle 50s to paying indirect taxes, culminating in a tax revolt in A.D. 58.[10]

These forces at work in the larger society may have led the Roman Christians to question their need to obey the government. Greatly exacerbating such tendencies was the indirect influence of the Jewish zealot movement. Some of the Christians in Rome were Jewish, and some may well have sympathized with the increasingly prominent and popular revolutionary program of the Zealots, who were seeking to rescue Israel from Roman oppression by violence.

In conclusion, what we know of the history of the period suggests that the Christians in Rome may have become imbalanced in their view of government, led by the unrest of their broader culture, the influence of the Zealots, and their own "world-renouncing" theology to regard governmental authority as something to be ignored at will. Romans 13:1–7 may well be an attempt to right this imbalance. In other words, Paul is not giving a careful, balanced teaching about the state; rather, he is deliberately focusing on only one side of the issue.

Our own context. It can be tempting to think of "context" as something that affects only the biblical authors. We must indeed recognize their cultural situation and allow for it as we interpret what they wrote. But if the biblical

---

10. Tacitus, *Ann.* 13.50ff.

authors *wrote* in a certain context, we also *read* in a specific context, and that context affects the way we read. With no issue is our own context more determinative than in this matter of submission to government.

(1) Most of us read the text within the tradition of the liberal democracies of the twentieth century. We are accustomed to governments elected by the people, following certain broad, humanitarian guidelines in their laws and procedures, susceptible to pressure brought on them by ordinary citizens. All this is completely foreign to Paul's context. Transferring what he and other biblical authors say about government from their political situation to ours is not easy. Christians who still live under autocratic and even repressive regimes can probably appreciate what Paul is teaching better than those of us who have never had to live in this kind of atmosphere.

(2) We read Romans 13 with the horrifying example of the Holocaust vivid in our memory. Here is a modern incarnation of a demonic governmental system at its worst. Almost every interpretation of Romans 13 written since 1945 explicitly brings the situation of Hitler's Germany into the discussion. It is pointless to claim that such experiences do not affect our interpretation. Would Karl Barth have argued as strongly that spiritual powers (potentially evil ones) are behind human rulers if he had not fled Nazi Germany before World War II? Would Ernst Käsemann have been as skeptical about the Pauline authorship of this passage if he had not almost been arrested and sent to a concentration camp for preaching the gospel during the war?

Few of us have so direct an experience of governmental evil. But some of us have; and all of us have imbedded deep within us the sense that human rulers can turn against God and his people and take on the attitudes and policies of the devil himself. We cannot divest ourselves of this knowledge; nor should we, because it counts as evidence about the world as it now functions under God. But we must also acknowledge the ways in which the broad culture and our own experiences perhaps prevent us from reading and applying Romans 13 as we should.

WHERE IS THE EXCEPTION? As we noted above, the key question most of us ask when we come to Romans 13 is not "What does it mean?" but "Where is the exception?" Since it is taught so consistently in Scripture, we do not have too much difficulty coming to grips with the idea that God has ordained all governing authorities and that we must recognize that we stand under them. But we do have difficulty with the apparent demand of Romans 13 that we always do whatever any governmental authority tells us to do. We know there are exceptions in Scripture itself, and we believe deeply that it was contrary to God's will for Germans to obey their rulers and help the Nazis kill millions of Jews, Poles, Russians, and so on. But how can we justify any exceptions in Romans 13? On what basis can we allow exceptions without doing violence to these verses? Seven possibilities deserve to be mentioned—listed here in the order of least probable to most probable.

(1) Paul does not demand submission to the government because Romans 13:1–7 is a late, non-Pauline, addition to the letter. We dismissed this possibility above.

(2) Paul is naive about human government. His own experience lead him to be far more optimistic about rulers than is justified. What he writes in 13:1–7 is his own prejudiced opinion, and we can ignore it. But not only does such a view deny a fundamental facet of the faith—the authority of Scripture—it also ignores the reality of Paul's own circumstances.

(3) Paul demands that Christians obey government only for a very short time, until Christ returns to establish his eternal kingdom. But, while Paul believes that Christ can come back at any time, he also teaches believers to be prepared for life in this world on a continuing basis.

(4) Paul insists that Christians obey governing authorities only as long these authorities, and the spiritual rulers standing behind them, remain in submission to Christ. As we noted on verse 1, however, a dual reference to both secular and spiritual rulers in this passage is unlikely.

(5) Paul is demanding obedience to the governing authorities as they exist in his time and place—not for rulers in other situations. As we have noted, there may have been good reason for Paul to write as he does to the Roman Christians because of their own special circumstances. He is writing, then, only to that situation, and we are wrong to extrapolate from that situation to others. This point must be taken seriously. Indeed, we think that Paul focuses only on the positive side of government here because of the need he faces to redress an imbalance in the Roman Christians' own perspective (see Bridging Contexts section). But while the circumstantial nature of Paul's writing limits *what* Paul says, it does not limit the *scope* of what he says. In verse 1 he extends his principle beyond the situation in first-century Rome to the situation of the world in general: "There is *no* authority except that which God has established" (italics added).

(6) In our interpretation of verses 3–4, we suggested Paul admits only of the possibility that states will reward good and punish evil because he is implicitly thinking of the ideal state—the state when it operates as God intends it to. Paul may, therefore, be calling on Christians to submit to governing authorities only as long as they are fulfilling their mission, under God,

to restrain evil and encourage good. When a state ceases to do so, Christians are free to disobey its mandates.[11]

The problem with this view is that Paul does not explicitly qualify his command with any such restriction. Yet this idea has merit, for it is difficult otherwise to explain why Paul ignores the possibility that the state may punish good and reward evil. He is describing how the state is supposed to function under God and is calling believers to submit to states that function in that way. Perhaps there is room in what he says to allow believers to turn against the state when it turns against God—as it does, for example, in Revelation.

(7) In demanding "submission" to the state, Paul is not necessarily demanding obedience to every mandate of the state. Key to this restriction is the recognition that the word "submit" (*hypotasso*) in Paul is not a simple equivalent to "obey" (*hypakouo*). To be sure, they overlap, and in some contexts, perhaps, they cannot be distinguished (cf. 1 Peter 3:1, 6). Moreover, submission is usually expressed through obedience.

Nevertheless, submission is broader and more basic than obedience. To submit is to recognize one's subordinate place in a hierarchy established by God. It is to acknowledge that certain institutions or people have been placed over us and have the right to our respect and deference. In addition to rulers (see also Titus 3:1), Paul also calls on believers to submit to their spiritual leaders (1 Cor. 16:16) and even to one another (Eph. 5:21; i.e., in the ways Paul outlines in 5:22–6:9). Christian slaves are to submit to their masters (Titus 2:9), Christian prophets to other prophets (1 Cor. 14:32), and Christian wives to their husbands (1 Cor. 14:35 [?]; Eph. 5:24; Col. 3:18; Titus 2:5). In each case, one person is to recognize the rightful leadership role that another human being has in his or her life.

But implicit always in the idea of submission is the need to recognize that God is at the pinnacle of any hierarchy. While not always explicit, Paul assumes that one's ultimate submission must be to God and that no human being can ever stand as the ultimate authority for a believer.

The parallel between a Christian's submitting to government and a wife's submitting to her husband is particularly helpful. The wife is to recognize that God has ordained her husband to be her "head," that is, her leader and guide. Thus, she must follow his leadership. But Paul would never think that a wife must always do whatever her husband demanded. I once counseled a Christian woman who took her need to submit to her husband so seriously that she felt obliged to obey him by engaging in sex with him and another woman at the same time. I urged her to recognize that her ultimate allegiance was

---

11. See, e.g., Paul Achtemeier, *Romans* (Atlanta: John Knox, 1985), 205; Franz Leenhardt, *The Epistle to the Romans* (London: Lutterworth, 1961), 323–25.

to God, the authority standing over her husband. She needed to follow the higher authority in this case and disobey her husband. But this did not mean that she was simply to dismiss her husband or to renounce his general authority over her.

In a similar way, it seems to me, we can also, as believers, continue to submit to governing authorities even as, in certain specific instances, we find that we cannot obey them. When they order us to do something incompatible with our allegiance to God, our higher authority, we must, as Peter and John put it, "obey God rather than men" (Acts 5:29).

Christians will, of course, disagree about what those specific occasions might be. At the time of Vietnam War, for instance, some Christians were convinced because of pacifist convictions along with doubts about the justness of the war itself that they would be denying their God by obeying the government's insistence that they serve in the military. Other Christians were equally convinced that serving in the military did not conflict with God's will. These kinds of conflicts are undoubtedly going to increase in our pluralistic, permissive society.

But it is our brothers and sisters living elsewhere who face these conflicts with particular intensity. For instance, believers living in countries ruled by Islamic governments face many difficult conflicts between God's will and the decree of their rulers. How should they decide to act on these issues? Those of us not faced by these choices and their consequences are not in a position to pontificate from a distance.

The burden of this text. Our final word on this issue, however, must respect the intention of this passage. Clearly, it does not intend to encourage disobedience to the government or even to lay the theological basis for such disobedience. It warns us against the danger of ignoring the rightful place government has in God's ordering of the world according to his purposes. Government—and each individual state and ruler—is appointed by God. Christians seeking to do God's will, therefore, recognize the right of the governing authorities to command them to do things, and they should, as much as possible, do what the government says.

This message is particularly appropriate in our current cultural climate, in which many are increasingly disrespectful of any authority. The various right-wing organizations rebelling against the United States government (sometimes in the name of Christ) are an obvious manifestation of this antiauthority tendency. But we see it just as clearly in the growing number of people who simply ignore the government's rules about speed limits on highways or paying taxes.

One of my sons works as a caddy over the summer. He is not only the only caddy he knows who actually reports his income, but he is the only one he knows (Christian or not) who even shows concern about what the tax law might be. The culture we live in tells us to make decisions based on what is convenient or profitable for ourselves (and avoid, of course, getting caught). But the Scriptures call us to place our lives under the lordship of God in Christ. God has ordained government as his instrument to order and run society.

Capital punishment. Recent movies (e.g., *Dead Man Walking*) and books (e.g., John Grisham's *The Chamber*) have brought forcefully before us some of the tangled issues involved in the death penalty. The growing use of DNA testing has added fuel to the fire of controversy by proving the innocence of a number of death-row inmates. The United States remains one of a few Western democracies that allows the death penalty. Arguably, one reason is the fading remnant of a general Christian ethic. But to what degree is the death penalty warranted from Scripture?

Christians who favor the death penalty usually cite the provisions of the Old Testament law, which required death for a number of offenses. However, as most sophisticated interpreters recognize, these legal texts are not conclusive. After all, it is not clear that the legal provisions of the Mosaic code, designed for Old Testament Israel, are still valid for the church—not to mention the modern state.

More pertinent, perhaps, is the principle enunciated by the Lord to Noah: "And for your lifeblood I will surely demand an accounting. I will demand an accounting from every animal. And from each man, too, I will demand an accounting for the life of his fellow man. Whoever sheds the blood of man, by man shall his blood be shed; for in the image of God has God made man" (Gen. 9:5–6). Here is a general principle, antedating the law of Moses and grounded in the theology of creation. Most Christian ethicists who favor the death penalty cite this text as critical for their position.

But other Christians think that the Old Testament principle of "blood for blood" is implicitly renounced in the New Testament. The "eye for an eye" method of retaliation is explicitly criticized (Matt. 5:33–48). Moreover, the overwhelming biblical emphasis on the sanctity of human life rules out the taking of a criminal's life as much as it rules out taking the life of an unborn baby.

For these reasons, Romans 13:4 becomes especially significant. For here we have a New Testament text that apparently says something about the state's right to execute people. The state, Paul claims, has the God-given task of punishing the wrongdoer, and, in describing that task, he asserts that the ruler "does not bear the sword for nothing." Is this not clear New Testament warrant for the death penalty?

A lot depends on what Paul means by "bearing the sword." Some interpreters claim that it refers to the Roman *ius gladii*, the authority (possessed by all magistrates) of inflicting the sentence of death.[12] But this practice seems to have been confined to the power of Roman provincial governors to condemn to death Roman citizens serving in the military.[13] Others think Paul is alluding to the authority of the police[14] or to the military.[15] We cannot be sure of the background. This makes it difficult to be sure how far to take Paul's statement. Certainly he accords to the state the right to punish evildoers, and that punishment in Paul's day certainly included death. But it is not finally clear that Paul is endorsing the death penalty. The debate will no doubt continue; what will be important is that believers seek to establish what they believe on the basis of all of Scripture, not just isolated texts.

---

12. See Tacitus, *Histories* 3.68; cf. Barrett, *The Epistle to the Romans*, 247.

13. A. N. Sherwin-White, *Roman Society and Roman Law in the New Testament* (Oxford: Clarendon, 1963), 8–11.

14. Philo refers to the police in Egypt as "sword-bearers" (*Special Laws* 2.92–95).

15. E.g., Cranfield, *The Epistle to the Romans*, 666–67.

Romans 13:8–10

L ET NO DEBT remain outstanding, except the continuing debt to love one another, for he who loves his fellow man has fulfilled the law. ⁹The commandments, "Do not commit adultery," "Do not murder," "Do not steal," "Do not covet," and whatever other commandment there may be, are summed up in this one rule: "Love your neighbor as yourself." ¹⁰Love does no harm to its neighbor. Therefore love is the fulfillment of the law.

WHILE PAUL'S CALL for believers to submit to governing authorities has a secure place in his outline of the "good . . . and perfect" will of God (12:2), it is a bit of a detour from the main line of his description of the believer's responsibilities. With 13:8–10, Paul returns to this main line, picking up the theme of love from 12:9–21. The earlier text gave an overview of ways in which believers should show sincere love. He now shows that this sincere love is the heart of new covenant ethics. All the commandments of the Old Testament law culminate in the demand that we love our neighbors as ourselves.

While 13:8–10 connect in substance to 12:9–21, Paul cleverly plays on the notion of "debt" that he introduced in 13:7 to create a transition back into the topic of love. Believers are to pay their "debts" (cf. v. 7); they are not to "be in debt" to anyone (cf. v. 8). But, Paul acknowledges, one debt will never be discharged: the debt of love we owe to other people. As the early church father Origen put it, "Let your only debt that is unpaid be that of love—a debt which you should always be attempting to discharge in full, but will never succeed in discharging."[1]

The second part of verse 8 explains ("for," *gar*) why we will never discharge this debt of love: love of "the other" (lit. trans.; NIV "fellow man") "fulfills" the law. The "one another" language used in the first part of the verse suggests Paul may be thinking of the need to love our fellow Christians (see 12:10, 16). But by using the more general "the other," Paul may be alluding to Jesus' insistence that love not be confined to those like us, but, as the good Samaritan illustrates, should be displayed to everyone we come into contact with—even those different from us.

---

1. Quoted in Sanday and Headlam, *The Epistle to the Romans*, 373.

In 13:9–10, Paul explains just how it is that loving others "fulfills" the law. The love command, found in Leviticus 19:18 and cited by Jesus himself when asked about the "greatest commandment" (Matt. 22:36–40), sums up all the other commandments. Paul cites as examples four of the most famous commandments from the Decalogue: the prohibitions against adultery, murder, stealing, and coveting.[2] But how does the love command sum up these other commands? The verb Paul uses here (*anakephalaioo*) is rare in the Bible, occurring elsewhere only in his assertion that God intends to "bring ... under one head" all things in Christ (Eph. 1:10). It was used in literary Greek to refer to the summation or conclusion of a book or speech,[3] but this meaning is not relevant to this text. Thus, we are left to draw our own conclusions from the context and from Paul's teaching elsewhere.

Two main possibilities emerge. (1) Paul may mean that love for others is the essential ingredient that must accompany obedience to all the other commandments.[4] We must still obey these commandments, but they cannot truly be obeyed without a loving spirit. (2) Paul may also mean that the demand of love for others replaces the other commandments.[5] When we truly love "the other," we automatically do what the other commandments of the law require. As Paul puts it in verse 10, "love does no harm to its neighbor." No one who truly loves another person will murder, commit adultery, steal, or covet.

We think the latter interpretation is closer to the truth. As we have argued, Paul elsewhere proclaims that believers are released from the binding authority of the Mosaic law (see 6:14–15; 7:4–6). Paul's use of "fulfillment" language in this paragraph (13:8, 10) also suggests that he views the love command as the eschatological "replacement" for the various commandments of the Mosaic law (see Gal. 5:13–15).

THE GREATEST COMMANDMENT. Paul's teaching in this paragraph cannot be understood apart from Jesus' teaching about the greatest commandment. That teaching, in turn, may reflect some Jewish traditions. The great emphasis the Jews placed on the law and

---

2. In both Ex. 20:1–17 and Deut. 5:6–21, the prohibition of murder comes before that of adultery. But Paul's order is found in an important manuscript of the LXX (uncial B) and is reflected elsewhere in early Jewish and Christian texts (e.g., Luke 18:20; James 2:11; Philo, etc.).

3. See H. Schlier, *TDNT*, 3:681–82.

4. See esp. Schreiner, *Romans*, 692–95.

5. See, e.g., Deidun, *New Covenant Morality*, 153; Westerholm, *Israel's Law*, 201–2.

large number of commandments and prohibitions in that law led to discussions among the rabbis about the most important commandment(s). Generally, however, these discussions were theoretical in nature: The rabbis wondered if a single commandment would serve as the "logical" starting point for all the others, the commandment from which all the others could be derived.[6]

Some Jews preceded Jesus in summarizing the essential obligation in terms of love of God and love of others.[7] Thus, when Jesus was asked about the "greatest" commandment in the law (Matt. 22:36), his response was not altogether new. But what separated Jesus from his Jewish contemporaries was a more radical approach to the law as a whole. In claiming to be "Lord ... of the Sabbath" (Mark 2:27–28) and to have sovereign authority to determine the meaning and application of the law (Matt. 5:17–48), Jesus demonstrated an authority that astonished the crowds and signaled his unique status as the One on whom the ages turned. With the coming of the kingdom and the preaching of the gospel to all the nations, the law no longer has the same authority as before.

Jesus, in other words, institutes a new law, built on the twin foundations of love for God and love for the neighbor and focused on his own teaching. When he commissions his followers to "make disciples of all nations," he charges them to teach all *he* taught them (Matt. 28:16–20).

Paul refers extensively (though implicitly) to Jesus' teaching throughout this part of Romans. Surely he builds his teaching in verses 8–10 on Jesus' reduction of the Mosaic law to love of God and love for one's neighbor. This means, among other things, that he probably does not intend love for the neighbor to be the sole criterion by which we are to judge right behavior. He focuses on that command because he is thinking in this context of the way we are to relate to other people. But he would not want to exclude the other commandment that Christ singled out: the need to love our God with all our heart, mind, soul, and body.

The believer's obligation emerges from both these commandments. Against the background of Jesus' teaching, we cannot imagine Paul suggesting that love for God, expressed in obedience to all his commandments, can ever be omitted when considering the ultimate responsibility of the believer.

---

6. See the discussion in E. E. Urbach, *The Sages: Their Concepts and Beliefs* (2 vols.; Jerusalem: Magnes, 1975), 1:349.

7. See, e.g., *T. Iss.* 5:1–2: "Keep the Law of God, my children; achieve integrity; live without malice, not tinkering with God's commands or your neighbor's affairs. Love the Lord and your neighbor; be compassionate toward poverty and sickness" (see also *T. Iss.* 7:6; *T. Dan* 5:3; Philo, *Abraham* 208; *Special Laws* 2.63).

DEBTS. AMERICANS LOVE DEBT. We borrow to buy houses, cars, stereos, food, medicine, clothes, appliances, lottery tickets. College students take on staggering debts to finance their education. Churches borrow immense sums to erect buildings. What does Romans 13:8—"Let no debt remain outstanding"—say to our debt-ridden society?

A few interpreters, taking a more literal rendering of the Greek—"Owe nothing to anyone"—think that the Bible here prohibits any form of borrowing at all. Individual believers should not borrow money, nor should churches. We should wait to build the building, buy the house or car, purchase the stereo, and so on, until we have the cash to pay for it up front. But this is probably not what verse 8 means. The NIV rendering gets the sense of what Paul is saying. He is not prohibiting us from borrowing money but demanding we pay back what we owe. If I have entered into an agreement with a bank to pay them $800 per month for thirty years to buy a house, I need to discharge my obligation by paying that money on time. So what the text calls on us to do is to be careful, prudent financial planners, not taking on any more debt that we are sure we can handle.

Yet even this principle is sadly neglected in our day—by believers as well as unbelievers. As an elder in my church, I frequently have to deal with people who have overextended themselves and are asking the church to help them pay their debts. Of course, some people have encountered unexpected circumstances for which they are not to blame—catastrophic illness or sudden loss of employment. But we have had to deal with believers who made bad decisions about debt so often that we have instituted a program of financial counseling that is tied to our charitable giving. We are extending the program to anyone in the church who is interested.

The age we live in seeks to conform us to its pleasure-oriented, present gratification spirit. Buy what you *want* now so that you can enjoy life; let the future worry about itself. Believers need to anchor themselves solidly in a contrasting worldview—one that reminds us that present pleasure should never be our focus in life and that God expects his people to manage prudently and for his glory the resources he has entrusted to us.

Love and law. One of the perennial issues among ethicists is the relationship between inner motivations and external law or commands—or, to put it in terms of our text, the relationship between love and law. Which is primary? Does one take precedence over the other? Am I to decide what to do in a given situation by looking for a commandment to guide me? Or should I do what seems to be the loving thing? The interpretation of this text given above may suggest that we subscribe to this last viewpoint. For we have suggested that Paul teaches that obeying the love command is itself the fulfillment of all the other commandments of the law. But we need to qualify the significance of our interpretation in two important ways.

(1) The commands Paul has in view here are the commandments of the *Mosaic law*. We must never forget the important point that he uses the word "law" (*nomos*) in a specific way, reflective of his own background and situation. *Nomos* in Paul does not mean (at least not usually) law in general but the law of Moses specifically—the Torah. So what the apostle claims in this paragraph is no more than that the other commandments of the Mosaic law are no longer directly applicable to the believer.

As we have noted elsewhere, however, Paul clearly believes that other commandments—those of Jesus and the apostles—do stand as an authority for believers. These commands embody many of the same moral principles found, for instance, in the Decalogue. Of course, Paul would insist that love for others is basic to these new covenant obligations as well. But we misread Romans 13:8–10 if we think Paul does away with commandments altogether. As we argued in our comments on 12:1–2, the primary motivation and direction of Christian motivation comes from within us, as the Spirit "renews our minds" and instills love for others within us.

Mere outward conformity to commandments is not what God wants. He wants "sincere love": an honest, consistent concern for other people that spills over into actions of all kinds. When we love rightly, with the love that the Spirit inspires in us, we cannot help but obey whatever commandments God has given us. For he does not speak with two voices. What he requires is what his Spirit inspires. But because our minds are not perfectly renewed and because we can misunderstand what love requires, we still need commandments to remind us of the absolute demands of God and to keep us on "the straight and narrow."

(2) This brings us to the second qualification. I do not want anyone to misread what I am saying as advocating what is called "situation ethics" (see comments in the Contemporary Significance section on 12:9–21). This approach to ethics argues that there are no moral absolutes at all, except the demand of love. Any other commandment we name must be interpreted in light of the situation. Whether we obey that commandment or how must be determined on a case-by-case basis, and love will decide the matter.

We are commanded, for instance, not to lie. But suppose a friend of mine asks if another friend really said something nasty about that person. By answering truthfully I may damage the relationship between these two. So love for them demands that I tell a falsehood. But I am perfectly ethical in doing so since I am following the dictates of love.

I do not think this is at all what Paul is suggesting. The idea that the demand of love has a hermeneutical function, enabling us to interpret the meaning of other commandments, is not taught in the New Testament. We must love others, and that love should be the touchstone of the way I conduct myself in relation to others. But that demand of love does not absolve me from obeying the other commandments God has given me.

Romans 13:11-14

AND DO THIS, understanding the present time. The hour has come for you to wake up from your slumber, because our salvation is nearer now than when we first believed. ¹²The night is nearly over; the day is almost here. So let us put aside the deeds of darkness and put on the armor of light. ¹³Let us behave decently, as in the daytime, not in orgies and drunkenness, not in sexual immorality and debauchery, not in dissension and jealousy. ¹⁴Rather, clothe yourselves with the Lord Jesus Christ, and do not think about how to gratify the desires of the sinful nature.

THIS SHORT PARAGRAPH concludes the survey of Christian lifestyle issues that Paul began in 12:1– 2. It brings us back full circle to our starting point, for again the apostle issues a general demand that believers take on a totally new way of life in light of the climax of history that has come in the work of Christ. In 12:1–2, he called on us to renounce the ways of "this world," judged and passing away in Christ, and to "be transformed" in all our thinking and conduct. Now he demands that we "clothe [ourselves] with the Lord Jesus Christ" (13:14) in light of the "day" that is almost here.

Eschatology, an understanding of the times in which we live, should govern our conduct. We need to recognize both what God is doing and what he plans to do and then live accordingly. The verses of the paragraph fall neatly into these two basic categories: Understanding the times (13:11–12a, the "indicative") leads to right living (13:12b–14, the "imperative").

Paul signals the summarizing nature of these verses with the transitional phrase "And do this" ("do" in the NIV, while not explicit in the Greek, is a legitimate addition). "This" (touto) refers to the command to love in 13:8–10,[1] but it probably includes all Paul has taught in 12:1–13:10.[2] We should be motivated all the more to do all these things—think of ourselves in the right way, exercise our gifts for the good of the body, display sincere love, obey the government, love others—as we "understand the present time."

---

1. Murray, *The Epistle to the Romans*, 2:165; Fitzmyer, *Romans*, 682.
2. Godet, *Commentary on Romans*, 449; Cranfield, *The Epistle to the Romans*, 680.

The Greek word for "time" is *kairos*, which connotes "appointed hour," as when we say, "It is time to play the game." So, Paul suggests, believers need to remember what time it is: "Salvation is nearer now then when we first believed." As he often does, Paul uses "salvation" (*soteria*) language to refer to the final accomplishment of God's plan in history (see his use of "save" [*sozo*] in 5:9–10 and comments there). That final day, the day of Christ's return and the glorification of the believer, is getting closer all the time.

Thus, we need to "wake up from [our] slumber." Why? Because "the night is nearly over; the day is almost here" (v. 12a). Paul skillfully blends two important strands of tradition using the imagery of day and night. The day/night contrast was popular in general moral teaching in the ancient world as a way of distinguishing good behavior from evil behavior. The night is the time when people indulge their passions and when thieves and other scoundrels do their work. But the Old Testament and Judaism also referred to the time when God would intervene to save and to judge as the "Day of the Lord" (see Bridging Contexts for further discussion). Paul reminds us that the Day of the Lord is near, which should motivate us to put away the kinds of behavior associated with the night of this present evil age (see 12:2).

Paul makes explicit these behavioral consequences in 13:12b–14. As is commonly done in the New Testament, the transition from one form of conduct to another is put in terms of "putting off" one set of clothes and "putting on" another (see also, e.g., Eph. 4:22, 25; Col. 3:8, 12; cf. Eph. 6:11, 14; 1 Thess. 5:8; James 1:21; 1 Peter 2:1). As we "put aside [off] the deeds of darkness," we are to "put on the armor of light." Why "armor" or "weapons" (*hopla*)? Because, as Calvin suggests, "we are to carry on a warfare for the Lord."[3]

Verse 13 carries on the contrast between the behavior typical of the daytime/the Day of the Lord and that characteristic of the nightime/this present evil age. The Day of the Lord may not have come yet, but it is so close that we should live as if it were here. We should "walk [*peripateo*; NIV, behave] decently," which suggests behavior that is careful, decorous, and restrained (see 1 Cor. 7:35; 12:23, 24; 14:40; 1 Thess. 4:12). We are to avoid, in contrast, those actions typical of the nightime: unrestrained sexual conduct and drinking to excess (i.e., what we today call partying). Interestingly, Paul concludes his list with some unexpected items: "dissension and jealousy." He probably adds these because he is thinking ahead to the next subject he will address: the divisions in the Roman community (ch. 14).

Paul concludes with a final contrast. Picking up the imagery of 13:12b, Paul commands: "Clothe yourselves with the Lord Jesus Christ" (v. 14). He

---

3. Calvin, *Epistle of Paul to the Romans,* 489.

is probably building on his earlier presentation of Christ as a corporate figure, the "new self" to whom believers have been joined by faith (5:12–21; 6:6). What has happened in principle must take place in reality: We who are in Christ must envelop ourselves with him in such a way that he directs all our thinking and conduct.

A few interpreters (and many preachers!) argue that this command is a once-for-all one: We must reach a point of crisis in which we determine to "put on" Christ for good. But this interpretation rests on a faulty understanding of the Greek aorist tense used here. The tense does not (in itself) denote "once-for-all" action but rather states simply and without adornment that the action is to take place. In light of what the New Testament says about the believer's continuing battle with sin, we must regularly make the decision to "put on" Christ.

As the negative counterpart to putting on Christ, we are also not to consider how we might "gratify the desires of the sinful nature." In typical NIV fashion, "sinful nature" translates *sarx* (flesh, see comments on 8:1–13), the word Paul uses to encapsulate the human condition apart from Christ. In commanding us not to "think about" (*pronoian*, i.e., foresight, concern) gratifying the flesh, Paul is urging us not to allow our human impulses to dominate our behavior.

ETHICS AND ESCHATOLOGY. Paul's ethical appeal in this paragraph grows out of eschatology. We are to live a certain way because we recognize the period of time in which we live. God superintends the course of human history, and we can live rightly only by knowing what phase of history we are now in. As noted above, Paul beautifully captures the relationship of eschatology and ethics by using the same imagery for both. Building on widespread traditions of his time, Paul uses "day," "daytime," and "light" imagery to denote both. Only by appreciating these traditions will we be able to understand what he is communicating in here.

The contrast between light and darkness is a natural way to express the contrast between good and evil, moral and immoral behavior. For whatever psychological and/or cultural reasons, human beings have always associated darkness with danger and evil. Bad things happen in the dark, and so human beings have sought to drive back the darkness by felling forests, closing doors and curtains after nightfall, and increasing the intensity and spread of light. The literature of almost all people—including Jews, Greeks, and Romans—freely uses darkness to characterize evil actions. As an inevitable counterpart, good deeds are related to the light. Examples are far too numerous to list, but typical is *Testament of Levi* 19:1: "Choose for yourselves either darkness or light, either the law of the Lord or the works of Belial."

But this moral strand in the imagery of light and darkness mixes quickly and sometimes seamlessly with an eschatological strand derived from the Old Testament and Jewish use of the term *day*. The "Day of the Lord" is a standard phrase to denote the time when God will intervene to save his people and to judge their enemies. Note, for instance, Obadiah 15–17:

> The day of the LORD is near for all nations.
> As you have done, it will be done to you;
>   your deeds will return upon your own head.
> Just as you drank on my holy hill,
>   so all the nations will drink continually;
> they will drink and drink
>   and be as if they had never been.
> But on Mount Zion will be deliverance;
>   it will be holy,
> and the house of Jacob
>   will possess its inheritance.

So common was the imagery that the phrase could be abbreviated and the sense still clearly communicated, as in Jeremiah 30:8–9:

> "In that day," declares the LORD Almighty,
>   "I will break the yoke off their necks
> and will tear off their bonds;
>   no longer will foreigners enslave them.
> Instead, they will serve the LORD their God
>   and David their king,
>   whom I will raise up for them."

Jewish writers continued the imagery, and we find it frequently in the New Testament as well. Here, however, the Christology of the early church affects the wording of the phrase. So, in addition to the "day of the Lord," we also find a variety of other expressions, such as "the day of our Lord Jesus Christ" (1 Cor. 1:8), "the day of Christ" (Phil. 1:10; 2:16), and so on.

As a natural progression, especially important for the imagery of Romans 13:8–10, the idea of the Day of the Lord was associated with light and, by contrast, the evil time in which the people lived with night and darkness. See, for instance, Amos 5:18: "Woe to you who long for the day of the LORD! Why do you long for the day of the LORD? That day will be darkness, not light." "Darkness" and "light" by themselves were used to contrast this age with the age to come (see *1 Enoch* 58:2–6):

The righteous ones shall be in the light of the sun and the elect ones in the light of eternal life which has no end.... The sun has shined upon the earth and the darkness is over. There shall be a light that has no end.... For already darkness has been destroyed, light shall be permanent before the Lord of the Spirits, and the light of uprightness shall stand firm forever and ever before the Lord of the Spirits.[4]

We must read Romans 13:12a in light of this tradition. According to Paul, this present evil age is ending soon and the time of God's final victory is at hand. But the immediate sequel—"So let us put aside the deeds of darkness and put on the armor of light"—reveals that the eschatological language is tied up with ethical nuances as well. "Dark" deeds are typical of this age ("the night"), while in the "day" of the Lord only deeds of light will be tolerated. Recognizing that dawn is upon us and that the Lord Jesus may return at any time to finalize his victory, we need to live even now as if that day has come.

Indeed, as Paul's teaching makes clear, that final age of sinlessness and salvation, while not yet here in full force, has already been introduced into history through the work of Christ and the presence of the Spirit. Paul is more explicit about this typical New Testament "inaugurated eschatology" in a closely related passage (1 Thess. 5:1–10):

> Now, brothers, about times and dates we do not need to write to you, for you know very well that the day of the Lord will come like a thief in the night. While people are saying, "Peace and safety," destruction will come on them suddenly, as labor pains on a pregnant woman, and they will not escape.
>
> But you, brothers, are not in darkness so that this day should surprise you like a thief. You are all sons of the light and sons of the day. We do not belong to the night or to the darkness. So then, let us not be like others, who are asleep, but let us be alert and self-controlled. For those who sleep, sleep at night, and those who get drunk, get drunk at night. But since we belong to the day, let us be self-controlled, putting on faith and love as a breastplate, and the hope of salvation as a helmet. For God did not appoint us to suffer wrath but to receive salvation through our Lord Jesus Christ. He died for us so that, whether we are awake or asleep, we may live together with him.

The "day of the Lord" is still on its way (1 Thess. 5:2), but believers even now are "sons of the light and sons of the day" (v. 5); we "belong to the day" (v. 8). What Paul hints at in Romans 13, then, he makes explicit here: We

---

4. For these references and a full discussion, see E. Lövestam, *Spiritual Wakefulness in the New Testament* (Lund: Gleerup, 1963), 10–24.

display the "deeds of light" not only because the day of the Lord is coming, but also because we already participate, by faith, in that day.

BEING AND LIVING. One of the most important points of application for the contemporary Christian is left unsaid in the paragraphs above, although it is presumed throughout: A great gap can exist between who we *are* and how we *live*. Paul has theologized about this fundamental tension in Romans 6, where he argues that our new relationship to Christ rescues us from slavery to sin. Being in Christ means that we now have the power to do what God tells us to do, to live Christianly from morning to night, day in and day out. But even in Romans 6 Paul tells us that this new power is not a magical potion that automatically makes us holy. We have to respond to God's offer of grace and allow his power in Christ to capture every part of our being at every moment of time. Holiness is both a gift and an accomplishment. God gives it, but we have to accept it and give it pride of place in our affections and intentions.

In 13:11—14 also Paul presumes that God is working in us. He writes to people who have believed and who are already saved (v. 11). But he can still tell us that we need to "clothe [ourselves] with the Lord Jesus Christ." In one sense, of course, we are already clothed with Christ (Gal. 3:27). By faith we belong to him. He is "in [us]" (Rom. 8:10), and we are "in [him]" (6:11). But Paul wants us to make Christ the focal point of everything we do. He should be like a suit of clothes that we wear all the time. His dominating presence should guide us to do things pleasing to God and restrain us from activity inconsistent with the Lord whom we represent.

Paul is especially concerned in this passage with activity typical of the night: immoral sexual practices, excessive drinking, coarse joking—the kind of partying that most of us are all too familiar with. At the risk of sounding like a Puritan (curiously, an expression of disapprobation even among Christians), I suggest that the contemporary church needs a "wake-up call" about these activities.

When I first came to the Lord, in the 1970s, what we might call the fundamentalist strand in evangelicalism was much stronger than it is today. Often indistinguishable in their theology from evangelicals, fundamentalists typically put much greater stress on separation from the world. Drinking, smoking, and dancing, of course, were frowned on; forms of dress and hairstyles that might resemble too closely the latest craze among the worldly minded were banned; and mingling with those who did not share the same moral emphases was discouraged. Many of the students I taught in seminary in the late 1970s and 1980s had been reared in the bosom of fundamentalism, but, as suggested by the fact they were at a broadly evangelical school like Trinity, they had turned their backs on this heritage. What often happened was that their new sense of freedom led to excess in the other direction.

In those years, I frequently found myself, as someone who found Christ only late in my college years, in the position C. S. Lewis described so poignantly: a converted pagan in the midst of lapsed puritans. I rejoiced that these students had turned away from what I thought was an overly negative and overly strict understanding of what it meant to be a Christian in the world. But I deplored what I thought was their failure to see that some of the things they did in reaction against their strict upbringing might open themselves to activities that were questionable in light of biblical standards of behavior.

As I look at my college-age children, talk to their friends, and visit the Christian colleges that a couple of them attend, I find that this general attitude is widespread. Why, I am not sure. But perhaps it is because the people influencing them in their faith—their parents, teachers, and administrators—in a continuing reaction against fundamentalism, put too much stress on our freedom in Christ and too little on our responsibilities in Christ. Young Christian people think nothing of watching movies that contain explicit sex and raunchy humor.

Do we have freedom in Christ to do so? Maybe, although Paul warns that "it is shameful even to mention what the disobedient do in secret" (Eph. 5:12). But I find that exposure to the values propagated in such movies almost inevitably leads those who watch them to become tolerant of some of those same values. Premarital sex is rampant among Christian young people—depending, of course, on what we mean by "sex." But even when they don't "go all the way," all too many young believers get involved in heavy petting before marriage. Paul warns about "unwholesome talk" and "coarse joking" (Eph. 4:29; 5:4), yet many Christian young people listen to and pass on the off-color humor that seems to pervade the Comedy Channel.

All these activities, it seems to me, fall under the heading of the "debauchery" that Paul in this passage claims to be incompatible with our status as children of the light. I have encouraged my own children (as I must regularly encourage myself) to ask not "*Can* I do this?" (i.e., are Christians allowed to do this?), but "*Should* I do this?"(i.e., does this activity glorify God and honor the Lord whom I represent?).

Romans 14:1–12

A CCEPT HIM WHOSE faith is weak, without passing judgment on disputable matters. ²One man's faith allows him to eat everything, but another man, whose faith is weak, eats only vegetables. ³The man who eats everything must not look down on him who does not, and the man who does not eat everything must not condemn the man who does, for God has accepted him. ⁴Who are you to judge someone else's servant? To his own master he stands or falls. And he will stand, for the Lord is able to make him stand.

⁵One man considers one day more sacred than another; another man considers every day alike. Each one should be fully convinced in his own mind. ⁶He who regards one day as special, does so to the Lord. He who eats meat, eats to the Lord, for he gives thanks to God; and he who abstains, does so to the Lord and gives thanks to God. ⁷For none of us lives to himself alone and none of us dies to himself alone. ⁸If we live, we live to the Lord; and if we die, we die to the Lord. So, whether we live or die, we belong to the Lord.

⁹For this very reason, Christ died and returned to life so that he might be the Lord of both the dead and the living. ¹⁰You, then, why do you judge your brother? Or why do you look down on your brother? For we will all stand before God's judgment seat. ¹¹It is written:

> "'As surely as I live,' says the Lord,
> 'every knee will bow before me;
>   every tongue will confess to God.'"

¹²So then, each of us will give an account of himself to God.

IN CHAPTER 14, Paul moves from the general to the particular. In 12:1–13:14 he has touched quickly on some of the basic components of the gospel lifestyle. Beginning in 14:1, he tackles at length one particular issue, rebuking Christians in Rome for standing in judgment over one another (14:2, 13). The community is divided into two groups, those who are "weak [in faith]" (cf. 14:1) and those who are "strong [in faith]"

(cf. 15:1). They criticize and condemn each other, and Paul insists this judgmental attitude must give way to tolerance and mutual recognition. As he puts it succinctly in 15:7, "Accept one another, then, just as Christ accepted you."

The apostle leads up to this climactic exhortation in three stages. In 14:1—12, he rebukes the two groups for looking down on one another and reminds them that it is to God, not to each other, that every believer must ultimately answer. In 14:13—23, he urges those who are strong in faith to act out of love rather than out of a selfish insistence on doing what they feel free to do. He continues to focus mainly on the strong in 15:1—6, identifying with them and calling on them to follow Christ's example of loving service for the good of the body. After his summarizing demand that believers "accept one another" (15:7), Paul reinforces his exhortation by showing how God himself has intended Gentiles and Jews to form one body for the praise of his name (15:8—13).

A few scholars think that 14:1—15:13 continues Paul's outline of basic gospel demands. They note that his discussion parallels at many points what he says in 1 Corinthians 8—10.[1] The parallels are obvious, but there are differences too. Moreover, most scholars agree that Paul writes 14:1—15:13 because he knows that the Roman church is divided. Why this church was divided is more difficult to determine, for Paul is not specific about the issues between the strong and the weak. He mentions debates about eating meat (14:2—3, 6; cf. 14:20—21) and observing some kind of holy days (14:5), and he alludes in passing to drinking wine (14:21), but that is all.

Differences over these matters may have arisen for a number of different reasons (see Bridging Contexts section). Most commentators conclude that the core of the dispute has to do with observance of the Jewish law. The weak were those—mainly Jewish Christians—who could not bring themselves to abandon the requirements of the law they had observed all their lives. They could not, as Christians, simply ignore the food laws, Sabbath observance, and so on. The strong, by contrast, felt no need to observe these laws. Most of them were undoubtedly Gentile Christians, although a few, like Paul himself (see the "we" in 15:1), were Jewish Christians. The weak condemned the strong for cavalierly dismissing God's laws, while the strong pooh-poohed the weak, looking down on them for clinging to the old ways when the new had come. Paul sides with the strong on the basic issues involved, but his main concern is to get each group to stop criticizing the other and to accept each other in a spirit of love and unity.

---

1. See Karris, "Romans 14:1—15:13 and the Occasion of Romans"; W. A. Meeks, "Judgment and the Brother: Romans 14:1—15:13," in *Tradition and Interpretation in the New Testament: Essays in Honor of E. Earle Ellis for his Sixtieth Birthday*, ed. G. F. Hawthorne and O. Betz (Grand Rapids: Eerdmans, 1987), 290—300; Sanday and Headlam, *The Epistle to the Romans*, 399—403.

Along with the NIV editors, I think the opening paragraph in Paul's rebuke of the Roman Christians (14:1–12) falls into three parts. But I divide it differently, using the two rhetorical questions as the markers of each new section: "Who are you to judge someone else's servant?" (v. 4), and "You, then, why do you judge your brother? Or why do you look down on your brother?" (v. 10). In verses 1–3, Paul introduces the issue; in verses 4–9 he insists that every believer must answer to the Lord and the Lord alone; and in verses 10–12 he reminds us that only God has the right to stand in judgment over the believer.

Stop Judging One Another (14:1–3)

WHILE PAUL WANTS both groups in the church to accept each other, he is clearly most concerned about the attitude of the strong. This probably reflects the fact that the strong, mainly Gentile Christians, are the dominant group in the church. Thus, we should not be surprised that he opens his exhortation by implicitly appealing to the strong: "Accept him whose faith is weak."

If we are to understand the point of this section as a whole, we must recognize that the phrase "whose faith is weak" (lit., "one who is weak with respect to faith") has a special nuance in this context. "Faith" refers not directly to one's belief generally but to one's convictions about what that faith allows him or her to do. The weak in faith are not necessarily lesser Christians than the strong. They are simply those who do not think their faith allows them to do certain things that the strong feel free to do.[2] What Paul wants the strong to do is not simply extend grudging tolerance to the weak, but to welcome them (the verb *proslambano*, used here, means to receive or accept into one's society, home, circle of acquaintance[3]). They should not allow differences over "disputable matters" to interfere with full fellowship in the body of Christ.

Verse 2 identifies one of these "disputable matters": the eating of meat. To be sure, Paul does not put it just that way here. He distinguishes between those who "eat only vegetables" and those who "eat everything." But, in light of verse 21, it is clear that the weak in faith are those who eat only vegetables while the strong eat meat as well.

In verse 3, Paul urges both groups to change their attitude toward the other. The strong should stop "looking down on" the weak.[4] This translation

---

2. See esp. Cranfield, *The Epistle to the Romans*, 699–700.

3. BAGD.

4. I say "stop" because I think this is a case in which *me* + present imperative connotes the need to stop an action that one is engaging in. But the tense itself does not indicate this (contrary to the impression given in some grammars); it is the context that reveals this nuance.

can be stronger, for the verb Paul uses here (*exoutheneo*) probably has in this context the nuance "reject with contempt" (see Acts 4:11; 1 Thess. 5:20). But the weak are also at fault. They must stop "condemning" (*krino*) the strong believers. *Krino* means to pronounce doom on a person, to deny someone one's right to salvation. Paul will later argue that only God has the right to make such a determination. But here he points to a more specific issue: God has accepted this strong believer. How can we reject from our fellowship one whom God has accepted? Here is the theological bottom line in Paul's critique of judgmentalism in the church.

Slaves of the Lord Jesus (14:4–9)

IN VERSES 4–9, Paul elaborates this fundamental principle. Paul singles out a specific person (the "you" in Greek is singular [*sy*]). He does this because he reverts again to the diatribe style he has used so effectively in Romans (see comments on 2:1–11). This "you" may include both weak and strong,[5] but is more likely confined to the weak.[6] "Who do you think you are?" is basically what Paul is asking this weak believer. In condemning the strong believer, the weak believer is, in effect, claiming to be that believer's master. But the Christian has only one "master": the Lord Jesus Christ.

The rhetorical quality of Paul's argument is not evident in English, because English obscures the fact that the Greek word for both "master" and "Lord" is the same: *kyrios*. This word is central to the argument of verses 4–9, and it is not always clear to whom Paul refers. But the NIV is correct, I think, to take the first occurrence in verse 4 to denote a "master" in general and the second in a theological sense: *the* Lord, probably Christ.[7] "Stand" (*histemi*) and "fall" (*pipto*) may be paraphrased to mean "stand in favor with" and "fall out of favor with."[8]

Paul now cites a second "disputable matter" (cf. v. 1) creating tension between the strong and the weak: judging certain days to be "more sacred" than other days.[9] What these days are is one of the key points of dispute in this passage (see below), but reference is probably to Jewish holy days, including various festivals and the Sabbath. In any case, Paul wants every believer to be firmly convinced (*plerophoreo*; cf. the use of this same verb in 4:21) in his or her own mind.

---

5. E.g., Käsemann, *Commentary on Romans*, 369.

6. E.g., Sanday and Headlam, *The Epistle to the Romans*, 385; Dunn, *Romans*, 803.

7. See, e.g., Murray, *The Epistle to the Romans*, 2:177.

8. Cf. 1 Cor. 10:12, where these two verbs are used in a similar manner: "So, if you think you are standing firm, be careful that you don't fall!"

9. The Greek uses the preposition *para*, which means here "more than." So Paul literally says, "One judges a day more important than [another] day."

With verse 6 Paul resumes the theological basis for his rebuke of the judgmental Roman believers that he began in verse 4. He first refers to the weak believer, who regards certain days "as special" (there is nothing corresponding in the Greek, but this must be the sense), then to the strong believer, who eats meat (cf. v. 2), and finally again to the weak believer, who abstains from eating meat. Each, Paul argues, acts out of sincere regard for God and a desire to please him. That is why it is wrong for them to be condemning each other. They may differ over specific practices, but each group needs to recognize the sincerity of the other.

The Christian, Paul has suggested, is a slave who owes allegiance to a master (vv. 4, 6). In verses 7–9 he underscores and elaborates this relationship. No Christian acts (or should act) out of regard to himself or herself alone. We always have to take into account not just our own interests, but the interests of the one who died for us and returned to life so that he might be our Lord (v. 9). In whatever state we find ourselves, therefore—whether in life or in death—Christ, our Lord, owns us and expects us to act in obedience to him. As Paul puts it in 2 Corinthians 5:15, "he died for all, that those who live should no longer live for themselves but for him who died for them and was raised again." The Roman Christians are presuming to dictate to one another what their behavior should be—what they should eat, or not eat, and what days to observe. But only the Lord has that right.

It Is God Who Judges (14:10–12)

PAUL NOW BRINGS home the theology of verses 7–9. In parallel rhetorical questions, he effectively rebukes the weak believer for condemning (*krino;* cf. v. 3b) the strong Christian and the strong Christian for "looking down on" (*exoutheneo;* cf. v. 3a) the weak believer. Both are engaged in an activity that is God's alone: "We will all stand before God's judgment seat." Paul may be warning these Christians that their judgmental attitudes will bring judgment on themselves when they appear before God at the end of history. In light of verses 7–9, however, it is more likely that he is teaching that every believer is ultimately answerable to God, not to other believers, for their conduct in this life.

In verse 11 Paul underscores the unique role God plays in the judgment by citing Isaiah 45:23. We can appreciate how apropos this text is when we turn to the Old Testament context and see that it is surrounded with affirmations of God's sovereignty: "I am God, and there is no other" (45:22); "in the LORD alone are righteousness and strength" (45:24). It is before this sovereign Lord that each of us will have to give an account. Whether we are right or wrong in what we choose to do or not to do is ultimately a matter between ourselves and God. Fellow Christians can sometimes help us understand God's will and direct us in the right paths, but God has the final say.

Bridging Contexts

THE WEAK IN ROME. As we will see below, Paul's plea for tolerance in 14:1–15:13 has sometimes been wrongly applied, primarily because of a failure to understand just what kind of issue he is discussing in these verses. This text affords a classic example of a passage in which the author and readers share intimate knowledge of a situation we do not have access to. The Roman Christians know what the problem is, and so does Paul. Thus, he does not have to spell it out to them, and we have to reconstruct the issue on the basis of the hints Paul gives in this text along with what we know of the first-century cultural and religious context. As one might expect when the evidence is not straightforward and explicit, scholars come up with different reconstructions of the exact situation. Six deserve mention.

(1) The weak are Gentile Christians who abstain from meat (and perhaps wine), especially on certain fast days, under the influence of pagan religious traditions.[10]

(2) The weak are Christians generally who are devoted, for whatever reason, to an ascetic lifestyle.[11]

(3) The weak are mainly Jewish Christians who think they need to observe certain rituals of the Mosaic law in order to be justified before God.[12]

(4) The weak are mainly Jewish Christians who, under the influence of widespread religious trends in the first century, are expressing their devotion to God by following an ascetic lifestyle (see Col. 2:16–23).[13]

(5) The weak are Jewish Christians who, like some of the Corinthians (see 1 Cor. 8–10), refuse to eat meat because it may have been tainted with idolatry in the marketplace.[14]

(6) The weak are mainly Jewish Christians who do not eat certain food and observe certain days (and perhaps do not drink wine) out of loyalty to the Mosaic law.[15]

Four specific arguments combine to make the last of these alternatives the most likely. (1) The dispute Paul refers to has its roots in the tension between Jews and Gentiles in Rome. Why else would Paul conclude his exhortation with a series of Old Testament quotations celebrating the unity of Jews and

---

10. See, in general, Käsemann, *Commentary on Romans*, 367–68.

11. Murray, *The Epistle to the Romans*, 2:172–74.

12. Barrett, *Epistle to the Romans*, 256–57.

13. Matthew Black, *Romans* (Grand Rapids: Eerdmans, 1973), 190–91.

14. Nygren, *Commentary on Romans*, 442.

15. This is by far the most popular view among modern commentators. See, e.g., Cranfield, *The Epistle to the Romans*, 694–97; Dunn, *Romans*, 799–802.

Gentiles in the people of God (15:8−12)? Moreover, Paul's use of the word "common" (*koinos*) in 14:14 to refer to what the NIV calls "unclean" food also suggests a Jewish basis for the position of the weak. This word was widely applied to food forbidden to God's people by the Mosaic law (cf. Mark 7:2, 5; Acts 10:14).

(2) Paul's exhortation to strong believers to accept the weak makes clear that the weak are not holding a view Paul thinks is antithetical to the gospel. As we know from his other letters (e.g., Galatians), Paul can be harsh toward Christians who hold views contrary to the gospel of God. If the weak thought their obedience to the law was necessary for their salvation (view 3), Paul would do more than simply urge the strong to accept them into Christian fellowship.

(3) Paul never suggests that the meat the weak believers refuse to eat has been sacrificed to idols. We do not have sufficient basis to read the situation of 1 Corinthians 8−10 into Romans. Moreover, had that been the problem, we cannot explain why the observance of days is also an issue.

(4) On a positive note, the practices Paul attributes to the weak in this passage are easily explained against the background of Jewish attempts to keep the Mosaic law in a Gentile environment. The observance of holy days, including the major festivals and the Sabbath, were important Jewish identity markers in the first-century world. The Mosaic law did not, of course, demand abstinence from meat or wine. But scrupulous Jews often avoided eating meat if they could not be sure it had been prepared in a kosher manner. They would similarly abstain from wine out of a concern that it had been tainted by the pagan practice of offering wine as a libation to the gods.

The classic biblical example of such care to avoid pagan contamination is Daniel, who "resolved not to defile himself with the royal food and wine" (Dan. 1:8; see also 10:3; Tobit 1:10−12; Judith 12:2, 19; Add. Esth. 14:17; *Joseph and Aseneth* 14). It would not be surprising if many, perhaps most, Jews in Rome, surrounded by pagans, had decided to adopt similar practices in order to maintain their purity before the Lord.

If this background makes this scenario plausible, the whole tenor of Romans confirms this direction of interpretation. For the letter is preoccupied from the beginning with the question of the Mosaic law and the relationship between Jews and Gentiles. In other words, the theology developed in Romans 1−11 perfectly applies to a situation in which Christians in Rome are divided over the continuing relevance of certain provisions of, or drawn from, the Mosaic law. This does not, of course, prove that this is the issue, but the "fit" between theology and practical exhortation does support this scenario.

If, then, the situation in Rome is as we have suggested, Paul is addressing an issue that we sometimes call a matter of the *adiaphora* ("things indifferent").

The Scripture commands us to do certain things (e.g., to worship God), and it forbids us from doing certain other things (e.g., to commit adultery). But many other things are neither commanded nor prohibited—God's people have the freedom to do them or not to do them. Should we use the King James Version of the Bible or the New International Version? Should we sing in church to an organ or with a guitar? The Bible does not say (though some Christians may think it does!).

As Paul makes clear elsewhere in his letters and in the book of Acts, he believes that Jewish Christians have the freedom to continue to observe the Mosaic law if they want to. But they must not think it is necessary for their salvation, and they cannot impose it on Gentile believers (Galatians). He also insists that believers have no obligation to continue obeying the law of Moses (see 6:14, 15; 7:4, 6). Therefore, observing the Sabbath and other special days and avoiding meat and wine to maintain ritual purity fall into the category of the *adiaphora*.

In other words, if Christians from a Jewish background want to keep the Sabbath and abstain from meat and wine, that is fine. But if other Christians neglect the Sabbath and eat meat and drink wine, that is fine too. Both positions are "acceptable" Christian positions, and believers who hold each position should not condemn the others.

Nevertheless—and this is a vital point—we cannot extend the tolerance Paul demands here to *all* issues. As we have noted, he takes a different approach toward people who are violating a clear teaching of the gospel. Such people are not to be tolerated but corrected, and, if they do not repent, are to be cut off from the life of the church (see 1 Cor. 5). We must, then, be careful to apply the tolerance of Romans 14:1—15:13 to issues similar to the one Paul treats here.

THE SABBATH COMMAND. As we have just hinted, Paul's teaching in this part of Romans has great significance for the practice of tolerance. Who and what views do we tolerate? Why? It is perhaps better to deal with this broader issue after we have seen more of Paul's argument on this matter (see the Contemporary Significance sections on 14:13—23 and 15:1—6). In the present section we will look at a minor matter in the text but one that continues to divide and perplex believers: the Sabbath.

In the history of Protestant Christianity especially, Sabbath observance has been a contentious issue. There are both theological and cultural reasons for the controversy. Our culture, until just recently, was deeply influenced by the Christian tradition, associated especially with the Puritans, of viewing

Sunday as the "Christian Sabbath" and therefore as a day of rest. When I was growing up, few stores were open on Sunday. Until fairly recently in the state of Illinois it was illegal for car dealers to be open on Sunday. And many Christians, though not always clear why they were doing so, were convinced that Sunday was a day on which normal activities should be suspended. It was not a day for car-washing or lawn-mowing or even for sports, but a day to spend in physical rest, spiritual refreshment, and worship.

All this probably sounds foreign to many younger believers, who cannot imagine a Sunday with malls closed or deserted baseball diamonds and soccer fields. Even worship is no longer a Sunday matter, for many attend one of the growing number of churches with Saturday night worship services. Attitudes toward Sunday have changed dramatically over the last twenty years. But whether the changes are good or ill has to be decided theologically.

Theologically, the Sabbath command became a lightning rod for the larger issue of the believer's relationship to the Old Testament law. In the Ten Commandments God commands his people to worship him and to rest on the Sabbath (Ex. 20:8–11; Deut. 5:12–15). A strong tradition within evangelical Protestantism, rooted in the teaching of Calvin especially and mediated to the modern church through the influence of the Puritans, holds that the Ten Commandments summarize God's eternal moral law. Must we then obey the Sabbath command? If so, how?

Seventh Day Adventists claim to be the only consistent Christians when it comes to Sabbath observance. They believe, with many other Christians, that the Decalogue contains God's eternal moral law. That being the case, worship and rest on the Sabbath is as much as a requirement for believers as is refraining from murder and stealing. God made "the seventh day" the Sabbath—our Saturday. We have no right to change the day God himself established.[16]

Many who view the Ten Commandments as having continuing authority for the church think, however, that the New Testament implies a change in the Sabbath command. The early Christians met on the "first day of the week" to break bread (Acts 20:7) and to take offerings for charity (1 Cor. 16:2). John received his famous vision on "the Lord's Day" (Rev. 1:10). Most interpreters think these texts suggest that what we can document from the post-New Testament church was already happening in the New Testament church: In honor of the resurrection, the day of worship was moved from Saturday to Sunday. Jesus, after all, claimed to be "Lord . . . of the Sabbath" (Mark 2:28), implying that he had the authority, as the fulfiller of the law, to change the Sabbath command.

---

16. A good summary of this perspective is found in Samuele Bacchiochi, *From Sabbath to Sunday* (Rome: Pontifical Gregorian Univ. Press, 1977).

But to what extent did he change it? Did he remove the obligation to cease from work on the Sabbath? The evidence here is not clear. To be sure, he and his disciples sometimes did things on the Sabbath that violated the Jewish interpretation of that day (Mark 2:23–28 and par.; 3:1–6 and par.; Luke 14:10–17; John 5). But none is clearly a violation of the Old Testament Sabbath rules.[17] More pertinent, perhaps, is Hebrews 4:1–11, which claims that "there remains ... a Sabbath-rest for the people of God" (4:9). But the author of this book appears to interpret that "rest" metaphorically, applying it to the salvific experience of God's people (see 4:10–11).[18]

The uncertain nature of this evidence leaves in doubt the continuing applicability of the Sabbath command's demand for "rest." But it is at this point that Romans 14:5, along with Colossians 2:16, may help. In the Colossians text, Paul urges believers not to succumb to false teachers. He tells them, "Do not let anyone judge you by what you eat or drink, or with regard to a religious festival, a New Moon celebration or a Sabbath day." Paul here appears to put Sabbath observance in the category of the *adiaphora*, a practice neither commanded nor forbidden.

The same seems to be true of Romans 14:5. To be sure, Paul does not mention the Sabbath explicitly. But debates about observance of special days, within a Jewish context, almost certainly included the Sabbath, the most prominent of Jewish holy days.[19] I think these specific texts, along with the attitude toward the Sabbath command as a whole in the New Testament, show that observance of the Sabbath is no longer incumbent on believers. This fits with my understanding of the authority of the law as a whole in the new covenant era.

What are the practical implications of this view? (1) Christians are not required to "rest" on Sunday. Taking a job that requires one to work on Sunday, washing one's car on Sunday, playing basketball on Sunday—none is prohibited to us. Yet Christians also have the liberty to rest on Sunday if they choose. I think that such a rest, while not mandated, is physically and spiritually wise. I do not usually do any of my usual work on Sunday—I do not prepare lectures, grade papers, or write books. Yes, emergencies sometimes arise when I have to work, and I often teach and preach in a church. But I find that establishing a rule for myself of not working on Sunday is intensely liberating. I feel no guilt about not being in my study, and I am certain that the break on Sunday enables me to be far more efficient on the other six days of

---

17. See Douglas J. Moo, "Jesus and the Authority of the Mosaic Law," *JSNT* 20 (1984), 15–18.

18. See, e.g. George Guthrie, *Hebrews* (NIVAC; Grand Rapids: Zondervan, 1998), 159–72.

19. See esp. Dunn, *Romans*, 805; Stuhlmacher, *Paul's Letter to the Romans*, 224. For a contrary opinion, see, e.g., Murray, *The Epistle to the Romans*, 2:177–78.

the week. Many theologians speculate that the essence of the Sabbath command is precisely this idea of a break from regular activities to rest and worship God.[20] The exact day may not finally matter all that much.

(2) This brings us to a second, in my mind more difficult, matter: the requirement of worship on the Sabbath. One might think that consistency would demand that worship be put in the same category as rest: Regular worship is required, but the day is optional. This may be right. But I hesitate because of the explicit New Testament references to the "the first day of the week" and to the "Lord's Day" noted above. Sunday worship is not mandated in the New Testament, but it does seem to be a pattern (although, admittedly, one attested in only a few texts). For this reason, I am not so sure we should jettison Sunday as the church's regular day of worship.

(3) This, in turn, brings up several other implications. (a) We should take a hard, theological look at the trend to establish Saturday evening worship services. Most churches adopt the Saturday worship for the sake of convenience: perhaps to relieve congestion on Sunday morning or to attract people who might not get up for Sunday morning. But do they establish solid biblical and theological justification for it? Do they deal seriously with what seems to be the pattern of New Testament worship timing? Perhaps a case can be made that anytime after sundown on Saturday counts as the Sabbath day, by Jewish reckoning. But few churches make this argument, nor would it work for most of the year in many northern hemisphere latitudes anyway.

(b) While believers are not required to rest on Sunday, they are required to attend worship—which is usually on Sunday. Some professions, to be sure, make consistent Sunday morning worship impossible—medicine, fire protection, law, athletics. But the vast majority of Christians have a clear choice to make, a choice that will reflect the priority we give to worship. My own children, following my example/law (I am not quite sure which category it belongs in!) have sometimes refused lucrative jobs because they would force them to work often on Sunday.

A friend of my third son, Lukas, had the opportunity to make his priorities clear to the whole community. In 1998, just after Tiger Woods rocketed to fame after his first Masters Tournament win, he came to our area to play golf with Michael Jordan. My son's friend was asked to caddy for them. He refused because it would have forced him to miss church. Most people in our area were simply flabbergasted; they could not even imagine someone making such a choice. But what a witness it was to the value this young man placed on worship!

---

20. See, e.g., Paul Jewett, *The Lord's Day: A Theological Guide to the Christian Day of Worship* (Grand Rapids: Eerdmans, 1971).

(c) As our culture has changed, we believers find ourselves pressured at yet another point to conform—to treat Sunday as a day to sleep in, to go to brunch, to read the newspaper, to take the kids to soccer games, and so on. At the least, we must hold high the primacy of worship as what, for us, Sunday is first of all for.

Romans 14:13-23

THEREFORE LET US stop passing judgment on one another. Instead, make up your mind not to put any stumbling block or obstacle in your brother's way. ¹⁴As one who is in the Lord Jesus, I am fully convinced that no food is unclean in itself. But if anyone regards something as unclean, then for him it is unclean. ¹⁵If your brother is distressed because of what you eat, you are no longer acting in love. Do not by your eating destroy your brother for whom Christ died. ¹⁶Do not allow what you consider good to be spoken of as evil. ¹⁷For the kingdom of God is not a matter of eating and drinking, but of righteousness, peace and joy in the Holy Spirit, ¹⁸because anyone who serves Christ in this way is pleasing to God and approved by men.

¹⁹Let us therefore make every effort to do what leads to peace and to mutual edification. ²⁰Do not destroy the work of God for the sake of food. All food is clean, but it is wrong for a man to eat anything that causes someone else to stumble. ²¹It is better not to eat meat or drink wine or to do anything else that will cause your brother to fall.

²²So whatever you believe about these things keep between yourself and God. Blessed is the man who does not condemn himself by what he approves. ²³But the man who has doubts is condemned if he eats, because his eating is not from faith; and everything that does not come from faith is sin.

Original Meaning

WHILE PAUL IN 14:1–12 addresses both parties in the dispute at Rome, his main criticism is directed at the weak, who stand in judgment over the strong. In 14:13–23, he redresses that imbalance by focusing on the strong. Negatively, Paul warns these believers not to use their liberty in a way that brings spiritual harm to their weaker brothers and sisters (the idea of stumbling; see vv. 13b, 20b–21; also vv. 15, 20a). Positively, he wants them to use their freedom on these matters in accordance with love in order to edify the body (vv. 15, 19).

Paul structures this exhortation to the strong much as he did verses 1–12. His key concern, that strong believers avoid being a "stumbling block" to the weak, is expressed at the beginning and the end (vv. 13b–16 and vv. 19–23). These two sections follow a chiastic order:

A Warning about stumbling blocks (v. 13b)
   B Nothing is unclean (v. 14a)
      C Don't destroy one for whom Christ died (v. 15b)
      C' Don't tear down the work of God (v. 20a)
   B' All things are clean (v. 20b)
A' Don't do anything to cause a believer to stumble (v. 21)

In between, we find the theological rationale for this concern: the nature of the kingdom of God (vv. 17–18).

Don't Be a Stumbling Block (14:13–16)

THE COMMAND "THEREFORE let us stop passing judgment on one another" is transitional, summing up the point Paul has made in 14:1–12 and preparing for what follows. (Paul may again here be quoting Jesus, who taught, "Do not judge, or you too will be judged" [Matt. 7:1].[1]) Both those who are weak and those who are strong in faith—that is, those who have scruples and those who do not—are to accept one another as fellow members of Christ's body.

Paul plays on the Greek verb *krino* as he moves from the first part of verse 13 to the second. In the opening exhortation, this verb means "pass judgment," but in the second part it means "decide, determine" (NIV "make up your mind"). Turning specifically to the strong, Paul warns them about putting "any stumbling block or obstacle" in the way of another believer. The vivid imagery of the "stumbling block" (*proskomma*) comes from the Old Testament (see esp. Isa. 8:14, quoted in Rom. 9:32); the same is true of the word *skandalon* (NIV "obstacle"). It refers literally to a trap, but was used widely in the LXX to refer to the cause of one's spiritual downfall (see esp. Lev. 19:14); it has this same sense throughout the New Testament (e.g., Matt. 13:41; 18:7; Rom. 9:33; 11:9; 16:17; 1 Peter 2:8). Paul's point is clear: Those who pride themselves on being strong should display their spiritual maturity by doing everything they can to avoid bringing spiritual downfall to a brother or sister.

In a deft rhetorical move, Paul tries to get the strong to listen to him by conceding that they are right on the basic issue: "No food in unclean in itself" (v. 14). "Unclean" translates *koinos* (lit., common), which Jews used to describe things that, by virtue of their contact with the ordinary, secular world, were considered to be defiled (see, e.g., 1 Macc. 1:47, 62; Mark 7:2, 5; Acts 10:14,

---

1. See, e.g., M. Thompson, *Clothed with Christ: The Example and Teaching of Jesus in Romans 12.1–15.13* (Sheffield: JSOT, 1991), 163–73.

15, 28; 11:8, 9; Heb. 10:29). In other words, Paul emphasizes that all food is kosher. He follows the lead of Jesus, whose teaching about "true defilement" had the same import (Mark 7:19; cf. also Acts 10:9–23, 28).

But while the strong have the theory right, they must come to grips with the practice. Although God now pronounces all foods to be kosher, people who have always believed that avoiding certain foods is necessary to maintain their holiness are probably unable immediately to internalize this new perspective. They may not be convinced—at least emotionally and psychologically—that they can eat anything. For them certain foods are still "unclean."

Having explained how food can bring spiritual downfall to a person, Paul moves on in verse 15 to show that this is just what the strong are doing to the weak. Their eating food that weak believers feel convinced is unclean "distresses" (*lypeo*, to cause pain) them. More than that, it may even "destroy" (*apollymi*) them. This language is very strong. Some interpreters want to mitigate its strength by suggesting that *apollymi* refers to the weak Christian's own self-condemnation. But when Paul uses this verb with a personal object, it always means "bring to ultimate spiritual ruin" (Rom 2:12; 1 Cor. 1:18; 8:11; 10:9, 10; 15:18; 2 Cor. 2:15; 4:3, 9; 2 Thess. 2:10). In other words, the cavalier attitude of the strong may lead to the weak believer's damnation.

How? Paul does not explain, but there are two possibilities. (1) The "peer pressure" brought by the example of the strong believers may lead the weak believer to eat what he or she is still convinced is unclean, and so violate his or her conscience. Paul suggests again in verse 23 that a person "is condemned" when he or she eats while harboring doubts about whether it is proper.

(2) The strong believers' flaunting of their freedom to eat all food may so offend conservative Jewish Christians that they are driven from their faith altogether. Verse 16 perhaps supports this idea, since the "good" likely refers to the freedom believers enjoy. That freedom, Paul claims, can be considered an evil (lit., it will be "blasphemed") when it is abused and others are harmed because of it. Whatever the case, the strong are not acting out of love. Christ has given his life for these weak believers, and the strong are unwilling even to give up some food.

The Values of the Kingdom (14:17–18)

THE STRONG ARE not wrong to think they have freedom to eat whatever they want. Rather, they are wrong for using that freedom without regard to the effect it may have on their weaker brothers and sisters—people for whom Christ died. The strong need a reordering of priorities, in which kingdom values take precedence over selfish interest and pleasure. Thus, Paul now reminds us, God's kingdom is not about eating and drinking but about "righteousness, peace and joy in the Holy Spirit."

Since Paul typically uses "righteousness" language in Romans in a forensic sense to refer to our status before God, many interpreters think that *dikaiosyne* has that sense here.[2] But Paul also uses this word to refer to "ethical righteousness," that is, behavior pleasing to God (e.g., 6:16, 18, 19). This meaning fits the present context better.[3] "Peace" refers to the horizontal harmony that believers should manifest. When these blessings are present, "joy" results.

All three of these characteristics, however, are possible only where the Holy Spirit is at work. When believers serve Christ "in this way," they both please God and find approval with their fellow believers. The "this way" may refer to the virtues Paul has listed in verse 17.[4] But the singular "this" (*touto*) does not match the plurality of these virtues. Most likely Paul is referring to the kingdom focus as a whole described in verse 17: God approves believers who serve Christ by focusing on those matters that are truly central to the kingdom.

Don't Cause Your Fellow Believer to Stumble (14:19–23)

AFTER THE INDICATIVE interlude (vv. 17–18), Paul returns to the imperative. We must live out the values of the kingdom by acting in ways that lead to "peace" and "mutual edification." "Mutual edification" is a good rendering of an awkward Greek phrase (lit., "the things of edification that are for one another"). "Edification" translates a word that means "act of building" (cf. Matt. 24:1), though it is usually used in the New Testament with a spiritual sense: the process of building up individual believers or the church in faith (e.g., Rom. 15:2; 1 Cor. 14:3; Eph. 4:12, 16). The strong ought to be more concerned about the growth of the body as a whole rather than their own freedom and spiritual advancement.

In verse 20 Paul shifts from the positive to the negative: How foolish it would be to "destroy" (*katalyo*) this body, this "work of God for the sake of food." "Destroy" in the somewhat parallel verse 15 referred to the spiritual damnation of an individual. Here, applied to the church, it probably means "ruin"—disputes over food bring disunity, mutual distrust, and, eventually, the break up of a congregation.

Paul then reiterates his conviction that all food is "clean" (v. 20b) and continues (cf. v. 14) with a reference to a "man" who eats. The Greek leaves

2. E.g., Cranfield, *The Epistle to the Romans*, 718–19; Dunn, *Romans*, 823.

3. E.g., Godet, *Commentary on Romans*, 462; Murray, *The Epistle to the Romans*, 2:193–94.

4. So most commentators (e.g., Sanday and Headlam, *The Epistle to the Romans*, 392; Fitzmyer, *Romans*, 697).

unclear who this person is. In verse 14 the reference was to the weak believer, and the Greek here may have a similar sense.[5] But the grammar and context favor a reference to the strong Christian, as the NIV translates.[6] The strong Christian needs to recognize that it is wrong for him or her to eat food in such a way that spiritual harm comes to another believer.

Paul formalizes the point in a general principle in verse 21: Believers should avoid doing anything that brings spiritual harm to another believer. But why does Paul include "drinking wine" here as an example of a practice to avoid? He may simply be adding it as an illustration; "eating and drinking" form a natural pair (see v. 17). But most likely he introduces it because, along with eating meat and observing holy days, drinking wine is also an issue in the Roman church (see Bridging Contexts section of 14:1–12, where we noted that many Jews abstained from wine because they feared it had been tainted with idolatry through pagan practices).

In verses 22–23 Paul draws conclusions from his teaching for both the strong (v. 22) and weak (v. 23) Christians. Paul urges the strong to keep their convictions about the matters in dispute to themselves. There is no need for them to broadcast their views or to be continually trying to convince fellow believers how right they are. The blessing at the end of verse 22 is the bottom line for strong believers. They should act in such a way that they have no reason to "condemn" themselves with respect to the practices that they "approve" (*dokimazo*, consider to be right; cf. 12:2). Paul wants those who, like him, have internalized the truth about the freedom Christians have in the new era to have clear consciences about the ways they use that freedom—out of love and concern for the edification of the community.

But, Paul reminds us again, there are those who are presently unconvinced about freedom on these matters. Those believers, who still "doubt," should not eat. While the eating in itself may not be wrong, it is wrong to violate one's conscience. The weak believer who eats would not be eating "from faith"— that is, on the basis of a sincere conviction that eating meat is OK. Such eating then is sin, since "everything that does not come from faith is sin." Paul is again using "faith" (*pistis*) in the specific sense he gave the word at the beginning of the chapter (14:1–2): a conviction that one's faith allows one to engage in a certain activity. So, as true as it may be that any action that does not arise from faith in a general sense is sin,[7] this is not Paul's point here.

---

5. E.g., Godet, *Commentary on Romans*, 462–63; Murray, *The Epistle to the Romans*, 2:195. See, e.g., the NJB: "but all the same, any kind [of food] can be evil for someone to whom it is an offense to eat."

6. Käsemann, *Commentary on Romans*, 378; Cranfield, *The Epistle to the Romans*, 723–24.

7. Augustine, for instance, used this text to argue that any act of a non-Christian must be sinful (*Contra Julianum* 4.32).

TRADITION! TEVYE'S FAMOUS cry "Tradition!" in *Fiddler on the Roof* embodies an attitude shared by almost all people in every century. All of us have certain traditions we maintain that serve to link us with past generations and to bind us tightly with other people in our own social or religious group. We often do not even know where such traditions come from.

I am reminded of a story my pastor, Todd Habegger, tells. In a family he knows, a ham always had an inch or so sliced off from one side before it was put in the oven. He asked why this was done. The woman cooking the ham replied, "Because my mother always prepared ham that way." With her interest stimulated, she in turn asked her mother about the ham. Her mother said, "Because my mother always prepared ham that way." When she then asked her great-grandmother about it, she laughed and explained: "The oven in our first home was so small that a whole ham would not fit into it. So I had to cut off part of it."

Most of us probably have better reasons to maintain traditions. But, understandable or not, we all have them, and they have great value in giving us a sense of identity. We understand the issues in Romans 14 and their application to our own day better by fully recognizing the power of tradition. The Jews who lived in Rome in Paul's day were especially in need of identity-reinforcing traditions. They were a minority religious group trying to survive and preserve their identity in the midst of a pluralistic and often hostile environment. Like many other Jews in the centuries after the Exile, they put great emphasis on some of the religious traditions that helped to preserve their identity and to keep them separate from the world around them.

Faced with both persecution and dispersion, Jews magnified Old Testament-based traditions such as circumcision, the avoidance of unclean food, and the observance of ritual days, especially the Sabbath. We should not, therefore, be surprised that it was just these issues that repeatedly surfaced as points of tension between many Jewish Christians and Gentile Christians. Theology, of course, played a big role. The group of Jewish Christians known as Judaizers, for instance, argued that God's covenant with Abraham and its subsequent restatement under Moses made circumcision and obedience to the law essential components of what it meant to belong to God. Paul disagreed, as he reveals in Galatians.

But other Jewish Christians undoubtedly approached these issues from less of a theological or even theoretical perspective. They had been taught by parents and peers that certain practices were essential for all good Jews. Their acceptance of Jesus as their Messiah expanded their horizons, revealing to them that God had brought about a new era in salvation history in which Gentiles could join with them in worshiping the one true God. And, unlike the Judaizers, many of them acknowledged that the Gentiles did not need to follow those customs peculiar to Jews. Yet they had a hard time understanding why they personally should not continue to follow the rules they had been taught since childhood.

Even those who agreed in theory that the rules were no longer necessary probably had difficulty discarding what was so integral to their cultural and religious identity. These were *traditions*, and it is not always easy to throw them overboard, however persuasive the arguments for their abandonment might be. From his own background Paul knew well how powerful tradition was among the Jews. He sympathized with Jewish Christians who found it difficult to abandon overnight what was so ingrained in them. Thus, he wants the other Christians in Rome to "cut them some slack."

But tradition is not confined to Jews or to the ancient world. Traditions are alive and well, and modern people are just as much affected by them. In contextualizing Romans 14, then, we ought to take modern as well as ancient traditions into account. We must realize that people in our own day who accept the good news are embedded in cultures and religions with their own traditions and that those traditions will not always be easy to give up. To be sure, tradition is never an excuse for sin. Paul unapologetically calls on new converts to turn away from any traditions contrary to God's revealed will. But many traditions are not clearly sinful, and when this is the case, Romans 14 encourages us to take a slow and loving approach.

Theology, exegesis, and eternal security. Romans 14:15 is another one of those warning texts that create problems for those of us who believe in the perseverance of the saints (see comments on 11:21–22). Our final conclusions will again reflect our understanding of the overall biblical witness on this matter. A straightforward exegesis of the NIV seems to lead to the conclusion that a genuine Christian can lose his or her faith and be lost forever. Paul calls the person a "brother for whom Christ died." That person, he claims, can be "destroyed" by the uncaring attitudes of other believers.

As we noted above, some interpreters try to get around the problem by understanding "destroy" to mean the spiritual grief and self-condemnation that the weak believer experiences when she adopts, against her conscience, the practices of the strong.[8] But, as we also pointed out, Paul usually uses the verb "destroy" to refer to eternal damnation. A more promising approach is to ask the question whether the person Paul refers to here is truly a Christian. The NIV "brother" is a paraphrase; there is no *adelphos* in the Greek. To

---

8. See, e.g., Volf, *Paul and Perseverance*, 85–97.

be sure, the word does occur earlier in the verse, and it may be legitimate to bring the word over into this last statement. But the matter is not as clear as the NIV suggests.

Of course, if one believes in the doctrine of limited atonement, the issue is settled. Those who hold this view insist that Christ died only for the elect. "One for whom Christ died" then must be a Christian. But I am not sure that limited atonement is a biblical teaching, so this is not decisive for me.

When all legitimate qualifications are allowed for, however, I still think the text, on its own, could suggest that genuine Christians can lose their salvation forever. But the text is not "on its own." As a believer in the truthfulness and coherence of all of Scripture, I must bring to bear on this text what I see the Bible teaching elsewhere on the matter of a believer's eternal security. I still tend toward the opinion that texts teaching the finality and therefore unchangeableness of a believer's salvation in Christ are clearer and more dominant than those warning texts that may suggest the opposite.

Of course, I must always try to let each new "problem" text influence my view of what the Bible teaches. To simply impose my theology on every new text without sincerely letting that text have an impact on that theology is the epitome of eisegesis and a recipe for stagnation. Because we must be open to new truth that God may reveal to us through his Word, our theological conclusions must always be tentative and subject to change.

WHILE 15:1—13 REINFORCES Paul's plea for tolerance, all the key points he makes on the issue are now before us. This, then, is a good place to talk about the significance of his teaching for the contemporary church.

Dealing with the adiaphora. To begin, we must insist again that Paul's advice in this chapter can only be applied to issues that are similar to the ones he is dealing with here. As we showed in our discussion of 14:1–12, eating meat, drinking wine, and observing Jewish holy days belong in the category of the *adiaphora*: things neither commanded nor prohibited to Christians. Extending Paul's plea for tolerance to other issues is both wrong and dangerous.

In an approach typical of our times, a few interpreters have turned to Romans 14 as evidence that professing Christians, whatever their exact beliefs, need to "accept one another." Theological differences should be no bar to complete Christian recognition and unity. But such an approach not only unfairly extrapolates from the specific issues of this text to any issue; it also ignores the many texts in the New Testament that draw a line between acceptable Christian beliefs and unacceptable ones. People who insist on imposing the law on Christians, says Paul, are preaching another gospel (Gal. 1:6–10); anyone who does not believe that Christ came "in the flesh" is an "antichrist," denying both the Father and the Son (1 John 2:22–23; 4:1–6). Right doctrine matters—and matters eternally. Paul is not encouraging acceptance of any professing Christian, regardless of what he or she may believe.

Recognizing the need to distinguish between essential doctrines and the *adiaphora* raises another perplexing issue. How do we determine what belongs in which category? Roman Catholics have an advantage here: They can rely on papal authority to make that decision for them. But for Protestants the answer is not so easy. To be sure, Scripture is clear about some doctrinal matters. But the evidence on others is not so clear-cut. Thus, professing Christians take positions along a wide spectrum. Some are "minimalists," insisting on only a very few beliefs (or none at all) as essential to the faith. This impulse is found especially in the ecumenical movement. At the other end of the spectrum are "maximalists," who insist that any Christian who wants to enter into fellowship must cross the "t" and dot the "i" on an interminable list of doctrinal, ethical, and social issues. Some fundamentalists take this latter kind of an approach.

From the beginning of the church, Christians have written confessions and doctrinal statements to formulate what is essential to the faith. Our own ideas about what is essential should probably be grounded in these early ecumenical confessions (e.g., the Nicene Creed). Most churches and denominations will want to express their own distinctive approach to the faith by adding certain doctrines to the list. But we should be careful about insisting that such additions are essential to the faith and therefore a basis for fellowship with other believers. Paul's advice to the parties in Rome applies to denominations and churches in our day: Where our differences lie in nonessentials, we need to "accept each other."

Valuing and even trying to propagate our own perspective on the faith does not require that we refuse to acknowledge the genuineness of the faith of others. Paul serves as an outstanding model of what he himself would want each of us to exhibit: an unswerving commitment to the truth of the gospel combined with complete flexibility on the *adiaphora*.

Regarding the *adiaphora*, as Paul deals with the specific problems dividing the Roman church, he teaches several principles that should guide us as we deal with issues that divide believers in our own day.

(1) We must try to understand and respect where people are coming from. In the Arthur Conan Doyle story "Silver Blaze," Sherlock Holmes comments to Dr. Watson that the behavior of the dog is the key to the mystery. But, Watson responds, the dog didn't do anything. Precisely, Holmes responds, and the

dog's silence reveals that the intruder must have been known to the animal. Silence can be significant. One of the most important points in Romans 14 is something that Paul does *not* say: that the weak in faith must change their view. He makes clear that he does not agree with them, and by labeling them weak he implies also that they have room to grow on these matters. But he does not tell them to change their mind; he does not berate them for being "immature"; he does not tell them to "get with the program."

Yet this is usually our first reaction to someone who differs with us. We want to change their minds, to convince them we are right. Paul would undoubtedly support the church's efforts to educate its members as fully as possible about the gospel and its implications. But he is wise enough to know that there is a time and a place for such efforts. As we suggested above, all of us have our traditions, and they are not easy to give up. As long as they are not contrary to the gospel and hindering the work of the church, we should learn to tolerate these differences.

I need to preach to myself here. I have frequently, for instance, lost my cool in dealing with people who insist that the King James Bible is the only accurate English translation. (There is a "King James Bible church" here in the Chicago area, and I have relatives who attend it.) I immediately become irritated with their failure to grasp what seem to me obvious historical and textual facts. What I often fail to realize is that they are coming from a background in which adherence to the King James Version is bound up with their own identity and significance. It is not a matter simply of an intellectual issue but of a deep-seated social convention. I must learn to accept and value these folks as fellow believers, even as I pray that time will bring them to a more healthy perspective on translations.

(2) Christians who are not convinced in their own minds that something is right for them to do should not do it. Paul urges weak believers who still harbor doubts about eating meat not to eat, for they will be acting against their faith and thus sinning (v. 23). We may be placed in a situation in which most other Christians are doing something we have always considered wrong. We may be led by their example and arguments to rethink our own position on the matter. But until we are convinced, Paul suggests, we should refrain from acting.

Some of us bring baggage into our Christian experience from our background that we will never get away from. I know mature believers who refuse, for instance, to drink alcohol, dance, or play card games—not because they are sure such activities are wrong (they are often sure they are not wrong) but because they simply do not feel "comfortable" doing it themselves.

(3) When confronted with believers that have such scruples, those of us who do not have them need to *modify the expression of our freedom by the demands*

of love. Liberty is wonderful, but love is even greater. Paul spends most of his time elaborating this point. He never suggests that believers do not have freedom on matters that fall into the category of the *adiaphora*. No one can take that freedom from us. But he is insistent about our need to express that freedom in such a way that we do not bring spiritual harm to another believer.

"Bring spiritual harm" summarizes well the language Paul uses about this point (see vv. 13, 15, 20–21). On the negative side, he is *not* saying that we must refrain from activity that another believer may disagree with. I happen to believe I have freedom in Christ to play cards, for instance. I have relatives who don't think Christians should do that and are not happy when I do. But my playing cards is not, as far as I can see, bringing spiritual harm to them. I do not think, therefore, that I must refrain for their sake.

How might I, however, bring spiritual harm to another believer? Here, frustratingly, Paul is not clear. As we noted in our comments on verse 15, we can perhaps think of two main possibilities. (a) Our engaging in an activity that another believer thinks to be wrong may encourage that other believer to do it as well. They would then be sinning because they are not acting "from faith" (v. 23). We must be particularly careful about vaunting our liberty when the weak believer is in a minority. The peer pressure of most of the other Christians around him or her engaging in a particular action may be difficult to withstand. The strong believer must be sensitive to this problem and seek to identify with the weaker brother or sister—even at the expense of his or her own pleasure.

(b) An ostentatious flaunting of liberty on a particular matter may so deeply offend someone that he or she may turn from the faith altogether. A person may begin to think, *Well, if the Christian faith encourages that kind of behavior, I want nothing more to do with it*. To be sure, we want eventually to help people understand and enjoy the genuine freedom we have in Christ—the freedom to enjoy the world God has given us and the innocent pleasures of his common grace. But believers struggling on certain issues may not be ready for a display of our freedom on these matters.

(4) We should also note a point that Paul is *not* making in this text, although it is often read into it. The weak brother or sister is not someone who has a susceptibility to a particular vice, and Paul does not urge the strong believer to abstain because he is worried that our example may lead that individual to a life of degradation. This type of argument is especially brought up in connection with the drinking of alcohol. We are told that we ought to avoid drinking because our example may lead someone who has a weakness for alcohol to indulge to excess and so bring physical and perhaps even spiritual ruin to that person.

This concern may well be valid, but it is not what Paul is teaching here. The weak are not those who have a propensity to eat meat or to drink wine. Their weakness is spiritual: an inability to see that their faith allows them to drink. The potential problem is not that they may indulge to excess but that they may drink even when their faith is still telling them not to.[9]

In conclusion, we need to say again: The need to limit the expression of our liberty out of love for God and fellow believers is the key principle in this chapter. Our culture insists on rights, and it is easy for Christians to bring that attitude into the church. But the spiritual health of the body is far more important than our rights. The freedom God has purchased for us through his Son is a precious gift, but it is a freedom to live as God wants, not as we want. Luther put it well in his famous comment on Christian liberty: "A Christian man is a most free lord of all, subject to none. A Christian man is a most dutiful servant of all, subject to all."[10]

---

9. On this point, see Murray, *The Epistle to the Romans*, 2:260–61.
10. From *On the Freedom of a Christian Man*.

Romans 15:1-6

WE WHO ARE strong ought to bear with the failings of the weak and not to please ourselves. [2]Each of us should please his neighbor for his good, to build him up. [3]For even Christ did not please himself but, as it is written: "The insults of those who insult you have fallen on me." [4]For everything that was written in the past was written to teach us, so that through endurance and the encouragement of the Scriptures we might have hope.

[5]May the God who gives endurance and encouragement give you a spirit of unity among yourselves as you follow Christ Jesus, [6]so that with one heart and mouth you may glorify the God and Father of our Lord Jesus Christ.

AS THE REFERENCES to the "strong" and the "weak" in verse 1 show, Paul is continuing his rebuke of the Roman Christians for their judgmental attitudes. But what is the exact nature of the relationship between this paragraph and chapter 14? Some interpreters think that 15:1–6 is part of the specific exhortation to the strong that began in 14:20.[1] Others insist 15:1–6 moves away from the specific divisive issues at Rome to address any similar kind of issue that Christians may face.[2] The truth lies between these extremes. Paul does not abandon the specific issue he has been talking about since 14:1, but he is now at the point of wrapping up his discussion with some concluding exhortations. Specifically, he encourages those who are strong to follow the example of their Lord in putting the good of others before their own (15:1–4) and then urges the whole community to seek a unity that will enable them effectively to praise God (15:5–6).

Although Paul has indicated his agreement with the thinking of the strong group in Rome (14:14, 20), he now for the first time explicitly identifies with them, using the first person plural to include himself within the scope of his exhortation. He labels himself and the others who share his view as the *dynatoi* (lit., the powerful or able ones), that is, those who are "able" to see that

---

1. E.g., Ulrich Wilckens, *Der Brief an die Römer* (Neukirchen-Vluyn: Neukirchener, 1982), 3:100.

2. E.g., Godet, *Commentary on Romans*, 467; Käsemann, *Commentary on Romans*, 381.

their faith allows them to eat meat, drink wine, and so forth. The others are the *adynatoi*, believers who are "unable" to come to grips with this truth.

In urging the *dynatoi* to "bear with the failings of the weak," Paul is not asking them simply to "put up with" those who differ from them. The verb "bear" (*bastazo*) has the same force here that it does in Galatians 6:2, where Paul exhorts believers to "bear one another's burdens and so fulfill the law of Christ" (pers. trans.). The strong are actively and lovingly to assume the burden that the weak are not able to carry for themselves, moderating their own conduct to identify as much as possible with them. They will thus not seek to "please" themselves, but the "neighbor," hoping to "build . . . up" that fellow believer (v. 2). The sudden introduction of "neighbor" language suggests Paul is thinking of the love command that exhorts love for one's neighbor (Lev. 19:18; cf. Rom. 13:8—10).

When the *dynatoi* act in this way, they will be following the example of Christ, who "did not please himself" (v. 3). If Christ, "powerful" as he was, could give up his own right to life itself, these strong believers should certainly be able to give up their right to eat meat whenever they want or to drink wine or to ignore Jewish holy days. Paul puts the words of Psalm 69:9b on Christ's lips to illustrate the attitude he had: "The insults of those who insult you have fallen on me." "Me" in the quotation refers to Christ and "you" to God: Christ has received the scorn that people were directing at God.

Why does Paul use Psalm 69:9 to illustrate Jesus' attitude? He is probably drawn to it because this psalm is used so often in the New Testament to describe Jesus' suffering (see Matt. 27:34 par.; John 2:17; 15:25; Acts 1:20; Rom. 11:9). At a more specific level, he may also be thinking of the insults that the weak believers in Rome are heaping on the strong. Like Jesus, the strong in Rome should be willing to serve in love even those who are being nasty to them.

Verse 4 is parenthetical. Paul pauses to remind us why he can cite the Old Testament the way he doesus: "Everything that was written in the past was written to teach us." The Old Testament, while no longer a direct source of moral instruction (see 6:14, 15; 7:4—6), continues to play a central role in helping believers understand salvation history and their responsibilities as the new covenant people of God.

The ultimate goal of this instruction is "hope." Why bring hope into the discussion here? Perhaps the allusion to suffering in 15:3 leads Paul to remind us of the outcome of that suffering (see 8:20, 24—25). But he may also introduce the concept of hope as a subtle reminder to the strong at Rome—mainly Gentile Christians—that they were once "without hope" in the world (cf. Eph. 2:12) but have now been integrated into God's people by grace. In order to preserve their hope, they must work for the health and unity of God's people, the basis for their hope.

In verse 4 Paul cited "endurance" and "encouragement" as two specific traits fostered by the Scriptures that will culminate in hope. He picks up these two words in verse 5 at the beginning of his "prayer-wish" to God on behalf of the squabbling Roman believers. He prays specifically that God himself will grant to the community the ability "to think the same way" (lit. trans.; NIV "spirit of unity"). In light of his insistence that the weak not change their minds until their own faith leads them to do so (14:23), it is unlikely that Paul is praying here that all the Roman believers will come to the same opinion on the matters at issue. Rather, he is praying that they may possess a unity of purpose that transcends these differences.

It is a unity and way of thinking that is "according to Christ Jesus" (NIV "as you follow Christ Jesus")—that is, a unity founded on and modeled after Christ. But unity is not the ultimate goal. Unity is simply one stage on the way to the church's final purpose: to praise God (15:6). Only when believers cease to quarrel with one another and speak with one heart and one voice will they be able to praise God as they should.

PAUL'S USE OF TRADITION. In these verses Paul once again makes brief allusion to certain traditions that would have enhanced the Roman Christians' appreciation for what he is teaching.

(1) The reference to Psalm 69 would have triggered a series of associations. As we noted above, the Gospel writers allude to this psalm in their portrayal of Christ's sufferings. This psalm, attributed to David, is a lament psalm. In the typical pattern of these psalms, David both bemoans his unjust suffering (Ps. 69:1–12, 19–21) and calls on God to deliver him (69:13–18) and to punish his enemies (69:22–28), ending with praise to God for his faithfulness and certain salvation (69:29–36). The Evangelists portray Jesus as the "righteous sufferer" of these lament psalms (Ps. 22 is another) by picking up their language to describe his mockery and suffering.

All the Evangelists allude to Psalm 69:21 ("They put gall in my food and gave me vinegar for my thirst") when they describe the drink Jesus was offered as he hung on the cross (see. e.g., Matt. 27:34). According to John, Jesus himself quoted Psalm 69:4 to explain why people hated him "without reason" (John 15:25). The early Christians took their cue from this application of Psalm 69 to Jesus, using it to explain Judas's defection (Ps. 69:25 in Acts 1:20) and the spiritual hardness of the Jews (Ps. 69:22–23 in Rom. 11:9–10; see comments). The Roman Christians knew the Old Testament well and would have immediately discerned the echoes of all these other applications of Psalm 69 as they read this text.

(2) Paul cites the tradition about Jesus. Michael Thompson and others have shown how all of Romans 12−15 is suffused with allusions not only to Jesus' teaching but also to his example.[3] This "law of Christ" is the implicit source for much of what Paul teaches about the Christian life in these chapters. But it is only 15:3 that he actually refers to Jesus, quoting Jesus' own quotation of the Old Testament and citing his example of sacrificial giving.

Less obvious is a possible allusion to Jesus' example, via Old Testament language, in 15:1. Paul calls on "powerful" Christians to "bear [*bastazo*] the weaknesses [*astheneia*] of the unpowerful" (lit. trans.; see Original Meaning). This language is similar to the words about the suffering servant that Matthew quotes in Matthew 8:17: "He took our weaknesses [*astheneia*] and bore [*bastazo*] our diseases" (pers. trans.). Would the Roman Christians have heard this subtle allusion to the mission of their servant-Messiah? We cannot be sure, but we think that the later explicit allusions to Jesus' example may well have led them to discern this further allusion.

What Paul is doing, it appears, is crafting his appeal to the Roman Christians in such a way that the example of Jesus is subtly in the background throughout. Such allusions strengthen his appeal, as the Roman Christians are forced to compare their own arrogance toward the weaknesses of others with Christ's loving humility and service. They are clearly not following Jesus' admonition to be like him in serving rather than being served (cf. Mark 10:45).

(3) A third tradition that lies behind 15:1−6 is an early Christian pattern of exhortation that linked humility, unity, and the example of Jesus. This pattern is clearest in Philippians 2:1−11. Paul begins by urging the Philippian believers to be united in "thinking the same thing" (lit. trans. of v. 2). Such unity will come only when believers "consider others better than [themselves]" (v. 3) and look to "the interests of others" (v. 4). What they must do is to think as Christ thinks, for he "did not consider equality with God something to be grasped, but made himself nothing, taking the very nature of a servant" (vv. 6−7).

It is not hard to discern this same pattern of teaching in Romans 15:1−6. Paul urges the Roman Christians to be united (using the same construction as in Phil. 2:2, "think the same thing," in Rom. 15:5−6), recommends pleasing others rather than themselves as a way of achieving that unity (15:1−2), and cites Jesus' example as someone who did just that (15:3). It is not that Paul "quotes" Romans when he writes Philippians (or vice versa). Rather, what we have is an outcropping of what was probably a basic and widespread

---

3. See his monograph *Clothed with Christ.*

Christian catechism, giving instructions to converts on how they are to please the God who has redeemed them. Discerning such patterns contributes to our appreciation of the unity of Scripture and accentuates the importance of the unity and humility Paul calls for in these verses.

 THE OLD TESTAMENT. I want to visit again a point that emerges in passing in this paragraph: the enduring value of the Old Testament for Christian thought and life. The very fact that Paul can mention the value of the Old Testament in passing shows how ingrained that idea was in the early church. Yet the ignorance of the Old Testament among believers in our day is staggering. Average Christians, of course, are not entirely to blame. Calculate sometime the percentage of sermons you hear in your own church on the Old Testament in comparison with the New Testament. We can trace the problem one step further back. When students ask for recommendations for commentaries on New Testament books, I can usually name off the top of my head five or six excellent, contemporary treatments. But I am sometimes hard-pressed to name even one excellent commentary on certain Old Testament books.

I have taken a pretty strong discontinuous view of the Mosaic law. As I have said repeatedly, I do not think it remains a direct authoritative source for Christian ethics. But I have also made clear that we must not thereby conclude that the Old Testament is no longer of value for believers. Paul's "no" to the continuing *direct authority* of the law is combined with a resounding "yes" to the continuing *value* of the Old Testament—including the law.

Nowhere does he make this point clearer than in Romans 15:4: "For everything that was written in the past [*prographo*] was written to teach us, so that through endurance and the encouragement of the Scriptures we might have hope." Paul's use of *prographo* certifies he is referring to the Old Testament. Note that "everything" in the Old Testament is written for our benefit as new covenant believers.

Paul does not detail all the ways in which the Old Testament is of value to believers. But he does mention two points. (1) We gain "endurance" from reading the Old Testament. Perhaps Paul thinks here especially of the example of godly men and women who stood fast in the midst of persecution and apostasy—the people whom the author of Hebrews lists in his survey of the "heroes of faith" (ch. 11). Indeed, that author likewise ties his record of faith to the need for his readers to "persevere" or endure (10:36; cf. 12:1). The example of other believers who have endured and remained faithful is a great stimulus to our own perseverance.

(2) We also get "encouragement" (*paraklesis*) from the Old Testament. *Paraklesis* can mean "exhortation," but most commentators rightly prefer in this context "encouragement, comfort." Perhaps Paul is here thinking of God's faithfulness to his people, displayed throughout the Old Testament. How comforting it is to know that God never fails to fulfill his promises and remains committed to his people even when they are not as committed to him as they should be. We often stumble, we often fall. We persist in sinning, in failing to love others as we should, in putting too high a priority on our own pleasure and comfort. God is not pleased with our failures, but he is always willing to forgive and never turns his back on his own children.

In both these specific ways, then, contemplation of the Old Testament stimulates our "hope." We have in the Old Testament a record of God's dealings with his people that we must not neglect. We learn about God, about his purposes in history, and about his ways of dealing with his people. The modern church's impoverished understanding of the Old Testament cannot but breed an impoverished faith, hope, and love.

Unity. Paul's ultimate goal in this section of Romans, as his prayer in 15:5–6 reveals, is to create unity in the church at Rome. The bickering, distrust, and rejection of one another needs to be replaced with a unity of mind and spirit. Paul would write much the same thing were he living in our day. Church after church is wracked by dissension; churches quarrel with one another; Christian institutions criticize each other and bitterly compete with one another.

To be sure, there are fights that need to be fought. As we noted above, Paul is not for unity at any price. We can have *Christian* unity only where the essentials of what it means to be Christian are believed and lived. But so many of the fights that disfigure the body of Christ, harm our witness, and stifle our praise of God are not those kinds of fights. We quarrel about the instruments to be used in worship service, about the color of the choir robes, and about the style of our church building. Believers may have strong feelings on these kinds of matters—and there is nothing wrong with that. But we need to keep perspective. We need wisdom and a thorough grounding in God's Word to know which issues are essential to the life of the church and which are on the periphery.

Most of all, we need to fight our battles in a Christian spirit. Paul is not urging either group in Rome to give up their beliefs. He is not even telling them not to discuss their views with one another. Though the situation prevents him from saying so, he may even hope that solid teaching and the work of the Spirit will, over the years, transform weak believers into strong ones. Similarly, God is not necessarily displeased when we hold different views on issues in the church today. When honestly expressed and calmly debated, arguments about various issues can teach us all a great deal. God does not want a bland uniformity in the church or believers who do not have enough brains or gumption to hold and defend their own ideas.

But the key is that all this take place under the umbrella of a unified spirit (15:5). When everyone seeks the good of the others and the church as a whole, disagreements can strengthen rather than weaken the community. Ultimately, the Scriptures call on each one of us to bring together two personality traits that do not always go together: tenacity in holding to the essentials of the faith and infinite patience and tolerance toward people who hold differing ideas on the nonessentials, that is, on the *adiaphora*.

Romans 15:7–13

ACCEPT ONE ANOTHER, then, just as Christ accepted you, in order to bring praise to God. [8]For I tell you that Christ has become a servant of the Jews on behalf of God's truth, to confirm the promises made to the patriarchs [9]so that the Gentiles may glorify God for his mercy, as it is written:

> "Therefore I will praise you among the Gentiles;
> I will sing hymns to your name."

[10]Again, it says,

> "Rejoice, O Gentiles, with his people."

[11]And again,

> "Praise the Lord, all you Gentiles,
> and sing praises to him, all you peoples."

[12]And again, Isaiah says,

> "The Root of Jesse will spring up,
> one who will arise to rule over the nations;
> the Gentiles will hope in him."

[13]May the God of hope fill you with all joy and peace as you trust in him, so that you may overflow with hope by the power of the Holy Spirit.

Original Meaning

PAUL SIGNALS THAT he is concluding his plea for unity in the Roman church by returning to the characteristic vocabulary with which he began. Just as he exhorted the strong to "accept" the weak (14:1) and rebuked both weak and strong for rejecting each other when God had "accepted" them (14:3), so now he urges them to "accept one another ... just as Christ accepted you." Through such mutual acceptance God will be praised. For God sent Christ to the Jews so that Gentiles also might be able to praise God (15:8–9a), and the Old Testament likewise predicts that Gentiles will join with Jews in worshiping God (15:9b–12). The balanced emphasis on God's faithfulness to Jews along with the inclusion of the Gentiles sums up a key motif in Romans. In a sense, then, these verses

477

bring closure not only to the section on the strong and the weak, but to the entire body of the letter.[1]

To "accept" one another means not just to tolerate other believers but to welcome them as brothers and sisters in the body of Christ (see comments on 14:1). The "just as" (*kathos*) introducing the next clause in 15:7 may suggest Paul is drawing a comparison: We should accept one another *in the same way* as Christ has accepted us.[2] But *kathos* probably has a causal sense here: We are to welcome one another *because* Christ has welcomed each one of us.[3] What right do we have to refuse fellowship with a person whom Christ himself has accepted into the body? "In order to bring praise to God" may be the purpose of Christ's accepting people.[4] But this phrase more likely depends on the ruling idea of the verse, namely, that we accept one another.[5]

Paul draws attention to the significance of what he says next with the rhetorical opening "For I tell you." What he does in 15:8–9a is to summarize one of the key theological teachings of the letter: how the fulfillment of God's promises in the gospel brings blessing to both Jews and Gentiles. Precisely how Paul makes this point is debated. His syntax can be construed in two different ways.

(1) I say
    (a) that Christ has become a servant of the Jews on behalf of God's truth, to confirm the promises made to the patriarchs; and
    (b) that the Gentiles are glorifying God for his mercy.[6]

(2) I say that Christ has become a servant of the Jews on behalf of God's truth,
    (a) in order to confirm the promises made to the patriarchs; and
    (b) in order that the Gentiles might glorify God for his mercy.[7]

This second construction, reflected in most English translations (including the NIV) is better. It beautifully captures the fine balance Paul preserves in Romans between the priority of the Jew—Christ came as a "servant of the

---

1. See, e.g., Dunn, *Romans*, 844–45.
2. E.g., Dunn, *Romans*, 846.
3. E.g., Käsemann, *Commentary on Romans*, 385; Cranfield, *The Epistle to the Romans*, 739.
4. E.g., Murray, *The Epistle to the Romans*, 2:204.
5. E.g., Godet, *Commentary on Romans*, 470.
6. This reading takes the infinitive *doxasai* ("glorify") in v. 9 as parallel to the infinitive *gegenesthai* ("become") in v. 8, with both dependent on the verb *lego* ("I tell you"); see esp. Cranfield, *The Epistle to the Romans*, 742–44.
7. On this reading, *doxasai* ("glorify") is dependent, along with *bebaiosai* ("confirm"), on the *eis to* ("in order that") construction at the end of v. 8. Most commentators support this reading (see, e.g., Sanday and Headlam, *The Epistle to the Romans*, 398; Murray, *The Epistle to the Romans*, 2:205).

Jews"[8]—and the full inclusion of the Gentiles—Christ's ministry to the Jews fulfills God's promises and so enables Gentiles also to "glorify God for his mercy." As Paul puts it in the theme statement of the letter, the gospel is "first for the Jew, then for the Gentile" (1:16). The weak (mainly, if not entirely, Jewish Christians) need to accept Gentile Christians because God's ultimate purpose is to include them, and the strong (mainly Gentile Christians) need to remember that the Jews have always been at the center of God's concerns and promises.

Paul supports what he says in verses 8–9a with a series of Old Testament quotations (vv. 9b–12). God intends for his mercy to Israel to spill over to the Gentiles so that they can join together in praising his name. Paul cites each of the three sections of the Jewish Scriptures: the Torah (Deut. 32:43 in v. 10), the Prophets (Isa. 11:10 in v. 12), and the Writings (Ps. 18:49 in v. 9b; Ps. 117:1 in v. 11). Each quotation refers to the Gentiles, and two of them (vv. 10, 12) make clear that their presence in the people of God depends on the Jews. Two of them also speak of praising God (vv. 9, 11).

The quotation of Psalm 18:49 (see also 2 Sam. 22:50) serves Paul's purposes because it mentions God's being praised among the Gentiles. But if Paul thinks of the "I" as Christ, it may also suggest the Messiah's rule over the Gentiles (see Bridging Contexts section). But not only will God's name be praised among the Gentiles (v. 9); the Gentiles themselves are called on to "rejoice" (v. 10, quoting Deut. 32:43). Because the gospel breaks down "the dividing wall of hostility" between Jews and Gentiles (Eph. 2:14), this invitation can now be fulfilled.

In verse 11 Paul quotes yet another Old Testament verse that calls on Gentiles to join in praising God (Ps. 117:1). He rounds off the series by quoting the familiar messianic prophecy from Isaiah 11:10 about how the "the Root of Jesse" will rule over nations and be the object of hope for Gentiles.

Paul completes his exhortation to the weak and the strong with a final "prayer-wish": an appeal to God to work among the Romans in such a way that the unity he urges on them becomes a reality. Paul beautifully incorporates into this prayer some of the key ideas from the previous chapters. "The God of hope" (or "the God who gives hope" [REB]) reminds us of the immediately preceding quotation, with its promise that the Gentiles "will hope" in the Jewish Messiah. The "joy" and "peace" he wants them to experience are two of the essential values of God's kingdom that Paul has encouraged the strong to make a priority (14:17). The Holy Spirit, by whose "power" the Christians in Rome will be able to "overflow with hope," is the third of the kingdom essentials listed in 14:17. Only when Jew and Gentile at Rome rejoice together

---

8. The Greek here is *peritome,* "circumcision" (see NIV marginal note).

in their *common* hope will they be able to praise God as he wants to be praised—with the united hearts and voices of a *community* of believers (see 15:5–6).

ONCE AGAIN, **Old Testament quotations.** In this last series of Old Testament quotations in Romans (one more solitary quotation comes in 15:21), it is appropriate for us once again to dig behind the quotations to see what light they may shed on the meaning Paul gives them. As we have noted before, the apostle rarely simply lifts Old Testament verses out of their contexts. Their appropriateness for his own application usually arises not just from their own wording and meaning but from their function within the Old Testament context. We can see this procedure at work yet again in the quotations in 15:9–12.

If Paul uses Psalm 18:49 in Romans 15:9 simply because it mentions the praise of God along with the Gentiles, the text does not suit his purposes as well as it might, since it speaks only of God being praised "among" the Gentiles. But a closer look at the Old Testament context suggests a deeper and more appropriate significance. For the "I" in the quotation of Psalm 18:49 is David. Since Paul read many of the Davidic psalms typologically (see Ps. 69:9 in Rom. 15:3), he may intend us to identify this "I" as Christ.

In Psalm 18, David's praise of God stems from the fact that God has subdued the nations under him (see 18:43: "You have delivered me from the attacks of the people; you have made me the head of nations; people I did not know are subject to me"). We can assume, I think, that Paul's first readers knew Psalm 18 well enough to know this context. They would then have heard this quotation as a reminder of God's plan to bring Gentiles under the umbrella of the Messiah's rule. They would also have known that God had fulfilled this plan in Jesus of Nazareth. The weak in Rome are therefore reminded that Gentiles, as much as Jews, are now included in God's people and deserve acceptance and welcome.

The quotation of Deuteronomy 32:43 in Romans 15:10 is interesting for two reasons. (1) The wording follows closely the LXX, which differs significantly from the standard Hebrew text (the Masoretic). The Hebrew, translated literally, reads: "Praise his people, O Gentiles" (see NRSV note). But the LXX rendering finds support in at least one medieval Hebrew manuscript and possibly in a Qumran scroll.[9] This may, in fact, have been the original text of Deuteronomy 32:43—note that most English versions (including the NIV) follow this text in their translation. Thus, Paul is probably quoting the passage in its original form.

(2) This quotation comes from a chapter that Paul has used elsewhere to

---

9. The Qumran MS is 4QDeutᵃ; cf. Fitzmyer, *Romans*, 707.

support the idea of Gentile inclusion among God's people. Indeed, Deuteronomy 32:21, quoted in Romans 10:19, became the basis for Paul's whole development of the idea of the Jews being made jealous by the Gentiles (11:11–15). Again, Paul is not just quoting at random. He is deliberately drawing our attention to *passages* in the Old Testament that teach the inclusion of Gentiles. He is not engaged in mere prooftexting, but in contextually sensitive biblical-theological argument.

The quotation in 15:11 comes from a short, two-verse psalm (Ps. 117) that Paul quotes nowhere else. But even here we can spot elements in the context that may have drawn Paul to this verse. For the second verse of the psalm goes on to cite God's "love" (or "mercy," *eleos*) and "faithfulness" (or "truth," *aletheia*) as reasons why the Gentiles should praise the Lord. These are precisely the blessings Paul has cited in Romans 15:8–9a as reason to praise God.[10]

Paul's final quotation (v. 12) comes from Isaiah 11:10. Once again, the wording in Romans reflects the LXX, which differs from the standard Hebrew text. These differences become obvious when we set down side-by-side the NIV of Isaiah 11:10 and of Paul's quotation:

Isaiah 11:10	*Romans 15:12*
In that day the Root of Jesse will *stand* as a banner for the peoples; the nations will *rally* to him, and his place of rest will *be glorious*.	The Root of Jesse will *spring up*, one who will arise to *rule over* the nations; the Gentiles *will hope* in him. (italics added)

The key differences are found in the three verbs we have italicized. The Greek version suits Paul's argument better than the Hebrew. Nevertheless, the basic meaning of the text is the same. Either allows Paul to make the point he wants to make, namely, that the Gentiles' participation in the praise of God (vv. 9b–11) comes as a result of the work of "the shoot of Jesse," a messianic designation.[11] Again, Paul may cite this text partly because of its context: Isaiah 11 goes on to refer to God's gathering of the remnant of Israel from among the nations.[12]

SUMMARY OF PAUL'S ARGUMENT. Since this paragraph both completes the body of the letter that began in 1:18 and restates one of the letter's key themes, this is an appropriate place for some summary remarks about Paul's argument as a whole.

10. Hays, *Echoes of Scripture in the Letters of Paul*, 71.
11. See Jer. 23:5; 33:15; Sir. 47:22; 4QFlor 1:11; 4QPat 3–4; Rev. 5:5; 22:16.
12. Hays, *Echoes of Scripture in the Letters of Paul*, 73.

We must return one last time to one of the key issues in the modern interpretation of Romans: the tension between the personal focus and the community focus. Both are clearly present in Romans; both, Paul makes clear, are intrinsic to the gospel. Through the good news of Jesus Christ, God is both *transforming* individuals and *forming* a community.

The passage before us focuses on the latter, and many modern interpreters think this focus reflects Paul's real concern in the letter. I do not totally agree. I think Paul focuses on the community in 15:7–13 because these verses conclude a section (14:1–15:13) that is about the community. But however we decide this matter, we must read Romans in such a way that we focus on *both* transformation of the individual *and* formation of the community.

Interpreters in the past were sometimes guilty of seeing in Romans only the former, so that all they talked about were justification by faith, the sanctification of the believer, and one's duties as a believer. But some contemporary interpreters make the opposite mistake: Reading Romans in a culture obsessed with community and the need for reconciliation among races, ethnic groups, and nations, they emphasize only how we as God's people should function as a single, united body. Justification by faith and similar themes become minimized or reinterpreted.

We must keep things in balance. The heart of the gospel is the message of God's justifying work in Christ. The essential human problem is estrangement from God. Only when this estrangement is overcome and a person is reconciled to God by faith can we speak about God's good news having done its work. Our preaching and teaching must therefore confront people with sin and offer them redemption in Christ.

But God also wants to form people transformed by the gospel into communities that reflect the values of the gospel. Vertical reconciliation with God must lead to horizontal reconciliation with one another. Faithfulness to the gospel demands that any of us involved in ministry should seek to maintain a balance between the two perspectives. Some pastors are marvelous proclaimers of the gospel of individual transformation. They are passionate to save souls, rescuing people lost in sin and destined for hell. I commend their passion. But they need also to make clear—as Paul does in Romans—that the gospel not only rescues people from hell but also transforms whole persons, bringing reconciliation with other people as well as with God.

But the opposite problem also exists: pastors who think that "soul-saving" is too old-fashioned and spend all their time talking about racial reconciliation, mending marriages, restoring families, and the like. God, of course, wants to do these things too. But he has chosen the way of individual transformation through a new relationship with God as the means. Focusing on horizontal reconciliation without encouraging vertical reconciliation first is to put the cart before the horse.

At Rome in Paul's day, mutual distrust between Jews and Gentiles threatened the unity of the church. Naturally, therefore, Paul addresses these groups. The tension between Jew and Gentile is in some ways a unique one, rooted in God's revelatory focus in the Old Testament on Jews. But Paul's vision ultimately transcends the Jewish-Gentile debate. God wants his church to be a place that transcends any cultural, racial, or ethnic division in a unity based on the gospel.

That vision is far from being a reality. In too many ways, our praise of God is still muted by the divisions among us. Some of those divisions are based on theology. I know of anti-charismatic churches that refuse to join with charismatic churches in occasional worship services. On the other side, I have been treated as a second-class Christian (if Christian at all) in charismatic churches. Such issues of theology create the most difficult divisions to overcome.

Some theological issues, as we have argued earlier, are worth separating over. But if some churches err in including too many within the scope of those whom God has accepted, I think that many more have drawn those lines far too narrowly. We need to be willing to put our own cherished ecclesiological traditions to the test of Scripture. Even when we think Scripture validates them, we may have to admit that they are not as clear as we think or as important as we make them to be. Theological differences need not mean division in worship and service.

Race, of course, is another serious cause of disunity in the church. Churches in certain cultural contexts have been able to incorporate blacks and whites in a single congregation. But such integrated churches are rare. The church I attend is 95 percent white. I have a number of black Christian friends; they tell me that their churches are 95 percent black. There are many reasons, of course, for such segregation in our churches, and not all the reasons are bad ones. But I have to think that my own understanding of the faith and the quality of corporate worship is hampered by too homogenous a racial mix.

My church and churches like mine need to take a hard look at the underlying attitudes that foster this segregation. I still hear white Christians doing a lot of racial stereotyping, telling racial jokes, and so forth. By tolerating this kind of talk, we will not root out sinful attitudes that stand in the way of genuine racial harmony, mutual acceptance, and unified praise of God.

Romans 15:14–33

IMYSELF AM convinced, my brothers, that you yourselves are full of goodness, complete in knowledge and competent to instruct one another. ¹⁵I have written you quite boldly on some points, as if to remind you of them again, because of the grace God gave me ¹⁶to be a minister of Christ Jesus to the Gentiles with the priestly duty of proclaiming the gospel of God, so that the Gentiles might become an offering acceptable to God, sanctified by the Holy Spirit.

¹⁷Therefore I glory in Christ Jesus in my service to God. ¹⁸I will not venture to speak of anything except what Christ has accomplished through me in leading the Gentiles to obey God by what I have said and done—¹⁹by the power of signs and miracles, through the power of the Spirit. So from Jerusalem all the way around to Illyricum, I have fully proclaimed the gospel of Christ. ²⁰It has always been my ambition to preach the gospel where Christ was not known, so that I would not be building on someone else's foundation. ²¹Rather, as it is written:

"Those who were not told about him will see,
    and those who have not heard will understand."

²²This is why I have often been hindered from coming to you.

²³But now that there is no more place for me to work in these regions, and since I have been longing for many years to see you, ²⁴I plan to do so when I go to Spain. I hope to visit you while passing through and to have you assist me on my journey there, after I have enjoyed your company for a while. ²⁵Now, however, I am on my way to Jerusalem in the service of the saints there. ²⁶For Macedonia and Achaia were pleased to make a contribution for the poor among the saints in Jerusalem. ²⁷They were pleased to do it, and indeed they owe it to them. For if the Gentiles have shared in the Jews' spiritual blessings, they owe it to the Jews to share with them their material blessings. ²⁸So after I have completed this task and have made sure that they have received this fruit, I will go to Spain and visit you on the way. ²⁹I know that when I come to you, I will come in the full measure of the blessing of Christ.

³⁰I urge you, brothers, by our Lord Jesus Christ and by the love of the Spirit, to join me in my struggle by praying to God for me. ³¹Pray that I may be rescued from the unbelievers in Judea and that my service in Jerusalem may be acceptable to the saints there, ³²so that by God's will I may come to you with joy and together with you be refreshed. ³³The God of peace be with you all. Amen.

WITH THE PRAYER-WISH of 15:13, we reach the end of the body of Romans. What remains makes up the closing. Paul includes in 15:14–16:27 the elements typical of his letter closings:

Reference to travel plans (15:14–29)
Request for prayer (15:30–32)
Prayer-wish for peace (15:33)
Commendation of Paul's ministry associates (16:1–2)
Exhortation to greet one another (16:3–15)
The "holy kiss" (16:16a)
Concluding warning/exhortation (16:17–19)
Eschatological wish/promise (16:20a)
Concluding benediction (16:20b)
Greetings from Paul's associates (16:16b, 21–23)
Doxology (16:25–27)

As befitting the most complex of Paul's letters and in keeping with the letter opening, this letter closing is by far the longest in all Paul's letters. He goes into so much detail because he is writing to a church he has never visited.

Paul's travels are the motif that binds together 15:14–33. These verses divide into three parts, marked by the address "brothers" in verses 14 and 30 and the transitional "therefore" in verse 22 (not in NIV). Paul's focus in the first section (vv. 14–21) is on his special ministry calling and his past travels. In verses 22–29, his focus shifts to his future plans and their significance to the Romans. The section concludes with a prayer request for his impending visit to Jerusalem and the contribution for the Christians to be brought there (vv. 30–33).

Paul's Ministry and Its Past Expression (15:14–21)

PAUL IS ESPECIALLY concerned to explain to the Romans why he has taken the liberty to write to them so "boldly" (v. 15) about the gospel. As he explains, he has been called to convert and strengthen Gentiles so that he might present them as an acceptable offering to the Lord.

As in 1:11–12, Paul again displays his tact and diplomacy in writing to a church he has neither planted nor visited. Thus, he compliments the Roman Christians on being "full of goodness, complete in knowledge and competent to instruct one another." The word translated "goodness" (*agathosyne*) is rare (occurring elsewhere in the New Testament only in Gal. 5:22; Eph. 5:9; 2 Thess. 1:11). It denotes moral goodness of any kind.[1] Paul knows he is not writing to a novice community or to a deeply sinful one, but to one that both knows and practices the faith.

To be sure, Paul has written "quite boldly on some points" (i.e., in some parts of the letter). But he did so not to impart new knowledge but to "remind" the Roman Christians of truth they already knew. If Paul has not let his diplomacy here descend into insincere flattery—for surely the believers in Rome did not know everything Paul teaches in this letter!—he must mean by this that he has simply explicated gospel truth that they already know.

Paul's second excuse for writing so boldly is more important. It is introduced in the last phrase in verse 15—"because of the grace God gave me"— and elaborated in verses 17–21: Paul has been given by God the gracious ministry of bringing Gentiles into obedience to God. Since the Roman church is mainly Gentile in composition, it lies within the scope of the mandate God himself has given to Paul.

Paul's use of cultic language to describe this ministry is striking. He calls himself a *leitourgos* (servant; NIV "minister"), a word that in this context has priestly connotations.[2] This ministry consists in "proclaiming the gospel of God" as a "priestly duty," in order that "the offering of the Gentiles might be acceptable" (lit. trans.). Some interpreters think that the offering is not the Gentiles themselves (which presumes that *ton ethnon* ["of the Gentiles"] is an epexegetic genitive) but the praise or obedience that the Gentiles offer (a subjective genitive).[3] But the epexegetic genitive suits the context better. In other words, Paul pictures himself as a priest, using the gospel as the means by which he offers his Gentile converts as a sacrifice acceptable to God. But,

---

1. See, e.g., Murray, *The Epistle to the Romans*, 2:209; contra, e.g., Cranfield (*The Epistle to the Romans*, 752), who thinks it means "honesty in dealing with others."

2. The word can refer broadly to people who serve the Lord or his people in various ways (e.g., 2 Kings 4:43; Ps. 103:21; 104:4) and to court officials (e.g., 2 Sam. 13:18). In the New Testament it can refer generally to "ministry" of various kinds (2 Cor. 9:12; Phil. 2:25; Heb. 1:7). But it also often denotes those who serve in the temple (e.g., Num. 4:37, 41; 1 Sam. 2:11; cf. Heb. 8:2; 10:11), and the cognate *leitourgia* has cultic reference in Luke 1:23; Heb. 8:6; 9:21. *Leitourgos* refers directly to a priest in Neh. 10:39 (LXX 2 Esdr. 20:37); Isa. 61:6; and in many Jewish intertestamental books.

3. See, e.g., R. Dabelstein, *Die Beurteilung der 'Heiden' bei Paulus* (Frankfurt: Peter Lang, 1981), 112–14.

like the animal sacrifices of the old economy, these new sacrifices also must be "sanctified by the Holy Spirit" if they are to be acceptable.

Because God is the One who has given Paul this service, he can legitimately "glory" in it (v. 17). Glorying or boasting in something can be wrong when we are trying to take credit for our own achievement (cf. 2:17, 23; 3:27; 4:2—3), but it is appropriate when it is the product of God's own work (cf. 5:2, 3, 11).

In verse 18 Paul pursues this idea further, explaining just how it is that his glorying is "in Christ Jesus." Paul speaks "quite boldly" to the Romans (v. 15), but "he would not be so bold" (NIV "will not venture") as to say anything beyond what Christ himself has done in and through him. The goal of what Christ does through Paul is (lit.) "the obedience of the Gentiles," an important echo of the letter's opening (1:5). The means of Christ's work in Paul is both "word and deed" (lit. trans.; NIV "what I have said and done," 15:18).

Verse 19 elaborates this last point. It is tempting to arrange the two pairs in a chiastic structure, whereby "word" is related to "through the power of the Spirit" and "deed" to "by the power of signs and miracles." But Paul's actions as well as his words are certainly done in the Spirit's power, and his deeds include more than miracles. Therefore verse 19 continues Paul's description of his ministry. "Signs and wonders" (NIV "miracles") is standard biblical terminology for miraculous acts that accompany and give credence to God's Word. The phrase is especially prominent in Old Testament descriptions of the Exodus (e.g., Ex. 7:3, 9; 11:9—10; Deut. 4:34; Ps. 78:43) and in the book of Acts (e.g., Acts 2:22, 43; 4:30; 5:12; 14:3; 15:12). Paul perhaps uses this expression to signal his importance in salvation history. God works miracles through him because he is God's "point man" to open up the Gentile world to the gospel.[4]

Paul has identified the agent of his apostolic ministry (Christ) and its purpose (leading Gentiles to obey the Lord). In the second half of verse 19, he states the results of his ministry: "From Jerusalem all the way around to Illyricum, I have fully proclaimed the gospel of Christ." Illyricum was the Roman province that incorporated modern-day Albania and parts of the old Yugoslavia. The NIV "all the way around" translates a difficult word (*kyklo*), but it probably means "around" (see Mark 6:6 in a similar context).[5] Paul's journey from Jerusalem to Illyricum has not been a direct one but a circuitous one.

More important than geography is Paul's sense of having completed a significant phase of the ministry God has given him. The Greek word for "fully proclaimed" is *pleroo* (lit., fulfill), a word full of theological import in the

---

4. See, e.g., Dunn, *Romans*, 862—63; Peter T. O'Brien, *Consumed by Passion: Paul and the Logic of the Gospel* (Homebush West, Australia: Lancer, 1993), 31, 50—51.

5. See Cranfield, *The Epistle to the Romans*, 761.

New Testament. Paul has brought to the divinely ordained climax his commission to plant thriving, self-reproducing churches throughout the region he has described.[6] He is now, therefore, in a position to move on. For, as he explains in verse 20, his ministry is to "preach the gospel where Christ was not known." There is nothing wrong with building on someone else's foundations. Significant ministers like Apollos did just that (see 1 Cor. 3:3–11). But this is not the job God has given Paul. He sees himself carrying out the commission given to the servant of the Lord in Isaiah 52:15, revealing the good news to people who have not been told before and who have not heard before (Rom. 15:21).

Paul's Immediate Travel Plans (15:22–29)

PAUL GOES ON to mention his next three destinations (in order of visit): Jerusalem (vv. 25–27), Rome (vv. 22–24, 28–29), and Spain (vv. 24, 28). He is not interested is simply giving the Roman Christians his itinerary. His main concern is to explain why it has taken him so long to get to Rome (v. 22) and why, when he does get there, he does not plan to stay long (v. 28). He must fulfill his commission to bring the gospel where the name of Christ has not yet been heard, and Spain is a fertile field for pioneer church-planting. But a stop in Rome is necessary for the apostle to secure logistical support for this new outreach, so far from his original home base of Antioch. But before these plans can be carried out, Paul must first visit Jerusalem, where he hopes to bring to a successful climax his long-cherished project of collecting money from Gentile churches for the impoverished saints in the home city of the gospel.

The NIV makes verse 22 the concluding verse of the preceding paragraph. But it is better, following modern editions of the Greek text and most English versions (e.g., NRSV; TEV; NASB; NJB), to make it the first verse in the new paragraph. Because Paul has been "fully proclaiming" the gospel all the way from Jerusalem to Illyricum (vv. 18–19), therefore (Gk. *dio* in v. 22, untranslated in NIV) he has been hindered up to now from coming to Rome (cf. 1:13).

Now, however, things have changed. With his ministry in the east fulfilled, there is no longer a place for him in those regions. Because he has so long wanted to visit the Romans, he now plans to stop there on his way to Spain. The clause "I plan to do so [i.e., to see you]" in 15:24 does not occur in the Greek but helps clarify Paul's syntax, which he breaks off awkwardly in verse 24 (NASB preserves the incomplete sentence in vv. 23–24a and indicates the break with a dash). In other words, Paul has two reasons to come to Rome:

---

6. See esp. John Knox, "Romans 15:14–33 and Paul's Conception of His Apostolic Mission," *JBL* 83 (1964): 3.

a negative one (the hindrance of ministry in the east has been removed) and a positive one (he longs to see them).

Still, Rome is not his final destination. He will visit them and hopes to "enjoy [their] company," but he will not remain there long; he is "passing through" on his way to Spain. Parts of Spain had been occupied by the Romans since about 200 B.C. But the Romans had fully organized the area as a province only in Paul's lifetime. There may have been a significant Jewish community there, although the matter is debated.[7] Obviously, Paul thinks it a good place to embark in a fresh church-planting ministry.

Paul's plan to spend only a short time in Rome creates a certain tension with what he says in the introduction to the letter, where he speaks about preaching the gospel in Rome and says nothing about Spain (1:15). What is said here probably reflects a delicacy about seeking financial support. For the verb "assist" (*propempo*) that he uses in verse 24b has the regular New Testament connotation of missionary support (Acts 15:3; 20:38; 21:5; 1 Cor. 16:6, 11; 2 Cor. 1:16; Titus 3:13; 3 John 6). Paul hints, then, that he hopes to enlist the support of the Roman Christians for his new missionary effort in Spain. Spain is a long way from Antioch, his original sending church, and he knows he will need a new base of operations. In addition to financial support, the Romans can perhaps also help with translators and other specific needs.

One obstacle, however, still remains in the way of Paul's trip to the western part of the empire: He is on his way to Jerusalem "in the service of the saints there" (v. 25). "In the service" translates the Greek verb *diakoneo* (to serve, minister). This word refers to any kind of ministry, but the context reveals that Paul is referring to the specific ministry of "the collection" (words from this root refer to the collection also in 2 Cor. 8:4, 19, 20; 9:1, 12, 13).

Paul initiated this enterprise on his third missionary journey, requesting contributions from the Gentile churches he had planted to be sent to Jerusalem for the believers who were suffering from severe want (1 Cor. 16:1–2; 2 Cor. 8–9). In somewhat of a parenthesis, Paul now explains this "service" (Rom. 15:26–27) before continuing to discuss his plans to visit Rome (vv. 28–29). Macedonia is the Roman province that includes important Pauline churches like Philippi and Thessalonica, while Achaia includes Corinth. Paul has requested money from them, but he makes clear that they gave of their own free will: They were "pleased to make a contribution [*koinonia*]." *Koinonia* is the usual New Testament word for "fellowship" enjoyed by believers in Christ. The money sent by the Gentiles is a tangible expression of this fellowship.

---

7. For an assessment of the evidence, see W. P. Bowers, "Jewish Communities in Spain in the Time of Paul the Apostle," *JTS* 26 (1975): 395–402.

The recipients of this collection are "the poor among the saints in Jerusalem" (15:26). This NIV rendering (cf. also most modern versions) assumes a particular interpretation of the Greek phrase used here. Some commentators think that "the poor" may have a theological meaning, derived from the Old Testament and Jewish use of that word to denote the "pious." But since Paul gives no hint of this theological use of the word, the NIV interpretation is preferable.

In verse 27 we detect why the collection is so important to Paul. It is not just a charitable project; it is also designed to bring into closer fellowship Gentile and Jewish believers. The Gentiles, after all, have benefited spiritually from the Jews. As Paul explains in 11:17–18, Gentile Christians derive whatever spiritual blessing they experience from the Jewish Messiah and the fulfillment of God's promises to Israel (cf. also 4:13–16; 15:7–8). The Gentile Christians can partially repay this debt by sharing with the Jews their own material blessings.

Paul will only head for Rome and Spain when he has "completed this task" of bringing the collection to Jerusalem. Why must Paul himself accompany the collection? He hints at the reason in the phrase the NIV translates "I ... have made sure that they have received this fruit" (lit. trans.: "I have sealed for them this fruit"). The idea of "sealing" (*sphragizo*, affix a seal) often connotes an official affirmation of authenticity (see, e.g., Est. 8:8, 10; John 3:33; cf. also Paul's references to believers being sealed by the Holy Spirit in 2 Cor. 1:22; Eph. 1:13; 4:30). Paul, as the apostle to the Gentiles, must accompany the gift to Jerusalem in order to authenticate its purpose as a healing gesture.

In verse 29 Paul breathes "a sigh of relief."[8] For by the time he gets to Rome the tension over the collection will be over. He will therefore be able to come to them "in the full measure of the blessing of Christ." Paul probably refers here to the mutual ministry of edification he anticipates when he comes to Rome (cf. 1:12).

Request for Prayer (15:30–33)

SINCE PAUL HOPES that the collection will help to heal the growing rift between Jewish and Gentile Christians—a matter at the heart of his concern—he asks the Romans to join him in praying for the success of this venture. He strengthens his request by indicating that he makes it "by [the authority of] our Lord Jesus Christ" and on the basis of "the love of the Spirit." "Of the Spirit" may indicate the love the Spirit has for us (a subjective

---

8. Käsemann, *Commentary on Romans*, 402.

genitive),[9] but, in this context, probably means "the love the Spirit engenders among us" (a genitive of source).[10]

Why does Paul denote this ministry of prayer as a "struggle"? This word may suggest that prayer involves a wrestling with God[11] or that prayer must be especially diligent.[12] But frequent references to his own ministry as a "struggle" suggest rather that he invites the Roman Christians to participate with him, through their prayers, in his missionary work.[13]

Paul asks the Romans to pray for two things specifically (v. 31): that he will "be rescued from the unbelievers [lit., those who disobey] in Judea," and that the saints in Jerusalem will accept the offering of the collection. Unbelieving Jews were especially hostile to Paul for his opening the doors of God's people to Gentiles. His fears about them were justified, as the outcry against him when he does get to Jerusalem makes clear (Acts 21–22). But he is also concerned that Jewish Christians do not refuse the gift as being tainted by the "unclean" hands of Gentiles.

Only when these requests have been answered will Paul be able to come to Rome "with joy" and be spiritually refreshed with them (15:32). Paul concludes his request for the Romans' prayer with his own prayer for them: that "the God of peace," that is, the God who gives peace, may be with them (v. 33).

PRINCIPLES FOR DEFINING APPLICATION. Bridging the gap between Paul's travel plans and application today is not easy. Straightforwardly applying the main points of these verses—where Paul has been, where he is going, what he hopes to do in Rome, and what he wants the Roman Christians to do—is simply not helpful to us today. Yet God inspired these words for our benefit. What and how are we to learn from them? Most interpreters would argue that we can learn a lot from the principles that underlie Paul's words. We may not derive much spiritual benefit from knowing *that* Paul was going to Spain, but knowing *why* he is going there may shed light on New Testament principles of ministry.

But if most would agree that isolating principles in this kind of text is a valid procedure, not everyone agrees on what these principles are. By definition, we are isolating points in the text that are not explicitly applied to us

---

9. E.g., Murray, *The Epistle to the Romans,* 2:221; Fitzmyer, *Romans,* 725.

10. E.g., Cranfield, *The Epistle to the Romans,* 776; Dunn, *Romans,* 878.

11. Black, *Romans,* 177. He refers to the story of Jacob's wrestling with God (Gen. 32).

12. Murray, *The Epistle to the Romans,* 2:221–22; Cranfield, *The Epistle to the Romans,* 776–77.

13. See esp. V. C. Pfitzner, *Paul and the Agon Motif: Traditional Athletic Imagery in the Pauline Literature* (Leiden: Brill, 1967), 120–25.

by Paul. How, then, do we determine which apply and which do not? Two questions that we pose to each possible principle will be helpful, if not definitive. (1) Is the principle dependent on something distinct to that time, place, culture, or situation in salvation history? (2) Is the principle taught elsewhere, perhaps more clearly, in Scripture?

Two of the most potentially significant principles in these verses—Paul's description of his ministry (vv. 16–22) and the collection (vv. 25–27)—yield confusing answers. On the one hand, both contain elements unique to that time and place. Paul is not just *any* minister, but *the* apostle to the Gentiles. As we have see, Paul has a unique ministry, predicted in Scripture, to open the door of faith to the Gentiles. Some of what he says about his ministry, then, will not be transferable to us today. The same is true of the collection. Paul viewed this as a way that the Gentiles who shared in Israel's spiritual blessings could repay that debt to the Jerusalem Christians. No other charitable collection in history will have quite this significance. On the other hand, what Paul says here about his ministry also contains elements true for any ministry, and some find parallels in other New Testament passages. The same is true for the collection.

No clear answers await us as we raise these kind of hermeneutical questions. Good and sincere interpreters will sometimes disagree on just what we can carry over from a text like this. But we need to be aware that a problem exists and not make the mistake of finding all kinds of specific points of application in a text that simply are not there. Moreover, those points of application that we do isolate probably need to be taught somewhat tentatively—unless, of course, we can find clear Scriptural support for the idea elsewhere.

Paul himself sometimes uses Old Testament narratives in just this fashion (e.g., 1 Cor. 10:1–6), so perhaps we have good biblical basis for using the New Testament in a similar way. But before examining what principles we might be able to isolate in Romans 15:14–33, we must look more deeply into two specific contextual issues that will help our application.

The New Testament transformation of the cult (cf. 15:16). As we have noted elsewhere (see comments on 12:1–2), cultic worship, involving priest, sacrifice, and temple, was the focal point for the religious experience of many in the ancient Greco-Roman world. Paul picks up this language in 15:16, thereby tapping into one of the most basic religious elements of the ancient worldview. He calls himself a priest (*leitourgos*, NIV "minister"), describes his missionary activity as "the priestly duty of proclaiming the gospel of God," and claims that Gentile converts constitute the "offering" (*prosphora*) he makes to God. What are we to make of this language? For both Paul and the Roman Christians, of course, the cultic system taught in the Old Testament and practiced by the Jews is the key reference point. We can only appreciate what he is saying by exploring this tradition and its transformation in the New Testament.

We need not here detail the importance of the cult in the Old Testament. But we should note that the Old Testament itself suggests that the animal sacrifices, in and of themselves, are not efficacious to bring a worshiper into right relationship with God. The prophets frequently criticize the Israelites for making this very assumption (see comments on 12:1–2). During the intertestamental period and into the New Testament period, this criticism was sharpened under the influence of Hellenistic philosophy. A number of Greek philosophers scorned the notion of sacrifice, claiming that the cult deflected people from the true meaning of religion, which consisted in intellectual truth and moral living. Certain more radical Jewish thinkers, such as Philo of Alexandria, echoed this criticism, although in muted form.

Few Jews wanted to do away with sacrifices. But many wanted to validate them by finding spiritual significance behind them. Philo's famous allegorizing method of interpretation had precisely this purpose. He wanted to make Judaism both intelligible and palatable to sophisticated Greek thinkers by finding philosophical and moral truths behind the history and strange customs of his people, the Jews.

All this sets the stage for the early Christian church. Jesus himself did not speak against the cult, though he continued and even radicalized the prophetic critique of meaningless sacrifice (see, e.g., Matt. 12:7–8; 23:23). But in one famous saying, at least, he lays the foundation for a new way of viewing the cult. When asked to give a "sign" to justify his authority to cleanse the temple, Jesus responded, "Destroy this temple, and I will raise it again in three days" (John 2:19). While the Jews thought Jesus was talking about the physical temple, John explains Jesus was speaking about his own body (v. 21). Here, in the typical "replacement" motif of John's Gospel, Jesus suggests his own body takes the place of the temple as the focal point for worshiping God.

The early Christians eventually developed the notion of the church as "the body of Christ." The center of worship was transferred from a physical building in Jerusalem to the people of God. God lives in the midst of his people and no longer manifests himself in any special way in a temple. Christians, both individually and corporately, are now "God's temple" (see 1 Cor. 3:16–17; cf. 6:19; Eph. 2:21; 1 Peter 2:5; Rev. 21:22).

Along with the replacement of a physical temple goes a transformation in sacrifice and priesthood. As Hebrews reveals, Christ's own sacrifice climaxes and brings to an end the Old Testament sacrificial system. He is now our high priest, presenting his own sacrifice to God the Father on our behalf.

New covenant sacrifices, then, are obedient Christians (cf. Rom. 12:1) and the praise they offer God (Heb. 13:15). Every Christian, called to offer such praise, becomes a priest (1 Peter 2:5, 9). What the early Christians, did, then, was different from the spiritualization going on in the world at that time. They did not find a hidden, spiritual meaning in the cult. Rather, they announced that God had, in Jesus and in their community, brought his cult to its fulfillment. They transformed the cult through their eschatology.[14]

Paul builds on this world of metaphor in his allusions in verse 16. He is not claiming in any technical sense to be a priest. He picks up the concept of new covenant transformation of the cult as a way of describing what he does as a minister of the gospel. Nor is Paul claiming a monopoly on the priesthood. He is not denying that other Christians might also be priests.

Old Testament background to Paul's special ministry. The text we have just looked at carries eschatological overtones in another important sense. Paul, we must remember, is not here describing Christian ministry generally. He is characterizing his own apostolic ministry, "the grace God gave me" (v. 15). While not excluding other Christians from serving as priests, Paul does suggest that he was been given a unique priestly duty: to offer the Gentiles up to God.

Contributing to this notion are two interesting Old Testament allusions. (1) The characterization of the Gentiles as "sanctified by the Holy Spirit" (v. 16) probably alludes to the Old Testament prediction that God will sanctify his name among the Gentiles in the last days (see esp. Ezek. 36:22–28).[15] This allusion is particularly striking, since Ezekiel's prediction occurs in the same text in which Israel's exile is said to have caused God's name to be "profaned among the nations" (vv. 21, 22, 23). Paul uses this same language, perhaps from this same text, in Romans 2:24 to castigate Israel. The Ezekiel passage is also the text in which God promises to give to his people a new heart and a new spirit. Thus, Paul seems to imply, God has now reversed the profanation of his name among the Gentiles by sanctifying those Gentiles themselves.

(2) The second Old Testament text Paul may have in mind in verse 16 is Isaiah 66:20: "And they will bring all your brothers, from all the nations, to my holy mountain in Jerusalem as an offering to the LORD." If these "brothers" are Gentiles, then this verse fits well with Paul's understanding of his ministry. As one of the Jewish remnant who has experienced God's salvation, Paul brings in Gentiles converts "as an offering to the Lord."[16] The "brothers" may, however, be fellow Jews, in which case the allusion is not so evident.

---

14. See, e.g., O'Brien, *Consumed by Passion*, 31–32.

15. See ibid., 31, 50–51.

16. See esp. R. D. Aus, "Paul's Travel Plans to Spain and the 'Full Number of the Gentiles' of Rom. XI 25," *NovT* 21 (1979): 236–37; Arland J. Hultgren, *Paul's Gospel and Ministry* (Philadelphia: Fortress, 1985), 133–34.

Whether or not we can include the latter as an allusion, Paul clearly pictures his own ministry in eschatological terms. Without buying into the whole package presented by J. Munck in his picture of the eschatological ministry of Paul, the unique significance of Paul's own ministry must not be missed. He claims, according to Acts, to be fulfilling Israel's vocation as servant of the Lord to be "a light for the Gentiles" (Acts 13:47). As "the apostle to the Gentiles" par excellence, he carries out a priestly ministry with clear eschatological significance. With the coming of Christ, the barrier between Jew and Gentile represented by the cult is broken down. No longer are atonement, sacrifice, or worship Jewish-oriented or Jerusalem-centered. Through the priestly ministry of Paul, Gentiles such as those in Rome have heard the gospel and become an offering pleasing to God.

Several interpreters think that certain Old Testament traditions related to these verses in Isaiah may have influenced Paul at other points in this passage. Popular is the notion that Paul may have regarded the collection he was putting together from the Gentile churches as the fulfillment of the prophetic predictions that the wealth of the nations would flow to Jerusalem in the last days (e.g., Isa. 45:14; 60:5–17; 61:6; Mic. 4:13).[17]

A few have even thought that Paul chose Spain as his next missionary outreach through these same prophecies. In Isaiah 66:19, God through Isaiah predicts that in the last days, "I will set a sign among them, and I will send some of those who survive to the nations—to Tarshish, to the Libyans and Lydians (famous as archers), to Tubal and Greece, and to the distant islands that have not heard of my fame or seen my glory. They will proclaim my glory among the nations." There is some evidence that ancient people identified Tarshish with the area of Spain. Perhaps Paul's plans for Spain are thus the result of identifying his own ministry with the prophetic forecast of God's work to bring the Gentiles into fellowship with Jews.[18]

WHAT PRINCIPLES CAN we isolate from Paul's travel plans in 15:14–33 that are significant for the church today? I think three principles emerge clearly, and one other more tangentially.

Successful ministry. One clear principle is this: Successful ministry is always God's doing. Paul implicitly gives himself a significant role in salvation history as he describes his ministry in verses 16–22. Yet he gives all the credit for his ministry to the Lord, to "the grace God gave me." His role as

---

17. See, e.g., Dunn, *Romans*, 874.
18. See Aus, "Paul's Travel Plans," 242–46.

apostle to the Gentiles is not one he has earned through hard study or by virtue of intrinsic talent. God chose him, prepared him, gave him the ministry, and empowers it. All is of grace. The Gentile converts he offers as a sacrifice to God are acceptable only because they are "sanctified by the Holy Spirit" (v. 16). What Paul has done is no more than what "Christ has accomplished through me" (v. 18), as the "power of the Spirit" enabled both his deeds and his words (v. 19).

"Successful" ministers are prone to pride, one of the most basic of all sins. It is frighteningly easy to fall into a mode in which we begin taking credit for whatever positive spiritual impact we are having. The people with whom we minister will often be the innocent inducers to this pride. In an effort to be supportive and encouraging, they will often flatter us about the sermon preached, book written, or life changed. Our dutiful response, "Glory to God, it was his doing," can become both formulaic and insincere.

God, of course, has his own ways of humbling our pride. For every parishioner who flatters us, God sends two others to ask, after we preach, "Was your week particularly busy?" or "Did you lose your watch?" Yet the natural inclination for many of us is to listen to the flatterers far too much. Moreover, pride is not only wrong in itself, it can lead to so many other sins. I am positive that many prominent ministers fall into sexual sin precisely because they begin to think that they are immune to such ordinary temptations or, worse yet, they begin unconsciously thinking they are above the law.

How can one fight the temptation to pride and imitate Paul in giving all the glory to God? I have no magic formula, but I am convinced that interaction in a small group of peers to whom we are accountable can be a great help. Many ministers tend to be isolated, spending all their time with people to whom they minister and never developing any genuine peer relationships. Any isolated Christian is in a dangerous situation. That situation is doubly dangerous for the pastor who may be a special target of the evil one. All of us in ministry need at least one peer (in addition, of course, to our spouse!) who will feel free to "tell us off" when necessary.

Balancing spontaneity and obligation. A second principle we can validly derive from this text is the need to balance spontaneity and obligation in giving to the Lord and to his people. As Paul describes the collection for the saints in Jerusalem, he emphasizes that those who gave "were pleased" to do so (vv. 26–27). This verb (*eudokeo*) has the idea of free decision (cf. TEV, "their decision was their own"). Yet Paul can also say, in the same verse, that the Gentiles "owe it to the Jews to share with them."

Paul combines these same points in 2 Corinthians 8–9 when he talks about giving. In the famous words of 9:7, God loves "a cheerful giver," who does not give by compulsion (9:7; cf. also 8:2; 9:5). Yet the Corinthians' giving is also a matter of "obedience" (9:13). Of course, both Romans 15 and 2 Corinthians 8–9 are about the collection for the saints in Jerusalem, and that collection, as we pointed out above, has certain unique dimensions. But the motivation for giving is not attached to any unique feature of that collection, and 2 Corinthians 9:7 expresses a general truth about God's attitude toward the giver.

Each of us, then, must recognize that we are under a certain obligation to give back to the Lord a portion of what he has given us. We owe it to him in repayment for his grace, and we owe it to other believers who need our help. Yet, at the same time, our giving should be free and unconstrained.

How can these both be true at the same time? Perhaps an analogy will help. I know I am under obligation to be a good father to my children; I owe it to them. Yet I also delight in being a good father to them (most of the time). The key is the personal relationship. Because I love my children, my fathering is not an onerous obligation but a glad responsibility. I discharge the obligation with delight and gratitude. Our giving to the Lord must arise from the joy of our relationship with him so that it is also a glad obligation. The same can be said about our Christian giving. The more I get to know other believers who are in need, the more sincerely motivated I will be to share with them from the good things God has given to me.

Praying for people in ministry. Prayer for people involved in ministry is a third principle we can isolate in this text. Paul typically asks his churches to pray for him at the end of his letters. Romans is no exception. After informing the Christians in Rome about the collection he is bringing to Jerusalem (15:25–27), he asks them to pray for him and for the success of this venture. As we indicated in the Original Meaning section, the collection held great significance for Paul. He hoped it would become an important means of healing the growing rift between Gentile and Jewish Christians. The unity of the church was at stake. No wonder he asks for prayer.

Yet we should not miss the significance of this request. (1) It illustrates the humility and sense of need Paul has. Though he has a divinely given mission, unique in salvation history, he still needs other believers to pray for him. How much more, then, do the rest of us, engaged in far humbler tasks and with far less biblical confirmation, need the prayers of God's people. Pride can be an obstacle here as we can subtly begin depending on our own skills, talents, or resources rather than on the Lord, who empowers through the prayers of his people.

(2) Paul's call for prayer also illustrates the biblical tension between God's determination of events and the situation-changing power of prayer. Paul undoubtedly sensed that God himself had inaugurated and was empowering this collection. Yet he still asks people to pray for it. To be sure, we have no

evidence Paul saw the collection in terms of a divine prophecy, sure to succeed because God had said it would. But even if this were the case, evidence from other texts shows that he would still have asked prayer for it.

Our own enterprises come with no more (and usually considerably less) divine mandate than Paul's collection. We can fall into the error of assuming our own ministries or projects are so important for the cause of Christ that God, as it were, is bound to prosper them. We can fail to pray for them or to enlist others in prayer. No matter how hard we try to avoid it, the anti-supernaturalism of our culture exerts a strong pull on us. Particularly at a time when the business world is becoming more and more a paradigm for ministry, it is easy for us in ministry to put our projects in the same category as a business enterprise and assume that the keys to success are the same: hard work, careful planning, effective execution. Prayer can get left out.

Church planting. A point of application that I advance only hesitantly comes from Paul's description of his own ground-breaking church planting ministry. As he makes clear in verse 20, he made it his practice to "preach the gospel where Christ was not known." Many early American pioneers moved to a new log cabin whenever they could see the smoke from another person's chimney. Paul seems to have a been a bit like that, moving his ministry on whenever there were too many Christians around. His job, he was convinced, was to plant churches that could thrive and carry on the work of ministry on their own. Then he could leave for new, untilled gospel ground.

Nothing in our text justifies the conclusion that Paul is setting forth here a general way to "do missions." That is why our application must be tentative. But maybe we can learn a couple of things from Paul's example. (1) Obviously, God may today also be raising up people who have the difficult job of bringing the gospel to places it has not been heard before. Most of us know of missions organizations and missionaries dedicated just to this task—"New Tribes Missions," for example. But are there enough missionaries giving themselves to this task? The vast majority of Christian workers are serving a small minority of the world's population. We need more workers willing to follow Paul's example.

(2) Paul's example may also suggest that our missions work should have as its goal the planting of self-reproducing churches. Sometimes we do not stay long enough in a given area for a church to reach this critical mass. Perhaps more often, however, the missionary stays too long, beyond the time when the help of foreigners is any longer needed.

Romans 16:1–16

I COMMEND TO you our sister Phoebe, a servant of the church in Cenchrea. ²I ask you to receive her in the Lord in a way worthy of the saints and to give her any help she may need from you, for she has been a great help to many people, including me.

³ Greet Priscilla and Aquila, my fellow workers in Christ Jesus. ⁴They risked their lives for me. Not only I but all the churches of the Gentiles are grateful to them.
⁵ Greet also the church that meets at their house.
Greet my dear friend Epenetus, who was the first convert to Christ in the province of Asia.
⁶ Greet Mary, who worked very hard for you.
⁷ Greet Andronicus and Junias, my relatives who have been in prison with me. They are outstanding among the apostles, and they were in Christ before I was.
⁸ Greet Ampliatus, whom I love in the Lord.
⁹ Greet Urbanus, our fellow worker in Christ, and my dear friend Stachys.
¹⁰ Greet Apelles, tested and approved in Christ.
Greet those who belong to the household of Aristobulus.
¹¹ Greet Herodion, my relative.
Greet those in the household of Narcissus who are in the Lord.
¹² Greet Tryphena and Tryphosa, those women who work hard in the Lord.
Greet my dear friend Persis, another woman who has worked very hard in the Lord.
¹³ Greet Rufus, chosen in the Lord, and his mother, who has been a mother to me, too.
¹⁴ Greet Asyncritus, Phlegon, Hermes, Patrobas, Hermas and the brothers with them.
¹⁵ Greet Philologus, Julia, Nereus and his sister, and Olympas and all the saints with them.
¹⁶ Greet one another with a holy kiss.
All the churches of Christ send greetings.

PAUL CONTINUES WITH items typical of the conclusions of his letters (see comments on 15:14–33): commendation of a fellow-worker (16:1–2), exhortations to greet other Christians (16:3–16a), and greetings to the Roman Christians from others (16:16b). But what is not typical about this section is the number of greetings. He asks the Romans to greet twenty-six individuals, two families, and three house churches. This number is all the more surprising when we remember that Paul had never visited Rome.

In fact, some scholars have been so struck by this circumstance that they do not think Romans 16 could have been sent to Rome. They posit that it may have been part of a different letter or a separate letter of its own, sent perhaps to Ephesus. We found good reason to reject this theory in the Introduction. But as we noted there, many of these Roman Christians (like Priscilla and Aquila, v. 3) had spent years in exile away from Rome, where they had opportunity to get to know Paul. Perhaps, indeed, the relatively small number of Christians Paul knows in Rome enables him to send greetings to virtually everyone he is aware of in the city.

Commendation of a Prominent Christian Worker (16:1–2)

LETTERS OF COMMENDATION were important in the ancient world. People who traveled in an age with few public facilities (such as hotels or restaurants) depended on the assistance of people they had sometimes never met for their needs. Phoebe is apparently going to be traveling to Rome, and so Paul commends to the church this "sister" (*adelphe*, rare in the New Testament as a description of believer [1 Cor. 7:15; 9:5; Philem. 2; James 2:15]).

But Phoebe is more than a sister; she is also a "servant [*diakonos*] of the church in Cenchrea." *Diakonos* can be applied to any Christian, called to "serve" God and his people. This may be its sense here.[1] But the addition "of the church in Cenchrea" makes it more likely that Phoebe holds an official position in the church there. Phoebe is probably a "deacon," serving the church by ministering to the financial and material needs of the believers (see esp. 1 Tim. 3:8–12; cf. also Phil. 1:1).[2]

Paul gives a further hint of Phoebe's function in the church at the end of verse 2, where he calls her a *prostatis* "to many people, including me." *Prostatis* is derived from a verb that means both to care for, give aid to, and to direct, preside over. The former meaning is assumed in the NIV translation,

---

1. See, e.g., Murray, *The Epistle to the Romans*, 2:226.

2. So most commentators; see, e.g., Godet, *Commentary on Romans*, 488; Cranfield, *The Epistle to the Romans*, 781; Dunn, *Romans*, 886–87.

"she has been a great help." Others argue for the latter meaning, viewing Phoebe as the "leader" of the community.[3] Perhaps the best suggestion is to give *prostatis* the meaning it often has in secular Greek, "patron, benefactor."[4] Phoebe was probably a wealthy businesswoman, who used her wealth to support the church and its missionaries (like Paul). Her ministry in the church and beneficence to the church's workers make her worthy of a Christian greeting and any assistance the Roman church can give her.

Greetings (16:3–16)

PAUL OFTEN ENCOURAGES the Christians to whom he writes to "greet one another" (Phil. 4:21; Titus 3:15), sometimes by means of a "holy kiss" (Rom. 16:16a; 1 Cor. 16:20; 2 Cor. 13:12; 1 Thess. 5:26). But in verses 3–15 Paul also conveys individual greetings to a whole host of people. This feature is not unprecedented in his letters (cf. Col. 4:15; 2 Tim. 4:19), but its extent is. In addition to the reasons mentioned above and in the Introduction, a concern to establish good relations with the church in Rome may also have been a reason for all these greetings. Public recognition, as the letter was read aloud, of those Christians in Rome whom Paul already knew would help cement good relationships with the community.[5] The passage falls into three sections of unequal length:

> verses 3–15: a list of requests to greet specific individuals and groups
> verse 16a: an exhortation for the Christians in Rome to greet one another
> verse 16b: greetings to the Roman Christians from others

Priscilla[6] and Aquila (vv. 3–4) are a well-known couple in the New Testament. Luke tells us that they came to Corinth after fleeing Rome because of Emperor Claudius's expulsion order (Acts 18:2). Like Paul, they were tentmakers (18:3). They ministered with him in Corinth, then went to Ephesus and engaged in ministry there (18:18), where they were instrumental in bringing Apollos to a better understanding of the faith (18:26). They apparently served with Paul in Ephesus for some time (1 Cor. 16:19) before returning to Rome after Claudius's edict lapsed.

---

3. See, e.g., David M. Scholer, "Paul's Women Co-workers in the Ministry of the Church," *Daughters of Sarah* 6/4 (1980): 3–6.

4. E.g., Sanday and Headlam, *The Epistle to the Romans*, 417–18; Cranfield, *The Epistle to the Romans*, 782–83; Dunn, *Romans*, 888–89.

5. Peter Lampe, "The Roman Christians of Romans 16," in *The Romans Debate*, 218; Jeffrey A. D. Weima, *Neglected Endings: The Significance of the Pauline Letter Closings* (Sheffield: JSOT, 1994), 226–28.

6. NIV; the Greek actually has the shortened name "Prisca," but the NIV standardizes the spelling of names.

Paul commends Priscilla and Aquila as "fellow workers" (*synergos*), a term he uses regularly to refer to people who minister with him in all kinds of ways (see also vv. 9, 21; 2 Cor. 8:23; Phil. 2:25; 4:3; Col. 4:11; Philem. 1, 24). They have also "risked their lives" for Paul. When this happened we do not know, although it may have been at the time of the riot in Ephesus (Acts 19). They must have been fairly wealthy, owning a house large enough for a group of believers to meet there regularly for worship (a "house church") (Rom. 16:5a).

Epenetus (v. 5b) is mentioned only here in the New Testament. Paul may have known him well, since he calls him "my dear friend" (*agapetos*, lit., "beloved one"). Or this term may have become somewhat formalized as a way of referring to any brother or sister in Christ. In any case, Paul remembers him well, since he was the "first convert to Christ" (*aparche*; lit., "the firstfruits") in the province of Asia (which included Ephesus).

Mary was a common Jewish name, but it was also used by the Gentiles; thus, we cannot be sure of her ethnic background. Paul commends her for working "very hard for" the Roman Christians.

Andronicus and Junias (v. 7) are the most debated names in the list. They are relatives of Paul, they have been in prison with him (probably for the sake of the gospel), they were Christians before Paul, and they are "outstanding among the apostles." Andronicus is clearly a male name. But who was *Iounias*? The NIV translation (see also RSV; NASB; TEV; NJB) assumes that this Greek form is a contraction of a masculine name, Junianus.[7] But the Greek form can also reflect a feminine name, Junia (KJV; NRSV; REB). This may seem like a trivial matter, but the fact that this person is apparently called an "apostle" has turned this verse into a minor squall in the storm of controversy over women and ministry (see Contemporary Significance section). Here we simply note that the case for a feminine name is strong. *Iounia* (the feminine) is a common Greek name; the contracted form of *Iounianos* (the masculine) is apparently unknown.[8]

Andronicus and Junias, like Aquila and Priscilla (v. 3), were probably husband and wife. But how can Paul call them "apostles" (*apostolos*) when they were clearly not among the Twelve? Some interpreters have suggested that we translate "esteemed *by* the apostles,"[9] but this is unlikely. More to the point is to remember that Paul uses *apostolos* in ways other than as a reference to the

---

7. See, e.g., Godet, *Commentary on Romans*, 491; Sanday and Headlam, *The Epistle to the Romans*, 422–23.

8. See esp. Richard S. Cervin, "A Note Regarding the Name 'Junia(s)' in Romans 16.7," *NTS* 40 (1994): 464–70; see also Cranfield, *The Epistle to the Romans*, 788–89; Dunn, *Romans*, 894; Schreiner, *Romans*, 795–96; Fitzmyer, *Romans*, 737–38 (with a thorough historical survey).

9. E.g., Murray, *The Epistle to the Romans*, 2:229–30.

official, authoritative "twelve apostles." It can refer to a "messenger" (2 Cor. 8:23; Phil. 2:25) or a "commissioned missionary" (1 Cor. 9:5–6; 15:7[?]; Gal. 2:9; Acts 14:4, 14). In this context, this latter meaning is the most likely.[10]

Ampliatus (v. 8), Urbanus (v. 9), and Apelles (v. 10a) are unknown apart from this list. "Those who belong to the household of Aristobulus" is a fair paraphrase of the Greek, which, literally translated, says simply "those of Aristobulus." The reference is probably mainly to the slaves who work for Aristobulus. Aristobulus was the name of a brother of Herod Agrippa I who died in Rome in A.D. 48 or 49; those mentioned in this verse may be slaves who continued to serve in his household.[11]

"Herodion" (v. 11) is a name otherwise unattested. He was probably a freed slave who took the name of the Herodian family he served. Narcissus is also a freed slave—perhaps the same Narcissus who gained prominence as a servant of Emperor Claudius. We have no evidence that Narcissus had become a Christian, and the fact that he committed suicide shortly before Paul wrote Romans suggests he was not.[12] Tryphena, Tryphosa, and Persis (v. 12) are mentioned only here in the New Testament. Rufus (v. 13), by contrast, may be the same Rufus referred to in Mark 15:21 as the son of Simon of Cyrene, who was forced to carry Jesus' cross.[13] We know nothing about those mentioned in Romans 16:14–15. The "brothers with him" (i.e., Hermas) in verse 14b probably refers to Christians who meet in Hermas's house for worship, and Paul refers to another such house church at the end of verse 15.

Paul concludes his request for greetings with a catch-all request: "Greet one another with a holy kiss" (v. 16a). The kiss was a standard form of greeting in the ancient world generally and in Judaism in particular. By the time of the second century, the "kiss of peace" had become a part of the usual Christian liturgy. Perhaps Paul has in mind that the Roman Christians will conclude the public hearing of his letter with such a kiss.[14]

Paul ends this section by turning the tables and conveying greetings to the Roman Christians from "all the churches of Christ." This is clearly a hyperbole; the reference is probably to those churches he has planted "from Jerusalem all the way around to Illyricum" (15:19).

---

10. So most recent commentators (e.g., Käsemann, *Commentary on Romans*, 413; Cranfield, *The Epistle to the Romans*, 789; Dunn, *Romans*, 894–95; Schreiner, *Romans*, 796).

11. See the discussion about Roman Christianity in J. B. Lightfoot, *St. Paul's Epistle to the Philippians* (London: Macmillan, 1913), 174–75; cf. also Lampe, "Roman Christians," 222.

12. See Lightfoot, *Philippians*, 175.

13. Favoring the identification are, e.g., Lightfoot, *Philippians*, 176; Godet, *Commentary on Romans*, 493; Cranfield, *The Epistle to the Romans*, 793–94; Dunn, *Romans*, 897; skeptical is, e.g., Käsemann, *Commentary on Romans*, 414.

14. E.g., Cranfield, *The Epistle to the Romans*, 796.

Bridging Contexts

BRINGING THIS TEXT into the twenty-first century requires an approach similar to the one we outlined for 15:14–33. The explicit intention of the author, Paul, is to commend Phoebe and to convey greetings to the first-century church at Rome. These points are simply not relevant to our day. Faced with this dilemma, some interpreters resort to application by analogy: As Paul endorsed traveling Christians, so should we; as he greeted and commended fellow Christians, so should we. But nothing in this text suggests Paul is making his epistolary conventions a pattern for others to follow. Even if there were hermeneutical justification, the points are so banal as hardly to require exposition.

A more productive approach, as we suggested above, is to seek principles expressed or hinted at within the text that govern what Paul is saying. A text is often as interesting for what it assumes as for what it explicitly teaches. In 16:1–16, Paul touches on or implies three facets of the early Christian church that we can learn something from: its social composition, its organization, and the importance of women. Each, but particularly the last, requires some initial exploration here as a basis for any application.

Social composition of the early church. While the average believer does not find much of interest in the interminable list of names in Romans 16:3–15, the historian of early Christianity does. To the historian the names reveal a lot. Names in the ancient world conveyed data about the person. They were not mere handles chosen on the basis of euphony or fad. At the minimum, names usually enable us to pin down a person's ethnic origin. They can also indicate social class or occupation. "Onesimus," for instance, the escaped slave Paul writes about in Philemon, means "useful"; it was the kind of name often given to a slave, in the hopes that he would live up to it.

The historian Peter Lampe has done a thorough study of the names in Romans 16.[15] He concludes that most of the people whom Paul mentions are Gentiles or freedmen or are descendants of slaves and freedmen (*freedman* is the term given the class of freed slaves in the Roman empire). Note too that Paul specifically mentions at least two groups of slaves: the household (servants) of Aristobulus (v. 10) and those of Narcissus (v. 11).

The information of Romans 16 applies, of course, only to that church. We cannot extrapolate from it to other churches that may have been very different. But what little evidence we have suggests that most of the early Christians came from the "lower" classes. As Paul puts it in 1 Corinthians 1:26,

---

15. His major work is the monograph, *Die stadtrömischen Christen in den ersten beiden Jahrhunderten: Untersuchungen zur Socialgeschichte* (2d ed.; Tübingen: J. C. B. Mohr, 1989). A summary of some of his main points is found in his article, "Roman Christians."

"Brothers, think of what you were when you were called. Not many of you were wise by human standards; not many were influential; not many were of noble birth." This is not to say that other classes were not represented. The ease with which Priscilla and Aquila moved around the eastern Mediterranean and the fact that they hosted a church in their house suggests they were relatively wealthy.

Such information about the social composition of the church can be helpful to us because all people—Christians included—function within and are strongly influenced by social structures. New Testament scholars have given a lot of attention to this dimension of the early church in recent years. What we learn from such investigations can help us translate the explicit information of the text from the first century social context to ours.

Organization of the early church. What 16:1–16 reveals about the organization of the church is that it was apparently loose. Paul refers to at least three, and perhaps five, house churches (vv. 5, 14, 15 are clear; the "households" mentioned in vv. 10 and 11 may also represent house churches). The Christian community reflects the loose organization of the Jewish community, which was apparently also broken up into many independent synagogues.[16] It was probably the case, for instance, that certain house churches were composed entirely of believers "weak in faith" and others of believers "strong in faith" (see comments on 14:1–15:13). Paul's plea for acceptance of one another, then, is seeking reconciliation among various "churches" in Rome. We will suggest possible implications of this below.

Women in the early church. Of the twenty-seven Christians Paul greets or commends in verses 1–15, ten (more than one-third) are women. Six of them (Phoebe [vv. 1–2], Priscilla [v. 3], Junias [v. 7], Tryphena, [v. 12], Tryphosa [v. 12], and Persis [v. 12]) are commended for their labor "in the Lord." Junia is a "commissioned missionary" (*apostolos*; see comments on v. 7), and Phoebe is a benefactor and deacon of the church. What conclusions can we draw from these numbers? We can only answer that question after setting these references into the larger context of the New Testament teaching about "women in the church."

In what is a minefield of controversy, everybody at least agrees on three things: (1) women made up a significant part of the early Christian church (note the list above); (2) women were given the same access to God that men enjoyed (e.g., Gal. 3:28; 1 Peter 3:7); and (3) women engaged in significant ministry (see again the list above). What continues to divide believers is the extent to which the new covenant erased gender role distinctions in the home and in the church.

---

16. See Leon, *Jews*, 135–70.

Our text does not touch the issue of the home, so we will leave it aside here. But we can hardly come to final conclusions about the implications of Romans 16 for the role of women in the church without some sense of the teaching of the New Testament as a whole. We may never isolate one text apart from the larger canon in deciding its meaning. Especially is this important in a text like Romans 16, which does not directly teach about the role of women but makes indirect references to it. To be sure, such indirect evidence is important, giving us a window into the way the church actually operated. The importance of such evidence should not be unduly minimized. But it must finally be integrated with clear teaching passages.

Scholars are so divided over what the New Testament as a whole teaches on this matter that we simply have no consensus or agreed-on foundation on which to build our interpretation of Romans 16. All I can do here is briefly delineate my own understanding of New Testament teaching.[17] I do not think that the New Testament removes all restrictions on the ministry of women. Paul's claim that the husband is "head" (*kephale*) over his wife involves a claim that the husband has the role of loving, sacrificial leader—a role parallel to Christ's with respect to the church (Eph. 5:22–24). The wife responds to this relationship by joyful submission to the leadership of her husband (Eph. 5:22; Col. 3:18; 1 Peter 3:1–6).

Since the church imitates the family in the spiritual sphere, Paul extends this relationship of man and woman in marriage to the church. Women, he claims are not to "teach or to have authority" over men (1 Tim. 2:12). Paul effectively, then, prohibits women from ministries such as preaching or serving as "ruling elders." Accepting the Bible as a single book with one ultimate author means that I must bring these results into my study of Romans 16. But open and accurate understanding of the Bible also means that I must allow Romans 16 to modify my view of the biblical evidence. But we are moving into the area of contemporary significance (see below).

THE SOCIAL DIMENSION **of the church.** The social composition of the ancient Roman church is of interest to the historian and exegete, but I am not sure that it has much significance for the contemporary church. To argue, for instance, that our own churches should have the same social composition as the Roman church would be to indulge

---

17. For further explanation and justification of these points, see my article "What Does It Mean Not to Teach or Have Authority Over Men (1 Timothy 2:11–15)?" in *Recovering Biblical Manhood and Womanhood* (ed. J. Piper and W. Grudem; Westchester, Ill.: Crossway, 1991), 179–93.

in the worst form of analogical application. It is simply *not* always the case that "as it was then, so it must be now."

Nevertheless, it may, perhaps, be useful to remind ourselves that God has a special concern for the poor, for the downtrodden, for the helpless. This point emerges again and again in Luke's Gospel and is reaffirmed in the New Testament letters (see esp. James 2:5–6; 5:1–11). Many of the Roman Christians, as we have noted, were slaves or former slaves. It is often those who feel the most alienated in our world that are open to find status in the world to come.

Sociologists often explain virtually all religious affiliation along such lines. But we need not succumb to a reductionistic sociological explanation of religious affection to recognize the germ of truth in what they are teaching. The church, we may therefore infer, must be a place that intentionally sets out to offer solace to those in our world who most need it. Ministry to the poor, the down and out, and the homeless should be high on the agenda of the church's priorities.

The organization of the church. We must also be cautious in drawing conclusions from Romans 16 in this area. Once again, the fact that the Roman community was divided into house churches does not mean that the contemporary church should adopt a similar structure. Paul does not teach that the community *should* be divided into house churches. Indeed, house churches were probably a physical necessity in a time before church buildings existed and when other public buildings of any size would not have been available for Christians.

But there is one point we can draw from this circumstance, even if it is a bit tangential. *If* the Roman church met in a number of separate locations and rarely, perhaps never, met together in one place, and *if* Paul's plea for mutual acceptance in Romans 14:1–15:13 was directed to these churches, there may here be indirect encouragement for local churches to do a better job of getting along with one another. Local churches, even when they believe almost all the same things, tend all too easily to be in competition with each other— a competition that often leads to mutual distrust and even criticism. Churches try to justify their own existence and raise their own status by blackballing others. Paul would urge us to recognize each other even if we disagree about the nonessentials of the faith.

Women in the church. We can turn, now, to the third matter of potential significance for the contemporary church: the significance of women in Romans 16. Before we enter into the controversial part of our conclusions, we should emphasize two points that the text makes clear. (1) Women were an important and public part of the Roman Christian community. The term *public* in this assertion is especially important. In many religions in the ancient world, women were allowed to participate only by proxy—through their husbands—or were relegated to the outer fringes of worship. Romans 16 suggests, and the rest of the New Testament confirms, that the early church was different. Paul recognizes women along with men, implying their equality in the community and their participation together in worship.

(2) Women engaged in significant ministry. I cringe when I hear the modern debate put in terms of *women and ministry*—as if there is doubt about whether women can be *ministers*. Our unfortunate restriction of that term to a particular ministry (e.g., head pastor) blinds us to the New Testament insistence that every believer is a minister, that is, a servant of Christ and the church, with important contributions to make to the life of the body. Those of us who conclude that the New Testament imposes restrictions on certain ministries of women should take the lead in honoring women in ministry and in seeking to involve them in all the ministries that they are free to engage in. Much chauvinism still lurks in the corners of our churches. Women are too often relegated to menial duties in the church when the body is aching because of the absence of gifted, trained women to teach other women, to counsel, to evangelize, to organize, and so on.

What, finally, of the contribution of Romans 16 to the continuing debate about restrictions on women in ministry? This text has become an important skirmish in the larger battle. On the one side are those who insist that the New Testament imposes no restrictions whatever on ministry for women. They frequently appeal to three points in Romans 16 to support their view. (1) The word "coworker(s)" (*synergos*) that Paul applies to women in verses 3 and 9 implies that these women had ministries equal in significance and nature to Paul's; they were "leaders" in the church.[18] (2) Phoebe was a *prostatis*, a "lead preacher" or "ruler" of the church in Cenchrea (vv. 1–2). (3) Junia was an apostle of the same nature and rank as Paul and the Twelve (v. 7).

As I have asserted above, I tend to think that the New Testament as a whole upholds restrictions on the ministry of women, barring them from teaching men or having authority over them (see 1 Tim. 2:12). The first two of the points just mentioned pose no problem for that view, but the third is more troublesome.

(1) When Paul calls women his "coworkers," he is recognizing that they are carrying on ministries that are as significant as his own. But this word says nothing about the kind of ministry they are engaged in.

(2) Phoebe had an important ministry. But, as we argued in the Original Meaning section, Paul does not call her a pastor or leader but a deacon and

---

18. See, e.g., Elizabeth S. Fiorenza, "Missionaries, Apostles, Coworkers: Romans 16 and the Reconstruction of Women's Early Christian History," *Word and World* 6 (1986): 430.

benefactor. Both ministries (the former more "official" than the latter) were vital to the health of the church, but neither involved teaching or having authority over a man.

(3) But Junia is not so easy to explain away. Many scholars who take the position I hold on women in ministry insist that the name is Junias and that Paul is referring to a man. The lexical evidence, however, is decisively against this view. Indeed, the history of interpretation suggests that many interpreters have read their theology into this word. They assume that a woman cannot be an apostle, and so this individual cannot be a woman. Therefore, Romans 16:7 does, indeed, prove that women were "apostles" in the early church.

Must this verse force me to reconsider the position I hold? I should, of course, always go back to check the validity of my view against new findings. But in this case the situation is complicated by the different meanings that Paul gives to the term *apostle* (Gk. *apostolos*). As we argued above, it is at least as possible that Paul is using the word of these otherwise unknown early Christians in the sense of "commissioned missionary" rather than in the sense of "authoritative representative of Christ."

My own conclusion, then, is that Romans 16 does not overturn the view I think the New Testament elsewhere teaches about women in ministry. But I want to underscore the fact that I both understand the exegetical arguments for different conclusions and have tremendous respect for many of those who make those arguments. My good friend and former colleague, Walt Liefeld, and I have discussed this issue at length privately and in public forums. We come to different conclusions on the matter (see his NIV Application Commentary on 1 and 2 Timothy, Titus). But this in no way diminishes our regard for one another or the Christian fellowship we enjoy together.

Sadly, such relationships are not always maintained by people who take different sides on this issue. Moreover, I can sympathize with women especially who take a view such as mine as a personal threat to what they are doing. All I can do is plead that my own reading of the New Testament (always provisional) leads me to take the view that I do.

IURGE YOU, brothers, to watch out for those who cause divisions and put obstacles in your way that are contrary to the teaching you have learned. Keep away from them. ¹⁸For such people are not serving our Lord Christ, but their own appetites. By smooth talk and flattery they deceive the minds of naive people. ¹⁹Everyone has heard about your obedience, so I am full of joy over you; but I want you to be wise about what is good, and innocent about what is evil.

²⁰The God of peace will soon crush Satan under your feet. The grace of our Lord Jesus be with you.

²¹Timothy, my fellow worker, sends his greetings to you, as do Lucius, Jason and Sosipater, my relatives.

²²I, Tertius, who wrote down this letter, greet you in the Lord.

²³Gaius, whose hospitality I and the whole church here enjoy, sends you his greetings.

Erastus, who is the city's director of public works, and our brother Quartus send you their greetings.

²⁵Now to him who is able to establish you by my gospel and the proclamation of Jesus Christ, according to the revelation of the mystery hidden for long ages past, ²⁶but now revealed and made known through the prophetic writings by the command of the eternal God, so that all nations might believe and obey him—²⁷to the only wise God be glory forever through Jesus Christ! Amen.

WE GROUP THESE verses together for convenience sake. Paul touches quickly on many different topics as he brings the letter to its conclusion, most of which are common in the endings of Paul's letters (see comments on 15:14–33). But two are not: the warning about false teachers in 16:17–19 and the concluding doxology in 16:25–27. The former is certainly part of the text, and we will discuss just why Paul may have added it here.

The doxology, however, is textually uncertain. It is not found in a couple of manuscripts of Romans and is located elsewhere in other manuscripts.

Some claim that its vocabulary is not typical of Paul. Thus, many scholars conclude that it is not part of Paul's letter to the Romans but was added by someone else at a later date.[1] The vast majority of manuscripts, however, do include the doxology at the end of the letter, and the vocabulary is non-Pauline only if we think Paul did not write Ephesians. So the case for including these verses is strong.[2]

Paul does not elsewhere launch into a warning about false teachers in the conclusion of a letter. But he does issue exhortations and warnings that may presume their presence (e.g., 1 Cor. 16:13–14; 2 Cor. 13:11; Col. 4:17). It is a greater mystery why he waits until the very end of Romans to issue such a warning. Possibly he waits until now because the false teachers have not yet arrived on the scene, or because he only hears about the threat as he is finishing the letter.[3]

Various theories about who these false teachers may have been and what heresy they are propagating have been suggested. But Paul does not give us enough information to make a decision. All we know is what he here tells us. As with most false teachers, they "cause divisions" (*dichostasias*, a rare word [1 Macc. 3:29; Gal. 5:20]), putting "obstacles" or stumbling blocks (*skandala*; cf. 9:33; 11:9; 14:13) in the way of believers. They bring spiritual harm to believers by teaching doctrines contrary to the gospel. These people are not, then, serving Christ, "but their own appetites" (lit., their own belly [*koilia*]).

Paul uses the same language to brand false teachers in Philippians 3:19, creating a similar problem of identification. The language may be an ironical way of referring to Judaizers, that is, Christians who insisted, among other things, that the Jewish food laws must be obeyed.[4] But, lacking evidence for such an application of the word elsewhere, we cannot assume that the Roman Christians would have caught such an allusion. Probably, then, *koilia* is a synecdoche for sensual appetites generally.[5] The false teachers are interested in their own pleasure and ease, not in helping people know God.

---

1. E.g., Käsemann, *Commentary on Romans*, 422, 427–28; Cranfield, *The Epistle to the Romans*, 808; Dunn, *Romans*, 912–13; Fitzmyer, *Romans*, 753.

2. E.g., Murray, *The Epistle to the Romans*, 2:262–68; Stuhlmacher, *Paul's Letter to the Romans*, 244–46; Schreiner, *Romans*, 816–17; Larry Hurtado, "The Doxology at the End of Romans," in *New Testament Textual Criticism: Its Significance for Exegesis. Essays in Honor of Bruce M. Metzger* (ed. E. J. Epp and G. Fee; Oxford: Clarendon, 1981), 185–99; I. Howard Marshall, "Romans 16:25–27—An Apt Conclusion," in *Romans and the People of God: Essays in Honor of Gordon D. Fee on the Occasion of His 65th Birthday* (ed. Sven K. Soderlund and N. T. Wright; Grand Rapids: Eerdmans, 1999), 170–84.

3. E.g., Wilckens, *Römer 12–16*, 143.

4. E.g., Barrett, *The Epistle to the Romans*, 285.

5. E.g., Godet, *Commentary on Romans*, 496.

Again, in a way typical of false teachers, these people mask their lack of truth by employing persuasive speaking methods. People who are "naive" or innocent (*akakon*, v. 18) are susceptible to such an approach, and the Roman Christians themselves may fit in that category. Their very sincerity and desire to obey may make them easy prey for false teachers. So, in an ironic twist, Paul wants them to remain "innocent" (*akeraios*, v. 19) about evil.

Paul's promise that God will soon "crush Satan under your feet" (v. 20a) perhaps relates to the false teachers. More likely, however, the promise is a general one (cf. 1 Cor. 16:22; 1 Thess. 5:24). The language of the promise perhaps alludes to the famous *protoevangelium* of Genesis 3:15: "And I will put enmity between you and the woman, and between your offspring and hers; he will crush your head, and you will strike his heel."

Paul's grace wish in verse 20b finds a parallel in every other letter he writes. It acts as a kind of bookend with the beginning of the letter, since Paul there wishes the Romans "grace and peace to you from God our Father and from the Lord Jesus Christ" (1:7).

In 16:21–23, Paul conveys greetings to the Romans from some of his own associates and from other believers where he is staying. Timothy was Paul's closest fellow worker. He is identified as a cowriter with Paul in six of his letters (2 Corinthians, 1 and 2 Thessalonians, Philippians, Colossians, Philemon). Two other letters of Paul were written to him.

The Lucius in verse 21 may be the same as "Lucius of Cyrene" in Acts 13:1 or Luke the Evangelist.[6] Neither identification is likely, however. Jason is probably the same Jason who offered hospitality to Paul during his brief and tumultuous stay in Thessalonica (Acts 17:5–9). Sosipater is probably the same as the Sopater of Berea mentioned in Acts 20:4. The NIV "my relatives" leaves the wrong impression about the relationship of these three men to Paul. They were not close relatives but fellow Jews (cf. Rom. 9:3; 16:7, 11).

Tertius (v. 22) identifies himself as the amanuensis of the letter, that is, the trained scribe who "wrote down" what Paul dictated. He is otherwise unknown to us.

Gaius (v. 23) was a common name, but is probably the Gaius of Corinth (1 Cor. 1:14), since Paul is likely writing from Corinth. Gaius offers hospitality both to Paul and the "whole church," which may mean that a church is meeting in his house[7] or that he regularly offers to put up visiting believers.[8]

Erastus may be the same Erastus referred to in Acts 19:21–22 (cf. 2 Tim. 4:20). But an inscription has been discovered in Corinth that refers to an

---

6. For the former, see Godet, *Commentary on Romans*, 500; for the latter, see perhaps Dunn, *Romans*, 909, who states this view is "not impossible."

7. E.g., Dunn, *Romans*, 910–11; Fitzmyer, *Romans*, 749.

8. Käsemann, *Commentary on Romans*, 421.

Erastus who was an *aedile* of the city. This title may be equivalent to Paul's *oikonomos* (NIV "director of public works"). Even if the two are not identical, Erastus may have first served as *oikonomos* before being promoted to *aedile*.[9] Quartus is otherwise unknown.

Paul appropriately concludes his letter with a doxology in praise of God. He words the doxology in such a way as to echo many key ideas in the letter, especially its opening part:

who is able (who has power)	cf. 1:4, 16
establish you	1:11
my gospel	1:1, 9, 16; 2:16
revelation/revealed	1:17; cf. 3:21
prophetic writings	1:2; cf. 3:21
believe and obey	1:5
all nations (or Gentiles)	1:5
only God	3:29–30
wise God	11:33–36

While Paul (cf. 1:11) or others seek to establish believers in their faith, only God can ultimately do so. He works through the gospel, which Paul further defines as "the proclamation of [or about] Jesus Christ." This gospel is "according to the revelation of the mystery." As the apostle says elsewhere (cf. 1 Cor. 2:7; Eph. 3:3–9; Col. 1:26–27), the good news of redemption for all people in Christ is the climax of a plan of God, a "mystery " hidden in the past but now "revealed and made known" (v. 26) for all to see. Since the New Testament reveals this mystery, "the prophetic writings" may be a reference to the gospel.[10] But Paul has shown throughout Romans that the Old Testament as a whole is a prophetic book, pointing forward to Christ and the revelation of God's righteousness in him (cf. 1:2; 3:21). The fact and timing of the revelation of this mystery lay in God's plan; it was his "command" that put the gospel into effect.

God's purpose in doing so was that "all nations might believe and obey him." The Greek phrase is the same as we encountered in 1:5 (lit., "the obedience of faith"). As there, the phrase refers to the obedient lifestyle that must always be flowing from sincere faith in the Lord.

The concluding description of God (16:27) reminds us especially that he has instituted a "wise" and wonderful plan for the redemption of his creation (cf. 11:33–36). Surely our response should echo Paul, as we give glory to him through Jesus Christ!

---

9. See esp. A. D. Clarke, "Another Corinthian Erastus Inscription," *TynBul* 42 (1991): 146–51.

10. Godet, *Commentary on Romans*, 504.

FALSE TEACHERS. Our application of Paul's warning about false teachers (vv. 17–19) would gain precision if we could determine exactly what they were teaching. But, as we pointed out above, Paul gives us little help in making specific identification. Coming so suddenly at the end of the letter, the warning may be intended to reinforce earlier teaching. But Paul does not warn about specific false teachers anywhere else in this letter. The closest we get is the weak in faith in 14:1–15:13, and a few scholars have suggested it is this group, or a group allied with them, that Paul warns against here.[11] Paul, however, never treats the weak in faith as false teachers. Indeed, he calls on other Christians to accept them and even to respect their opinions.

Paul also alludes in passing to people who blasphemed him by accusing him of encouraging evil that good may come (3:8), but that reference is as obscure as this one. Taking their cue from the one specific issue that Paul does bring up—the false teachers "serve ... their own appetites [*koilia*]"—scholars have generally suggested two main identifications. If this refers to a preoccupation with Jewish food laws, the false teachers are probably Judaizers, Jewish-Christians who wanted to impose the law on Gentile Christians.[12] If, however, the phrase refers to a concern with satisfying one's own appetites, then the false teachers are perhaps libertines, people who see the gospel as an excuse for a licentious lifestyle.[13]

Both tendencies surfaced repeatedly in the early church, representing extreme positions on the value of "law" for believers. But serving the *koilia* is a phrase that eludes precise meaning; thus, as we concluded above, we simply cannot know just what these false teachers were saying. But if our inability to identify them prevents us from making specific application to similar teachers today, it has the advantage of allowing us to apply the language of this passage to virtually any threat of false teaching in our own day.

FALSE TEACHERS **then and now.** The truth of Christianity is, of course, formally opposed by adherents of other religions, philosophies, and worldviews. Buddhists, Muslims, animists, Marxists, atheists, and so forth propagate worldviews that are explicitly set in

---

11. E.g., Black, *Romans*, 212–13.

12. E.g., Godet, *Commentary on Romans*, 496; Sanday and Headlam, *The Epistle to the Romans*, 429; Stuhlmacher, *Paul's Letter to the Romans*, 252–53.

13. E.g., Dodd, *Epistle to the Romans*, 242–43.

contrast to Christianity. The battle lines are drawn, and we understand the need to oppose these worldviews with a vigorous and reasoned defense of our own.

But Christians must also deal with false teachers—people *within* the church who claim to be Christians but who deviate in some way from an essential truth of the gospel. False teachers have always plagued the church, and they are not going away. What Paul says in verses 17–19 may help us spot these false teachers and deal with them once we have identified them.

Paul's message about the false teachers reiterates what is said almost everywhere in the New Testament on such people. What we have is a stock profile of typical false teachers. In addition to errors in doctrine, Paul says three things about them: (1) They serve themselves rather than Christ; (2) they are crafty and effective speakers; and (3) they create divisions in the church. Paul, in other words, describes the motives, the means, and the results of their ministry.

False teachers often go wrong at the level of motivation. Instead of focusing on the glory of God and the good of the church, they become preoccupied with themselves. Pride is often their root sin. More status, prestige, and publicity come to people who teach new or strange things than to those who plod along, following the lines of truth laid down in Scripture and in the history of the church. *Time* magazine does not run articles on orthodox theologians. Only what is new and different is newsworthy. Thus, people can drift into false teaching out of a concern to stand out from others around them. And once a teacher has gone public with a new view, it is humiliating to back down in the face of opposition. One gets a vested interest in the view. Each of us needs, then, to make sure that we teach and minister for the right reasons. We need to evaluate, as best we can, what it is that motivates those who teach us.

By definition, the views that false teachers propagate are contrary to biblical teaching. They are often illogical as well. They will mask these problems in a flurry of rhetoric. False teachers are usually glib and convincing. They pull out every rhetorical trick in the book to try to win converts. Paul himself often faced these kinds of people, and some of his converts compared his own rhetorical abilities rather unfavorably with those of his opponents (see esp. 1 Cor. 1–2; 2 Cor. 10–13). But Paul prided himself on being a plain speaker, seeking to convey the truth of the gospel as clearly and straightforwardly as he could. He wanted people to be convicted by the truth of what he said, not moved for the moment by a slick presentation.

Which methods do we use? Carefully crafted sermons are certainly not wrong, but the preacher must always be careful not to substitute fancy words or illustrations or rhetorical devices for truth. The old adage about the preacher's notes—"weak point, speak more loudly"—is too often close to the truth. Those of us who listen to Christian teaching and preaching—in our churches, Sunday school classes, on the radio, and on TV—need to evaluate what is being said on the basis of its content, not just its style. False teachers often gain a hearing because they can be so engaging and so much fun to listen to. They disguise a lack of truth with smooth words.

Divisions, of course, can be created by people who proclaim the truth of the gospel in situations where that truth has not been carefully preserved. The zealous evangelical pastor who comes into a church that has drifted from orthodoxy over the years is bound to stir up dissension. Some people are not going to like the "new" ideas, and they will resist them. Factions in the church, and even permanent divisions, may result.

But false teachers are especially prone to create divisions. They are often guilty of singling out one point of doctrine, distorting it and then exaggerating it until it stands out from others. In their zeal for their "new" idea, they make converts who are equally zealous. The upshot is a group within the church who follow the lead of these false teachers and try to force their view on everyone else. We ought, therefore, to be suspicious of teachers in the church who encourage such devoted followings and who focus exclusively on one doctrine.

Theology and doxology. The wonderful doxology in 16:25–27 is an appropriate way to end a letter that so beautifully sets forth the truth of the gospel. All theology has its ultimate goal in the glory of God, and any true theology will always lead to this end. Theology, the "study of God," is not an intellectual pastime. Nor is it only for the good of the church. Its ultimate purpose is to enable God's people to glorify him more effectively and more passionately because they have learned more about him. We noted above how Paul weaves into this doxology so many of the motifs of the letter. It is as if he himself is led to burst out in spontaneous praise to God as he reflects on the marvelous truths he has taught in the letter. May our "bottom line" also be *sola dei gloria*—"to God alone be the glory."

Scripture Index

Subject Index

Bring ancient truth to modern life with the
NIV Application Commentary *series*

Covering both the Old and New Testaments, the **NIV Application Commentary** series is a staple reference for pastors seeking to bring the Bible's timeless message into a modern context. It explains not only what the Bible means but also how that meaning impacts the lives of believers today.

Genesis
This commentary demonstrates how the text charts a course of theological affirmation that results in a simple but majestic account of an ordered, purposeful cosmos with God at the helm, masterfully guiding it, and what this means to us today.

John H. Walton   ISBN: 978-0-310-20617-0

Exodus
The truth of Christ's resurrection and its resulting impact on our lives mean that to Christians, the application of Exodus is less about how to act than it is about what God has done and what it means to be his children.

Peter Enns   ISBN: 978-0-310-20607-1

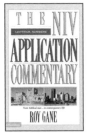

Leviticus, Numbers
Roy Gane's commentary on Leviticus and Numbers helps readers understand how the message of these two books, which are replete with what seem to be archaic laws, can have a powerful impact on Christians today.

Roy Gane   ISBN: 978-0-310-21088-7

Judges, Ruth
This commentary helps readers learn how the messages of Judges and Ruth can have the same powerful impact today that they did when they were first written. Judges reveals a God who employs very human deliverers but refuses to gloss over their sins and the consequences of those sins. Ruth demonstrates the far-reaching impact of a righteous character.

K. Lawson Younger Jr.   ISBN: 978-0-310-20636-1

1&2 Samuel

In Samuel, we meet Saul, David, Goliath, Jonathan, Bathsheba, the witch of Endor, and other unforgettable characters. And we encounter ourselves. For while the culture and conditions of Israel under its first kings are vastly different from our own, the basic issues of humans in relation to God, the Great King, have not changed. Sin, repentance, forgiveness, adversity, prayer, faith, and the promises of God—these continue to play out in our lives today.

Bill T. Arnold   ISBN: 978-0-310-21086-3

1&2 Chronicles

First and Second Chronicles are a narrative steeped in the best and worst of the human heart—but they are also a revelation of Yahweh at work, forwarding his purposes in the midst of fallible people, but a people who trust in the Lord and his word through the prophets. God has a plan to which he is committed.

Andrew E. Hill   ISBN: 978-0-310-20610-1

Esther

Karen H. Jobes shows what a biblical narrative that never mentions God tells Christians about him today.

Karen H. Jobes   ISBN: 978-0-310-20672-9

Psalms Volume 1

Gerald Wilson examines Books 1 and 2 of the Psalter. His seminal work on the shaping of the Hebrew Psalter has opened a new avenue of psalms research by shifting focus from exclusive attention to individual psalms to the arrangement of the psalms into groups.

Gerald H. Wilson   ISBN: 978-0-310-20635-4

Proverbs

Few people can remember when they last heard a sermon from Proverbs or looked together at its chapters. In this NIV Application Commentary on Proverbs, Paul Koptak gives numerous aids to pastors and church leaders on how to study, reflect on, and apply this book on biblical wisdom as part of the educational ministry of their churches.

Paul Koptak   ISBN: 978-0-310-21852-4

Ecclesiastes, Song of Songs
Ecclesiastes and Songs of Songs have always presented particular challenges to their readers, especially if those readers are seeking to understand them as part of Christian Scripture. Revealing the links between the Scriptures and our own times, Iain Provan shows how these wisdom books speak to us today with relevance and conviction.

Iain Provan   ISBN: 978-0-310-21372-7

Isaiah
Isaiah wrestles with the realities of people who are not convicted by the truth but actually hardened by it, and with a God whose actions sometimes seem unintelligible, or even worse, appears to be absent. Yet Isaiah penetrates beyond these experiences to an even greater reality. Isaiah sees God's rule over history and his capacity to take the worst of human actions and use it for good. He declares the truth that even in the darkest hours, the Holy One of Israel is infinitely trustworthy.

John N. Oswalt   ISBN: 978-0-310-20613-2

Jeremiah/Lamentations
These two books cannot be separated from the political conditions of ancient Judah. Beginning with the time of King Josiah, who introduced religious reform, Jeremiah reflects the close link between spiritual and political prosperity or disaster for the nation as a whole.

J. Andrew Dearman   ISBN: 978-0-310-20616-3

Ezekiel
Discover how, properly understood, this mysterious book with its obscure images offers profound comfort to us today.

Iain M. Duguid   ISBN: 978-0-310-21047-4

Daniel
Tremper Longman III reveals how the practical stories and spellbinding apocalyptic imagery of Daniel contain principles that are as relevant now as they were in the days of the Babylonian Captivity.

Tremper Longman III   ISBN: 978-0-310-20608-8

Hosea, Amos, Micah

Scratch beneath the surface of today's culture and you'll find we're not so different from ancient Israel. Revealing the links between Israel eight centuries B.C. and our own times, Gary V. Smith shows how the prophetic writings of Hosea, Amos, and Micah speak to us today with relevance and conviction.

Gary V. Smith   ISBN: 978-0-310-20614-9

Jonah, Nahum, Habakkuk, Zephaniah

James Bruckner shows how the messages of these four Old Testament prophets, who lived during some of Israel and Judah's most turbulent times, are as powerful in today's turbulent times as when first written.

James Bruckner   ISBN: 978-0-310-20637-8

Joel, Obadiah, Malachi

David Baker shows how these three short prophetic books contain both a message of impending judgment (for Israel's enemies and for Israel herself) and a message of great hope — of the outpouring of God's Spirit, of restoration and renewal, and of a coming Messiah. We need to hear that same message today.

David W. Baker   ISBN: 978-0-310-20723-8

Haggai, Zechariah

This commentary on Haggai and Zechariah helps readers learn how the message of these two prophets who challenged and encouraged the people of God after the return from Babylon can have the same powerful impact on the community of faith today.

Mark J. Boda   ISBN: 978-0-310-20615-6

Matthew
Matthew helps readers learn how the message of Matthew's gospel can have the same powerful impact today that it did when the author first wrote it.

Michael J. Wilkins   ISBN: 978-0-310-49310-5

Mark
Learn how the challenging gospel of Mark can leave recipients with the same powerful questions and answers it did when it was written.

David E. Garland   ISBN: 978-0-310-49350-1

Luke
Focus on the most important application of all: "the person of Jesus and the nature of God's work through him to deliver humanity."

Darrell L. Bock   ISBN: 978-0-310-49330-3

John
Learn both halves of the interpretive task. Gary M. Burge shows readers how to bring the ancient message of John into a modern context. He also explains not only what the book of John meant to its original readers but also how it can speak powerfully today.

Gary M. Burge   ISBN: 978-0-310-49750-9

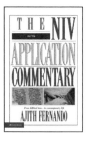

Acts
Study the first portraits of the church in action around the world with someone whose ministry mirrors many of the events in Acts. Biblical scholar and worldwide evangelist Ajith Fernando applies the story of the church's early development to the global mission of believers today.

Ajith Fernando   ISBN: 978-0-310-49410-2

Romans

Paul's letter to the Romans remains one of the most important expressions of Christian truth ever written. Douglas Moo comments on the text and then explores issues in Paul's culture and in ours that help us understand the ultimate meaning of each paragraph.

Douglas J. Moo   ISBN: 978-0-310-49400-3

1 Corinthians

Is your church struggling with the problem of divisiveness and fragmentation? See the solution Paul gave the Corinthian Christians over 2,000 years ago. It still works today!

Craig Blomberg   ISBN: 978-0-310-48490-5

2 Corinthians

Often recognized as the most difficult of Paul's letters to understand, 2 Corinthians can have the same powerful impact today that it did when it was first written.

Scott J. Hafemann   ISBN: 978-0-310-49420-1

Galatians

A pastor's message is true not because of his preaching or people-management skills, but because of Christ. Learn how to apply Paul's example of visionary church leadership to your own congregation.

Scot McKnight   ISBN: 978-0-310-48470-7

Ephesians

Explore what the author calls "a surprisingly comprehensive statement about God and his work, about Christ and the gospel, about life with God's Spirit, and about the right way to live."

Klyne Snodgrass   ISBN: 978-0-310-49340-2

Philippians

The best lesson Philippians provides is how to encourage people who actually are doing quite well. Learn why not all the New Testament letters are reactions to theological crises.

Frank Thielman   ISBN: 978-0-310-49300-6

Colossians/Philemon

The temptation to trust in the wrong things has always been strong. Use this commentary to learn the importance of trusting only in Jesus, God's Son, in whom all the fullness of God lives. No message is more important for our post-modern culture.

David E. Garland   ISBN: 978-0-310-48480-6

1&2 Thessalonians

Paul's letters to the Thessalonians say as much to us today about Christ's return and our resurrection as they did in the early church. This volume skillfully reveals Paul's answers to these questions and how they address the needs of contemporary Christians.

Michael W. Holmes   ISBN: 978-0-310-49380-8

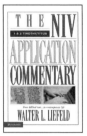

1&2 Timothy, Titus

Reveals the context and meanings of Paul's letters to two leaders in the early Christian Church and explores their present-day implications to help you to accurately apply the principles they contain to contemporary issues.

Walter L. Liefeld   ISBN: 978-0-310-50110-7

Hebrews

The message of Hebrews can be summed up in a single phrase: "God speaks effectively to us through Jesus." Unpack the theological meaning of those seven words and learn why the gospel still demands a hearing today.

George H. Guthrie   ISBN: 978-0-310-49390-7

James

Give your church the best antidote for a culture of people who say they believe one thing but act in ways that either ignore or contradict their belief. More than just saying, "Practice what you preach," James gives solid reasons why faith and action must coexist.

David P. Nystrom   ISBN: 978-0-310-49360-0

1 Peter

The issue of the church's relationship to the state hits the news media in some form nearly every day. Learn how Peter answered the question for Christians surviving under Roman rule and how it applies similarly to believers living amid the secular institutions of the modern world.

Scot McKnight   ISBN: 978-0-310-49290-0

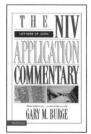

2 Peter, Jude

Introduce your modern audience to letters they may not be familiar with and show why they'll want to get to know them.

Douglas J. Moo   ISBN: 978-0-310-20104-5

Letters of John

Like the community in John's time, which faced disputes over erroneous "secret knowledge," today's church needs discernment in affirming new ideas supported by Scripture and weeding out harmful notions. This volume will help you show today's Christians how to use John's example.

Gary M. Burge   ISBN: 978-0-310-48620-6

Revelation

Craig Keener offers a "new" approach to the book of Revelation by focusing on the "old." He stresses the need for believers to prepare for the possibility of suffering for the sake of Jesus.

Craig S. Keener   ISBN: 978-0-310-23192-9

Praise for the NIV Application Commentary Series

"This series promises to become an indispensable tool for every pastor and teacher who seeks to make the Bible's timeless message speak to this generation."
—Billy Graham

"It is encouraging to find a commentary that is not only biblically trustworthy but also contemporary in its application. **The NIV Application Commentary** series will prove to be a helpful tool in the pastor's sermon preparation. I use it and recommend it."
—Charles F. Stanley, Pastor, First Baptist Church of Atlanta

"**The NIV Application Commentary** is an outstanding resource for pastors and anyone else who is serious about developing 'doers of the Word.'"
—Rick Warren, Pastor, Saddleback Valley Community
Church, Author, *The Purpose-Driven Church*

"**The NIV Application Commentary** series shares the same goal that has been the passion of my own ministry—communicating God's Word to a contemporary audience so that they feel the full impact of its message."
—Bill Hybels, Willow Creek Community Church

"**The NIV Application Commentary** series helps pastors and other Bible teachers with one of the most neglected elements in good preaching—accurate, useful application. Most commentaries tell you a few things that are helpful and much that you do not need to know. By dealing with the original meaning and contemporary significance of each passage, **The NIV Application Commentary** series promises to be helpful all the way around."
—Dr. James Montgomery Boice, Tenth Presbyterian Church

"If you want to avoid hanging applicational elephants from interpretive threads, then **The NIV Application Commentary** is for you! This series excels at both original meaning and contemporary signficance. I support it one hundred percent."
—Howard G. Hendricks, Dallas Theological Seminary

"**The NIV Application Commentary** series doesn't fool around: It gets right down to business, bringing this ancient and powerful Word of God into the present so that it can be heard and delivered with all the freshness of a new day, with all the immediacy of a friend's embrace."
—Eugene H. Peterson, Regent College

"This series dares to go where few scholars have gone before—into the real world of biblical application faced by pastors and teachers every day. This is everything a good commentary series should be."
—Leith Anderson, Pastor, Wooddale Church

"This is THE pulpit commentary for the 21ˢᵗ century."
—George K. Brushaber, President, Bethel College & Seminary

"Here, at last, is a commentary that makes the proper circuit from the biblical world to main street. **The NIV Application Commentary** is a magnificent gift to the church."
—R. Kent Hughes, Pastor, College Church, Wheaton, IL

Look for the NIV Application Commentary *at your local Christian bookstore*

"Academically well informed ... this series helps the contemporary reader hear God's Word and consider its implications; scholarship in the service of the Church."

—Arthur Rowe, Spurgeon's College

"The NIV Application Commentary series promises to be of very great service to all who preach and teach the Word of God."

—J. I. Packer, Regent College

"The NIV Application Commentary series will be a great help for readers who want to understand what the Bible means, how it applies, and what they should do in response."

—Stuart Briscoe, Pastor, Elmbrook Church

"The NIV Application Commentary meets the urgent need for an exhaustive and authoritative commentary based on the New International Version. This series will soon be found in libraries and studies throughout the evangelical community."

—Dr. James Kennedy, Ph.D., Senior Minister,
Coral Ridge Presbyterian Church

"... for readers who want a reliable synthesis with a strong emphasis on application.... [Provides a] freshness that can benefit students, teachers, and (especially) church leaders ... makes good devotional reading, precisely because it emphasizes the contemporary application.... This approach refreshes and challenges the reader, and would make helpful material for sermon-preparation or Bible study.... At a time when many pastors are deeply in need of inspiration and encouragement, these volumes ... would be a good investment for congregations, even if it means adding a line to the annual budget."

—Christianity Today

"This commentary needs to be given full marks for what it is attempting to do. This is to provide a commentary for the English reader that takes exegesis seriously and still has space left for considerations of what the text is saying in today's world.... One will understand everything that one reads. May its tribe increase!"

—Journal of the Evangelical Theological Society

"... a useful, nontechnical commentary.... In the application section are illustrations, which, to pastors seeking a fresh approach, are worth the price of the book.... Other useful features include same-page footnotes; Greek words transliterated in the text of the commentary; and an attractive, user-friendly layout. Pastors and Bible teachers who want to emphasize contemporary application will find this commentary a useful tool."

—Bookstore Journal

"... one of the most helpful commentary sets from recent years."

—Alabama Southern Baptist Convention

"Some commentaries build walls that isolate you back in the ancient world. The NIV Application Commentary builds bridges that make the Bible come alive with meaning for contemporary life—and the series does so concisely, clearly and accurately. No wasted words or academic detours—just solid help and practical truth!"

—Warren Wiersbe

Look for the NIV Application Commentary *at your local Christian bookstore*